STATISTICAL HANDBOOK ON POVERTY IN THE DEVELOPING WORLD

Edited by
Chandrika Kaul and Valerie Tomaselli-Moschovitis

Oryx Press
1999

The rare Arabian Oryx is believed to have inspired the myth of the unicorn. This desert antelope became virtually extinct in the early 1960s. At that time, several groups of international conservationists arranged to have nine animals sent to the Phoenix Zoo to be the nucleus of a captive breeding herd. Today, the Oryx population is over 1,000, and over 500 have been returned to the Middle East.

Library of Congress Cataloging-in-Publication Data

Statistical handbook on poverty in the developing world / edited by
Chandrika Kaul and Valerie Tomaselli-Moschovitis.
    p. cm.
  Includes bibliographical references and index.
  ISBN 1-57356-249-1 (alk. paper)
    1. Poverty—Developing countries—Statistics. I. Kaul,
Chandrika. II. Tomaselli-Moschovitis, Valerie.
HC59.72.P6S73 1999   99-29114
339.4'6'091724—dc21   CIP

Contents

Introduction

Poverty in developing countries is a profoundly disturbing problem. In a world where resources are plentiful and imbalances in the distribution of material goods are vast, the huge number of individuals who suffer under poverty—one-quarter of the world's population, according to *United Nations Human Development Report 1997*—strains credibility. Poverty results in a wide variety of human deprivations and can affect not only an individual's chances for survival and economic well-being, but a person's health, education, and social status; in the developing world, these effects deepen. Moreover, the poverty of developing countries has global implications, affecting international economic and political stability, as the poverty suffered in these countries strains national resources and creates pressure on political systems and policy apparatus.

Given the importance of these issues, of both the absolute and relative effects of poverty throughout the developing world, the need for understandable statistical material for the student and layperson is considerable. Indeed, statistics abound on the subject; however, data are frequently hard to access and understand, are presented in formats that are difficult to comprehend, and are scattered across a huge array of resources. The purpose of this volume, then, is to compile a comprehensive set of statistics from a wide variety of sources that explore the causes, effects, ramifications, and policies concerning poverty in developing countries in an organized format accessible to the non-specialist. It presents explanations for each indicator included in the volume in language that is clear and organizes those indicators in such a way as to make a comprehensive portrait of poverty in the developing world understandable to the user.

Definition and Scope

The title of this volume reveals its focus: it looks at poverty as a worldwide phenomenon but with particular emphasis on developing nations. The book employs a relative scale based on the full scope of human deprivation existing throughout the world and targets the poverty suffered by those underdeveloped populations throughout the world that fall considerably short of the standard witnessed in "developed" countries. Employing this relative scale, the data therefore focus on statistics in less wealthy "developing" countries. To accomplish this task, we include data mostly on low- and middle-income countries, as classified by the World Bank.

Admittedly, profound instances of poverty exist in wealthy industrialized countries. The poverty experienced by pockets of people in industrialized countries—the rural or inner city poor in the United States, for example—might be as extreme as the poverty in some of the poorer developing countries of the world. Nevertheless, such poverty can be seen as deviations against higher norms than those in less-developed countries. And the issues resulting from poverty in developed countries are less global in nature, as wealthier countries often have the means of addressing poverty within their own boundaries. Therefore, such instances of poverty lie beyond the scope of this book.

Organization and Content

Although developing countries are the focus of this volume, Section A will present a comprehensive international backdrop made up of key indicators involving land area, population, economic output, health, and education for over 190 countries of the world. This first section presents indicators for countries in tables organized by continents, allowing for regional comparisons between indicators, and is meant to serve as a touchstone for the targeted examination of poverty in the remaining sections.

In the rest of the book, tables of indicators are organized by 1998 World Bank income levels to facilitate an analysis of the variations between developing countries; included are separate tables for low-income, lower middle-income, and upper middle-income countries. Interspersed throughout the tables of data on countries are graphs that show cross-regional or income-level summaries. These graphs are meant to help users expand their analysis to include broad-sweep comparisons of individual countries against appropriate aggregated data. This organization holds throughout the book.

The World Bank's classification system was used due to its universal acceptance and the simplicity of its criteria: it is based solely on GNP per capita. The World Bank's 1998 classifications use GNP per capita for 1996. The levels are listed here:

- Low-income countries have a GNP per capita of $785 or less.
- Lower middle-income countries have a GNP per capita of between $786 and $3115.
- Upper middle-income countries have a GNP per capita of between $3116 and $9635.
- High-income countries have a GNP per capita of over $9636.

Section K deviates slightly from this format. In addition to presenting tables of countries in income-level categories along with comparative graphs, it also presents data tables for cities in low- and middle-income countries covering population, health, education, and other indicators. Included is any city whose population is greater than four million.

Other classification systems—primarily that of the United Nations' Development Programme (UNDP)—are available to help organize data, yet they are more complex. The UNDP system employed in that agency's annual *Human Development Report* uses a two-tier approach: it first categorizes countries as either developing or industrial, and then within each of these two general categories, ranks each country as either a high- medium- or low-human development country. The human development measure takes into account indicators beyond income, including data on education and health, for instance. While more purposeful relating to the full range of causes and effects of poverty, the UNDP system was judged to be too complex for the simple purpose of organizing countries into reasonable and manageable groups.

Each section of the book begins with an introductory overview and explanations of each indicator. This introductory material is included to help the user make sense of the data and to offer a quick snapshot of the material presented in the section.

Each table or graph is followed by notes on sources, along with an explanation and/or definition of the indicator presented. The definitions are based on those found in the source material. However, they are not taken verbatim, and may include information not found in the original sources if we thought the explanations needed further clarification. Notes repeat on all tables that cover the same or similar indicators. This is done for ease of use, so that the user will not have to flip back and forth to find pertinent definitions or sources.

Notes on Data and Sources

All data are taken from internationally recognized official agencies and sources including publications of the World Bank, the United Nations Development Programme, UNICEF, the World Health Organization, and the Food and Agriculture Organization. In using such sources, consistency and a high level of standardization of data are ensured.

Although care has been taken to include the latest available data for all indicators, many of the data included here are from 1996, with some indicators slightly more recent and some slightly older. While this may seem a bit old when compared to the timeliness of statistical material available for the United States, these international data were the most recent available as this book went to print. Consistent data for all countries and economies of the world, taken from reliable sources, often have a one- to two-year delay in preparation and publication. Such delays are understandable when researching countries whose government systems, language, and institutional structures vary.

Also, some statistics are not updated annually; in those cases, we have included data from the most recent compilation available. For instance, data on women in Section I and throughout the other sections come from the United Nations' report *The World's Women 1995: Trends and Statistics*, which is not issued annually.

Finally, in amassing such a large volume of data, mistakes and omissions can occur. It is our hope that, if such mistakes are uncovered, they will be communicated to us so that corrections can be made in future editions of this *Handbook*.

List of Tables and Figures

C. ECONOMICS

1. Gross Domestic Product

2. Gross Domestic Product per Capita

3. Consumer Price Index

4. Commodity Price Index

5. Economic Activity Rates

6. Earned Income, Share by Male and Female

7. Domestic Credit

8. Percentage Share of Income or Consumption

A. Key Indicators

GENERAL OVERVIEW

A collection of key indicators—involving land area, population, economic output, health, and education—sets the stage for this statistical investigation of poverty by outlining basic aspects of each country's material, geographic, demographic, and social features and prospects. Figures summarizing the indicator according to total world performance and income-level categories lead off the presentation for each type of indicator. Tables follow, which list all countries in alphabetical order for ease of research. These comprehensive alphabetical lists are followed by another set of tables organized by continent so that a more comparative analysis can be conducted if needed.

All countries of the world are presented in the tables and figures in Section A. This is done to provide a worldwide backdrop to the data given on poverty in later chapters, when indicators specifically representing the causes, effects, features, and policy aspects of poverty in less developed countries become the focus.

EXPLANATION OF INDICATORS

The indicators used in this chapter help to outline the material and human capacity of a country to provide for its people. The most basic indicators—land area, population, and gross national product—present data on the three arenas of greatest concern in analyzing the material health of a society

Land Area: Land area is a crude but crucial indicator. It represents the land mass available within the political boundaries of a country, and therefore indicates potential capacity for production of physical resources to satisfy human needs. However, such raw data obviously offers an incomplete picture. Answers to questions such as how much of that land is arable and what specific material resources (minerals, forests, etc.) the land hosts offer further details about the satisfaction of human needs, or lack thereof (A1.1–A1.6).

Population: Population is another raw but vital statistic in this introductory portrait. It represents the number of people within the physical boundaries of a country and under the jurisdiction of that country's political control. It can be interpreted both as a potential resource—as individuals convert physical resources to material goods to satisfy human needs—as well as a designation of potential need, as individual requirements for survival (food, clothing, shelter), health and education, etc., absorb physical resources (A2.1–A2.5).

Population Density: Population density brings the two top-level indicators in this chapter—land area and population—into relationship with each other. It distributes the total land area of a country across its population. As presented here, it is an even, or "averaged," distribution, without attempts to account for internal variations (rural vs. urban, regional differences, etc.). Therefore, while it is a good measure of available land in relationship to the specific human needs of a country, it is limited because of its generalized character. The three largest countries of the world, in terms of land mass, illustrate the meaning of this indicator. Russia is ranked as the largest country in the world, yet it has a very low population density of 8.7. Canada, ranked as the second largest country, has an even lower population density of 3.2. Yet China, the third largest country in the world, with vast land reserves, has a population density of 130.3, putting it within the top quarter of the most densely populated countries (A3.1–A3.6).

Gross National Product (GNP): This indicator, presented in two permutations (total and per capita), helps to convey a society's total capacity for material production. As a measure of the total goods and services produced by a country, it singlehandedly frames the economic outlook of that country. Certain factors, of course, affect a country's economic output level, such as natural and human resources. Other factors are also crucial, including the productivity of specific industries, the extent of mechanization available to all sectors of economic activity (agriculture, industry, and service), and the skill level of the labor force (A4.1–A4.6).

GNP per Capita: This indicator applies a country's aggregate economic output to the size of its population. Similar to population density in its limitations, GNP per capita is only an "averaged" indication of economic output per individual. Although the calculation includes only the GNP and the total population, with no measure of exactly what portion of the population produces how much, it provides a more than adequate indicator of the size of the economy in relationship to the size of the population and it helps to explain how countries with large outputs in absolute terms do not perform well in terms of the size of its population. China may be the best example of such a country. With a GNP of 906.1 billion dollars (seventh in the world) and a population of 1.2 billion (first in the world), its GNP per capita is $520, 99th among the world's countries (A5.1–A5.5).

To round out this introductory worldwide portrait, other statistical materials supplement these basic indicators. These include information on aspects of health (life expectancy and infant mortality) and education (literacy rates).

Life Expectancy: Life expectancy is a broad-based measure of the health status of a population. Many factors affect this statistic: availability of adequate nutrition, general economic well-being, and the accessibility of health care services, to name a few. In general, the more developed countries have better life expectancy prospects, due to generally better standards of living. For instance, Japan has the highest life expectancy at 79.8 years, while Sierra Leone in Africa ranks near the lowest with 36.9 years, less than half of Japan's. Such low life expectancy figures relate not just to lower standards of living but to the presence of war and civil unrest in certain countries, where life is threatened not just by lack of adequate food, water, etc., but by violence and other social stresses (A6.1–A6.6).

Infant Mortality Rates: Infant mortality is considered one of the most important measurements of the health status of a country. It directly represents the quality of life factors—food, clothing, and shelter—that affect the health of mothers and consequently the viability of newborns, as well as the accessibility of health care services to pregnant mothers and their newborns. As with life expectancy, infant mortality rates are often highest in least developed countries. Further, these indicators are often not widely available in countries whose health care systems and government structures are not equipped to keep track of birth and death records on a systematic and comprehensive basis (A7.1–A7.6).

Literacy Rates: Literacy is an extremely important and basic indicator of a population's educational status. As a measure of what share of a country's people can read and write basic sentences concerning their everyday life, it represents the most basic requirements for educational attainment. In later chapters, more detailed indicators of educational attainment and achievement are included that help to explore education in more depth—as a factor and feature of poverty (A8.1–A8.6).

A1.1 Land and Population Summary—Comparison by Income Level per World Bank

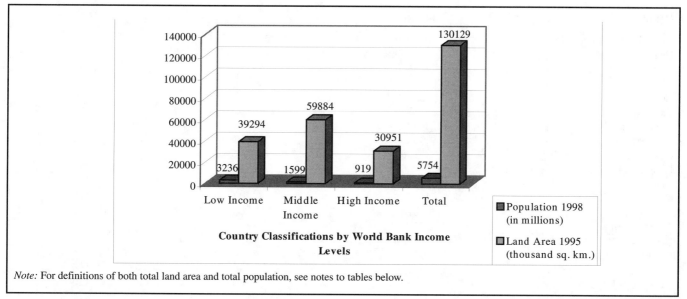

Note: For definitions of both total land area and total population, see notes to tables below.

Source: World Bank, *World Development Indicators 1998,* Table 1.1

A1.2 Land Area, 1995

Country	Sq. Km.	Sq. Miles	Rank
Afghanistan	652090	251771.9	40
Albania	27400	10579	142
Algeria	2381740	919590	10
Andorra	450	174	176
Angola	1246700	481351	22
Antigua and Barbuda	440	170	178
Argentina	2736690	1056636	8
Armenia	28200	10888	137
Australia	7682300	2966136	6
Austria	82730	31942	113
Azerbaijan	86600	33436	111
Bahamas	10010	3865	158
Bahrain	690	266	173
Bangladesh	130170	50259	93
Barbados	430	166	179
Belarus	207480	80108	81
Belgium	32820	12672	135
Belize	22800	8803	147
Benin	110620	42710	98
Bhutan	47000	18147	128
Bolivia	1084380	418679	25
Bosnia and Herzegovina	51000	19691	125
Botswana	566730	218814	46
Brazil	8456510	3265059	5
Brunei	5270	2035	161
Bulgaria	110550	42683	99
Burkina Faso	273600	105637	72
Burundi	25680	9915	143
Cambodia	176520	68154	87
Cameroon	465400	179691	52
Canada	9220970	3560217	3
Cape Verde	4030	1556	163

A1.2 Land Area, 1995 *(continued)*

Country	Sq. Km.	Sq. Miles	Rank
Central African Republic	622980	240533	42
Chad	1259200	486177	21
Chile	748800	289112	37
China	9326410	3600927	2
Colombia	1038700	401042	26
Comoros	2230	861	166
Congo, Dem. Rep. (Zaire)	2267050	875308	12
Congo, Rep.	341500	131853	62
Costa Rica	51060	19714	124
Cote d'Ivoire	318000	122780	65
Croatia	55920	21591	122
Cuba	109820	42402	100
Cyprus	9240	3568	160
Czech Republic	77280	29838	114
Denmark	42430	16382	129
Djibouti	23180	8950	146
Dominica	750	290	169
Dominican Republic	48380	18680	126
Ecuador	276840	106888	71
Egypt	995450	384343	29
El Salvador	20720	8000	148
Equatorial Guinea	28050	10830	139
Eritrea	101000	38996	103
Estonia	42270	16320	130
Ethiopia	1000000	386100	28
Fiji	18270	7054	151
Finland	304590	117602	67
France	550100	212394	47
Gabon	257670	99486	74
Gambia	10000	3861	159
Georgia	69700	26911	117
Germany	349270	134853	61
Ghana	227540	87853	79
Greece	128900	49768	94
Grenada	340	131	182
Guatemala	108430	41865	101
Guinea	245720	94872	75
Guinea-Bissau	28120	10857	138
Guyana	196850	76004	83
Haiti	27560	10641	141
Honduras	111890	43201	97
Hungary	92340	35652	108
Iceland	100250	38707	104
India	2973190	1147949	7
Indonesia	1811570	699447	15
Iran	1622000	626254	17
Iraq	437370	168869	55
Ireland	68890	26598	118
Israel	20620	7961	149
Italy	294060	113537	70
Jamaica	10830	4181	156
Japan	376520	145374	60
Jordan	88930	34336	110
Kazakhstan	2670730	1031169	9
Kenya	569140	219745	45
Kiribati	730	282	170
Kuwait	17820	6880	152
Kyrgyzstan	191800	74054	85

A1.2 Land Area, 1995 *(continued)*

Country	Sq. Km.	Sq. Miles	Rank
Laos	230800	89112	77
Latvia	62050	23958	121
Lebanon	10230	3950	157
Lesotho	30350	11718	136
Liberia	96320	37189	106
Libya	1759540	679358	16
Liechtenstein	160	62	186
Lithuania	64800	25019	119
Luxembourg	2586	998	165
Macedonia, FYRO	25430	9819	144
Madagascar	581540	224533	43
Malawi	94080	36324	107
Malaysia	328550	126853	63
Maldives	300	116	184
Mali	1220190	471115	24
Malta	320	124	183
Marshall Islands	181	70	185
Mauritania	1025220	395837	27
Mauritius	2030	784	167
Mexico	1908690	736945	14
Micronesia	702	271	172
Moldova	32970	12730	134
Monaco	2	1	190
Mongolia	1566500	604826	18
Morocco	446300	172316	54
Mozambique	784090	302737	34
Myanmar (Burma)	657550	253880	39
Namibia	823290	317872	33
Nauru	21	8	189
Nepal	143000	55212	91
Netherlands	33920	13097	133
New Zealand	267990	103471	73
Nicaragua	121400	46873	95
Niger	1266700	489073	20
Nigeria	910770	351648	30
North Korea, Dem. Rep.	120410	46490	96
Norway	306830	118467	66
Oman	212460	82031	80
Pakistan	770880	297637	35
Palau	1	1	191
Panama	74430	28737	115
Papua New Guinea	452860	174849	53
Paraguay	397300	153398	58
Peru	1280000	494208	19
Philippines	298170	115123	69
Poland	304420	117537	68
Portugal	91500	35328	109
Qatar	11000	4247	155
Romania	230340	88934	78
Russia	16888500	6520650	1
Rwanda	24670	9525	145
Samoa	2830	1093	164
San Marino	60	23	187
Sao Tome and Principe	960	371	168
Saudi Arabia	2149690	829995	13
Senegal	192530	74336	84
Seychelles	450	174	177
Sierra Leone	71620	27652	116

A1.2   Land Area, 1995 *(continued)*

Country	Sq. Km.	Sq. Miles	Rank
Singapore	610	236	174
Slovakia	48080	18564	127
Slovenia	20120	7768	150
Solomon Islands	27990	10807	140
Somalia	627340	242216	41
South Africa	1221040	471444	23
South Korea, Rep.	98730	38120	105
Spain	499440	192834	50
Sri Lanka	64630	24954	120
St. Kitts & Nevis	360	139	181
St. Lucia	610	236	175
St. Vincent and the Grenadines	390	151	180
Sudan	2376000	917374	11
Suriname	156000	60232	89
Swaziland	17200	6641	153
Sweden	411620	158926	57
Switzerland	39550	15270	131
Syria	183780	70957	86
Taiwan	35980	13892	132
Tajikistan	140600	54286	92
Tanzania	883590	341154	31
Thailand	510890	197255	49
Togo	54390	21000	123
Tonga	720	278	171
Trinidad & Tobago	5130	1981	162
Tunisia	155360	59984	90
Turkey	769630	297154	36
Turkmenistan	469930	181440	51
Tuvalu	26	10	188
Uganda	199650	77085	82
Ukraine	579350	223687	44
United Arab Emirates	83600	32278	112
United Kingdom	241600	93282	76
United States	9159120	3536336	4
Uruguay	174810	67494	88
Uzbekistan	414240	159938	56
Vanuatu	12190	4707	154
Venezuela	882050	340560	32
Vietnam	325490	125672	64
Yemen	527970	203849	48
Yugoslavia	102000	39382	102
Zambia	743390	287023	38
Zimbabwe	386850	149363	59

Note: Land area is a country's total area, within its international borders, excluding areas under inland bodies of water; in most cases definition of inland water bodies includes major rivers and lakes.

Source: World Bank, *World Development Indicators 1998*, Table 1.1 (AG.LND.TOTL.K2); Central Intelligence Agency, *World Factbook 1998*

A1.3 Land Area, 1995—Africa

Country	Sq. Km.	Sq. Miles	World Rank
Algeria	2381740	919590	10
Angola	1246700	481351	22
Benin	110620	42710	98
Botswana	566730	218814	46
Burkina Faso	273600	105637	72
Burundi	25680	9915	143
Cameroon	465400	179691	52
Cape Verde	4030	1556	163
Central African Republic	622980	240533	42
Chad	1259200	486177	21
Comoros	2230	861	166
Congo, Dem. Rep. (Zaire)	2267050	875308	12
Congo, Rep.	341500	131853	62
Cote d'Ivoire	318000	122780	65
Egypt	995450	384343	29
Equatorial Guinea	28050	10830	139
Eritrea	101000	38996	103
Ethiopia	1000000	386100	28
Gabon	257670	99486	74
Gambia	10000	3861	159
Ghana	227540	87853	79
Guinea	245720	94872	75
Guinea-Bissau	28120	10857	138
Kenya	569140	219745	45
Lesotho	30350	11718	136
Liberia	96320	37189	106
Libya	1759540	679358	16
Madagascar	581540	224533	43
Malawi	94080	36324	107
Mali	1220190	471115	24
Mauritania	1025220	395837	27
Mauritius	2030	784	167
Morocco	446300	172316	54
Mozambique	784090	302737	34
Namibia	823290	317872	33
Niger	1266700	489073	20
Nigeria	910770	351648	30
Rwanda	24670	9525	145
Sao Tome and Principe	960	371	168
Senegal	192530	74336	84
Seychelles	450	174	177
Sierra Leone	71620	27652	116
Somalia	627340	242216	41
South Africa	1221040	471444	23
Sudan	2376000	917374	11
Swaziland	17200	6641	153
Tanzania	883590	341154	31
Togo	54390	21000	123
Tunisia	155360	59984	90
Uganda	199650	77085	82
Zambia	743390	287023	38
Zimbabwe	386850	149363	59

Note: Land area is a country's total area, within its international borders, excluding areas under inland bodies of water; in most cases definition of inland water bodies includes major rivers and lakes.

Source: World Bank, *World Development Indicators 1998,* Table 1.1 (AG.LND.TOTL.K2); Central Intelligence Agency, *World Factbook 1998*

A1.4   Land Area, 1995—Americas

Country	Sq. Km.	Sq. Miles	World Rank
Antigua and Barbuda	440	170	178
Argentina	2736690	1056636	8
Bahamas	10010	3865	158
Barbados	430	166	179
Belize	22800	8803	147
Bolivia	1084380	418679	25
Brazil	8456510	3265059	5
Canada	9220970	3560217	3
Chile	748800	289112	37
Colombia	1038700	401042	26
Costa Rica	51060	19714	124
Cuba	109820	42402	100
Dominica	750	290	169
Dominican Republic	48380	18680	126
Ecuador	276840	106888	71
El Salvador	20720	8000	148
Grenada	340	131	182
Guatemala	108430	41865	101
Guyana	196850	76004	83
Haiti	27560	10641	141
Honduras	111890	43201	97
Jamaica	10830	4181	156
Mexico	1908690	736945	14
Nicaragua	121400	46873	95
Panama	74430	28737	115
Paraguay	397300	153398	58
Peru	1280000	494208	19
St. Kitts & Nevis	360	139	181
St. Lucia	610	236	175
St. Vincent and the Grenadines	390	151	180
Suriname	156000	60232	89
Trinidad & Tobago	5130	1981	162
United States	9159120	3536336	4
Uruguay	174810	67494	88
Venezuela	882050	340560	32

Note: Land area is a country's total area, within its international borders, excluding areas under inland bodies of water; in most cases definition of inland water bodies includes major rivers and lakes.

Source: World Bank, *World Development Indicators 1998,* Table 1.1 (AG.LND.TOTL.K2); Central Intelligence Agency, *World Factbook 1998*

A1.5 Land Area, 1995—Asia and Oceania

Country	Sq. Km.	Sq. Miles	World Rank
Afghanistan	652090	251771.9	40
Australia	7682300	2966136	6
Azerbaijan	86600	33436	111
Bahrain	690	266	173
Bangladesh	130170	50259	93
Bhutan	47000	18147	128
Brunei	5270	2035	161
Cambodia	176520	68154	87
China	9326410	3600927	2
Djibouti	23180	8950	146
Fiji	18270	7054	151
India	2973190	1147949	7
Indonesia	1811570	699447	15
Iran	1622000	626254	17
Iraq	437370	168869	55
Israel	20620	7961	149
Japan	376520	145374	60
Jordan	88930	34336	110
Kazakhstan	2670730	1031169	9
Kiribati	730	282	170
Kuwait	17820	6880	152
Kyrgyzstan	191800	74054	85
Laos	230800	89112	77
Lebanon	10230	3950	157
Malaysia	328550	126853	63
Maldives	300	116	184
Marshall Islands	181	70	185
Micronesia	702	271	172
Mongolia	1566500	604826	18
Myanmar (Burma)	657550	253880	39
Nauru	21	8	189
Nepal	143000	55212	91
New Zealand	267990	103471	73
North Korea, Dem. Rep.	120410	46490	96
Oman	212460	82031	80
Pakistan	770880	297637	35
Palau	1	0	191
Papua New Guinea	452860	174849	53
Philippines	298170	115123	69
Qatar	11000	4247	155
Samoa	2830	1093	164
Saudi Arabia	2149690	829995	13
Singapore	610	236	174
Solomon Islands	27990	10807	140
South Korea, Rep.	98730	38120	105
Sri Lanka	64630	24954	120
Syria	183780	70957	86
Taiwan	35980	13892	132
Tajikistan	140600	54286	92
Thailand	510890	197255	49
Tonga	720	278	171
Turkey	769630	297154	36
Turkmenistan	469930	181440	51
Tuvalu	26	10	188
United Arab Emirates	83600	32278	112
Uzbekistan	414240	159938	56
Vanuatu	12190	4707	154

A1.5 Land Area, 1995—Asia and Oceania *(continued)*

Country	Sq. Km.	Sq. Miles	World Rank
Vietnam	325490	125672	64
Yemen	527970	203849	48

Note: Land area is a country's total area, within its international borders, excluding areas under inland bodies of water; in most cases definition of inland water bodies includes major rivers and lakes.

Source: World Bank, *World Development Indicators 1998,* Table 1.1 (AG.LND.TOTL.K2); Central Intelligence Agency, *World Factbook 1998*

A1.6 Land Area, 1995—Europe

Country	Sq. Km.	Sq. Miles	World Rank
Albania	27400	10579	142
Andorra	450	174	176
Armenia	28200	10888	137
Austria	82730	31942	113
Belarus	207480	80108	81
Belgium	32820	12672	135
Bosnia and Herzegovina	51000	19691	125
Bulgaria	110550	42683	99
Croatia	55920	21591	122
Cyprus	9240	3568	160
Czech Republic	77280	29838	114
Denmark	42430	16382	129
Estonia	42270	16320	130
Finland	304590	117602	67
France	550100	212394	47
Georgia	69700	26911	117
Germany	349270	134853	61
Greece	128900	49768	94
Hungary	92340	35652	108
Iceland	100250	38707	104
Ireland	68890	26598	118
Italy	294060	113537	70
Latvia	62050	23958	121
Liechtenstein	160	62	186
Lithuania	64800	25019	119
Luxembourg	2586	998	165
Macedonia, FYRO	25430	9819	144
Malta	320	124	183
Moldova	32970	12730	134
Monaco	2	1	190
Netherlands	33920	13097	133
Norway	306830	118467	66
Poland	304420	117537	68
Portugal	91500	35328	109
Romania	230340	88934	78
Russia	16888500	6520650	1
San Marino	60	23	187
Slovakia	48080	18564	127
Slovenia	20120	7768	150
Spain	499440	192834	50
Sweden	411620	158926	57
Switzerland	39550	15270	131
Ukraine	579350	223687	44
United Kingdom	241600	93282	76
Yugoslavia	102000	39382	102

Note: Land area is a country's total area, within its international borders, excluding areas under inland bodies of water; in most cases definition of inland water bodies includes major rivers and lakes.

Source: World Bank, *World Development Indicators 1998,* Table 1.1 (AG.LND.TOTL.K2); Central Intelligence Agency, *World Factbook 1998*

A2.1 Population: 1998, 2025 (projection)

Country	1998 (mid-year)	2025 (proj.)	Rank (by 1998)
Afghanistan	24,792,375	48,044,542	39
Albania	3,330,754	4,306,000	127
Algeria	30,480,793	47,675,820	35
Andorra	64,716	88,229	182
Angola	10,865,000	21,598,322	68
Antigua and Barbuda	64,006	65,413	183
Argentina	36,265,463	48,351,219	31
Armenia	3,421,775	3,433,747	124
Australia	18,613,087	22,190,652	52
Austria	8,133,611	7,822,446	84
Azerbaijan	7,855,576	9,429,191	87
Bahamas	279,833	368,670	167
Bahrain	616,342	922,902	156
Bangladesh	127,567,002	180,560,502	8
Barbados	259,025	278,611	169
Belarus	10,409,050	10,248,170	71
Belgium	10,174,922	9,533,170	74
Belize	230,160	383,496	170
Benin	6,100,799	13,541,352	94
Bhutan	1,908,307	3,340,681	142
Bolivia	7,826,352	12,007,028	88
Bosnia and Herzegovina	3,365,727	3,470,613	126
Botswana	1,448,454	1,633,683	144
Brazil	169,806,557	209,586,835	5
Brunei	315,292	529,595	165
Bulgaria	8,240,426	7,292,242	83
Burkina Faso	11,266,393	21,360,037	65
Burundi	5,537,387	10,468,908	100
Cambodia	11,339,562	22,817,359	64
Cameroon	15,029,433	29,108,181	59
Canada	30,675,398	37,987,471	33
Cape Verde	399,857	531,633	163
Central African Republic	3,375,771	5,544,579	125
Chad	7,359,512	14,359,716	90
Chile	14,787,781	17,942,290	60
China	1,236,914,658	1,407,739,146	1
Colombia	38,580,949	58,287,171	30
Comoros	545,528	1,160,486	157
Congo, Dem. Rep. (Zaire)	49,000,511	105,737,162	24
Congo, Rep.	2,658,123	4,246,447	131
Costa Rica	3,604,642	5,327,331	120
Cote d'Ivoire	15,446,231	27,840,275	58
Croatia	4,671,584	4,348,133	109
Cuba	11,050,729	11,697,123	66
Cyprus	748,982	967,114	153
Czech Republic	10,286,470	10,127,921	72
Denmark	5,333,617	5,333,705	102
Djibouti	440,727	840,724	160
Dominica	65,777	66,962	181
Dominican Republic	7,998,766	11,780,544	85
Ecuador	12,336,572	17,799,981	62
Egypt	66,050,004	97,431,183	16
El Salvador	5,752,067	8,381,567	97
Equatorial Guinea	454,001	876,225	158
Eritrea	3,842,436	8,437,639	117
Estonia	1,421,335	1,237,013	145
Ethiopia	58,390,351	98,762,736	21
Fiji	802,611	1,084,937	152

A2.1   Population: 1998, 2025 (projection) *(continued)*

Country	1998 (mid-year)	2025 (proj.)	Rank (by 1998)
Finland	5,149,242	5,009,347	105
France	58,804,944	57,806,479	20
Gabon	1,207,844	1,799,727	147
Gambia	1,291,858	2,678,362	146
Georgia	5,108,527	4,718,035	106
Germany	82,079,454	75,372,295	12
Ghana	18,497,206	28,191,005	53
Greece	10,662,138	10,473,429	69
Grenada	96,217	154,361	178
Guatemala	12,007,580	22,344,183	63
Guinea	7,477,110	13,135,320	89
Guinea-Bissau	1,206,311	2,102,298	148
Guyana	707,954	710,266	154
Haiti	6,780,501	10,170,748	93
Honduras	5,861,955	8,612,256	96
Hungary	10,208,127	9,374,100	73
Iceland	271,033	298,018	168
India	984,003,683	1,408,320,301	2
Indonesia	212,941,810	287,985,072	4
Iran	68,959,931	111,891,148	15
Iraq	21,722,287	52,615,035	46
Ireland	3,619,480	3,913,417	119
Israel	5,643,966	7,778,332	99
Italy	56,782,748	50,351,674	22
Jamaica	2,634,678	3,354,566	132
Japan	125,931,533	119,864,560	9
Jordan	4,434,978	8,222,996	114
Kazakhstan	16,846,808	18,564,593	54
Kenya	28,337,071	34,773,605	37
Kiribati	83,976	98,764	179
Kuwait	1,913,285	3,558,774	141
Kyrgyzstan	4,522,281	6,066,461	112
Laos	5,260,842	9,804,562	104
Latvia	2,385,396	1,964,902	135
Lebanon	3,505,794	4,831,388	122
Lesotho	2,089,829	2,724,163	138
Liberia	2,771,901	6,524,316	129
Libya	5,690,727	14,185,462	98
Liechtenstein	31,717	36,052	187
Lithuania	3,600,158	3,417,198	121
Luxembourg	425,017	447,368	162
Macedonia, FYRO	2,009,387	2,171,241	139
Madagascar	14,462,509	29,306,165	61
Malawi	9,840,474	10,911,225	77
Malaysia	20,932,901	34,248,134	48
Maldives	290,211	623,150	166
Mali	10,108,569	22,646,955	75
Malta	379,563	390,832	164
Marshall Islands	63,031	170,829	184
Mauritania	2,511,473	5,445,945	134
Mauritius	1,168,256	1,488,342	149
Mexico	98,552,776	141,592,523	11
Micronesia	129,658	142,869	175
Moldova	4,457,729	4,830,277	113
Monaco	32,035	33,832	186
Mongolia	2,578,530	3,555,370	133
Morocco	29,114,497	43,227,753	36
Mozambique	18,641,469	33,308,035	51

A2.1 Population: 1998, 2025 (projection) *(continued)*

Country	1998 (mid-year)	2025 (proj.)	Rank (by 1998)
Myanmar (Burma)	47,305,319	68,106,967	25
Namibia	1,622,328	2,309,815	143
Nauru	10,501	11,888	190
Nepal	23,698,421	42,576,135	41
Netherlands	15,731,112	15,851,599	57
New Zealand	3,625,388	4,445,272	118
Nicaragua	4,583,379	8,112,068	111
Niger	9,671,848	20,423,708	79
Nigeria	110,532,242	203,423,396	10
North Korea, Dem. Rep.	21,234,387	26,054,682	47
Norway	4,419,955	4,591,906	115
Oman	2,363,591	5,307,157	136
Pakistan	135,135,195	211,675,333	7
Palau	18,110	21,259	189
Panama	2,735,943	3,796,038	130
Papua New Guinea	4,599,785	7,597,486	110
Paraguay	5,291,020	9,929,121	103
Peru	26,111,110	39,157,814	38
Philippines	77,725,862	120,519,345	13
Poland	38,606,922	40,116,796	29
Portugal	9,927,556	9,011,799	76
Qatar	697,126	1,208,407	155
Romania	22,395,848	21,416,886	43
Russia	146,861,022	138,841,556	6
Rwanda	7,956,172	12,158,817	86
Samoa	224,713	367,080	171
San Marino	24,894	27,034	188
Sao Tome and Principe	150,123	330,843	174
Saudi Arabia	20,785,955	50,374,341	49
Senegal	9,723,149	22,456,276	78
Seychelles	78,641	90,959	180
Sierra Leone	5,080,004	11,010,156	107
Singapore	3,490,356	4,230,872	123
Slovakia	5,392,982	5,718,296	101
Slovenia	1,971,739	1,864,211	140
Solomon Islands	441,039	840,044	159
Somalia	6,841,695	15,192,344	92
South Africa	42,834,520	49,851,312	27
South Korea, Rep.	46,416,796	54,256,166	26
Spain	39,133,996	36,841,084	28
Sri Lanka	18,933,558	24,087,501	50
St. Kitts & Nevis	42,291	59,737	185
St. Lucia	152,335	202,605	173
St. Vincent and the Grenadines	119,818	151,154	176
Sudan	33,550,552	64,757,210	32
Suriname	427,980	459,991	161
Swaziland	966,462	1,589,457	151
Sweden	8,886,738	9,158,022	82
Switzerland	7,260,357	7,063,794	91
Syria	16,673,282	31,683,963	55
Taiwan	21,908,135	25,897,118	45
Tajikistan	6,020,095	9,634,047	95
Tanzania	30,608,769	50,660,932	34
Thailand	60,037,366	70,315,728	18
Togo	4,905,827	11,712,282	108
Tonga	108,207	132,642	177
Trinidad & Tobago	1,116,595	1,083,470	150
Tunisia	9,380,404	12,760,316	81

A2.1   Population: 1998, 2025 (projection) *(continued)*

Country	1998 (mid-year)	2025 (proj.)	Rank (by 1998)
Turkey	64,566,511	89,727,479	17
Turkmenistan	4,297,629	6,513,742	116
Tuvalu	10,444	15,475	191
Uganda	22,167,195	33,505,309	44
Ukraine	50,125,108	45,096,294	23
United Arab Emirates	2,303,088	3,443,758	137
United Kingdom	58,970,119	56,439,944	19
United States	270,311,758	335,359,714	3
Uruguay	3,284,841	3,916,227	128
Uzbekistan	23,784,321	34,348,391	40
Vanuatu	185,204	282,279	172
Venezuela	22,803,409	32,474,216	42
Vietnam	76,236,259	103,908,883	14
Yemen	16,387,963	40,438,981	56
Yugoslavia	10,526,135	10,551,826	70
Zambia	9,460,736	16,156,233	80
Zimbabwe	11,044,147	12,365,776	67

Note: Total population is the number of all residents regardless of legal status or citizenship, living within the boundaries of a country, in a given year. Refugees not permanently settled in the country of asylum are generally considered to be part of the population of their country of origin.

Source: World Bank, *World Development Indicators 1998,* Table 3.1; World Bank, *World Development Indicators 1998,* CD-ROM, Series: Population, total (SP.POP.TOTL); US Census International Database, http://www.census.gov/ipc/www/idbsum.html.

A2.2 Population: 1998, 2025 (projection)—Africa

Country	1998	2025 (proj.)	World Rank (by 1998)
Algeria	30,480,793	47,675,820	35
Angola	10,865,000	21,598,322	68
Benin	6,100,799	13,541,352	94
Botswana	1,448,454	1,633,683	144
Burkina Faso	11,266,393	21,360,037	65
Burundi	5,537,387	10,468,908	100
Cameroon	15,029,433	29,108,181	59
Cape Verde	399,857	531,633	163
Central African Republic	3,375,771	5,544,579	125
Chad	7,359,512	14,359,716	90
Comoros	545,528	1,160,486	157
Congo, Dem. Rep. (Zaire)	49,000,511	105,737,162	24
Congo, Rep.	2,658,123	4,246,447	131
Cote d'Ivoire	15,446,231	27,840,275	58
Egypt	66,050,004	97,431,183	16
Equatorial Guinea	454,001	876,225	158
Eritrea	3,842,436	8,437,639	117
Ethiopia	58,390,351	98,762,736	21
Gabon	1,207,844	1,799,727	147
Gambia	1,291,858	2,678,362	146
Ghana	18,497,206	28,191,005	53
Guinea	7,477,110	13,135,320	89
Guinea-Bissau	1,206,311	2,102,298	148
Kenya	28,337,071	34,773,605	37
Lesotho	2,089,829	2,724,163	138
Liberia	2,771,901	6,524,316	129
Libya	5,690,727	14,185,462	98
Madagascar	14,462,509	29,306,165	61
Malawi	9,840,474	10,911,225	77
Mali	10,108,569	22,646,955	75
Mauritania	2,511,473	5,445,945	134
Mauritius	1,168,256	1,488,342	149
Morocco	29,114,497	43,227,753	36
Mozambique	18,641,469	33,308,035	51
Namibia	1,622,328	2,309,815	143
Niger	9,671,848	20,423,708	79
Nigeria	110,532,242	203,423,396	10
Rwanda	7,956,172	12,158,817	86
Sao Tome and Principe	150,123	330,843	174
Senegal	9,723,149	22,456,276	78
Seychelles	78,641	90,959	180
Sierra Leone	5,080,004	11,010,156	107
Somalia	6,841,695	15,192,344	92
South Africa	42,834,520	49,851,312	27
Sudan	33,550,552	64,757,210	32
Swaziland	966,462	1,589,457	151
Tanzania	30,608,769	50,660,932	34
Togo	4,905,827	11,712,282	108
Tunisia	9,380,404	12,760,316	81
Uganda	22,167,195	33,505,309	44
Zambia	9,460,736	16,156,233	80
Zimbabwe	11,044,147	12,365,776	67

Note: Total population is the number of all residents regardless of legal status or citizenship, living within the boundaries of a country, in a given year. Refugees not permanently settled in the country of asylum are generally considered to be part of the population of their country of origin.

Source: World Bank, *World Development Indicators 1998,* Table 3.1; World Bank, *World Development Indicators 1998,* CD-ROM, Series: Population, total (SP.POP.TOTL); US Census International Database, http://www.census.gov/ipc/www/idbsum.html.

A2.3   Population: 1998, 2025 (projection)—Americas

Country	1998	2025 (proj.)	World Rank (by 1998)
Antigua and Barbuda	64,006	65,413	183
Argentina	36,265,463	48,351,219	31
Bahamas	279,833	368,670	167
Barbados	259,025	278,611	169
Belize	230,160	383,496	170
Bolivia	7,826,352	12,007,028	88
Brazil	169,806,557	209,586,835	5
Canada	30,675,398	37,987,471	33
Chile	14,787,781	17,942,290	60
Colombia	38,580,949	58,287,171	30
Costa Rica	3,604,642	5,327,331	120
Cuba	11,050,729	11,697,123	66
Dominica	65,777	66,962	181
Dominican Republic	7,998,766	11,780,544	85
Ecuador	12,336,572	17,799,981	62
El Salvador	5,752,067	8,381,567	97
Grenada	96,217	154,361	178
Guatemala	12,007,580	22,344,183	63
Guyana	707,954	710,266	154
Haiti	6,780,501	10,170,748	93
Honduras	5,861,955	8,612,256	96
Jamaica	2,634,678	3,354,566	132
Mexico	98,552,776	141,592,523	11
Nicaragua	4,583,379	8,112,068	111
Panama	2,735,943	3,796,038	130
Paraguay	5,291,020	9,929,121	103
Peru	26,111,110	39,157,814	38
St. Kitts & Nevis	42,291	59,737	185
St. Lucia	152,335	202,605	173
St. Vincent and the Grenadines	119,818	151,154	176
Suriname	427,980	459,991	161
Trinidad & Tobago	1,116,595	1,083,470	150
United States	270,311,758	335,359,714	3
Uruguay	3,284,841	3,916,227	128
Venezuela	22,803,409	32,474,216	42

Note: Total population is the number of all residents regardless of legal status or citizenship, living within the boundaries of a country, in a given year. Refugees not permanently settled in the country of asylum are generally considered to be part of the population of their country of origin.

Series: World Bank, *World Development Indicators 1998,* Table 3.1; World Bank, *World Development Indicators 1998,* CD-ROM, Series: Population, total (SP.POP.TOTL); US Census International Database, http://www.census.gov/ipc/www/idbsum.html.

A2.4   Population: 1998, 2025 (projection)—Asia and Oceania

Country	1998	2025 (proj.)	World Rank (by 1998)
Afghanistan	24,792,375	48,044,542	39
Australia	18,613,087	22,190,652	52
Azerbaijan	7,855,576	9,429,191	87
Bahrain	616,342	922,902	156
Bangladesh	127,567,002	180,560,502	8
Bhutan	1,908,307	3,340,681	142
Brunei	315,292	529,595	165
Cambodia	11,339,562	22,817,359	64
China	1,236,914,658	1,407,739,146	1
Djibouti	440,727	840,724	160
Fiji	802,611	1,084,937	152
India	984,003,683	1,408,320,301	2

A2.4 Population: 1998, 2025 (projection)—Asia and Oceania *(continued)*

Country	1998	2025 (proj.)	World Rank (by 1998)
Indonesia	212,941,810	287,985,072	4
Iran	68,959,931	111,891,148	15
Iraq	21,722,287	52,615,035	46
Israel	5,643,966	7,778,332	99
Japan	125,931,533	119,864,560	9
Jordan	4,434,978	8,222,996	114
Kazakhstan	16,846,808	18,564,593	54
Kiribati	83,976	98,764	179
Kuwait	1,913,285	3,558,774	141
Kyrgyzstan	4,522,281	6,066,461	112
Laos	5,260,842	9,804,562	104
Lebanon	3,505,794	4,831,388	122
Malaysia	20,932,901	34,248,134	48
Maldives	290,211	623,150	166
Marshall Islands	63,031	170,829	184
Micronesia	129,658	142,869	175
Mongolia	2,578,530	3,555,370	133
Myanmar (Burma)	47,305,319	68,106,967	25
Nauru	10,501	11,888	190
Nepal	23,698,421	42,576,135	41
New Zealand	3,625,388	4,445,272	118
North Korea, Dem. Rep.	21,234,387	26,054,682	47
Oman	2,363,591	5,307,157	136
Pakistan	135,135,195	211,675,333	7
Palau	18,110	21,259	189
Papua New Guinea	4,599,785	7,597,486	110
Philippines	77,725,862	120,519,345	13
Qatar	697,126	1,208,407	155
Samoa	224,713	367,080	171
Saudi Arabia	20,785,955	50,374,341	49
Singapore	3,490,356	4,230,872	123
Solomon Islands	441,039	840,044	159
South Korea, Rep.	46,416,796	54,256,166	26
Sri Lanka	18,933,558	24,087,501	50
Syria	16,673,282	31,683,963	55
Taiwan	21,908,135	25,897,118	45
Tajikistan	6,020,095	9,634,047	95
Thailand	60,037,366	70,315,728	18
Tonga	108,207	132,642	177
Turkey	64,566,511	89,727,479	17
Turkmenistan	4,297,629	6,513,742	116
Tuvalu	10,444	15,475	191
United Arab Emirates	2,303,088	3,443,758	137
Uzbekistan	23,784,321	34,348,391	40
Vanuatu	185,204	282,279	172
Vietnam	76,236,259	103,908,883	14
Yemen	16,387,963	40,438,981	56

Note: Total population is the number of all residents regardless of legal status or citizenship, living within the boundaries of a country, in a given year. Refugees not permanently settled in the country of asylum are generally considered to be part of the population of their country of origin.

Source: World Bank, *World Development Indicators 1998,* Table 3.1; World Bank, *World Development Indicators 1998,* CD-ROM, Series: Population, total (SP.POP.TOTL); US Census International Database, http://www.census.gov/ipc/www/idbsum.html.

A2.5   Population: 1998, 2025 (projection)—Europe

Country	1998	2025 (proj.)	World Rank (by 1998)
Albania	3,330,754	4,306,000	127
Andorra	64,716	88,229	182
Armenia	3,421,775	3,433,747	124
Austria	8,133,611	7,822,446	84
Belarus	10,409,050	10,248,170	71
Belgium	10,174,922	9,533,170	74
Bosnia and Herzegovina	3,365,727	3,470,613	126
Bulgaria	8,240,426	7,292,242	83
Croatia	4,671,584	4,348,133	109
Cyprus	748,982	967,114	153
Czech Republic	10,286,470	10,127,921	72
Denmark	5,333,617	5,333,705	102
Estonia	1,421,335	1,237,013	145
Finland	5,149,242	5,009,347	105
France	58,804,944	57,806,479	20
Georgia	5,108,527	4,718,035	106
Germany	82,079,454	75,372,295	12
Greece	10,662,138	10,473,429	69
Hungary	10,208,127	9,374,100	73
Iceland	271,033	298,018	168
Ireland	3,619,480	3,913,417	119
Italy	56,782,748	50,351,674	22
Latvia	2,385,396	1,964,902	135
Liechtenstein	31,717	36,052	187
Lithuania	3,600,158	3,417,198	121
Luxembourg	425,017	447,368	162
Macedonia, FYRO	2,009,387	2,171,241	139
Malta	379,563	390,832	164
Moldova	4,457,729	4,830,277	113
Monaco	32,035	33,832	186
Netherlands	15,731,112	15,851,599	57
Norway	4,419,955	4,591,906	115
Poland	38,606,922	40,116,796	29
Portugal	9,927,556	9,011,799	76
Romania	22,395,848	21,416,886	43
Russia	146,861,022	138,841,556	6
San Marino	24,894	27,034	188
Slovakia	5,392,982	5,718,296	101
Slovenia	1,971,739	1,864,211	140
Spain	39,133,996	36,841,084	28
Sweden	8,886,738	9,158,022	82
Switzerland	7,260,357	7,063,794	91
Ukraine	50,125,108	45,096,294	23
United Kingdom	58,970,119	56,439,944	19
Yugoslavia	10,526,135	10,551,826	70

Note: Total population is the number of all residents regardless of legal status or citizenship, living within the boundaries of a country, in a given year. Refugees not permanently settled in the country of asylum are generally considered to be part of the population of their country of origin.

Source: World Bank, *World Development Indicators 1998,* Table 3.1; World Bank, *World Development Indicators 1998,* CD-ROM, Series: Population, total (SP.POP.TOTL); US Census International Database, http://www.census.gov/ipc/www/idbsum.html.

A3.1 Population Density Summary—Comparison by Income Level per World Bank

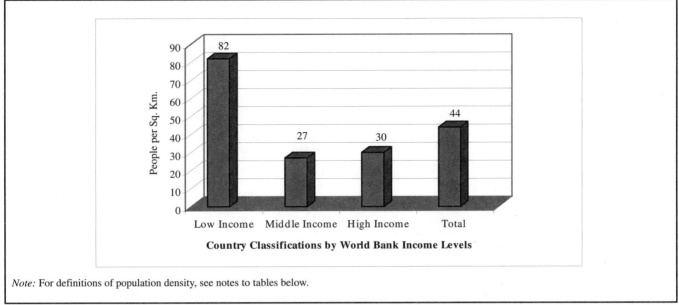

Note: For definitions of population density, see notes to tables below.

Source: World Bank, *World Development Indicators 1998,* Table 1.1

A3.2 Population Density, 1996—People per Sq. Km.

Country	People/Sq. Km.	Rank	Country	People/Sq. Km.	Rank
Afghanistan	37.1	114	Cape Verde	96.6	65
Albania	119.9	46	Central African Republic	5.4	166
Algeria	12.1	152	Chad	5.3	167
Andorra	na	na	Chile	19.3	137
Angola	8.9	159	China	130.3	42
Antigua and Barbuda	149.4	36	Colombia	36.1	116
Argentina	12.9	149	Comoros	226.3	28
Armenia	133.8	39	Congo, Dem. Rep. (Zaire)	20.0	136
Australia	2.4	175	Congo, Rep.	7.9	162
Austria	97.4	64	Costa Rica	67.4	81
Azerbaijan	87.5	68	Cote d'Ivoire	45.1	104
Bahamas	28.4	127	Croatia	85.3	69
Bahrain	868.1	4	Cuba	100.3	59
Bangladesh	934.7	3	Cyprus	80.1	72
Barbados	614.7	6	Czech Republic	133.5	40
Belarus	49.6	99	Denmark	124.0	45
Belgium	na	na	Djibouti	26.7	129
Belize	9.8	156	Dominica	98.2	62
Benin	50.9	98	Dominican Republic	164.6	34
Bhutan	15.2	143	Ecuador	42.3	107
Bolivia	7.0	164	Egypt	59.5	88
Bosnia and Herzegovina	na	Na	El Salvador	280.4	16
Botswana	2.6	174	Equatorial Guinea	14.6	144
Brazil	19.1	138	Eritrea	36.6	115
Brunei	54.9	94	Estonia	34.7	118
Bulgaria	75.6	79	Ethiopia	58.2	90
Burkina Faso	39.0	110	Fiji	44.0	106
Burundi	250.1	22	Finland	16.8	141
Cambodia	58.2	91	France	106.1	56
Cameroon	29.4	123	Gabon	4.4	168
Canada	3.2	170	Gambia	114.7	48

A3.2   Population Density, 1996—People per Sq. Km. *(continued)*

Country	People/Sq. Km.	Rank	Country	People/Sq. Km.	Rank
Georgia	77.6	77	Netherlands	457.5	9
Germany	234.5	26	New Zealand	13.6	148
Ghana	77.0	78	Nicaragua	37.1	113
Greece	81.3	71	Niger	7.4	163
Grenada	291.2	13	Nigeria	125.8	44
Guatemala	100.8	58	North Korea, Dem. Rep.	186.5	30
Guinea	27.5	128	Norway	14.3	145
Guinea-Bissau	38.9	111	Oman	10.2	154
Guyana	4.3	169	Pakistan	173.2	32
Haiti	266.2	19	Palau	na	na
Honduras	54.5	95	Panama	35.9	117
Hungary	110.4	52	Papua New Guinea	9.7	157
Iceland	2.7	173	Paraguay	12.5	150
India	317.9	12	Peru	19.0	139
Indonesia	108.8	53	Philippines	241.1	24
Iran	38.5	112	Poland	126.9	43
Iraq	48.9	100	Portugal	108.5	54
Ireland	52.6	97	Qatar	59.8	87
Israel	276.0	17	Romania	98.2	63
Italy	195.1	29	Russia	8.7	160
Jamaica	235.1	25	Rwanda	272.7	18
Japan	334.0	11	Samoa	60.7	85
Jordan	48.5	102	San Marino	na	na
Kazakhstan	6.2	165	Sao Tome and Principe	140.9	37
Kenya	48.1	103	Saudi Arabia	9.0	158
Kiribati	111.8	50	Senegal	44.3	105
Kuwait	89.2	66	Seychelles	170.4	33
Kyrgyzstan	23.9	131	Sierra Leone	64.6	83
Laos	20.5	135	Singapore	4990.2	1
Latvia	40.1	109	Slovakia	111.1	51
Lebanon	398.7	10	Slovenia	99.0	60
Lesotho	66.7	82	Solomon Islands	13.9	147
Liberia	29.2	124	Somalia	15.6	142
Libya	2.9	171	South Africa	30.8	120
Liechtenstein	na	na	South Korea, Rep.	461.3	8
Lithuania	57.2	92	Spain	78.6	74
Luxembourg	na	na	Sri Lanka	283.2	15
Macedonia, FYRO	77.9	75	St. Kitts & Nevis	113.6	49
Madagascar	23.6	132	St. Lucia	258.8	20
Malawi	106.5	55	St. Vincent and the Grenadines	286.4	14
Malaysia	62.6	84	Sudan	11.5	153
Maldives	851.8	5	Suriname	2.8	172
Mali	8.2	161	Swaziland	53.8	96
Malta	1165.6	2	Sweden	21.5	134
Marshall Islands	na	na	Switzerland	178.9	31
Mauritania	2.3	176	Syria	78.9	73
Mauritius	558.6	7	Taiwan	na	na
Mexico	48.8	101	Tajikistan	42.2	108
Micronesia	na	na	Tanzania	34.5	119
Moldova	131.2	41	Thailand	117.4	47
Monaco	na	na	Togo	77.8	76
Mongolia	1.6	178	Tonga	135.3	38
Morocco	60.5	86	Trinidad & Tobago	252.8	21
Mozambique	23.0	133	Tunisia	58.8	89
Myanmar (Burma)	69.8	80	Turkey	81.5	70
Namibia	1.9	177	Turkmenistan	9.8	155
Nauru	na	na	Tuvalu	na	na
Nepal	154.1	35	Uganda	98.9	61

A3.2 Population Density, 1996—People per Sq. Km. *(continued)*

Country	People/Sq. Km.	Rank	Country	People/Sq. Km.	Rank
Ukraine	87.5	67	Venezuela	25.3	130
United Arab Emirates	30.3	121	Vietnam	231.5	27
United Kingdom	243.3	23	Yemen	29.9	122
United States	29.0	126	Yugoslavia	103.7	57
Uruguay	18.3	140	Zambia	12.4	151
Uzbekistan	56.1	93	Zimbabwe	29.1	125
Vanuatu	14.2	146			

Note: Population density is midyear population divided by land area in square kilometers. Total population is based on the de facto definition of population, which counts all residents regardless of legal status or citizenship. Refugees not permanently settled in the country of asylum are generally considered to be part of the population of their country of origin. Land area is a country's total area, excluding area under inland water bodies. In most cases the definition of inland water bodies includes major rivers and lakes.

Source: World Bank, *World Development Indicators 1998,* Table 1.6; US Census International, http://www.census.gov/cgi-bin/ipc/idbsprd

A3.3 Population Density, Africa, 1996—People per Sq. Km.

Country	Population Density, 1996	World Rank	Country	Population Density, 1996	World Rank
Algeria	12.1	152	Libya	2.9	171
Angola	8.9	159	Madagascar	23.6	132
Benin	50.9	98	Malawi	106.5	55
Botswana	2.6	174	Mali	8.2	161
Burkina Faso	39.0	110	Mauritania	2.3	176
Burundi	250.1	22	Mauritius	558.6	7
Cameroon	29.4	123	Morocco	60.5	86
Cape Verde	96.6	65	Mozambique	23.0	133
Central African Republic	5.4	166	Namibia	1.9	177
Chad	5.3	167	Niger	7.4	163
Comoros	226.3	28	Nigeria	125.8	44
Congo, Dem. Rep. (Zaire)	20.0	136	Rwanda	272.7	18
Congo, Rep.	7.9	162	Sao Tome and Principe	140.9	37
Cote d'Ivoire	45.1	104	Senegal	44.3	105
Egypt	59.5	88	Seychelles	170.4	33
Equatorial Guinea	14.6	144	Sierra Leone	64.6	83
Eritrea	36.6	115	Somalia	15.6	142
Ethiopia	58.2	90	South Africa	30.8	120
Gabon	4.4	168	Sudan	11.5	153
Gambia	114.7	48	Swaziland	53.8	96
Ghana	77.0	78	Tanzania	34.5	119
Guinea	27.5	128	Togo	77.8	76
Guinea-Bissau	38.9	111	Tunisia	58.8	89
Kenya	48.1	103	Uganda	98.9	61
Lesotho	66.7	82	Zambia	12.4	151
Liberia	29.2	124	Zimbabwe	29.1	125

Note: Population density is midyear population divided by land area in square kilometers. Total population is based on the de facto definition of population, which counts all residents regardless of legal status or citizenship. Refugees not permanently settled in the country of asylum are generally considered to be part of the population of their country of origin. Land area is a country's total area, excluding area under inland water bodies. In most cases the definition of inland water bodies includes major rivers and lakes.

Source: World Bank, *World Development Indicators 1998,* Table 1.6; US Census International, http://www.census.gov/cgi-bin/ipc/idbsprd

A3.4   Population Density, Americas, 1996—People per Sq. Km.

Country	Population Density, 1996	World Rank	Country	Population Density, 1996	World Rank
Antigua and Barbuda	149.4	36	Guatemala	100.8	58
Argentina	12.9	149	Guyana	4.3	169
Bahamas	28.4	127	Haiti	266.2	19
Barbados	614.7	6	Honduras	54.5	95
Belize	9.8	156	Jamaica	235.1	25
Bolivia	7.0	164	Mexico	48.8	101
Brazil	19.1	138	Nicaragua	37.1	113
Canada	3.2	170	Panama	35.9	117
Chile	19.3	137	Paraguay	12.5	150
Colombia	36.1	116	Peru	19.0	139
Costa Rica	67.4	81	St. Kitts & Nevis	113.6	49
Cuba	100.3	59	St. Lucia	258.8	20
Dominica	98.2	62	St. Vincent and the Grenadines	286.4	14
Dominican Republic	164.6	34	Suriname	2.8	172
Ecuador	42.3	107	Trinidad & Tobago	252.8	21
El Salvador	280.4	16	United States	29.0	126
Grenada	291.2	13	Uruguay	18.3	140
			Venezuela	25.3	130

Note: Population density is midyear population divided by land area in square kilometers. Total population is based on the de facto definition of population, which counts all residents regardless of legal status or citizenship. Refugees not permanently settled in the country of asylum are generally considered to be part of the population of their country of origin. Land area is a country's total area, excluding area under inland water bodies. In most cases the definition of inland water bodies includes major rivers and lakes.

Source: World Bank, *World Development Indicators 1998,* Table 1.6; US Census International, http://www.census.gov/cgi-bin/ipc/idbsprd

A3.5 Population Density, Asia and Oceania, 1996—People per Sq. Km.

Country	Population Density, 1996	World Rank	Country	Population Density, 1996	World Rank
Afghanistan	37.1	114	Nauru	na	na
Australia	2.4	175	Nepal	154.1	35
Azerbaijan	87.5	68	New Zealand	13.6	148
Bahrain	868.1	4	North Korea, Dem. Rep.	186.5	30
Bangladesh	934.7	3	Oman	10.2	154
Bhutan	15.2	143	Pakistan	173.2	32
Brunei	54.9	94	Palau	na	na
Cambodia	58.2	91	Papua New Guinea	9.7	157
China	130.3	42	Philippines	241.1	24
Djibouti	26.7	129	Qatar	59.8	87
Fiji	44.0	106	Samoa	60.7	85
India	317.9	12	Saudi Arabia	9.0	158
Indonesia	108.8	53	Singapore	4990.2	1
Iran	38.5	112	Solomon Islands	13.9	147
Iraq	48.9	100	South Korea, Rep.	461.3	8
Israel	276.0	17	Sri Lanka	283.2	15
Japan	334.0	11	Syria	78.9	73
Jordan	48.5	102	Taiwan	na	na
Kazakhstan	6.2	165	Tajikistan	42.2	108
Kiribati	111.8	50	Thailand	117.4	47
Kuwait	89.2	66	Tonga	135.3	38
Kyrgyzstan	23.9	131	Turkey	81.5	70
Laos	20.5	135	Turkmenistan	9.8	155
Lebanon	398.7	10	Tuvalu	na	na
Malaysia	62.6	84	United Arab Emirates	30.3	121
Maldives	851.8	5	Uzbekistan	56.1	93
Marshall Islands	na	na	Vanuatu	14.2	146
Micronesia	na	na	Vietnam	231.5	27
Mongolia	1.6	178	Yemen	29.9	122
Myanmar (Burma)	69.8	80			

Note: Population density is midyear population divided by land area in square kilometers. Total population is based on the de facto definition of population, which counts all residents regardless of legal status or citizenship. Refugees not permanently settled in the country of asylum are generally considered to be part of the population of their country of origin. Land area is a country's total area, excluding area under inland water bodies. In most cases the definition of inland water bodies includes major rivers and lakes.

Source: World Bank, *World Development Indicators 1998*, Table 1.6; US Census International, http://www.census.gov/cgi-bin/ipc/idbsprd

A3.6 Population Density, Europe, 1996—People per Sq. Km.

Country	Population Density, 1996	World Rank	Country	Population Density, 1996	World Rank
Albania	119.9	46	Liechtenstein	na	na
Andorra	na	na	Lithuania	57.2	92
Armenia	133.8	39	Luxembourg	na	na
Austria	97.4	64	Macedonia, FYRO	77.9	75
Belarus	49.6	99	Malta	1165.6	2
Belgium	na	na	Moldova	131.2	41
Bosnia and Herzegovina	na	na	Monaco	na	na
Bulgaria	75.6	79	Netherlands	457.5	9
Croatia	85.3	69	Norway	14.3	145
Cyprus	80.1	72	Poland	126.9	43
Czech Republic	133.5	40	Portugal	108.5	54
Denmark	124.0	45	Romania	98.2	63
Estonia	34.7	118	Russia	8.7	160
Finland	16.8	141	San Marino	na	Na
France	106.1	56	Slovakia	111.1	51
Georgia	77.6	77	Slovenia	99.0	60
Germany	234.5	26	Spain	78.6	74
Greece	81.3	71	Sweden	21.5	134
Hungary	110.4	52	Switzerland	178.9	31
Iceland	2.7	173	Ukraine	87.5	67
Ireland	52.6	97	United Kingdom	243.3	23
Italy	195.1	29	Yugoslavia	103.7	57
Latvia	40.1	109			

Note: Population density is midyear population divided by land area in square kilometers. Total population is based on the de facto definition of population, which counts all residents regardless of legal status or citizenship. Refugees not permanently settled in the country of asylum are generally considered to be part of the population of their country of origin. Land area is a country's total area, excluding area under inland water bodies. In most cases the definition of inland water bodies includes major rivers and lakes.

A4.1 Gross National Product, 1996 Summary—Comparison by Income Level per World Bank

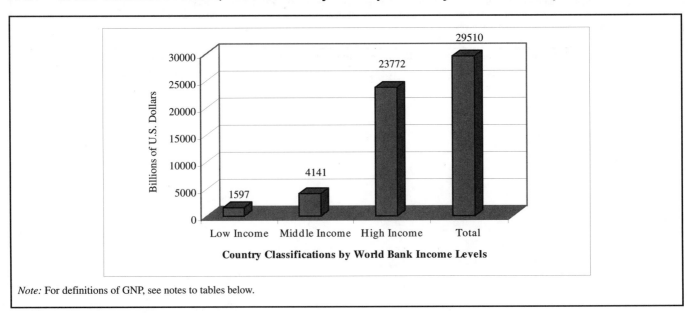

Note: For definitions of GNP, see notes to tables below.

Source: World Bank, *World Development Indicators 1998,* Table 1.1

A4.2 Gross National Product (GNP), 1996—Billions of U.S. Dollars

Country	GNP	Rank	Country	GNP	Rank
Afghanistan	na	na	Finland	119.1	30
Albania	2.7	105	France	1,533.6	4
Algeria	43.7	47	Gabon	4.4	93
Andorra	na	na	Gambia	na	na
Angola	3.0	104	Georgia	4.6	91
Antigua and Barbuda	0.5	134	Germany	2,364.6	3
Argentina	295.1	18	Ghana	6.2	81
Armenia	2.4	108	Greece	120.0	29
Australia	367.8	13	Grenada	0.3	139
Austria	226.5	21	Guatemala	16.0	64
Azerbaijan	3.6	99	Guinea	3.8	98
Bahamas	na	na	Guinea-Bissau	0.3	140
Bahrain	na	na	Guyana	0.6	132
Bangladesh	31.2	50	Haiti	2.3	111
Barbados	na	na	Honduras	4.0	97
Belarus	22.5	53	Hungary	44.3	46
Belgium	268.6	19	Iceland	7.2	77
Belize	0.6	131	India	357.8	14
Benin	2.0	112	Indonesia	213.4	22
Bhutan	0.3	138	Iran	na	na
Bolivia	6.3	80	Iraq	na	na
Bosnia and Herzegovina	na	na	Ireland	62.0	41
Botswana	na	na	Israel	90.3	33
Brazil	709.6	8	Italy	1,140.5	6
Brunei	na	na	Jamaica	4.1	96
Bulgaria	9.9	68	Japan	5,149.2	2
Burkina Faso	2.4	109	Jordan	7.1	78
Burundi	1.1	124	Kazakhstan	22.2	54
Cambodia	3.1	103	Kenya	8.7	73
Cameroon	8.4	75	Kiribati	0.1	151
Canada	569.9	9	Kuwait	na	na
Cape Verde	0.4	136	Kyrgyzstan	2.5	106
Central African Republic	1.0	127	Laos	1.9	115
Chad	1.0	128	Latvia	5.7	85
Chile	70.1	37	Lebanon	12.1	67
China	906.1	7	Lesotho	1.3	121
Colombia	80.2	36	Liberia	na	na
Comoros	0.2	144	Libya	na	na
Congo, Dem. Rep. (Zaire)	5.7	84	Liechtenstein	na	na
Congo, Rep.	1.8	117	Lithuania	8.5	74
Costa Rica	9.1	71	Luxembourg	18.9	56
Cote d'Ivoire	9.4	70	Macedonia, FYRO	2.0	113
Croatia	18.1	60	Madagascar	3.4	101
Cuba	na	na	Malawi	1.8	118
Cyprus	na	na	Malaysia	89.8	34
Czech Republic	48.9	45	Maldives	0.3	141
Denmark	168.9	25	Mali	2.4	110
Djibouti	na	na	Malta	na	na
Dominica	na	na	Marshall Islands	0.1	152
Dominican Republic	12.8	66	Mauritania	1.1	125
Ecuador	17.5	62	Mauritius	4.2	95
Egypt	64.3	39	Mexico	341.7	16
El Salvador	9.9	69	Micronesia	0.2	146
Equatorial Guinea	0.2	145	Moldova	2.5	107
Eritrea	na	na	Monaco	na	na
Estonia	4.5	92	Mongolia	0.9	129
Ethiopia	6.0	82	Morocco	34.9	49
Fiji	na	na	Mozambique	1.5	120

A4.2 Gross National Product (GNP), 1996—Billions of U.S. Dollars *(continued)*

Country	GNP	Rank	Country	GNP	Rank
Myanmar (Burma)	na	na	South Korea, Rep.	483.1	11
Namibia	3.6	100	Spain	563.2	10
Nauru	na	na	Sri Lanka	13.5	65
Nepal	4.7	90	St. Kitts & Nevis	0.2	148
Netherlands	402.6	12	St. Lucia	0.6	133
New Zealand	57.1	44	St. Vincent and the Grenadines	0.3	143
Nicaragua	1.7	119	Sudan	na	na
Niger	1.9	116	Suriname	0.4	137
Nigeria	27.6	51	Swaziland	1.1	126
North Korea, Dem. Rep.	na	na	Sweden	227.3	20
Norway	151.2	26	Switzerland	313.7	17
Oman	na	na	Syria	16.8	63
Pakistan	63.6	40	Taiwan	na	na
Palau	na	na	Tajikistan	2.0	114
Panama	8.2	76	Tanzania	5.2	86
Papua New Guinea	5.0	87	Thailand	177.5	23
Paraguay	9.0	72	Togo	1.3	123
Peru	58.7	43	Tonga	0.2	149
Philippines	83.3	35	Trinidad & Tobago	5.0	88
Poland	124.7	28	Tunisia	17.6	61
Portugal	100.9	31	Turkey	177.5	24
Qatar	na	na	Turkmenistan	4.3	94
Romania	36.2	48	Tuvalu	na	na
Russia	356.0	15	Uganda	5.8	83
Rwanda	1.3	122	Ukraine	60.9	42
Samoa	0.2	147	United Arab Emirates	na	na
San Marino	na	na	United Kingdom	1,152.1	5
Sao Tome and Principe	0.1	153	United States	7,433.5	1
Saudi Arabia	na	na	Uruguay	18.5	57
Senegal	4.9	89	Uzbekistan	23.5	52
Seychelles	0.5	135	Vanuatu	0.2	150
Sierra Leone	0.9	130	Vatican City	na	na
Singapore	93.0	32	Venezuela	67.3	38
Slovakia	18.2	58	Vietnam	21.9	55
Slovenia	18.2	59	Yemen	na	na
Solomon Islands	0.3	142	Yugoslavia	na	na
Somalia	na	na	Zambia	3.4	102
South Africa	132.5	27	Zimbabwe	6.8	79

Note: Gross National Product (GNP) is the sum of gross value added by all resident producers plus any taxes (less subsidies) that are not included in the valuation of output plus net receipts of primary income (employee compensation and property income) from nonresident sources.

Source: World Bank, *World Development Indicators 1998*, Table 1.1; World Bank, *World Development Indicators 1998*, CD-ROM, 1 Series: GNP (NY.GNP.KD.87)

A4.3   Gross National Product (GNP), 1996, Africa—Billions of U.S. Dollars

Country	1996	World Rank	Country	1996	World Rank
Algeria	43.7	47	Libya	na	na
Angola	3.0	104	Madagascar	3.4	101
Benin	2.0	112	Malawi	1.8	118
Botswana	na	na	Mali	2.4	110
Burkina Faso	2.4	109	Mauritania	1.1	125
Burundi	1.1	124	Mauritius	4.2	95
Cameroon	8.4	75	Morocco	34.9	49
Cape Verde	0.4	136	Mozambique	1.5	120
Central African Republic	1.0	127	Namibia	3.6	100
Chad	1.0	128	Niger	1.9	116
Comoros	0.2	144	Nigeria	27.6	51
Congo, Dem. Rep. (Zaire)	5.7	84	Rwanda	1.3	122
Congo, Rep.	1.8	117	Sao Tome and Principe	0.1	153
Cote d'Ivoire	9.4	70	Senegal	4.9	89
Egypt	64.3	39	Seychelles	0.5	135
Equatorial Guinea	0.2	145	Sierra Leone	0.9	130
Eritrea	na	na	Somalia	na	na
Ethiopia	6.0	82	South Africa	132.5	27
Gabon	4.4	93	Sudan	na	na
Gambia	na	na	Swaziland	1.1	126
Ghana	6.2	81	Tanzania	5.2	86
Guinea	3.8	98	Togo	1.3	123
Guinea-Bissau	0.3	140	Tunisia	17.6	61
Kenya	8.7	73	Uganda	5.8	83
Lesotho	1.3	121	Zambia	3.4	102
Liberia	na	na	Zimbabwe	6.8	79

Note: Gross National Product (GNP) is the sum of gross value added by all resident producers plus any taxes (less subsidies) that are not included in the valuation of output plus net receipts of primary income (employee compensation and property income) from nonresident sources.

Source: World Bank, *World Development Indicators 1998,* Table 1.1; World Bank, *World Development Indicators 1998,* CD-ROM, 1 Series: GNP (NY.GNP.KD.87)

A4.4   Gross National Product (GNP), 1996, Americas—Billions of U.S. Dollars

Country	1996	World Rank	Country	1996	World Rank
Antigua and Barbuda	0.5	134	Guyana	0.6	132
Argentina	295.1	18	Haiti	2.3	111
Bahamas	na	na	Honduras	4.0	97
Barbados	na	na	Jamaica	4.1	96
Belize	0.6	131	Mexico	341.7	16
Bolivia	6.3	80	Nicaragua	1.7	119
Brazil	709.6	8	Panama	8.2	76
Canada	569.9	9	Paraguay	9.0	72
Chile	70.1	37	Peru	58.7	43
Colombia	80.2	36	St. Kitts & Nevis	0.2	148
Costa Rica	9.1	71	St. Lucia	0.6	133
Cuba	na	na	St. Vincent and the Grenadines	0.3	143
Dominica	na	na	Suriname	0.4	137
Dominican Republic	12.8	66	Trinidad & Tobago	5.0	88
Ecuador	17.5	62	United States	7,433.5	1
El Salvador	9.9	69	Uruguay	18.5	57
Grenada	0.3	139	Venezuela	67.3	38
Guatemala	16.0	64			

Note: Gross National Product (GNP) is the sum of gross value added by all resident producers plus any taxes (less subsidies) that are not included in the valuation of output plus net receipts of primary income (employee compensation and property income) from nonresident sources.

Source: World Bank, *World Development Indicators 1998,* Table 1.1; World Bank, *World Development Indicators 1998,* CD-ROM, 1 Series: GNP (NY.GNP.KD.87)

A4.5   Gross National Product (GNP), 1996, Asia and Oceania—Billions of U.S. Dollars

Country	1996	World Rank	Country	1996	World Rank
Afghanistan	na	na	Nauru	na	Na
Australia	367.8	13	Nepal	4.7	90
Azerbaijan	3.6	99	New Zealand	57.1	44
Bahrain	na	na	North Korea, Dem. Rep.	na	na
Bangladesh	31.2	50	Oman	na	na
Bhutan	0.3	138	Pakistan	63.6	40
Brunei	na	na	Palau	na	na
Cambodia	3.1	103	Papua New Guinea	5.0	87
China	906.1	7	Philippines	83.3	35
Djibouti	na	na	Qatar	na	na
Fiji	na	na	Samoa	0.2	147
India	357.8	14	Saudi Arabia	na	na
Indonesia	213.4	22	Singapore	93.0	32
Iran	na	na	Solomon Islands	0.3	142
Iraq	na	na	South Korea, Rep.	483.1	11
Israel	90.3	33	Sri Lanka	13.5	65
Japan	5,149.2	2	Syria	16.8	63
Jordan	7.1	78	Taiwan	na	na
Kazakhstan	22.2	54	Tajikistan	2.0	114
Kiribati	0.1	151	Thailand	177.5	23
Kuwait	na	na	Tonga	0.2	149
Kyrgyzstan	2.5	106	Turkey	177.5	24
Laos	1.9	115	Turkmenistan	4.3	94
Lebanon	12.1	67	Tuvalu	na	na
Malaysia	89.8	34	United Arab Emirates	na	na
Maldives	0.3	141	Uzbekistan	23.5	52
Marshall Islands	0.1	152	Vanuatu	0.2	150
Micronesia	0.2	146	Vietnam	21.9	55
Mongolia	0.9	129	Yemen	na	na
Myanmar (Burma)	na	na			

Note: Gross National Product (GNP) is the sum of gross value added by all resident producers plus any taxes (less subsidies) that are not included in the valuation of output plus net receipts of primary income (employee compensation and property income) from nonresident sources.

Source: World Bank, *World Development Indicators 1998,* Table 1.1; World Bank, *World Development Indicators 1998,* CD-ROM, 1 Series: GNP (NY.GNP.KD.87)

A4.6 Gross National Product (GNP), 1996, Europe—Billions of U.S. Dollars

Country	1996	World Rank	Country	1996	World Rank
Albania	2.7	105	Liechtenstein	na	na
Andorra	na	na	Lithuania	8.5	74
Armenia	2.4	108	Luxembourg	18.9	56
Austria	226.5	21	Macedonia, FYRO	2.0	113
Belarus	22.5	53	Malta	na	na
Belgium	268.6	19	Moldova	2.5	107
Bosnia and Herzegovina	na	na	Monaco	na	na
Bulgaria	9.9	68	Netherlands	402.6	12
Croatia	18.1	60	Norway	151.2	26
Cyprus	na	na	Poland	124.7	28
Czech Republic	48.9	45	Portugal	100.9	31
Denmark	168.9	25	Romania	36.2	48
Estonia	4.5	92	Russia	356.0	15
Finland	119.1	30	San Marino	na	na
France	1,533.6	4	Slovakia	18.2	58
Georgia	4.6	91	Slovenia	18.2	59
Germany	2,364.6	3	Spain	563.2	10
Greece	120.0	29	Sweden	227.3	20
Hungary	44.3	46	Switzerland	313.7	17
Iceland	7.2	77	Ukraine	60.9	42
Ireland	62.0	41	United Kingdom	1,152.1	5
Italy	1,140.5	6	Yugoslavia	na	na
Latvia	5.7	85			

Note: Gross National Product (GNP) is the sum of gross value added by all resident producers plus any taxes (less subsidies) that are not included in the valuation of output plus net receipts of primary income (employee compensation and property income) from nonresident sources.

Source: World Bank, *World Development Indicators 1998*, Table 1.1; World Bank, *World Development Indicators 1998*, CD-ROM, 1 Series: GNP (NY.GNP.KD.87)

A5.1   Gross National Product (GNP) per Capita, 1996—U.S. Dollars (Constant Valuation Based on 1987)

Country	GNP 1996	World Rank	Country	GNP 1996	World Rank
Afghanistan	na	na	Fiji	1,937	50
Albania	na	na	Finland	18,394	10
Algeria	2,278	44	France	18,146	12
Andorra	na	na	Gabon	3,954	27
Angola	465	102	Gambia	na	na
Antigua and Barbuda	5,323	25	Georgia	na	na
Argentina	3,828	28	Germany	na	na
Armenia	311	117	Ghana	420	105
Australia	14,408	17	Greece	6,580	22
Austria	18,196	11	Grenada	1,928	52
Azerbaijan	384	110	Guatemala	901	77
Bahamas	na	na	Guinea	420	106
Bahrain	na	na	Guinea-Bissau	219	126
Bangladesh	209	128	Guyana	437	104
Barbados	na	na	Haiti	162	132
Belarus	1,697	61	Honduras	868	79
Belgium	16,961	13	Hungary	2,259	45
Belize	2,034	46	Iceland	21,558	6
Benin	362	113	India	454	103
Bhutan	531	96	Indonesia	727	85
Bolivia	787	81	Iran	3,054	34
Bosnia and Herzegovina	na	na	Iraq	na	na
Botswana	na	na	Ireland	8,826	21
Brazil	2,028	47	Israel	na	na
Brunei	na	na	Italy	15,185	15
Bulgaria	2,394	43	Jamaica	1,346	64
Burkina Faso	264	120	Japan	25,244	4
Burundi	154	135	Jordan	1,914	53
Cambodia	na	na	Kazakhstan	976	71
Cameroon	674	87	Kenya	370	111
Canada	15,597	14	Kiribati	676	86
Cape Verde	333	114	Kuwait	na	na
Central African Republic	364	112	Kyrgyzstan	257	121
Chad	162	131	Laos	400	108
Chile	2,635	39	Latvia	1,932	51
China	520	99	Lebanon	na	na
Colombia	1,331	65	Lesotho	485	101
Comoros	415	107	Liberia	na	na
Congo, Dem. Rep. (Zaire)	95	137	Libya	na	na
Congo, Rep.	778	83	Liechtenstein	na	na
Costa Rica	1,835	56	Lithuania	1,940	49
Cote d'Ivoire	780	82	Luxembourg	30,245	1
Croatia	na	na	Macedonia, FYRO	na	na
Cuba	na	na	Madagascar	200	129
Cyprus	na	na	Malawi	160	133
Czech Republic	3,648	30	Malaysia	3,108	33
Denmark	22,120	5	Maldives	634	91
Djibouti	na	na	Mali	255	122
Dominica	na	na	Malta	na	na
Dominican Republic	954	72	Marshall Islands	na	na
Ecuador	1,157	67	Mauritania	487	100
Egypt	987	70	Mauritius	2,642	38
El Salvador	996	69	Mexico	1,823	58
Equatorial Guinea	817	80	Micronesia	na	na
Eritrea	na	na	Moldova	na	na
Estonia	2,834	36	Monaco	na	na
Ethiopia	164	130	Mongolia	na	na

A5.1 Gross National Product (GNP) per Capita, 1996—U.S. Dollars (Constant Valuation Based on 1987) *(continued)*

Country	GNP 1996	World Rank	Country	GNP 1996	World Rank
Morocco	928	73	South Africa	2,419	42
Mozambique	121	136	South Korea, Rep.	5,898	23
Myanmar (Burma)	na	na	Spain	9,183	20
Namibia	1,824	57	Sri Lanka	520	98
Nauru	na	na	St. Kitts & Nevis	3,669	29
Nepal	216	127	St. Lucia	2,687	37
Netherlands	18,434	9	St. Vincent and the Grenadines	1,790	60
New Zealand	9,214	19	Sudan	na	na
Nicaragua	771	84	Suriname	na	na
Niger	268	119	Swaziland	923	75
Nigeria	301	118	Sweden	20,231	8
North Korea, Dem. Rep.	na	na	Switzerland	28,046	2
Norway	25,431	3	Syria	1,262	66
Oman	na	na	Taiwan	na	na
Pakistan	387	109	Tajikistan	228	124
Palau	na	na	Tanzania	na	na
Panama	2,624	40	Thailand	1,855	55
Papua New Guinea	1,001	68	Togo	321	116
Paraguay	926	74	Tonga	901	76
Peru	323	115	Trinidad & Tobago	3,544	31
Philippines	659	88	Tunisia	1,362	63
Poland	1,795	59	Turkey	1,965	48
Portugal	5,351	24	Turkmenistan	na	na
Qatar	na	na	Tuvalu	na	na
Romania	1,400	62	Uganda	586	94
Russia	1,875	54	Ukraine	522	97
Rwanda	220	125	United Arab Emirates	na	na
Samoa	646	90	United Kingdom	13,722	18
San Marino	na	na	United States	20,934	7
Sao Tome and Principe	na	na	Uruguay	2,878	35
Saudi Arabia	na	na	Uzbekistan	587	93
Senegal	648	89	Vanuatu	876	78
Seychelles	4,578	26	Vatican City	na	na
Sierra Leone	156	134	Venezuela	2,499	41
Singapore	14,787	16	Vietnam	na	na
Slovakia	3,251	32	Yemen	na	na
Slovenia	na	na	Yugoslavia	na	na
Solomon Islands	598	92	Zambia	241	123
Somalia	na	na	Zimbabwe	582	95

Note: Gross National Product (GNP) per capita is the gross national product divided by the midyear population. GNP is the sum of the gross value added by all resident producers plus any taxes (less subsidies) that are not included in the valuation of output plus net receipts of primary income (employee compensation and property income) from nonresident sources. Data are in constant 1987 U.S. dollars, reflecting adjustments to level out the effects of inflation.

Source: World Bank, *World Development Indicators 1998,* Table 1.1; World Bank, *World Development Indicators 1998,* CD-ROM, l Series: GNP per capita (constant 1987 US$) (NY.GNP.PCAP.KD.87)

A5.2   Gross National Product (GNP) per Capita, 1996, Africa—U.S. Dollars (Constant Valuation Based on 1987)

Country	GNP 1996	World Rank	Country	GNP 1996	World Rank
Algeria	2,278	44	Libya	na	na
Angola	465	102	Madagascar	200	129
Benin	362	113	Malawi	160	133
Botswana	na	na	Mali	255	122
Burkina Faso	264	120	Mauritania	487	100
Burundi	154	135	Mauritius	2,642	38
Cameroon	674	87	Morocco	928	73
Cape Verde	333	114	Mozambique	121	136
Central African Republic	364	112	Namibia	1,824	57
Chad	162	131	Niger	268	119
Comoros	415	107	Nigeria	301	118
Congo, Dem. Rep. (Zaire)	95	137	Rwanda	220	125
Congo, Rep.	778	83	Sao Tome and Principe	na	na
Cote d'Ivoire	780	82	Senegal	648	89
Egypt	987	70	Seychelles	4,578	26
Equatorial Guinea	817	80	Sierra Leone	156	134
Eritrea	na	na	Somalia	na	na
Ethiopia	164	130	South Africa	2,419	42
Gabon	3,954	27	Sudan	na	na
Gambia	na	na	Swaziland	923	75
Ghana	420	105	Tanzania	na	na
Guinea	420	106	Togo	321	116
Guinea-Bissau	219	126	Tunisia	1,362	63
Kenya	370	111	Uganda	586	94
Lesotho	485	101	Zambia	241	123
Liberia	na	na	Zimbabwe	582	95

Note: Gross National Product (GNP) per capita is the gross national product divided by the midyear population. GNP is the sum of the gross value added by all resident producers plus any taxes (less subsidies) that are not included in the valuation of output plus net receipts of primary income (employee compensation and property income) from nonresident sources. Data are in constant 1987 U.S. dollars, reflecting adjustments to level out the effects of inflation.

Source: World Bank, *World Development Indicators 1998,* Table 1.1; World Bank, *World Development Indicators 1998,* CD-ROM, 1 Series: GNP per capita (constant 1987 US $) (NY.GNP.PCAP.KD.87)

A5.3 Gross National Product (GNP) per Capita, 1996, Americas—U.S. Dollars (Constant Valuation Based on 1987)

Country	GNP 1996	World Rank	Country	GNP 1996	World Rank
Antigua and Barbuda	5,323	25	Guyana	437	104
Argentina	3,828	28	Haiti	162	132
Bahamas	na	na	Honduras	868	79
Barbados	na	na	Jamaica	1,346	64
Belize	2,034	46	Mexico	1,823	58
Bolivia	787	81	Nicaragua	771	84
Brazil	2,028	47	Panama	2,624	40
Canada	15,597	14	Paraguay	926	74
Chile	2,635	39	Peru	323	115
Colombia	1,331	65	St. Kitts & Nevis	3,669	29
Costa Rica	1,835	56	St. Lucia	2,687	37
Cuba	na	na	St. Vincent and the Grenadines	1,790	60
Dominica	na	na	Suriname	na	na
Dominican Republic	954	72	Trinidad & Tobago	3,544	31
Ecuador	1,157	67	United States	20,934	7
El Salvador	996	69	Uruguay	2,878	35
Grenada	1,928	52	Venezuela	2,499	41
Guatemala	901	77			

Note: Gross National Product (GNP) per capita is the gross national product divided by the midyear population. GNP is the sum of the gross value added by all resident producers plus any taxes (less subsidies) that are not included in the valuation of output plus net receipts of primary income (employee compensation and property income) from nonresident sources. Data are in constant 1987 U.S. dollars, reflecting adjustments to level out the effects of inflation.

Source: World Bank, *World Development Indicators 1998,* Table 1.1; World Bank, *World Development Indicators 1998,* CD-ROM, 1 Series: GNP per capita (constant 1987 US $) (NY.GNP.PCAP.KD.87)

A5.4   Gross National Product (GNP) per Capita, 1996, Asia and Oceania—U.S. Dollars (Constant Valuation Based on 1987)

Country	GNP 1996	World Rank	Country	GNP 1996	World Rank
Afghanistan	na	na	Nauru	na	na
Australia	14,408	17	Nepal	216	127
Azerbaijan	384	110	New Zealand	9,214	19
Bahrain	na	na	North Korea, Dem. Rep.	na	Na
Bangladesh	209	128	Oman	na	na
Bhutan	531	96	Pakistan	387	109
Brunei	na	na	Palau	na	na
China	520	99	Papua New Guinea	1,001	68
Djibouti	na	na	Philippines	659	88
Fiji	1,937	50	Qatar	na	na
India	454	103	Samoa	646	90
Indonesia	727	85	Saudi Arabia	na	na
Iran	3,054	34	Singapore	14,787	16
Iraq	na	na	Solomon Islands	598	92
Israel	15,870	20	South Korea, Rep.	5,898	23
Japan	25,244	4	Sri Lanka	520	98
Jordan	1,914	53	Syria	1,262	66
Kazakhstan	976	71	Taiwan	na	na
Kiribati	676	86	Tajikistan	228	124
Kuwait	na	na	Thailand	1,855	55
Kyrgyzstan	257	121	Tonga	901	76
Laos	400	108	Turkey	1,965	48
Lebanon	na	na	Turkmenistan	na	na
Malaysia	3,108	33	Tuvalu	na	na
Maldives	634	91	United Arab Emirates	na	na
Marshall Islands	na	na	Uzbekistan	587	93
Micronesia	na	na	Vanuatu	876	78
Mongolia	na	na	Vietnam	na	na
Myanmar (Burma)	na	na	Yemen	na	na

Note: Gross National Product (GNP) per capita is the gross national product divided by the midyear population. GNP is the sum of the gross value added by all resident producers plus any taxes (less subsidies) that are not included in the valuation of output plus net receipts of primary income (employee compensation and property income) from nonresident sources. Data are in constant 1987 U.S. dollars, reflecting adjustments to level out the effects of inflation.

Source: World Bank, *World Development Indicators 1998,* Table 1.1; World Bank, *World Development Indicators 1998,* CD-ROM, l Series: GNP per capita (constant 1987 US$) (NY.GNP.PCAP.KD.87).

A5.5 Gross National Product (GNP) per Capita, 1996, Europe—U.S. Dollars (Constant Valuation Based on 1987)

Country	GNP 1996	World Rank	Country	GNP 1996	World Rank
Albania	na	na	Liechtenstein	na	na
Andorra	na	na	Lithuania	1,940	49
Armenia	311	117	Luxembourg	30,245	1
Austria	18,196	11	Macedonia, FYRO	na	na
Belarus	1,697	61	Malta	na	na
Belgium	16,961	13	Moldova	na	na
Bosnia and Herzegovina	na	na	Monaco	na	na
Bulgaria	2,394	43	Netherlands	18,434	9
Croatia	na	na	Norway	25,431	3
Cyprus	na	na	Poland	1,795	59
Czech Republic	3,648	30	Portugal	5,351	24
Denmark	22,120	5	Romania	1,400	62
Estonia	2,834	36	Russia	1,875	54
Finland	18,394	10	San Marino	na	na
France	18,146	12	Slovakia	3,251	32
Georgia	na	na	Slovenia	na	na
Germany	na	na	Spain	9,183	20
Greece	6,580	22	Sweden	20,231	8
Hungary	2,259	45	Switzerland	28,046	2
Iceland	21,558	6	Ukraine	522	97
Ireland	8,826	21	United Kingdom	13,722	18
Italy	15,185	15	Yugoslavia	na	na
Latvia	1,932	51			

Note: Gross National Product (GNP) per capita is the gross national product divided by the midyear population. GNP is the sum of the gross value added by all resident producers plus any taxes (less subsidies) that are not included in the valuation of output plus net receipts of primary income (employee compensation and property income) from nonresident sources. Data are in constant 1987 U.S. dollars, reflecting adjustments to level out the effects of inflation.

Source: World Bank, *World Development Indicators 1998,* Table 1.1; World Bank, *World Development Indicators 1998,* CD-ROM, 1 Series: GNP per capita (NY.GNP.PCAP.KD.87)

A6.1 Life Expectancy at Birth, 1996 Summary—Comparison by Income Level per World Bank

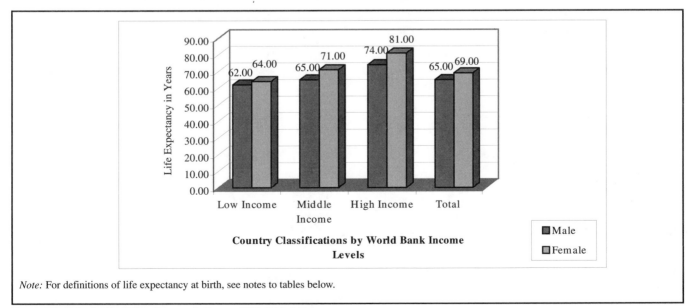

Note: For definitions of life expectancy at birth, see notes to tables below.

Source: World Bank, *World Development Indicators 1998,* Table 1.2

A6.2   Life Expectancy at Birth, 1996—Number of Years

Country	1996	World Rank	Country	1996	World Rank
Afghanistan	45.1	128	France	78.1	7
Albania	71.7	38	Gabon	54.7	102
Algeria	70.0	49	Gambia	52.7	112
Andorra	na	na	Georgia	72.5	32
Angola	46.5	126	Germany	76.5	16
Antigua and Barbuda	75.2	21	Ghana	58.9	90
Argentina	72.9	29	Greece	78.0	8
Armenia	72.7	30	Grenada	na	na
Australia	78.2	6	Guatemala	66.0	72
Austria	77.0	11	Guinea	46.1	127
Azerbaijan	69.2	55	Guinea-Bissau	43.6	130
Bahamas	73.5	28	Guyana	64.1	80
Bahrain	72.9	29	Haiti	55.2	101
Bangladesh	58.0	94	Honduras	66.9	68
Barbados	75.9	19	Hungary	69.8	50
Belarus	68.6	61	Iceland	78.6	4
Belgium	76.7	14	India	62.7	84
Belize	74.5	24	Indonesia	64.6	78
Benin	54.5	104	Iran	69.8	50
Bhutan	52.7	112	Iraq	61.6	85
Bolivia	61.0	86	Ireland	76.2	18
Bosnia and Herzegovina	na	na	Israel	77.2	10
Botswana	51.0	113	Italy	78.0	8
Brazil	67.0	67	Jamaica	74.3	25
Brunei	75.5	20	Japan	79.8	1
Bulgaria	70.8	43	Jordan	70.6	45
Burkina Faso	46.1	127	Kazakhstan	65.0	76
Burundi	46.6	125	Kenya	58.3	92
Cambodia	53.5	108	Kiribati	59.9	87
Cameroon	56.4	98	Kuwait	76.6	15
Canada	78.7	3	Kyrgyzstan	66.5	69
Cape Verde	66.1	71	Laos	53.0	110
Central African Republic	48.6	122	Latvia	69.3	54
Chad	48.2	123	Lebanon	69.6	52
Chile	75.1	22	Lesotho	58.4	91
China	69.5	53	Liberia	49.1	121
Colombia	70.0	49	Libya	68.2	62
Comoros	59.3	89	Liechtenstein	na	na
Congo, Dem. Rep. (Zaire)	52.7	112	Lithuania	70.4	46
Congo, Rep.	51.0	113	Luxembourg	76.6	15
Costa Rica	76.8	13	Macedonia, FYRO	72.2	34
Cote d'Ivoire	53.9	107	Madagascar	58.1	93
Croatia	72.4	33	Malawi	43.1	131
Cuba	75.9	19	Malaysia	71.9	37
Cyprus	77.5	9	Maldives	64.2	79
Czech Republic	73.5	28	Mali	50.0	117
Denmark	75.2	21	Malta	77.0	11
Djibouti	49.9	118	Marshall Islands	na	na
Dominica	73.7	27	Mauritania	53.1	109
Dominican Republic	70.7	44	Mauritius	71.3	40
Ecuador	70.0	49	Mexico	71.7	37
Egypt	65.5	74	Micronesia	66.5	69
El Salvador	69.1	56	Moldova	67.4	66
Equatorial Guinea	49.6	119	Monaco	na	na
Eritrea	54.6	103	Mongolia	65.3	75
Estonia	69.0	57	Morocco	66.2	70
Ethiopia	49.5	120	Mozambique	45.1	128
Fiji	72.4	33	Myanmar (Burma)	59.6	88
Finland	76.7	14	Namibia	55.7	100

A6.2 Life Expectancy at Birth, 1996—Number of Years (continued)

Country	1996	World Rank	Country	1996	World Rank
Nauru	na	na	Spain	77.2	10
Nepal	56.8	97	Sri Lanka	72.9	29
Netherlands	77.5	9	St. Kitts & Nevis	69.6	52
New Zealand	76.4	17	St. Lucia	70.3	47
Nicaragua	67.7	64	St. Vincent and the Grenadines	72.6	31
Niger	46.8	124	Sudan	54.2	105
Nigeria	52.9	111	Suriname	71.2	41
North Korea, Dem. Rep.	63.0	83	Swaziland	57.4	96
Norway	78.2	6	Sweden	78.9	2
Oman	70.8	43	Switzerland	78.5	5
Pakistan	63.5	82	Syria	68.6	61
Palau	na	na	Taiwan	na	na
Panama	73.8	26	Tajikistan	68.8	59
Papua New Guinea	57.5	95	Tanzania	50.5	114
Paraguay	70.9	42	Thailand	69.1	56
Peru	68.2	62	Togo	50.3	116
Philippines	66.0	72	Tonga	71.6	39
Poland	72.1	35	Trinidad & Tobago	72.5	32
Portugal	75.1	22	Tunisia	69.7	51
Qatar	72.4	33	Turkey	68.7	60
Romania	69.1	56	Turkmenistan	65.7	73
Russia	66.0	72	Tuvalu	na	na
Rwanda	40.6	132	Uganda	43.1	131
Samoa	68.9	58	Ukraine	67.5	65
San Marino	na	na	United Arab Emirates	74.9	23
Sao Tome and Principe	63.8	81	United Kingdom	76.9	12
Saudi Arabia	70.1	48	United States	77.2	10
Senegal	50.4	115	Uruguay	73.5	28
Seychelles	71.3	40	Uzbekistan	69.2	55
Sierra Leone	36.9	133	Vanuatu	64.2	79
Singapore	76.2	18	Venezuela	72.6	31
Slovakia	72.7	30	Vietnam	68.0	63
Slovenia	74.5	24	Yemen	54.0	106
Solomon Islands	62.7	84	Yugoslavia	72.1	35
Somalia	48.6	122	Zambia	44.5	129
South Africa	64.8	77	Zimbabwe	56.2	99
South Korea, Rep.	72.0	36			

Note: Life expectancy at birth is the number of years a newborn infant would live if prevailing patterns of mortality at the time of its birth were to stay the same throughout its life. The rankings noted in the "World Rank" column indicate the order in which the data flowed, from highest life expectancy to lowest; in most instances, the rankings are not unique, as countries share rankings with other countries that have the same life expectancy.

Source: World Bank, *World Development Indicators 1998,* Table 1.2; World Bank, *World Development Indicators 1998,* CD-ROM, Series: Life expectancy at birth (SP.DYN.LE00.IN)

A6.3   Life Expectancy at Birth, Africa, 1996—Number of Years

Country	Number of Years, 1996	World Rank	Country	Number of Years, 1996	World Rank
Algeria	70.0	49	Libya	68.2	62
Angola	46.5	126	Madagascar	58.1	93
Benin	54.5	104	Malawi	43.1	131
Botswana	51.0	113	Mali	50.0	117
Burkina Faso	46.1	127	Mauritania	53.1	109
Burundi	46.6	125	Mauritius	71.3	40
Cameroon	56.4	98	Morocco	66.2	70
Cape Verde	66.1	71	Mozambique	45.1	128
Central African Republic	48.6	122	Namibia	55.7	100
Chad	48.2	123	Niger	46.8	124
Comoros	59.3	89	Nigeria	52.9	111
Congo, Dem. Rep. (Zaire)	52.7	112	Rwanda	40.6	132
Congo, Rep.	51.0	113	Sao Tome and Principe	63.8	81
Cote d'Ivoire	53.9	107	Senegal	50.4	115
Egypt	65.5	74	Seychelles	71.3	40
Equatorial Guinea	49.6	119	Sierra Leone	36.9	133
Eritrea	54.6	103	Somalia	48.6	122
Ethiopia	49.5	120	South Africa	64.8	77
Gabon	54.7	102	Sudan	54.2	105
Gambia	52.7	112	Swaziland	57.4	96
Ghana	58.9	90	Tanzania	50.5	114
Guinea	46.1	127	Togo	50.3	116
Guinea-Bissau	43.6	130	Tunisia	69.7	51
Kenya	58.3	92	Uganda	43.1	131
Lesotho	58.4	91	Zambia	44.5	129
Liberia	49.1	121	Zimbabwe	56.2	99

Note: Life expectancy at birth is the number of years a newborn infant would live if prevailing patterns of mortality at the time of its birth were to stay the same throughout its life. The rankings noted in the "World Rank" column indicate the order in which the data flowed, from highest life expectancy to lowest; in most instances, the rankings are not unique, as countries share rankings with other countries that have the same life expectancy.

Source: World Bank, *World Development Indicators 1998,* Table 1.2; World Bank, *World Development Indicators 1998,* CD-ROM, Series: Life expectancy at birth (SP.DYN.LE00.IN)

A6.4   Life Expectancy at Birth, Americas, 1996—Number of Years

Country	Number of Years, 1996	World Rank	Country	Number of Years, 1996	World Rank
Antigua and Barbuda	75.2	21	Guyana	64.1	80
Argentina	72.9	29	Haiti	55.2	101
Bahamas	73.5	28	Honduras	66.9	68
Barbados	75.9	19	Jamaica	74.3	25
Belize	74.5	24	Mexico	71.7	37
Bolivia	61.0	86	Nicaragua	67.7	64
Brazil	67.0	67	Panama	73.8	26
Canada	78.7	3	Paraguay	70.9	42
Chile	75.1	22	Peru	68.2	62
Colombia	70.0	49	St. Kitts & Nevis	69.6	52
Costa Rica	76.8	13	St. Lucia	70.3	47
Cuba	75.9	19	St. Vincent and the Grenadines	72.6	31
Dominica	73.7	27	Suriname	71.2	41
Dominican Republic	70.7	44	Trinidad & Tobago	72.5	32
Ecuador	70.0	49	United States	77.2	10
El Salvador	69.1	56	Uruguay	73.5	28
Grenada	na	na	Venezuela	72.6	31
Guatemala	66.0	72			

Note: Life expectancy at birth is the number of years a newborn infant would live if prevailing patterns of mortality at the time of its birth were to stay the same throughout its life. The rankings noted in the "World Rank" column indicate the order in which the data flowed, from highest life expectancy to lowest; in most instances, the rankings are not unique, as countries share rankings with other countries that have the same life expectancy.

Source: World Bank, *World Development Indicators 1998,* Table 1.2; World Bank, *World Development Indicators 1998,* CD-ROM, Series: Life Expectancy at Birth (SP.DYN.LE00.IN)

A6.5 Life Expectancy at Birth, Asia and Oceania, 1996—Number of Years

Country	Number of Years, 1996	World Rank	Country	Number of Years, 1996	World Rank
Afghanistan	45.1	128	Myanmar (Burma)	59.6	88
Australia	78.2	6	Nauru	na	na
Azerbaijan	69.2	55	Nepal	56.8	97
Bahrain	72.9	29	New Zealand	76.4	17
Bangladesh	58.0	94	North Korea, Dem. Rep.	63.0	83
Bhutan	52.7	112	Oman	70.8	43
Brunei	75.5	20	Pakistan	63.5	82
Cambodia	53.5	108	Palau	na	na
China	69.5	53	Papua New Guinea	57.5	95
Djibouti	49.9	118	Philippines	66.0	72
Fiji	72.4	33	Qatar	72.4	33
India	62.7	84	Samoa	68.9	58
Indonesia	64.6	78	Saudi Arabia	70.1	48
Iran	69.8	50	Singapore	76.2	18
Iraq	61.6	85	Solomon Islands	62.7	84
Israel	77.2	10	South Korea, Rep.	72.0	36
Japan	79.8	1	Sri Lanka	72.9	29
Jordan	70.6	45	Syria	68.6	61
Kazakhstan	65.0	76	Taiwan	na	na
Kiribati	59.9	87	Tajikistan	68.8	59
Kuwait	76.6	15	Thailand	69.1	56
Kyrgyzstan	66.5	69	Tonga	71.6	39
Laos	53.0	110	Turkey	68.7	60
Lebanon	69.6	52	Turkmenistan	65.7	73
Malaysia	71.9	37	Tuvalu	na	na
Maldives	64.2	79	United Arab Emirates	74.9	23
Marshall Islands	na	na	Uzbekistan	69.2	55
Micronesia	66.5	69	Vanuatu	64.2	79
Mongolia	65.3	75	Vietnam	68.0	63
			Yemen	54.0	106

Note: Life expectancy at birth is the number of years a newborn infant would live if prevailing patterns of mortality at the time of its birth were to stay the same throughout its life. The rankings noted in the "World Rank" column indicate the order in which the data flowed, from highest life expectancy to lowest; in most instances, the rankings are not unique, as countries share rankings with other countries that have the same life expectancy.

Source: World Bank, *World Development Indicators 1998,* Table 1.2; World Bank, *World Development Indicators 1998,* CD-ROM, Series: Life expectancy at birth (SP.DYN.LE00.IN)

A6.6 Life Expectancy at Birth, Europe, 1996—Number of Years

Country	Number of Years, 1996	World Rank	Country	Number of Years, 1996	World Rank
Albania	71.7	38	Liechtenstein	na	na
Andorra	na	na	Lithuania	70.4	46
Armenia	72.7	30	Luxembourg	76.6	15
Austria	77.0	11	Macedonia, FYRO	72.2	34
Belarus	68.6	61	Malta	77.0	11
Belgium	76.7	14	Moldova	67.4	66
Bosnia and Herzegovina	na	na	Monaco	na	na
Bulgaria	70.8	43	Netherlands	77.5	9
Croatia	72.4	33	Norway	78.2	6
Cyprus	77.5	9	Poland	72.1	35
Czech Republic	73.5	28	Portugal	75.1	22
Denmark	75.2	21	Romania	69.1	56
Estonia	69.0	57	Russia	66.0	72
Finland	76.7	14	San Marino	na	na
France	78.1	7	Slovakia	72.7	30
Georgia	72.5	32	Slovenia	74.5	24
Germany	76.5	16	Spain	77.2	10
Greece	78.0	8	Sweden	78.9	2
Hungary	69.8	50	Switzerland	78.5	5
Iceland	78.6	4	Ukraine	67.5	65
Ireland	76.2	18	United Kingdom	76.9	12
Italy	78.0	8	Yugoslavia	72.1	35
Latvia	69.3	54			

Note: Life expectancy at birth is the number of years a newborn infant would live if prevailing patterns of mortality at the time of its birth were to stay the same throughout its life. The rankings noted in the "World Rank" column indicate the order in which the data flowed, from highest life expectancy to lowest; in most instances, the rankings are not unique, as countries share rankings with other countries that have the same life expectancy.

Source: World Bank, *World Development Indicators 1998,* Table 1.2, World Bank, *World Development Indicators 1998,* CD-ROM, Series: Life expectancy at birth (SP.DYN.LE00.IN)

A7.1 Infant Mortality Rates, 1996 Summary—Comparison by Income Level per World Bank

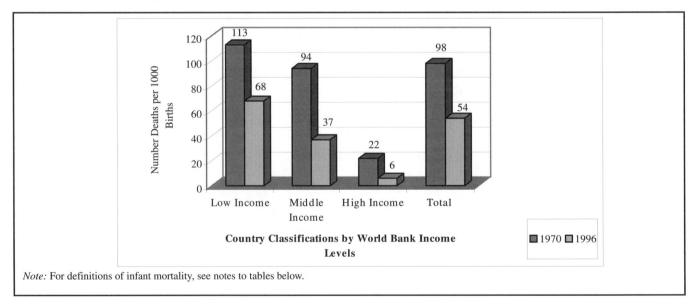

Note: For definitions of infant mortality, see notes to tables below.

Source: World Bank, *World Development Indicators 1998,* Table 1.3

A7.2 Infant Mortality Rates, 1996—Per 1,000 Live Births

Country	1996	World Rank	Country	1996	World Rank
Afghanistan	na	na	Finland	4	1
Albania	37	27	France	5	2
Algeria	32	23	Gabon	87	55
Andorra	na	na	Gambia	79	50
Angola	124	73	Georgia	17	14
Antigua and Barbuda	na	na	Germany	5	2
Argentina	22	17	Ghana	71	45
Armenia	16	13	Greece	8	5
Australia	6	3	Grenada	na	na
Austria	5	2	Guatemala	41	29
Azerbaijan	20	16	Guinea	122	71
Bahamas	na	na	Guinea-Bissau	134	76
Bahrain	na	na	Guyana	na	na
Bangladesh	77	48	Haiti	72	46
Barbados	na	na	Honduras	44	33
Belarus	13	10	Hungary	11	8
Belgium	7	4	Iceland	na	na
Belize	na	na	India	65	43
Benin	87	55	Indonesia	49	34
Bhutan	na	na	Iran	36	26
Bolivia	67	44	Iraq	101	64
Bosnia and Herzegovina	na	na	Ireland	5	2
Botswana	56	37	Israel	6	3
Brazil	36	26	Italy	6	3
Brunei	na	na	Jamaica	12	9
Bulgaria	16	13	Japan	4	1
Burkina Faso	98	62	Jordan	30	21
Burundi	97	61	Kazakhstan	25	19
Cambodia	105	65	Kenya	57	38
Cameroon	54	36	Kiribati	na	na
Canada	6	3	Kuwait	11	8
Cape Verde	na	na	Kyrgyzstan	26	20
Central African Republic	96	60	Laos	101	64
Chad	115	68	Latvia	16	13
Chile	12	9	Lebanon	31	22
China	33	24	Lesotho	74	47
Colombia	25	19	Liberia	na	na
Comoros	na	na	Libya	25	19
Congo, Dem. Rep. (Zaire)	90	57	Liechtenstein	na	na
Congo, Rep.	90	58	Lithuania	10	7
Costa Rica	12	9	Luxembourg	na	na
Cote d'Ivoire	84	52	Macedonia, FYRO	16	13
Croatia	9	6	Madagascar	88	56
Cuba	8	5	Malawi	133	75
Cyprus	na	na	Malaysia	11	8
Czech Republic	6	3	Maldives	na	na
Denmark	6	3	Mali	120	70
Djibouti	na	na	Malta	na	na
Dominica	na	na	Marshall Islands	na	na
Dominican Republic	40	28	Mauritania	94	59
Ecuador	34	25	Mauritius	17	14
Egypt	53	35	Mexico	32	23
El Salvador	34	25	Micronesia	na	na
Equatorial Guinea	na	na	Moldova	20	16
Eritrea	64	42	Monaco	na	na
Estonia	10	7	Mongolia	53	35
Ethiopia	109	66	Morocco	53	35
Fiji	na	na	Mozambique	123	72

A7.2   Infant Mortality Rates, 1996—Per 1,000 Live Births *(continued)*

Country	1996	World Rank	Country	1996	World Rank
Myanmar (Burma)	80	51	South Korea, Rep.	9	6
Namibia	61	40	Spain	5	2
Nauru	na	na	Sri Lanka	15	12
Nepal	85	53	St. Kitts & Nevis	na	na
Netherlands	5	2	St. Lucia	na	na
New Zealand	6	3	St. Vincent and the Grenadines	na	na
Nicaragua	44	33	Sudan	74	47
Niger	118	69	Suriname	na	na
Nigeria	78	49	Swaziland	na	na
North Korea, Dem. Rep.	56	37	Sweden	4	1
Norway	4	1	Switzerland	5	2
Oman	18	15	Syria	31	22
Pakistan	88	56	Taiwan	na	na
Palau	na	na	Tajikistan	32	23
Panama	22	17	Tanzania	86	54
Papua New Guinea	62	41	Thailand	34	25
Paraguay	24	18	Togo	87	55
Peru	42	30	Tonga	na	na
Philippines	37	27	Trinidad & Tobago	13	10
Poland	12	9	Tunisia	30	21
Portugal	7	4	Turkey	42	30
Qatar	na	na	Turkmenistan	41	29
Romania	22	17	Tuvalu	na	na
Russia	17	14	Uganda	99	63
Rwanda	129	74	Ukraine	14	11
Samoa	na	na	United Arab Emirates	15	12
San Marino	na	na	United Kingdom	6	3
Sao Tome and Principe	na	na	United States	7	4
Saudi Arabia	22	17	Uruguay	18	15
Senegal	60	39	Uzbekistan	24	18
Seychelles	na	na	Vanuatu	na	na
Sierra Leone	174	77	Venezuela	22	17
Singapore	4	1	Vietnam	40	28
Slovakia	11	8	Yemen	98	62
Slovenia	5	2	Yugoslavia	14	11
Solomon Islands	na	na	Zambia	112	67
Somalia	na	na	Zimbabwe	56	37
South Africa	49	34			

Note: Infant mortality rate is the number of deaths of infants under one year of age during the indicated year per 1,000 live births in the same year. The rankings noted in the "World Rank" column indicate the order in which the data flowed, from lowest mortality rate to highest; in most instances, the rankings are not unique, as countries share rankings with other countries that have the same mortality rates.

Source: World Bank, *World Development Indicators 1998,* Table 1.3

A7.3 Infant Mortality Rates, Africa, 1996—Per 1,000 Live Births

Country	1996	World Rank	Country	1996	World Rank
Algeria	32	23	Libya	25	19
Angola	124	73	Madagascar	88	56
Benin	87	55	Malawi	133	75
Botswana	56	37	Mali	120	70
Burkina Faso	98	62	Mauritania	94	59
Burundi	97	61	Mauritius	17	14
Cameroon	54	36	Morocco	53	35
Cape Verde	na	na	Mozambique	123	72
Central African Republic	96	60	Namibia	61	40
Chad	115	68	Niger	118	69
Comoros	na	na	Nigeria	78	49
Congo, Dem. Rep. (Zaire)	90	57	Rwanda	129	74
Congo, Rep.	90	58	Sao Tome and Principe	na	na
Cote d'Ivoire	84	52	Senegal	60	39
Egypt	53	35	Seychelles	na	na
Equatorial Guinea	na	na	Sierra Leone	174	77
Eritrea	64	42	Somalia	na	na
Ethiopia	109	66	South Africa	49	34
Gabon	87	55	Sudan	74	47
Gambia	79	50	Swaziland	na	na
Ghana	71	45	Tanzania	86	54
Guinea	122	71	Togo	87	55
Guinea-Bissau	134	76	Tunisia	30	21
Kenya	57	38	Uganda	99	63
Lesotho	74	47	Zambia	112	67
Liberia	na	na	Zimbabwe	56	37

Note: Infant mortality rate is the number of deaths of infants under one year of age during the indicated year per 1,000 live births in the same year. The rankings noted in the "World Rank" column indicate the order in which the data flowed, from lowest mortality rate to highest; in most instances, the rankings are not unique, as countries share rankings with other countries that have the same mortality rates.

Source: World Bank, *World Development Indicators 1998,* Table 1.3

A7.4 Infant Mortality Rates, Americas, 1996—Per 1,000 Live Births

Country	1996	World Rank	Country	1996	World Rank
Antigua and Barbuda	na	na	Guyana	na	na
Argentina	22	17	Haiti	72	46
Bahamas	na	na	Honduras	44	33
Barbados	na	na	Jamaica	12	9
Belize	na	na	Mexico	32	23
Bolivia	67	44	Nicaragua	44	33
Brazil	36	26	Panama	22	17
Canada	6	3	Paraguay	24	18
Chile	12	9	Peru	42	30
Colombia	25	19	St. Kitts & Nevis	na	na
Costa Rica	12	9	St. Lucia	na	na
Cuba	8	5	St. Vincent and the Grenadines	na	na
Dominica	na	na	Suriname	na	na
Dominican Republic	40	28	Trinidad & Tobago	13	10
Ecuador	34	25	United States	7	4
El Salvador	34	25	Uruguay	18	15
Grenada	na	na	Venezuela	22	17
Guatemala	41	29			

Note: Infant mortality rate is the number of deaths of infants under one year of age during the indicated year per 1,000 live births in the same year. The rankings noted in the "World Rank" column indicate the order in which the data flowed, from lowest mortality rate to highest; in most instances, the rankings are not unique, as countries share rankings with other countries that have the same mortality rates.

Source: World Bank, *World Development Indicators 1998,* Table 1.3

A7.5 Infant Mortality Rates, Asia and Oceania, 1996—Per 1,000 Live Births

Country	1996	World Rank	Country	1996	World Rank
Afghanistan	na	na	Nauru	na	na
Australia	6	3	Nepal	85	53
Azerbaijan	20	16	New Zealand	6	3
Bahrain	na	na	North Korea, Dem. Rep.	56	37
Bangladesh	77	48	Oman	18	15
Bhutan	na	na	Pakistan	88	56
Brunei	na	na	Palau	na	na
Cambodia	105	65	Papua New Guinea	62	41
China	33	24	Philippines	37	27
Djibouti	na	na	Qatar	na	na
Fiji	na	na	Samoa	na	na
India	65	43	Saudi Arabia	22	17
Indonesia	49	34	Singapore	4	1
Iran	36	26	Solomon Islands	na	na
Iraq	101	64	South Korea, Rep.	9	6
Israel	6	3	Sri Lanka	15	12
Japan	4	1	Syria	31	22
Jordan	30	21	Taiwan	na	na
Kazakhstan	25	19	Tajikistan	32	23
Kiribati	na	na	Thailand	34	25
Kuwait	11	8	Tonga	na	na
Kyrgyzstan	26	20	Turkey	42	30
Laos	101	64	Turkmenistan	41	29
Lebanon	31	22	Tuvalu	na	na
Malaysia	11	8	United Arab Emirates	15	12
Maldives	na	na	Uzbekistan	24	18
Marshall Islands	na	na	Vanuatu	na	na
Micronesia	na	na	Vietnam	40	28
Mongolia	53	35	Yemen	98	62
Myanmar (Burma)	80	51			

Note: Infant mortality rate is the number of deaths of infants under one year of age during the indicated year per 1,000 live births in the same year. The rankings noted in the "World Rank" column indicate the order in which the data flowed, from lowest mortality rate to highest; in most instances, the rankings are not unique, as countries share rankings with other countries that have the same mortality rates.

Source: World Bank, *World Development Indicators 1998,* Table 1.3

A7.6   Infant Mortality Rates, Europe, 1996—Per 1,000 Live Births

Country	1996	World Rank	Country	1996	World Rank
Albania	37	27	Liechtenstein	na	na
Andorra	na	na	Lithuania	10	7
Armenia	16	13	Luxembourg	na	na
Austria	5	2	Macedonia, FYRO	16	13
Belarus	13	10	Malta	na	na
Belgium	7	4	Moldova	20	16
Bosnia and Herzegovina	na	na	Monaco	na	na
Bulgaria	16	13	Netherlands	5	2
Croatia	9	6	Norway	4	1
Cyprus	na	na	Poland	12	9
Czech Republic	6	3	Portugal	7	4
Denmark	6	3	Romania	22	17
Estonia	10	7	Russia	17	14
Finland	4	1	San Marino	na	na
France	5	2	Slovakia	11	8
Georgia	17	14	Slovenia	5	2
Germany	5	2	Spain	5	2
Greece	8	5	Sweden	4	1
Hungary	11	8	Switzerland	5	2
Iceland	na	na	Ukraine	14	11
Ireland	5	2	United Kingdom	6	3
Italy	6	3	Yugoslavia	14	11
Latvia	16	13			

Note: Infant mortality rate is the number of deaths of infants under one year of age during the indicated year per 1,000 live births in the same year. The rankings noted in the "World Rank" column indicate the order in which the data flowed, from lowest mortality rate to highest; in most instances, the rankings are not unique, as countries share rankings with other countries that have the same mortality rates.

Source: World Bank, *World Development Indicators,* Table 1.3

A8.1   Adult Illiteracy Rate, 1995 Summary—Comparison by Income Level per World Bank

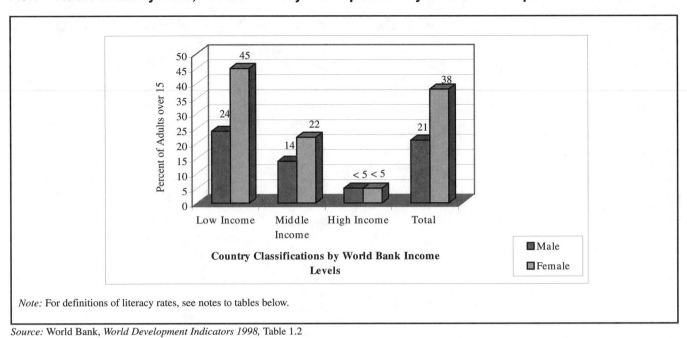

Note: For definitions of literacy rates, see notes to tables below.

Source: World Bank, *World Development Indicators 1998,* Table 1.2

A8.2   Literacy Rate, 1995—Percent of Total Adults

Country	Literacy rate %, 1995	World Rank	Country	Literacy rate %, 1995	World Rank
Afghanistan	32	153	Central African Republic	60	119
Albania	na	na	Chad	48	132
Algeria	62	115	Chile	95	41
Andorra	na	na	China	82	80
Angola	42	138	Colombia	91	55
Antigua and Barbuda	95	41	Comoros	57	122
Argentina	96	38	Congo, Dem. Rep. (Zaire)	77	93
Armenia	100	1	Congo, Rep.	75	97
Australia	na	na	Costa Rica	95	41
Austria	na	na	Cote d'Ivoire	40	140
Azerbaijan	100	1	Croatia	98	19
Bahamas	98	19	Cuba	96	38
Bahrain	85	69	Cyprus	94	46
Bangladesh	38	143	Czech Republic	na	na
Barbados	97	32	Denmark	na	na
Belarus	99	8	Djibouti	46	133
Belgium	na	na	Dominica	na	na
Belize	80	86	Dominican Republic	82	80
Benin	37	147	Ecuador	90	61
Bhutan	42	138	Egypt	51	131
Bolivia	83	75	El Salvador	72	99
Bosnia and Herzegovina	na	na	Equatorial Guinea	79	87
Botswana	70	104	Eritrea	na	na
Brazil	83	75	Estonia	98	19
Brunei	88	67	Ethiopia	36	148
Bulgaria	98	19	Fiji	92	52
Burkina Faso	19	158	Finland	na	na
Burundi	35	150	France	na	na
Cambodia	65	109	Gabon	63	112
Cameroon	63	112	Gambia	39	142
Canada	97	32	Georgia	99	8
Cape Verde	72	99	Germany	na	na

A8.2 Literacy Rate, 1995—Percent of Total Adults *(continued)*

Country	Literacy rate %, 1995	World Rank	Country	Literacy rate %, 1995	World Rank
Ghana	65	109	Nicaragua	66	108
Greece	97	32	Niger	14	159
Grenada	96	38	Nigeria	57	122
Guatemala	56	126	North Korea, Dem. Rep.	na	na
Guinea	36	148	Norway	na	na
Guinea-Bissau	55	128	Oman	59	120
Guyana	98	19	Pakistan	38	143
Haiti	45	136	Palau	98	19
Honduras	73	98	Panama	91	55
Hungary	99	8	Papua New Guinea	72	99
Iceland	na	na	Paraguay	92	52
India	52	129	Peru	89	66
Indonesia	84	72	Philippines	95	41
Iran	69	105	Poland	na	na
Iraq	58	121	Portugal	90	61
Ireland	na	na	Qatar	79	87
Israel	95	41	Romania	98	19
Italy	98	19	Russia	99	8
Jamaica	85	69	Rwanda	61	118
Japan	na	na	Samoa	98	19
Jordan	87	68	San Marino	na	na
Kazakhstan	100	1	Sao Tome and Principe	57	122
Kenya	78	91	Saudi Arabia	63	112
Kiribati	93	49	Senegal	33	151
Kuwait	79	87	Seychelles	84	72
Kyrgyzstan	97	32	Sierra Leone	31	154
Laos	57	122	Singapore	91	55
Latvia	100	1	Slovakia	na	na
Lebanon	92	52	Slovenia	99	8
Lesotho	71	102	Solomon Islands	62	115
Liberia	38	143	Somalia	24	157
Libya	76	95	South Africa	82	80
Liechtenstein	100	1	South Korea, Rep.	98	19
Lithuania	99	8	Spain	97	32
Luxembourg	na	na	Sri Lanka	90	61
Macedonia, FYRO	na	na	St. Kitts & Nevis	90	61
Madagascar	46	133	St. Lucia	na	na
Malawi	56	126	St. Vincent and the Grenadines	82	80
Malaysia	84	72	Sudan	46	133
Maldives	93	49	Suriname	93	49
Mali	31	154	Swaziland	77	93
Malta	91	55	Sweden	na	na
Marshall Islands	91	55	Switzerland	na	na
Mauritania	38	143	Syria	71	102
Mauritius	83	75	Taiwan	na	na
Mexico	90	61	Tajikistan	100	1
Micronesia	81	85	Tanzania	68	106
Moldova	99	8	Thailand	94	46
Monaco	na	na	Togo	52	129
Mongolia	83	75	Tonga	99	8
Morocco	44	137	Trinidad & Tobago	98	19
Mozambique	40	140	Tunisia	67	107
Myanmar (Burma)	83	75	Turkey	82	80
Namibia	76	95	Turkmenistan	98	19
Nauru	na	na	Tuvalu	99	8
Nepal	28	156	Uganda	62	115
Netherlands	na	na	Ukraine	99	8
New Zealand	na	na	United Arab Emirates	79	87

A8.2 Literacy Rate, 1995—Percent of Total Adults *(continued)*

Country	Literacy rate %, 1995	World Rank	Country	Literacy rate %, 1995	World Rank
United Kingdom	na	na	Vietnam	94	46
United States	99	8	Yemen	33	151
Uruguay	97	32	Yugoslavia	98	19
Uzbekistan	100	1	Zambia	78	91
Vanuatu	64	111	Zimbabwe	85	69
Venezuela	91	55			

Note: Adult literacy rate is the proportion of adults aged 15 and above who can, with some understanding, read and write a short, simple statement on their everyday life. This does not include people who can read but not write. Number of 15 years and over adults is expressed as percentage of population of the same age group.

Source: The State of the World's Children 1998, Table 1, UNICEF web site, http://www.unicef.org/sowc98

A8.3 Literacy Rate, Africa, 1995—Percent of Total Adults

Country	Literacy Rate %, 1995	World Rank	Country	Literacy Rate %, 1995	World Rank
Algeria	62	115	Libya	76	95
Angola	42	138	Madagascar	46	133
Benin	37	147	Malawi	56	126
Botswana	70	104	Mali	31	154
Burkina Faso	19	158	Mauritania	38	143
Burundi	35	150	Mauritius	83	75
Cameroon	63	112	Morocco	44	137
Cape Verde	72	99	Mozambique	40	140
Central African Republic	60	119	Namibia	76	95
Chad	48	132	Niger	14	159
Comoros	57	122	Nigeria	57	122
Congo, Dem.Rep. (Zaire)	77	93	Rwanda	61	118
Congo, Rep.	75	97	Sao Tome and Principe	57	122
Cote d'Ivoire	40	140	Senegal	33	151
Egypt	51	131	Seychelles	84	72
Equatorial Guinea	79	87	Sierra Leone	31	154
Eritrea	na	na	Somalia	24	157
Ethiopia	36	148	South Africa	82	80
Gabon	63	112	Sudan	46	133
Gambia	39	142	Swaziland	77	93
Ghana	65	109	Tanzania	68	106
Guinea	36	148	Togo	52	129
Guinea-Bissau	55	128	Tunisia	67	107
Kenya	78	91	Uganda	62	115
Lesotho	71	102	Zambia	78	69
Liberia	38	143	Zimbabwe	85	na

Note: Adult literacy rate is the proportion of adults aged 15 and above who can, with some understanding, read and write a short, simple statement on their everyday life. This does not include people who can read but not write. Number of 15 years and over adults is expressed as percentage of population of the same age group.

Source: The State of the World's Children 1998, Table 1, UNICEF web site, http://www.unicef.org/sowc98

A8.4   Literacy Rate, Americas, 1995—Percent of Total Adults

Country	Literacy Rate %, 1995	World Rank	Country	Literacy Rate %, 1995	World Rank
Antigua and Barbuda	95	41	Guatemala	56	126
Argentina	96	38	Guyana	98	19
Bahamas	98	19	Haiti	45	136
Barbados	97	32	Honduras	73	98
Belize	80	86	Jamaica	85	69
Bolivia	83	75	Mexico	90	61
Brazil	83	75	Nicaragua	66	108
Canada	97	32	Panama	91	55
Chile	95	41	Paraguay	92	52
Colombia	91	55	Peru	89	66
Costa Rica	95	41	St. Kitts & Nevis	90	61
Cuba	96	38	St. Lucia	na	na
Dominica	na	na	St. Vincent and the Grenadines	82	80
Dominican Republic	82	80	Suriname	93	49
Ecuador	90	61	Trinidad & Tobago	98	19
El Salvador	72	99	United States	99	8
Grenada	96	38	Uruguay	97	32
			Venezuela	91	46

Note: Adult literacy rate is the proportion of adults aged 15 and above who can, with some understanding, read and write a short, simple statement on their everyday life. This does not include people who can read but not write. Number of 15 years and over adults is expressed as percentage of population of the same age group.

Source: The State of the World's Children 1998, Table 1, UNICEF web site, http://www.unicef.org/sowc98

A8.5   Literacy Rate, Asia and Oceania, 1995—Percent of Total Adults

Country	Literacy Rate %, 1995	World Rank	Country	Literacy Rate %, 1995	World Rank
Afghanistan	32	153	Nauru	na	na
Australia	na	na	Nepal	28	156
Azerbaijan	100	1	New Zealand	na	na
Bahrain	85	69	North Korea, Dem. Rep.	na	na
Bangladesh	38	143	Oman	59	120
Bhutan	42	138	Pakistan	38	143
Brunei	88	67	Palau	98	19
Cambodia	65	109	Papua New Guinea	72	99
China	82	80	Philippines	95	41
Djibouti	46	133	Qatar	79	87
Fiji	92	52	Samoa	98	19
India	52	129	Saudi Arabia	63	112
Indonesia	84	72	Singapore	91	55
Iran	69	105	Solomon Islands	62	115
Iraq	58	121	South Korea, Rep.	98	19
Israel	95	41	Sri Lanka	90	61
Japan	na	na	Syria	71	102
Jordan	87	68	Taiwan	na	na
Kazakhstan	100	1	Tajikistan	100	1
Kiribati	93	49	Thailand	94	46
Kuwait	79	87	Tonga	99	8
Kyrgyzstan	97	32	Turkey	82	80
Laos	57	122	Turkmenistan	98	19
Lebanon	92	52	Tuvalu	99	8
Malaysia	84	72	United Arab Emirates	79	87
Maldives	93	49	Uzbekistan	100	1
Marshall Islands	91	55	Vanuatu	64	111
Micronesia	81	85	Vietnam	94	151
Mongolia	83	75	Yemen	33	19
Myanmar (Burma)	83	75			

Note: Adult literacy rate is the proportion of adults aged 15 and above who can, with some understanding, read and write a short, simple statement on their everyday life. This does not include people who can read but not write. Number of 15 years and over adults is expressed as percentage of population of the same age group.

Source: The State of the World's Children 1998, Table 1, UNICEF web site, http://www.unicef.org/sowc98

A8.6 Literacy Rate, Europe, 1995—Percent of Total Adults

Country	Literacy Rate %, 1995	World Rank	Country	Literacy Rate %, 1995	World Rank
Albania	na	na	Liechtenstein	100	1
Andorra	na	na	Lithuania	99	8
Armenia	100	1	Luxembourg	na	na
Austria	na	na	Macedonia, FYRO	na	na
Belarus	99	8	Malta	91	55
Belgium	na	na	Moldova	99	8
Bosnia and Herzgovina	na	na	Monaco	na	na
Bulgaria	98	19	Netherlands	na	na
Croatia	98	19	Norway	na	na
Cyprus	94	46	Poland	na	na
Czech Republic	na	na	Portugal	90	61
Denmark	na	na	Romania	98	19
Estonia	98	19	Russia	99	8
Finland	na	na	San Marino	na	na
France	na	na	Slovakia	na	na
Georgia	99	8	Slovenia	99	8
Germany	na	na	Spain	97	32
Greece	97	32	Sweden	na	na
Hungary	99	8	Switzerland	na	na
Iceland	na	na	Ukraine	99	8
Ireland	na	na	United Kingdom	na	na
Italy	98	19	Vatican City	na	55
Latvia	100	1	Yugoslavia	98	91

Note: Adult literacy rate is the proportion of adults aged 15 and above who can, with some understanding, read and write a short, simple statement on their everyday life. This does not include people who can read but not write. Number of 15 years and over adults is expressed as percentage of population of the same age group.

Source: The State of the World's Children 1998, Table 1, UNICEF web site, http://www.unicef.org/sowc98

B. Poverty Measures

GENERAL OVERVIEW

This section gathers data concerning standardized measures of poverty, including the human poverty index and people living below poverty lines. These measurements help to quantify poverty by establishing international standards below which individuals are considered poor. These international scales have only been recently developed by international organizations such as the United Nations and the World Bank in order to more fully understand, measure, and address the problems of worldwide poverty.

As the subject of this volume is poverty in developing countries, we have chosen to focus the scope of this and succeeding sections on countries that the World Bank classifies as low and middle income.

For many of these countries, some of the poverty measures included in this section are unavailable; however, we have chosen to include tables on these indicators even when many countries are missing and the tables appear to be sketchy. We believe that it is better to include material, even though it may not be comprehensive across all subject countries, than to exclude it.

EXPLANATION OF INDICATORS

Human Poverty Index for Developing Countries: The United Nations Development Programme introduced the concept of the Human Poverty Index for Developing Countries in their *Human Development Report 1997* ". . . to bring together in a composite index the different dimensions of deprivation in human life." It covers three areas of human existence—limitation of life expectancy, illiteracy, and overall standard of living. And as a quantifier of such human deprivation, it helps to identify those countries and people in most need of international help and technical assistance (B1.1–B1.4).

People Living Below National Poverty Lines: These indicators—including the total, rural, and urban data—show the part of a population of a country that lives below nationally accepted norms of adequate living standards (B2.1–B2.9).

International Poverty Line: The International Poverty Line helps to establish an international standard upon which poverty can be measured. The World Bank established two international poverty lines—at one and two U.S. dollars per person per day (of consumption, not income)—to allow for meaningful comparison between countries. The indicators in this chapter measure the number of people falling below the poverty lines and therefore reflect the extent of poverty within an individual country (B3.1–B3.6).

Poverty Gap: The poverty gap measures presented at the end of this chapter are based on the World Bank's International Poverty Lines (people living below one or two dollars per day) and measure the extent to which, on an average basis, the poverty suffered by individual households falls below the poverty lines. As such, the poverty gap measures not just the extent of poverty, but its depth—how deeply deprived the poor in a country are (B4.1–B4.6).

B1.1 Human Poverty Index for Developing Countries (HP-1), Value and Rank, 1998—Low-Income Countries per World Bank

Country	World Rank	Percent	Country	World Rank	Percent
Afghanistan	na	na	Laos	39.4	49
Angola	na	na	Lesotho	25.7	30
Armenia	na	na	Liberia	na	na
Azerbaijan	na	na	Madagascar	47.7	66
Bangladesh	46.5	65	Malawi	47.7	67
Benin	na	na	Mali	52.8	73
Bhutan	44.9	61	Mauritania	45.9	62
Bosnia and Herzegovina	na	na	Moldova	na	na
Burkina Faso	58.2	76	Mongolia	14.0	13
Burundi	49.5	72	Mozambique	48.5	68
Cambodia	39.9	52	Myanmar (Burma)	27.5	36
Cameroon	30.9	43	Nepal	na	na
Central African Republic	40.7	55	Nicaragua	26.2	32
Chad	na	na	Niger	62.1	77
China	17.1	16	Nigeria	40.5	54
Comoros	na	na	Pakistan	46.0	63
Congo, Dem.Rep. (Zaire)	41.1	56	Rwanda	na	na
Congo, Rep.	31.5	44	Sao Tome and Principe	na	na
Cote d'Ivoire	46.4	64	Senegal	48.6	69
Equatorial Guinea	na	na	Sierra Leone	58.2	75
Eritrea	na	na	Somalia	na	na
Ethiopia	55.5	74	Sri Lanka	20.6	22
Gambia	na	na	Sudan	42.5	58
Ghana	31.8	45	Tajikistan	na	na
Guinea	49.1	71	Tanzania	39.8	51
Guinea-Bissau	42.9	59	Togo	39.8	50
Guyana	na	na	Uganda	42.1	57
Haiti	44.5	60	Vietnam	26.1	31
Honduras	21.8	25	Yemen	48.9	70
India	35.9	47	Zambia	36.9	48
Kenya	27.1	35	Zimbabwe	25.2	29
Kyrgyzstan	na	na			

Note: The human poverty index for developing countries (HPI-1) measures deprivation in terms of basic human development. A composite statistic, the HPI focuses on three areas of human existence: longevity, knowledge, and standard of living. The factor of longevity is represented by the percentage of people expected to die before age 40, and the knowledge factor is represented by the percentage of illiterate adults. The standard of living factor includes three variables: the percentage of people without access to health services, the percentage of people without access to safe water, and the percentage of underweight children under five.

Source: United Nations Development Programme, *Human Development Report 1998,* Table 1.7

B1.2   Human Poverty Index for Developing Countries (HP-1), Value and Rank, 1998—Lower Middle-Income Countries per World Bank

Country	World Rank	Percent	Country	World Rank	Percent
Albania	na	na	Macedonia, FYRO	na	na
Algeria	27.1	34	Maldives	na	na
Belarus	na	na	Marshall Islands	na	na
Belize	na	na	Micronesia	na	na
Bolivia	21.6	24	Morocco	40.2	53
Botswana	27.0	33	Namibia	30.0	41
Bulgaria	na	na	North Korea, Dem. Rep.	na	na
Cape Verde	na	na	Panama	11.1	9
Colombia	11.1	8	Papua New Guinea	29.8	40
Costa Rica	6.6	5	Paraguay	19.1	20
Cuba	na	na	Peru	23.1	27
Djibouti	na	na	Philippines	17.7	19
Dominica	na	na	Romania	na	na
Dominican Republic	17.4	18	Russia	na	na
Ecuador	15.3	15	Samoa	na	na
Egypt	34.0	46	Solomon Islands	na	na
El Salvador	27.8	37	St. Vincent and the Grenadines	na	na
Estonia	na	na	Suriname	na	na
Fiji	na	na	Swaziland	na	na
Georgia	na	na	Syria	20.9	23
Grenada	na	na	Thailand	11.9	11
Guatemala	29.3	39	Tonga	na	na
Indonesia	20.2	21	Tunisia	23.3	28
Iran	22.2	26	Turkey	na	na
Iraq	30.1	42	Turkmenistan	na	na
Jamaica	11.8	10	Ukraine	na	na
Jordan	10.0	6	Uzbekistan	na	na
Kazakhstan	na	na	Vanuatu	na	na
Kiribati	na	na	Venezuela	na	na
Latvia	na	na	Yugoslavia	na	na
Lebanon	na	na			
Lithuania	na	na			

Note: The human poverty index for developing countries (HPI-1) measures deprivation in terms of basic human development. A composite statistic, the HPI focuses on three areas of human existence: longevity, knowledge, and standard of living. The factor of longevity is represented by the percentage of people expected to die before age 40, and the knowledge factor is represented by the percentage of illiterate adults. The standard of living factor includes three variables: the percentage of people without access to health services, the percentage of people without access to safe water, and the percentage of underweight children under five.

Source: United Nations Development Programme, *Human Development Report 1998,* Table 1.7

B1.3 Human Poverty Index for Developing Countries (HP-1), Value and Rank, 1998—Upper Middle-Income Countries per World Bank

Country	World Rank	Percent	Country	World Rank	Percent
Antigua and Barbuda	na	na	Palau	na	na
Argentina	na	na	Poland	na	na
Bahrain	na	na	Saudi Arabia	na	na
Barbados	na	na	Seychelles	na	na
Brazil	na	na	Slovakia	na	na
Chile	4.1	2	Slovenia	na	na
Croatia	na	na	South Africa	na	na
Czech Republic	na	na	St. Kitts & Nevis	na	na
Gabon	na	na	St. Lucia	na	na
Hungary	na	na	Trinidad & Tobago	3.3	1
Libya	17.4	17	Uruguay	4.1	3
Malaysia	na	na	Nauru	na	na
Malta	na	na	San Marino	na	na
Mauritius	12.1	12	Taiwan	na	na
Mexico	10.7	7	Tuvalu	na	na
Oman	28.9	38			

Note: The human poverty index for developing countries (HPI-1) measures deprivation in terms of basic human development. A composite statistic, the HPI focuses on three areas of human existence: longevity, knowledge, and standard of living. The factor of longevity is represented by the percentage of people expected to die before age 40, and the knowledge factor is represented by the percentage of illiterate adults. The standard of living factor includes three variables: the percentage of people without access to health services, the percentage of people without access to safe water, and the percentage of underweight children under five.

Source: United Nations Development Programme, *Human Development Report 1998,* Table 1.7

B1.4 Components of Human Poverty Index for Developing Countries (HPI-1)—by U.N. Development Program Country Classifications

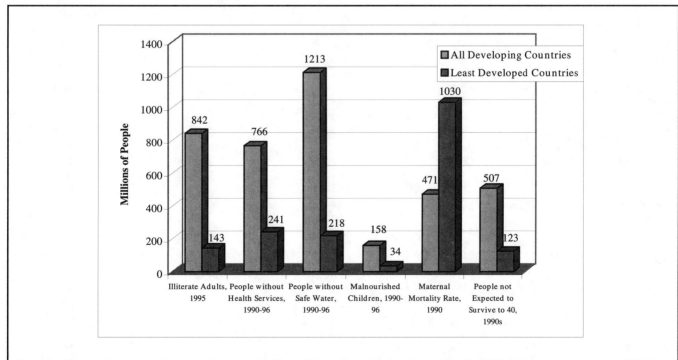

Note: The above graph represents the component parts of the Human Poverty Index for Developing Countries (HPI-1). For an explanation of the HPI-1, see notes for above tables.

Source: United Nations Development Programme, *Human Development Report 1997,* Table 2.1

B2.1   Population below National Poverty Line—Low-Income Countries per World Bank, Two-Year Comparison, Percent of Total Population

Country	Survey Year 1	Percent for Survey Year 1	Survey Year 2	Percent for Survey Year 2
Afghanistan		na		na
Angola		na		na
Armenia		na		na
Azerbaijan		na		na
Bangladesh	1991–92	42.7	1995–96	35.6
Benin	1995	33		na
Bhutan		na		na
Bosnia and Herzegovina		na		na
Burkina Faso		na		na
Burundi	1990	36.2		na
Cambodia		na		na
Cameroon	1984	40.0		na
Central African Republic		na		na
Chad		na		na
China	1994	8.4	1995	6.5
Comoros		na		na
Congo, Dem. Rep. (Zaire)		na		na
Congo, Rep.		na		na
Cote d'Ivoire		na		na
Equatorial Guinea		na		na
Eritrea		na		na
Ethiopia		na		na
Gambia	1992	64.0		na
Ghana	1992	31.4		na
Guinea		na		na
Guinea-Bissau	1991	48.8		na
Guyana		na		na
Haiti	1987	65		na
Honduras	1992	50		na
India	1992	40.9	1994	35
Kenya	1992	42.0		na
Kyrgyzstan	1993	40.0		na
Laos	1993	46.1		na
Lesotho	1993	49.2		na
Liberia		na		na
Madagascar		na		na
Malawi	1990–91	54.0		na
Mali		na		na
Mauritania	1990	57.0		na
Moldova		na		na
Mongolia	1995	36.3		na
Mozambique		na		na
Myanmar (Burma)		na		na
Nepal	1995–96	42.0		na
Nicaragua	1993	50.3		na
Niger		na		na
Nigeria	1985	43.0	1992–93	34.1
Pakistan	1991	34.0		na
Rwanda	1993	51.2		na
Sao Tome and Principe		na		na
Senegal		na		na
Sierra Leone	1989	68.0		na
Somalia		na		na
Sri Lanka	1985–86	40.6	1990–91	35.3
Sudan		na		na

B2.1 Population below National Poverty Line—Low-Income Countries per World Bank, Two-Year Comparison, Percent of Total Population (continued)

Country	Survey Year 1	Percent for Survey Year 1	Survey Year 2	Percent for Survey Year 2
Tajikistan		na		na
Tanzania	1991	51.1		na
Togo	1987–89	32.3		na
Uganda	1993	55.0		na
Vietnam	1993	50.9		na
Yemen	1992	19.1		na
Zambia	1991	68.0	1993	86.0
Zimbabwe	1990–91	25.5		na

Note: National poverty rate is the percentage of the population living below the national poverty line, which has been established by each individual country based upon the specific economic and social circumstances of that country. National estimates of those living below the poverty line are derived from household surveys and then based on estimates of population-weighted subgroup from the surveys. The survey year is the year for which the data were collected.

Source: World Bank, *World Development Indicators 1998*, Table 2.7, Poverty

B2.2 Population below National Poverty Line—Lower Middle-Income Countries per World Bank, Two-Year Comparison, Percent of Total Population

Country	Survey Year 1	Percent for Survey Year 1	Survey Year 2	Percent for Survey Year 2
Albania	1996	19.6		na
Algeria	1988	12.2	1995	22.6
Belarus		na		na
Belize		na		na
Bolivia		na		na
Botswana		na		na
Bulgaria		na		na
Cape Verde		na		na
Colombia	1991	16.9	1992	17.7
Costa Rica		na		na
Cuba		na		na
Djibouti		na		na
Dominica		na		na
Dominican Republic	1989	24.5	1992	20.6
Ecuador	1994	35.0	1995	na
Egypt		na		na
El Salvador	1992	48.3		na
Estonia	1994	8.9		na
Fiji		na		na
Georgia		na		na
Grenada		na		na
Guatemala		na		na
Indonesia	1987	17.4	1990	15.1
Iran		na		na
Iraq		na		na
Jamaica	1992	34.2		na
Jordan	1991	15.0		na
Kazakhstan		na		na
Kiribati		na		na
Latvia		na		na
Lebanon		na		na
Lithuania		na		na
Macedonia, FYRO		na		na

B2.2   Population below National Poverty Line—Lower Middle-Income Countries per World Bank, Two-Year Comparison, Percent of Total Population *(continued)*

Country	Survey Year 1	Percent for Survey Year 1	Survey Year 2	Percent for Survey Year 2
Maldives		na		na
Marshall Islands		na		na
Micronesia		na		na
Morocco	1984–85	26.0	1990-91	13.1
Namibia		na		na
North Korea, Dem. Rep.		na		na
Panama		na		na
Papua New Guinea		na		na
Paraguay	1991	21.8		na
Peru	1986	52.0	1991	54.0
Philippines	1985	52.0	1991	54.0
Romania	1994	21.5		na
Russia	1994	30.9		na
Samoa		na		na
Solomon Islands		na		na
St. Vincent and the Grenadines		na		na
Suriname		na		na
Swaziland		na		na
Syria		na		na
Thailand	1990	18	1992	13.1
Tonga		na		na
Tunisia	1985	19.9	1990	14.1
Turkey		na		na
Turkmenistan		na		na
Ukraine	1995	31.7		na
Uzbekistan		na		na
Vanuatu		na		na
Venezuela	1989	31.3		na
Yugoslavia		na		na

Note: National poverty rate is the percentage of the population living below the national poverty line, which has been established by each individual country based upon the specific economic and social circumstances of that country. National estimates of those living below the poverty line are derived from household surveys and then based on estimates of population-weighted subgroup from the surveys. The survey year is the year for which the data were collected. In some survey years, data for particular indicators were not available.

Source: World Bank, *World Development Indicators 1998,* Table 2.7, Poverty

B2.3   Population below National Poverty Line—Upper Middle-Income Countries per World Bank, Two-Year Comparison, Percent of Total Population

Country	Survey Year 1	Percent for Survey Year 1	Survey Year 2	Percent for Survey Year 2
Antigua and Barbuda				
Argentina	1991	25.5		na
Bahrain		na		na
Barbados		na		na
Brazil	1990	17.4		na
Chile	1992	21.6	1994	20.5
Croatia		na		na
Czech Republic		na		na
Gabon		na		na
Hungary	1993	25.3		na
Libya		na		na
Malaysia	1989	15.5		na
Malta		na		na

B2.3   Population below National Poverty Line—Upper Middle-Income Countries per World Bank, Two-Year Comparison, Percent of Total Population *(continued)*

Country	Survey Year 1	Percent for Survey Year 1	Survey Year 2	Percent for Survey Year 2
Mauritius	1992	10.6		na
Mexico	1988	10.1		na
Oman		na		na
Palau		na		na
Poland	1993	23.8		na
Saudi Arabia		na		na
Seychelles		na		na
Slovakia		na		na
Slovenia		na		na
South Africa		na		na
St. Kitts & Nevis		na		na
St. Lucia		na		na
Trinidad & Tobago	1992	21		na
Uruguay		na		na
Nauru		na		na
San Marino		na		na
Taiwan		na		na
Tuvalu		na		na

Note: National poverty rate is the percentage of the population living below the national poverty line, which has been established by each individual country based upon the specific economic and social circumstances of that country. National estimates of those living below the poverty line are derived from household surveys and then based on estimates of population-weighted subgroup from the surveys. The survey year is the year for which the data were collected.

Source: World Bank, *World Development Indicators 1998,* Table 2.7 Poverty

B2.4   Rural Population below National Rural Poverty Line—Low-Income Countries per World Bank, Two-Year Comparison, Percent of Total Population

Country	Survey Year 1	Percent for Survey Year 1	Survey Year 2	Percent for Survey Year 2
Afghanistan		na		na
Angola		na		na
Armenia		na		na
Azerbaijan		na		na
Bangladesh	1991–92	46.0	1995–96	39.8
Benin	1995	na		na
Bhutan		na		na
Bosnia and Herzegovina		na		na
Burkina Faso		na		na
Burundi	1990	na		na
Cambodia		na		na
Cameroon	1984	32.4		na
Central African Republic		na		na
Chad		na		na
China	1994	11.8	1995	9.2
Comoros		na		na
Congo, Dem. Rep. (Zaire)		na		na
Congo, Rep.		na		na
Cote d'Ivoire		na		na
Equatorial Guinea		na		na
Eritrea		na		na
Ethiopia		na		na
Gambia	1992	na		na
Ghana	1992	34.3		na

B2.4   Rural Population below National Rural Poverty Line—Low-Income Countries per World Bank, Two-Year Comparison, Percent of Total Population *(continued)*

Country	Survey Year 1	Percent for Survey Year 1	Survey Year 2	Percent for Survey Year 2
Guinea		na		na
Guinea-Bissau	1991	60.9		na
Guyana		na		na
Haiti	1987	na		na
Honduras	1992	46.0		na
India	1992	43.5	1994	36.7
Kenya	1992	46.4		na
Kyrgyzstan	1993	48.1		na
Laos	1993	53.0		na
Lesotho	1993	53.9		na
Liberia		na		na
Madagascar		na		na
Malawi		na		na
Mali		na		na
Mauritania	1990	na		na
Moldova		na		na
Mongolia	1995	33.1		na
Mozambique		na		na
Myanmar (Burma)		na		na
Nepal	1995–96	44.0		na
Nicaragua	1993	76.1		na
Niger		na		na
Nigeria	1985	49.5	1992–93	36.4
Pakistan	1991	36.9		na
Rwanda	1993	na		na
Sao Tome and Principe		na		na
Senegal		na		na
Sierra Leone	1989	76		na
Somalia		na		na
Sri Lanka	1985–86	45.5	1990–91	38.1
Sudan		na		na
Tajikistan		na		na
Tanzania	1991	na		na
Togo		na		na
Uganda	1993	na		na
Vietnam	1993	57.2		na
Yemen	1992	19.2		na
Zambia	1991	88.0	1993	na
Zimbabwe		na		na

Note: National rural poverty rate is the percentage of the population living below the national rural poverty line, which has been established by each individual country based upon the specific economic and social circumstances of that country. National estimates of those living below the poverty line are derived from household surveys and then based on estimates of population-weighted subgroup from the surveys. The survey year is the year for which the data were collected. In some survey years, data for particular indicators were not available.

Source: World Bank, *World Development Indicators 1998,* Table 2.7, Poverty

B2.5 Rural Population below National Rural Poverty Line—Lower Middle-Income Countries per World Bank, Two-Year Comparison, Percent of Total Population

Country	Survey Year 1	Percent for Survey Year 1	Survey Year 2	Percent for Survey Year 2
Albania	1996	na		na
Algeria	1988	16.6	1995	30.3
Belarus		na		na
Belize		na		na
Bolivia		na		na
Botswana		na		na
Bulgaria		na		na
Cape Verde		na		na
Colombia	1991	29.0	1992	31.2
Costa Rica		na		na
Cuba		na		na
Djibouti		na		na
Dominica		na		na
Dominican Republic	1989	27.4	1992	29.8
Ecuador	1994	47	1995	na
Egypt		na		na
El Salvador	1992	55.7		na
Estonia	1994	14.7		na
Fiji		na		na
Georgia		na		na
Grenada		na		na
Guatemala		na		na
Indonesia	1987	16.4	1990	14.3
Iran		na		na
Iraq		na		na
Jamaica	1992	na		na
Jordan	1991	na		na
Kazakhstan		na		na
Kiribati		na		na
Latvia		na		na
Lebanon		na		na
Lithuania		na		na
Macedonia, FYRO		na		na
Maldives		na		na
Marshall Islands		na		na
Micronesia		na		na
Morocco	1984–85	32.6	1990-91	18.0
Namibia		na		na
North Korea, Dem. Rep.		na		na
Panama		na		na
Papua New Guinea		na		na
Paraguay	1991	28.5		na
Peru	1986	64.0	1991	68.0
Philippines	1985	58.0	1991	71.0
Romania	1994	27.9		na
Russia	1994	na		na
Samoa		na		na
Solomon Islands		na		na
St. Vincent and the Grenadines		na		na
Suriname		na		na
Swaziland		na		na
Syria		na		na
Thailand	1990	na	1992	15.5
Tonga		na		na
Tunisia	1985	29.2	1990	21.6
Turkey		na		na

B2.5   Rural Population below National Rural Poverty Line—Lower Middle-Income Countries per World Bank, Two-Year Comparison, Percent of Total Population *(continued)*

Country	Survey Year 1	Percent for Survey Year 1	Survey Year 2	Percent for Survey Year 2
Turkmenistan		na		na
Ukraine	1995	na		na
Uzbekistan		na		na
Vanuatu		na		na
Venezuela	1989	na		na
Yugoslavia		na		na

Note: National rural poverty rate is the percentage of the population living below the national rural poverty line, which has been established by each individual country based upon the specific economic and social circumstances of that country. National estimates of those living below the poverty line are derived from household surveys and then based on estimates of population-weighted subgroup from the surveys. The survey year is the year for which the data were collected. In some survey years, data for particular indicators were not available.

Source: World Bank, *World Development Indicators 1998,* Table 2.7, Poverty

B2.6   Rural Population below National Rural Poverty Line—Upper Middle-Income Countries per World Bank, Two-Year Comparison, Percent of Total Population

Country	Survey Year 1	Percent for Survey Year 1	Survey Year 2	Percent for Survey Year 2
Antigua and Barbuda		na		na
Argentina	1991	na		na
Bahrain		na		na
Barbados		na		na
Brazil	1990	32.6		na
Chile	1992	na	1994	na
Croatia		na		na
Czech Republic		na		na
Gabon		na		na
Hungary	1993	na		na
Libya		na		na
Malaysia	1989	na		na
Malta		na		na
Mauritius	1992	na		na
Mexico	1988	na		na
Oman		na		na
Palau		na		na
Poland	1993	na		na
Saudi Arabia		na		na
Seychelles		na		na
Slovakia		na		na
Slovenia		na		na
South Africa		na		na
St. Kitts & Nevis		na		na
St. Lucia		na		na
Trinidad & Tobago	1992	na		na
Uruguay		na		na
Nauru		na		na
San Marino		na		na
Taiwan		na		na
Tuvalu		na		na

Note: National rural poverty rate is the percentage of the population living below the national rural poverty line, which has been established by each individual country based upon the specific economic and social circumstances of that country. National estimates of those living below the poverty line are derived from household surveys and then based on estimates of population-weighted subgroup from the surveys. The survey year is the year for which the data were collected. In some survey years, data for particular indicators were not available.

Source: World Bank, *World Development Indicators 1998,* Table 2.7, Poverty

B2.7   Urban Population below National Urban Poverty Line—Low-Income Countries per World Bank, Two-Year Comparison, Percent of Total Population

Country	Survey Year 1	Percent for Survey Year 1	Survey Year 2	Percent for Survey Year 2
Afghanistan		na		na
Angola		na		na
Armenia		na		na
Azerbaijan		na		na
Bangladesh	1991–92	23.3	1995–96	14.3
Benin	1995	na		na
Bhutan		na		na
Bosnia and Herzegovina		na		na
Burkina Faso		na		na
Burundi	1990	na		na
Cambodia		na		na
Cameroon	1984	44.4		na
Central African Republic		na		na
Chad		na		na
China	1994	<2.0	1995	<2.0
Comoros		na		na
Congo, Dem. Rep. (Zaire)		na		na
Congo, Rep.		na		na
Cote d'Ivoire		na		na
Equatorial Guinea		na		na
Eritrea		na		na
Ethiopia		na		na
Gambia	1992	na		na
Ghana	1992	26.7		na
Guinea		na		na
Guinea-Bissau	1991	24.1		na
Guyana		na		na
Haiti	1987	na		na
Honduras	1992	56.0		na
India	1992	33.7	1994	30.5
Kenya	1992	29.3		na
Kyrgyzstan	1993	28.7		na
Laos	1993	24.0		na
Lesotho	1993	27.8		na
Liberia		na		na
Madagascar		na		na
Malawi		na		na
Mali		na		na
Mauritania	1990	na		na
Moldova		na		na
Mongolia	1995	38.5		na
Mozambique		na		na
Myanmar (Burma)		na		na
Nepal	1995–96	23.0		na
Nicaragua	1993	31.9		na
Niger		na		na
Nigeria	1985	31.7	1992–93	30.4
Pakistan	1991	28		na
Rwanda	1993	na		na
Sao Tome and Principe		na		na
Senegal		na		na
Sierra Leone	1989	53.0		na
Somalia		na		na
Sri Lanka		26.8	1990–91	28.4
Sudan		na		na
Tajikistan		na		na
Tanzania	1991	na		na

B2.7   Urban Population below National Urban Poverty Line—Low-Income Countries per World Bank, Two-Year Comparison, Percent of Total Population *(continued)*

Country	Survey Year 1	Percent for Survey Year 1	Survey Year 2	Percent for Survey Year2
Togo		na		na
Uganda	1993	na		na
Vietnam	1993	25.9		na
Yemen	1992	18.6		na
Zambia	1991	46.0	1993	na
Zimbabwe		na		na

Note: National urban poverty rate is the percentage of the population living below the national urban poverty line, which has been established by each individual country based upon the specific economic and social circumstances of that country. National estimates of those living below the poverty line are derived from household surveys and then based on estimates of population-weighted subgroup from the surveys. The survey year is the year for which the data were collected. In some survey years, data for particular indicators were not available.

Source: World Bank, *World Development Indicators 1998,* Table 2.7

B2.8   Urban Population below National Urban Poverty Line—Lower Middle-Income Countries per World Bank, Two-Year Comparison, Percent of Total Population

Country	Survey Year 1	Percent for Survey Year 1	Survey Year 2	Percent for Survey Year 2
Albania	1996	na		na
Algeria	1988	7.3	1995	14.7
Belarus		na		na
Belize		na		na
Bolivia		na		na
Botswana		na		na
Bulgaria		na		na
Cape Verde		na		na
Colombia	1991	7.8	1992	8.0
Costa Rica		na		na
Cuba		na		na
Djibouti		na		na
Dominica		na		na
Dominican Republic	1989	23.3	1992	10.9
Ecuador	1994	25	1995	na
Egypt		na		na
El Salvador	1992	43.1		na
Estonia	1994	6.8		na
Fiji		na		na
Georgia		na		na
Grenada		na		na
Guatemala		na		na
Indonesia	1987	20.1	1990	16.8
Iran		na		na
Iraq		na		na
Jamaica	1992	na		na
Jordan	1991	na		na
Kazakhstan		na		na
Kiribati		na		na
Latvia		na		na
Lebanon		na		na
Lithuania		na		na
Macedonia, FYRO		na		na
Maldives		na		na
Marshall Islands		na		na
Micronesia		na		na

B2.8   Urban Population below National Urban Poverty Line—Lower Middle-Income Countries per World Bank, Two-Year Comparison, Percent of Total Population *(continued)*

Country	Survey Year 1	Percent for Survey Year 1	Survey Year 2	Percent for Survey Year 2
Morocco	1984–85	17.3	1990–91	7.6
Namibia		na		na
North Korea, Dem. Rep.		na		na
Panama		na		na
Papua New Guinea		na		na
Paraguay	1991	19.7		na
Peru	1986	45.0	1991	50.3
Philippines	1985	42.0	1991	39.0
Romania	1994	20.4		na
Russia	1994	na		na
Samoa		na		na
Solomon Islands		na		na
St. Vincent and the Grenadines		na		na
Suriname		na		na
Swaziland		na		na
Syria		na		na
Thailand	1990	na	1992	10.2
Tonga		na		na
Tunisia	1985	12.0	1990	8.9
Turkey		na		na
Turkmenistan		na		na
Ukraine	1995	na		na
Uzbekistan		na		na
Vanuatu		na		na
Venezuela	1989	na		na
Yugoslavia		na		na

Note: National urban poverty rate is the percentage of the population living below the national urban poverty line, which has been established by each individual country based upon the specific economic and social circumstances of that country. National estimates of those living below the poverty line are derived from household surveys and then based on estimates of population-weighted subgroup from the surveys. The survey year is the year for which the data were collected. In some survey years, data for particular indicators were not available.

Source: World Bank, *World Development Indicators 1998*, Table 2.7

B2.9   Urban Population below National Urban Poverty Line—Upper Middle-Income Countries per World Bank, Two-Year Comparison, Percent of Total Population

Country	Survey Year 1	Percent for Survey Year 1	Survey Year 2	Percent for Survey Year 2
Antigua and Barbuda		na		na
Argentina	1991	na		na
Bahrain		na		na
Barbados		na		na
Brazil	1990	13.1		na
Chile	1992	na	1994	na
Croatia		na		na
Czech Republic		na		na
Gabon		na		na
Hungary	1993	na		na
Libya		na		na
Malaysia	1989	na		na
Malta		na		na
Mauritius	1992	na		na
Mexico	1988	na		na
Oman		na		na

B2.9   Urban Population below National Urban Poverty Line—Upper Middle-Income Countries per World Bank, Two-Year Comparison, Percent of Total Population *(continued)*

Country	Survey Year 1	Percent for Survey Year 1	Survey Year 2	Percent for Survey Year 2
Palau		na		na
Poland	1993	na		na
Saudi Arabia		na		na
Seychelles		na		na
Slovakia		na		na
Slovenia		na		na
South Africa		na		na
St. Kitts & Nevis		na		na
St. Lucia		na		na
Trinidad & Tobago	1992	na		na
Uruguay		na		na
Nauru		na		na
San Marino		na		na
Taiwan		na		na
Tuvalu		na		na

Note: National urban poverty rate is the percentage of the population living below the national urban poverty line, which has been established by each individual country based upon the specific economic and social circumstances of that country. National estimates of those living below the poverty line are derived from household surveys and then based on estimates of population-weighted subgroup from the surveys. The survey year is the year for which the data were collected. In some survey years, data for particular indicators were not available.

Source: World Bank, *World Development Indicators 1998,* Table 2.7

B3.1   International Poverty Line-Population Living below One Dollar per Day—Low-Income Countries per World Bank, Percent of Population

Country	Survey Year	Percent Living below $1/day	Country	Survey Year	Percent Living below $1/day
Afghanistan		na	Haiti		na
Angola		na	Honduras	1992	46.9
Armenia		na	India	1992	52.5
Azerbaijan		na	Kenya	1992	50.2
Bangladesh		na	Kyrgyzstan	1993	18.9
Benin		na	Laos		na
Bhutan		na	Lesotho		48.8
Bosnia and Herzegovina		na	Liberia		na
Burkina Faso		na	Madagascar	1993	72.3
Burundi		na	Malawi		na
Cambodia		na	Mali		na
Cameroon		na	Mauritania	1988	31.4
Central African Republic		na	Moldova	1992	6.8
Chad		na	Mongolia		na
China	1995	22.2	Mozambique		na
Comoros		na	Myanmar (Burma)		na
Congo, Dem. Rep. (Zaire)		na	Nepal	1995	50.3
Congo, Rep.		na	Nicaragua	1993	43.8
Cote d'Ivoire	1988	17.7	Niger	1992	61.5
Equatorial Guinea		na	Nigeria	1992–93	31.1
Eritrea		na	Pakistan	1991	11.6
Ethiopia	1981–82	46.0	Rwanda	1983–85	45.7
Gambia		na	Sao Tome and Principe		na
Ghana		na	Senegal	1991–92	54.0
Guinea	1991	26.3	Sierra Leone		na
Guinea-Bissau	1991	88.2	Somalia		na
Guyana		na	Sri Lanka	1990	4.0

B3.1   International Poverty Line-Population Living below One Dollar per Day—Low-Income Countries per World Bank, Percent of Population *(continued)*

Country	Survey Year	Percent Living below $1/day	Country	Survey Year	Percent Living below $1/day
Sudan		na	Vietnam		na
Tajikistan		na	Yemen		na
Tanzania	1993	10.5	Zambia	1993	84.6
Togo		na	Zimbabwe	1990–91	41.0
Uganda	1989–90	69.3			

Note: The population below one dollar a day represents the portion of a country's population existing on less than one dollar a day. It is stated as a percent and based on 1985 international prices, which is adjusted for purchasing power parity (PPP). The World Bank uses a poverty line of one dollar a day for international comparison and is based on the consumption, not income, of households. International poverty lines are developed from household surveys that are representative of national circumstances. The survey year is the year for which the data were collected.

Source: World Bank, *World Development Indicators 1998,* Table 2.7

B3.2   International Poverty Line-Population Living below One Dollar per Day—Lower Middle-Income Countries per World Bank, Percent of Population

Country	Survey Year	Percent Living below $1/day	Country	Survey Year	Percent Living below $1/day
Albania		na	Lithuania	1993	<2.0
Algeria	1995	<2.0	Macedonia, FYRO		na
Belarus	1993	<2.0	Maldives		na
Belize		na	Marshall Islands		na
Bolivia		na	Micronesia		na
Botswana	1985–86	33.0	Morocco	1990–91	<2.0
Bulgaria	1992	2.6	Namibia		na
Cape Verde		na	North Korea, Dem. Rep.		na
Colombia	1991	7.4	Panama	1989	25.6
Costa Rica	1989	18.9	Papua New Guinea		na
Cuba		na	Paraguay		na
Djibouti		na	Peru		na
Dominica		na	Philippines	1991	28.6
Dominican Republic	1989	19.9	Romania	1992	17.7
Ecuador	1994	30.4	Russia	1993	<2.0
Egypt	1990–91	7.6	Samoa		na
El Salvador		na	Solomon Islands		na
Estonia	1993	6.0	St. Vincent and the Grenadines		na
Fiji		na	Suriname		na
Georgia		na	Swaziland		na
Grenada		na	Syria		na
Guatemala	1989	53.3	Thailand	1992	<2.0
Indonesia	1995	11.8	Tonga		na
Iran		na	Tunisia	1990	3.9
Iraq		na	Turkey		na
Jamaica	1993	4.3	Turkmenistan	1993	4.9
Jordan	1992	2.5	Ukraine		na
Kazakhstan	1993	<2.0	Uzbekistan		na
Kiribati		na	Vanuatu		na
Latvia		na	Venezuela	1991	11.8
Lebanon		na	Yugoslavia		na

Note: The population below one dollar a day represents the portion of a country's population existing on less than one dollar a day. It is stated as a percent and based on 1985 international prices, which is adjusted for purchasing power parity (PPP). The World Bank uses a poverty line of one dollar a day for international comparison and is based on the consumption, not income, of households. International poverty lines are developed from household surveys that are representative of national circumstances. The survey year is the year for which the data were collected.

Source: World Bank, *World Development Indicators 1998,* Table 2.7

B3.3   International Poverty Line-Population Living below One Dollar per Day—Upper Middle-Income Countries per World Bank, Percent of Population

Country	Survey Year	Percent Living below $1/day	Country	Survey Year	Percent Living below $1/day
Antigua and Barbuda		na	Palau		na
Argentina		na	Poland	1993	6.8
Bahrain		na	Saudi Arabia		na
Barbados		na	Seychelles		na
Brazil	1995	23.6	Slovakia	1992	12.8
Chile	1992	15.0	Slovenia		na
Croatia		na	South Africa	1993	23.7
Czech Republic	1993	3.1	St. Kitts & Nevis		na
Gabon		na	St. Lucia		na
Hungary	1993	<2.0	Trinidad & Tobago		na
Libya		na	Uruguay		na
Malaysia	1989	5.6	Nauru		na
Malta		na	San Marino		na
Mauritius		na	Taiwan		na
Mexico	1992	14.9	Tuvalu		na
Oman		na			

Note: The population below one dollar a day represents the portion of a country's population existing on less than one dollar a day. It is stated as a percent and based on 1985 international prices, which is adjusted for purchasing power parity (PPP). The World Bank uses a poverty line of one dollar a day for international comparison and is based on the consumption, not income, of households. International poverty lines are developed from household surveys that are representative of national circumstances. The survey year is the year for which the data were collected.

Source: World Bank, *World Development Indicators 1998,* Table 2.7

B3.4   International Poverty Line-Population Living below Two Dollars per Day—Low-Income Countries per World Bank, Percent of Population

Country	Survey Year	Percent Living below $2/day	Country	Survey Year	Percent Living below $2/day
Afghanistan		na	Guyana		na
Angola		na	Haiti		na
Armenia		na	Honduras	1992	75.7
Azerbaijan		na	India	1992	88.8
Bangladesh		na	Kenya	1992	78.1
Benin		na	Kyrgyzstan	1993	55.3
Bhutan		na	Laos		na
Bosnia and Herzegovina		na	Lesotho	1986–87	74.1
Burkina Faso		na	Liberia		na
Burundi		na	Madagascar	1993	93.2
Cambodia		na	Malawi		na
Cameroon		na	Mali		na
Central African Republic		na	Mauritania	1988	68.4
Chad		na	Moldova	1992	30.6
China	1995	57.8	Mongolia		na
Comoros		na	Mozambique		na
Congo, Dem. Rep. (Zaire)		na	Myanmar (Burma)		na
Congo, Rep.		na	Nepal	1995	86.7
Cote d'Ivoire	1988	54.8	Nicaragua	1993	74.5
Equatorial Guinea		na	Niger	1992	92.0
Eritrea		na	Nigeria	1992–93	59.9
Ethiopia		89	Pakistan	1991	57.0
Gambia		na	Rwanda	1983–85	88.7
Ghana		na	Sao Tome and Principe		na
Guinea	1991	50.2	Senegal	1991–92	79.6
Guinea-Bissau	1991	96.7	Sierra Leone		na

B3.4 International Poverty Line-Population Living below Two Dollars per Day—Low-Income Countries per World Bank, Percent of Population *(continued)*

Country	Survey Year	Percent Living below $2/day	Country	Survey Year	Percent Living below $2/day
			Uganda	1989–90	92.2
Somalia		na	Vietnam		na
Sri Lanka	1990	41.2	Yemen		na
Sudan		na	Zambia	1993	98.1
Tajikistan		na	Zimbabwe	1990–91	68.2
Tanzania	1993	45.5			
Togo		na			

Note: The population below two dollars a day represents the portion of a country's population existing on less than two dollars a day. It is stated as a percent and based on 1985 international prices, which is adjusted for purchasing power parity (PPP). The World Bank uses a poverty line of two dollars a day for international comparison and is based on the consumption, not income, of households. International poverty lines are developed from household surveys that are representative of national circumstances. The survey year is the year for which the data were collected.

Source: World Bank, *World Development Indicators 1998,* Table 2.7

B3.5 International Poverty Line-Population Living below Two Dollars per Day—Lower Middle-Income Countries per World Bank, Percent of Population

Country	Survey Year	Percent Living below $2/day	Country	Survey Year	Percent Living below $2/day
Albania		na	Lithuania	1993	18.9
Algeria	1995	17.6	Macedonia, FYRO		na
Belarus	1993	6.4	Maldives		na
Belize		na	Marshall Islands		na
Bolivia		na	Micronesia		na
Botswana	1985–86	61.0	Morocco	1990–91	19.6
Bulgaria	1992	23.5	Namibia		na
Cape Verde		na	North Korea, Dem. Rep.		na
Colombia	1991	21.7	Panama	1989	46.2
Costa Rica	1989	43.8	Papua New Guinea		na
Cuba		na	Paraguay		na
Djibouti		na	Peru		na
Dominica		na	Philippines	1991	64.5
Dominican Republic	1989	47.7	Romania	1992	70.9
Ecuador	1994	65.8	Russia	1993	10.9
Egypt	1990–91	51.9	Samoa		na
El Salvador		na	Solomon Islands		na
Estonia	1993	32.5	St. Vincent and the Grenadines		na
Fiji		na	Suriname		na
Georgia		na	Swaziland		na
Grenada		na	Syria		na
Guatemala	1989	76.8	Thailand	1992	23.5
Indonesia	1995	58.7	Tonga		na
Iran		na	Tunisia	1990	22.7
Iraq		na	Turkey		na
Jamaica	1993	24.9	Turkmenistan	1993	25.8
Jordan	1992	23.5	Ukraine		na
Kazakhstan	1993	12.1	Uzbekistan		na
Kiribati		na	Vanuatu		na
Latvia		na	Venezuela	1991	32.2
Lebanon		na	Yugoslavia		na

Note: Population below two dollars a day is the percentage of the population living on less than two dollars a day at 1985 international prices, adjusted for purchasing power parity (PPP). A poverty line set at two dollars (1985 PPP$) a day per person is used by the World Bank for international comparison and is based on the consumption, not income, of households. International poverty lines are developed from household surveys that are representative of national circumstances. The survey year is the year for which the data were collected.

Source: World Bank, *World Development Indicators 1998,* Table 2.7

B3.6 International Poverty Line-Population Living below Two Dollars per Day—Upper Middle-Income Countries per World Bank, Percent of Population

Country	Survey Year	Percent Living below $2/day	Country	Survey Year	Percent Living below $2/day
Antigua and Barbuda		na	Palau		na
Argentina		na	Poland	1993	15.1
Bahrain		na	Saudi Arabia		na
Barbados		na	Seychelles		na
Brazil	1995	43.5	Slovakia	1992	85.1
Chile	1992	38.5	Slovenia		na
Croatia		na	South Africa	1993	50.2
Czech Republic	1993	55.1	St. Kitts & Nevis		na
Gabon		na	St. Lucia		na
Hungary	1993	10.7	Trinidad & Tobago		na
Libya		na	Uruguay		na
Malaysia	1989	26.6	Nauru		na
Malta		na	San Marino		na
Mauritius		na	Taiwan		na
Mexico	1992	40.0	Tuvalu		na
Oman		na			

Note: Population below two dollars a day is the percentage of the population living on less than two dollars a day at 1985 international prices, adjusted for purchasing power parity (PPP). A poverty line set at two dollars (1985 PPP$) a day per person is used by the World Bank for international comparison and is based on the consumption, not income, of households. International poverty lines are developed from household surveys that are representative of national circumstances. The survey year is the year for which the data were collected.

Source: World Bank, *World Development Indicators 1998,* Table 2.7

B4.1   International Poverty Line, Poverty Gap below One Dollar per Day—Low-Income Countries per World Bank, Percent of Population

Country	Survey Year	Percent	Country	Survey Year	Percent
Afghanistan		na	Laos		na
Angola		na	Lesotho	1986–87	23.8
Armenia		na	Liberia		na
Azerbaijan		na	Madagascar	1993	33.2
Bangladesh		na	Malawi		na
Benin		na	Mali		na
Bhutan		na	Mauritania	1988	15.2
Bosnia and Herzegovina		na	Moldova	1992	1.2
Burkina Faso		na	Mongolia		na
Burundi		na	Mozambique		na
Cambodia		na	Myanmar (Burma)		na
Cameroon		na	Nepal	1995	16.2
Central African Republic		na	Nicaragua	1993	18.0
Chad		na	Niger	1992	22.2
China	1995	6.9	Nigeria		12.9
Comoros		na	Pakistan	1991	2.6
Congo, Dem. Rep. (Zaire)		na	Rwanda		11.3
Congo, Rep.		na	Sao Tome and Principe		na
Cote d'Ivoire	1988	4.3	Senegal	1991–92	25.5
Equatorial Guinea		na	Sierra Leone		na
Eritrea		na	Somalia		na
Ethiopia	1981–82	12.4	Sri Lanka	1990	0.7
Gambia		na	Sudan		na
Ghana		na	Tajikistan		na
Guinea	1991	12.4	Tanzania	1993	2.1
Guinea-Bissau	1991	59.5	Togo		na
Guyana		na	Uganda	1989–90	29.1
Haiti		na	Vietnam		na
Honduras	1992	20.4	Yemen		na
India	1992	15.6	Zambia	1993	53.8
Kenya	1992	22.2	Zimbabwe	1990–91	14.3
Kyrgyzstan	1993	5.0			

Note: The poverty gap is the average shortfall of household consumption below the poverty line of one or two dollars per day; it is stated as a percentage of the poverty line. (The non-poor population has a zero shortfall.) For definitions of one or two dollars per day poverty lines, see notes to tables above. The survey year is the year for which the data were collected.

Source: World Bank, *World Development Indicators 1998,* Table 2.7

B4.2   International Poverty Line, Poverty Gap below One Dollar per Day—Lower Middle-Income Countries per World Bank, Percent of Population

Country	Survey Year	Percent	Country	Survey Year	Percent
Albania		na	Macedonia, FYRO		na
Algeria	1995	na	Maldives		na
Belarus	1993	na	Marshall Islands		na
Belize		na	Micronesia		na
Bolivia		na	Morocco		na
Botswana	1985–86	12.4	Namibia		na
Bulgaria	1992	0.8	North Korea, Dem. Rep.		na
Cape Verde		na	Panama	1989	12.6
Colombia	1991	2.3	Papua New Guinea		na
Costa Rica	1989	7.2	Paraguay		na
Cuba		na	Peru		na
Djibouti		na	Philippines	1991	7.7
Dominica		na	Romania	1992	4.2
Dominican Republic	1989	6.0	Russia	1993	na
Ecuador	1994	9.1	Samoa		na
Egypt	1990–91	1.1	Solomon Islands		na
El Salvador		na	St. Vincent and the Grenadines		na
Estonia	1993	1.6	Suriname		na
Fiji		na	Swaziland		na
Georgia		na	Syria		na
Grenada		na	Thailand	1992	na
Guatemala	1989	28.5	Tonga		na
Indonesia	1995	1.8	Tunisia	1990	0.9
Iran		na	Turkey		na
Iraq		na	Turkmenistan	1993	0.5
Jamaica	1993	0.5	Ukraine		na
Jordan	1992	0.5	Uzbekistan		na
Kazakhstan	1993	na	Vanuatu		na
Kiribati		na	Venezuela	1991	3.1
Latvia		na	Yugoslavia		na
Lebanon		na			
Lithuania	1993	na			

Note: The poverty gap is the average shortfall of household consumption below the poverty line of one or two dollars per day; it is stated as a percentage of the poverty line. (The non-poor population has a zero shortfall.) For definitions of one or two dollars per day poverty lines, see notes to tables above. The survey year is the year for which the data were collected. In some survey years, data for particular indicators were not available.

Source: World Bank, *World Development Indicators 1998*, Table 2.7

B4.3   International Poverty Line, Poverty Gap below One Dollar per Day—Upper Middle-Income Countries per World Bank, Percent of Population

Country	Survey Year	Percent	Country	Survey Year	Percent
Antigua and Barbuda		na	Palau		na
Argentina		na	Poland	1993	4.7
Bahrain		na	Saudi Arabia		na
Barbados		na	Seychelles		na
Brazil	1995	10.7	Slovakia	1992	2.2
Chile	1992	4.9	Slovenia		na
Croatia		na	South Africa	1993	6.6
Czech Republic	1993	0.4	St. Kitts & Nevis		na
Gabon		na	St. Lucia		na
Hungary	1993	na	Trinidad & Tobago		na
Libya		na	Uruguay		na
Malaysia	1989	0.9	Nauru		na
Malta		na	San Marino		na
Mauritius		na	Taiwan		na
Mexico	1992	3.8	Tuvalu		na
Oman		na			

Note: The poverty gap is the average shortfall of household consumption below the poverty line of one or two dollars per day; it is stated as a percentage of the poverty line. (The non-poor population has a zero shortfall.) For definitions of one or two dollars per day poverty lines, see notes to tables above. The survey year is the year for which the data were collected. In some survey years, data for particular indicators were not available.

Source: World Bank, *World Development Indicators 1998,* Table 2.7

B4.4   International Poverty Line, Poverty Gap below Two Dollars per Day—Low-Income Countries per World Bank, Percent of Population

Country	Survey Year	Percent	Country	Survey Year	Percent
Afghanistan		na	India	1992	45.8
Angola		na	Kenya	1992	44.4
Armenia		na	Kyrgyzstan	1993	21.4
Azerbaijan		na	Laos		na
Bangladesh		na	Lesotho	1986–87	43.5
Benin		na	Liberia		na
Bhutan		na	Madagascar	1993	59.6
Bosnia and Herzegovina		na	Malawi		na
Burkina Faso		na	Mali		na
Burundi		na	Mauritania	1988	33.0
Cambodia		na	Moldova	1992	9.7
Cameroon		na	Mongolia		na
Central African Republic		na	Mozambique		na
Chad		na	Myanmar (Burma)		na
China	1995	24.1	Nepal	1995	44.6
Comoros		na	Nicaragua	1993	39.7
Congo, Dem. Rep. (Zaire)		na	Niger	1992	51.8
Congo, Rep.		na	Nigeria	1992–93	29.8
Cote d'Ivoire	1988	20.4	Pakistan	1991	18.6
Equatorial Guinea		na	Rwanda	1983–85	42.3
Eritrea		na	Sao Tome and Principe		na
Ethiopia	1981–82	42.7	Senegal	1991–92	47.2
Gambia		na	Sierra Leone		na
Ghana		na	Somalia		na
Guinea	1991	25.6	Sri Lanka	1990	11.0
Guinea-Bissau	1991	76.6	Sudan		na
Guyana		na	Tajikistan		na
Haiti		na	Tanzania	1993	15.3
Honduras	1992	41.9	Togo		na

B4.4   International Poverty Line, Poverty Gap below Two Dollars per Day—Low-Income Countries per World Bank, Percent of Population (continued)

Country	Survey Year	Percent	Country	Survey Year	Percent
Uganda	1989–90	56.6	Zambia	1993	73.4
Vietnam		na	Zimbabwe	1990–91	35.5
Yemen		na			

Note: The poverty gap is the average shortfall of household consumption below the poverty line of one or two dollars per day; it is stated as a percentage of the poverty line. (The non-poor population has a zero shortfall.) For definitions of one or two dollars per day poverty lines, see notes to tables above. The survey year is the year for which the data were collected.

Source: World Bank, *World Development Indicators 1998*, Table 2.7

B4.5   International Poverty Line, Poverty Gap below Two Dollars per Day—Lower Middle-Income Countries per World Bank, Percent of Population

Country	Survey Year	Percent	Country	Survey Year	Percent
Albania		na	Macedonia, FYRO		na
Algeria	1995	4.4	Maldives		na
Belarus	1993	0.8	Marshall Islands		na
Belize		na	Micronesia		na
Bolivia		na	Morocco	1990–91	4.6
Botswana	1985–86	30.4	Namibia		na
Bulgaria	1992	6.0	North Korea, Dem. Rep.		na
Cape Verde		na	Panama	1989	24.5
Colombia	1991	8.4	Papua New Guinea		na
Costa Rica	1989	19.4	Paraguay		na
Cuba		na	Peru		na
Djibouti		na	Philippines	1991	28.2
Dominica		na	Romania	1992	24.7
Dominican Republic	1989	20.2	Russia	1993	2.3
Ecuador	1994	29.6	Samoa		na
Egypt	1990–91	15.3	Solomon Islands		na
El Salvador		na	St. Vincent and the Grenadines		na
Estonia	1993	10	Suriname		na
Fiji		na	Swaziland		na
Georgia		na	Syria		na
Grenada		na	Thailand	1992	5.4
Guatemala	1989	47.6	Tonga		na
Indonesia	1995	19.3	Tunisia	1990	6.8
Iran		na	Turkey		na
Iraq		na	Turkmenistan	1993	7.6
Jamaica	1993	7.5	Ukraine		na
Jordan	1992	6.3	Uzbekistan		na
Kazakhstan	1993	2.5	Vanuatu		na
Kiribati		na	Venezuela	1991	12.2
Latvia		na	Yugoslavia		na
Lebanon		na			
Lithuania	1993	4.1			

Note: The poverty gap is the average shortfall of household consumption below the poverty line of one or two dollars per day; it is stated as a percentage of the poverty line. (The non-poor population has a zero shortfall.) For definitions of one or two dollars per day poverty lines, see notes to tables above. The survey year is the year for which the data were collected.

Source: World Bank, *World Development Indicators 1998*, Table 2.7

B4.6 International Poverty Line, Poverty Gap below Two Dollars per Day—Upper Middle-Income Countries per World Bank, Percent of Population

Country	Survey Year	Percent	Country	Survey Year	Percent
Antigua and Barbuda		na	Oman		na
Argentina		na	Palau		na
Bahrain		na	Poland	1993	7.7
Barbados		na	Saudi Arabia		na
Brazil	1995	22.4	Seychelles		na
Chile	1992	16.0	Slovakia	1992	27.5
Croatia		na	Slovenia		na
Czech Republic	1993	14.0	South Africa	1993	22.5
Gabon		na	St. Kitts & Nevis		na
Hungary	1993	2.1	St. Lucia		na
Libya		na	Trinidad & Tobago		na
Malaysia	1989	8.5	Uruguay		na
Malta		na	Nauru		na
Mauritius		na	San Marino		na
Mexico	1992	15.9	Taiwan		na
			Tuvalu		na

Note: The poverty gap is the average shortfall of household consumption below the poverty line of one or two dollars per day; it is stated as a percentage of the poverty line. (The non-poor population has a zero shortfall.) For definitions of one or two dollars per day poverty lines, see notes to tables above. The survey year is the year for which the data were collected.

Source: World Bank, *World Development Indicators 1998,* Table 2.7

C. Economics

GENERAL OVERVIEW

Economic indicators—such as gross domestic product and inflation rates—provide analysts, policymakers, and students of poverty with basic information about the economic viability of an economy. They signify a country's capacity to satisfy the material needs of its people, such as its ability to produce products and services for consumption, to provide individuals with livelihoods, and to provide stable price arenas within which to produce products and sustain life.

For a study of poverty, the value of these indicators is crucial. The economic concerns they cover are vital to poor people throughout the developing world. For instance, the Consumer Price Index (CPI), which measures the change in prices consumers pay over periods of time, has a direct impact on the capacity of individuals to satisfy their material needs: if an increase in prices outstrips an increase in income, a lessening of the standard of living may result.

But the picture of deprivation suffered by the poor throughout the world cannot always be reduced to dollars and cents. Economic data must be supplemented by an investigation into demographic trends, health concerns, and educational issues in order to derive a fully human portrait of poverty. Indicators analyzing these types of data are presented in other sections in this book.

EXPLANATION OF INDICATORS

Gross Domestic Product (GDP): As a measure of the total output of goods and services of a country, the GDP is a benchmark in analyzing any country's economic health. It shows the economic capacity of a country. It is a complex indicator, determined by various factors including the physical wealth (land, minerals, forests, etc.), human resources (employees, employers, and their skill levels), and capital development (internal infrastructure, production-related machinery, etc.). Given the factors that go into the GDP, it is easy to see why many poor coun-

tries tally low GDP statistics: with limited and/or underperforming physical, human, and capital resources, a capacity for healthy economic development will be limited as well.

GDP growth rates help to measure the progress of economic development over time. Growth in GDP for all countries in the designated income categories shows that, on the whole, economic capacity is on the rise. Clearly, as summary totals, the growth rates only average out the change in GDP; therefore, the upward trends can mask the economic performance of individual countries (C1.1).

The sectoral breakdown on GDP is a measure of the components of a country or group of countries' economic output. Least-developed countries often have a higher share of their GDP rooted in agriculture than higher-income or more-developed countries do. Analyzing the sectoral breakdown helps analysts to understand, in raw terms, what drives economic activity and growth (C1.2).

Gross Domestic Product per Capita: GDP per Capita is the GDP of a country divided by its population; it helps to relate a country's economic output to the size of its population and therefore acts as an important qualifier to the cruder GDP measurement. Consequently, it is a more valuable tool in analyzing the economic well-being of a country: it can tell us whether a country's output is in proportion to its population (C2.1–C2.6).

Consumer Price Index (CPI): CPI represents the volatility of prices experienced by the population within a country. As a measure of the change in the price of a "basket" of goods deemed vital to all people, it measures the extent to which individual income is threatened by economic erosion due to price increases. As with many indicators in this book, it is averaged out across all regions within a country and therefore has limitations: it does not tell us whether it is less expensive to live in urban areas than rural areas, for instance. Nevertheless, it helps to gauge an important aspect of economies of poorer countries—whether their production capacities (supply) and consumption capabilities (demand) are stable. In many poorer countries, an unfavorable supply-and-demand situation frequently exists: with increases in demand for basic goods expanding due to rapidly growing populations, and supply lagging behind demand due to inefficient production capacity, the upward pressure on prices exists (C3.1–C3.3).

Commodity Price Index: This indicator represents the change in prices of primary commodities (agricultural products, metals, minerals, etc.) from 1980 to 1997. The worldwide index is graphed here, showing price fluctuation against a base year of 1990. The price of commodities is important to all countries, as production of final products relies on the primary goods market. For developing countries, this market is especially important, as their economies focus heavily on the production and export of primary goods. Stability in international commodity prices are therefore crucial to the internal economic stability of these countries (C4.1).

Economic Activity Rates: This indicator tells us what part of a population is working—as employees, employers, or self-employed family workers, etc. It helps to highlight the capacity of the economy to provide livelihoods for its people. Although it does not give specific information concerning the nature of the economic activity people are engaged in, and the amount of income such work generates, it is a measure of a country's economic viability. This measure is more helpful than unemployment figures for lower- and middle-income countries, because their economies rely less on jobs at firms in the marketplace, and more on self-employment and subsistence work, both situations not typically measured by unemployment figures (C5.1–C5.3).

Earned Income Share for Women and Men: The earned income share for men and women indicates what portion of the total income earned in a country is attributed to men and to women. It helps to point out the disparity between the sexes in income-earning capabilities. More male-female gaps such as this one are included in Section I: Women and Poverty, where the deprivation and inequalities particular to poor women are explored (C6.1–C6.3).

Domestic Credit Provided by Banking Sector: This domestic credit indicator reflects the health, viability, and development of the banking sector of a country. An advanced feature of a market economy, domestic credit helps economic enterprises to grow, and an increasing availability of credit, efficiently and fairly administered, helps poorer countries to expand the economic opportunities available to their people (C7.1–C7.3).

Percentage Share of Income or Consumption: The percentage share of a country's total income and consumption at various levels of the income-earning scale helps to point out economic inequalities in a society. Nearly always, those ranked poorest receive and consume a disproportionately tiny portion of the total income of a country, and those at the top receive and consume a disproportionately large share of the income. In other words, the lowest one-fifth of a country's income scale usually accounts for less than one-fifth of its income. And the top one-fifth usually accounts for more than one-fifth. This tendency toward unequal distribution of income is a feature in nearly all countries of the world; and in poorer countries, it can be exacerbated by the fact that small elites frequently own or have access to the material and capital resources of a country. Such indicators of income inequality help policymakers in planning income transference mechanisms such as a country's tax structure and the features of its welfare system (C8.1–C8.3).

C1.1   GDP Average Annual Growth, 1980–1990 and 1990–1996—Comparison by Income Level per World Bank

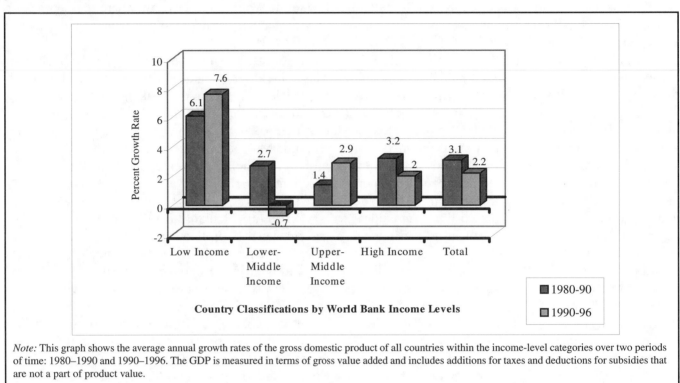

Note: This graph shows the average annual growth rates of the gross domestic product of all countries within the income-level categories over two periods of time: 1980–1990 and 1990–1996. The GDP is measured in terms of gross value added and includes additions for taxes and deductions for subsidies that are not a part of product value.

Source: World Bank, *World Development Indicators 1998*, Table 4.1

C1.2   GDP Sectoral Breakdown, 1996—Comparison by Income Level per World Bank

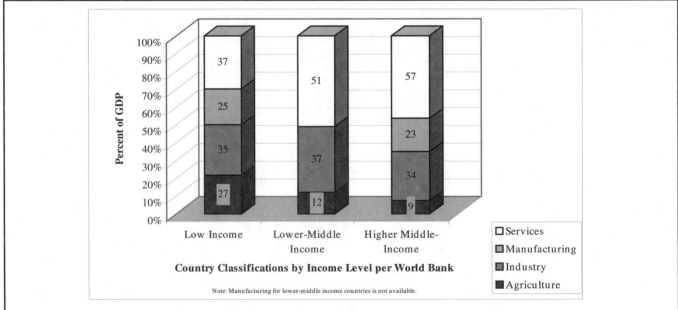

Note: This graph shows the share of Gross Domestic Product arising from each of the four sectors of economic activity: agriculture, industry, manufacturing, and services for the entire group of low and middle income countries (as categorized by the World Bank). The calculations for GDP sectoral breakdowns are based on value added in each sector, which is each sectors net output (total of all outputs less intermediate inputs).

Source: World Bank, *World Development Indicators 1998*, Table 4.2

C2.1 GDP per Capita, Current International U.S. Dollars, 1980–1996, In Purchasing Power Parity (PPP)—Low-Income Countries per World Bank

Country	1980	1985	1990	1995	1996
Afghanistan	na	na	na	na	na
Angola	na	1,258	1,492	2,055	2,004
Armenia	2,900	4,190	5,077	2,005	na
Azerbaijan	na	na	3,760	1,493	1,515
Bangladesh	390	543	744	971	1,010
Benin	641	878	970	1,207	1,254
Bhutan	na	na	na	na	na
Bosnia and Herzegovina	na	na	na	na	na
Burkina Faso	463	623	782	914	954
Burundi	419	559	740	657	597
Cambodia	na	na	na	na	na
Cameroon	1,256	2,067	1,993	1,812	1,930
Central African Republic	1,007	1,221	1,412	1,521	1,463
Chad	392	645	792	889	910
China	500	907	1,556	3,072	3,364
Comoros	1,096	1,445	1,735	1,772	1,767
Congo, Dem. Rep. (Zaire)	1,149	1,281	1,362	916	902
Congo, Rep.	907	1,522	1,723	1,642	1,793
Cote d'Ivoire	1,397	1,327	1,547	1,655	1,724
Equatorial Guinea	na	na	1,030	2,432	3,165
Eritrea	na	na	na	na	na
Ethiopia	na	291	403	465	504
Gambia	787	983	1,201	1,273	na
Ghana	1,034	1,058	1,417	1,767	1,831
Guinea	na	na	1,427	1,734	1,788
Guinea-Bissau	392	593	818	1,007	1,049
Guyana	1,645	1,591	1,758	2,640	2,465
Haiti	1,193	1,242	1,433	1,129	1,135
Honduras	1,342	1,476	1,902	2,120	2,133
India	519	724	1,116	1,515	1,606
Kenya	640	726	1,034	1,125	1,162
Kyrgyzstan	na	na	3,440	1,959	2,065
Laos	na	na	860	1,190	1,250
Lesotho	709	761	1,126	1,479	1,713
Liberia	na	na	na	na	na
Madagascar	789	764	925	941	937
Malawi	413	472	563	619	705
Mali	424	457	621	719	727
Mauritania	1,098	1,202	1,507	1,850	1,908
Moldova	na	na	3,640	1,599	1,466
Mongolia	na	1,540	2,026	1,825	1,855
Mozambique	na	239	412	537	556
Myanmar (Burma)	na	na	na	na	na
Nepal	437	582	805	1,037	1,074
Nicaragua	1,784	1,926	1,594	2,039	2,075
Niger	902	764	911	930	934
Nigeria	560	539	757	877	894
Pakistan	607	860	1,227	1,558	1,605
Rwanda	559	652	774	577	636
Sao Tome and Principe	na	na	na	na	na
Senegal	952	1,136	1,487	1,632	1,693
Sierra Leone	472	489	628	503	520
Somalia	na	na	na	na	na
Sri Lanka	805	1,195	1,652	2,274	2,324
Sudan	na	na	na	na	na

C2.1   GDP per Capita, Current International U.S. Dollars, 1980–1996, In Purchasing Power Parity (PPP)—Low-Income Countries per World Bank *(continued)*

Country	1980	1985	1990	1995	1996
Tajikistan	na	na	2,440	835	901
Tanzania	na	na	na	na	na
Togo	1,378	1,408	1,732	1,626	1,687
Uganda	na	508	713	970	1,038
Vietnam	na	na	na	1,450	1,570
Yemen	na	na	na	799	899
Zambia	756	805	933	853	884
Zimbabwe	1,328	1,636	2,042	2,156	2,298

Note: Gross Domestic Product (GDP) is a measure of a country's total economic output—the total of goods and services it produces within its territory, whether it is attributed to domestic or foreign claims. It is a gross measure, excluding deductions for depreciation or depletion of resources. As stated in purchasing power parity (PPP), it is translated to international U.S. dollars, which have equivalent purchasing power as does the U.S. dollar in the United States. This table presents Gross Domestic Product per capita, that is, the total goods and services for the year divided by a country's population for that same year. The data in this table are stated in current terms, that is, without adjustments to deflate the effect of inflation.

Source: World Bank, *World Development Indicators 1998*, Table 4.1, 4.2, 4.10, and 4.11; World Bank, *World Development Indicators 1998*, CD-ROM, Series GDP per capita, PPP (NY.GDP.PCAP.PP.CD)

C2.2   GDP per Capita, Current International U.S. Dollars, 1980–1996, In Purchasing Power Parity (PPP)—Lower Middle-Income Countries per World Bank

Country	1980	1985	1990	1995	1996
Albania	na	na	na	na	na
Algeria	3,067	4,070	4,554	4,743	4,870
Belarus	na	na	5,860	4,223	4,393
Belize	1,838	1,994	3,488	4,344	4,355
Bolivia	1,785	1,792	2,304	2,913	na
Botswana	2,170	3,546	6,094	7,695	7,663
Bulgaria	2,357	3,473	4,855	4,815	4,455
Cape Verde	494	988	1,818	1,943	1,994
Colombia	2,959	3,628	5,230	6,915	7,000
Costa Rica	3,498	3,726	5,048	6,618	6,479
Cuba	na	na	na	na	na
Djibouti	na	na	na	na	na
Dominica	1,283	2,030	3,324	na	na
Dominican Republic	2,107	2,562	3,297	4,244	4,527
Ecuador	2,799	3,314	4,094	4,970	5,099
Egypt	1,036	1,546	2,241	2,746	2,853
El Salvador	1,546	1,568	2,033	2,798	2,816
Estonia	na	na	5,270	4,377	4,658
Fiji	2,162	2,424	3,458	4,119	4,249
Georgia	3,610	5,170	4,910	1,639	na
Grenada	1,568	2,279	3,729	4,466	4,476
Guatemala	2,494	2,463	3,093	3,518	3,877
Indonesia	897	1,285	2,096	3,230	3,456
Iran	2,951	3,954	4,229	5,351	na
Iraq	na	na	na	na	na
Jamaica	1,892	2,120	3,186	3,670	3,564
Jordan	2,198	2,827	2,790	3,520	3,649
Kazakhstan	na	na	4,930	3,168	3,244
Kiribati	na	na	na	na	na
Latvia	2,840	3,924	5,714	3,476	3,649
Lebanon	na	na	na	5,573	5,928
Lithuania	na	na	5,220	4,239	4,442
Macedonia, FYRO	na	na	na	na	na
Maldives	na	1,326	2,337	3,231	3,392

C2.2 GDP per Capita, Current International U.S. Dollars, 1980–1996, In Purchasing Power Parity (PPP)—Lower Middle-Income Countries per World Bank *(continued)*

Country	1980	1985	1990	1995	1996
Marshall Islands	na	na	na	na	na
Micronesia	na	na	na	na	na
Morocco	1,580	1,999	2,807	3,104	3,433
Namibia	3,004	3,385	4,107	5,139	5,232
North Korea, Dem. Rep.	na	na	na	na	na
Panama	3,638	4,669	5,150	7,046	7,209
Papua New Guinea	1,362	1,619	1,945	3,006	3,045
Paraguay	2,230	2,473	3,316	3,530	3,520
Peru	2,716	2,913	2,886	4,518	4,523
Philippines	2,054	2,047	2,846	3,270	3,416
Romania	2,783	3,828	4,073	4,362	4,632
Russia	3,404	4,611	6,162	4,439	4,269
Samoa	na	na	na	na	na
Solomon Islands	893	1,240	1,884	2,424	2,292
St. Vincent and the Grenadines	1,229	1,919	3,232	4,226	na
Suriname	920	na	na	na	na
Swaziland	1,375	1,661	2,902	3,303	3,335
Syria	1,569	1,841	2,126	3,139	
Thailand	1,472	2,096	4,000	6,492	6,873
Tonga					
Tunisia	2,214	2,870	3,744	4,751	4,811
Turkey	2,298	3,078	4,591	5,643	5,977
Turkmenistan	na	na	na	2,080	1,993
Ukraine	na	na	4,260	2,444	2,259
Uzbekistan	na	na	2,870	2,456	2,582
Vanuatu		2,248	2,698	2,807	2,841
Venezuela	5,624	5,603	7,071	8,544	8,321
Yugoslavia	na	na	na	na	na

Note: Gross Domestic Product (GDP) is a measure of a country's total economic output—the total of goods and services it produces within its territory, whether it is attributed to domestic or foreign claims. It is a gross measure, excluding deductions for depreciation or depletion of resources. As stated in purchasing power parity (PPP), it is translated to international U.S. dollars, which have equivalent purchasing power as does the U.S. dollar in the United States. This table presents Gross Domestic Product per capita, that is, the total goods and services for the year divided by a country's population for that same year. The data in this table are stated in current terms, that is, without adjustments to deflate the effect of inflation.

Source: World Bank, *World Development Indicators 1998*, Table 4.1, 4.2, 4.10, and 4.11; World Bank, *World Development Indicators 1998*, CD-ROM, Series GDP per capita, PPP (NY.GDP.PCAP.PP.CD)

C2.3   GDP per Capita, Current International U.S. Dollars, 1980–1996, In Purchasing Power Parity (PPP)—Upper Middle-Income Countries per World Bank

Country	1980	1985	1990	1995	1996
Antigua and Barbuda	2,706	5,567	7,306	9,093	na
Argentina	5,579	5,579	6,725	9,287	9,652
Bahrain	11,649	9,944	11,684	15,462	na
Barbados	4,987	6,598	9,357	10,586	na
Brazil	3,598	4,109	5,390	5,986	6,491
Chile	3,926	4,601	7,255	11,162	12,013
Croatia	na	na	na	4,252	4,300
Czech Republic	na	6,890	9,390	10,313	11,006
Gabon	5,294	6,244	6,358	7,428	7,451
Hungary	3,532	4,677	6,477	6,761	6,952
Libya	na	na	na	na	na
Malaysia	3,174	4,285	6,588	10,261	10,905
Malta	4,017	5,529	9,192	13,373	
Mauritius	2,491	3,598	6,208	8,579	9,109
Mexico	4,613	5,447	6,721	7,592	7,983
Oman	3,082	6,369	8,332	9,814	na
Palau	na	na	na	na	'na
Poland	3,161	3,641	4,623	5,620	6,016
Saudi Arabia	11,212	7,694	9,385	9,908	na
Seychelles	na	na	na	na	na
Slovakia	na	5,346	7,115	6,946	7,478
Slovenia	na	na	na	11,351	12,010
South Africa	4,821	5,414	6,749	7,438	7,623
St. Kitts & Nevis	1,961	2,977	5,250	7,207	7,785
St. Lucia		2,153	3,872	5,208	5,312
Trinidad & Tobago	4,515	5,123	5,520	6,437	6,678
Uruguay	4,678	3,792	5,450	7,246	7,841

Note: Gross Domestic Product (GDP) is a measure of a country's total economic output—the total of goods and services it produces within its territory, whether it is attributed to domestic or foreign claims. It is a gross measure, excluding deductions for depreciation or depletion of resources. As stated in purchasing power parity (PPP), it is translated to international U.S. dollars, which have equivalent purchasing power as does the U.S. dollar in the United States. This table presents Gross Domestic Product per capita, that is, the total goods and services for the year divided by a country's population for that same year. The data in this table are stated in current terms, that is, without adjustments to deflate the effect of inflation.

Source: World Bank, *World Development Indicators 1998*, Table 4.1, 4.2, 4.10, and 4.11; World Bank, *World Development Indicators 1998*, CD-ROM, Series GDP per capita, PPP (NY.GDP.PCAP.PP.CD)

C2.4 GDP per Capita, Constant International U.S. Dollars, 1980–1996, In Purchasing Power Parity (PPP)—Low-Income Countries per World Bank

Country	1980	1985	1990	1995	1996
Afghanistan	na	na	na	na	na
Angola		1,335	1,321	1,582	1,514
Armenia	4,080	4,435	4,483	1,545	na
Azerbaijan	na	na	3,314	1,151	1,150
Bangladesh	544	574	654	754	767
Benin	905	924	854	932	948
Bhutan	na	na	na	na	'na
Bosnia and Herzegovina	na	na	na	na	na
Burkina Faso	652	661	691	710	719
Burundi	591	595	658	503	448
Cambodia	na	na	na	na	na
Cameroon	1,765	2,191	1,757	1,395	1,461
Central African Republic	1,413	1,288	1,242	1,172	1,103
Chad	546	686	699	691	686
China	700	957	1,376	2,370	2,546
Comoros	1,541	1,526	1,536	1,363	1,340
Congo, Dem. Rep. (Zaire)	1,619	1,356	1,203	711	682
Congo, Rep.	1,272	1,608	1,522	1,272	1,363
Cote d'Ivoire	1,963	1,409	1,367	1,281	1,306
Equatorial Guinea	na	na	907	1,871	2,391
Eritrea	na	na	na	na	na
Ethiopia	na	305	355	361	381
Gambia	1,103	1,037	1,065	979	
Ghana	1,451	1,123	1,250	1,366	1,390
Guinea	na	na	1,262	1,338	1,350
Guinea-Bissau	552	624	722	780	796
Guyana	2,316	1,688	1,558	2,038	1,870
Haiti	1,680	1,309	1,268	868	854
Honduras	1,891	1,562	1,683	1,637	1,614
India	725	768	982	1,172	1,210
Kenya	904	769	909	865	878
Kyrgyzstan	na	na	3,040	1,516	1,560
Laos	na	na	761	914	943
Lesotho	998	803	996	1,142	1,298
Liberia	na	na	na	na	na
Madagascar	1,114	811	813	731	706
Malawi	576	496	500	474	534
Mali	599	484	546	556	550
Mauritania	1,542	1,277	1,328	1,427	1,441
Moldova	na	na	3,213	1,232	1,106
Mongolia	na	1,629	1,792	1,405	1,404
Mozambique	na	258	360	414	415
Myanmar (Burma)	na	na	na	na	na
Nepal	617	615	709	799	815
Nicaragua	2,506	2,043	1,411	1,578	1,571
Niger	1,263	803	805	714	710
Nigeria	788	573	665	675	679
Pakistan	855	914	1,083	1,198	1,217
Rwanda	788	688	679	446	481
Sao Tome and Principe	na	na	na	na	na
Senegal	1,336	1,199	1,314	1,260	1,284
Sierra Leone	659	517	559	383	395
Somalia	na	na	na	na	na
Sri Lanka	1,133	1,267	1,457	1,755	1,755
Sudan	na	na	na	na	na

C2.4   GDP per Capita, Constant International U.S. Dollars, 1980-1996—In Purchasing Power Parity (PPP), Low-Income Countries per World Bank *(continued)*

Country	1980	1985	1990	1995	1996
Tajikistan	na	na	2,149	642	678
Tanzania	na	na	na	na	na
Togo	1,938	1,493	1,531	1,256	1,276
Uganda	na	540	625	749	787
Vietnam	na	na	na	1,122	1,190
Yemen	na	na	na	611	684
Zambia	1,063	854	824	656	672
Zimbabwe	1,862	1,734	1,802	1,669	1,737

Note: Gross Domestic Product (GDP) is a measure of a country's total economic output—the total of goods and services it produces within its territory, whether it is attributed to domestic or foreign claims. It is a gross measure, excluding deductions for depreciation or depletion of resources. As stated in purchasing power parity (PPP), it is translated to international U.S. dollars, which have equivalent purchasing power as does the U.S. dollar in the United States. This table presents Gross Domestic Product per capita, that is, the total goods and services for the year divided by a country's population for that same year. The data in this table are stated in constant terms, that is, with adjustments to counter the effect of inflation.

Source: World Bank, *World Development Indicators 1998*, Table 4.1, 4.2, 4.10, and 4.11; World Bank, *World Development Indicators 1998*, CD-ROM, Series GDP per capita, PPP (NY.GDP.PCAP.PP.CD)

C2.5   GDP per Capita, Constant International U.S. Dollars, 1980–1996, In Purchasing Power Parity (PPP)—Lower Middle-Income Countries per World Bank

Country	1980	1985	1990	1995	1996
Albania	na	na	na	na	na
Algeria	4,307	4,302	4,023	3,664	3,688
Belarus	na	na	5,167	3,261	3,322
Belize	2,579	2,108	3,079	3,354	3,290
Bolivia	2,506	1,897	2,038	2,250	na
Botswana	3,045	3,749	5,379	5,935	5,793
Bulgaria	3,314	3,673	4,287	3,717	3,375
Cape Verde	696	1,045	1,607	1,497	1,512
Colombia	4,158	3,839	4,616	5,336	5,299
Costa Rica	4,912	3,945	4,455	5,111	4,903
Cuba	na	na	na	na	na
Djibouti	na	na	na	na	na
Dominica	1,803	2,148	2,934	na	na
Dominican Republic	2,959	2,715	2,905	3,276	3,426
Ecuador	3,936	3,511	3,616	3,838	3,860
Egypt	1,460	1,637	1,977	2,118	2,163
El Salvador	2,171	1,659	1,798	2,155	2,126
Estonia	na	na	4,649	3,375	3,527
Fiji	3,038	2,561	3,049	3,175	3,215
Georgia	5,076	5,471	4,331	1,269	na
Grenada	2,204	2,408	3,295	3,443	3,382
Guatemala	3,506	2,607	2,725	2,713	2,937
Indonesia	1,256	1,364	1,853	2,496	2,612
Iran	4,149	4,179	3,737	4,129	na
Iraq	na	na	na	na	na
Jamaica	2,657	2,241	2,809	2,830	2,699
Jordan	3,086	2,988	2,458	2,717	2,763
Kazakhstan	na	na	4,347	2,440	2,449
Kiribati	na	na	na	na	na
Latvia	3,993	4,154	5,039	2,678	2,759

C2.5 GDP per Capita, Constant International U.S. Dollars, 1980–1996, In Purchasing Power Parity (PPP)—Lower Middle-Income Countries per World Bank *(continued)*

Country	1980	1985	1990	1995	1996
Lebanon	na	na	na	4,305	4,481
Lithuania	na	na	4,612	3,266	3,356
Macedonia, FYRO	na	na	na	na	na
Maldives	na	1,400	2,060	2,498	2,561
Marshall Islands	na	na	na	na	na
Micronesia	na	na	na	na	na
Morocco	2,223	2,118	2,477	2,399	2,596
Namibia	4,218	3,587	3,625	3,969	3,960
North Korea, Dem. Rep.	na	na	na	na	na
Panama	5,114	4,940	4,547	5,439	5,452
Papua New Guinea	1,919	1,711	1,717	2,322	2,308
Paraguay	3,131	2,618	2,923	2,719	2,663
Peru	3,815	3,080	2,550	3,488	3,422
Philippines	2,890	2,165	2,510	2,519	2,588
Romania	3,909	4,054	3,593	3,363	3,507
Russia	4,786	4,873	5,437	3,420	3,231
Samoa	na	na	na	na	na
Solomon Islands	1,255	1,309	1,659	1,871	1,732
St. Vincent and the Grenadines	1,729	2,028	2,848	3,261	na
Suriname	1,297	na	na	na	na
Swaziland	1,928	1,758	2,559	2,545	2,522
Syria	2,206	1,952	1,881	2,424	na
Thailand	2,073	2,219	3,527	5,005	5,197
Tonga	na	na	na	na	na
Tunisia	3,111	3,034	3,306	3,667	3,644
Turkey	3,225	3,256	4,057	4,357	4,525
Turkmenistan	na	na	3,227	1,603	1,509
Ukraine	na	na	3,761	1,886	1,713
Uzbekistan	na	na	2,536	1,898	1,959
Vanuatu	na	2,379	2,377	2,167	2,153
Venezuela	7,899	5,925	6,237	6,598	6,292
Yugoslavia	na	na	na	na	na

Note: Gross Domestic Product (GDP) is a measure of a country's total economic output—the total of goods and services it produces within its territory, whether it is attributed to domestic or foreign claims. It is a gross measure, excluding deductions for depreciation or depletion of resources. As stated in purchasing power parity (PPP), it is translated to international U.S. dollars, which have equivalent purchasing power as does the U.S. dollar in the United States. This table presents Gross Domestic Product per capita, that is, the total goods and services for the year divided by a country's population for that same year. The data in this table are stated in constant terms, that is, with adjustments to counter the effect of inflation.

Source: World Bank, *World Development Indicators 1998*, Table 4.1, 4.2, 4.10, and 4.11; World Bank, *World Development Indicators 1998*, CD-ROM, Series GDP per capita, PPP (NY.GDP.PCAP.PP.CD)

C2.6   GDP per Capita, Constant International U.S. Dollars, 1980–1996, In Purchasing Power Parity (PPP)—Upper Middle-Income Countries per World Bank

Country	1980	1985	1990	1995	1996
Antigua and Barbuda	3,802	5,891	6,453	7,017	na
Argentina	7,843	5,907	5,934	7,167	7,299
Bahrain	16,367	10,522	10,315	11,930	na
Barbados	7,009	6,980	8,258	8,168	na
Brazil	5,060	4,348	4,758	4,622	4,911
Chile	5,521	4,871	6,403	8,612	9,089
Croatia	na	na	na	na	na
Czech Republic	na	7,293	8,289	7,959	8,331
Gabon	7,444	6,601	5,615	5,737	5,633
Hungary	4,963	4,946	5,716	5,220	5,259
Libya	na	na	na	na	na
Malaysia	4,465	4,530	5,817	7,918	8,246
Malta	5,644	5,849	8,112	10,320	na
Mauritius	3,498	3,801	5,476	6,617	6,896
Mexico	6,488	5,765	5,934	5,863	6,041
Oman	4,334	6,739	7,357	7,570	na
Palau	na	na	na	na	na
Poland	4,439	3,855	4,079	4,334	4,554
Saudi Arabia	15,755	8,143	8,281	7,649	na
Seychelles	na	na	na	na	na
Slovakia	na	5,660	6,282	5,362	5,652
Slovenia	na	na	na	8,759	9,086
South Africa	6,779	5,732	5,956	5,739	5,763
St. Kitts & Nevis	2,758	3,147	4,637	5,566	5,893
St. Lucia	na	2,273	3,416	4,023	4,017
Trinidad & Tobago	6,343	5,415	4,877	4,966	5,048
Uruguay	6,571	4,013	4,813	5,587	5,932

Note: Gross Domestic Product (GDP) is a measure of a country's total economic output—the total of goods and services it produces within its territory, whether it is attributed to domestic or foreign claims. It is a gross measure, excluding deductions for depreciation or depletion of resources. As stated in purchasing power parity (PPP), it is translated to international U.S. dollars, which have equivalent purchasing power as does the U.S. dollar in the United States. This table presents Gross Domestic Product per capita, that is, the total goods and services for the year divided by a country's population for that same year. The data in this table are stated in constant terms, that is, with adjustments to counter the effect of inflation.

Source: World Bank, *World Development Indicators 1998*, Table 4.1, 4.2, 4.10, and 4.11; World Bank, *World Development Indicators 1998*, CD-ROM, Series GDP per capita, PPP (NY.GDP.PCAP.PP.CD)

C3.1 Consumer Price Index, Annual Average Percent Change, 1980–1990 and 1990–1996—Low-Income Countries per World Bank

Country	1980–90	1990–96	Country	1980–90	1990–96
Afghanistan	na	na	Laos	na	na
Angola	na	na	Lesotho	13.6	12.1
Armenia	na	na	Liberia	na	na
Azerbaijan	na	na	Madagascar	16.6	23.9
Bangladesh	10.5	3.6	Malawi	16.9	34.2
Benin	na	na	Mali	na	na
Bhutan	na	na	Mauritania	7.1	7.0
Bosnia and Herzegovina	na	na	Moldova	na	na
Burkina Faso	3.4	7.0	Mongolia	na	na
Burundi	7.1	12.6	Mozambique	na	48.5
Cambodia	na	na	Myanmar (Burma)	11.5	25.5
Cameroon	8.7	8.9	Nepal	10.2	10.4
Central African Republic	3.2	7.4	Nicaragua	536	63.2
Chad	0.6	8.7	Niger	0.7	7.2
China	na	13.5	Nigeria	21.5	48.8
Comoros	na	na	Pakistan	6.3	11.1
Congo, Dem.Rep. (Zaire)	57.1	2,824.80	Rwanda	3.9	22.6
Congo, Rep.	6.1	15.3	Sao Tome and Principe	na	na
Cote d'Ivoire	5.4	9.4	Senegal	6.2	7.6
Equatorial Guinea	na	na	Sierra Leone	72.4	37.5
Eritrea	na	na	Somalia	na	na
Ethiopia	4.0	8.9	Sri Lanka	10.9	10.7
Gambia	20.0	5.7	Sudan	37.6	114.3
Ghana	39.1	29.8	Tajikistan	na	na
Guinea	na	na	Tanzania	31.0	26.8
Guinea-Bissau	na	44.5	Togo	2.5	9.8
Guyana	na	na	Uganda	102.5	16.9
Haiti	5.2	26.8	Vietnam	na	na
Honduras	6.3	19.6	Yemen	na	na
India	8.6	9.9	Zambia	72.5	93.3
Kenya	11.1	23.5	Zimbabwe	13.8	26.8
Kyrgyzstan	na	na			

Note: The Consumer Price Index (CPI), a common measure of inflation, reflects the change in price over a period of time for a standard "basket" of goods and services. The above indicators show an average annual rate of change in the CPI for the given time periods.

Source: World Bank, *World Development Indicators 1998*, Table 4.15

C3.2   Consumer Price Index, Annual Average Percent Change, 1980–1990 and 1990–1996—Lower Middle-Income Countries per World Bank

Country	1980–90	1990–96	Country	1980–90	1990–96
Albania	na	na	Lithuania	na	na
Algeria	9.1	27.0	Macedonia, FYRO	na	na
Belarus	na	na	Maldives	na	na
Belize	na	na	Marshall Islands	na	na
Bolivia	322.6	11.1	Micronesia	na	na
Botswana	10.0	12.4	Morocco	7.0	5.5
Bulgaria	na	na	Namibia	12.6	11.2
Cape Verde	na	na	North Korea, Dem. Rep.	na	na
Colombia	22.7	23.9	Panama	1.4	1.1
Costa Rica	23.0	17.8	Papua New Guinea	5.6	7.4
Cuba	na	na	Paraguay	21.9	17.0
Djibouti	na	na	Peru	246.3	54.3
Dominica	na	na	Philippines	14.4	9.5
Dominican Republic	22.4	10.9	Romania	na	na
Ecuador	35.8	36.6	Russia	na	na
Egypt	17.4	12.4	Samoa	na	na
El Salvador	19.6	12.6	Solomon Islands	na	na
Estonia	na	na	St. Vincent and the Grenadines	na	na
Fiji	na	na	Suriname	na	na
Georgia	na	na	Swaziland	na	na
Grenada	na	na	Syria	23.2	11.3
Guatemala	14.0	12.7	Thailand	3.5	4.8
Indonesia	8.3	8.8	Tonga	na	na
Iran	18.2	29.3	Tunisia	7.4	5.3
Iraq	na	na	Turkey	44.9	80.2
Jamaica	15.1	36.5	Turkmenistan	na	na
Jordan	5.7	4.2	Ukraine	na	na
Kazakhstan	na	na	Uzbekistan	na	na
Kiribati	na	na	Vanuatu	na	na
Latvia	na	na	Venezuela	20.9	50.6
Lebanon	75.5	36.8	Yugoslavia	na	na

Note: The Consumer Price Index (CPI), a common measure of inflation, reflects the change in price over a period of time for a standard "basket" of goods and services. The above indicators show an average annual rate of change in the CPI for the given time periods.

Source: World Bank, *World Development Indicators 1998*, Table 4.15

C3.3 Consumer Price Index, Annual Average Percent Change, 1980–1990 and 1990–1996— Upper Middle-Income Countries per World Bank

Country	1980–90	1990–96	Country	1980–90	1990–96
Antigua and Barbuda	na	na	Mexico	73.8	18.2
Argentina	390.6	20.1	Oman	na	na
Bahrain	na	na	Palau	na	na
Barbados	na	na	Poland	50.9	37.5
Brazil	371.1	643.9	Saudi Arabia	-0.8	1.8
Chile	20.6	12.5	Seychelles	na	na
Croatia	304.1	232.3	Slovakia	na	na
Czech Republic	na	na	Slovenia	na	na
Gabon	5.1	6.6	South Africa	14.8	10.4
Hungary	9.6	24.1	St. Kitts & Nevis	na	na
Libya	na	na	St. Lucia	na	na
Malaysia	2.6	4.2	Trinidad & Tobago	10.7	7
Malta	na	na	Uruguay	61.1	53.7
Mauritius	6.9	7.2			

Note: The Consumer Price Index (CPI), a common measure of inflation, reflects the change in price over a period of time for a standard "basket" of goods and services. The above indicators show an average annual rate of change in the CPI for the given time periods.

Source: World Bank, *World Development Indicators 1998*, Table 4.15

C4.1 Commodity Price Index, 1980–1997—World Summary (1990=100)

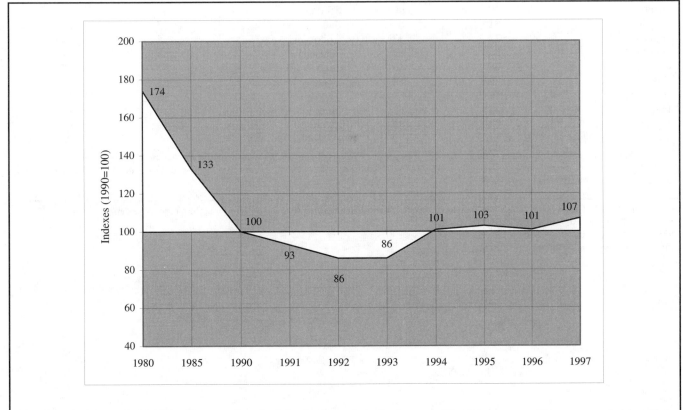

Note: This graph shows the World Bank's commodity price index for all non-fuel primary commodities. Primary commodities are raw materials, such as metals, minerals, and crops, that are used in the process of making finished products. Presented as an index, the indicator for each year shows the extent of variation from the base year of 1990, which equals 100%, or one unit value.

Source: World Bank, *World Development Indicators 1998*, Table 6.5

C5.1   Adult Economic Activity Rate, Percent of Total, Men and Women, 1995—Low-Income Countries per World Bank

Country	Women	Men	Country	1980–90	1990–96
Afghanistan	47	86	Kyrgyzstan	60	74
Angola	73	90	Laos	75	89
Armenia	62	73	Lesotho	47	85
Azerbaijan	53	74	Liberia	54	84
Bangladesh	66	87	Madagascar	69	89
Benin	75	83	Malawi	79	87
Bhutan	58	90	Mali	72	90
Bosnia and Herzegovina	44	75	Mauritania	64	87
Burkina Faso	77	90	Moldova	60	73
Burundi	83	93	Mongolia	73	84
Cambodia	83	87	Mozambique	83	91
Cameroon	48	86	Myanmar (Burma)	66	88
Central African Republic	69	87	Nepal	57	86
Chad	67	88	Nicaragua	44	86
China	74	86	Niger	70	93
Comoros	63	87	Nigeria	48	87
Congo, Dem. Rep. (Zaire)	62	85	Pakistan	32	85
Congo, Rep.	58	83	Rwanda	83	94
Cote d'Ivoire	44	88	Sao Tome and Principe	37	77
Equatorial Guinea	45	88	Senegal	61	86
Eritrea	75	87	Sierra Leone	44	84
Ethiopia	58	86	Somalia	63	87
Gambia	69	90	Sri Lanka	41	78
Ghana	81	82	Sudan	33	86
Guinea	78	87	Tajikistan	55	74
Guinea-Bissau	57	91	Tanzania	83	89
Guyana	40	85	Togo	53	87
Haiti	57	82	Uganda	81	91
Honduras	37	86	Vietnam	75	84
India	41	85	Yemen	29	82
Kenya	74	89	Zambia	66	86
			Zimbabwe	67	86

Note: This indicator reflects the number of adult men and women (over 15 years of age) who participate in the production of goods and services, whether employees, employers, the self-employed, members of producer-cooperatives, or unpaid family workers (in the case of subsistence work). The rate is stated as a percentage of total men and total women.

Source: The World's Women 1995: Trends and Statistics, Table 5.1; United Nations Web site, http://www.un.org/Depts/unsd/gender/5.1afr.htm
http://www.un.org/Depts/unsd/gender/5.1dev.htm
http://www.un.org/Depts/unsd/gender/5.1lat.htm
http://www.un.org/Depts/unsd/gender/5.1asi.htm

C5.2   Adult Economic Activity Rate, Percent of Total, Men and Women, 1995—Lower Middle-Income Countries per World Bank

Country	Women	Men	Country	Women	Men
Albania	59	83	Lithuania	58	74
Algeria	24	76	Macedonia, FYRO	50	72
Belarus	59	74	Maldives	65	83
Belize	26	84	Marshall Islands	na	na
Bolivia	47	83	Micronesia	na	na
Botswana	65	83	Morocco	40	79
Bulgaria	58	66	Namibia	54	81
Cape Verde	44	88	North Korea, Dem. Rep.	62	82
Colombia	46	80	Panama	41	79
Costa Rica	35	82	Papua New Guinea	na	na
Cuba	47	77	Paraguay	35	87
Djibouti	na	na	Peru	32	79
Dominica	43	75	Philippines	48	82
Dominican Republic	37	86	Romania	51	67
Ecuador	30	85	Russia	59	74
Egypt	33	79	Samoa	na	na
El Salvador	41	84	Solomon Islands	na	na
Estonia	62	76	St. Vincent and the Grenadines	44	81
Fiji	na	na	Suriname	35	76
Georgia	55	73	Swaziland	41	80
Grenada	57	71	Syria	26	78
Guatemala	32	88	Thailand	74	86
Indonesia	53	82	Tonga	na	na
Iran	25	79	Tunisia	35	79
Iraq	17	75	Turkey	47	82
Jamaica	69	81	Turkmenistan	61	78
Jordan	22	76	Ukraine	55	71
Kazakhstan	60	76	Uzbekistan	61	74
Kiribati	na	na	Vanuatu	na	na
Latvia	62	76	Venezuela	40	81
Lebanon	27	76	Yugoslavia	50	70

Note: This indicator reflects the amount of adult men and women (over 15 years of age) who participate in the production of goods and services, whether employees, employers, the self-employed, members of producer-cooperatives, and unpaid family workers (in the case of subsistence work). The rate is stated as a percentage of total men and total women.

Source: The World's Women 1995: Trends and Statistics, Table 5.1; United Nations Web site
http://www.un.org/Depts/unsd/gender/5.1afr.htm
http://www.un.org/Depts/unsd/gender/5.1dev.htm
http://www.un.org/Depts/unsd/gender/5.1lat.htm
http://www.un.org/Depts/unsd/gender/5.1asi.htm

C5.3   Adult Economic Activity Rate, Percent of Total, Men and Women, 1995—Upper Middle-Income Countries per World Bank

Country	Women	Men	Country	Women	Men
Antigua and Barbuda	na	na	Mexico	37	83
Argentina	32	77	Oman	16	80
Bahrain	31	87	Palau	na	na
Barbados	60	76	Poland	57	73
Brazil	44	85	Saudi Arabia	18	82
Chile	35	78	Seychelles	57	79
Croatia	48	69	Slovakia	63	74
Czech Republic	62	73	Slovenia	54	68
Gabon	63	84	South Africa	46	79
Hungary	48	67	St. Kitts & Nevis	na	na
Libya	23	78	St. Lucia	49	79
Malaysia	47	81	Trinidad & Tobago	42	76
Malta	25	72	Uruguay	46	73
Mauritius	36	80			

Note: This indicator reflects the amount of adult men and women (over 15 years of age) who participate in the production of goods and services, whether employees, employers, the self-employed, members of producer-cooperatives, and unpaid family workers (in the case of subsistence work). The rate is stated as a percentage of total men and total women.

Source: The World's Women 1995: Trends and Statistics, Table 5.1; United Nations Web site, http://www.un.org/Depts/unsd/gender/5.1afr.htm
http://www.un.org/Depts/unsd/gender/5.1dev.htm
http://www.un.org/Depts/unsd/gender/5.1lat.htm
http://www.un.org/Depts/unsd/gender/5.1asi.htm

C6.1   Earned Income, Share by Male and Female, Percent of Total, 1995—Low-Income Countries per World Bank

Country	Female	Male	Country	Female	Male
Afghanistan	na	na	Laos	39.6	60.4
Angola	39.2	60.8	Lesotho	30.5	69.5
Armenia	40.9	59.1	Liberia	na	na
Azerbaijan	36.8	63.2	Madagascar	37.5	62.5
Bangladesh	23.1	76.9	Malawi	42.0	58.0
Benin	41.8	58.2	Mali	39.1	60.9
Bhutan	32.3	67.7	Mauritania	36.7	63.3
Bosnia and Herzegovina	na	na	Moldova	41.4	58.6
Burkina Faso	39.6	60.4	Mongolia	39.7	60.4
Burundi	42.3	57.7	Mozambique	41.9	58.1
Cambodia	45.2	54.8	Myanmar (Burma)	42.3	57.7
Cameroon	30.4	69.6	Nepal	33.4	66.6
Central African Republic	38.8	61.2	Nicaragua	28.3	71.7
Chad	37.2	62.8	Niger	37.1	62.9
China	38.1	61.9	Nigeria	30.0	70.0
Comoros	35.0	65.0	Pakistan	20.6	79.4
Congo, Dem. Rep. (Zaire)	36.2	63.8	Rwanda	na	na
Congo, Rep.	36.4	63.7	Sao Tome and Principe	na	na
Cote d'Ivoire	25.8	74.2	Senegal	35.1	64.9
Equatorial Guinea	28.9	71.1	Sierra Leone	29.2	70.8
Eritrea	34.3	65.7	Somalia	na	na
Ethiopia	33.3	66.7	Sri Lanka	35.5	64.5
Gambia	37.5	62.5	Sudan	22.4	77.6
Ghana	43.3	56.7	Tajikistan	36.6	63.4
Guinea	40.2	59.8	Tanzania	47.3	52.7
Guinea-Bissau	33.0	67.0	Togo	32.3	67.7
Guyana	26.9	73.1	Uganda	40.6	59.4
Haiti	36.0	64.0	Vietnam	42.0	58.0
Honduras	24.4	75.6	Vietnam	na	na
India	25.4	74.6	Yemen	21.3	78.7
Kenya	41.8	58.2	Zambia	39.3	60.7
Kyrgyzstan	39.6	60.4			

Note: Share of earned income is the percentage of total earned income attributed to men and attributed to women.

Source: Gender-Related Development Index; United Nations Development Program Web site, http://www.undp.org/undp/hdro/98gdi.htm

C6.2   Earned Income, Share by Male and Female, Percent of Total, 1995—Lower Middle-Income Countries per World Bank

Country	Female	Male	Country	Female	Male
Albania	34.1	65.9	Lithuania	40.9	59.1
Algeria	19.1	80.9	Macedonia, FYRO	34.0	66.0
Belarus	41.5	58.5	Maldives	35.3	64.7
Belize	18.5	81.5	Marshall Islands	na	na
Bolivia	26.8	73.2	Micronesia	na	na
Botswana	38.9	61.1	Morocco	27.8	72.2
Bulgaria	41.1	58.9	Namibia	34.0	66.0
Cape Verde	32.3	67.7	North Korea, Dem. Rep.	36.6	63.4
Colombia	33.5	66.5	Panama	27.8	72.2
Costa Rica	26.9	73.1	Papua New Guinea	34.9	65.1
Cuba	31.5	68.5	Paraguay	23.2	76.8
Djibouti	na	na	Peru	23.8	76.2
Dominica	na	na	Philippines	35.0	65.0
Dominican Republic	24.0	76.0	Romania	37.5	62.5
Ecuador	18.6	81.4	Russia	41.3	58.7
Egypt	25.0	75.0	Samoa	na	na
El Salvador	33.6	66.4	Solomon Islands	39.4	60.6
Estonia	41.9	58.1	St. Vincent and the Grenadines	na	na
Fiji	22.0	78.0	Suriname	26.1	73.9
Georgia	39.3	60.7	Swaziland	32.6	67.4
Grenada	na	na	Syria	19.8	80.2
Guatemala	21.3	78.7	Thailand	36.7	63.3
Indonesia	33.0	67.0	Tunisia	24.7	75.3
Iran	18.9	81.1	Turkey	35.5	64.5
Iraq	13.9	86.1	Turkmenistan	38.3	61.7
Jamaica	39.2	60.8	Ukraine	42.4	57.6
Jordan	19.1	80.9	United Arab Emirates	10.2	89.8
Kazakhstan	39.3	60.7	Uzbekistan	39.1	60.9
Kiribati	na	na	Vanuatu	na	na
Latvia	44.0	56.0	Venezuela	27.1	72.9
Lebanon	22.7	77.3	Yugoslavia	na	na

Note: Share of earned income is the percentage of total earned income attributed to men and attributed to women.

Source: Gender-Related Development Index; United Nations Development Program Web site, http://www.undp.org/undp/hdro/98gdi.htm

C6.3   Earned Income, Share by Male and Female, Percent of Total, 1995—Upper Middle-Income Countries per World Bank

Country	Female	Male	Country	Female	Male
Antigua and Barbuda	na	na	Mexico	25.7	74.3
Argentina	22.1	77.9	Oman	10.6	89.4
Bahrain	15.0	85.0	Palau	na	na
Barbados	39.6	60.4	Poland	39.0	61.0
Brazil	29.3	70.7	Saudi Arabia	10.0	90.0
Chile	22.0	78.0	Seychelles	na	na
Croatia	36.6	63.4	Slovakia	40.7	59.3
Czech Republic	39.0	61.0	Slovenia	39.3	60.7
Gabon	37.1	62.9	South Africa	30.9	69.1
Hungary	38.5	61.5	St. Kitts & Nevis	na	na
Libya	16.3	83.7	St. Lucia	na	na
Malaysia	30.4	69.6	Trinidad & Tobago	26.8	73.2
Malta	21.1	78.9	Uruguay	33.7	66.3
Mauritius	25.6	74.4			

Note: Share of earned income is the percentage of total earned income attributed to men and attributed to women.

Source: Gender-Related Development Index; United Nations Development Program Web site, http://www.undp.org/undp/hdro/98gdi.htm

C7.1 Domestic Credit Provided by Banking Sector, Percent of GDP, 1990 and 1996—Low-Income Countries per World Bank

Country	1990	1996	Country	1990	1996
Afghanistan	na	na	Laos	5.1	8.7
Angola	na	na	Lesotho	30.1	-15.2
Armenia	62.3	9.1	Liberia	na	na
Azerbaijan	57.2	11.3	Madagascar	26.8	14.6
Bangladesh	32.5	30.7	Malawi	19.9	9.1
Benin	22.4	10.8	Mali	13.4	10.1
Bhutan	na	na	Mauritania	54.7	14
Bosnia and Herzegovina	na	na	Moldova	62.8	22
Burkina Faso	13.7	6.7	Mongolia	68.5	17.5
Burundi	24.5	21.1	Mozambique	29.5	2.8
Cambodia	na	6.9	Myanmar (Burma)	32.7	na
Cameroon	31.2	16.4	Nepal	28.9	36.0
Central African Republic	13.1	11.2	Nicaragua	206.6	144.8
Chad	14.4	15.3	Niger	16.2	8.8
China	90.0	98.0	Nigeria	23.7	16.3
Comoros	na	na	Pakistan	50.9	52.5
Congo, Dem. Rep. (Zaire)	25.3	1.6	Rwanda	17	10.6
Congo, Rep.	29.1	16.2	Sao Tome and Principe	na	na
Cote d'Ivoire	44.5	29.1	Senegal	33.7	21.8
Equatorial Guinea	na	na	Sierra Leone	26.3	52.3
Eritrea	na	na	Somalia	na	na
Ethiopia	67.5	45.1	Sri Lanka	43.0	35.0
Gambia	3.6	8.2	Sudan	29.9	18.9
Ghana	13.2	21.4	Tajikistan	na	na
Guinea	5.5	8.2	Tanzania	39.2	17.4
Guinea-Bissau	0.7	0.1	Togo	21.3	25.8
Guyana	na	na	Uganda	17.7	4.6
Haiti	32.9	27.4	Vietnam	15.9	20.8
Honduras	40.9	26.0	Yemen	62	29.0
India	54.7	49.8	Zambia	64.5	56.2
Kenya	52.9	52.8	Zimbabwe	53.8	55.3
Kyrgyzstan	na	na			

Note: This indicator reflects all credit granted to all sectors of a country's economy and includes credit given by monetary authorities, deposit money banks, savings, mortgage loan, and building and loan institutions. It includes all credit on a gross basis, except for that given to the central government, which is calculated on a net basis. The total credit is stated in terms of percent of GDP.

Source: World Bank, *World Development Indicators 1998*, Table 5.4

C7.2   Domestic Credit Provided by Banking Sector, Percent of GDP, 1990 and 1996—Lower Middle-Income Countries per World Bank

Country	1990	1996	Country	1990	1996
Albania	na	44.9	Macedonia, FYRO	na	na
Algeria	74.7	42.4	Maldives	na	na
Belarus	na	16.1	Marshall Islands	na	na
Belize	na	na	Micronesia	na	na
Bolivia	33.3	57.5	Morocco	60.1	74.8
Botswana	-49.7	-37.7	Namibia	19.2	60.1
Bulgaria	126.8	150.6	North Korea, Dem. Rep.	na	na
Cape Verde	na	na	Panama	52.7	74.4
Colombia	36.2	45.5	Papua New Guinea	35.8	28.0
Costa Rica	29.9	33.1	Paraguay	14.9	28.2
Cuba	na	na	Peru	16.2	12.1
Djibouti	na	na	Philippines	26.9	72.2
Dominica	na	na	Romania	79.7	4.2
Dominican Republic	31.3	29.5	Russia	na	24.8
Ecuador	17.2	31.7	Samoa	na	na
Egypt	106.8	82.8	Solomon Islands	na	na
El Salvador	32	41.4	St. Vincent and the Grenadines	na	na
Estonia	65	20.1	Suriname	na	na
Fiji	na	na	Swaziland	na	na
Georgia	na	na	Syria	56.6	45.7
Grenada	na	na	Thailand	90.7	98.8
Guatemala	17.4	19.4	Tonga	na	na
Indonesia	45.5	54.6	Tunisia	62.5	65.4
Iran	70.8	45.7	Turkey	25.9	34.4
Iraq	na	na	Turkmenistan	na	1.7
Jamaica	34.8	33.5	Ukraine	83.2	15
Jordan	117.9	86.1	Uzbekistan	na	na
Kazakhstan	na	9.5	Vanuatu	na	na
Kiribati	na	na	Venezuela	37.4	19.9
Latvia	na	13	Yugoslavia	na	na
Lebanon	132.6	104.2			
Lithuania	na	11.5			

Note: This indicator reflects all credit granted to all sectors of a country's economy and includes credit given by monetary authorities, deposit money banks, savings, mortgage loan, and building and loan institutions. It includes all credit on a gross basis, except for that given to the central government, which is calculated on a net basis. The total credit is stated in terms of percent of GDP.

Source: World Bank, *World Development Indicators 1998*, Table 5.4

C7.3 Domestic Credit Provided by Banking Sector, Percent of GDP, 1990 and 1996—Upper Middle-Income Countries per World Bank

Country	1990	1996	Country	1990	1996
Antigua and Barbuda	na	na	Mexico	42.5	40.6
Argentina	32.4	26.0	Oman	16.6	29.2
Bahrain	na	na	Palau	na	na
Barbados	na	na	Poland	19.5	35.4
Brazil	87.2	36.8	Saudi Arabia	58.7	38
Chile	72.9	59.6	Seychelles	na	na
Croatia	na	46.4	Slovakia	na	60.1
Czech Republic	na	78.6	Slovenia	36.8	36.0
Gabon	20.0	15.0	South Africa	102.7	160.2
Hungary	82.6	49.1	St. Kitts & Nevis	na	na
Libya	na	na	St. Lucia	na	na
Malaysia	77.9	131.9	Trinidad & Tobago	58.5	54.2
Malta	na	na	Uruguay	60.7	39.8
Mauritius	45.1	63.9			

Note: This indicator reflects all credit granted to all sectors of a country's economy and includes credit given by monetary authorities, deposit money banks, savings, mortgage loan, and building and loan institutions. It includes all credit on a gross basis, except for that given to the central government, which is calculated on a net basis. The total credit is stated in terms of percent of GDP.

Source: World Bank, *World Development Indicators 1998*, Table 5.4

C8.1 Percentage Share of Income or Consumption, Lower Tenth and In Quintiles, Applicable Survey Year—Low-Income Countries per World Bank

Country	Lowest 10%	Lowest 20%	Second Lowest 20%	Third Lowest 20%	Fourth Lowest 20%	Top 20%
Afghanistan	na	na	na	na	na	na
Angola	na	na	na	na	na	na
Armenia	na	na	na	na	na	na
Azerbaijan	na	na	na	na	na	na
Bangladesh	4.1	9.4	13.5	17.2	22.0	37.9
Benin	na	na	na	na	na	na
Bhutan	na	na	na	na	na	na
Bosnia and Herzegovina	na	na	na	na	na	na
Burkina Faso	na	na	na	na	na	na
Burundi	na	na	na	na	na	na
Cambodia	na	na	na	na	na	na
Cameroon	na	na	na	na	na	na
Central African Republic	na	na	na	na	na	na
Chad	na	na	na	na	na	na
China	2.2	5.5	9.8	14.9	22.3	47.5
Comoros	na	na	na	na	na	na
Congo, Dem. Rep. (Zaire)	na	na	na	na	na	na
Congo, Rep.	na	na	na	na	na	na
Cote d'Ivoire	2.8	6.8	11.2	15.8	22.2	44.1
Equatorial Guinea	na	na	na	na	na	na
Eritrea	na	na	na	na	na	na
Ethiopia	na	na	na	na	na	na
Gambia	na	na	na	na	na	na
Ghana	3.4	7.9	12	16.1	21.8	42.2
Guinea	0.9	3.0	8.3	14.6	23.9	50.2
Guinea-Bissau	0.5	2.1	6.5	12	20.6	58.9
Guyana	2.4	6.3	10.7	15	21.2	46.9
Haiti	na	na	na	na	na	na
Honduras	1.2	3.4	7.1	11.7	19.7	58
India	4.1	9.2	13.0	16.8	21.7	39.3

C8.1 Percentage Share of Income or Consumption, Lower Tenth and In Quintiles, Applicable Survey Year—Low-Income Countries per World Bank *(continued)*

Country	Lowest 10%	Lowest 20%	Second Lowest 20%	Third Lowest 20%	Fourth Lowest 20%	Top 20%
Kenya	1.2	3.4	6.7	10.7	17.0	62.1
Kyrgyzstan	2.7	6.7	11.5	16.4	23.1	42.3
Laos	4.2	9.6	12.9	16.3	21	40.2
Lesotho	0.9	2.8	6.5	11.2	19.4	60.1
Liberia	na	na	na	na	na	na
Madagascar	2.3	5.8	9.9	14.0	20.3	50.0
Malawi	na	na	na	na	na	na
Mali	na	na	na	na	na	na
Mauritania	0.7	3.6	10.6	16.2	23.0	46.5
Moldova	2.7	6.9	11.9	16.7	23.1	41.5
Mongolia	2.9	7.3	12.2	16.6	23	40.9
Mozambique	na	na	na	na	na	na
Myanmar (Burma)	na	na	na	na	na	na
Nepal	3.2	7.6	11.5	15.1	21	44.8
Nicaragua	1.6	4.2	8.0	12.6	20	55.2
Niger	3	7.5	11.8	15.5	21.1	44.1
Nigeria	1.3	4	8.9	14.4	23.4	49.4
Pakistan	3.4	8.4	12.9	16.9	22.2	39.7
Rwanda	4.2	9.7	13.2	16.5	21.6	39.1
Sao Tome and Principe	na	na	na	na	na	na
Senegal	1.4	3.5	7.0	11.6	19.3	58.6
Sierra Leone	0.5	1.1	2.0	9.8	23.7	63.4
Somalia	na	na	na	na	na	na
Sri Lanka	3.8	8.9	13.1	16.9	21.7	39.3
Sudan	na	na	na	na	na	na
Tajikistan	na	na	na	na	na	na
Tanzania	2.9	6.9	10.9	15.3	21.5	45.4
Togo	na	na	na	na	na	na
Uganda	3	6.8	10.3	14.4	20.4	48.1
Vietnam	3.5	7.8	11.4	15.4	21.4	44
Yemen	2.3	6.1	10.9	15.3	21.6	46.1
Zambia	1.5	3.9	8	13.8	23.8	50.4
Zimbabwe	1.8	4	6.3	10	17.4	62.3

Note: These indicators reflect the fact that income and consumption are distributed unevenly throughout a country. They represent the shares of a country's total income or consumption earned or used by the lowest 10%, 20%, next lowest 20%, etc. It is possible that percentage shares in quintiles might not sum to 100 due to rounding.

Source: World Bank, *World Development Indicators 1998*, Table 2.8

C8.2 Percentage Share of Income or Consumption, Lower Tenth and In Quintiles, Applicable Survey Year—Lower Middle-Income Countries per World Bank

Country	Lowest 10%	Lowest 20%	Second Lowest 20%	Third Lowest 20%	Fourth Lowest 20%	Top 20%
Albania	na	na	na	na	na	na
Algeria	2.8	7.0	11.6	16.1	22.7	42.6
Belarus	4.9	11.1	15.3	18.5	22.2	32.9
Belize	na	na	na	na	na	na
Bolivia	2.3	5.6	9.7	14.5	22.0	48.2
Botswana	na	na	na	na	na	na
Bulgaria	3.3	8.3	13	17.0	22.3	39.3
Cape Verde	na	na	na	na	na	na
Colombia	1.0	3.1	6.8	10.9	17.6	61.5
Costa Rica	1.3	4.0	8.8	13.7	21.7	51.8
Cuba	na	na	na	na	na	na
Djibouti	na	na	na	na	na	na
Dominica	na	na	na	na	na	na
Dominican Republic	1.6	4.2	7.9	12.5	19.7	55.7
Ecuador	2.3	5.4	8.9	13.2	19.9	52.6
Egypt	3.9	8.7	12.5	16.3	21.4	41.1
El Salvador	1.2	3.7	8.3	13.1	20.5	54.4
Estonia	2.4	6.6	10.7	15.1	21.4	46.3
Fiji	na	na	na	na	na	na
Georgia	na	na	na	na	na	na
Grenada	na	na	na	na	na	na
Guatemala	0.6	2.1	5.8	10.5	18.6	63
Indonesia	3.6	8.4	12.0	15.5	21.0	43.1
Iran	na	na	na	na	na	na
Iraq	na	na	na	na	na	na
Jamaica	2.4	5.8	10.2	14.9	21.6	47.5
Jordan	2.4	5.9	9.8	13.9	20.3	50.1
Kazakhstan	3.1	7.5	12.3	16.9	22.9	40.4
Kiribati	na	na	na	na	na	na
Latvia	4.3	9.6	13.6	17.5	22.6	36.7
Lebanon	na	na	na	na	na	na
Lithuania	3.4	8.1	12.3	16.2	21.3	42.1
Macedonia, FYRO	na	na	na	na	na	na
Maldives	na	na	na	na	na	na
Marshall Islands	na	na	na	na	na	na
Micronesia	na	na	na	na	na	na
Morocco	2.8	6.6	10.5	15.0	21.7	46.3
Namibia	na	na	na	na	na	na
North Korea, Dem. Rep.	na	na	na	na	na	na
Panama	0.5	2.0	6.3	11.3	20.3	60.1
Papua New Guinea	1.7	4.5	7.9	11.9	19.2	56.5
Paraguay	0.7	2.3	5.9	10.7	18.7	62.4
Peru	1.9	4.9	9.2	14.1	21.4	50.4
Philippines	2.4	5.9	9.6	13.9	21.1	49.6
Romania	3.8	9.2	14.4	18.4	23.2	34.8
Russia	3	7.4	12.6	17.7	24.2	38.2
Samoa	na	na	na	na	na	na
Solomon Islands	na	na	na	na	na	na
St. Vincent and the Grenadines	na	na	na	na	na	na
Suriname	na	na	na	na	na	na
Swaziland	na	na	na	na	na	na
Syria	na	na	na	na	na	na
Thailand	2.5	5.6	8.7	13.0	20.0	52.7
Tonga	na	na	na	na	na	na
Tunisia	2.3	5.9	10.4	15.3	22.1	46.3
Turkey	na	na	na	na	na	na

C8.2   Percentage Share of Income or Consumption, Lower Tenth and In Quintiles, Applicable Survey Year—Lower Middle-Income Countries per World Bank *(continued)*

Country	Lowest 10%	Lowest 20%	Second Lowest 20%	Third Lowest 20%	Fourth Lowest 20%	Top 20%
Turkmenistan	2.7	6.7	11.4	16.3	22.8	42.8
Ukraine	4.1	9.5	14.1	18.1	22.9	35.4
Uzbekistan	na	na	na	na	na	na
Vanuatu	na	na	na	na	na	na
Venezuela	1.5	4.3	8.8	13.8	21.3	51.8
Yugoslavia	na	na	na	na	na	na

Note: These indicators reflect the fact that income and consumption are distributed unevenly throughout a country. They represent the shares of a country's total income or consumption earned or used by the lowest 10%, 20%, next lowest 20%, etc. It is possible that percentage shares in quintiles might not sum to 100 due to rounding.

Source: World Bank, *World Development Indicators 1998*, Table 2.8

C8.3   Percentage Share of Income or Consumption, Lower Tenth and In Quintiles, Applicable Survey Year—Upper Middle-Income Countries per World Bank

Country	Lowest 10%	Lowest 20%	Second Lowest 20%	Third Lowest 20%	Fourth Lowest 20%	Top 20%
Antigua and Barbuda	na	na	na	na	na	na
Argentina	na	na	na	na	na	na
Bahrain	na	na	na	na	na	na
Barbados	na	na	na	na	na	na
Brazil	0.8	2.5	5.7	9.9	17.7	64.2
Chile	1.4	3.5	6.6	10.9	18.1	61
Croatia	na	na	na	na	na	na
Czech Republic	4.6	10.5	13.9	16.9	21.3	37.4
Gabon	na	na	na	na	na	na
Hungary	4.1	9.7	13.9	16.9	21.4	38.1
Libya	na	na	na	na	na	na
Malaysia	1.9	4.6	8.3	13	20.4	53.7
Malta	na	na	na	na	na	na
Mauritius	na	na	na	na	na	na
Mexico	1.6	4.1	7.8	12.5	20.2	55.3
Oman	na	na	na	na	na	na
Palau	na	na	na	na	na	na
Poland	4	9.3	13.8	17.7	22.6	36.6
Saudi Arabia	na	na	na	na	na	na
Seychelles	na	na	na	na	na	na
Slovakia	5.1	11.9	15.8	18.8	22.2	31.4
Slovenia	4	9.3	13.3	16.9	21.9	38.6
South Africa	1.4	3.3	5.8	9.8	17.7	63.3
St. Kitts & Nevis	na	na	na	na	na	na
St. Lucia	na	na	na	na	na	na
Trinidad & Tobago	na	na	na	na	na	na
Uruguay	na	na	na	na	na	na

Note: These indicators reflect the fact that income and consumption are distributed unevenly throughout a country. They represent the shares of a country's total income or consumption earned or used by the lowest 10%, 20%, next lowest 20%, etc. It is possible that percentage shares in quintiles might not sum to 100 due to rounding.

Source: World Bank, *World Development Indicators 1998*, Table 2.8

D. Demographics

GENERAL OVERVIEW

The indicators included in this section outline the most basic human dimensions of poverty throughout the world: demographics. They include such statistics as total population, population growth rates, population density, urban population share, gender breakdowns, birth rates, share of population over age 60, death rates, and mortality rates.

These demographic statistics are indicators of the past, current, and projected characteristics of a population's structure—its size, its size in relation to land, its component ratios between young and old and male and female, its past growth trends, and its future growth prospects. Demographics help students, researchers, and policymakers analyze the current and potential impacts that a society's people have on its physical resources, environmental situation, social needs, and economic prospects.

EXPLANATION OF INDICATORS

Total Population: Total population in poverty studies is a double-sided indicator. It indicates the breadth of a society's human resources, but at the same time can represent the scope of a country's responsibility towards its people. As it is a simple head count, it is most often used with other indicators to arrive at more sophisticated measurements, such as population density (land area divided by population) and gross domestic product per capita (GDP/capita), both of which add further dimension to a raw count of the people within the boundaries of an individual country (D1.1–D1.4).

Population Growth Rates: Growth rates in population show the change over a designated period of time in the size of a country's population. For the students and policymakers concerned with poverty, they are a crucial indicator of the pressure exerted on a country's natural, economic, and social resources (health care and education, for instance). Controlling rapidly accelerating growth rates is one of the primary concerns of policymakers in developing countries (D2.1–D2.3).

Population Density: As a measure of the number of people per unit of land area, population density is one of the most basic indicators of the human pressure on natural resources. As population growth rates (see above) accelerate—and the land area of a country remains the same—population density increases. Increasing pressure on existing land resources may engender health and environmental concerns, such as inadequate food supply and unhealthy sanitation, if the growth of appropriate infrastructure lags behind (D3.1–D3.3).

Rural Population Density: The rural component of population density helps analysts and students monitor the potential population pressure on rural communities. This demographic pressure is important, as some rural environments are already strained to accommodate existing populations, and accelerating rural population density trends indicate potential increased threats to the survival (outstripping of food supply, for instance), health concerns, and infrastructure in these communities (D4.1–D4.4).

Urban Population and Growth Rates: Often in developing countries, urban population growth rates are higher than those in rural areas and continue to accelerate at an astronomical rate, as economic needs push people towards centers of population where economic opportunity is most often the highest. Pressures on existing infrastructure in cities—sanitation, water supply, utilities, and others—is a grave concern, as urban planners in developing countries often struggle to keep up with rapid growth (D5.1–D5.7).

Male and Female Population Breakdowns: A basic indicator of the make-up of a country's population, such figures help policymakers plan for services that meet the needs of each segment of the population. In particular, projecting future trends in the size of the female population helps analysts to plan for health services particular to women's health needs, especially those relating to reproductive concerns—pregnancy and prenatal care, labor and delivery needs, and postnatal, infant-care concerns (D6.1–D6.3).

Birth Rates and Fertility Rates: The birth rate and fertility rate are benchmark statistics that help to illuminate potential future trends in the size of a country's population. The birth rate, which is the number of births per 1000 people and the fertility rate, which estimates the number of children each women is likely to give birth to throughout her reproductive years, both help to analyze past trends and forecast future trends not just in the number of people in a country, but the number of children in a population at various points in the future. Nearly always, birth rates and fertility rates in developing countries are higher than those in industrial, or developed, countries, because there is a need for as many children as possible to undertake subsistence work and contribute economically to their families and households. Further, reliable birth control is less available and less easily obtainable in poorer countries, where most health services are often inaccessible (D7.1–D7.7).

Death Rates and Mortality Rates: The opposite of birth and fertility rates, death and mortality rates reveal trends in the number of deaths measured against the total population. Not only do these statistics (along with birth and fertility rates) help to project the size of a population at future points in time; they also serve as indicators of the adequacy of a country's health care services. Generally in poorer countries whose health care systems are less developed, higher death and mortality rates are typical (D8.1–D8.10).

Population Age 60 and Over: Population age 60 and over is an indicator of the number of elderly people within a population, and therefore an indicator of the scope of the needs and services particular to the elderly, such as elder nursing care and retirement income and support (D9.1–D9.3).

D1.1 Total Population, 1970–2050 (projected)—Low-Income Countries per World Bank

Country	1970	1980	1990	1998	2025	2050
Afghanistan	12,457,000	15,950,000	20,445,000	24,792,375	48,044,542	76,230,578
Angola	5,588,000	7,019,000	9,229,000	10,865,000	21,598,322	34,465,137
Armenia	2,520,000	3,096,000	3,545,000	3,421,775	3,433,747	3,428,146
Azerbaijan	5,172,000	6,166,000	7,159,000	7,855,576	9,429,191	10,584,994
Bangladesh	66,671,000	86,700,000	110,368,000	127,567,002	180,560,502	210,624,418
Benin	2,657,000	3,464,000	4,737,000	6,100,799	13,541,352	22,171,075
Bhutan	408,560	487,880	600,110	1,908,307	3,340,681	4,935,375
Bosnia and Herzegovina	3,703,000	4,092,000	4,450,000	3,365,727	3,470,613	2,833,491
Burkina Faso	5,633,000	6,962,000	9,016,000	11,266,393	21,360,037	34,956,159
Burundi	3,514,000	4,130,000	5,487,000	5,537,387	10,468,908	17,303,804
Cambodia	6,938,000	6,498,000	8,695,000	11,339,562	22,817,359	37,300,574
Cameroon	6,506,000	8,701,000	11,484,000	15,029,433	29,108,181	48,605,757
Central African Republic	1,849,000	2,313,000	2,929,000	3,375,771	5,544,579	7,915,342
Chad	3,652,000	4,477,000	5,680,000	7,359,512	14,359,716	22,503,896
China	818,315,000	981,235,000	1,135,160,000	1,236,914,658	1,407,739,146	1,322,434,932
Comoros	na	335,000	432,000	545,528	1,160,486	1,953,253
Congo, Dem. Rep. (Zaire)	20,270,000	27,009,000	37,405,000	49,000,511	105,737,162	184,455,832
Congo, Rep.	1,263,000	1,669,000	2,276,000	2,658,123	4,246,447	6,080,975
Cote d'Ivoire	5,510,000	8,194,000	11,974,000	15,446,231	27,840,275	44,509,074
Equatorial Guinea	291,000	217,000	352,000	454,001	876,225	1,393,582
Eritrea	na	na	3,139,000	3,842,436	8,437,639	13,735,785
Ethiopia	28,937,000	37,717,000	51,180,000	58,390,351	98,762,736	159,170,225
Gambia	464,000	641,000	921,000	1,291,858	2,678,362	4,037,592
Ghana	8,614,000	10,740,000	14,870,000	18,497,206	28,191,005	34,324,026
Guinea	3,851,000	4,461,000	5,755,000	7,477,110	13,135,320	20,034,447
Guinea-Bissau	525,000	809,000	965,000	1,206,311	2,102,298	2,970,216
Guyana	670,000	760,000	795,000	707,954	710,266	726,356
Haiti	4,520,000	5,353,000	6,473,000	6,780,501	10,170,748	12,745,695
Honduras	2,627,000	3,662,000	5,105,000	5,861,955	8,612,256	11,001,319
India	547,569,000	687,332,000	849,515,000	984,003,683	1,408,320,301	1,694,785,676
Kenya	11,498,000	16,560,000	23,354,000	28,337,071	34,773,605	43,851,963
Kyrgyzstan	2,964,000	3,632,000	4,395,000	4,522,281	6,066,461	7,394,167
Laos	2,713,000	3,205,000	4,033,000	5,260,842	9,804,562	13,843,859
Lesotho	1,064,000	1,367,000	1,783,000	2,089,829	2,724,163	3,532,841
Liberia	1,385,000	1,879,000	2,435,000	2,771,901	6,524,316	10,992,106
Madagascar	6,745,000	8,714,000	11,672,000	14,462,509	29,306,165	48,327,070
Malawi	4,518,000	6,138,000	8,507,000	9,840,474	10,911,225	14,787,877
Mali	5,335,000	6,590,000	8,460,000	10,108,569	22,646,955	40,433,240
Mauritania	1,221,000	1,551,000	2,003,000	2,511,473	5,445,945	9,328,651
Moldova	3,595,000	4,002,000	4,364,000	4,457,729	4,830,277	4,810,648
Mongolia	1,256,000	1,663,000	2,216,000	2,578,530	3,555,370	4,057,444
Mozambique	9,395,000	12,095,000	14,151,000	18,641,469	33,308,035	47,805,294
Myanmar (Burma)	27,102,000	33,821,000	41,354,000	47,305,319	68,106,967	87,777,673
Nepal	11,350,000	14,498,000	18,772,000	23,698,421	42,576,135	60,661,284
Nicaragua	2,063,000	2,802,000	3,750,000	4,583,379	8,112,068	10,816,954
Niger	4,146,000	5,515,000	7,666,000	9,671,848	20,423,708	33,895,881
Nigeria	53,215,000	71,148,000	96,203,000	110,532,242	203,423,396	337,590,809
Pakistan	60,607,000	82,581,000	112,351,000	135,135,195	211,675,333	260,246,716
Rwanda	3,728,000	5,163,000	6,954,000	7,956,172	12,158,817	19,607,335
Sao Tome and Principe	73,000	89,000	115,000	150,123	330,843	518,320
Senegal	4,158,000	5,538,000	7,327,000	9,723,149	22,456,276	39,689,503
Sierra Leone	2,656,000	3,236,000	3,999,000	5,080,004	11,010,156	18,369,471
Somalia	4,791,000	6,713,000	8,623,000	6,841,695	15,192,344	26,242,585
Sri Lanka	12,516,000	14,738,000	16,993,000	18,933,558	24,087,501	26,145,911
Sudan	13,859,000	18,681,000	24,061,000	33,550,552	64,757,210	93,624,886
Tajikistan	2,941,000	3,966,000	5,303,000	6,020,095	9,634,047	13,261,267
Tanzania	13,694,000	18,581,000	25,483,000	30,608,769	50,660,932	76,500,098
Togo	2,020,000	2,615,000	3,524,000	4,905,827	11,712,282	20,725,195

D1.1 Total Population, 1970–2050 (projected)—Low-Income Countries per World Bank *(continued)*

Country	1970	1980	1990	1998	2025	2050
Uganda	9,812,000	12,806,900	16,330,000	22,167,195	33,505,309	53,886,447
Vietnam	42,729,000	53,700,000	66,233,300	76,236,259	103,908,883	119,463,548
Yemen	6,332,000	8,538,000	11,876,000	16,387,963	40,438,981	76,008,463
Zambia	4,189,000	5,738,000	7,784,000	9,460,736	16,156,233	26,967,305
Zimbabwe	5,249,000	7,009,000	9,747,000	11,044,147	12,365,776	16,064,009

Definition: Total population is the number of all residents, regardless of legal status or citizenship, living within the borders of a country.

Source: World Bank, *World Development Indicators 1998*, Table 3.1; World Bank, *World Development Indicators 1998*, CD-ROM, Series: Population, total (SP.POP.TOTL); US Census International database, http://www.census.gov/cgi-bin/ipc/idbsprd

D1.2 Total Population, 1970–2050 (projected)—Lower Middle-Income Countries per World Bank

Country	1970	1980	1990	1998	2025	2050
Albania	2,136,000	2,671,000	3,282,000	3,330,754	4,306,000	4,609,063
Algeria	13,746,000	18,669,170	25,010,000	30,480,793	47,675,820	58,879,798
Belarus	9,040,000	9,643,000	10,260,000	10,409,050	10,248,170	9,100,128
Belize	119,970	146,000	189,300	230,160	383,496	489,105
Bolivia	4,212,000	5,355,000	6,573,000	7,826,352	12,007,028	15,240,486
Botswana	623,500	901,500	1,277,000	1,448,454	1,633,683	2,146,199
Bulgaria	8,490,000	8,862,000	8,718,000	8,240,426	7,292,242	5,904,941
Cape Verde	267,000	289,000	341,400	399,857	531,633	545,012
Colombia	22,001,000	27,894,000	33,634,000	38,580,949	58,287,171	73,348,764
Costa Rica	1,731,000	2,284,000	3,035,000	3,604,642	5,327,331	6,320,781
Cuba	8,551,000	9,724,000	10,625,000	11,050,729	11,697,123	10,565,062
Djibouti	148,000	281,000	517,000	440,727	840,724	1,329,419
Dominica	68,400	73,350	72,260	65,777	66,962	69,398
Dominican Republic	4,423,000	5,697,000	7,110,000	7,998,766	11,780,544	14,586,298
Ecuador	5,970,000	7,961,000	10,264,000	12,336,572	17,799,981	21,059,233
Egypt	33,053,000	40,875,000	52,442,000	66,050,004	97,431,183	117,121,038
El Salvador	3,598,000	4,547,000	5,031,000	5,752,067	8,381,567	10,813,591
Estonia	1,365,000	1,480,000	1,571,000	1,421,335	1,237,013	1,046,945
Fiji	520,000	634,000	736,000	802,611	1,084,937	1,284,973
Georgia	4,708,000	5,073,000	5,460,100	5,108,527	4,718,035	4,364,895
Grenada	94,000	89,000	91,000	96,217	154,361	210,239
Guatemala	5,246,000	6,917,000	9,197,000	12,007,580	22,344,183	32,184,770
Indonesia	117,537,000	148,303,000	178,232,000	212,941,810	287,985,072	330,566,219
Iran	28,429,000	39,124,000	53,730,000	68,959,931	111,891,148	142,335,748
Iraq	9,356,000	13,007,000	18,078,000	21,722,287	52,615,035	85,536,508
Jamaica	1,869,000	2,133,000	2,403,500	2,634,678	3,354,566	3,712,019
Jordan	1,508,000	2,181,000	3,170,000	4,434,978	8,222,996	11,303,292
Kazakhstan	13,110,000	14,905,000	16,742,000	16,846,808	18,564,593	20,426,414
Kiribati	48,900	58,100	72,340	83,976	98,764	99,959
Latvia	2,374,000	2,544,000	2,670,700	2,385,396	1,964,902	1,658,642
Lebanon	2,617,140	3,002,350	3,635,000	3,505,794	4,831,388	5,598,489
Lithuania	3,140,000	3,413,000	3,722,000	3,600,158	3,417,198	3,062,885
Macedonia, FYRO	1,630,000	1,889,000	1,903,000	2,009,387	2,171,241	1,977,235
Maldives	121,000	158,000	215,000	290,211	623,150	949,475
Marshall Islands	23,000	31,000	46,200	63,031	170,829	348,080
Micronesia	na	71,000	96,000	129,658	142,869	142,951
Morocco	15,310,000	19,382,000	24,043,000	29,114,497	43,227,753	52,068,646
Namibia	792,000	1,030,000	1,352,000	1,622,328	2,309,815	3,757,130
North Korea, Dem. Rep.	14,263,000	17,666,000	20,363,000	21,234,387	26,054,682	26,305,274
Panama	1,531,000	1,956,000	2,398,000	2,735,943	3,796,038	4,418,388
Papua New Guinea	2,422,000	3,086,000	3,839,000	4,599,785	7,597,486	10,049,378
Paraguay	2,351,000	3,136,000	4,219,000	5,291,020	9,929,121	15,000,657
Peru	13,193,000	17,295,000	21,512,000	26,111,110	39,157,814	47,855,437

D1.2 Total Population, 1970–2050 (projected)—Lower Middle-Income Countries per World Bank (continued)

Country	1970	1980	1990	1998	2025	2050
Philippines	37,540,000	48,317,000	62,598,000	77,725,862	120,519,345	150,271,797
Romania	20,253,000	22,201,000	23,207,000	22,395,848	21,416,886	18,483,404
Russia	130,404,000	139,010,000	148,292,000	146,861,022	138,841,556	121,776,572
Samoa	142,820	155,000	160,000	224,713	367,080	470,961
Solomon Islands	164,000	233,000	320,000	441,039	840,044	1,157,823
St. Vincent and the Grenadines	88,000	97,800	107,050	119,818	151,154	163,447
Suriname	372,000	356,210	405,000	427,980	459,991	379,698
Swaziland	419,000	565,000	770,000	966,462	1,589,457	3,059,288
Syria	6,257,000	8,704,000	12,116,000	16,673,282	31,683,963	43,463,336
Thailand	35,745,000	46,718,000	55,580,000	60,037,366	70,315,728	69,740,733
Tonga	86,000	94,000	96,000	108,207	132,642	156,183
Tunisia	5,127,000	6,384,000	8,162,000	9,380,404	12,760,316	14,398,877
Turkey	35,321,000	44,484,000	56,126,000	64,566,511	89,727,479	103,648,860
Turkmenistan	2,189,000	2,861,000	3,668,000	4,297,629	6,513,742	8,422,237
Ukraine	47,371,000	50,043,000	51,892,000	50,125,108	45,096,294	39,096,194
Uzbekistan	11,973,000	15,952,000	20,515,000	23,784,321	34,348,391	42,761,562
Vanuatu	83,000	115,060	147,300	185,204	282,279	346,817
Venezuela	10,721,000	14,871,000	19,502,000	22,803,409	32,474,216	37,772,517
Yugoslavia	8,901,000	9,780,000	10,529,000	10,526,135	10,551,826	9,194,839

Definition: Total population is the number of all residents, regardless of legal status or citizenship, living in the borders of a country.

Source: World Bank, *World Development Indicators 1998*, Table 3.1; World Bank, *World Development Indicators 1998*, CD-ROM, Series: Population, total (SP.POP.TOTL); US Census International database, http://www.census.gov/cgi-bin/ipc/idbsprd

D1.3 Total Population, 1970–2050 (projected)—Upper Middle-Income Countries per World Bank

Country	1970	1980	1990	1998	2025	2050
Antigua and Barbuda	65,850	61,000	64,000	64,006	65,413	51,396
Argentina	23,962,000	28,114,000	32,527,000	36,265,463	48,351,219	56,258,478
Bahrain	210,000	334,000	503,000	616,342	922,902	1,097,951
Barbados	239,200	249,100	258,000	259,025	278,611	265,925
Brazil	95,847,000	121,286,000	148,002,000	169,806,557	209,586,835	228,144,875
Chile	9,494,000	11,143,000	13,099,000	14,787,781	17,942,290	18,300,865
Croatia	4,411,000	4,588,000	4,778,000	4,671,584	4,348,133	3,486,259
Czech Republic	9,775,000	10,232,000	10,363,000	10,286,470	10,127,921	8,626,046
Gabon	504,000	691,000	960,000	1,207,844	1,799,727	2,517,913
Hungary	10,337,000	10,707,000	10,365,000	10,208,127	9,374,100	7,683,724
Libya	1,986,000	3,043,000	4,434,000	5,690,727	14,185,462	26,625,309
Malaysia	10,853,000	13,763,000	17,891,000	20,932,901	34,248,134	47,288,747
Malta	326,000	364,000	354,200	379,563	390,832	324,798
Mauritius	829,000	966,000	1,057,000	1,168,256	1,488,342	1,613,972
Mexico	50,328,000	66,561,630	83,488,310	98,552,776	141,592,523	167,479,483
Oman	723,000	1,101,000	1,627,000	2,363,591	5,307,157	8,453,172
Palau	na	na	na	18,110	21,259	24,090
Poland	32,526,000	35,578,000	38,118,800	38,606,922	40,116,796	36,465,185
Saudi Arabia	5,745,000	9,372,000	15,803,000	20,785,955	50,374,341	97,119,774
Seychelles	53,600	64,400	70,000	78,641	90,959	95,424
Slovakia	4,528,500	4,984,300	5,283,400	5,392,982	5,718,296	5,214,883
Slovenia	1,726,500	1,901,200	1,998,100	1,971,739	1,864,211	1,483,952
South Africa	21,710,000	27,149,000	33,957,000	42,834,520	49,851,312	58,971,685
St. Kitts & Nevis	44,900	44,400	42,030	42,291	59,737	68,825
St. Lucia	101,000	123,770	149,000	152,335	202,605	223,705
Trinidad & Tobago	971,000	1,082,000	1,236,000	1,116,595	1,083,470	1,057,366
Uruguay	2,808,000	2,914,000	3,094,000	3,284,841	3,916,227	4,255,955

Definition: Total population is the number of all residents regardless of legal status or citizenship, living in the borders of a country.

Source: World Bank, *World Development Indicators 1998*, Table 3.1; World Bank, *World Development Indicators 1998*, CD-ROM, Series: Population, total (SP.POP.TOTL); US Census International database, http://www.census.gov/cgi-bin/ipc/idbsprd

D1.4 Total Population—Comparison by Income Level per World Bank

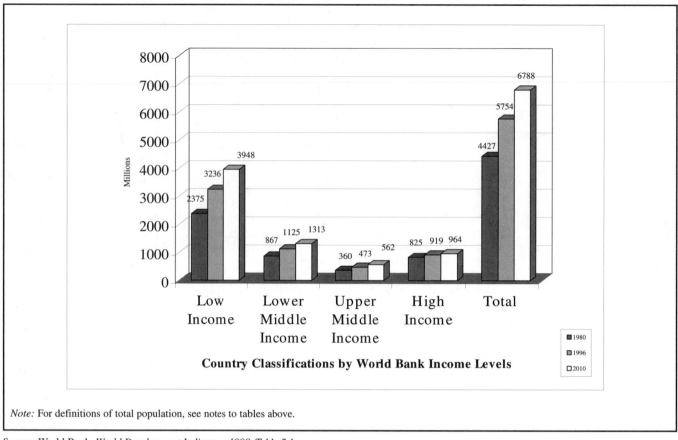

Note: For definitions of total population, see notes to tables above.

Source: World Bank, *World Development Indicators 1998*, Table 2.1

D2.1 Population Growth Rates, Annual Percent Change, 1980–2010 (projected)—Low-Income Countries per World Bank

Country	1980	1985	1990	1995	1996	Average Annual 1980–96	Average Annual 1996–2010 (proj.)
Afghanistan	2.56	2.48	2.44	2.99	2.88	na	na
Angola	2.75	2.60	3.15	3.05	3.00	2.9	2.7
Armenia	1.59	1.42	1.79	0.32	0.37	1.2	0.4
Azerbaijan	1.49	1.60	1.05	0.69	0.93	1.3	0.5
Bangladesh	2.46	2.49	1.99	1.57	1.58	2.1	1.5
Benin	2.86	3.18	3.11	2.78	2.82	3.0	2.7
Bhutan	2.16	1.96	2.12	2.94	2.87	na	na
Bosnia and Herzegovina	0.68	1.19	0.23	na	na	na	na
Burkina Faso	2.39	2.57	2.76	2.85	2.77	2.7	2.4
Burundi	2.63	2.87	2.89	2.49	2.50	2.8	2.4
Cambodia	0.85	3.17	3.16	2.63	2.48	2.9	1.8
Cameroon	3.00	2.63	2.94	2.91	2.88	2.8	2.4
Central African Republic	2.35	2.30	2.48	2.07	2.08	2.3	1.9
Chad	2.17	2.37	2.52	2.53	2.49	2.4	2.3
China	1.25	1.36	1.47	1.04	1.00	1.3	0.7
Comoros	na	2.55	2.62	2.56	2.54	na	na
Congo, Dem. Rep. (Zaire)	3.09	3.28	3.28	3.11	3.11	3.2	3.0
Congo, Rep.	2.90	3.12	3.20	2.72	2.71	3.0	2.4
Cote d'Ivoire	3.86	3.86	3.65	2.72	2.61	3.5	2.1
Equatorial Guinea	3.81	5.65	0.98	2.56	2.55	na	na

D2.1 Population Growth Rates, Annual Percent Change, 1980–2010 (projected)—Low-Income Countries per World Bank *(continued)*

Country	1980	1985	1990	1995	1996	Average Annual 1980–96	Average Annual 1996–2010 (proj.)
Eritrea	na	na	na	2.60	3.42	na	3.0
Ethiopia	2.74	2.80	3.67	2.72	3.19	2.7	3.0
Gambia	2.94	3.55	4.70	3.18	3.00	3.6	2.3
Ghana	2.25	3.65	3.04	2.59	2.58	3.1	2.3
Guinea	1.71	2.57	2.95	2.57	2.52	2.6	2.6
Guinea-Bissau	3.84	1.81	1.64	2.32	2.29	1.9	2.2
Guyana	0.74	0.49	0.13	0.98	1.02	na	na
Haiti	1.72	1.89	2.04	2.24	2.32	2.0	1.6
Honduras	3.58	3.39	2.90	2.98	2.95	3.2	2.4
India	2.25	2.04	2.02	1.71	1.68	2.0	1.3
Kenya	3.79	3.54	2.85	2.55	2.50	3.1	2.0
Kyrgyzstan	1.89	1.97	1.54	0.93	1.34	1.4	1.1
Laos	1.50	2.82	2.30	2.62	2.58	2.4	2.4
Lesotho	2.83	2.60	2.73	2.14	2.14	2.4	2.0
Liberia	3.24	2.68	1.80	2.65	2.79	na	na
Madagascar	2.72	2.93	3.12	2.84	3.00	2.8	2.8
Malawi	3.15	3.32	3.41	2.74	2.62	3.1	2.3
Mali	2.21	2.47	2.87	2.67	2.98	2.6	2.8
Mauritania	2.54	2.57	2.50	2.57	2.54	2.6	2.3
Moldova	0.90	0.89	0.32	-0.26	-0.28	0.5	0.0
Mongolia	2.75	2.94	2.66	2.12	2.10	2.6	1.9
Mozambique	2.75	1.42	1.16	4.75	3.41	2.5	2.4
Myanmar (Burma)	2.09	2.07	1.80	1.69	1.71	1.9	1.3
Nepal	2.52	2.64	2.54	2.76	2.67	2.6	2.3
Nicaragua	2.73	2.86	3.27	2.96	2.89	3.0	2.4
Niger	3.39	3.33	3.04	3.35	3.35	3.3	3.0
Nigeria	3.09	3.05	2.84	2.97	2.92	3.0	2.6
Pakistan	3.01	3.08	3.12	2.75	2.74	3.0	2.5
Rwanda	3.28	3.36	2.37	2.69	4.98	1.7	3.5
Sao Tome and Principe	na	2.63	2.86	2.56	2.45	na	na
Senegal	2.83	2.82	2.76	2.62	2.64	2.7	2.3
Sierra Leone	2.00	2.09	2.26	2.49	2.63	2.2	2.2
Somalia	3.96	2.64	1.29	5.16	3.26	na	na
Sri Lanka	1.83	1.51	1.11	1.38	1.02	1.4	1.0
Sudan	3.01	2.57	2.14	2.05	2.09	2.4	2.2
Tajikistan	2.76	2.86	2.39	1.47	1.55	2.5	1.3
Tanzania	3.16	3.18	3.10	2.92	2.82	3.1	2.2
Togo	2.82	2.99	3.05	2.96	2.88	3.0	2.5
Uganda	2.30	1.98	3.49	3.01	2.94	2.7	2.4
Vietnam	2.12	2.02	2.23	1.98	1.87	2.1	1.6
Yemen	3.88	3.06	3.71	3.24	3.26	3.8	3.3
Zambia	3.33	2.98	3.10	2.70	2.58	3.0	1.9
Zimbabwe	3.15	3.43	2.94	2.18	2.13	3.0	1.5

Definition: This indicator represents the change in a country's population. Nearly always an upward change, indicating growth, it is calculated as an annual average.

Source: World Bank, *World Development Indicators 1998*, Table 2.; World Bank, *World Development Indicators 1998*, CD-ROM, Series: Population growth (SP.POP.GROW)

D2.2 Population Growth Rates, Annual Percent Change, 1980-2010 (projected)—Lower Middle-Income Countries per World Bank

Country	1980	1985	1990	1995	1996	Average Annual 1980–96	Average Annual 1996–2010 (proj.)
Albania	2.04	2.05	1.60	1.46	1.13	1.3	0.9
Algeria	3.08	3.13	2.51	2.30	2.20	2.7	1.9
Belarus	0.61	0.65	0.30	-0.26	-0.30	0.4	-0.3
Belize	2.67	2.59	2.61	2.72	2.60	na	na
Bolivia	2.16	1.96	2.31	2.42	2.32	2.2	2.1
Botswana	3.52	3.57	3.24	2.07	2.05	3.1	1.4
Bulgaria	0.41	0.18	-1.81	-0.42	-0.53	-0.4	-0.9
Cape Verde	0.98	1.68	2.01	2.36	2.42	na	na
Colombia	2.06	1.87	1.81	1.82	1.72	1.8	1.3
Costa Rica	3.00	2.90	2.61	2.10	2.00	2.6	1.4
Cuba	0.04	1.04	0.97	0.19	0.18	0.8	0.4
Djibouti	6.56	6.42	4.86	3.01	2.90	na	na
Dominica	0.89	-0.37	-0.36	0.77	0.87	na	na
Dominican Republic	2.34	2.23	2.12	1.77	1.78	2.1	1.4
Ecuador	2.79	2.58	2.28	2.15	2.06	2.4	1.6
Egypt	2.53	2.57	2.29	1.94	1.86	2.3	1.6
El Salvador	1.38	0.68	1.98	2.62	2.58	1.5	2
Estonia	0.68	0.75	-0.44	-1.01	-1.22	-0.1	-1
Fiji	2.07	1.59	1.37	1.27	1.13	na	na
Georgia	na	0.85	0.21	-0.11	-0.02	0.4	0
Grenada	na	na	na	3.21	4.12	na	na
Guatemala	2.78	2.85	2.89	2.86	2.85	2.9	2.3
Indonesia	2.07	1.83	1.79	1.63	1.57	1.8	1.3
Iran	3.38	3.25	2.76	2.49	2.15	2.9	1.9
Iraq	3.30	3.33	3.22	2.49	2.79	3.1	2.8
Jamaica	1.35	1.36	1.20	1.04	0.97	1.1	0.8
Jordan	3.82	3.57	3.66	3.25	2.74	4.3	2.6
Kazakhstan	1.19	1.41	0.77	-1.19	-0.85	0.6	0.1
Kiribati	2.05	2.24	2.08	1.98	1.98	na	na
Latvia	0.59	0.61	-0.50	-1.24	-1.04	-0.1	-0.7
Lebanon	1.02	1.96	1.97	1.90	1.82	1.9	1.4
Lithuania	0.23	0.88	0.84	-0.16	-0.16	0.5	-0.2
Macedonia, FYRO	1.39	0.66	-4.87	0.97	0.71	0.3	0.7
Maldives	2.96	3.11	3.06	2.86	2.59	na	na
Marshall Islands	3.28	5.56	3.84	3.64	1.77	na	na
Micronesia	na	2.95	2.08	2.36	1.85	na	na
Morocco	2.24	2.18	2.04	1.91	1.85	2.1	1.6
Namibia	2.70	2.72	2.76	2.61	2.52	2.7	2.1
North Korea, Dem. Rep.	1.42	1.41	1.46	1.75	1.59	1.5	0.9
Panama	2.14	2.04	2.02	1.75	1.62	2.0	1.3
Papua New Guinea	2.37	2.18	2.22	2.34	2.28	2.2	2.0
Paraguay	3.28	3.03	2.51	2.82	2.60	2.9	2.2
Peru	2.50	2.17	2.04	2.03	1.95	2.1	1.5
Philippines	2.10	2.64	2.58	2.31	2.30	2.5	1.8
Romania	0.69	0.44	0.24	-0.22	-0.32	0.1	-0.3
Russia	0.71	0.78	0.45	-0.10	-0.31	0.4	-0.2
Samoa	0.65	0.03	0.57	1.05	1.00	na	na
Solomon Islands	3.73	3.15	3.07	3.02	2.91	na	na
St. Vincent and the Grenadines	0.99	0.90	0.88	0.57	0.61	na	na
Suriname	-2.43	2.80	-0.27	1.15	1.19	na	na
Swaziland	3.16	3.08	3.13	3.11	2.86	na	na
Syria	3.27	3.49	3.33	2.86	2.72	3.2	2.3
Thailand	2.18	1.50	1.78	1.16	1.01	1.6	0.6
Tonga	0.93	-0.26	0.52	-0.01	0.41	na	na

D2.2 Population Growth Rates, Annual Percent Change, 1980–2010 (projected)—Lower Middle-Income Countries per World Bank *(continued)*

Country	1980	1985	1990	1995	1996	Average Annual 1980–96	Average Annual 1996–2010 (proj.)
Tunisia	2.68	3.05	2.43	1.59	1.60	2.2	1.4
Turkey	2.23	2.43	2.20	1.75	1.69	2.1	1.3
Turkmenistan	2.41	2.38	2.48	2.29	1.98	3.0	1.5
Ukraine	0.38	0.32	0.23	-0.75	-1.59	0.1	-0.6
Uzbekistan	2.36	2.33	2.60	1.80	1.93	2.3	1.6
Vanuatu	2.29	1.72	2.61	2.53	2.64	na	na
Venezuela	2.99	2.74	2.48	2.16	2.12	2.5	1.6
Yugoslavia	na	0.71	0.53	0.23	0.28	0.5	0.2

Definition: This indicator represents the change in a country's population. Nearly always an upward change, indicating growth, it is calculated as an annual average.

Source: World Bank, *World Development Indicators 1998*, CD-ROM, Table 2.; World Bank, *World Development Indicators 1998*, CD-ROM, Series: Population growth (SP.POP.GROW)

D2.3 Population Growth Rates, Percent Change, 1980–2010 (projected)—Upper Middle-Income Countries per World Bank

Country	1980	1985	1990	1995	1996	Average Annual 1980–96	Average Annual 1996–2010 (proj.)
Antigua and Barbuda	-0.26	0.32	0.61	0.37	0.84	na	na
Argentina	1.51	1.49	1.34	1.33	1.29	1.4	1.0
Bahrain	4.59	4.25	2.82	3.53	3.74	na	na
Barbados	1.05	0.16	0.60	-0.04	0.04	na	na
Brazil	2.29	2.05	1.64	1.34	1.34	1.8	1.2
Chile	1.50	1.61	1.72	1.53	1.46	1.6	1.1
Croatia	0.38	0.45	0.23	-0.02	-0.11	0.2	-0.3
Czech Republic	0.00	0.13	0.01	-0.05	-0.15	0.1	-0.2
Gabon	3.13	3.36	3.16	2.49	2.43	3.0	2.1
Hungary	0.08	-0.46	-0.32	-0.30	-0.36	-0.3	-0.4
Libya	4.40	4.35	2.87	2.45	2.42	3.3	2.3
Malaysia	2.35	2.69	2.58	2.21	2.30	2.5	1.6
Malta	0.98	-1.98	0.96	0.81	0.54	na	na
Mauritius	1.83	0.46	0.80	0.81	1.06	1.0	1.0
Mexico	2.35	2.30	2.12	1.76	1.71	2.1	1.5
Oman	5.37	3.77	3.17	2.80	1.76	4.2	3.8
Palau	na	na	na	na	na	na	na
Poland	1.00	0.78	0.41	0.12	0.08	0.5	0.2
Saudi Arabia	5.51	5.33	4.45	3.38	2.24	4.6	3.3
Seychelles	1.27	0.74	0.88	1.85	1.80	na	na
Slovakia	0.11	0.60	-0.27	-0.29	0.21	0.4	0.2
Slovenia	1.02	1.55	-0.07	0.06	0.05	0.3	-0.1
South Africa	2.58	2.32	1.84	1.59	1.84	2.0	1.4
St. Kitts & Nevis	1.61	-2.13	-0.33	-0.46	-0.29	na	na
St. Lucia	1.99	1.99	0.54	1.17	1.19	na	na
Trinidad & Tobago	1.59	1.46	0.70	0.88	0.77	1.1	0.9
Uruguay	0.62	0.63	0.55	0.54	0.59	0.6	0.6

Definition: This indicator represents the change in a country's population. Nearly always an upward change, indicating growth, it is calculated as an annual average.

Source: World Bank, *World Development Indicators 1998*, Table 2.; World Bank, *World Development Indicators 1998*, CD-ROM, Series: Population growth (SP.POP.GROW)

D3.1 Population Density, 1980–1996—Low-Income Countries per World Bank

Country	1980	1985	1990	1995	1996
Afghanistan	24.5	27.7	31.4	36.0	37.1
Angola	5.6	6.4	7.4	8.6	8.9
Armenia	na	na	na	133.3	133.8
Azerbaijan	na	na	na	86.7	87.5
Bangladesh	666.1	753.1	847.9	920.1	934.7
Benin	31.3	36.5	42.8	49.5	50.9
Bhutan	10.4	11.5	12.8	14.8	15.2
Bosnia and Herzegovina	na	na	na	na	na
Burkina Faso	25.4	28.8	33.0	37.9	39.0
Burundi	160.8	185.0	213.7	243.9	250.1
Cambodia	36.8	42.0	49.3	56.8	58.2
Cameroon	18.7	21.4	24.7	28.6	29.4
Central African Republic	3.7	4.2	4.7	5.3	5.4
Chad	3.6	4.0	4.5	5.1	5.3
China	105.2	112.7	121.7	129.0	130.3
Comoros	150.2	170.0	193.7	220.6	226.3
Congo, Dem. Rep. (Zaire)	11.9	14.0	16.5	19.3	20.0
Congo, Rep.	4.9	5.7	6.7	7.7	7.9
Cote d'Ivoire	25.8	31.2	37.7	44.0	45.1
Equatorial Guinea	7.7	11.1	12.5	14.3	14.6
Eritrea	na	na	na	35.4	36.6
Ethiopia	na	na	na	56.4	58.2
Gambia	64.1	74.5	92.1	111.3	114.7
Ghana	47.2	55.5	65.4	75.0	77.0
Guinea	18.2	20.3	23.4	26.8	27.5
Guinea-Bissau	28.8	31.5	34.3	38.0	38.9
Guyana	3.9	4.0	4.0	4.2	4.3
Haiti	194.2	212.7	234.9	260.1	266.2
Honduras	32.7	39.2	45.6	52.9	54.5
India	231.2	257.3	285.7	312.6	317.9
Kenya	29.1	35.1	41.0	46.9	48.1
Kyrgyzstan	na	na	na	23.5	23.9
Laos	13.9	15.6	17.5	20.0	20.5
Lesotho	45.0	51.5	58.7	65.2	66.7
Liberia	19.5	22.8	25.3	28.4	29.2
Madagascar	15.0	17.2	20.1	22.9	23.6
Malawi	65.2	76.4	90.4	103.7	106.5
Mali	5.4	6.1	6.9	8.0	8.2
Mauritania	1.5	1.7	2.0	2.2	2.3
Moldova	na	na	na	131.6	131.2
Mongolia	1.1	1.2	1.4	1.6	1.6
Mozambique	15.4	17.3	18.0	22.2	23.0
Myanmar (Burma)	51.4	57.1	62.9	68.6	69.8
Nepal	101.4	115.4	131.3	150.0	154.1
Nicaragua	23.1	26.4	30.9	36.0	37.1
Niger	4.4	5.2	6.1	7.1	7.4
Nigeria	78.1	91.3	105.6	122.2	125.8
Pakistan	107.1	124.8	145.7	168.5	173.2
Rwanda	209.3	245.5	281.9	259.4	272.7
Sao Tome and Principe	92.7	104.2	119.8	137.5	140.9
Senegal	28.8	33.1	38.1	43.2	44.3
Sierra Leone	45.2	50.1	55.8	63.0	64.6
Somalia	10.7	12.6	13.7	15.1	15.6
Sri Lanka	228.0	245.0	262.9	280.3	283.2
Sudan	7.9	9.0	10.1	11.2	11.5
Tajikistan	na	na	na	41.5	42.2
Tanzania	21.0	24.7	28.8	33.6	34.5
Togo	48.1	55.7	64.8	75.6	77.8

D3.1 Population Density, 1980–1996—Low-Income Countries per World Bank *(continued)*

Country	1980	1985	1990	1995	1996
Uganda	64.1	70.8	81.8	96.0	98.9
Vietnam	165.0	180.9	203.5	227.2	231.5
Yemen	16.2	19.1	22.5	28.9	29.9
Zambia	7.7	9.0	10.5	12.1	12.4
Zimbabwe	18.1	21.5	25.2	28.5	29.1

Definition: Population density indicates the number of people (from midyear population figures) per square kilometer of land area. It is based on the above definitions of population and land area.

Source: US Census International; http://www.census.gov/cgi-bin/ipc/idbsprd; World Bank, *World Development Indicators 1998*, Table 1.1 and Table 1.6;

D3.2 Population Density, 1980–1996—Lower Middle-Income Countries per World Bank

Country	1980	1985	1990	1995	1996
Albania	97.5	107.9	119.8	118.6	119.9
Algeria	7.8	9.2	10.5	11.8	12.1
Belarus	na	na	na	49.8	49.6
Belize	6.4	7.3	8.3	9.5	9.8
Bolivia	4.9	5.4	6.1	6.8	7.0
Botswana	1.6	1.9	2.3	2.6	2.6
Bulgaria	80.2	80.9	78.9	76.0	75.6
Cape Verde	71.7	76.9	84.7	94.3	96.6
Colombia	26.9	29.6	32.4	35.4	36.1
Costa Rica	44.7	51.7	59.4	66.1	67.4
Cuba	88.5	92.0	96.7	100.2	100.3
Djibouti	12.1	16.9	22.3	25.9	26.7
Dominica	97.8	98.1	96.3	97.3	98.2
Dominican Republic	117.8	131.8	147.0	161.7	164.6
Ecuador	28.8	32.9	37.1	41.4	42.3
Egypt	41.1	46.7	52.7	58.4	59.5
El Salvador	219.4	225.7	242.8	273.3	280.4
Estonia	na	na	na	35.1	34.7
Fiji	34.7	38.1	40.3	43.5	44.0
Georgia	na	na	na	77.6	77.6
Grenada	261.8	264.7	267.6	279.4	291.2
Guatemala	63.8	73.4	84.8	98.0	100.8
Indonesia	81.9	90.0	98.4	107.1	108.8
Iran	24.1	28.6	33.1	37.7	38.5
Iraq	29.7	35.0	41.3	47.5	48.9
Jamaica	197.0	213.4	221.9	232.9	235.1
Jordan	24.5	29.7	35.6	47.2	48.5
Kazakhstan	na	na	na	6.2	6.2
Kiribati	79.6	89.0	99.1	109.6	111.8
Latvia	na	na	na	40.5	40.1
Lebanon	293.5	320.1	355.3	391.5	398.7
Lithuania	na	na	na	57.3	57.2
Macedonia, FYRO	na	na	na	77.3	77.9
Maldives	526.7	613.3	716.7	830.0	851.8
Marshall Islands	na	na	na	na	na
Micronesia	na	na	na	na	na
Morocco	43.4	48.5	53.9	59.4	60.5
Namibia	1.3	1.4	1.6	1.9	1.9
North Korea, Dem. Rep.	146.7	157.3	169.1	183.5	186.5
Panama	26.3	29.1	32.2	35.3	35.9
Papua New Guinea	6.8	7.6	8.5	9.5	9.7
Paraguay	7.9	9.3	10.6	12.2	12.5
Peru	13.5	15.1	16.8	18.6	19.0

D3.2 Population Density, 1980–1996—Lower Middle-Income Countries per World Bank *(continued)*

Country	1980	1985	1990	1995	1996
Philippines	162.0	183.3	209.9	235.7	241.1
Romania	96.4	98.7	100.8	98.5	98.2
Russia	na	na	na	8.8	8.7
Samoa	54.8	55.5	56.5	60.1	60.7
Solomon Islands	8.3	9.8	11.4	13.5	13.9
St. Vincent and the Grenadines	250.8	262.3	274.5	284.6	286.4
Suriname	2.3	2.6	2.6	2.7	2.8
Swaziland	32.8	38.3	44.8	52.3	53.8
Syria	47.4	56.3	65.9	76.8	78.9
Thailand	91.4	100.1	108.8	116.3	117.4
Tonga	130.6	131.9	133.3	134.7	135.3
Tunisia	41.1	46.8	52.5	57.8	58.8
Turkey	57.8	65.3	72.9	80.1	81.5
Turkmenistan	na	na	na	9.6	9.8
Ukraine	na	na	na	88.9	87.5
Uzbekistan	na	na	na	55.0	56.1
Vanuatu	9.4	10.6	12.1	13.8	14.2
Venezuela	16.9	19.4	22.1	24.8	25.3
Yugoslavia				103.4	103.7

Definition: Population density indicates the number of people (from midyear population figures) per square kilometer of land area. It is based on the above definitions of population and land area.

Source: US Census International; http://www.census.gov/cgi-bin/ipc/idbsprd; World Bank, *World Development Indicators 1998*, Table 1.1 and Table 1.6

D3.3 Population Density, 1980–1996—Upper Middle-Income Countries per World Bank

Country	1980	1985	1990	1995	1996
Antigua and Barbuda	138.6	140.9	145.5	148.1	149.4
Argentina	10.3	11.1	11.9	12.7	12.9
Bahrain	484.1	615.9	729.0	836.2	868.1
Barbados	579.3	588.4	600.0	614.4	614.7
Brazil	14.3	16.0	17.5	18.8	19.1
Chile	14.9	16.1	17.5	19.0	19.3
Croatia	na	na	na	85.4	85.3
Czech Republic	na	na	na	133.7	133.5
Gabon	2.7	3.2	3.7	4.3	4.4
Hungary	116.0	114.6	112.2	110.8	110.4
Libya	1.7	2.2	2.5	2.9	2.9
Malaysia	41.9	47.7	54.5	61.2	62.6
Malta	1137.5	1075.0	1106.9	1159.4	1165.6
Mauritius	475.9	500.5	520.7	552.7	558.6
Mexico	34.9	39.2	43.7	48.0	48.8
Oman	5.2	6.6	7.7	10.0	10.2
Palau	na	na	na	na	na
Poland	116.8	122.2	125.2	126.8	126.9
Saudi Arabia	4.4	5.8	7.4	8.8	9.0
Seychelles	143.1	149.8	155.6	167.3	170.4
Slovakia	na	na	na	110.9	111.1
Slovenia	na	na	na	98.9	99.0
South Africa	22.2	25.1	27.8	30.3	30.8
St. Kitts & Nevis	123.3	118.8	116.8	113.9	113.6
St. Lucia	202.9	224.2	244.3	255.7	258.8
Trinidad & Tobago	210.9	229.6	240.9	250.9	252.8
Uruguay	16.7	17.2	17.7	18.2	18.3

Definition: Population density indicates the number of people (from midyear population figures) per square kilometer of land area. It is based on the above definitions of population and land area.

Source: US Census International; http://www.census.gov/cgi-bin/ipc/idbsprd; World Bank, *World Development Indicators 1998*, Table 1.1 and Table 1.6;

D4.1 Rural Population Density, 1980–1995—Low-Income Countries per World Bank

Country	People/Sq. Km. 1980	People/Sq. Km. 1985	People/Sq. Km. 1990	People/Sq. Km. 1995
Afghanistan	170.2	190.0	211.4	237.8
Angola	191.4	209.2	230.4	247.8
Armenia	na	na	na	197.8
Azerbaijan	na	na	na	208.0
Bangladesh	862.8	957.5	974.9	1157.2
Benin	186.5	201.3	220.1	235.8
Bhutan	450.8	468.0	503.5	502.6
Bosnia and Herzegovina	na	na	na	516.3
Burkina Faso	229.8	231.1	221.3	255.1
Burundi	395.2	450.3	530.0	623.0
Cambodia	284.6	274.9	191.0	208.9
Cameroon	101.0	108.5	115.4	123.3
Central African Republic	80.3	87.1	95.3	103.3
Chad	115.6	127.7	140.0	154.4
China	813.3	861.7	898.0	913.2
Comoros	343.0	371.5	399.3	439.0
Congo, Dem. Rep. (Zaire)	273.2	317.4	372.0	429.4
Congo, Rep.	734.9	726.8	736.5	755.4
Cote d'Ivoire	273.3	260.4	293.7	272.3
Equatorial Guinea	121.2	168.5	174.1	177.8
Eritrea	na	na	na	673.4
Ethiopia	na	na	na	421.3
Gambia	324.1	341.6	365.9	451.6
Ghana	388.9	356.0	364.0	390.9
Guinea	611.7	635.2	701.0	666.6
Guinea-Bissau	263.6	249.3	257.3	279.0
Guyana	110.0	112.6	110.6	111.7
Haiti	749.4	783.2	830.4	873.0
Honduras	152.8	173.4	188.0	196.4
India	320.8	349.7	381.6	409.6
Kenya	365.6	400.9	443.1	476.4
Kyrgyzstan	na	na	na	336.2
Laos	414.3	356.9	394.2	417.3
Lesotho	405.4	429.3	449.4	470.3
Liberia	969.3	1059.4	1101.5	1183.6
Madagascar	283.6	312.6	346.1	379.4
Malawi	425.3	446.0	457.2	505.4
Mali	262.4	282.0	308.4	208.0
Mauritania	586.5	579.7	560.2	541.3
Moldova	na	na	na	118.4
Mongolia	67.4	63.4	67.2	73.2
Mozambique	368.8	381.6	358.2	391.0
Myanmar (Burma)	268.5	297.4	325.9	350.8
Nepal	591.9	661.6	737.1	658.7
Nicaragua	113.4	89.7	77.6	67.5
Niger	135.7	159.3	178.4	147.7
Nigeria	186.7	202.3	211.7	221.7
Pakistan	297.0	334.2	373.5	405.5
Rwanda	647.4	695.7	774.8	710.0
Sao Tome and Principe	6167.7	3260.0	3513.3	3768.6
Senegal	151.6	169.4	187.0	208.4
Sierra Leone	545.8	551.7	576.0	619.0
Somalia	530.8	599.4	639.6	706.1
Sri Lanka	1328.1	1386.8	1445.8	1548.9
Sudan	120.9	132.2	137.7	142.0
Tajikistan	na	na	na	482.5

D4.1 Rural Population Density, 1980–1995—Low-Income Countries per World Bank *(continued)*

Country	People/Sq. Km. 1980	People/Sq. Km. 1985	People/Sq. Km. 1990	People/Sq. Km. 1995
Tanzania	719.6	787.2	667.2	728.4
Togo	100.8	111.3	122.9	137.6
Uganda	286.3	259.9	290.0	331.5
Vietnam	730.5	842.8	996.2	1082.1
Yemen	498.8	555.3	612.8	701.9
Zambia	67.7	76.4	85.8	97.2
Zimbabwe	220.9	230.5	256.6	243.8

Definition: Rural population density is found by dividing the rural population of a country by the total arable land area, which includes land under crops, temporary meadows for mowing or pasture, and land under market and kitchen gardens.

Source: World Bank, *World Development Indicators 1998*, Table 3.1; World Bank, *World Development Indicators 1998*, Series: Population density, rural (EN.RUR.DNST)

D4.2 Rural Population Density, 1980–1995—Lower Middle-Income Countries per World Bank

Country	People/Sq. Km. 1980	People/Sq. Km. 1985	People/Sq. Km. 1990	People/Sq. Km. 1995
Albania	302.3	327.3	364.5	353.6
Algeria	153.7	166.2	169.9	164.7
Belarus	na	na	na	49.2
Belize	164.2	199.1	198.8	193.2
Bolivia	155.7	142.3	139.0	137.5
Botswana	191.3	201.0	177.4	167.6
Bulgaria	89.8	83.3	75.7	66.6
Cape Verde	581.8	546.6	464.6	445.3
Colombia	271.3	267.3	336.3	419.2
Costa Rica	459.2	510.8	563.3	600.2
Cuba	117.9	111.3	106.9	70.8
Djibouti	na	na	na	na
Dominica	383.5	416.8	466.8	747.0
Dominican Republic	263.6	269.3	282.4	220.9
Ecuador	273.6	279.3	287.3	299.2
Egypt	1004.9	1132.0	1288.1	1144.2
El Salvador	474.2	474.2	499.5	572.4
Estonia	na	na	na	35.5
Fiji	438.2	357.2	279.2	235.8
Georgia	na	na	na	290.5
Grenada	1194.4	1200.6	1197.6	1524.8
Guatemala	340.9	381.6	438.6	478.9
Indonesia	641.0	617.9	610.7	731.5
Iran	151.9	145.0	145.4	147.8
Iraq	85.5	91.0	97.1	96.3
Jamaica	630.4	743.1	742.5	659.7
Jordan	292.5	312.2	327.2	374.9
Kazakhstan	na	na	na	21.0
Kiribati	na	na	na	na
Latvia	na	na	na	40.0
Lebanon	367.3	324.3	276.1	236.1
Lithuania	na	na	na	35.3
Macedonia, FYRO	na	na	na	130.1
Maldives	4092.2	4569.3	5310.5	6067.3
Marshall Islands	na	na	na	na
Micronesia	na	na	na	na
Morocco	151.6	152.2	140.1	148.2
Namibia	121.4	131.2	141.3	121.2
North Korea, Dem. Rep.	472.9	469.0	480.3	504.3

D4.2 Rural Population Density, 1980–1995—Lower Middle-Income Countries per World Bank *(continued)*

Country	People/Sq. Km. 1980	People/Sq. Km. 1985	People/Sq. Km. 1990	People/Sq. Km. 1995
Panama	223.0	223.2	222.5	233.6
Papua New Guinea	13424.1	10571.9	9323.3	6022.8
Paraguay	112.9	106.9	102.6	104.9
Peru	190.1	190.0	196.8	182.4
Philippines	580.3	582.4	584.9	585.6
Romania	114.9	110.6	113.9	107.1
Russia	na	na	na	27.3
Samoa	222.1	225.5	229.8	244.2
Solomon Islands	521.3	600.1	683.2	747.0
St. Vincent and the Grenadines	1424.0	1698.2	1589.7	1440.2
Suriname	491.6	417.8	378.0	381.3
Swaziland	251.0	322.1	301.4	331.6
Syria	88.7	106.0	111.6	134.5
Thailand	234.8	237.2	258.3	278.1
Tonga	448.3	396.2	366.5	336.6
Tunisia	97.1	109.4	118.1	120.5
Turkey	98.6	97.1	88.4	77.0
Turkmenistan	na	na	na	177.4
Ukraine	na	na	na	46.1
Uzbekistan	na	na	na	327.3
Vanuatu	524.8	529.3	602.5	682.9
Venezuela	107.9	107.0	104.7	114.9
Yugoslavia	na	na	na	122.7

Definition: Rural population density is found by dividing the rural population of a country by the total arable land area, which includes land under crops, temporary meadows for mowing or pasture, and land under market and kitchen gardens.

Source: World Bank, *World Development Indicators 1998*, Table 3.1; World Bank, *World Development Indicators 1998*, CD-ROM, Series: Population density, rural (EN.RUR.DNST)

D4.3 Rural Population Density, 1980–1995—Upper Middle-Income Countries per World Bank

Country	People/Sq. Km. 1980	People/Sq. Km. 1985	People/Sq. Km. 1990	People/Sq. Km. 1995
Antigua and Barbuda	498.7	503.8	516.8	523.1
Argentina	19.2	18.4	17.6	16.5
Bahrain	6513.0	6715.0	6237.2	5596.9
Barbados	931.0	909.2	890.1	870.2
Brazil	106.1	93.4	82.1	64.6
Chile	52.1	50.9	54.1	57.5
Croatia	na	na	na	189.0
Czech Republic	na	na	na	113.7
Gabon	157.3	170.9	180.3	168.6
Hungary	91.8	85.1	77.7	75.4
Libya	53.3	49.4	44.7	40.8
Malaysia	798.3	662.6	529.4	512.4
Malta	512.6	415.7	366.0	397.0
Mauritius	556.4	595.4	628.9	667.6
Mexico	97.5	98.2	99.2	94.8
Oman	5801.4	4982.6	3854.0	3255.9
Palau	na	na	na	na
Poland	102.0	102.6	101.2	98.6
Saudi Arabia	169.1	133.0	100.2	88.2
Seychelles	3864.0	3720.5	3514.0	3433.7
Slovakia	na	na	na	148.4

D4.3 Rural Population Density, 1980–1995—Upper Middle-Income Countries per World Bank *(continued)*

Country	People/Sq. Km. 1980	People/Sq. Km. 1985	People/Sq. Km. 1990	People/Sq. Km. 1995
Slovenia	na	na	na	414.2
South Africa	113.3	128.4	129.1	125.0
St. Kitts & Nevis	355.8	346.3	343.6	338.3
St. Lucia	1552.1	1715.1	1871.4	1959.4
Trinidad & Tobago	570.4	553.0	516.1	485.6
Uruguay	30.7	30.1	27.3	24.5

Definition: Rural population density is found by dividing the rural population of a country by the total arable land area, which includes land under crops, temporary meadows for mowing or pasture, and land under market and kitchen gardens.

Source: World Bank, *World Development Indicators 1998*, Table 3.1; World Bank, *World Development Indicators 1998*, CD-ROM, Series: Population density, rural (EN.RUR.DNST)

D4.4 Rural Population Density Summary, 1995—Comparison by Income Level per World Bank

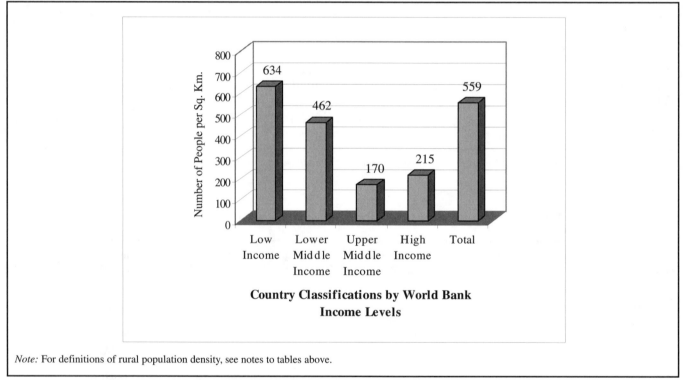

Note: For definitions of rural population density, see notes to tables above.

Source: World Bank, *World Development Indicators 1998*, Table 3.1

D5.1 Urban Population, 1980–1996—Low-Income Countries per World Bank

Country	% of Total 1980	% of Total 1985	% of Total 1990	% of Total 1995	% of Total 1996
Afghanistan	15.6	16.9	18.2	19.9	20.3
Angola	20.9	24.2	27.6	31.0	31.64
Armenia	65.7	66.6	67.5	68.6	68.88
Azerbaijan	52.8	53.6	54.4	55.7	56.02
Bangladesh	11.3	13.4	15.7	18.3	18.88
Benin	27.3	30.8	34.5	38.4	39.18
Bhutan	3.9	4.4	5.2	6.0	6.22
Bosnia and Herzegovina	35.5	37.6	39.3	41.1	41.5

D5.1 Urban Population, 1980–1996—Low-Income Countries per World Bank *(continued)*

Country	% of Total 1980	% of Total 1985	% of Total 1990	% of Total 1995	% of Total 1996
Burkina Faso	8.5	11.4	13.6	15.9	16.42
Burundi	4.3	5.2	6.3	7.5	7.8
Cambodia	12.4	14.8	17.5	20.4	21.02
Cameroon	31.4	35.7	40.3	44.7	45.54
Central African Republic	35.1	36.3	37.5	39.1	39.52
Chad	18.8	19.9	21.1	22.2	22.52
China	19.6	22.6	26.2	30.2	31.02
Comoros	23.2	25.5	27.9	30.4	30.96
Congo, Dem. Rep. (Zaire)	28.7	27.9	27.9	28.7	29.02
Congo, Rep.	41.0	47.5	53.4	58.4	59.22
Cote d'Ivoire	34.8	37.6	40.4	43.4	44.02
Equatorial Guinea	27.4	29.8	35.7	42.2	43.4
Eritrea	13.5	14.8	15.8	17.1	17.42
Ethiopia	10.5	11.7	13.4	15.4	15.84
Gambia	19.6	22.5	25.7	29.0	29.7
Ghana	31.2	32.3	33.9	35.9	36.4
Guinea	19.1	22.3	25.7	29.2	29.92
Guinea-Bissau	16.9	18.4	20.0	21.7	22.1
Guyana	30.5	31.6	33.2	35.4	35.96
Haiti	23.7	26.1	28.8	31.8	32.42
Honduras	34.9	37.7	40.7	43.8	44.42
India	23.1	24.3	25.5	26.8	27.12
Kenya	16.1	19.8	24.1	28.6	29.5
Kyrgyzstan	38.3	38.2	38.2	38.8	39.06
Laos	13.4	15.6	18.1	20.7	21.26
Lesotho	13.4	16.5	20.1	24.0	24.8
Liberia	35.0	39.3	42.1	45.0	45.58
Madagascar	18.3	20.8	23.5	26.4	27.02
Malawi	9.1	10.4	11.8	13.5	13.88
Mali	18.5	21.0	23.8	26.8	27.44
Mauritania	27.4	35.0	43.5	51.2	52.5
Moldova	39.9	43.8	47.8	51.6	52.32
Mongolia	52.1	55.0	58.0	60.8	61.34
Mozambique	13.1	19.4	26.6	33.8	35.08
Myanmar (Burma)	24.0	24.0	24.6	25.8	26.18
Nepal	6.5	7.8	8.9	10.3	10.62
Nicaragua	53.4	56.4	59.4	62.1	62.62
Niger	12.6	14.3	16.1	18.2	18.68
Nigeria	26.9	30.7	35.0	39.5	40.4
Pakistan	28.1	29.8	31.9	34.3	34.84
Rwanda	4.7	5.0	5.3	5.7	5.8
Sao Tome and Principe	30.7	34.8	38.9	42.9	43.66
Senegal	35.9	37.9	40.4	43.7	44.36
Sierra Leone	24.1	26.9	30.0	33.3	33.96
Somalia	22.2	23.2	24.2	25.6	25.98
Sri Lanka	21.6	21.1	21.3	22.1	22.4
Sudan	20.0	22.4	26.6	31.3	32.26
Tajikistan	34.3	33.2	32.2	32.2	32.34
Tanzania	14.8	17.6	20.8	24.2	24.92
Togo	22.9	26.5	28.5	30.7	31.22
Uganda	8.8	9.9	11.2	12.5	12.84
Vietnam	19.2	19.6	19.7	19.4	19.46
Yemen	20.2	24.4	28.9	33.5	34.4
Zambia	39.8	40.9	42.0	43.0	43.3
Zimbabwe	22.3	25.2	28.4	31.8	32.5

Definition: Urban population is the population at midyear of areas considered urban, such as towns, cities, metropolitan areas, etc.

Source: World Bank, *World Development Indicators 1998*, Table 3.10; World Bank, *World Development Indicators 1998*, CD-ROM, Series: Urban population (SP.URB.TOTL.IN.ZS)

D5.2 Urban Population, 1980–1996—Lower Middle-Income Countries per World Bank

Country	% of Total 1980	% of Total 1985	% of Total 1990	% of Total 1995	% of Total 1996
Albania	33.8	34.8	35.7	37.2	37.58
Algeria	43.4	47.5	51.7	55.7	56.42
Belarus	56.5	61.8	66.8	71.0	71.68
Belize	49.4	48.5	47.5	46.5	46.50
Bolivia	45.5	50.5	55.6	60.5	61.36
Botswana	15.1	25.2	41.5	60.0	62.72
Bulgaria	61.2	64.5	66.5	68.3	68.66
Cape Verde	23.5	33.0	44.2	54.3	55.88
Colombia	63.9	67.0	70.0	72.6	73.06
Costa Rica	43.1	44.9	47.1	49.3	49.82
Cuba	68.1	71.0	73.5	75.8	76.22
Djibouti	73.6	77.5	80.2	82.1	82.34
Dominica	63.4	66.0	67.7	69.3	69.64
Dominican Republic	50.5	54.6	58.3	61.9	62.56
Ecuador	47.0	51.2	55.1	58.9	59.60
Egypt	43.8	43.9	43.9	44.6	44.86
El Salvador	41.6	42.7	43.9	45.0	45.32
Estonia	69.7	70.8	71.8	73.0	73.26
Fiji	37.8	38.5	39.3	40.6	40.94
Georgia	51.6	53.9	56.0	58.3	58.78
Grenada	32.9	33.3	34.2	35.8	36.22
Guatemala	37.4	37.7	38.0	38.9	39.20
Indonesia	22.2	26.1	30.6	35.4	36.36
Iran	49.6	53.4	56.3	59.0	59.52
Iraq	65.5	68.8	71.8	74.5	74.96
Jamaica	46.8	49.2	51.5	53.7	54.18
Jordan	59.9	64.1	68.0	71.4	71.96
Kazakhstan	54.0	55.8	57.6	59.6	60.02
Kiribati	31.7	33.5	34.6	35.7	36.02
Latvia	68.2	69.8	71.2	72.8	73.10
Lebanon	73.7	79.4	84.2	87.5	87.94
Lithuania	61.2	65.1	68.8	72.0	72.54
Macedonia, FYRO	53.5	55.7	57.8	59.9	60.32
Maldives	22.3	25.5	25.9	26.9	27.18
Marshall Islands	na	na	na	na	na
Micronesia	25.0	25.3	26.2	27.7	28.10
Morocco	41.1	44.6	48.2	51.8	52.50
Namibia	22.8	26.5	31.0	36.0	36.98
North Korea, Dem. Rep.	56.9	58.9	59.9	61.2	61.52
Panama	50.4	52.1	53.7	55.6	56.02
Papua New Guinea	13.0	14.0	15.0	16.0	16.28
Paraguay	41.7	45.0	48.7	52.4	53.12
Peru	64.6	66.9	68.9	70.9	71.28
Philippines	37.5	43.0	48.8	54.0	54.92
Romania	49.1	51.4	53.6	55.9	56.36
Russia	69.8	71.9	74.0	75.9	76.26
Samoa	21.2	21.1	21.0	21.0	21.10
Solomon Islands	10.5	12.4	14.6	17.0	17.54
St. Vincent and the Grenadines	27.2	33.6	40.6	48.1	49.44
Suriname	44.8	45.4	46.8	49.1	49.72
Swaziland	17.8	21.8	26.4	31.1	32.02
Syria	46.7	48.4	50.2	52.2	52.66
Thailand	17.0	17.9	18.7	20.0	20.32
Tonga	23.7	29.1	35.1	41.0	42.00
Tunisia	51.5	53.8	57.9	61.9	62.62
Turkey	43.8	52.5	61.2	69.2	70.42
Turkmenistan	47.1	46.0	44.9	44.9	45.02

D5.2 Urban Population, 1980–1996—Lower Middle-Income Countries per World Bank *(continued)*

Country	% of Total 1980	% of Total 1985	% of Total 1990	% of Total 1995	% of Total 1996
Ukraine	61.7	64.7	67.5	70.2	70.66
Uzbekistan	40.8	40.7	40.6	41.1	41.36
Vanuatu	17.9	18.0	18.2	18.9	19.12
Venezuela	79.4	81.9	84.0	85.8	86.12
Yugoslavia	46.3	49.7	53.2	56.6	57.26

Definition: Urban population is the population at midyear of areas considered urban, such as towns, cities, metropolitan areas, etc.).

Source: World Bank, *World Development Indicators 1998*, Table 3.10; World Bank, *World Development Indicators 1998*, CD-ROM, Series: Urban population (SP.URB.TOTL.IN.ZS)

D5.3 Urban Population, 1980–1996—Upper Middle-Income Countries per World Bank

Country	% of Total 1980	% of Total 1985	% of Total 1990	% of Total 1995	% of Total 1996
Antigua and Barbuda	34.6	35.0	35.4	35.8	36.00
Argentina	82.9	84.8	86.5	88.1	88.36
Bahrain	80.5	84.2	87.6	90.3	90.68
Barbados	40.2	42.5	44.8	47.3	47.84
Brazil	66.2	70.7	74.7	78.3	78.90
Chile	81.2	82.6	83.3	83.9	84.04
Croatia	50.1	52.3	54.0	55.8	56.18
Czech Republic	63.6	64.5	64.9	65.4	65.58
Gabon	34.0	39.2	44.6	50.1	51.12
Hungary	56.9	59.5	62.1	64.6	65.06
Libya	69.3	76.7	81.8	85.3	85.76
Malaysia	42.0	45.9	49.7	53.6	54.34
Malta	83.1	85.5	87.6	89.3	89.54
Mauritius	42.4	41.4	40.5	40.5	40.66
Mexico	66.3	69.6	72.5	73.4	73.6
Oman	31.5	46.5	62.1	75.6	77.28
Palau	na	na	na	na	na
Poland	58.1	60.0	61.8	63.7	64.08
Saudi Arabia	65.9	72.6	78.5	82.8	83.38
Seychelles	40.0	44.8	49.8	54.4	55.22
Slovakia	51.6	54.2	56.5	58.8	59.26
Slovenia	48.0	49.6	50.5	51.3	51.56
South Africa	48.1	48.3	48.8	49.3	49.52
St. Kitts & Nevis	35.9	35.2	34.6	34	34.02
St. Lucia	37.3	37.3	37.2	37.2	37.32
Trinidad & Tobago	63.1	66.2	69.1	71.7	72.18
Uruguay	85.2	87.2	88.9	90.3	90.50

Definition: Urban population is the population at midyear of areas considered urban, such as towns, cities, metropolitan areas, etc.

Source: World Bank, *World Development Indicators 1998*, Table 3.10; World Bank, *World Development Indicators 1998*, CD-ROM, Series: Urban population (SP.URB.TOTL.IN.ZS)

D5.4 Urban Population, Percent of Total, Summary 1980 and 1996—Comparison by Income Level per World Bank

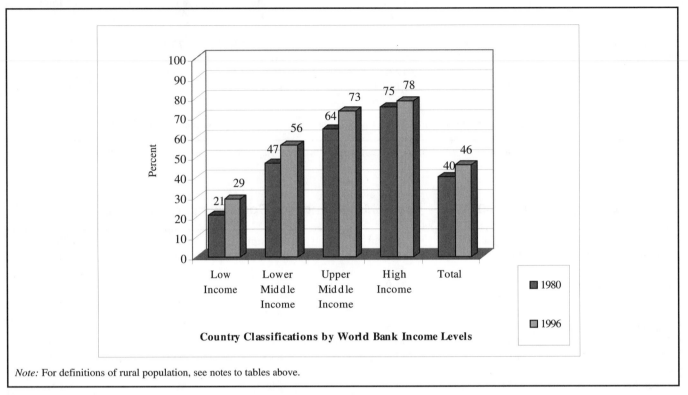

Country Classifications by World Bank Income Levels

■ 1980

■ 1996

Note: For definitions of rural population, see notes to tables above.

Source: World Bank, *World Development Indicators 1998*, Table 3.10

D5.5 Urban Population Growth Rate, Percent, 1980–1996—Low-Income Countries per World Bank

Country	1980	1985	1990	1995	1996	Average Annual 1960–80	Average Annual 1980–96
Afghanistan	5.55	4.03	3.88	4.71	4.87	5.3	3.3
Angola	5.76	5.36	5.65	5.27	5.04	5.4	5.5
Armenia	2.42	1.69	2.06	0.64	0.78	3.4	1.3
Azerbaijan	1.98	1.90	1.35	1.16	1.50	2.5	1.7
Bangladesh	6.06	5.67	4.97	4.45	4.70	6.7	5.2
Benin	6.89	5.48	5.28	4.83	4.83	7.6	5.2
Bhutan	4.24	4.26	5.24	5.64	6.47	4.4	5.2
Bosnia and Herzegovina	3.08	2.31	1.10	0.88	1.39	3.9	0.7
Burkina Faso	7.71	7.79	6.05	5.78	5.99	5.6	6.9
Burundi	7.88	6.39	6.44	5.74	6.42	6.2	6.3
Cambodia	4.30	6.47	6.30	5.52	5.47	1.3	6.2
Cameroon	5.91	5.07	5.24	4.90	4.74	6.9	5.2
Central African Republic	3.15	2.96	3.12	2.89	3.15	4.0	3.1
Chad	5.64	3.48	3.66	3.52	3.93	6.9	3.5
China	4.36	-0.39	1.47	4.23	3.68	2.8	4.2
Comoros	na	4.37	4.36	4.22	4.37	5.5	4.9
Congo, Dem. Rep. (Zaire)	2.53	2.71	3.28	3.67	4.22	3.5	3.5
Congo, Rep.	5.97	5.89	5.44	4.45	4.10	4.3	5.2
Cote d'Ivoire	5.42	5.36	5.05	4.11	4.02	6.7	4.8
Equatorial Guinea	4.03	7.28	4.34	5.69	5.36	-1.2	6.9
Eritrea	na	na	na	4.13	5.28	4.8	3.6
Ethiopia	4.67	4.87	6.24	5.35	6.01	4.5	5.6

D5.5 Urban Population Growth Rate, Percent, 1980–1996—Low-Income Countries per World Bank *(continued)*

Country	1980	1985	1990	1995	1996	Average Annual 1960–80	Average Annual 1980–96
Gambia	5.63	6.17	7.22	5.48	5.38	5.5	6.2
Ghana	2.96	4.33	3.98	3.71	3.97	3.3	4.1
Guinea	4.68	5.48	5.64	4.99	4.96	4.9	6.0
Guinea-Bissau	5.03	3.46	3.25	3.90	4.12	3.9	3.6
Guyana	1.07	1.19	1.09	2.23	2.59	1.4	1.6
Haiti	3.42	3.74	3.93	4.15	4.25	3.7	3.9
Honduras	5.20	4.88	4.38	4.41	4.35	5.1	4.6
India	3.82	3.04	2.96	2.69	2.87	3.6	3.0
Kenya	7.85	7.35	6.49	5.74	5.60	7.7	7.0
Kyrgyzstan	2.10	1.92	1.54	1.24	2.01	2.7	1.4
Laos	4.53	5.68	5.11	5.16	5.25	5.0	5.7
Lesotho	6.78	6.43	6.37	5.44	5.42	7.3	6.5
Liberia	5.96	4.89	3.14	3.95	4.07	6.1	3.1
Madagascar	5.15	5.36	5.44	5.06	5.32	5.3	5.8
Malawi	6.27	5.85	5.81	5.29	5.40	7.1	5.6
Mali	4.73	4.88	5.25	4.93	5.34	4.8	5.5
Mauritania	7.86	7.01	6.48	5.62	5.05	9.7	6.7
Moldova	2.98	2.68	2.01	1.22	1.11	3.7	2.3
Mongolia	4.06	4.00	3.70	3.05	2.98	4.2	3.6
Mozambique	9.87	8.13	6.72	9.11	7.13	9.5	8.6
Myanmar (Burma)	2.17	2.07	2.29	2.63	3.17	3.1	2.5
Nepal	7.24	6.03	5.04	5.52	5.73	6.5	5.7
Nicaragua	3.89	3.93	4.28	3.83	3.72	4.6	3.6
Niger	6.62	5.74	5.30	5.68	5.95	6.9	5.8
Nigeria	5.73	5.55	5.33	5.28	5.17	5.7	5.5
Pakistan	4.22	4.22	4.45	4.16	4.30	3.8	4.5
Rwanda	6.31	4.56	3.51	4.11	6.72	6.8	1.9
Sao Tome and Principe	na	5.02	4.99	4.45	4.20	5.3	4.4
Senegal	3.78	3.88	4.00	4.14	4.14	3.4	4.0
Sierra Leone	4.26	4.19	4.35	4.49	4.59	5.5	4.0
Somalia	4.77	3.51	2.12	6.26	4.73	3.9	3.4
Sri Lanka	1.46	1.04	1.29	2.11	2.37	2.4	1.5
Sudan	4.12	4.73	5.35	5.10	5.11	5.6	5.4
Tajikistan	2.06	2.20	1.77	1.47	1.98	2.9	2.2
Tanzania	9.72	6.41	6.23	5.77	5.75	9.9	6.5
Togo	8.75	5.75	4.46	4.41	4.56	7.9	4.9
Uganda	3.44	4.23	5.84	5.24	5.63	5.3	5.1
Vietnam	2.54	2.43	2.33	1.67	2.17	3.3	2.2
Yemen	7.72	6.56	6.87	6.03	5.91	6.3	7.4
Zambia	5.87	3.52	3.62	3.17	3.28	6.6	2.8
Zimbabwe	5.60	5.76	5.22	4.35	4.31	6.0	5.3

Definition: Urban population is the population at midyear of areas considered urban (towns, cities, metropolitan areas, etc.) The urban population growth rate is the annual change in the population attributed to urban areas for a given point in time.

Source: World Bank, *World Development Indicators 1998*, Table 3.10; World Bank, *World Development Indicators 1998*, CD-ROM, Series: Urban Population Growth; UNICEF, http://www.unicef.org/sowc98/, Table 5: Demographic indicators - 1965–80 & 1980–96

D5.6 Urban Population Growth Rate, Percent, 1980–1996—Lower Middle-Income Countries per World Bank

Country	1980	1985	1990	1995	1996	Average Annual 1960–80	Average Annual 1980–96
Gambia	5.63	6.17	7.22	5.48	5.38	5.5	6.2
Albania	2.64	2.63	2.10	2.27	2.15	2.9	2.2
Algeria	4.52	4.88	4.15	3.74	3.48	4.0	4.3
Belarus	2.83	2.38	2.27	0.93	0.65	3.4	1.9
Belize	2.34	2.22	2.19	2.29	2.60	1.7	2.2
Bolivia	3.93	3.96	4.16	4.05	3.73	3.2	4.1
Botswana	7.72	11.93	11.43	8.44	6.48	12.5	12.0
Bulgaria	1.62	1.21	-1.20	0.11	0.00	2.4	0.4
Cape Verde	2.79	7.61	7.22	6.15	5.29	3.4	7.4
Colombia	3.06	2.80	2.67	2.54	2.35	3.6	2.8
Costa Rica	3.84	3.71	3.55	2.99	3.05	3.7	3.6
Cuba	1.19	1.86	1.66	0.80	0.73	2.6	1.5
Djibouti	7.95	7.44	5.53	3.48	3.19	8.4	5.6
Dominica	3.48	0.42	0.14	1.23	1.36	2.8	0.3
Dominican Republic	4.42	3.74	3.40	2.94	2.84	5.1	3.4
Ecuador	4.77	4.24	3.71	3.45	3.24	4.5	3.9
Egypt	2.66	2.62	2.29	2.25	2.44	2.7	2.5
El Salvador	1.96	1.19	2.53	3.11	3.28	3.2	2.1
Estonia	1.28	1.06	-0.17	-0.68	-0.86	1.7	0.3
Fiji	2.66	1.96	1.78	1.91	1.96	3.1	1.9
Georgia	na	1.71	0.97	0.68	0.80	1.7	1.3
Grenada	na	na	na	4.11	5.29	-0.2	1.0
Guatemala	3.16	3.01	3.05	3.32	3.62	3.4	3.2
Indonesia	4.63	4.87	4.78	4.38	4.25	4.6	4.9
Iran	4.93	4.69	3.79	3.41	3.03	4.9	4.8
Iraq	4.56	4.30	4.06	3.22	3.40	5.0	3.8
Jamaica	2.51	2.34	2.09	1.86	1.86	2.7	1.9
Jordan	5.37	4.89	4.82	4.21	3.53	4.4	5.2
Kazakhstan	1.86	2.06	1.39	-0.52	-0.15	2.4	1.4
Kiribati	3.07	3.32	2.72	2.60	2.87	5.0	2.6
Latvia	1.42	1.07	-0.10	-0.80	-0.63	1.6	0.4
Lebanon	2.86	3.41	3.11	2.65	2.32	4.1	2.0
Lithuania	2.05	2.08	1.92	0.73	0.59	3.0	1.6
Macedonia, FYRO	2.48	1.46	-4.14	1.67	1.41	3.2	1.9
Maldives	6.89	5.65	3.36	3.60	3.62	6.6	4.5
Marshall Islands	na	na	na	na	na	2.4	4.3
Micronesia	na	3.19	2.77	3.45	3.29	3.7	3.4
Morocco	3.91	3.77	3.55	3.31	3.20	4.2	3.6
Namibia	4.64	5.55	5.70	5.43	5.20	4.6	5.7
North Korea, Dem. Rep.	1.50	2.09	1.80	2.18	2.11	4.1	2.0
Panama	2.69	2.69	2.62	2.43	2.37	3.5	2.6
Papua New Guinea	4.07	3.61	3.56	3.60	4.02	8.6	3.6
Paraguay	4.59	4.51	4.04	4.24	3.96	3.6	4.4
Peru	3.46	2.86	2.62	2.60	2.48	4.2	2.6
Philippines	3.12	5.23	4.99	4.26	3.99	3.9	4.7
Romania	1.88	1.34	1.06	0.61	0.50	2.8	1.0
Russia	1.69	1.36	1.02	0.40	0.17	1.8	1.0
Samoa	0.84	-0.06	0.48	1.05	1.47	1.9	0.5
Solomon Islands	6.43	6.26	6.13	5.89	6.04	4.6	6.6
St. Vincent and the Grenadines	5.96	4.79	4.39	3.74	3.36	5.4	4.6
Suriname	-2.43	3.07	0.33	2.10	2.44	0.1	1.9
Swaziland	7.52	6.82	6.67	6.18	5.77	9.5	6.5
Syria	3.96	4.19	4.05	3.63	3.60	4.3	4.0
Thailand	4.44	2.51	2.64	2.46	2.60	4.7	2.5

D5.6 Urban Population Growth Rate, Percent, 1980–1996—Lower Middle-Income Countries per World Bank *(continued)*

Country	1980	1985	1990	1995	1996	Average Annual 1960-80	Average Annual 1980-96
Tonga	3.84	3.52	4.00	2.91	2.82	2.6	3.9
Tunisia	3.30	3.90	3.86	2.89	2.76	4.0	3.4
Turkey	3.24	5.80	5.09	4.09	3.44	4.0	5.0
Turkmenistan	2.19	1.90	2.00	2.29	2.24	2.8	2.1
Ukraine	1.03	-1.21	0.53	0.02	-0.94	2.0	1.0
Uzbekistan	3.20	2.29	2.55	2.05	2.56	3.9	2.4
Vanuatu	4.78	1.83	2.83	3.27	3.79	6.4	2.8
Venezuela	3.90	3.35	2.98	2.58	2.49	4.5	3.0
Yugoslavia	na	2.09	1.86	1.44	1.44	3.0	1.8

Definition: Urban population is the population at midyear of areas considered urban (towns, cities, metropolitan areas, etc.) The urban population growth rate is the annual change in the population attributed to urban areas for a given point in time.

Source: World Bank, *World Development Indicators 1998*, Table 3.10; Series: Urban Population Growth; UNICEF, http://www.unicef.org/sowc98/, Table 5: Demographic indicators - 1965-80 & 1980-96

D5.7 Urban Population Growth Rate, Percent, 1980–1996—Upper Middle-Income Countries per World Bank

Country	1980	1985	1990	1995	1996	Average Annual 1960-80	Average Annual 1980-96
Antigua and Barbuda	-0.03	0.55	0.84	0.59	1.40	0.3	0.8
Argentina	2.04	1.94	1.74	1.69	1.59	2.1	1.8
Bahrain	4.92	5.13	3.60	4.13	4.16	3.8	3.8
Barbados	1.85	1.25	1.63	1.02	1.17	1.1	1.4
Brazil	3.81	3.33	2.72	2.26	2.10	4.3	2.9
Chile	2.19	1.95	1.89	1.67	1.62	2.6	1.8
Croatia	2.40	1.29	0.86	0.63	0.57	2.8	0.9
Czech Republic	1.84	0.41	0.13	0.10	0.12	2.1	0.2
Gabon	5.99	6.05	5.61	4.71	4.44	5.5	5.5
Hungary	1.54	0.42	0.52	0.47	0.35	1.8	0.4
Libya	6.85	6.30	4.13	3.28	2.96	10.4	5.2
Malaysia	4.42	4.41	4.12	3.67	3.67	4.7	4.1
Malta	1.63	-1.42	1.45	1.19	0.81	1.2	1.3
Mauritius	1.36	-0.02	0.36	0.81	1.46	2.6	0.7
Mexico	3.41	3.25	2.92	2.00	1.98	4.2	2.6
Oman	13.22	10.43	8.32	6.44	3.96	14.6	10.1
Palau	na	na	na	na	na	3.1	2.5
Poland	1.93	1.42	0.99	0.71	0.67	1.8	1.1
Saudi Arabia	7.81	7.19	5.97	4.43	2.94	8.2	5.7
Seychelles	4.67	2.91	2.90	3.56	3.30	4.9	3.1
Slovakia	2.18	1.56	0.55	0.50	0.99	3.1	1.3
Slovenia	3.39	2.20	0.29	0.37	0.56	3.4	0.7
South Africa	2.62	2.40	2.05	1.80	2.29	2.7	2.5
St. Kitts & Nevis	2.11	-2.53	-0.68	-0.81	-0.23	0.4	-0.8
St. Lucia	1.30	1.99	0.48	1.17	1.51	1.0	1.4
Trinidad & Tobago	1.62	2.40	1.55	1.61	1.44	1.2	2.0
Uruguay	1.11	1.09	0.93	0.85	0.82	0.9	1.0

Definition: Urban population is the population at midyear of areas considered urban (towns, cities, metropolitan areas, etc.) The urban population growth rate is the annual change in the population attributed to urban areas for a given point in time.

Source: World Bank, *World Development Indicators 1998*, Table 3.10; Series: Urban Population Growth; UNICEF, http://www.unicef.org/sowc98/, Table 5: Demographic indicators - 1965-80 & 1980-96

D6.1 Population, Female and Male Breakdown in Thousands, 1997—Low-Income Countries per World Bank

Country	Female (thousands)	Male (thousands)	Country	Female (thousands)	Male (thousands)
Afghanistan	10790	11342	Laos	2629	2566
Angola	5855	5715	Lesotho	1080	1051
Armenia	1872	1770	Liberia	1225	1243
Azerbaijan	3902	3753	Madagascar	7953	7892
Bangladesh	59391	62622	Malawi	5097	4990
Benin	2909	2811	Mali	5826	5654
Bhutan	926	936	Mauritania	1207	1185
Bosnia and Herzegovina	1911	1873	Moldova	2322	2126
Burkina Faso	5559	5528	Mongolia	1281	1288
Burundi	3276	3122	Mozambique	9244	9021
Cambodia	5430	5085	Myanmar (Burma)	23468	23297
Cameroon	7014	6923	Nepal	11154	11438
Central African Republic	1762	1654	Nicaragua	2180	2171
Chad	3392	3310	Niger	4949	4838
China	na	na	Nigeria	59674	58695
Comoros	321	331	Pakistan	69501	74330
Congo, Dem. Rep. (Zaire)	24281	23759	Rwanda	2981	2902
Congo, Rep.	1404	1341	Sao Tome and Principe	59	58
Cote d'Ivoire	7008	7291	Senegal	4376	4386
Equatorial Guinea	213	207	Sierra Leone	2257	2171
Eritrea	1717	1692	Somalia	5157	5060
Ethiopia	29891	30257	Sri Lanka	9210	9063
Gambia	591	577	Sudan	13900	13998
Ghana	9231	9107	Tajikistan	3036	3009
Guinea	3786	3828	Tanzania	15904	15602
Guinea-Bissau	565	547	Togo	2177	2139
Guyana	429	418	Uganda	10461	10330
Haiti	3765	3630	Vietnam	38805	37743
Honduras	2967	3014	Yemen	8098	8196
India	464316	495862	Zambia	4301	4177
Kenya	14181	14233	Zimbabwe	5884	5798
Kyrgyzstan	2284	2196			

Definition: Population figures by gender give estimates of numbers of residents in a country at mid-year. Typically, they are derived from a country's population census data with adjustments made for the subject year; such adjustments are based on birth, death and migration rates. The figures for female and male populations represent the number of each gender in the total population and are derived from similar census data adjustments.

Source: United Nations Web site: http://www.un.org/Depts/unsd/gender/1-1asi.htm; http://www.un.org/Depts/unsd/gender/1-1dev.htm; http://www.un.org/Depts/unsd/gender/1-1lat.htm; http://www.un.org/Depts/unsd/gender/1-1afr.htm; Series: 1-1

D6.2 Population, Female and Male Breakdown in Thousands, 1997—Lower Middle-Income Countries per World Bank

Country	Female (thousands)	Male (thousands)	Country	Female (thousands)	Male (thousands)
Albania	1671	1751	Lithuania	1960	1759
Algeria	14557	14916	Macedonia, FYRO	1086	1103
Belarus	5477	4861	Maldives	133	140
Belize	111	113	Marshall Islands	22	23
Bolivia	3911	3863	Micronesia	51	54
Botswana	773	745	Morocco	13742	13776
Bulgaria	4313	4115	Namibia	810	803
Cape Verde	215	191	North Korea, Dem. Rep.	11396	11441
Colombia	18673	18394	Panama	1347	1375
Costa Rica	1767	1808	Papua New Guinea	2180	2320
Cuba	5518	5550	Paraguay	2524	2564
Djibouti	322	312	Peru	12276	12091
Dominica	36	36	Philippines	35111	35613
Dominican Republic	3981	4116	Romania	11484	11122
Ecuador	5941	5997	Russia	78573	69136
Egypt	31745	32721	Samoa	80	88
El Salvador	3020	2907	Solomon Islands	196	208
Estonia	771	684	St. Vincent and the Grenadines	53	53
Fiji	398	411	Suriname	220	217
Georgia	2839	2596	Swaziland	471	435
Grenada	46	43	Syria	7395	7556
Guatemala	5567	5674	Thailand	29596	29563
Indonesia	101969	101510	Tonga	46	47
Iran	35145	36373	Tunisia	4602	4723
Iraq	10402	10775	Turkey	31032	31742
Jamaica	1253	1262	Turkmenistan	2140	2095
Jordan	2820	2954	Ukraine	27526	23898
Kazakhstan	8647	8185	Uzbekistan	11917	11739
Kiribati	37	36	Vanuatu	89	89
Latvia	1343	1132	Venezuela	11310	11467
Lebanon	1609	1535	Yugoslavia	5208	5142

Definition: Population figures by gender give estimates of numbers of residents in a country at mid-year. Typically, they are derived from a country's population census data with adjustments made for the subject year; such adjustments are based on birth, death, and migration rates. The figures for female and male populations represent the number of each gender in the total population and are derived from similar census data adjustments.

Source: United Nations Web site: http://www.un.org/Depts/unsd/gender/1-1asi.htm; http://www.un.org/Depts/unsd/gender/1-1dev.htm; http://www.un.org/Depts/unsd/gender/1-1lat.htm; http://www.un.org/Depts/unsd/gender/1-1afr.htm; Series: 1-1

D6.3 Population, Female and Male Breakdown in Thousands, 1997—Upper Middle-Income Countries per World Bank

Country	Female (thousands)	Male (thousands)	Country	Female (thousands)	Male (thousands)
Antigua and Barbuda	na	na	Mexico	47577	46703
Argentina	18174	17497	Oman	1125	1276
Bahrain	249	333	Palau	7	8
Barbados	135	127	Poland	19838	18798
Brazil	82446	80686	Saudi Arabia	8661	10833
Chile	7387	7237	Seychelles	37	37
Croatia	2322	2175	Slovakia	2747	2607
Czech Republic	5234	5004	Slovenia	991	931
Gabon	576	562	South Africa	21812	21525
Hungary	5214	4775	St. Kitts & Nevis	22	23
Libya	2778	3006	St. Lucia	70	66
Malaysia	10412	10606	Trinidad & Tobago	619	689
Malta	187	184	Uruguay	1652	1570
Mauritius	571	570			

Definition: Population figures by gender give estimates of numbers of residents in a country at mid-year. Typically, they are derived from a country's population census data with adjustments made for the subject year; such adjustments are based on birth, death, and migration rates. The figures for female and male populations represent the number of each gender in the total population and are derived from similar census data adjustments.

Source: United Nations Web site: http://www.un.org/Depts/unsd/gender/1-1asi.htm; http://www.un.org/Depts/unsd/gender/1-1dev.htm; http://www.un.org/Depts/unsd/gender/1-1lat.htm; http://www.un.org/Depts/unsd/gender/1-1afr.htm; Series: 1-1

D7.1 Birth Rate, Recent Trends, 1980–1996—Low-Income Countries per World Bank

Country	1980	1990	1996	Country	1980	1990	1996
Afghanistan	49.7	48.6	46.7	Laos	45.1	45.2	39.8
Angola	50.4	51.0	48.1	Lesotho	41.0	34.2	31.9
Armenia	23.0	22.5	12.8	Liberia	47.3	47.8	46.4
Azerbaijan	25.2	26.4	17.1	Madagascar	45.7	44.2	40.9
Bangladesh	44.1	32.7	28.3	Malawi	56.8	50.6	45.6
Benin	49.3	45.5	42.1	Mali	49.2	50.7	48.8
Bhutan	na	na	41.4	Mauritania	43.3	40.1	38.1
Bosnia and Herzegovina	18.8	14.2	na	Moldova	19.8	17.7	12.0
Burkina Faso	47.0	47.4	45.3	Mongolia	38.2	30.7	27.5
Burundi	45.5	46.1	42.5	Mozambique	45.6	45.2	43.8
Cambodia	39.5	40.6	34.4	Myanmar (Burma)	36.3	29.7	27.3
Cameroon	46.9	41.0	39.8	Nepal	42.6	39.7	36.6
Central African Republic	42.5	40.3	38.1	Nicaragua	44.8	37.0	32.7
Chad	44.2	43.9	41.7	Niger	51.4	51.9	50.6
China	18.2	20.2	17.0	Nigeria	49.8	43.8	41.0
Comoros	na	40.3	35.3	Pakistan	47.1	41.4	36.6
Congo, Dem. Rep. (Zaire)	48.1	47.3	45.2	Rwanda	51.4	42.0	40.5
Congo, Rep.	45.9	47.0	42.7	Sao Tome and Principe	38.5	40.4	34.6
Cote d'Ivoire	50.8	43.0	36.6	Senegal	46.1	42.4	40.3
Equatorial Guinea	43.1	43.9	41.5	Sierra Leone	48.9	48.6	48.1
Eritrea	na	na	39.8	Somalia	49.8	48.9	49.9
Ethiopia	46.8	49.9	48.1	Sri Lanka	28.4	21.2	18.7
Gambia	48.4	44.7	40.3	Sudan	44.9	35.9	33.7
Ghana	45.2	41.5	36.2	Tajikistan	37.0	38.8	22.0
Guinea	46.5	46.4	42.8	Tanzania	46.9	43.8	41.0
Guinea-Bissau	42.9	44.6	44.3	Togo	45.0	44.5	41.9
Guyana	30.3	26.1	22.4	Uganda	49.1	50.3	48.6
Haiti	36.7	35.8	32.1	Vietnam	36.1	28.8	25.4
Honduras	42.9	38.3	34.5	Yemen	53.2	49.6	47.4
India	34.9	29.5	25.0	Zambia	50.0	45.7	42.8
Kenya	51.3	38.5	33.9	Zimbabwe	49.3	36.1	30.9
Kyrgyzstan	29.6	29.3	23.6				

Definition: The birth rate reflects the number of life births stated against each 1,000 people in the population; it is also referred to as the crude birth rate.

Source: World Bank, *World Development Indicators 1998*, CD-ROM, Series: Birth Rate, crude (per 1,000 people) (SP.DYN.CBRT.IN)

D7.2 Birth Rate, Recent Trends, 1980–1996—Lower Middle-Income Countries per World Bank

Country	1980	1990	1996	Country	1980	1990	1996
Albania	28.8	25.2	20.3	Macedonia, FYRO	21.1	18.8	16.1
Algeria	42.4	31.1	25.7	Maldives	41.8	39.2	34.1
Belarus	16.3	13.9	9.3	Marshall Islands	na	na	26.1
Belize		35.1	31.1	Micronesia	na	34.6	29.0
Bolivia	39.3	36.2	33.5	Morocco	38.1	31.2	25.4
Botswana	48.3	37.1	33.4	Namibia	40.9	38.7	36.4
Bulgaria	14.5	12.1	8.7	North Korea, Dem. Rep.	22.4	21.7	21.6
Cape Verde	37.1	35.9	32.4	Panama	29.2	25.6	22.1
Colombia	30.3	25.6	22.8	Papua New Guinea	37.1	34.6	31.9
Costa Rica	30.3	27.3	23.2	Paraguay	35.6	33.6	29.8
Cuba	14.0	17.6	13.5	Peru	34.6	28.2	25.4
Djibouti	44.8	40.4	38.1	Philippines	35.3	31.1	28.5
Dominica	24.8	23.0	19.1	Romania	17.9	13.6	10.3
Dominican Republic	32.9	28.0	25.8	Russia	15.9	13.4	8.8
Ecuador	36.2	29.4	25.6	Samoa	na	33.2	30.6
Egypt	39.0	31.1	25.5	Solomon Islands	43.8	38.4	36.0
El Salvador	38.7	33.1	31.1	St. Vincent and the Grenadines	28.3	21.2	21.0
Estonia	15.4	14.2	9.4	Suriname	27.6	29.0	23.0
Fiji	29.6	25.0	23.2	Swaziland	44.3	39.2	37.6
Georgia	17.6	17.0	11.1	Syria	45.8	37.0	30.2
Grenada	na	na	21.3	Thailand	27.7	19.9	16.5
Guatemala	43.3	38.5	34.5	Tonga	29.4	30.1	30.6
Indonesia	33.5	25.4	22.7	Tunisia	34.8	27.1	22.7
Iran	43.6	37.6	26.2	Turkey	31.5	24.8	22.0
Iraq	41.4	38.4	36.8	Turkmenistan	34.3	34.2	24.0
Jamaica	27.6	25.2	20.9	Ukraine	14.7	12.7	9.1
Jordan	na	35.8	31.4	Uzbekistan	33.9	33.7	27.3
Kazakhstan	23.9	21.7	15.2	Vanuatu	na	37.3	32.6
Kiribati	na	32.2	32.0	Venezuela	32.7	27.7	24.5
Latvia	14.7	14.2	7.9	Yugoslavia	17.7	14.9	13.0
Lebanon	29.6	27.7	24.0				
Lithuania	15.6	15.3	10.6				

Definition: The birth rate reflects the number of life births stated against each 1,000 people in the population; it is also referred to as the crude birth rate.

Source: World Bank, *World Development Indicators 1998*, CD-ROM, Series: Birth Rate, crude (per 1,000 people) (SP.DYN.CBRT.IN)

D7.3 Birth Rate, Recent Trends, 1980–1996—Upper Middle-Income Countries per World Bank

Country	1980	1990	1996	Country	1980	1990	1996
Antigua and Barbuda	16.5	20.1	17.1	Mexico	33.4	28.5	25.6
Argentina	24.1	21.0	19.4	Oman	45.2	43.7	42.4
Bahrain	34.1	27.5	22.1	Palau	na	na	na
Barbados	16.6	15.7	14.4	Poland	19.4	14.5	11.2
Brazil	30.7	24.0	20.8	Saudi Arabia	42.7	36.3	35.4
Chile	24.0	23.5	18.9	Seychelles	28.9	23.7	20.9
Croatia	na	11.6	10.6	Slovakia	19.1	15.2	11.2
Czech Republic	15.4	12.7	9.0	Slovenia	15.5	11.2	9.5
Gabon	32.6	37.0	36.0	South Africa	36.2	31.9	26.6
Hungary	13.9	12.1	10.4	St. Kitts & Nevis	26.8	22.0	20.0
Libya	46.3	33.2	28.4	St. Lucia	30.6	27.0	24.0
Malaysia	31.4	28.9	26.8	Trinidad & Tobago	28.6	21.9	16.2
Malta	15.4	15.2	12.2	Uruguay	19.1	17.8	16.9
Mauritius	24.0	20.0	18.0				

Definition: The birth rate reflects the number of life births stated against each 1000 people in the population; it is also referred to as the crude birth rate.

Source: World Bank, *World Development Indicators 1998*, CD-ROM, Series: Birth Rate, crude (per 1,000 people) (SP.DYN.CBRT.IN)

D7.4 Total Fertility Rates, Recent Trends, 1980–1996—Low-Income Countries per World Bank

Country	1980	1990	1996	Country	1980	1990	1996
Afghanistan	7.0	6.9	6.9	Laos	6.7	6.3	5.7
Angola	6.9	7.2	6.8	Lesotho	5.6	5.0	4.6
Armenia	2.3	2.6	1.6	Liberia	6.8	6.8	6.4
Azerbaijan	3.2	2.7	2.1	Madagascar	6.5	6.2	5.7
Bangladesh	6.1	4.2	3.4	Malawi	7.6	7.1	6.5
Benin	7.0	6.5	5.9	Mali	7.1	na	6.7
Bhutan	na	na	5.9	Mauritania	6.3	5.5	5.1
Bosnia and Herzegovina	2.1	1.7	na	Moldova	2.4	2.4	1.9
Burkina Faso	7.5	7.0	6.7	Mongolia	5.4	4.1	3.3
Burundi	6.8	6.8	6.4	Mozambique	6.5	6.5	6.1
Cambodia	4.7	4.9	4.6	Myanmar (Burma)	5.1	3.9	3.4
Cameroon	6.5	5.8	5.5	Nepal	6.1	5.6	5.0
Central African Republic	5.8	5.5	5.0	Nicaragua	6.2	4.7	4.0
Chad	5.9	5.9	5.6	Niger	7.4	7.4	7.4
China	2.5	2.1	1.9	Nigeria	6.9	6.0	5.4
Comoros	7.2	5.8	4.7	Pakistan	7.0	5.8	5.1
Congo, Dem. Rep. (Zaire)	6.6	6.7	6.3	Rwanda	8.3	6.7	6.1
Congo, Rep.	6.2	6.3	6.0	Sao Tome and Principe	na	5.1	4.7
Cote d'Ivoire	7.4	6.1	5.1	Senegal	6.7	6.1	5.7
Equatorial Guinea	5.7	5.9	5.6	Sierra Leone	6.5	6.5	6.5
Eritrea	na	6.7	5.9	Somalia	7.0	7.0	7.0
Ethiopia	6.6	7.0	7.0	Sri Lanka	3.5	2.5	2.3
Gambia	6.5	5.8	5.3	Sudan	6.5	5.2	4.7
Ghana	6.5	5.8	5.0	Tajikistan	5.6	5.1	3.7
Guinea	6.1	5.9	5.7	Tanzania	6.7	6.3	5.6
Guinea-Bissau	6.0	6.0	6.0	Togo	6.6	6.6	6.2
Guyana	3.5	2.6	2.4	Uganda	7.2	7.0	6.7
Haiti	5.9	5.1	4.3	Vietnam	5.0	3.6	3.0
Honduras	6.5	5.1	4.5	Yemen	7.9	7.5	7.2
India	5.0	3.7	3.1	Zambia	7.0	6.3	5.8
Kenya	7.8	5.6	4.6	Zimbabwe	6.8	4.7	3.9
Kyrgyzstan	4.1	3.7	3.0				

Total fertility rate signifies the total amount of children projected to be born to a woman if she lived through the end of an expected childbearing period (usually from age 15 to 49 years) and if she bore children at a rate in accordance with prevailing fertility rates corresponding to specific age groups.

Source: World Bank, *World Development Indicators 1998*, Table 2.2, Series: Fertility rate, total (SP.DYN.TFRT.IN)

D7.5 Total Fertility Rates, Recent Trends, 1980–1996—Lower Middle-Income Countries per World Bank

Country	1980	1990	1996	Country	1980	1990	1996
Albania	3.6	3.0	2.6	Macedonia, FYRO	2.5	2.1	2.1
Algeria	6.7	4.5	3.4	Maldives	6.9	6.1	5.4
Belarus	2.0	1.9	1.3	Marshall Islands	na	na	na
Belize	na	4.4	3.8	Micronesia	na	4.8	4.1
Bolivia	5.5	4.9	4.4	Morocco	5.4	4.0	3.3
Botswana	6.7	4.9	4.3	Namibia	5.9	5.4	4.9
Bulgaria	2.1	1.8	1.2	North Korea, Dem. Rep.	3.0	2.3	2.1
Cape Verde	6.5	4.2	3.6	Panama	3.7	3.0	2.6
Colombia	3.8	3.1	2.7	Papua New Guinea	5.7	5.1	4.7
Costa Rica	3.7	3.2	2.7	Paraguay	4.8	4.5	3.9
Cuba	2.0	1.8	1.6	Peru	4.5	3.5	3.1
Djibouti	6.6	6.0	5.5	Philippines	4.8	4.0	3.6
Dominica	na	2.7	2.3	Romania	2.4	1.8	1.3
Dominican Republic	4.2	3.4	3.1	Russia	1.9	1.9	1.3
Ecuador	5.0	3.6	3.1	Samoa	na	4.9	4.6
Egypt	5.1	4.0	3.3	Solomon Islands	6.7	5.7	5.1
El Salvador	5.3	4.0	3.5	St. Vincent and the Grenadines	na	2.6	2.2
Estonia	2.0	2.0	1.3	Suriname	4.6	3.1	2.6
Fiji	3.5	3.1	2.8	Swaziland	6.2	5.0	4.5
Georgia	2.3	2.2	1.5	Syria	7.4	5.3	4.0
Grenada	na	na	na	Thailand	3.5	2.2	1.8
Guatemala	6.2	5.3	4.6	Tonga	4.8	4.2	4.0
Indonesia	4.3	3.0	2.6	Tunisia	5.2	3.5	2.8
Iran	6.1	5.5	3.8	Turkey	4.3	3.0	2.6
Iraq	6.4	5.9	5.3	Turkmenistan	4.9	4.2	3.3
Jamaica	3.7	2.8	2.3	Ukraine	2.0	1.8	1.3
Jordan	6.8	5.4	4.4	Uzbekistan	4.8	4.1	3.4
Kazakhstan	2.9	2.7	2.1	Vanuatu	na	5.5	4.9
Kiribati	4.6	4.0	4.4	Venezuela	4.1	3.4	3.0
Latvia	2.0	2.0	1.2	Yugoslavia	2.3	2.1	1.9
Lebanon	4.0	3.2	2.7				
Lithuania	2.0	2.0	1.4				

Total fertility rate signifies the total amount of children projected to be born to a woman if she lived through the end of an expected childbearing period (usually from age 15 to 49 years) and if she bore children at a rate in accordance with prevailing fertility rates corresponding to specific age groups.

Source: World Bank, *World Development Indicators 1998*, Table 2.2, Series: Fertility rate, total (SP.DYN.TFRT.IN)

D7.6 Total Fertility Rates, Recent Trends, 1980–1996—Upper Middle-Income Countries per World Bank

Country	1980	1990	1996	Country	1980	1990	1996
Antigua and Barbuda	2.1	1.8	1.7	Mexico	4.5	3.3	2.9
Argentina	3.3	2.9	2.7	Oman	9.9	7.7	7.0
Bahrain	5.2	3.8	3.1	Palau	na	na	na
Barbados	2.0	1.8	1.8	Poland	2.3	2.0	1.6
Brazil	3.9	2.8	2.4	Saudi Arabia	7.3	6.6	6.2
Chile	2.8	2.6	2.3	Seychelles	na	2.8	2.4
Croatia	na	1.6	1.6	Slovakia	2.3	2.1	1.5
Czech Republic	2.1	1.9	1.2	Slovenia	2.1	1.5	1.3
Gabon	4.5	5.0	5.0	South Africa	4.6	3.3	2.9
Hungary	1.9	1.8	1.5	St. Kitts & Nevis	na	2.7	2.4
Libya	7.3	5.0	4.0	St. Lucia	4.4	3.3	2.6
Malaysia	4.2	3.8	3.4	Trinidad & Tobago	3.3	2.4	2.1
Malta	na	2.1	1.8	Uruguay	2.7	2.4	2.2
Mauritius	2.7	2.3	2.1				

Total fertility rate signifies the total amount of children projected to be born to a woman if she lived through the end of an expected childbearing period (usually from age 15 to 49 years) and if she bore children at a rate in accordance with prevailing fertility rates corresponding to specific age groups.

Source: World Bank, *World Development Indicators 1998*, Table 2.2, Series: Fertility rate, total (SP.DYN.TFRT.IN)

D7.7 Total Fertility Rates, Births per Woman, Summary 1980 and 1996—Comparison by Income Level per World Bank

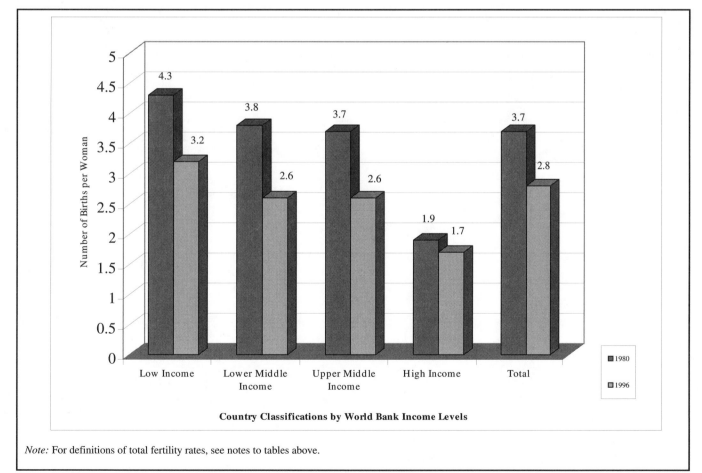

Note: For definitions of total fertility rates, see notes to tables above.

Source: World Bank, *World Development Indicators 1998*, Table 2.15

D8.1 Death Rate, Recent Trends, 1980–1996—Low-Income Countries per World Bank

Country	1980	1990	1996	Country	1980	1990	1996
Afghanistan	23.4	22.0	19.8	Laos	19.5	15.9	13.8
Angola	23.4	20.0	18.7	Lesotho	14.9	11.5	10.5
Armenia	5.6	6.2	6.6	Liberia	17.3	21.2	17.3
Azerbaijan	7.0	6.2	6.4	Madagascar	15.9	12.7	10.8
Bangladesh	18.1	12.4	9.9	Malawi	23.0	20.5	20.4
Benin	18.7	15.5	12.8	Mali	22.3	18.3	16.2
Bhutan	na	na	14.0	Mauritania	19.1	14.9	13.7
Bosnia and Herzegovina	6.7.0	6.9	na	Moldova	10.1	9.7	11.5
Burkina Faso	20.5	18.4	18.0	Mongolia	10.6	7.9	7.0
Burundi	18.1	18.3	17.1	Mozambique	20.4	18.8	18.3
Cambodia	26.6	15.0	12.5	Myanmar (Burma)	14.4	11.4	9.9
Cameroon	15.4	12.0	11.3	Nepal	17.1	13.4	11.4
Central African Republic	19.4	17.2	16.7	Nicaragua	10.6	7.2	5.6
Chad	22.1	18.8	17.2	Niger	23.3	19.7	18.2
China	6.3	7.0	7.0	Nigeria	17.7	14.6	12.7
Comoros	na	12.4	9.3	Pakistan	14.7	10.6	8.3
Congo, Dem. Rep. (Zaire)	16.7	14.8	13.9	Rwanda	19.2	22.6	20.7
Congo, Rep.	15.7	15.6	15.0	Sao Tome and Principe	10.2	9.1	9.4
Cote d'Ivoire	16.4	13.1	12.3	Senegal	19.8	15.6	13.9
Equatorial Guinea	21.7	18.7	16.7	Sierra Leone	28.8	28.7	26.5
Eritrea	na	na	12.7	Somalia	22.0	18.8	17.7
Ethiopia	20.0	18.3	16.6	Sri Lanka	6.2	6.1	5.5
Gambia	23.8	19.8	14.2	Sudan	16.6	13.8	12.0
Ghana	14.7	11.7	9.9	Tajikistan	8.1	6.2	5.1
Guinea	24.3	20.0	17.6	Tanzania	15.4	13.6	14.1
Guinea-Bissau	25.3	24.2	22.0	Togo	16.4	14.4	14.9
Guyana	7.3	8.2	7.6	Uganda	17.7	18.0	19.4
Haiti	15.1	12.4	12.2	Vietnam	8.4	7.3	6.6
Honduras	9.8	7.2	6.2	Yemen	19.1	14.2	12.5
India	13.3	10.3	9.0	Zambia	15.5	14.7	18.1
Kenya	13.5	10.1	9.3	Zimbabwe	13.0	8.1	10.4
Kyrgyzstan	8.9	7.0	7.6				

Definition: The death rate reflects the number of deaths stated against each 1,000 people in the population; it is also referred to as the crude death rate.

Source: World Bank, *World Development Indicators 1998*, CD-ROM, Series: Death rate, crude (per 1,000 people) (SP.DYN.CDRT.IN)

D8.2 Death Rate, Recent Trends, 1980–1996—Lower Middle-Income Countries per World Bank

Country	1980	1990	1996	Country	1980	1990	1996
Albania	6.1	5.6	6.1	Macedonia, FYRO	7.2	7.7	8.1
Algeria	11.8	6.9	5.3	Maldives	12.6	8.9	7.6
Belarus	9.9	10.7	13.0	Marshall Islands	na	na	4.0
Belize		5.5	4.5	Micronesia	na	6.7	6.7
Bolivia	14.5	10.7	9.2	Morocco	12.0	8.4	6.9
Botswana	13.9	9.2	12.7	Namibia	14.1	11.9	11.7
Bulgaria	11.1	12.4	14.0	North Korea, Dem. Rep.	5.7	6.1	8.6
Cape Verde	10.8	9.2	7.3	Panama	5.6	5.0	4.9
Colombia	6.9	6.5	6.5	Papua New Guinea	13.5	11.0	9.9
Costa Rica	4.1	3.6	3.9	Paraguay	6.8	5.8	4.8
Cuba	5.7	6.8	7.2	Peru	11.0	7.7	6.4
Djibouti	19.7	16.7	15.2	Philippines	8.5	7.2	6.6
Dominica	5.3	8.6	7.7	Romania	10.4	10.7	12.6
Dominican Republic	7.4	5.6	5.2	Russia	11.0	11.2	14.3
Ecuador	8.7	6.4	5.8	Samoa	na	7.2	6.2
Egypt	13.3	9.5	7.9	Solomon Islands	10.2	7.7	7.2
El Salvador	11.2	7.4	6.0	St. Vincent and the Grenadines	6.7	6.2	6.1
Estonia	12.2	12.4	12.9	Suriname	7.8	6.7	5.7
Fiji	6.3	5.0	4.7	Swaziland	14.7	11.4	10.4
Georgia	8.5	8.4	7.1	Syria	8.8	6.2	5.0
Grenada	na	na	7.9	Thailand	7.5	6.2	6.5
Guatemala	11.1	8.0	6.7	Tonga	8.8	6.9	6.0
Indonesia	12.1	8.5	7.7	Tunisia	9.0	6.7	5.7
Iran	11.4	7.7	5.4	Turkey	9.7	7.4	6.5
Iraq	8.6	9.2	9.1	Turkmenistan	8.3	7.0	7.0
Jamaica	6.7	6.6	5.9	Ukraine	11.4	12.1	15.2
Jordan	na	5.6	4.5	Uzbekistan	7.5	6.1	6.2
Kazakhstan	8.0	7.7	10.0	Vanuatu	na	8.0	7.7
Kiribati	na	10.5	8.7	Venezuela	5.7	4.9	4.5
Latvia	12.6	13.0	13.7	Yugoslavia	9.1	9.3	10.5
Lebanon	8.8	8.0	6.8				
Lithuania	9.5	10.6	11.6				

Definition: The death rate reflects the number of deaths stated against each 1,000 people in the population; it is also referred to as the crude death rate.

Source: World Bank, *World Development Indicators 1998*, CD-ROM, Death rate, crude (per 1,000 people) (SP.DYN.CDRT.IN)

D8.3 Death Rate, Recent Trends, 1980–1996—Upper Middle-Income Countries per World Bank

Country	1980	1990	1996	Country	1980	1990	1996
Antigua and Barbuda	5.6	6.8	4.8	Mexico	6.8	5.4	5.0
Argentina	8.7	8.3	7.8	Oman	9.8	4.9	4.1
Bahrain	5.9	4.5	3.8	Palau	na	na	na
Barbados	8.0	8.9	9.2	Poland	9.8	10.2	10.0
Brazil	8.5	7.7	7.3	Saudi Arabia	9.0	5.1	4.6
Chile	6.8	6.0	5.5	Seychelles	7.0	7.3	6.8
Croatia	na	10.9	11.0	Slovakia	10.1	10.3	9.5
Czech Republic	12.7	12.5	11.0	Slovenia	10.1	9.3	9.4
Gabon	18.4	15.9	14.5	South Africa	11.6	9.2	7.7
Hungary	13.6	14.0	14.1	St. Kitts & Nevis	11.3	10.8	10.9
Libya	11.6	3.5	5.0	St. Lucia	6.8	6.4	6.4
Malaysia	6.5	4.9	4.5	Trinidad & Tobago	7.1	6.4	6.9
Malta	9.1	7.7	7.5	Uruguay	10.0	9.7	9.8
Mauritius	6.1	6.6	6.5				

Definition: The death rate reflects the number of deaths stated against each 1,000 people in the population; it is also referred to as the crude death rate.

Source: World Bank, *World Development Indicators 1998*, CD-ROM, Series: Death rate, crude (per 1,000 people) (SP.DYN.CDRT.IN)

D8.4 Mortality Rates, Adult Female, Recent Trends, 1980–1995—Low-Income Countries per World Bank

Country	1980	1990	1995	Country	1980	1990	1995
Afghanistan	435	404	384	Laos	439	389	375
Angola	458	420	406	Lesotho	279	276	258
Armenia	85	119	108	Liberia	185	198	198
Azerbaijan	127	96	91	Madagascar	278	377	384
Bangladesh	388	308	292	Malawi	349	436	487
Benin	397	369	399	Mali	362	351	326
Bhutan	na	na	na	Mauritania	416	365	396
Bosnia and Herzegovina	108	109	na	Moldova	173	146	128
Burkina Faso	362	338	340	Mongolia	273	211	182
Burundi	400	379	403	Mozambique	361	321	339
Cambodia	355	319	298	Myanmar (Burma)	313	267	252
Cameroon	415	361	341	Nepal	395	376	354
Central African Republic	424	381	406	Nicaragua	189	147	130
Chad	449	397	385	Niger	453	413	401
China	148	135	130	Nigeria	453	401	377
Comoros	na	307	286	Pakistan	291	247	228
Congo, Dem. Rep. (Zaire)	na	na	na	Rwanda	409	409	461
Congo, Rep.	298	273	313	Sao Tome and Principe		104	84
Cote d'Ivoire	346	294	333	Senegal	516	506	496
Equatorial Guinea	440	400	392	Sierra Leone	527	492	470
Eritrea	na	347	342	Somalia	412	337	313
Ethiopia	401	358	352	Sri Lanka	152	120	108
Gambia	466	432	419	Sudan	462	398	378
Ghana	334	270	253	Tajikistan	129	106	197
Guinea	507	495	497	Tanzania	370	373	417
Guinea-Bissau	517	533	572	Togo	375	321	311
Guyana	210	172	154	Uganda	395	461	558
Haiti	275	291	329	Vietnam	204	153	136
Honduras	237	141	111	Yemen	304	336	331
India	279	241	219	Zambia	413	377	494
Kenya	339	287	295	Zimbabwe	321	270	393
Kyrgyzstan	131	143	120				

Definition: The adult female mortality rate is an indicator of the probability of a female dying between the ages of 15 and 60. It is stated per 1,000 of the female population, ages 15 to 60.

Source: World Bank, *World Development Indicators 1998*, CD-ROM, Series: Mortality rate, adult, female (SP.DYN.AMRT.FE)

D8.5 Mortality Rates, Adult Female, Recent Trends, 1980–1995—Lower Middle-Income Countries per World Bank

Country	1980	1990	1995	Country	1980	1990	1995
Albania	82	70	65	Lithuania	92	92	97
Algeria	197	156	133	Macedonia, FYRO	na	100	92
Belarus	95	98	100	Maldives	322	284	262
Belize	na	123	100	Marshall Islands	na	na	na
Bolivia	273	250	237	Micronesia	na	256	236
Botswana	278	158	153	Morocco	207	184	163
Bulgaria	106	107	106	Namibia	366	318	304
Cape Verde	249	218	206	North Korea, Dem. Rep.	156	116	102
Colombia	162	127	118	Panama	117	94	88
Costa Rica	100	73	68	Papua New Guinea	478	386	339
Cuba	94	83	78	Paraguay	144	117	108
Djibouti	428	387	373	Peru	229	173	157
Dominica	na	113	98	Philippines	259	208	189
Dominican Republic	138	109	100	Romania	116	114	119
Ecuador	176	120	110	Russia	120	107	172
Egypt	204	248	238	Samoa	na	202	158
El Salvador	178	165	154	Solomon Islands	na	273	268
Estonia	110	106	95	St. Vincent and the Grenadines	na	119	93
Fiji	152	115	105	Suriname	187	137	106
Georgia	94	90	77	Swaziland	232	196	191
Grenada	na	na	na	Syria	na	177	154
Guatemala	266	191	166	Thailand	210	123	119
Indonesia	308	219	205	Tonga	na	194	156
Iran	190	174	149	Tunisia	224	174	148
Iraq	191	154	143	Turkey	98	118	111
Jamaica	121	97	90	Turkmenistan	154	135	122
Jordan	na	152	120	Ukraine	112	105	112
Kazakhstan	140	136	120	Uzbekistan	116	109	101
Kiribati	na	na	na	Vanuatu	na	241	219
Latvia	106	108	102	Venezuela	123	101	94
Lebanon	181	150	135	Yugoslavia	106	101	99

Definition: The adult female mortality rate is an indicator of the probability of a female dying between the ages of 15 and 60. It is stated per 1,000 of the female population, ages 15 to 60.

Source: World Bank, *World Development Indicators 1998*, CD-ROM, Series: Mortality rate, adult, female (SP.DYN.AMRT.FE)

D8.6 Mortality Rates, Adult Female, Recent Trends, 1980–1995—Upper Middle-Income Countries per World Bank

Country	1980	1990	1995	Country	1980	1990	1995
Antigua and Barbuda	na	85	72	Mexico	121	96	89
Argentina	102	90	84	Oman	326	157	134
Bahrain	175	147	109	Palau	na	na	na
Barbados	98	82	74	Poland	105	102	92
Brazil	161	135	123	Saudi Arabia	241	158	149
Chile	120	92	82	Seychelles	237	113	90
Croatia	106	96	78	Slovakia	105	100	93
Czech Republic	102	99	83	Slovenia	105	91	81
Gabon	387	332	322	South Africa	na	na	na
Hungary	130	135	138	St. Kitts & Nevis	na	165	133
Libya	218	185	166	St. Lucia	na	144	126
Malaysia	149	125	110	Trinidad & Tobago	166	160	130
Malta	101	81	72	Uruguay	91	90	83
Mauritius	181	126	116				

Definition: The adult female mortality rate is an indicator of the probability of a female dying between the ages of 15 and 60. It is stated per 1,000 of the female population, ages 15 to 60.

Source: World Bank, *World Development Indicators 1998*, CD-ROM, Series: Mortality rate, adult, female (SP.DYN.AMRT.FE)

D8.7 Mortality Rates, Adult Male, Recent Trends, 1980–1995—Low-Income Countries per World Bank

Country	1980	1990	1995	Country	1980	1990	1995
Afghanistan	501	480	455	Laos	531	464	444
Angola	569	514	493	Lesotho	371	384	347
Armenia	158	216	209	Liberia	268	254	252
Azerbaijan	262	216	231	Madagascar	353	434	445
Bangladesh	383	322	314	Malawi	429	479	553
Benin	486	447	472	Mali	454	434	412
Bhutan	na	na	na	Mauritania	505	441	467
Bosnia and Herzegovina	181	186	na	Moldova	289	269	275
Burkina Faso	467	429	426	Mongolia	320	251	221
Burundi	489	460	481	Mozambique	468	418	431
Cambodia	473	392	370	Myanmar (Burma)	384	326	308
Cameroon	489	430	413	Nepal	376	350	327
Central African Republic	540	485	505	Nicaragua	277	220	177
Chad	556	487	470	Niger	562	515	510
China	185	160	155	Nigeria	535	476	450
Comoros	na	365	354	Pakistan	283	232	208
Congo, Dem. Rep. (Zaire)	na	na	na	Rwanda	503	493	542
Congo, Rep.	408	370	405	Sao Tome and Principe	na	153	149
Cote d'Ivoire	421	352	392	Senegal	586	579	561
Equatorial Guinea	543	488	474	Sierra Leone	540	601	589
Eritrea	na	433	429	Somalia	500	426	399
Ethiopia	491	448	442	Sri Lanka	210	184	172
Gambia	584	530	511	Sudan	537	464	445
Ghana	400	334	320	Tajikistan	190	168	200
Guinea	589	529	498	Tanzania	451	444	485
Guinea-Bissau	535	544	584	Togo	457	389	377
Guyana	294	263	245	Uganda	463	526	622
Haiti	348	353	391	Vietnam	262	215	206
Honduras	306	202	166	Yemen	382	363	384
India	261	236	229	Zambia	482	434	534
Kenya	417	357	362	Zimbabwe	389	305	391
Kyrgyzstan	296	291	276				

Definition: The adult male mortality rate is an indicator of the probability of a male dying between the ages of 15 and 60. It is stated per 1,000 of the male population, ages 15 to 60.

Source: World Bank, *World Development Indicators 1998*, CD-ROM, Series: Mortality rate, adult, male (SP.DYN.AMRT.MA)

D8.8 Mortality Rates, Adult Male, Recent Trends, 1980–1995—Lower Middle-Income Countries per World Bank

Country	1980	1990	1995	Country	1980	1990	1995
Albania	140	127	122	Lithuania	243	246	304
Algeria	226	193	177	Macedonia, FYRO	na	147	144
Belarus	255	254	301	Maldives	247	208	207
Belize	na	194	194	Marshall Islands	na	na	na
Bolivia	357	307	292	Micronesia	na	316	295
Botswana	341	218	212	Morocco	264	234	213
Bulgaria	190	211	213	Namibia	427	373	356
Cape Verde	292	245	234	North Korea, Dem. Rep.	270	223	215
Colombia	237	222	214	Panama	172	146	139
Costa Rica	159	122	115	Papua New Guinea	514	425	371
Cuba	135	125	122	Paraguay	198	169	158
Djibouti	527	472	452	Peru	287	228	211
Dominica	na	154	144	Philippines	323	273	254
Dominican Republic	183	157	155	Romania	216	237	270
Ecuador	229	183	179	Russia	341	298	472
Egypt	257	289	278	Samoa	na	262	222
El Salvador	410	284	229	Solomon Islands	na	299	300
Estonia	291	286	284	St. Vincent and the Grenadines	na	202	187
Fiji	209	173	162	Suriname	250	216	205
Georgia	210	195	189	Swaziland	321	260	248
Grenada	na	na	na	Syria	na	237	217
Guatemala	336	264	245	Thailand	280	207	199
Indonesia	368	275	262	Tonga	na	260	231
Iran	221	170	158	Tunisia	227	190	171
Iraq	207	193	182	Turkey	153	165	158
Jamaica	186	155	144	Turkmenistan	263	250	250
Jordan	na	205	171	Ukraine	282	268	294
Kazakhstan	312	306	296	Uzbekistan	219	207	209
Kiribati	na	na	na	Vanuatu	na	288	275
Latvia	281	295	328	Venezuela	219	186	173
Lebanon	241	210	191	Yugoslavia	164	168	170

Definition: The adult male mortality rate is an indicator of the probability of a male dying between the ages of 15 and 60. It is stated per 1,000 of the male population, ages 15 to 60.

Source: World Bank, *World Development Indicators 1998*, CD-ROM, Series: Mortality rate, adult, male (SP.DYN.AMRT.MA)

D8.9 Mortality Rates, Adult Male, Recent Trends, 1980–1995—Upper Middle-Income Countries per World Bank

Country	1980	1990	1995	Country	1980	1990	1995
Antigua and Barbuda	na	142	137	Mexico	205	173	162
Argentina	205	188	176	Oman	389	217	201
Bahrain	215	201	170	Palau	na	na	na
Barbados	167	140	128	Poland	253	263	179
Brazil	221	193	181	Saudi Arabia	283	192	181
Chile	218	165	155	Seychelles	299	221	203
Croatia	233	207	176	Slovakia	226	247	221
Czech Republic	225	230	195	Slovenia	250	211	188
Gabon	474	402	386	South Africa	na	na	na
Hungary	270	290	330	St. Kitts & Nevis	na	227	204
Libya	276	234	215	St. Lucia		205	200
Malaysia	230	198	182	Trinidad & Tobago	234	180	170
Malta	162	134	118	Uruguay	176	178	174
Mauritius	277	241	222				

Definition: The adult male mortality rate is an indicator of the probability of a male dying between the ages of 15 and 60. It is stated per 1,000 of the male population, ages 15 to 60.

Source: World Bank, *World Development Indicators 1998*, CD-ROM, Series: Mortality rate, adult, male (SP.DYN.AMRT.MA)

D8.10 Adult Mortality Rates, Births per Women, Summary, 1980 and 1996—Comparison by Income Level per World Bank

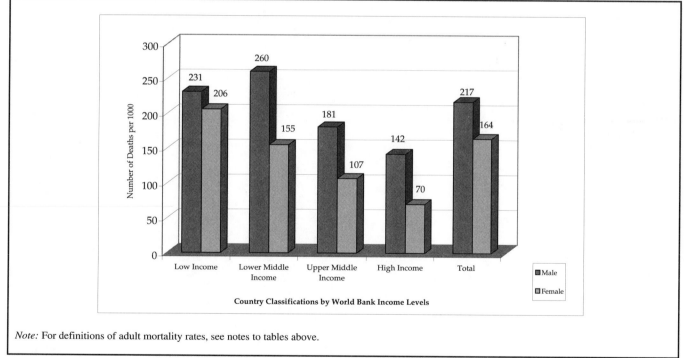

Note: For definitions of adult mortality rates, see notes to tables above.

Source: World Bank, *World Development Indicators 1998*, Table 2.17

D9.1 Population Age 60 and Over, 1996 and 2010 (projected)—Low-Income Countries per World Bank

Country	1996	2010	Country	1996	2010
Afghanistan	na	na	Laos	5.6	5.0
Angola	4.6	4.3	Lesotho	6.0	6.6
Armenia	11.7	14	Liberia	na	na
Azerbaijan	9.5	10.2	Madagascar	4.7	4.8
Bangladesh	5.0	6.0	Malawi	4.2	4.0
Benin	4.4	4.6	Mali	4.2	3.9
Bhutan	na	na	Mauritania	5.1	5.2
Bosnia and Herzegovina	na	na	Moldova	13.6	14.8
Burkina Faso	4.7	3.8	Mongolia	5.8	5.9
Burundi	4.3	3.4	Mozambique	4.1	4.2
Cambodia	4.8	5.8	Myanmar (Burma)	6.8	7.2
Cameroon	5.5	4.9	Nepal	5.5	5.7
Central African Republic	6.1	5.2	Nicaragua	4.5	5.1
Chad	5.7	5.2	Niger	3.9	3.7
China	9.8	11.9	Nigeria	4.1	4.3
Comoros	na	na	Pakistan	4.9	5.5
Congo, Dem. Rep. (Zaire)	4.5	4.3	Rwanda	3.6	3.1
Congo, Rep.	5.6	4.1	Sao Tome and Principe	na	na
Cote d'Ivoire	4.6	4.8	Senegal	4.6	3.9
Equatorial Guinea	na	na	Sierra Leone	4.4	4.2
Eritrea	4.8	4.7	Somalia	na	na
Ethiopia	4.5	4.3	Sri Lanka	8.9	11.8
Gambia	4.8	5.7	Sudan	4.9	5.7
Ghana	4.8	5.1	Tajikistan	6.5	6.4
Guinea	4.2	4.1	Tanzania	4.1	3.9
Guinea-Bissau	6.4	5.7	Togo	4.9	4.4
Guyana	na	na	Uganda	3.6	2.5
Haiti	5.9	5.8	Vietnam	7.2	6.8
Honduras	4.9	4.9	Yemen	3.9	3.4
India	7.3	8.6	Zambia	3.7	3.3
Kenya	4.2	3.8	Zimbabwe	4.7	4.3
Kyrgyzstan	8.5	7.8			

Source: World Bank, *World Development Indicators 1998*, Table 2.1

D9.2 Population Age 60 and Over, 1996 and 2010 (projected)—Lower Middle-Income Countries per World Bank, Percent of Total Population

Country	1996	2010	Country	1996	2010
Albania	9.3	11.5	Lithuania	17.6	20.0
Algeria	5.8	6.5	Macedonia, FYRO	12.7	15.5
Belarus	18.1	19.0	Maldives	na	na
Belize	na	na	Marshall Islands	na	na
Bolivia	6.0	6.4	Micronesia	na	na
Botswana	3.7	3.5	Morocco	6.3	7.1
Bulgaria	20.7	24.4	Namibia	5.7	5.5
Cape Verde	na	na	North Korea, Dem. Rep.	7.4	9.6
Colombia	7.8	9.2	Panama	7.6	9.6
Costa Rica	7.1	9.5	Papua New Guinea	4.9	5.8
Cuba	12.6	17.2	Paraguay	5.2	6.0
Djibouti	na	na	Peru	6.7	7.8
Dominica	na	na	Philippines	5.4	6.8
Dominican Republic	6.3	7.9	Romania	17.4	19.2
Ecuador	6.5	7.6	Russia	17.1	18.3
Egypt	6.6	7.7	Samoa	na	na
El Salvador	6.5	6.7	Solomon Islands	na	na
Estonia	18.6	23.9	St. Vincent and the Grenadines	na	na
Fiji	na	na	Suriname	na	na
Georgia	16.7	18.7	Swaziland	na	na
Grenada	na	na	Syria	4.6	4.9
Guatemala	5.3	5.3	Thailand	7.8	9.8
Indonesia	6.7	8.4	Tonga	na	na
Iran	6.4	6.5	Tunisia	7.1	7.8
Iraq	4.7	5.6	Turkey	8.2	9.7
Jamaica	8.8	9.3	Turkmenistan	6.3	6.2
Jordan	4.6	5.6	Ukraine	19.4	20.9
Kazakhstan	10.2	11.8	Uzbekistan	6.6	6.5
Kiribati	na	na	Vanuatu	na	na
Latvia	19.1	23.3	Venezuela	6.2	8.4
Lebanon	8.3	8.3	Yugoslavia	18	19.1

Source: World Bank, *World Development Indicators 1998*, Table 2.1

D9.3 Population Age 60 and Over, 1996 and 2010 (projected)—Upper Middle-Income Countries per World Bank, Percent of Total Population

Country	1996	2010	Country	1996	2010
Antigua and Barbuda	na	na	Mexico	6.2	8.1
Argentina	13.2	14.1	Oman	3.9	4.8
Bahrain	na	na	Palau	na	na
Barbados	na	na	Poland	15.8	18.2
Brazil	7.2	9.0	Saudi Arabia	4.4	5.6
Chile	9.7	12.6	Seychelles	na	na
Croatia	21.3	23.3	Slovakia	15.0	17.6
Czech Republic	17.4	22.6	Slovenia	17.8	22.3
Gabon	8.9	8.0	South Africa	6.5	7.3
Hungary	19.3	21.5	St. Kitts & Nevis	na	na
Libya	4.9	6.3	St. Lucia	na	na
Malaysia	6.0	7.9	Trinidad & Tobago	9.0	11.1
Malta	na	na	Uruguay	17.0	17.2
Mauritius	8.5	11.0			

Source: World Bank, *World Development Indicators 1998*, Table 2.1

E. Health

GENERAL OVERVIEW

The health statistics presented in this section and in Section F, which focuses on AIDS, illustrate both the effects of poverty on the health status of a country and the features of the health care system in poorer countries that contribute to increased health risks. Unlike the simple demographic indicators related to health presented in Sections A and D—such as life expectancy, fertility rates, and mortality rates—these indicators are more specifically targeted at health concerns and issues, and they attempt to more thoroughly quantify the details of a population's health status and its health care system.

EXPLANATION OF INDICATORS

People Not Expected to Survive to Age 40: This statistic helps to signify the extent of deprivation suffered by populations in poorer countries. People who die before age 40 often have experienced extreme malnutrition throughout much of their lives. Also, in countries where international and civil conflict exist, death before the age of forty might be more widespread, especially among males. This "short life cycle" is a significant feature of human poverty and one that is closely monitored by policymakers and students of poverty (E1.1–E1.3).

Tuberculosis Cases per 100,000: Tuberculosis (TB) is an infectious disease that affects the lungs and respiratory system. The number of tuberculosis cases is increasing, especially within the poorer populations of the world. Because the disease is so contagious, highly-urbanized developing countries whose sanitation and healthcare systems are underdeveloped and overburdened are the most threatened. The incidence of TB is also increasing in countries affected by the AIDS epidemic, as individuals who are HIV-positive are less likely to recover from TB (E2.1–E2.3).

Malaria Cases per 100,000: Malaria is a chronic disease transmitted through mosquito bites. Its symptoms include regular bouts of fever and chills. It is most common in tropical and sub-tropical regions of the world, in particular Central America, the Caribbean and northern South America, sub-Saharan Africa, and South and Southeast Asia. Its prevalence in developing countries indicates inadequate and inaccessible health care services, since malaria can be diagnosed by examining blood smears and it can be treated with a variety of drugs. It also can be prevented by use of screens and mosquito netting and through the implementation of community programs such as the draining of mosquito-infested swamps. Again, however, developing countries whose populations often lack the resources for simple survival needs may also lack the capacity to undertake such preventive measures (E3.1–E3.3).

Access to Health Services: This indicator measures the extent of available health care in a country. Lack of accessibility to health services is a major problem in poorer, developing countries. With inadequate facilities, curable diseases and conditions go untreated. (It should be noted here that even developed countries, such as the United States, may have inadequate health care services for certain portions of their population due to lack of geographic accessibility or prohibitive costs.) (E4.1–E4.3).

Access to Safe Water: Access to safe water is an important factor in maintaining the basic conditions required for human health. According to the World Health Organization (WHO), access to safe water means that a household member need not spend a disproportionate amount of their day obtaining it. In developing countries, water treatment facilities in rural areas are often nonexistent, and in urban areas are often inadequate for the size of the population (E5.1–E5.10).

Access to Sanitation: Access to sanitation indicates the extent of the means to effectively dispose of excreta in ways that will prevent human, animal, and insect contact with it. Including a variety of methods and devices, such as pit latrines and flush toilets with sewage hookups, these sanitation systems constitute one of the most important aspects of maintaining basic health standards. Developing countries often lack the resources to develop and maintain such infrastructure (E6.1–E6.3).

Hospital Beds, Physicians, and Nurses per Population: These three statistics compose a three-way snapshot of the level of development of the health care system in a country. Hospital beds per units of population measures one of the most advanced features of the health care system in a developing country, as it indicates the extent of actual physical facilities dedicated to inpatient-health care needs. Healthcare personnel, including physicians and nurses, are even more important in developing countries than in developed ones, as such professionals can administer tests and treatment outside of a hospital setting (E7.1–E7.11).

Total Health Expenditure per Capita and as Percent of GDP: These two indicators present a picture of the financial resources—both private and public—allotted to a country's health care system. Stated in per capita terms, it relates a country's health care spending to its population, presenting an average expenditure per individual. As with GDP per capita, it is limited: it says nothing about what part of a population actually spends what portion of the total health care expenditure or what part of a population reaps the most benefits from a country's health care system (E8.1–E8.4).

Stated as a share of the GDP, total health expenditure relates health care spending to overall economic output. The money spent on health care relative to the rest of a country's economic activity is usually small in developing countries as compared to developed countries, since poorer countries are often focused on a wide variety of concerns such as infrastructure development—sanitation projects, highways, and mass transit—as well as building up military capacity and other aspects of developing national institutions. Indeed, one reason that international stability is such a pressing global concern is that national policymakers in developing countries need to free public moneys spent on the military to use in satisfying human development needs (E8.5–E8.8).

E1.1 People Not Expected to Survive to Age 40, Percent of Population, 1990—Low-Income Countries per World Bank

Countries	Percent	Countries	Percent
Afghanistan	na	Laos	32.7
Angola	38.9	Lesotho	23.9
Armenia	6.9	Liberia	na
Azerbaijan	7.3	Madagascar	32.1
Bangladesh	26.4	Malawi	38.3
Benin	29.5	Mali	28.4
Bhutan	33.2	Mauritania	31.7
Bosnia and Herzegovina	na	Moldova	10.0
Burkina Faso	36.1	Mongolia	16.0
Burundi	33.8	Mozambique	43.8
Cambodia	31.9	Myanmar (Burma)	25.6
Cameroon	25.4	Nepal	19.9
Central African Republic	35.4	Nicaragua	13.6
Chad	34.0	Niger	43.2
China	9.1	Nigeria	33.8
Comoros	26.3	Pakistan	22.6
Congo, Dem. Rep. (Zaire)	22.1	Rwanda	42.1
Congo, Rep.	30.0	Sao Tome and Principe	na
Cote d'Ivoire	23.1	Senegal	25.3
Equatorial Guinea	36.5	Sierra Leone	52.1
Eritrea	34.1	Somalia	na
Ethiopia	35.7	Sri Lanka	7.9
Gambia	40.6	Sudan	25.2
Ghana	24.9	Tajikistan	11.4
Guinea	41.3	Tanzania	30.6
Guinea-Bissau	43.2	Togo	28.4
Guyana	15.8	Uganda	39.0
Haiti	27.1	Vietnam	12.1
Honduras	10.8	Yemen	25.6
India	19.4	Zambia	35.1
Kenya	22.3	Zimbabwe	18.4
Kyrgyzstan	9.9		

Note: People expected to die before age 40 is an estimate based on current trends in current conditions and accessibility of health care. It is calculated as a percent of the total population.

Source: United Nations Development Programme, *Human Development Report 1997,* Table A2.1 Profile of Human Poverty

E1.2 People Not Expected to Survive to Age 40, Percent of Population, 1990—Lower Middle-Income Countries per World Bank

Countries	Percent	Countries	Percent
Albania	6.1	Lithuania	6.5
Algeria	10.6	Macedonia, FYRO	6.6
Belarus	5.9	Maldives	18
Belize	4.9	Marshall Islands	na
Bolivia	19.6	Micronesia	na
Botswana	15.9	Morocco	12.3
Bulgaria	6.2	Namibia	21.1
Cape Verde	14.6	North Korea, Dem. Rep.	7.0
Colombia	6.3	Panama	6.2
Costa Rica	4.1	Papua New Guinea	28.6
Cuba	6.2	Paraguay	9.2
Djibouti	35.6	Peru	13.4
Dominica	na	Philippines	12.8
Dominican Republic	10.2	Romania	7.1
Ecuador	9.9	Russia	9.6
Egypt	16.6	Samoa	11.2
El Salvador	11.7	Solomon Islands	7.7
Estonia	7.3	St. Vincent and the Grenadines	na
Fiji	6.6	Suriname	7.8
Georgia	5.6	Swaziland	23.9
Grenada	na	Syria	10.3
Guatemala	14.5	Thailand	8.9
Indonesia	14.8	Tonga	na
Iran	11.7	Tunisia	10.5
Iraq	15.4	Turkey	13.1
Jamaica	4.3	Turkmenistan	13.6
Jordan	9.2	Ukraine	6.3
Kazakhstan	9.3	Uzbekistan	9.9
Kiribati	na	Vanuatu	14.0
Latvia	8.1	Venezuela	6.1
Lebanon	8.4	Yugoslavia	na

Note: People expected to die before age 40 is an estimate based on current trends in current conditions and accessibility of health care. It is calculated as a percent of the total population.

Source: United Nations Development Programme, *Human Development Report 1997,* Table A2.1 Profile of Human Poverty

E1.3   People Not Expected to Survive to Age 40, Percent of Population, 1990—Upper Middle-Income Countries per World Bank

Countries	Percent	Countries	Percent
Antigua and Barbuda	na	Mexico	8.3
Argentina	6.3	Oman	8.8
Bahrain	6.5	Palau	na
Barbados	4.2	Poland	5.0
Brazil	14.0	Saudi Arabia	8.8
Chile	4.6	Seychelles	na
Croatia	4.5	Slovakia	4.1
Czech Republic	3.7	Slovenia	na
Gabon	29.0	South Africa	17.0
Hungary	8.2	St. Kitts & Nevis	na
Libya	16.2	St. Lucia	na
Malaysia	7.2	Trinidad & Tobago	5.4
Malta	4.0	Uruguay	5.4
Mauritius	6.2		

Note: People expected to die before age 40 is an estimate based on current trends in current conditions and accessibility of health care. It is calculated as a percent of the total population.

Source: United Nations Development Programme, *Human Development Report 1997,* Table A2.1 Profile of Human Poverty

E2.1 Tuberculosis Cases per 100,000 Population, 1995—Low-Income Countries per World Bank

Country	Cases per 100,000	Country	Cases per 100,000
Afghanistan	na	Laos	235
Angola	225	Lesotho	250
Armenia	40	Liberia	na
Azerbaijan	47	Madagascar	310
Bangladesh	220	Malawi	173
Benin	135	Mali	289
Bhutan	na	Mauritania	220
Bosnia and Herzegovina	80	Moldova	70
Burkina Faso	289	Mongolia	100
Burundi	367	Mozambique	189
Cambodia	235	Myanmar (Burma)	189
Cameroon	194	Nepal	167
Central African Republic	139	Nicaragua	110
Chad	167	Niger	144
China	85	Nigeria	222
Comoros	na	Pakistan	150
Congo, Dem. Rep. (Zaire)	333	Rwanda	260
Congo, Rep.	250	Sao Tome and Principe	na
Cote d'Ivoire	196	Senegal	166
Equatorial Guinea	na	Sierra Leone	167
Eritrea	155	Somalia	na
Ethiopia	155	Sri Lanka	49
Gambia	166	Sudan	211
Ghana	222	Tajikistan	133
Guinea	166	Tanzania	187
Guinea-Bissau	220	Togo	244
Guyana	na	Uganda	300
Haiti	333	Vietnam	166
Honduras	133	Yemen	96
India	220	Zambia	345
Kenya	140	Zimbabwe	207
Kyrgyzstan	68		

Note: This indicator estimates the number of new tuberculosis cases (all forms) per 100,000 in the population as reported by the World Health Organization (WHO).

Source: World Bank, *World Development Indicators 1998,* Table 2.16 Health: risk factors and future challenges

E2.2 Tuberculosis Cases per 100,000 Population, 1995—Lower Middle-Income Countries per World Bank

Country	Cases per 100,000	Country	Cases per 100,000
Albania	40	Lithuania	82
Algeria	53	Macedonia, FYRO	60
Belarus	50	Maldives	na
Belize	na	Marshall Islands	na
Bolivia	335	Micronesia	na
Botswana	400	Morocco	125
Bulgaria	40	Namibia	400
Cape Verde	na	North Korea, Dem. Rep.	162
Colombia	67	Panama	90
Costa Rica	15	Papua New Guinea	275
Cuba	20	Paraguay	166
Djibouti	na	Peru	250
Dominica	na	Philippines	400
Dominican Republic	110	Romania	120
Ecuador	166	Russia	99
Egypt	78	Samoa	na
El Salvador	110	Solomon Islands	na
Estonia	60	St. Vincent and the Grenadines	na
Fiji	na	Suriname	na
Georgia	70	Swaziland	na
Grenada	na	Syria	58
Guatemala	110	Thailand	173
Indonesia	220	Tonga	na
Iran	50	Tunisia	55
Iraq	150	Turkey	57
Jamaica	10	Turkmenistan	72
Jordan	14	Ukraine	50
Kazakhstan	77	Uzbekistan	55
Kiribati	na	Vanuatu	na
Latvia	70	Venezuela	44
Lebanon	35	Yugoslavia	50

Note: This indicator estimates the number of new tuberculosis cases (all forms) per 100,000 in the population as reported by the World Health Organization (WHO).

Source: World Bank, *World Development Indicators 1998*, Table 2.16 Health: risk factors and future challenges

E2.3 Tuberculosis Cases per 100,000 Population, 1995—Upper Middle-Income Countries per World Bank

Country	Cases per 100,000	Country	Cases per 100,000
Antigua and Barbuda	na	Mexico	60
Argentina	50	Oman	20
Bahrain	na	Palau	na
Barbados	na	Poland	50
Brazil	80	Saudi Arabia	22
Chile	67	Seychelles	na
Croatia	65	Slovakia	40
Czech Republic	25	Slovenia	35
Gabon	100	South Africa	222
Hungary	50	St. Kitts & Nevis	na
Libya	12	St. Lucia	na
Malaysia	67	Trinidad & Tobago	20
Malta	na	Uruguay	20
Mauritius	50		

Note: This indicator estimates the number of new tuberculosis cases (all forms) per 100,000 in the population as reported by the World Health Organization (WHO).

Source: World Bank, *World Development Indicators 1998*, Table 2.16 Health: risk factors and future challenges

E3.1 Malaria Cases per 100,000 Population, 1994—Low-Income Countries per World Bank

Country	Cases per 100,000	Country	Cases per 100,000
Afghanistan	na	Laos	1,111
Angola	6,377	Lesotho	na
Armenia	na	Liberia	na
Azerbaijan	na	Madagascar	na
Bangladesh	143	Malawi	49,410
Benin	10,398	Mali	na
Bhutan	2,238	Mauritania	na
Bosnia and Herzegovina	na	Moldova	na
Burkina Faso	4,637	Mongolia	na
Burundi	14,022	Mozambique	na
Cambodia	870	Myanmar (Burma)	1,582
Cameroon	1,065	Nepal	45
Central African Republic	2,562	Nicaragua	1,035
Chad	na	Niger	9,238
China	6	Nigeria	na
Comoros	na	Pakistan	82
Congo, Dem. Rep. (Zaire)	na	Rwanda	na
Congo, Rep.	1,428	Sao Tome and Principe	na
Cote d'Ivoire	na	Senegal	na
Equatorial Guinea	3,812	Sierra Leone	na
Eritrea	na	Somalia	na
Ethiopia	na	Sri Lanka	1,540
Gambia	na	Sudan	na
Ghana	na	Tajikistan	na
Guinea	8,567	Tanzania	27,343
Guinea-Bissau	na	Togo	8,274
Guyana	4,819	Uganda	na
Haiti	331	Vietnam	1,189
Honduras	949	Yemen	260
India	243	Zambia	44,498
Kenya	23,068	Zimbabwe	2,964
Kyrgyzstan	na		

Note: Malaria, caused by parasites in red blood cells, is transmitted by the bite of mosquitoes. Its symptoms include periodic attacks of chills and fever. This indicator represents the number of malaria cases per 100,000 in the population.

Source: United Nations Development Programme, *Human Development Report 1998,* Tables 13 and 30

E3.2 Malaria Cases per 100,000 Population, 1994—Lower Middle-Income Countries per World Bank

Country	Cases per 100,000	Country	Cases per 100,000
Albania	na	Lithuania	na
Algeria	1	Macedonia, FYRO	na
Belarus	na	Maldives	7
Belize	4,787	Marshall Islands	na
Bolivia	480	Micronesia	na
Botswana	2,089	Morocco	1
Bulgaria	na	Namibia	27,209
Cape Verde	6	North Korea, Dem. Rep.	na
Colombia	362	Panama	26
Costa Rica	133	Papua New Guinea	14,974
Cuba	na	Paraguay	12
Djibouti	1,050	Peru	528
Dominica	na	Philippines	345
Dominican Republic	22	Romania	na
Ecuador	267	Russia	na
Egypt	na	Samoa	na
El Salvador	51	Solomon Islands	35,980
Estonia	na	St. Vincent and the Grenadines	na
Fiji	na	Suriname	1,115
Georgia	na	Swaziland	na
Grenada	na	Syria	4
Guatemala	214	Thailand	177
Indonesia	na	Tonga	na
Iran	77	Tunisia	na
Iraq	500	Turkey	7
Jamaica	na	Turkmenistan	na
Jordan	na	Ukraine	na
Kazakhstan	na	Uzbekistan	na
Kiribati	na	Vanuatu	2,285
Latvia	na	Venezuela	64
Lebanon	na	Yugoslavia	na

Note: Malaria, caused by parasites in red blood cells, is transmitted by the bite of mosquitoes. Its symptoms include periodic attacks of chills and fever. This indicator represents the number of malaria cases per 100,000 in the population.

Source: United Nations Development Programme, *Human Development Report 1998,* Tables 13 and 30

E3.3 Malaria Cases per 100,000 Population, 1994—Upper Middle-Income Countries per World Bank

Country	Cases per 100,000	Country	Cases per 100,000
Antigua and Barbuda	na	Mexico	14
Argentina	3	Oman	341
Bahrain	na	Palau	na
Barbados	na	Poland	na
Brazil	360	Saudi Arabia	56
Chile	na	Seychelles	na
Croatia	na	Slovakia	na
Czech Republic	na	Slovenia	na
Gabon	na	South Africa	25
Hungary	na	St. Kitts & Nevis	na
Libya	1	St. Lucia	na
Malaysia	299	Trinidad & Tobago	2
Malta	na	Uruguay	na
Mauritius	3		

Note: Malaria, caused by parasites in red blood cells, is transmitted by the bite of mosquitoes. Its symptoms include periodic attacks of chills and fever. This indicator represents the number of malaria cases per 100,000 in the population.

Source: United Nations Development Programme, *Human Development Report 1998,* Tables 13 and 30

E4.1 Population Without Access to Health Services, Percent of Total, 1995—Low-Income Countries per World Bank

Country	Percent	Country	Percent
Afghanistan	na	Laos	33
Angola	na	Lesotho	20
Armenia	na	Liberia	na
Azerbaijan	na	Madagascar	62
Bangladesh	55	Malawi	65
Benin	82	Mali	60
Bhutan	35	Mauritania	37
Bosnia and Herzegovina	na	Moldova	na
Burkina Faso	10	Mongolia	5
Burundi	20	Mozambique	61
Cambodia	47	Myanmar (Burma)	40
Cameroon	20	Nepal	na
Central African Republic	48	Nicaragua	17
Chad	70	Niger	na
China	12	Nigeria	49
Comoros	na	Pakistan	45
Congo, Dem. Rep. (Zaire)	17	Rwanda	20
Congo, Rep.	74	Sao Tome and Principe	na
Cote d'Ivoire	na	Senegal	10
Equatorial Guinea	na	Sierra Leone	62
Eritrea	na	Somalia	na
Ethiopia	54	Sri Lanka	na
Gambia	na	Sudan	30
Ghana	40	Tajikistan	na
Guinea	20	Tanzania	58
Guinea-Bissau	60	Togo	na
Guyana	na	Uganda	51
Haiti	40	Vietnam	10
Honduras	31	Yemen	62
India	15	Zambia	na
Kenya	23	Zimbabwe	15
Kyrgyzstan	na		

Note: Percentage of population without access to health care reflects the portion of a country's population without access to care for common diseases and injuries, including drugs listed as essential by a country's healthcare authority; such care must be available within one hour of an individual's home.

Source: United Nations Development Programme, *Human Development Report 1997,* Table A2.1 Profile of Human Poverty

E4.2 Population Without Access to Health Services, Percent of Total, 1995—Lower Middle-Income Countries per World Bank

Country	Percent	Country	Percent
Albania	na	Lithuania	na
Algeria	2	Macedonia, FYRO	na
Belarus	na	Maldives	na
Belize	na	Marshall Islands	na
Bolivia	33	Micronesia	na
Botswana	na	Morocco	30
Bulgaria	na	Namibia	41
Cape Verde	na	North Korea, Dem. Rep.	na
Colombia	19	Panama	30
Costa Rica	na	Papua New Guinea	4
Cuba	0	Paraguay	37
Djibouti	na	Peru	56
Dominica	na	Philippines	29
Dominican Republic	22	Romania	na
Ecuador	na	Russia	na
Egypt	1	Samoa	0
El Salvador	60	Solomon Islands	na
Estonia	na	St. Vincent and the Grenadines	na
Fiji	na	Suriname	na
Georgia	na	Swaziland	na
Grenada	na	Syria	10
Guatemala	43	Thailand	10
Indonesia	7	Tonga	na
Iran	12	Tunisia	na
Iraq	7	Turkey	na
Jamaica	10	Turkmenistan	0
Jordan	na	Ukraine	na
Kazakhstan	na	Uzbekistan	na
Kiribati	na	Vanuatu	na
Latvia	na	Venezuela	na
Lebanon	5	Yugoslavia	na

Note: Percentage of population without access to health care reflects the portion of a country's population without access to care for common diseases and injuries, including drugs listed as essential by a country's healthcare authority; such care must be available within one hour of an individual's home.

Source: United Nations Development Programme, *Human Development Report 1997,* Table A2.1 Profile of Human Poverty

E4.3 Population Without Access to Health Services, Percent of Total, 1995—Upper Middle-Income Countries per World Bank

Country	Percent	Country	Percent
Antigua and Barbuda	na	Mexico	7
Argentina	29	Oman	4
Bahrain	na	Palau	na
Barbados	na	Poland	na
Brazil	na	Saudi Arabia	3
Chile	3	Seychelles	na
Croatia	na	Slovakia	na
Czech Republic	na	Slovenia	na
Gabon	na	South Africa	na
Hungary	na	St. Kitts & Nevis	na
Libya	5	St. Lucia	na
Malaysia	na	Trinidad & Tobago	0
Malta	na	Uruguay	18
Mauritius	0		

Note: Percentage of population without access to health care reflects the portion of a country's population without access to care for common diseases and injuries, including drugs listed as essential by a country's healthcare authority; such care must be available within one hour of an individual's home.

Source: United Nations Development Programme, *Human Development Report 1997,* Table A2.1 Profile of Human Poverty

E5.1 Population with Access to Safe Water and Sanitation, Summary, 1995—Comparison by Income Level per World Bank

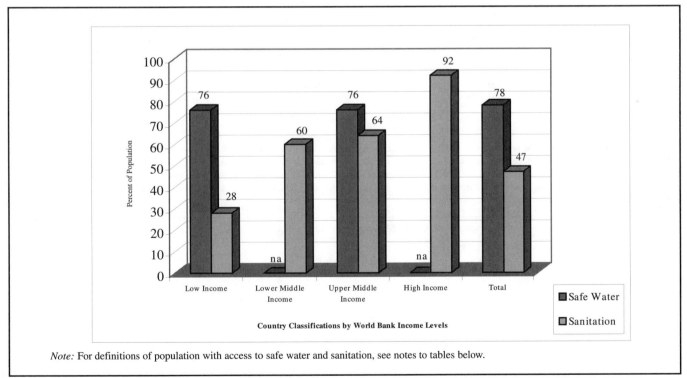

Note: For definitions of population with access to safe water and sanitation, see notes to tables below.

Source: World Bank, *World Development Indicators 1998,* Table 2.14

E5.2 Population With Access to Safe Water, Percent of Total, 1985 and 1995—Low-Income Countries per World Bank

Country	1985	1995	Country	1985	1995
Afghanistan	20.0	na	Laos	na	39
Angola	28.0	32	Lesotho	na	52
Armenia	na	na	Liberia	37.3	na
Azerbaijan	na	na	Madagascar	31.4	29
Bangladesh	40.0	79	Malawi	31.9	45
Benin	14.4	50	Mali	na	37
Bhutan	na	na	Mauritania	37.1	na
Bosnia and Herzegovina	na	na	Moldova	na	na
Burkina Faso	35.0	78	Mongolia	100.0	na
Burundi	23.4	na	Mozambique	na	32
Cambodia	na	13	Myanmar (Burma)	27.0	38
Cameroon	35.9	41	Nepal	23.9	48
Central African Republic	na	18	Nicaragua	50.0	61
Chad	31.0	24	Niger	36.5	53
China	na	90	Nigeria	36.3	39
Comoros	na	na	Pakistan	44.0	60
Congo, Dem. Rep. (Zaire)	na	na	Rwanda	na	na
Congo, Rep.	na	47	Sao Tome and Principe	na	na
Cote d'Ivoire	na	72	Senegal	43.5	50
Equatorial Guinea	na	na	Sierra Leone	24.0	34
Eritrea	na	na	Somalia	31.0	na
Ethiopia	na	27	Sri Lanka	37.0	na
Gambia	45.0	76	Sudan	40.0	50
Ghana	na	56	Tajikistan	na	na
Guinea	19.8	62	Tanzania	52.1	49
Guinea-Bissau	31.0	23	Togo	34.8	na
Guyana	80.0	na	Uganda	16.0	34
Haiti	38.0	28	Vietnam	na	36
Honduras	50.0	65	Yemen	na	52
India	54.0	81	Zambia	48.0	43
Kenya	27.0	53	Zimbabwe	52.0	74
Kyrgyzstan	na	75			

Note: This indicator represents the proportion of the population with reasonable access to an appropriate amount of safe water (including treated surface water and untreated but uncontaminated water, such as from springs, sanitary wells, and protected boreholes). In urban areas acceptable sources include public fountains or standposts located less than 200 meters from an individual's home. In rural areas the definition implies that household members do not have to spend an "unreasonable" and disproportionate part of the day getting water. About 20 liters of safe water for each person is deemed sufficient to satisfy daily metabolic, hygienic, and domestic needs.

Source: World Bank, *World Development Indicators 1998,* CD-ROM, Series: Safe water (SH.H2O.SAFE.ZS)

E5.3 Population With Access to Safe Water, Percent of Total, 1985 and 1995—Lower Middle-Income Countries per World Bank

Country	1985	1995	Country	1985	1995
Albania	96.6	na	Lithuania	na	na
Algeria	na	na	Macedonia, FYRO	na	na
Belarus	100.0	na	Maldives	na	na
Belize	67.0	na	Marshall Islands	31.1	na
Bolivia	53.0	60	Micronesia	na	na
Botswana	77.0	70	Morocco	57.0	52
Bulgaria	na	na	Namibia	na	na
Cape Verde	31.2	na	North Korea, Dem. Rep.	100.0	100
Colombia	91.0	76	Panama	82.0	83
Costa Rica	93.0	na	Papua New Guinea	na	28
Cuba	82.0	93	Paraguay	23.0	na
Djibouti	43.0	na	Peru	53.0	60
Dominica	na	na	Philippines	64.5	na
Dominican Republic	49.0	71	Romania	96.4	na
Ecuador	58.0	70	Russia	na	na
Egypt	na	64	Samoa	na	na
El Salvador	51.0	55	Solomon Islands	62.9	na
Estonia	na	na	St. Vincent and the Grenadines	na	na
Fiji	na	na	Suriname	97.0	na
Georgia	na	na	Swaziland	53.5	na
Grenada	85.0	na	Syria	71.0	85
Guatemala	58.0	60	Thailand	66.0	81
Indonesia	33.0	62	Tonga	95.0	na
Iran	71.0	na	Tunisia	89.0	na
Iraq	80.0	44	Turkey	81.7	92
Jamaica	96.0	70	Turkmenistan	na	85
Jordan	94.0	89	Ukraine	100.0	97
Kazakhstan	na	na	Uzbekistan	na	na
Kiribati	68.0	na	Vanuatu	45.0	na
Latvia	na	na	Venezuela	84.0	79
Lebanon	98.0	na	Yugoslavia	na	na

Note: This indicator represents the proportion of the population with reasonable access to an appropriate amount of safe water (including treated surface water and untreated but uncontaminated water, such as from springs, sanitary wells, and protected boreholes). In urban areas acceptable sources include public fountains or standposts located less than 200 meters from an individual's home. In rural areas the definition implies that household members do not have to spend an "unreasonable" and disproportionate part of the day getting water. About 20 liters of safe water for each person is deemed sufficient to satisfy daily metabolic, hygienic, and domestic needs.

Source: World Bank, *World Development Indicators 1998,* CD-ROM, Series: Safe water (SH.H2O.SAFE.ZS)

E5.4 Population With Access to Safe Water, Percent of Total, 1985 and 1995—Upper Middle-Income Countries per World Bank

Country	1985	1995	Country	1985	1995
Antigua and Barbuda	95.0	na	Mexico	82.0	83
Argentina	55.0	64	Oman	58.0	na
Bahrain	100.0	na	Palau	na	na
Barbados	100.0	na	Poland	89.0	na
Brazil	75.0	72	Saudi Arabia	93.0	93
Chile	86.0	na	Seychelles	95.0	na
Croatia	na	96	Slovakia	na	na
Czech Republic	100.0	na	Slovenia	na	na
Gabon	50.0	67	South Africa	na	70
Hungary	98.0	na	St. Kitts & Nevis	100.0	na
Libya	90.0	90	St. Lucia	na	na
Malaysia	71.0	88	Trinidad & Tobago	98.0	82
Malta	100.0	na	Uruguay	83.0	83
Mauritius	99.0	98			

Note: This indicator represents the proportion of the population with reasonable access to an appropriate amount of safe water (including treated surface water and untreated but uncontaminated water, such as from springs, sanitary wells, and protected boreholes). In urban areas acceptable sources include public fountains or standposts located less than 200 meters from an individual's home. In rural areas the definition implies that household members do not have to spend an "unreasonable" and disproportionate part of the day getting water. About 20 liters of safe water for each person is deemed sufficient to satisfy daily metabolic, hygienic, and domestic needs.

Source: World Bank, *World Development Indicators 1998,* CD-ROM, Series: Safe water (SH.H2O.SAFE.ZS)

E5.5 Rural Population With Access to Safe Water, Percent of Total Rural, 1985 and 1995—Low-Income Countries per World Bank

Country	1985	1995	Country	1985	1995
Afghanistan	17.0	na	Kyrgyzstan	na	na
Angola	14.8	15	Laos	na	39
Armenia	na	na	Lesotho	14.0	64
Azerbaijan	na	na	Liberia	24.0	na
Bangladesh	43.0	80	Madagascar	17.2	10
Benin	na	53	Malawi	26.9	44
Bhutan	14.0	na	Mali	na	38
Bosnia and Herzegovina	na	na	Mauritania	16.0	na
Burkina Faso	26.0	na	Moldova	na	na
Burundi	22.0	na	Mongolia	100.0	na
Cambodia	na	12	Mozambique	na	40
Cameroon	30.0	24	Myanmar (Burma)	21.0	39
Central African Republic	na	18	Nepal	19.8	49
Chad	na	17	Nicaragua	13.0	27
China	na	89	Niger	34.2	55
Comoros	na	na	Nigeria	30.0	26
Congo, Dem. Rep. (Zaire)	5.0	na	Pakistan	28.0	52
Congo, Rep.	7.0	na	Rwanda	60.0	na
Cote d'Ivoire	na	81	Sao Tome and Principe	na	na
Equatorial Guinea	na	na	Senegal	27.0	28
Eritrea	na	na	Sierra Leone	8.0	21
Ethiopia	42.0	20	Somalia	22.0	na
Gambia	33.0	na	Sri Lanka	26.0	na
Ghana	40.3	49	Sudan	na	45
Guinea	na	62	Tajikistan	na	na
Guinea-Bissau	37.0	27	Tanzania	47.0	45
Guyana	60.0	na	Togo	26.0	na
Haiti	32.0	23	Uganda	12.0	32
Honduras	49.0	53	Vietnam	30.0	32
India	47.0	79	Yemen	na	17
Kenya	21.0	49	Zambia	32.0	27
			Zimbabwe	10.0	65

Note: This indicator represents the proportion of the rural population with reasonable access to an appropriate amount of safe water (including treated surface water and untreated but uncontaminated water, such as from springs, sanitary wells, and protected boreholes). In rural areas the definition implies that household members do not have to spend an "unreasonable" and disproportionate part of the day getting water. About 20 liters of safe water for each person is deemed sufficient to satisfy daily metabolic, hygienic, and domestic needs.

Source: World Bank, *World Development Indicators 1998,* CD-ROM, Series: Safe water, rural (SH.H2O.SAFE.RU.ZS); 1995 data are from World Bank, *World Development Indicators 1998,* Table 3.5

E5.6 Rural Population With Access to Safe Water, Percent of Total Rural, 1985 and 1995—Lower Middle-Income Countries per World Bank

Country	1985	1995	Country	1985	1995
Albania	95.0	na	Lithuania	na	na
Algeria	na	na	Macedonia, FYRO	na	na
Belarus	100.0	na	Maldives	8.0	na
Belize	38.0	na	Marshall Islands	na	na
Bolivia	27.0	27	Micronesia	na	na
Botswana	na	53	Morocco	na	14
Bulgaria	na	na	Namibia	na	na
Cape Verde	21.0	na	North Korea, Dem. Rep.	100.0	100
Colombia	76.0	48	Panama	64.0	na
Costa Rica	82.0	na	Papua New Guinea	10.0	17
Cuba	na	85	Paraguay	8.0	17
Djibouti	21.0	na	Peru	17.0	24
Dominica	na	na	Philippines	na	na
Dominican Republic	24.0	67	Romania	90.0	na
Ecuador	33.0	55	Russia	na	na
Egypt	na	50	Samoa	na	na
El Salvador	47.0	37	Solomon Islands	59.8	na
Estonia	na	na	St. Vincent and the Grenadines	na	na
Fiji	na	na	Suriname	94.0	na
Georgia	na	na	Swaziland	7.0	na
Grenada	na	na	Syria	65.0	78
Guatemala	39.0	43	Thailand	na	72
Indonesia	30.5	54	Tonga	na	na
Iran	52.0	na	Tunisia	79.0	na
Iraq	46.0	na	Turkey	70.0	85
Jamaica	93.0	48	Turkmenistan	na	na
Jordan	88.0	na	Ukraine	100.0	na
Kazakhstan	na	na	Uzbekistan	na	na
Kiribati	na	na	Vanuatu	na	na
Latvia	na	na	Venezuela	65.0	75
Lebanon	98.0	na	Yugoslavia	na	na

Note: This indicator represents the proportion of the rural population with reasonable access to an appropriate amount of safe water (including treated surface water and untreated but uncontaminated water, such as from springs, sanitary wells, and protected boreholes). In rural areas the definition implies that household members do not have to spend an "unreasonable" and disproportionate part of the day getting water. About 20 liters of safe water for each person is deemed sufficient to satisfy daily metabolic, hygienic, and domestic needs.

Source: World Bank, *World Development Indicators 1998* CD-ROM, Series: Safe water, rural (SH.H2O.SAFE.RU.ZS); 1995 data are from World Bank, *World Development Indicators 1998,* Table 3.5

E5.7 Rural Population With Access to Safe Water, Percent of Total Rural, 1985 and 1995—Upper Middle-Income Countries per World Bank

Country	1985	1995	Country	1985	1995
Antigua and Barbuda	na	na	Mexico	50.0	62
Argentina	17.0	17	Oman	55.0	na
Bahrain	100.0	na	Palau	na	na
Barbados	100.0	na	Poland	82.0	na
Brazil	52.0	31	Saudi Arabia	68.0	na
Chile	22.0	na	Seychelles	na	na
Croatia	na	80	Slovakia	na	na
Czech Republic	100.0	na	Slovenia	na	na
Gabon	na	30	South Africa	na	na
Hungary	95.0	na	St. Kitts & Nevis	100.0	na
Libya	75.0	na	St. Lucia	na	na
Malaysia	na	74	Trinidad & Tobago	93.0	80
Malta	100.0	na	Uruguay	27.0	na
Mauritius	98.0	100			

Note: This indicator represents the proportion of the population with reasonable access to an appropriate amount of safe water (including treated surface water and untreated but uncontaminated water, such as from springs, sanitary wells, and protected boreholes). In rural areas the definition implies that household members do not have to spend an "unreasonable" and disproportionate part of the day getting water. About 20 liters of safe water for each person is deemed sufficient to satisfy daily metabolic, hygienic, and domestic needs.

Source: World Bank, *World Development Indicators 1998*, CD-ROM, Series: Safe water, rural (SH.H2O.SAFE.RU.ZS); 1995 data are from World Bank, *World Development Indicators 1998,* Table 3.5

E5.8 Urban Population With Access to Safe Water, Percent of Total Urban, 1985 and 1995—Low-Income Countries per World Bank

Country	1985	1995	Country	1985	1995
Afghanistan	38.0	na	Honduras	51.0	81
Angola	79.8	69	India	80.0	85
Armenia	na	na	Kenya	61.0	67
Azerbaijan	na	na	Kyrgyzstan	na	na
Bangladesh	29.0	42	Laos	na	40
Benin	45.0	41	Lesotho	na	14
Bhutan	40.0	na	Liberia	50.0	na
Bosnia and Herzegovina	na	na	Madagascar	81.4	83
Burkina Faso	50.0	na	Malawi	69.6	52
Burundi	32.8	na	Mali	na	36
Cambodia	na	20	Mauritania	80.0	na
Cameroon	46.0	71	Moldova	na	na
Central African Republic	24.0	18	Mongolia	100.0	na
Chad	na	48	Mozambique	na	17
China	na	93	Myanmar (Burma)	36.0	36
Comoros	na	na	Nepal	78.4	64
Congo, Dem. Rep. (Zaire)	43.0	na	Nicaragua	77.0	81
Congo, Rep.	42.0	na	Niger	48.0	46
Cote d'Ivoire	na	59	Nigeria	60.0	63
Equatorial Guinea	47.0	na	Pakistan	84.0	77
Eritrea	na	na	Rwanda	55.0	na
Ethiopia	93.0	90	Sao Tome and Principe	na	na
Gambia	100.0	na	Senegal	63.0	82
Ghana	57.0	70	Sierra Leone	58.0	58
Guinea	91.0	61	Somalia	57.0	na
Guinea-Bissau	21.0	18	Sri Lanka	76.0	na
Guyana	100.0	na	Sudan	na	66
Haiti	59.0	37	Tajikistan	na	na
			Tanzania	85.0	65

E5.8 Urban Population With Access to Safe Water, Percent of Total Urban, 1985 and 1995—Low-Income Countries per World Bank *(continued)*

Country	1985	1995	Country	1985	1995
Togo	68.0	na	Yemen	na	88
Uganda	45.0	47	Zambia	70.0	64
Vietnam	90.0	53	Zimbabwe	100.0	99

Definition: This indicator represents the proportion of the urban population with reasonable access to an appropriate amount of safe water (including treated surface water and untreated but uncontaminated water, such as from springs, sanitary wells, and protected boreholes). In urban areas the source may be a public fountain or standpost located not more than 200 meters away. About 20 liters of safe water for each person is deemed sufficient to satisfy daily metabolic, hygienic, and domestic needs.

Source: World Bank, *World Development Indicators 1998* CD-ROM, Series: Safe water, rural (SH.H2O.SAFE.UR.ZS); 1995 data are from World Bank, *World Development Indicators 1998*, Table 3.5

E5.9 Urban Population With Access to Safe Water, Percent of Total Urban, 1985 and 1995—Lower Middle-Income Countries per World Bank

Country	1985	1995	Country	1985	1995
Albania	100.0	na	Lithuania	na	na
Algeria	na	na	Macedonia, FYRO	na	na
Belarus	100.0	na	Maldives	53.0	na
Belize	100.0	na	Marshall Islands	na	na
Bolivia	81.0	75	Micronesia	na	na
Botswana	98.0	100	Morocco	na	98
Bulgaria	na	na	Namibia	na	na
Cape Verde	na	na	North Korea, Dem. Rep.	100.0	100
Colombia	na	88	Panama	100.0	na
Costa Rica	100.0	na	Papua New Guinea	54.0	84
Cuba	na	96	Paraguay	49.0	na
Djibouti	50.0	na	Peru	73.0	74
Dominica	na	na	Philippines	na	na
Dominican Republic	72.0	74	Romania	100.0	na
Ecuador	na	82	Russia	na	na
Egypt	na	82	Samoa	na	na
El Salvador	76.0	78	Solomon Islands	90.9	na
Estonia	na	na	St. Vincent and the Grenadines	na	na
Fiji	na	na	Suriname	100.0	na
Georgia	na	na	Swaziland	100.0	na
Grenada	na	na	Syria	77.0	92
Guatemala	89.0	91	Thailand	na	89
Indonesia	40.0	78	Tonga	na	na
Iran	90.0	na	Tunisia	98.0	na
Iraq	100.0	na	Turkey	100.0	98
Jamaica	99.0	92	Turkmenistan	na	na
Jordan	100.0	na	Ukraine	100.0	na
Kazakhstan	na	na	Uzbekistan	na	na
Kiribati	na	na	Vanuatu	na	na
Latvia	na	na	Venezuela	88.0	80
Lebanon	98.0	na	Yugoslavia	na	na

Definition: This indicator represents the proportion of the urban population with reasonable access to an appropriate amount of safe water (including treated surface water and untreated but uncontaminated water, such as from springs, sanitary wells, and protected boreholes). In urban areas the source may be a public fountain or standpost located not more than 200 meters away. About 20 liters of safe water for each person is deemed sufficient to satisfy daily metabolic, hygienic, and domestic needs.

Source: World Bank, *World Development Indicators 1998* CD-ROM, Series: Safe water, rural (SH.H2O.SAFE.UR.ZS); 1995 data are from World Bank, *World Development Indicators 1998*, Table 3.5

E5.10 Urban Population With Access to Safe Water, Percent of Total Urban, 1985 and 1995—Upper Middle-Income Countries per World Bank

Country	1985	1995	Country	1985	1995
Antigua and Barbuda	na	na	Mauritius	100.0	95
Argentina	63.0	73	Mexico	95.0	91
Bahrain	100.0	na	Oman	90.0	na
Barbados	100.0	na	Palau	na	na
Brazil	na	85	Poland	94.0	na
Chile	97.0	na	Saudi Arabia	100.0	na
Croatia	na	98	Seychelles	na	na
Czech Republic	100.0	na	Slovakia	na	na
Gabon	na	80	Slovenia	na	na
Hungary	100.0	na	South Africa	na	na
Libya	92.0	na	St. Kitts & Nevis	100.0	na
Malaysia	na	100	St. Lucia	na	na
Malta	100.0	na	Trinidad & Tobago	100.0	83
			Uruguay	95.0	na

Definition: This indicator represents the proportion of the urban population with reasonable access to an appropriate amount of safe water (including treated surface water and untreated but uncontaminated water, such as from springs, sanitary wells, and protected boreholes). In urban areas the source may be a public fountain or standpost located not more than 200 meters away. About 20 liters of safe water for each person is deemed sufficient to satisfy daily metabolic, hygienic, and domestic needs.

Source: World Bank, *World Development Indicators 1998* CD-ROM, Series: Safe water, rural (SH.H2O.SAFE.UR.ZS); 1995 data are from World Bank, *World Development Indicators 1998,* Table 3.5

E6.1 Population with Access to Sanitation, 1985 and 1995—Low-Income Countries per World Bank

Country	1985	1995	Country	1985	1995
Afghanistan	2	na	India	8	29
Angola	18	16	Kenya	44	77
Armenia	na	na	Kyrgyzstan	na	53
Azerbaijan	na	na	Laos	na	19
Bangladesh	4	35	Lesotho	na	6
Benin	10	20	Liberia	21	na
Bhutan	na	na	Madagascar	na	3
Bosnia and Herzegovina	na	na	Malawi	60	53
Burkina Faso	9	18	Mali	21	31
Burundi	52	na	Mauritania	na	na
Cambodia	na	na	Moldova	na	50
Cameroon	36	40	Mongolia	50	na
Central African Republic	19	na	Mozambique	na	21
Chad	14	21	Myanmar (Burma)	24	41
China	na	21	Nepal	1	20
Comoros	na	na	Nicaragua	27	31
Congo, Dem. Rep. (Zaire)	na	na	Niger	9	15
Congo, Rep.	40	9	Nigeria	na	36
Cote d'Ivoire	na	54	Pakistan	19	30
Equatorial Guinea	na	na	Rwanda	na	na
Eritrea	na	na	Sao Tome and Principe	15	na
Ethiopia	na	10	Senegal	na	58
Gambia	na	37	Sierra Leone	21	11
Ghana	26	27	Somalia	15	na
Guinea	na	70	Sri Lanka	66	na
Guinea-Bissau	25	20	Sudan	5	22
Guyana	95	na	Tajikistan	na	62
Haiti	19	24	Tanzania	na	86
Honduras	32	62	Togo	14	22

E6.1 Population with Access to Sanitation, 1985 and 1995—Low-Income Countries per World Bank (continued)

Uganda	13	57	Zambia	47	23
Vietnam	30	21	Zimbabwe	26	58
Yemen	na	51			

Defintion: Access to sanitation indicates the percent of the population with adequate facilities for the sanitary discarding of excreta. Such facilities must be able to prevent human, animal, and insect contact with excreta; they include simple but protected pit latrines, flush toilets with sewage hookups, pit privies, pour-flush latrines, septic tanks, and other adequate disposal devices.

Source: World Bank, *World Development Indicators 1998*, CD-ROM, Series: Sanitation (SH.STA.ACSN)

E6.2 Population with Access to Sanitation, 1985 and 1995—Lower Middle-Income Countries per World Bank

Country	1985	1995	Country	1985	1995
Albania	100	na	Lithuania	na	na
Algeria	na	na	Macedonia, FYRO	na	na
Belarus	na	100	Maldives	15	na
Belize	na	na	Marshall Islands	37	na
Bolivia	36	44	Micronesia	na	na
Botswana	36	55	Morocco	46	40
Bulgaria	na	99	Namibia	na	34
Cape Verde	10	na	North Korea, Dem. Rep.	100	100
Colombia	68	63	Panama	81	87
Costa Rica	95	na	Papua New Guinea	na	22
Cuba	na	66	Paraguay	49	30
Djibouti	37	na	Peru	48	44
Dominica	na	na	Philippines	57	na
Dominican Republic	66	78	Romania	98	49
Ecuador	57	64	Russia	na	na
Egypt	na	11	Samoa	80	na
El Salvador	62	68	Solomon Islands	na	na
Estonia	na	na	St. Vincent and the Grenadines	na	na
Fiji	na	na	Suriname	na	na
Georgia	na	na	Swaziland	na	na
Grenada	na	na	Syria	na	78
Guatemala	54	66	Thailand	47	70
Indonesia	30	51	Tonga	40	na
Iran	65	na	Tunisia	52	na
Iraq	69	87	Turkey	93	94
Jamaica	91	74	Turkmenistan	na	60
Jordan	na	100	Ukraine	na	49
Kazakhstan	na	na	Uzbekistan	na	18
Kiribati	63	na	Vanuatu	30	na
Latvia	na	na	Venezuela	45	58
Lebanon	75	na	Yugoslavia	na	100

Defintion: Access to sanitation indicates the percent of the population with adequate facilities for the sanitary discarding of excreta. Such facilities must be able to prevent human, animal, and insect contact with excreta; they include simple but protected pit latrines, flush toilets with sewage hookups, pit privies, pour-flush latrines, septic tanks, and other adequate disposal devices.

Source: World Bank, *World Development Indicators 1998*, CD-ROM, Series: Sanitation (SH.STA.ACSN)

E6.3 Population with Access to Sanitation, 1985 and 1995—Upper Middle-Income Countries per World Bank

Country	1985	1995	Country	1985	1995
Antigua and Barbuda	100	na	Mauritius	97	100
Argentina	69	89	Mexico	57	66
Bahrain	100	na	Oman	39	79
Barbados	na	na	Palau	na	na
Brazil	24	41	Poland	100	100
Chile	67	83	Saudi Arabia	na	86
Croatia	67	68	Seychelles	99	na
Czech Republic	na	na	Slovakia	46	51
Gabon	50	76	Slovenia	na	90
Hungary	100	94	South Africa	na	46
Libya	91	na	St. Kitts & Nevis	96	na
Malaysia	na	91	St. Lucia	na	na
Malta	100	na	Trinidad & Tobago	na	56
			Uruguay	59	82

Defintion: Access to sanitation indicates the percent of the population with adequate facilities for the sanitary discarding of excreta. Such facilities must be able to prevent human, animal, and insect contact with excreta; they include simple but protected pit latrines, flush toilets with sewage hookups, pit privies, pour-flush latrines, septic tanks, and other adequate disposal devices.

Source: World Bank, *World Development Indicators 1998*, CD-ROM, Series: Sanitation (SH.STA.ACSN)

E7.1 Hospital Beds per 1,000 in Population, 1980–1995—Low-Income Countries per World Bank

Country	1980	1985	1990	1995
Afghanistan	na	na	0.25	na
Angola	na	na	1.29	na
Armenia	8.40	8.42	8.60	7.63
Azerbaijan	9.73	9.88	9.90	9.93
Bangladesh	0.21	0.29	0.30	na
Benin	1.46	0.36	0.83	na
Bhutan	na	na	0.85	na
Bosnia and Herzegovina	na	na	4.49	na
Burkina Faso	na	na	0.29	na
Burundi	na	na	na	na
Cambodia	na	na	2.07	na
Cameroon	na	na	2.55	na
Central African Republic	1.56	na	0.88	na
Chad	na	na	na	na
China	2.00	1.98	2.30	na
Comoros	na	na	2.76	na
Congo, Dem. Rep. (Zaire)	na	na	1.43	na
Congo, Rep.	na	na	3.27	na
Cote d'Ivoire	na	na	0.79	na
Equatorial Guinea	na	na	na	na
Eritrea	na	na	na	na
Ethiopia	0.30	na	0.24	na
Gambia	na	1.67	0.61	na
Ghana	na	1.57	1.46	na
Guinea	na	na	0.55	na
Guinea-Bissau	1.78	na	1.49	na
Guyana	na	3.33	na	na
Haiti	0.74	0.72	0.76	na
Honduras	1.29	1.25	1.01	na
India	0.77	0.77	na	na
Kenya	na	1.70	1.66	na

E7.1 Hospital Beds per 1,000 in Population, 1980–1995—Low-Income Countries per World Bank *(continued)*

Country	1980	1985	1990	1995
Kyrgyzstan	12.03	12.06	11.96	9.01
Laos	na	na	2.57	na
Lesotho	na	na	na	na
Liberia	na	na	na	na
Madagascar	na	na	0.93	na
Malawi	na	na	1.55	na
Mali	na	na	na	na
Mauritania	na	na	0.67	na
Moldova	11.99	12.29	13.14	12.21
Mongolia	11.20	na	na	na
Mozambique	1.09	na	0.87	na
Myanmar (Burma)	0.85	na	0.64	na
Nepal	0.18	0.18	0.24	na
Nicaragua	na	2.56	1.82	na
Niger	na	na	na	na
Nigeria	0.87	na	1.67	na
Pakistan	0.57	na	0.64	na
Rwanda	1.53	na	1.65	na
Sao Tome and Principe	na	na	na	na
Senegal	na	na	0.73	na
Sierra Leone	1.21	na	na	na
Somalia	na	na	0.68	na
Sri Lanka	2.94	na	2.74	na
Sudan	0.92	na	1.09	na
Tajikistan	9.98	10.59	10.66	na
Tanzania	1.40	na	1.02	na
Togo	na	na	1.51	na
Uganda	na	na	na	na
Vietnam	3.50	na	3.83	na
Yemen	na	na	0.84	na
Zambia	na	na	na	na
Zimbabwe	3.06	1.44	0.51	na

Note: Hospital beds per 1,000 in population refers to inpatient beds at all types of medical institutions, such as public, private, general, specialized hospitals and rehabilitation centers. For most countries and in most cases, both acute and chronic care facilities are included in the bed count.

Source: World Bank, *World Development Indicators 1998*, CD-ROM, Series: Hospital Beds (per 1,000 people) (SH.MED.BEDS.ZS)

E7.2 Hospital Beds per 1,000 in Population, 1980–1995—Lower Middle-Income Countries per World Bank

Country	1980	1985	1990	1995
Albania	na	na	4.03	3.19
Algeria	na	na	2.50	na
Belarus	12.53	13.05	13.16	12.32
Belize	na	na	2.70	na
Bolivia	na	na	1.32	na
Botswana	2.37	na	1.57	na
Bulgaria	11.07	na	10.10	10.62
Cape Verde	2.19	na	na	na
Colombia	1.60	na	1.37	na
Costa Rica	3.31	na	2.50	na
Cuba	na	na	5.42	na
Djibouti	na	na	2.54	na
Dominica	na	na	3.00	na
Dominican Republic	na	na	1.88	na
Ecuador	1.91	na	1.64	na
Egypt	2.03	na	2.07	na
El Salvador	na	na	1.47	na
Estonia	12.43	12.43	11.60	8.08
Fiji	2.81	na	na	na
Georgia	10.66	10.48	9.73	6.62
Grenada	5.84	na	8.00	na
Guatemala	na	na	1.10	na
Indonesia	na	0.56	0.67	na
Iran	1.48	na	1.43	na
Iraq	1.95	na	1.66	na
Jamaica	na	3.33	2.20	na
Jordan	1.26	1.21	1.80	na
Kazakhstan	13.14	13.53	13.61	11.60
Kiribati	5.09	na	4.27	na
Latvia	13.72	na	14.04	11.05
Lebanon	na	na	1.65	na
Lithuania	12.07	12.78	12.41	10.84
Macedonia, FYRO	na	na	6.34	5.41
Maldives	na	na	0.76	na
Marshall Islands	na	na	2.27	na
Micronesia	na	na	na	na
Morocco	na	1.27	1.29	na
Namibia	na	na	na	na
North Korea, Dem. Rep.	na	na	na	na
Panama	na	3.35	2.52	na
Papua New Guinea	5.54	4.84	4.02	na
Paraguay	na	na	0.93	na
Peru	na	1.69	1.41	na
Philippines	1.70	1.74	1.39	na
Romania	8.77	8.81	8.92	7.64
Russia	12.96	13.47	13.02	11.70
Samoa	4.50	na	na	na
Solomon Islands	na	na	0.83	na
St. Vincent and the Grenadines	na	na	4.70	na
Suriname	8.90	na	5.70	na
Swaziland	na	na	na	na
Syria	1.10	na	1.09	na
Thailand	1.54	na	1.63	na
Tonga	3.45	na	na	na
Tunisia	2.13	na	1.92	na
Turkey	2.25	2.05	2.10	na
Turkmenistan	10.59	10.65	11.50	na

E7.2 Hospital Beds per 1,000 in Population, 1980–1995—Lower Middle-Income Countries per World Bank *(continued)*

Country	1980	1985	1990	1995
Ukraine	12.53	13.14	12.95	11.83
Uzbekistan	11.46	12.34	12.43	8.35
Vanuatu	6.18	na	na	na
Venezuela	0.34	2.69	2.68	na
Yugoslavia	13.64	na	5.92	5.31

Note: Hospital beds per 1,000 in population refers to inpatient beds at all types of medical institutions, such as public, private, general, specialized hospitals and rehabilitation centers. For most countries and in most cases, both acute and chronic care facilities are included in the bed count.

Source: World Bank, *World Development Indicators 1998*, CD-ROM, Series: Hospital Beds (per 1,000 people) (SH.MED.BEDS.ZS)

E7.3 Hospital Beds per 1,000 in Population, 1980–1995—Upper Middle-Income Countries per World Bank

Country	1980	1985	1990	1995
Antigua and Barbuda	na	na	6.59	na
Argentina	na	na	4.59	na
Bahrain	3.31	na	na	na
Barbados	8.53	na	8.37	na
Brazil	na	na	na	3.00
Chile	3.41	na	3.16	na
Croatia	na	na	7.38	na
Czech Republic	na	na	8.11	6.92
Gabon	na	1.53	3.19	na
Hungary	9.06	na	10.14	9.05
Libya	na	na	4.17	na
Malaysia	na	2.56	2.13	na
Malta	na	na	na	5.43
Mauritius	3.12	3.35	na	na
Mexico	na	na	0.80	1.20
Oman	1.62	na	2.11	na
Palau	na	na	na	na
Poland	5.62	5.65	6.60	6.30
Saudi Arabia	na	na	2.50	na
Seychelles	na	4.82	na	na
Slovakia	na	89.55	7.45	7.61
Slovenia	7.00	6.00	6.05	5.74
South Africa	na	na	na	na
St. Kitts & Nevis	8.54	na	9.21	na
St. Lucia	na	na	4.04	na
Trinidad & Tobago	na	na	4.00	na
Uruguay	na	3.25	4.52	na

Note: Hospital beds per 1,000 in population refers to inpatient beds at all types of medical institutions, such as public, private, general, specialized hospitals and rehabilitation centers. For most countries and in most cases, both acute and chronic care facilities are included in the bed count.

Source: World Bank, *World Development Indicators 1998*, CD-ROM, Series: Hospital Beds (per 1,000 people) (SH.MED.BEDS.ZS)

E7.4 Hospital Beds per 1,000 in Population, Summary, 1980 and 1994—Comparison by Income Level per World Bank

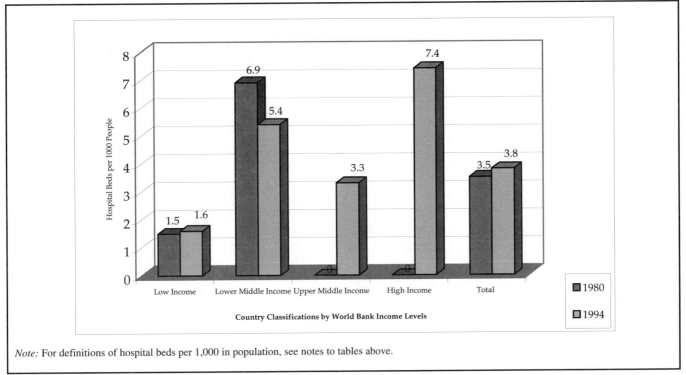

Note: For definitions of hospital beds per 1,000 in population, see notes to tables above.

Source: World Bank, *World Development Indicators 1998*, Table 2.13

E7.5 Physicians per 1,000 Population, 1980–1994—Low-Income Countries per World Bank

Country	1980	1985	1990	1994
Afghanistan	na	na	0.11	na
Angola	na	na	0.04	0
Armenia	3.52	3.83	3.71	3.1
Azerbaijan	3.36	3.79	3.76	3.8
Bangladesh	0.12	0.15	0.18	0.2
Benin	0.06	0.07	0.05	0.1
Bhutan	na	na	0.33	na
Bosnia and Herzegovina	na	na	1.58	0.6
Burkina Faso	0.02	na	na	na
Burundi	na	na	0.06	0.1
Cambodia	na	na	na	0.1
Cameroon	na	na	0.08	0.1
Central African Republic	0.04	na	0.04	na
Chad	na	na	na	na
China	0.91	0.99	1.54	1.6
Comoros	na	na	0.11	na
Congo, Dem. Rep. (Zaire)	na	na	0.07	0.1
Congo, Rep.	na	0.25	0.27	0.3
Cote d'Ivoire	na	0.07	0.09	0.1
Equatorial Guinea	na	na	0.28	na
Eritrea	na	na	na	na
Ethiopia	0.01	na	na	0
Gambia	na	0.08	na	na
Ghana	na	na	na	na
Guinea	na	0.03	0.13	0.2
Guinea-Bissau	0.13	0.14	na	na

E7.5 Physicians per 1,000 Population, 1980–1994—Low-Income Countries per World Bank (continued)

Country	1980	1985	1990	1994
Guyana	na	0.16	0.17	na
Haiti	na	0.14	0.08	0.1
Honduras	na	na	0.70	0.4
India	0.37	na	na	0.4
Kenya	na	0.15	0.05	0
Kyrgyzstan	2.92	3.38	3.35	3.1
Laos	na	0.73	0.23	0.2
Lesotho	na	0.07	0.04	0
Liberia	na	na	na	na
Madagascar	na	0.10	0.12	0.1
Malawi	na	na	0.02	0
Mali	0.04	0.04	0.05	0.1
Mauritania	na	0.11	0.06	0.1
Moldova	3.12	3.72	3.55	3.6
Mongolia	na	na	2.54	2.7
Mozambique	0.03	0.02	na	na
Myanmar (Burma)	na	0.27	0.08	0.1
Nepal	0.03	0.03	0.05	0.1
Nicaragua	0.43	na	0.66	0.7
Niger	na	na	0.02	0
Nigeria	0.11	0.19	na	0.2
Pakistan	0.29	na	0.46	0.5
Rwanda	0.03	0.03	na	0
Sao Tome and Principe	0.44	na	0.53	na
Senegal	na	na	0.05	0.1
Sierra Leone	0.06	na	na	na
Somalia	0.04	na	na	na
Sri Lanka	0.14	0.18	na	0.1
Sudan	0.11	na	na	na
Tajikistan	2.37	2.71	2.55	2.1
Tanzania	na	0.04	na	na
Togo	0.05	na	na	0.1
Uganda	na	na	na	na
Vietnam	0.24	na	0.40	0.4
Yemen	na	0.17	0.10	0.1
Zambia	0.08	0.14	0.09	0.1
Zimbabwe	0.16	0.17	0.14	0.1

Note: This indicator includes physicians who are graduates of any school of medicine (including primary-care physicians, family doctors, specialized doctors, surgeons, and others) and who are working in any medical field (practice, teaching, research). Data for some countries and in some cases include medical assistants.

Source: World Bank, *World Development Indicators 1998*, CD-ROM, Series: Physicians (per 1,000 people) (SH.MED.PHYS.ZS)

E7.6 Physicians per 1,000 Population, 1980–1994—Lower Middle-Income Countries per World Bank

Country	1980	1985	1990	1994
Albania	0.9	na	1.38	1.3
Algeria	na	na	0.94	0.8
Belarus	3.39	3.89	3.86	4.1
Belize	na	na	0.64	na
Bolivia	na	na	0.45	0.4
Botswana	0.12	na	na	0.2
Bulgaria	2.46	na	3.27	3.3
Cape Verde	0.18	na	na	na
Colombia	na	na	1.09	0.9
Costa Rica	na	na	1.26	0.9
Cuba	na	na	3.64	3.6
Djibouti	na	na	0.16	na
Dominica	na	na	0.46	na
Dominican Republic	na	na	1.49	1.1
Ecuador	na	na	1.53	1.5
Egypt	1.07	na	0.76	1.8
El Salvador	0.33	na	0.84	0.7
Estonia	4.19	4.62	3.66	3.1
Fiji	0.45	na	na	na
Georgia	4.81	5.33	4.89	4.2
Grenada	na	na	0.51	na
Guatemala	na	na	0.78	0.3
Indonesia	na	na	0.14	0.2
Iran	na	na	na	0.3
Iraq	0.56	na	0.20	0.6
Jamaica	na	na	0.57	0.5
Jordan	0.79	na	na	1.6
Kazakhstan	3.21	3.70	3.96	3.8
Kiribati	0.52	na	0.19	na
Latvia	4.13	na	4.11	3.0
Lebanon	na	na	na	1.9
Lithuania	3.93	4.34	4.00	4.0
Macedonia, FYRO	na	na	2.31	2.3
Maldives	na	na	0.07	na
Marshall Islands	na	na	na	na
Micronesia	na	na	na	na
Morocco	na	na	na	0.4
Namibia	na	na	na	0.2
North Korea, Dem. Rep.	na	na	na	na
Panama	na	1.01	1.65	1.8
Papua New Guinea	0.06	0.17	0.07	0.1
Paraguay	na	0.66	0.65	0.3
Peru	0.72	0.93	1.06	1.0
Philippines	0.13	0.15	0.12	0.1
Romania	1.48	1.76	1.80	1.8
Russia	4.03	4.50	4.06	3.8
Samoa	0.36	na	na	na
Solomon Islands	na	na	na	na
St. Vincent and the Grenadines	na	na	0.46	na
Suriname	na	na	0.75	na
Swaziland	na	na	0.11	na
Syria	0.45	na	0.83	0.8
Thailand	0.15	0.17	0.22	0.2
Tonga	0.36	na	na	na
Tunisia	0.27	na	0.53	0.6
Turkey	0.61	0.72	0.90	1.1
Turkmenistan	2.87	3.31	3.60	3.2

E7.6 Physicians per 1,000 Population, 1980–1994—Lower Middle-Income Countries per World Bank *(continued)*

Country	1980	1985	1990	1994
Ukraine	3.65	4.14	4.27	4.4
Uzbekistan	2.88	3.42	3.37	3.3
Vanuatu	0.19	na	na	na
Venezuela	0.84	1.20	1.56	1.6
Yugoslavia	3.36	na	2.02	2.0

Note: This indicator includes physicians who are graduates of any school of medicine (including primary-care physicians, family doctors, specialized doctors, surgeons, and others) and who are working in any medical field (practice, teaching, research). Data for some countries and in some cases include medical assistants.

Source: World Bank, *World Development Indicators 1998*, CD-ROM, Series: Physicians (per 1,000 people) (SH.MED.PHYS.ZS)

E7.7 Physicians per 1,000 Population, 1980–1994—Upper Middle-Income Countries per World Bank

Country	1980	1985	1990	1994
Antigua and Barbuda	na	na	0.77	na
Argentina	na	2.71	2.68	2.7
Bahrain	1.09	1.22	na	na
Barbados	na	na	1.14	na
Brazil	na	1.47	1.36	1.4
Chile	na	na	1.11	1.1
Croatia	na	na	2.12	2.0
Czech Republic	na	na	2.77	2.9
Gabon	na	0.51	na	0.5
Hungary	2.50	3.29	3.27	3.6
Libya	1.33	na	1.07	1.1
Malaysia	0.26	0.32	0.39	0.4
Malta	na	na	2.26	na
Mauritius	0.52	0.53	0.81	0.8
Mexico	na	na	1.10	1.3
Oman	0.47	0.52	0.61	0.9
Palau	na	na	na	na
Poland	1.79	1.97	2.14	2.3
Saudi Arabia	na	na	1.43	1.3
Seychelles	na	0.45	na	na
Slovakia	na	3.52	2.95	2.8
Slovenia	na	na	2.06	2.2
South Africa	na	na	na	na
St. Kitts & Nevis	0.36	na	0.90	na
St. Lucia	na	na	0.36	na
Trinidad & Tobago	0.73	na	0.72	0.7
Uruguay	na	1.95	3.68	3.2

Note: This indicator includes physicians who are graduates of any school of medicine (including primary-care physicians, family doctors, specialized doctors, surgeons, and others) and who are working in any medical field (practice, teaching, research). Data for some countries and in some cases include medical assistants.

Source: World Bank, *World Development Indicators 1998*, CD-ROM, Series: Physicians (per 1,000 people) (SH.MED.PHYS.ZS)

E7.8 Physicians per 1,000 in Population, Summary, 1980 and 1994—Comparison by Income Level per World Bank

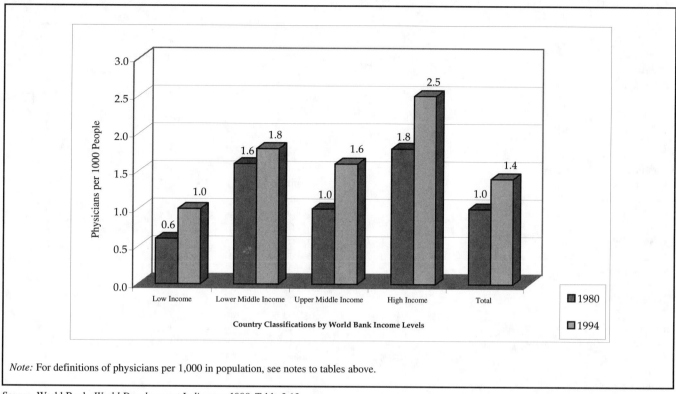

Note: For definitions of physicians per 1,000 in population, see notes to tables above.

Source: World Bank, *World Development Indicators 1998*, Table 2.13

E7.9 Nurses per 100,000 Population, 1993—Low-Income Countries per World Bank

Country	Nurses per 100,000	Country	Nurses per 100,000
Afghanistan	na	Kyrgyzstan	na
Angola	na	Laos	na
Armenia	na	Lesotho	33
Azerbaijan	na	Liberia	na
Bangladesh	5	Madagascar	55
Benin	33	Malawi	6
Bhutan	6	Mali	9
Bosnia and Herzegovina	na	Mauritania	27
Burkina Faso	na	Moldova	na
Burundi	17	Mongolia	452
Cambodia	136	Mozambique	na
Cameroon	na	Myanmar (Burma)	43
Central African Republic	45	Nepal	5
Chad	6	Nicaragua	56
China	88	Niger	17
Comoros	33	Nigeria	142
Congo, Dem. Rep. (Zaire)	na	Pakistan	32
Congo, Rep.	49	Rwanda	na
Cote d'Ivoire	na	Sao Tome and Principe	na
Equatorial Guinea	34	Senegal	35
Eritrea	na	Sierra Leone	na
Ethiopia	8	Somalia	na
Gambia	25	Sri Lanka	112
Ghana	na	Sudan	70
Guinea	3	Tajikistan	na
Guinea-Bissau	45	Tanzania	46
Guyana	88	Togo	31
Haiti	13	Uganda	28
Honduras	17	Vietnam	na
India	na	Yemen	51
Kenya	23	Zambia	na
		Zimbabwe	164

Note: This indicator includes nurses who have completed a program of basic nursing education and are authorized by the country to supply dependable and skilled services covering health promotion, prevention of illness, sick care, and rehabilitation services.

Source: United Nations Development Programme, *Human Development Report 1998,* Tables 13 and 30

E7.10 Nurses per 100,000 Population, 1993—Lower Middle-Income Countries per World Bank

Country	Nurses per 100,000	Country	Nurses per 100,000
Albania	na	Lithuania	na
Algeria	na	Macedonia, FYRO	na
Belarus	na	Maldives	13
Belize	76	Marshall Islands	na
Bolivia	25	Micronesia	na
Botswana	na	Morocco	94
Bulgaria	na	Namibia	81
Cape Verde	57	North Korea, Dem. Rep.	na
Colombia	49	Panama	98
Costa Rica	95	Papua New Guinea	97
Cuba	752	Paraguay	10
Djibouti	na	Peru	49
Dominica	263	Philippines	43
Dominican Republic	20	Romania	na
Ecuador	34	Russia	na
Egypt	222	Samoa	186
El Salvador	38	Solomon Islands	141
Estonia	na	St. Vincent and the Grenadines	187
Fiji	215	Suriname	227
Georgia	na	Swaziland	na
Grenada	239	Syria	212
Guatemala	30	Thailand	99
Indonesia	67	Tonga	na
Iran	na	Tunisia	283
Iraq	64	Turkey	151
Jamaica	69	Turkmenistan	na
Jordan	224	Ukraine	na
Kazakhstan	na	Uzbekistan	na
Kiribati	na	Vanuatu	na
Latvia	na	Venezuela	77
Lebanon	122	Yugoslavia	na

Note: This indicator includes nurses who have completed a program of basic nursing education and are authorized by the country to supply dependable and skilled services covering health promotion, prevention of illness, sick care, and rehabilitation services.

Source: United Nations Development Programme, *Human Development Report 1998,* Tables 13 and 30

E7.11 Nurses per 100,000 Population, 1993—Upper Middle-Income Countries per World Bank

Country	Nurses per 100,000	Country	Nurses per 100,000
Antigua and Barbuda	233	Mexico	40
Argentina	54	Oman	290
Bahrain	289	Palau	na
Barbados	323	Poland	na
Brazil	41	Saudi Arabia	348
Chile	42	Seychelles	417
Croatia	na	Slovakia	na
Czech Republic	na	Slovenia	na
Gabon	56	South Africa	175
Hungary	na	St. Kitts & Nevis	590
Libya	366	St. Lucia	177
Malaysia	160	Trinidad & Tobago	168
Malta	na	Uruguay	61
Mauritius	241		

Note: This indicator includes nurses who have completed a program of basic nursing education and are authorized by the country to supply dependable and skilled services covering health promotion, prevention of illness, sick care, and rehabilitation services.

Source: United Nations Development Programme, *Human Development Report 1998,* Tables 13 and 30

E8.1 Health Expenditure per Capita, Current U.S. Dollars, 1990–1995—Low-Income Countries per World Bank

Country	U.S. Dollars	Country	U.S. Dollars
Afghanistan	na	Laos	8
Angola	na	Lesotho	na
Armenia	10	Liberia	na
Azerbaijan	3	Madagascar	na
Bangladesh	5	Malawi	na
Benin	na	Mali	11
Bhutan	na	Mauritania	35
Bosnia and Herzegovina	na	Moldova	na
Burkina Faso	22	Mongolia	158
Burundi	na	Mozambique	na
Cambodia	18	Myanmar (Burma)	na
Cameroon	7	Nepal	9
Central African Republic	na	Nicaragua	34
Chad	6	Niger	na
China	23	Nigeria	5
Comoros	na	Pakistan	17
Congo, Dem. Rep. (Zaire)	na	Rwanda	na
Congo, Rep.	102	Sao Tome and Principe	na
Cote d'Ivoire	22	Senegal	na
Equatorial Guinea	na	Sierra Leone	18
Eritrea	na	Somalia	na
Ethiopia	na	Sri Lanka	12
Gambia	na	Sudan	29
Ghana	4	Tajikistan	na
Guinea	na	Tanzania	na
Guinea-Bissau	na	Togo	20
Guyana	na	Uganda	10
Haiti	8	Vietnam	na
Honduras	34	Yemen	39
India	24	Zambia	362
Kenya	13	Zimbabwe	86
Kyrgyzstan	na		

Note: Total health expenditure is cited in current United States dollars, as opposed to constant inflation-adjusted dollars, and is the sum of public and private health expenditures expressed as a share of the total population. It covers health services (preventive and curative), family planning activities, nutrition activities, and emergency aid designated for health; and it does not include provision of safe water and proper sanitation.

Source: World Bank, *World Development Indicators 1998*, CD-ROM, Series: Health Expenditure per capita (current US$) (SH.XPD.PCAP)

E8.2 Health Expenditure per Capita, Current U.S. Dollars, 1990–1995—Lower Middle-Income Countries per World Bank

Country	U.S. Dollars	Country	U.S. Dollars
Albania	na	Lithuania	na
Algeria	109	Macedonia, FYRO	na
Belarus	245	Maldives	na
Belize	na	Marshall Islands	na
Bolivia	38	Micronesia	na
Botswana	109	Morocco	36
Bulgaria	197	Namibia	153
Cape Verde	na	North Korea, Dem. Rep.	na
Colombia	138	Panama	201
Costa Rica	214	Papua New Guinea	na
Cuba	na	Paraguay	72
Djibouti	na	Peru	106
Dominica	na	Philippines	22
Dominican Republic	71	Romania	na
Ecuador	78	Russia	96
Egypt	na	Samoa	na
El Salvador	74	Solomon Islands	na
Estonia	na	St. Vincent and the Grenadines	na
Fiji	na	Suriname	na
Georgia	na	Swaziland	na
Grenada	na	Syria	na
Guatemala	33	Thailand	111
Indonesia	17	Tonga	na
Iran	1,343	Tunisia	104
Iraq	na	Turkey	100
Jamaica	91	Turkmenistan	na
Jordan	118	Ukraine	na
Kazakhstan	na	Uzbekistan	na
Kiribati	na	Vanuatu	na
Latvia	na	Venezuela	202
Lebanon	na	Yugoslavia	na

Note: Total health expenditure is cited in current United States dollars, as opposed to constant inflation-adjusted dollars, and is the sum of public and private health expenditures expressed as a share of the total population. It covers health services (preventive and curative), family planning activities, nutrition activities, and emergency aid designated for health; and it does not include provision of safe water and proper sanitation.

Source: World Bank, *World Development Indicators 1998*, CD-ROM, Series: Health Expenditure per capita (current US$) (SH.XPD.PCAP)

E8.3 Health Expenditure per Capita, Current U.S. Dollars, 1990–1995—Upper Middle-Income Countries per World Bank

Country	U.S. Dollars	Country	U.S. Dollars
Antigua and Barbuda	na	Mauritius	109
Argentina	877	Mexico	223
Bahrain	na	Oman	na
Barbados	na	Palau	na
Brazil	261	Poland	226
Chile	241	Saudi Arabia	159
Croatia	302	Seychelles	na
Czech Republic	383	Slovakia	na
Gabon	na	Slovenia	na
Hungary	295	South Africa	257
Libya	na	St. Kitts & Nevis	na
Malaysia	85	St. Lucia	na
Malta	na	Trinidad & Tobago	151
		Uruguay	439

Note: Total health expenditure is cited in current United States dollars, as opposed to constant inflation-adjusted dollars, and is the sum of public and private health expenditures expressed as a share of the total population. It covers health services (preventive and curative), family planning activities, nutrition activities, and emergency aid designated for health; and it does not include provision of safe water and proper sanitation.

Source: World Bank, *World Development Indicators 1998*, CD-ROM, Series: Health Expenditure per capita (current US$) (SH.XPD.PCAP)

E8.4 Health Expenditure per Capita, Summary, 1990–1995—Comparison by Income Level per World Bank

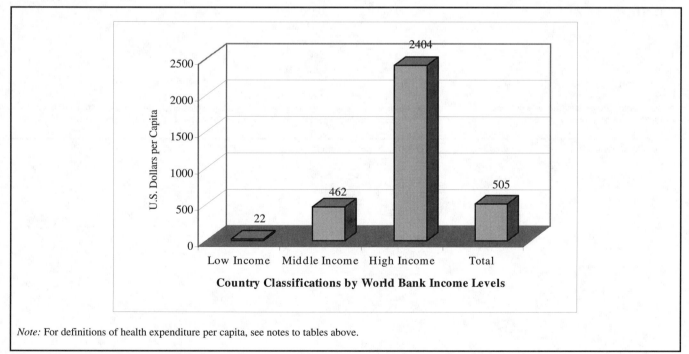

Note: For definitions of health expenditure per capita, see notes to tables above.

Source: World Bank, *World Development Indicators 1998*, Table 2.13

E8.5 Health Expenditure as Percent of GDP, 1990–1995—Low-Income Countries per World Bank

Country	Percent of GDP	Country	Percent of GDP
Afghanistan	na	Laos	2.6
Angola	na	Lesotho	na
Armenia	7.8	Liberia	na
Azerbaijan	7.5	Madagascar	na
Bangladesh	2.4	Malawi	na
Benin	na	Mali	2.9
Bhutan	na	Mauritania	5.2
Bosnia and Herzegovina	na	Moldova	na
Burkina Faso	5.5	Mongolia	6.7
Burundi	na	Mozambique	na
Cambodia	7.2	Myanmar (Burma)	na
Cameroon	1.4	Nepal	5
Central African Republic	na	Nicaragua	7.8
Chad	3.5	Niger	na
China	3.8	Nigeria	1.4
Comoros	na	Pakistan	3.5
Congo, Dem. Rep. (Zaire)	na	Rwanda	na
Congo, Rep.	6.3	Sao Tome and Principe	na
Cote d'Ivoire	3.4	Senegal	na
Equatorial Guinea	na	Sierra Leone	3.6
Eritrea	2.0	Somalia	na
Ethiopia	na	Sri Lanka	1.9
Gambia	na	Sudan	0.3
Ghana	1.4	Tajikistan	na
Guinea	na	Tanzania	na
Guinea-Bissau	na	Togo	3.4
Guyana	na	Uganda	3.9
Haiti	3.6	Vietnam	5.2
Honduras	5.6	Yemen	2.6
India	5.6	Zambia	3.3
Kenya	2.5	Zimbabwe	6.5
Kyrgyzstan	na		

Note: Total health expenditure as a percent of GDP is the total of all spending in a country—including both private and public moneys—stated as a percent of the GDP, or total output of a country. The total expenditure excludes moneys spent for the development of safe water and sanitation facilities.

Source: World Bank, *World Development Indicators 1998*, CD-ROM, Series: Health Expenditure, total (SH.XPD.TOTL.ZS)

E8.6 Health Expenditure as Percent of GDP, 1990–1995—Lower Middle-Income Countries per World Bank

Country	Percent of GDP	Country	Percent of GDP
Albania	na	Lithuania	na
Algeria	4.6	Macedonia, FYRO	8.3
Belarus	6.4	Maldives	na
Belize	na	Marshall Islands	na
Bolivia	5.0	Micronesia	na
Botswana	3.1	Morocco	3.4
Bulgaria	6.9	Namibia	7.6
Cape Verde	na	North Korea, Dem. Rep.	na
Colombia	7.4	Panama	7.5
Costa Rica	8.5	Papua New Guinea	na
Cuba	na	Paraguay	4.3
Djibouti	na	Peru	4.9
Dominica	na	Philippines	2.4
Dominican Republic	5.3	Romania	na
Ecuador	5.3	Russia	4.8
Egypt	3.7	Samoa	na
El Salvador	5.0	Solomon Islands	na
Estonia	na	St. Vincent and the Grenadines	na
Fiji	na	Suriname	na
Georgia	na	Swaziland	na
Grenada	na	Syria	na
Guatemala	2.7	Thailand	5.3
Indonesia	1.8	Tonga	na
Iran	4.8	Tunisia	5.9
Iraq	na	Turkey	4.2
Jamaica	5.4	Turkmenistan	na
Jordan	7.9	Ukraine	na
Kazakhstan	na	Uzbekistan	na
Kiribati	na	Vanuatu	na
Latvia	na	Venezuela	7.1
Lebanon	5.3	Yugoslavia	na

Note: Total health expenditure is the sum of public and private health expenditures and reflects the help government and private health sector gives to people in a country. Expressed as a percentage of gross domestic product (GDP), it covers health services (preventive and curative), family planning activities, nutrition activities, and emergency aid designated for health; this does not include provision of safe water and proper sanitation.

Source: World Bank, *World Development Indicators 1998*, CD-ROM, Series: Health Expenditure, total (SH.XPD.TOTL.ZS)

E8.7 Health Expenditure as Percent of GDP, 1990–1995—Upper Middle-Income Countries per World Bank

Country	Percent of GDP	Country	Percent of GDP
Antigua and Barbuda	na	Mexico	5.3
Argentina	10.6	Oman	na
Bahrain	na	Palau	na
Barbados	na	Poland	6.0
Brazil	7.4	Saudi Arabia	na
Chile	6.5	Seychelles	na
Croatia	10.1	Slovakia	na
Czech Republic	9.6	Slovenia	na
Gabon	na	South Africa	7.9
Hungary	7.3	St. Kitts & Nevis	na
Libya	na	St. Lucia	na
Malaysia	2.5	Trinidad & Tobago	3.9
Malta	na	Uruguay	8.5
Mauritius	3.4		

Note: Total health expenditure is the sum of public and private health expenditures and reflects the help government and private health sector gives to people in a country. Expressed as a percentage of gross domestic product (GDP), it covers health services (preventive and curative), family planning activities, nutrition activities, and emergency aid designated for health; this does not include provision of safe water and proper sanitation.

Source: World Bank, *World Development Indicators 1998*, CD-ROM, Series: Health Expenditure, total (SH.XPD.TOTL.ZS)

E8.8 Health Expenditure as Percent of GDP, Summary, 1990–1995—Comparison by Income Level per World Bank

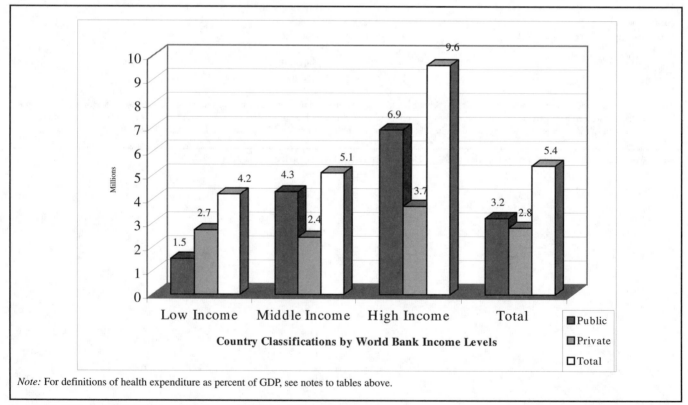

Note: For definitions of health expenditure as percent of GDP, see notes to tables above.

Source: World Bank, *World Development Indicators 1998*, Table 2.13

F. AIDS

GENERAL OVERVIEW

Acquired immune deficiency syndrome (AIDS), a fatal condition resulting in the suppression of the body's immune system, is the late stage of infection by the human immunodeficiency virus (HIV). Its known means of transmission are intravenous drug use and exchange of bodily fluids (which can include blood transfusion, unprotected sexual contact, or mother-fetus transfer in pregnant women.) AIDS first emerged in the early 1980s, reaching epidemic proportions soon after in most communities and regions of the world. Many sub-Saharan African nations have been particularly hard hit by it, due especially to the lack of access to methods of birth control (some of which also provide protection against the transmission of HIV) and the lack of education concerning the virus's modes of transmission.

This section on AIDS is separated from the rest of the health indicators for two reasons. The first is that the number of statistics available on the subject of AIDS—as a factor and ramification of poverty—is voluminous and the size alone would require separate treatment for organizational purposes. Second, AIDS has become such a major concern to impoverished countries, whose already inadequate and strained infrastructure cannot begin to address the problems it poses, that a separate section is warranted. Further, its effects on the poverty of children alone, as parents succumb to complications from AIDS and leave orphaned children behind, argues for special consideration.

All data on reported AIDS cases are subject to significant limitations, as people are reluctant to report their infection to health authorities. Therefore, the number of reported cases is usually much lower than estimates, which attempt to compensate for underreporting.

EXPLANATION OF INDICATORS

Estimated AIDS Cases, End of 1997, Worldwide Summary: The graphs at the beginning of this chapter offer a snapshot of the recent state of the AIDS epidemic region by region. These graphs are meant to be used as a touchstone against which to measure the statistics from individual countries in the tables that follow (F1.1–F1.4).

Estimated AIDS Cases and AIDS Deaths, Cumulative Total: As measures of the total number of cases and deaths since the beginning of the epidemic, these indicators help analysts to estimate the scope of the epidemic and which countries have been hardest hit, i.e., which countries need the most assistance in developing health and educational policies aimed at preventing HIV transmission (F2.1–F2.6).

Estimated AIDS Deaths, Adults and Children, Compared with Population, 1997: This indicator gives an estimate of the number of cases in one recent year, 1997, with comparison to the total population. It gives a snapshot of the proportion of AIDS deaths against the total population and therefore represents the extent to which a population is at risk, if current patterns of infection rates and prevention efforts continue (F3.1–F3.3).

Cumulative Number of Orphans, Compared with 1997 Population: This statistic helps to measure the extent of the effect of AIDS on children. As adults succumb to the disease, their children are left behind. Without primary care-givers, and often infected themselves due to fetal transmission, the deprivation suffered by AIDS orphans is immense. Further, the burden to poorer countries, whose welfare capacities are already strained, is enormous (F4.1–F4.3).

Sex Distribution of Reported AIDS Cases: The sex distribution of reported cases—what portion of the cases are attributed to men and women—reflects the make-up of the AIDS-affected population. As such, the data can help policymakers plan education, health care, and prevention programs. A caution concerning these data exists, however: as it only reports the sex of the person affected if the gender was known to begin with, the percentage breakdown indicated by the data may not accurately reflect the AIDS population as a whole (F5.1–F5.3).

Year of First Reported AIDS Case: This table is included to convey an idea of the length of time a country has been faced with the problems posed by the AIDS epidemic. For the most part, the earlier the first case was reported, the longer a country has dealt with the epidemic, although the epidemic developed at different rates in different countries, depending, for instance, on the segments of the population infected and the primary modes of transmission (F6.1–F6.3).

F1.1 Estimated AIDS Cases, End of 1997, Worldwide Summary—Percent of Total Adults

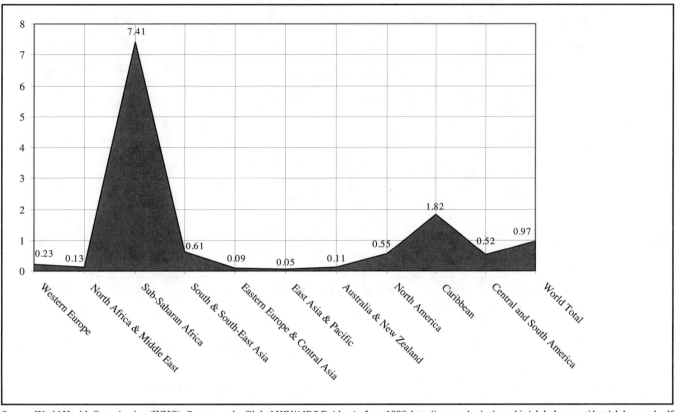

Source: World Health Organization (WHO), *Report on the Global HIV/AIDS Epidemic*, June 1998, http://www.who.int/emc-hiv/global_report/data/globrep_e4.pdf

F1.2 Estimated AIDS Cases, End of 1997, Worldwide Summary—Total and Adult

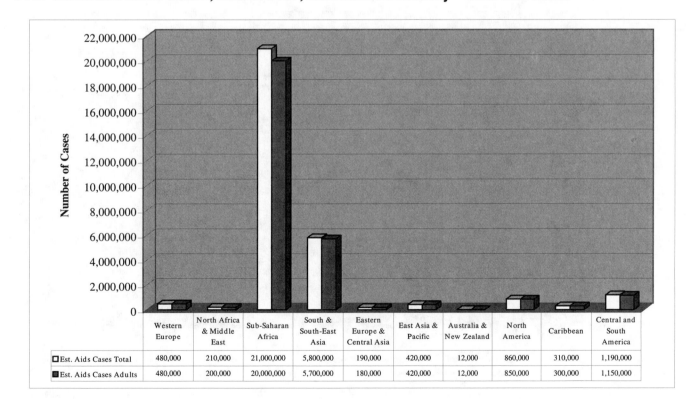

	Western Europe	North Africa & Middle East	Sub-Saharan Africa	South & South-East Asia	Eastern Europe & Central Asia	East Asia & Pacific	Australia & New Zealand	North America	Caribbean	Central and South America
☐ Est. Aids Cases Total	480,000	210,000	21,000,000	5,800,000	190,000	420,000	12,000	860,000	310,000	1,190,000
■ Est. Aids Cases Adults	480,000	200,000	20,000,000	5,700,000	180,000	420,000	12,000	850,000	300,000	1,150,000

Source: World Health Organization (WHO), *Report on the Global HIV/AIDS Epidemic*, June 1998, http://www.who.int/emc-hiv/global_report/data/globrep_e4.pdf

F1.3 Estimated AIDS Cases, End of 1997, Worldwide Summary—Total and Children

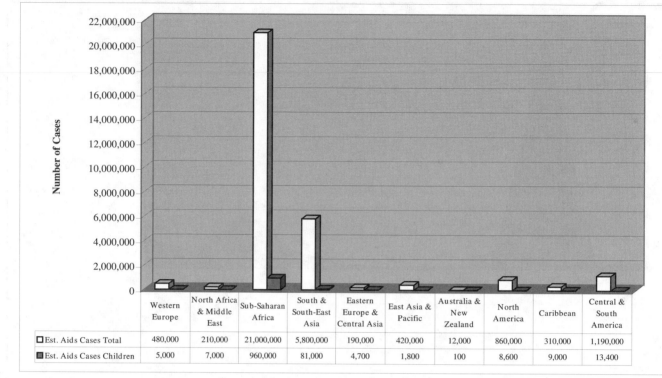

	Western Europe	North Africa & Middle East	Sub-Saharan Africa	South & South-East Asia	Eastern Europe & Central Asia	East Asia & Pacific	Australia & New Zealand	North America	Caribbean	Central & South America
☐ Est. Aids Cases Total	480,000	210,000	21,000,000	5,800,000	190,000	420,000	12,000	860,000	310,000	1,190,000
◼ Est. Aids Cases Children	5,000	7,000	960,000	81,000	4,700	1,800	100	8,600	9,000	13,400

Source: World Health Organization (WHO), *Report on the Global HIV/AIDS Epidemic*, June 1998, http://www.who.int/emc-hiv/global_report/data/globrep_e4.pdf

F1.4 Estimated AIDS Cases, End of 1997, Worldwide Summary—Total and Women

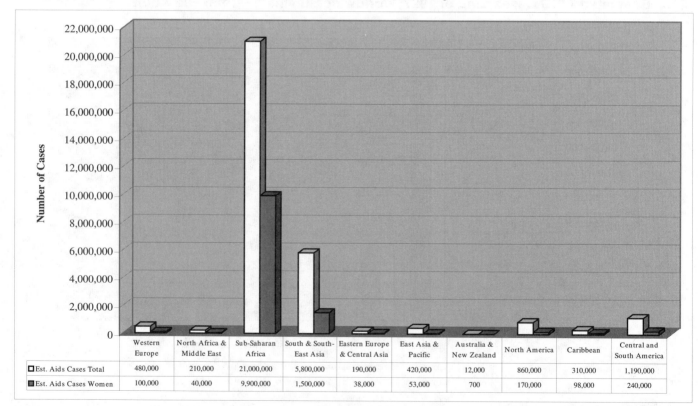

	Western Europe	North Africa & Middle East	Sub-Saharan Africa	South & South-East Asia	Eastern Europe & Central Asia	East Asia & Pacific	Australia & New Zealand	North America	Caribbean	Central and South America
☐ Est. Aids Cases Total	480,000	210,000	21,000,000	5,800,000	190,000	420,000	12,000	860,000	310,000	1,190,000
◼ Est. Aids Cases Women	100,000	40,000	9,900,000	1,500,000	38,000	53,000	700	170,000	98,000	240,000

Source: World Health Organization (WHO), *Report on the Global HIV/AIDS Epidemic*, June 1998, http://www.who.int/emc-hiv/global_report/data/globrep_e4.pdf

F2.1 Estimated AIDS Cases, Cumulative Total Since Beginning of Epidemic (Early 1980s)—Low-Income Countries per World Bank

Country	Total Cases	Country	Total Cases
Afghanistan	na	Kyrgyzstan	na
Angola	28,000	Laos	240
Armenia	na	Lesotho	17,000
Azerbaijan	<100	Liberia	26,000
Bangladesh	4,900	Madagascar	2,200
Benin	16,000	Malawi	480,000
Bhutan	na	Mali	44,000
Bosnia and Herzegovina	na	Mauritania	2,100
Burkina Faso	270,000	Moldova	<100
Burundi	220,000	Mongolia	na
Cambodia	18,000	Mozambique	290,000
Cameroon	110,000	Myanmar (Burma)	100,000
Central African Republic	100,000	Nepal	2,100
Chad	75,000	Nicaragua	380
China	9,000	Niger	27,000
Comoros	na	Nigeria	590,000
Congo, Dem. Rep. (Zaire)	510,000	Pakistan	17,000
Congo, Rep.	85,000	Rwanda	180,000
Cote d'Ivoire	450,000	Sao Tome and Principe	na
Equatorial Guinea	2,100	Senegal	60,000
Eritrea	na	Sierra Leone	57,000
Ethiopia	1,100,000	Somalia	na
Gambia	11,000	Sri Lanka	1,900
Ghana	180,000	Sudan	na
Guinea	25,000	Tajikistan	na
Guinea-Bissau	1,800	Tanzania	1,000,000
Guyana	2,300	Togo	140,000
Haiti	91,000	Uganda	1,900,000
Honduras	16,000	Vietnam	8,700
India	430,000	Yemen	na
Kenya	660,000	Zambia	630,000
		Zimbabwe	650,000

Note: This indicator shows an estimated number of AIDS cases (in both adults and children) as a cumulative total since the beginning of the epidemic. It should be noted that owing to underreporting of AIDS, the number of actual cases is higher than the totals given.

Source: World Health Organization (WHO), *Report on the Global HIV/AIDS Epidemic*, June 1998, http://www.who.int/emc-hiv/global_report/data/globrep_e4.pdf

F2.2 Estimated AIDS Cases, Cumulative Total Since Beginning of Epidemic (Early 1980s)— Lower Middle-Income Countries per World Bank

Country	Total Cases	Country	Total Cases
Albania	<100	Lithuania	<100
Algeria	na	Macedonia, FYRO	<100
Belarus	<100	Maldives	na
Belize	960	Marshall Islands	na
Bolivia	940	Micronesia	na
Botswana	50,000	Morocco	na
Bulgaria	na	Namibia	16,000
Cape Verde	na	North Korea, Dem. Rep.	na
Colombia	12,000	Panama	4,000
Costa Rica	3,400	Papua New Guinea	2,400
Cuba	690	Paraguay	1,500
Djibouti	7,900	Peru	7,200
Dominica	na	Philippines	1,600
Dominican Republic	11,000	Romania	na
Ecuador	8,300	Russia	290
Egypt	5,800	Samoa	na
El Salvador	6,900	Solomon Islands	na
Estonia	<100	St. Vincent and the Grenadines	na
Fiji	<100	Suriname	1,200
Georgia	<100	Swaziland	16,000
Grenada	na	Syria	na
Guatemala	9,100	Thailand	260,000
Indonesia	4,800	Tonga	na
Iran	na	Tunisia	na
Iraq	na	Turkey	na
Jamaica	5,700	Turkmenistan	na
Jordan	na	Ukraine	590
Kazakhstan	<100	Uzbekistan	<100
Kiribati	na	Vanuatu	na
Latvia	<100	Venezuela	7,900
Lebanon	na	Yugoslavia	690

Note: This indicator shows an estimated number of AIDS cases (in both adults and children) as a cumulative total since the beginning of the epidemic. It should be noted that owing to underreporting of AIDS, the number of actual cases is higher than the totals given.

Source: World Health Organization (WHO), *Report on the Global HIV/AIDS Epidemic*, June 1998, http://www.who.int/emc-hiv/global_report/data/globrep_e4.pdf

F2.3 Estimated AIDS Cases, Cumulative Total Since Beginning of Epidemic (Early 1980s)— Upper Middle-Income Countries per World Bank

Country	Total Cases	Country	Total Cases
Antigua and Barbuda	na	Mexico	98,000
Argentina	15,000	Oman	na
Bahrain	na	Palau	na
Barbados	2,300	Poland	840
Brazil	310,000	Saudi Arabia	na
Chile	3,200	Seychelles	na
Croatia	na	Slovakia	<100
Czech Republic	110	Slovenia	<100
Gabon	7,900	South Africa	420,000
Hungary	300	St. Kitts & Nevis	na
Libya	na	St. Lucia	na
Malaysia	6,900	Trinidad & Tobago	2,700
Malta	<100	Uruguay	2,400
Mauritius	na		

Note: This indicator shows an estimated number of AIDS cases (in both adults and children) as a cumulative total since the beginning of the epidemic. It should be noted that owing to underreporting of AIDS, the number of actual cases is higher than the totals given.

Source: World Health Organization (WHO), *Report on the Global HIV/AIDS Epidemic*, June 1998, http://www.who.int/emc-hiv/global_report/data/globrep_e4.pdf

F2.4 Estimated AIDS Deaths, Cumulative Total Since Beginning of Epidemic (Early 1980s)— Low-Income Countries per World Bank

Country	Total Cases	Country	Total Cases
Afghanistan	na	Laos	210
Angola	25,000	Lesotho	15,000
Armenia	na	Liberia	24,000
Azerbaijan	<100d	Madagascar	1,900
Bangladesh	4,200	Malawi	450,000
Benin	15,000	Mali	40,000
Bhutan	na	Mauritania	1,900
Bosnia and Herzegovina	na	Moldova	<100d
Burkina Faso	250,000	Mongolia	na
Burundi	200,000	Mozambique	250,000
Cambodia	15,000	Myanmar (Burma)	86,000
Cameroon	100,000	Nepal	1,700
Central African Republic	92,000	Nicaragua	320
Chad	70,000	Niger	25,000
China	6,400	Nigeria	530,000
Comoros	na	Pakistan	15,000
Congo, Dem. Rep. (Zaire)	470,000	Rwanda	170,000
Congo, Rep.	80,000	Sao Tome and Principe	na
Cote d'Ivoire	420,000	Senegal	na
Equatorial Guinea	2,000	Sierra Leone	54,000
Eritrea	na	Somalia	na
Ethiopia	1,000,000	Sri Lanka	1,700
Gambia	11,000	Sudan	na
Ghana	170,000	Tajikistan	na
Guinea	23,000	Tanzania	940,000
Guinea-Bissau	1,600	Togo	130,000
Guyana	2,100	Uganda	1,800,000
Haiti	85,000	Vietnam	7,200
Honduras	15,000	Yemen	na
India	350,000	Zambia	590,000
Kenya	600,000	Zimbabwe	590,000
Kyrgyzstan	na		

Note: This indicator shows an estimated number of AIDS deaths (of both adults and children) as a cumulative total since the beginning of the epidemic. It should be noted that owing to underreporting of AIDS, the number of actual cases is higher than the totals given.

Source: World Health Organization (WHO), *Report on the Global HIV/AIDS Epidemic*, June 1998, http://www.who.int/emc-hiv/global_report/data/globrep_e4.pdf

F2.5 Estimated AIDS Deaths, Cumulative Total Since Beginning of Epidemic (Early 1980s) —Lower Middle-Income Countries per World Bank

Country	Total Cases	Country	Total Cases
Albania	<100d	Lithuania	<100d
Algeria	na	Macedonia, FYRO	<100d
Belarus	<100d	Maldives	na
Belize	880	Marshall Islands	na
Bolivia	850	Micronesia	na
Botswana	43,000	Morocco	na
Bulgaria	na	Namibia	14,000
Cape Verde	na	North Korea, Dem. Rep.	na
Colombia	10,000	Panama	3,700
Costa Rica	3,100	Papua New Guinea	2,200
Cuba	640	Paraguay	1,300
Djibouti	7,000	Peru	6,000
Dominica	na	Philippines	1,300
Dominican Republic	9,300	Romania	4,100d
Ecuador	7,700	Russia	190d
Egypt	5,400	Samoa	na
El Salvador	6,300	Solomon Islands	na
Estonia	<100d	St. Vincent and the Grenadines	na
Fiji	<100	Suriname	1,100
Georgia	<100d	Swaziland	14,000
Grenada	na	Syria	na
Guatemala	8,300	Thailand	230,000
Indonesia	3,900	Tonga	na
Iran	na	Tunisia	na
Iraq	na	Turkey	na
Jamaica	5,200	Turkmenistan	na
Jordan	na	Ukraine	240d
Kazakhstan	<100d	Uzbekistan	<100d
Kiribati	na	Vanuatu	na
Latvia	<100d	Venezuela	6,600
Lebanon	na	Yugoslavia	na

Note: This indicator shows an estimated number of AIDS deaths (of both adults and children) as a cumulative total since the beginning of the epidemic. It should be noted that owing to underreporting of AIDS, the number of actual cases is higher than the totals given.

Source: World Health Organization (WHO), *Report on the Global HIV/AIDS Epidemic,* June 1998, http://www.who.int/emc-hiv/global_report/data/globrep_e4.pdf

F2.6 Estimated AIDS Deaths, Cumulative Total Since Beginning of Epidemic (Early 1980s)— Upper Middle-Income Countries per World Bank

Country	Total Cases	Country	Total Cases
Antigua and Barbuda	na	Mexico	91,000
Argentina	12,000	Oman	na
Bahrain	na	Palau	na
Barbados	2,100	Poland	490d
Brazil	290,000	Saudi Arabia	na
Chile	2,900	Seychelles	na
Croatia	<100d	Slovakia	<100d
Czech Republic	<200d	Slovenia	<100d
Gabon	7,100	South Africa	360,000
Hungary	200d	St. Kitts & Nevis	na
Libya	na	St. Lucia	na
Malaysia	5,700	Trinidad & Tobago	2,500
Malta	<100d	Uruguay	2,200
Mauritius	na		

Note: This indicator shows an estimated number of AIDS deaths (of both adults and children) as a cumulative total since the beginning of the epidemic. It should be noted that owing to underreporting of AIDS, the number of actual cases is higher than the totals given.

Source: World Health Organization (WHO), *Report on the Global HIV/AIDS Epidemic,* June 1998, http://www.who.int/emc-hiv/global_report/data/globrep_e4.pdf

F3.1 Estimated AIDS Deaths, Adults and Children, Compared with Population, 1997—Low-Income Countries per World Bank

Country	Deaths	Population (thous.)	Deaths/Thousand in Population
Afghanistan	na	22,132	na
Angola	7,200	11,569	0.6
Armenia	na	3,642	na
Azerbaijan	na	7,655	na
Bangladesh	1,300	122,013	0.0
Benin	3,900	5,720	0.7
Bhutan	na	1,862	na
Bosnia and Herzegovina	na	3,784	na
Burkina Faso	42,000	11,087	3.8
Burundi	30,000	6,398	4.7
Cambodia	6,300	10,516	0.6
Cameroon	24,000	13,937	1.7
Central African Republic	17,000	3,416	5.0
Chad	10,000	6,702	1.5
China	4,000	1,243,738	0.0
Comoros	na	651	na
Congo, Dem. Rep. (Zaire)	93,000	48,040	1.9
Congo, Rep.	11,000	2,745	4.0
Cote d'Ivoire	72,000	14,300	5.0
Equatorial Guinea	280	420	0.7
Eritrea	na	3,409	na
Ethiopia	250,000	60,148	4.2
Gambia	1,500	1,169	1.3
Ghana	24,000	18,338	1.3
Guinea	5,700	7,614	0.7
Guinea-Bissau	580	1,112	0.5
Guyana	490	847	0.6
Haiti	13,000	7,395	1.8
Honduras	3,100	5,981	0.5
India	140,000	960,178	0.1
Kenya	140,000	28,414	4.9

F3.1 Estimated AIDS Deaths, Adults and Children, Compared with Population, 1997—Low-Income Countries per World Bank *(continued)*

Country	Deaths	Population (thous.)	Deaths/Thousand in Population
Kyrgyzstan	na	4,481	na
Laos	<100	5,194	na
Lesotho	5,200	2,131	2.4
Liberia	4,600	2,467	1.9
Madagascar	600	15,845	0.0
Malawi	80,000	10,086	7.9
Mali	8,300	11,480	0.7
Mauritania	480	2,392	0.2
Moldova	na	4,448	na
Mongolia	na	2,568	na
Mozambique	83,000	18,265	4.5
Myanmar (Burma)	29,000	46,765	0.6
Nepal	840	22,591	0.0
Nicaragua	120	4,351	0.0
Niger	5,800	9,788	0.6
Nigeria	150,000	118,369	1.3
Pakistan	4,500	143,831	0.0
Rwanda	36,000	5,883	6.1
Sao Tome and Principe	na	na	na
Senegal	na	8,762	na
Sierra Leone	8,400	4,428	1.9
Somalia	na	10,217	na
Sri Lanka	400	18,273	0.0
Sudan	na	27,899	na
Tajikistan	na	6,046	na
Tanzania	150,000	31,507	4.8
Togo	20,000	4,317	4.6
Uganda	160,000	20,791	7.7
Vietnam	2,700	76,548	0.0
Yemen	na	16,294	na
Zambia	97,000	8,478	11.4
Zimbabwe	130,000	11,682	11.1

Note: This indicator shows an estimated number of AIDS deaths (of both adults and children) during 1997. This is measured against the 1997 total population and calculated as a proportion of that total.

Source: World Health Organization (WHO), *Report on the Global HIV/AIDS Epidemic,* June 1998, http://www.who.int/emc-hiv/global_report/data/globrep_e4.pdf

F3.2 Estimated AIDS Deaths, Adults and Children, Compared with Population, 1997—Lower Middle-Income Countries per World Bank

Country	Deaths	Population (thous.)	Deaths/Thousand in Population
Albania	na	3,422	na
Algeria	na	29,473	na
Belarus	na	10,339	na
Belize	160	224	0.7
Bolivia	180	7,774	0.0
Botswana	15,000	1,518	9.9
Bulgaria	na	8,427	na
Cape Verde	na	na	na
Colombia	3,000	37,068	0.1
Costa Rica	630	3,575	0.2
Cuba	100	11,068	0.0
Djibouti	2,200	634	3.5
Dominica	na	na	na
Dominican Republic	2,900	8,097	0.4
Ecuador	1,200	11,937	0.1
Egypt	930	64,465	0.0
El Salvador	1,100	5,928	0.2
Estonia	na	1,455	na
Fiji	<100	809	na
Georgia	na	5,434	na
Grenada	na	na	na
Guatemala	1,700	11,241	0.2
Indonesia	1,600	203,480	0.0
Iran	na	71,518	na
Iraq	na	21,177	na
Jamaica	990	2,515	0.4
Jordan	na	5,774	na
Kazakhstan	na	16,832	na
Kiribati	na	na	na
Latvia	na	2,474	na
Lebanon	na	3,144	na
Lithuania	na	3,719	na
Macedonia, FYRO	na	2,190	na
Maldives	na	273	na
Marshall Islands	na	na	na
Micronesia	na	na	na
Morocco	na	27,518	na
Namibia	6,400	1,613	4.0
North Korea, Dem. Rep.	na	22,837	na
Panama	650	2,722	0.2
Papua New Guinea	440	4,500	0.1
Paraguay	240	5,088	0.0
Peru	2,200	24,367	0.1
Philippines	630	70,724	0.0
Romania	na	22,606	na
Russia	na	147,708	na
Samoa	na	na	na
Solomon Islands	na	na	na
St. Vincent and the Grenadines	na	na	na
Suriname	210	437	0.5
Swaziland	5,000	906	5.5
Syria	na	14,951	na
Thailand	60,000	59,159	1.0
Tonga	na	na	na
Tunisia	na	9,326	na
Turkey	na	62,774	na

F3.2 Estimated AIDS Deaths, Adults and Children, Compared with Population, 1997—Lower Middle-Income Countries per World Bank (continued)

Country	Deaths	Population (thous.)	Deaths/Thousand in Population
Turkmenistan	na	4,235	na
Ukraine	na	51,424	na
Uzbekistan	na	23,656	na
Vanuatu	na	na	na
Venezuela	2,500	22,777	0.1
Yugoslavia	na	10,350	na

Note: This indicator shows an estimated number of AIDS deaths (of both adults and children) during 1997. This is measured against the 1997 total population and calculated as a proportion of that total.

Source: World Health Organization (WHO), *Report on the Global HIV/AIDS Epidemic,* June 1998, http://www.who.int/emc-hiv/global_report/data/globrep_e4.pdf

F3.3 Estimated AIDS Deaths, Adults and Children, Compared with Population, 1997—Upper Middle-Income Countries per World Bank

Country	Deaths	Population (thous.)	Deaths/Thousand in Population
Antigua and Barbuda			
Argentina	4,300	35,671	0.1
Bahrain	na	582	na
Barbados	330	262	1.3
Brazil	44,000	163,132	0.3
Chile	740	14,625	0.1
Croatia	na	4,498	na
Czech Republic	na	10,237	na
Gabon	1,700	1,138	1.5
Hungary	na	9,990	na
Libya	na	5,784	na
Malaysia	2,300	21,018	0.1
Malta	na	371	na
Mauritius	na	1,141	na
Mexico	14,000	94,281	0.1
Oman	na	2,401	na
Palau	na	na	na
Poland	na	38,635	na
Saudi Arabia	na	19,494	na
Seychelles	na	na	na
Slovakia	na	5,355	na
Slovenia	na	1,922	na
South Africa	140,000	43,336	3.2
St. Kitts & Nevis	na	na	na
St. Lucia	na	na	na
Trinidad & Tobago	480	1,307	0.4
Uruguay	390	3,221	0.1

Note: This indicator shows an estimated number of AIDS deaths (of both adults and children) during 1997. This is measured against the 1997 total population and calculated as a proportion of that total.

Source: World Health Organization (WHO), *Report on the Global HIV/AIDS Epidemic,* June 1998, http://www.who.int/emc-hiv/global_report/data/globrep_e4.pdf

F4.1 Cumulative Number of Orphans, Compared with 1997 Population—Low-Income Countries per World Bank

Country	Orphans	1997 Population (thous.)	Orphans/Thousand in Population
Afghanistan	na	22,132	1.6
Angola	19,000	11,569	na
Armenia	na	3,642	na
Azerbaijan	na	7,655	0.0
Bangladesh	810	122,013	1.9
Benin	11,000	5,720	na
Bhutan	na	1,862	na
Bosnia and Herzegovina	na	3,784	18.0
Burkina Faso	200,000	11,087	25.0
Burundi	160,000	6,398	0.7
Cambodia	7,300	10,516	5.3
Cameroon	74,000	13,937	19.0
Central African Republic	65,000	3,416	8.2
Chad	55,000	6,702	0.0
China	720	1,243,738	na
Comoros	na	651	8.5
Congo, Dem. Rep. (Zaire)	410,000	48,040	23.3
Congo, Rep.	64,000	2,745	22.4
Cote d'Ivoire	320,000	14,300	3.8
Equatorial Guinea	1,600	420	na
Eritrea	na	3,409	14.0
Ethiopia	840,000	60,148	7.2
Gambia	8,400	1,169	7.1
Ghana	130,000	18,338	2.4
Guinea	18,000	7,614	0.9
Guinea-Bissau	990	1,112	0.8
Guyana	660	847	5.4
Haiti	40,000	7,395	1.0
Honduras	6,100	5,981	0.1
India	120,000	960,178	15.5
Kenya	440,000	28,414	na
Kyrgyzstan	na	4,481	0.0
Laos	150	5,194	4.5
Lesotho	9,500	2,131	8.5
Liberia	21,000	2,467	0.1
Madagascar	1,300	15,845	35.7
Malawi	360,000	10,086	2.9
Mali	33,000	11,480	0.6
Mauritania	1,400	2,392	na
Moldova	na	4,448	na
Mongolia	na	2,568	9.3
Mozambique	170,000	18,265	0.3
Myanmar (Burma)	14,000	46,765	0.0
Nepal	750	22,591	0.0
Nicaragua	120	4,351	2.0
Niger	20,000	9,788	3.5
Nigeria	410,000	118,369	0.0
Pakistan	5,000	143,831	20.4
Rwanda	120,000	5,883	na
Sao Tome and Principe	na	na	5.6
Senegal	49,000	8,762	10.6
Sierra Leone	47,000	4,428	na
Somalia	na	10,217	0.0
Sri Lanka	450	18,273	na
Sudan	na	27,899	na
Tajikistan	na	6,046	23.2

F4.1 Cumulative Number of Orphans, Compared with 1997 Population—Low-Income Countries per World Bank *(continued)*

Country	Orphans	1997 Population (thous.)	Orphans/Thousand in Population
Tanzania	730,000	31,507	25.5
Togo	110,000	4,317	81.8
Uganda	1,700,000	20,791	0.0
Vietnam	1,900	76,548	na
Yemen	na	16,294	55.4
Zambia	470,000	8,478	38.5
Zimbabwe	450,000	11,682	na

Note: The cumulative number of orphans is the estimated number of children below age 15 having lost their mother or both parents to AIDS from the start of the epidemic. This is measured against the 1997 total population and calculated as a proportion of that total.

Source: World Health Organization (WHO), *Report on the Global HIV/AIDS Epidemic,* June 1998, http://www.who.int/emc-hiv/global_report/data/globrep_e4.pdf

F4.2 Cumulative Number of Orphans, Compared with 1997 Population—Lower Middle-Income Countries per World Bank

Country	Orphans	1997 Population (thous.)	Orphans/Thousand in Population
Albania	na	3,422	na
Algeria	na	29,473	na
Belarus	na	10,339	1.5
Belize	340	224	0.0
Bolivia	150	7,774	18.4
Botswana	28,000	1,518	na
Bulgaria	na	8,427	na
Cape Verde	na	na	0.0
Colombia	1,500	37,068	0.3
Costa Rica	940	3,575	0.0
Cuba	160	11,068	6.2
Djibouti	3,900	634	na
Dominica	na	na	0.5
Dominican Republic	3,700	8,097	0.1
Ecuador	1,100	11,937	0.0
Egypt	750	64,465	0.4
El Salvador	2,200	5,928	na
Estonia	na	1,455	na
Fiji	<100	809	na
Georgia	na	5,434	na
Grenada	na	na	0.3
Guatemala	3,600	11,241	0.0
Indonesia	1,000	203,480	na
Iran	na	71,518	na
Iraq	na	21,177	0.1
Jamaica	180	2,515	na
Jordan	na	5,774	na
Kazakhstan	na	16,832	na
Kiribati	na	na	na
Latvia	na	2,474	na
Lebanon	na	3,144	na
Lithuania	na	3,719	na
Macedonia, FYRO	na	2,190	na
Maldives	na	273	na
Marshall Islands	na	na	na
Micronesia	na	na	na

F4.2 Cumulative Number of Orphans, Compared with 1997 Population—Lower Middle-Income Countries per World Bank *(continued)*

Country	Orphans	1997 Population (thous.)	Orphans/Thousand in Population
Morocco	na	27,518	4.8
Namibia	7,800	1,613	na
North Korea, Dem. Rep.	na	22,837	0.4
Panama	1,000	2,722	0.3
Papua New Guinea	1,300	4,500	0.1
Paraguay	340	5,088	0.0
Peru	990	24,367	0.0
Philippines	480	70,724	na
Romania	na	22,606	na
Russia	na	147,708	na
Samoa	na	na	na
Solomon Islands	na	na	na
St. Vincent and the Grenadines	na	na	0.9
Suriname	390	437	8.8
Swaziland	8,000	906	na
Syria	na	14,951	0.8
Thailand	48,000	59,159	na
Tonga	na	na	na
Tunisia	na	9,326	na
Turkey	na	62,774	na
Turkmenistan	na	4,235	na
Ukraine	na	51,424	na
Uzbekistan	na	23,656	na
Vanuatu	na	na	0.1
Venezuela	1,200	22,777	na
Yugoslavia	na	10,350	na

Note: The cumulative number of orphans is the estimated number of children below age 15 having lost their mother or both parents to AIDS from the start of the epidemic. This is measured against the 1997 total population and calculated as a proportion of that total.

Source: World Health Organization (WHO), *Report on the Global HIV/AIDS Epidemic,* June 1998, http://www.who.int/emc-hiv/global_report/data/globrep_e4.pdf

F4.3 Cumulative Number of Orphans, Compared with 1997 Population—Upper Middle-Income Countries per World Bank

Country	Orphans	1997 Population (thous.)	Orphans/Thousand in Population
Antigua and Barbuda	na	na	0.1
Argentina	2,400	35,671	na
Bahrain	na	582	1.8
Barbados	470	262	na
Brazil	na	163,132	0.0
Chile	530	14,625	na
Croatia	na	4,498	na
Czech Republic	na	10,237	4.2
Gabon	4,800	1,138	na
Hungary	na	9,990	na
Libya	na	5,784	0.1
Malaysia	1,500	21,018	na
Malta	na	371	na
Mauritius	na	1,141	0.2
Mexico	16,000	94,281	na
Oman	na	2,401	na
Palau	na	na	na
Poland	na	38,635	na
Saudi Arabia	na	19,494	na
Seychelles	na	na	na
Slovakia	na	5,355	na
Slovenia	na	1,922	4.6
South Africa	200,000	43,336	na
St. Kitts & Nevis	na	na	na
St. Lucia	na	na	0.6
Trinidad & Tobago	760	1,307	0.1
Uruguay	340	3,221	na

Note: The cumulative number of orphans is the estimated number of children below age 15 having lost their mother or both parents to AIDS from the start of the epidemic. This is measured against the 1997 total population and calculated as a proportion of that total.

Source: World Health Organization (WHO), *Report on the Global HIV/AIDS Epidemic,* June 1998, http://www.who.int/emc-hiv/global_report/data/globrep_e4.pdf

F5.1 Sex Distribution of Reported AIDS Cases—Low-Income Countries per World Bank

Country	Percent of Female Cases	Percent of Male Cases	Years Reported
Afghanistan	na	na	na
Angola	52	48	1985–96
Armenia	na	na	na
Azerbaijan	na	na	na
Bangladesh	na	na	na
Benin	36	64	1985–97
Bhutan	na	na	na
Bosnia and Herzegovina	na	na	na
Burkina Faso	43	57	1994–96
Burundi	na	na	na
Cambodia	na	na	na
Cameroon	50	50	95
Central African Republic	55	45	1987–97
Chad	na	na	na
China	6	94	1985–96
Comoros	na	na	na
Congo, Dem. Rep. (Zaire)	na	na	na
Congo, Rep.	na	na	na
Cote d'Ivoire	38	62	1985–95
Equatorial Guinea	58	42	1988–96
Eritrea	na	na	na
Ethiopia	39	61	1986–97
Gambia	38	62	1989–96
Ghana	33	67	1986–96
Guinea	na	na	na
Guinea-Bissau	46	54	1989–96
Guyana	41	59	1994–97
Haiti	na	na	na
Honduras	58	42	1994–97
India	na	na	na
Kenya	46	54	1986–96
Kyrgyzstan	na	na	na
Laos	40	60	1991–96
Lesotho	56	44	1986–96
Liberia	39	61	1995–97
Madagascar	na	na	na
Malawi	50	50	1995–97
Mali	na	na	na
Mauritania	na	na	na
Moldova	na	na	na
Mongolia	na	na	na
Mozambique	48	52	1986–96
Myanmar (Burma)	19	81	1995–97
Nepal	42	58	1995–96
Nicaragua	11	89	1994–97
Niger	na	na	na
Nigeria	na	na	na
Pakistan	13	87	1987–97
Rwanda	na	na	na
Sao Tome and Principe	na	na	na
Senegal	na	na	na
Sierra Leone	41	59	1987–96
Somalia	na	na	na
Sri Lanka	31	69	1986–97
Sudan	22	78	1995–97
Tajikistan	na	na	na
Tanzania	na	na	na

F5.1 Sex Distribution of Reported AIDS Cases—Low-Income Countries per World Bank *(continued)*

Country	Percent of Female Cases	Percent of Male Cases	Years Reported
Togo	43	57	1987–97
Uganda	na	na	na
Vietnam	12	88	1993–96
Yemen	40	60	1995–96
Zambia	52	48	1984–97
Zimbabwe	44	56	1987–97

Defintion: This indicator represents the percent of female and male AIDS cases, as a percentage of total reported cases, for countries with 25 cases or more. However, this set of data excludes cases for which sexual identity was unknown; therefore, it might not be an accurate representation of the total AIDS population of the country.

Source: World Health Organization (WHO), *Report on the Global HIV/AIDS Epidemic,* June 1998, http://www.who.int/emc-hiv/global_report/data/globrep_e4.pdf

F5.2 Sex Distribution of Reported AIDS Cases—Lower Middle-Income Countries per World Bank

Country	Percent of Female Cases	Percent of Male Cases	Years Reported
Albania	na	na	na
Algeria	25	75	1985–97
Belarus	na	na	na
Belize	32	68	1994–96
Bolivia	26	74	1994–97
Botswana	49	51	1988–97
Bulgaria	na	na	na
Cape Verde	na	na	na
Colombia	9	91	1994–97
Costa Rica	11	89	1994–97
Cuba	26	74	1994–97
Djibouti	52	48	1995–96
Dominica	na	na	na
Dominican Republic	35	65	1994–97
Ecuador	16	84	1994–97
Egypt	7	93	1995–97
El Salvador	26	74	1994–97
Estonia	na	na	na
Fiji	na	na	na
Georgia	na	na	na
Grenada	na	na	na
Guatemala	22	78	1994–96
Indonesia	22	78	1995–97
Iran	7	93	1995–96
Iraq	na	na	na
Jamaica	41	59	1994–97
Jordan	na	na	na
Kazakhstan	na	na	na
Kiribati	na	na	na
Latvia	na	na	na
Lebanon	na	na	na
Lithuania	na	na	na
Macedonia, FYRO	na	na	na
Maldives	na	na	na
Marshall Islands	na	na	na
Micronesia	na	na	na
Morocco	33	67	1995–96
Namibia	na	na	na

F5.2 Sex Distribution of Reported AIDS Cases—Lower Middle-Income Countries per World Bank *(continued)*

Country	Percent of Female Cases	Percent of Male Cases	Years Reported
North Korea, Dem. Rep.	na	na	na
Panama	24	76	1994–97
Papua New Guinea	50	50	1987–97
Paraguay	25	75	1994–97
Peru	20	80	1994–97
Philippines	35	65	1985–96
Romania	44	56	95
Russia	21	79	1995–97
Samoa	na	na	na
Solomon Islands	na	na	na
St. Vincent and the Grenadines	na	na	na
Suriname	36	64	1994–96
Swaziland	50	50	1991–97
Syria	na	na	na
Thailand	19	81	1985–97
Tonga	na	na	na
Tunisia	18	82	1995–96
Turkey	16	84	1995–97
Turkmenistan	na	na	na
Ukraine	26	74	1995–97
Uzbekistan	na	na	na
Vanuatu	na	na	na
Venezuela	11	89	1994–96
Yugoslavia	28	72	1995–97

Defintion: This indicator represents the percent of female and male AIDS cases, as a percentage of total reported cases, for countries with 25 cases or more. However, this set of data excludes cases for which sexual identity was unknown; therefore, it might not be an accurate representation of the total AIDS population of the country.

Source: World Health Organization (WHO), *Report on the Global HIV/AIDS Epidemic,* June 1998, http://www.who.int/emc-hiv/global_report/data/globrep_e4.pdf

F5.3 Sex Distribution of Reported AIDS Cases—Upper Middle-Income Countries per World Bank

Country	Percent of Female Cases	Percent of Male Cases	Years Reported
Antigua and Barbuda	100	na	na
Argentina	29	71	1994–97
Bahrain	na	na	na
Barbados	8	92	1994–96
Brazil	25	75	1994–97
Chile	10	90	1994–97
Croatia	23	77	1995–97
Czech Republic	5	95	1995–97
Gabon	na	na	na
Hungary	10	90	1994–97
Libya	na	na	na
Malaysia	6	94	1987–96
Malta	na	na	na
Mauritius	17	83	1987–97
Mexico	13	87	1994–97
Oman	na	na	na
Palau	na	na	na
Poland	18	82	1995–97
Saudi Arabia	42	58	1995–96
Seychelles	na	na	na
Slovakia	na	na	na
Slovenia	16	84	1995–97
South Africa	52	48	1982–96
St. Kitts & Nevis	na	na	na
St. Lucia	na	na	na
Trinidad & Tobago	34	66	1994–96
Uruguay	24	76	1994–97

Defintion: This indicator represents the percent of female and male AIDS cases, as a percentage of total reported cases, for countries with 25 cases or more. However, this set of data excludes cases for which sexual identity was unknown; therefore, it might not be an accurate representation of the total AIDS population of the country.

Source: World Health Organization (WHO), *Report on the Global HIV/AIDS Epidemic,* June 1998, http://www.who.int/emc-hiv/global_report/data/globrep_e4.pdf

F6.1 Year of First Reported AIDS Case—Low-Income Countries per World Bank

Country	Year	Country	Year
Afghanistan	na	Laos	na
Angola	1985	Lesotho	1986
Armenia	1992	Liberia	na
Azerbaijan	1987	Madagascar	1987
Bangladesh	1989	Malawi	1985
Benin	1985	Mali	na
Bhutan	na	Mauritania	na
Bosnia and Herzegovina	na	Moldova	1986
Burkina Faso	1986	Mongolia	na
Burundi	1983	Mozambique	1986
Cambodia	1991	Myanmar (Burma)	1988
Cameroon	1985	Nepal	1988
Central African Republic	1984	Nicaragua	na
Chad	na	Niger	1987
China	1985	Nigeria	1986
Comoros	1988	Pakistan	1987
Congo, Dem. Rep. (Zaire)	1985	Rwanda	1983
Congo, Rep.	1986	Sao Tome and Principe	na
Cote d'Ivoire	1985	Senegal	1986
Equatorial Guinea	1988	Sierra Leone	1987
Eritrea	na	Somalia	na
Ethiopia	1984	Sri Lanka	1986
Gambia	1986	Sudan	1986
Ghana	1986	Tajikistan	na
Guinea	na	Tanzania	1983
Guinea-Bissau	1989	Togo	1987
Guyana	na	Uganda	1983
Haiti	na	Vietnam	1990
Honduras	1985	Yemen	1989
India	1986	Zambia	1985
Kenya	1980	Zimbabwe	1985
Kyrgyzstan	1990		

Note: This indicator represents the year during which each country reported its first AIDS case.

Source: World Health Organization (WHO), *Report on the Global HIV/AIDS Epidemic,* June 1998, http://www.who.int/emc-hiv/global_report/data/globrep_e4.pdf

F6.2 Year of First Reported AIDS Case—Lower Middle-Income Countries per World Bank

Country	Year	Country	Year
Albania	1994	Lithuania	1988
Algeria	1985	Macedonia, FYRO	1989
Belarus	1991	Maldives	1991
Belize	1985	Marshall Islands	na
Bolivia	1985	Micronesia	na
Botswana	1985	Morocco	1986
Bulgaria	1987	Namibia	1986
Cape Verde	na	North Korea, Dem. Rep.	na
Colombia	1983	Panama	1984
Costa Rica	1983	Papua New Guinea	1987
Cuba	na	Paraguay	1986
Djibouti	1986	Peru	na
Dominica	na	Philippines	1985
Dominican Republic	1983	Romania	1985
Ecuador	na	Russia	1986
Egypt	1986	Samoa	na
El Salvador	1988	Solomon Islands	na
Estonia	1992	St. Vincent and the Grenadines	na
Fiji	1989	Suriname	na
Georgia	1988	Swaziland	1986
Grenada	na	Syria	1986
Guatemala	1984	Thailand	1985
Indonesia	1987	Tonga	na
Iran	1987	Tunisia	1985
Iraq	1991	Turkey	1985
Jamaica	1982	Turkmenistan	1985
Jordan	1986	Ukraine	1987
Kazakhstan	1989	Uzbekistan	1992
Kiribati	na	Vanuatu	na
Latvia	1987	Venezuela	1982
Lebanon	1984	Yugoslavia	1985

Note: This indicator represents the year during which each country reported its first AIDS case.

Source: World Health Organization (WHO), *Report on the Global HIV/AIDS Epidemic,* June 1998, http://www.who.int/emc-hiv/global_report/data/globrep_e4.pdf

F6.3 Year of First Reported AIDS Case—Upper Middle-Income Countries per World Bank

Country	Year	Country	Year
Antigua and Barbuda	na	Mexico	na
Argentina	1982	Oman	na
Bahrain	na	Palau	na
Barbados	1984	Poland	1986
Brazil	1980	Saudi Arabia	1986
Chile	1984	Seychelles	na
Croatia	1986	Slovakia	1985
Czech Republic	1985	Slovenia	1986
Gabon	1986	South Africa	na
Hungary	1985	St. Kitts & Nevis	na
Libya	1986	St. Lucia	na
Malaysia	1986	Trinidad & Tobago	1983
Malta	1984	Uruguay	1983
Mauritius	1987		

Note: This indicator represents the year during which each country reported its first AIDS case.

Source: World Health Organization (WHO), *Report on the Global HIV/AIDS Epidemic,* June 1998, http://www.who.int/emc-hiv/global_report/data/globrep_e4.pdf

G. Education

GENERAL OVERVIEW

The statistics presented in this section paint a picture of the status of education in the developing countries of the world. They present data on educational attainment, accessibility, and public resources devoted to education—information that is vital to understanding the ways in which education affects the quality of life in poorer countries of the world.

Education helps individuals in developing countries in a wide variety of ways, not the least of which is through expansion of individual economic opportunity. As the global economy brings the consumer markets of western, industrial countries to the doorsteps of the labor markets in developing countries, an education becomes vital to individuals in those labor pools seeking employment and economic advancement. In many cases, simple literacy skills are necessary for factory work, and as the service economy expands in developing countries, literacy becomes even more important. Educational attainment beyond primary schooling offers possible advancement in such environments and may offer the only escape from a long-term cycle of poverty and under-development.

Lack of education for women is clearly linked to the propagation of poverty. Educated and literate women, as the primary caregivers of children, can improve the quality of life for their children in many ways. For instance, they set an example for their children, can teach their children language skills and transmit other knowledge they themselves have gained, and are more equipped to handle the health care concerns that face them throughout their family's lives. In most developing countries, women underperform, compared with men, in basic literacy standards. This performance gap is due primarily to imbalances in accessibility to educational opportunities. As the link between women's education and poverty becomes clearer, public policy in developing countries has become more focused on correcting the male-female gap in educational accessibility and attainment.

EXPLANATION OF INDICATORS

Illiteracy: Illiteracy is one of the most important indicators of human development in poorer countries. Literacy—the ability to read and write simple sentences—provides a basic tool of formalized communication, one needed for virtually all social functions; without literacy, individuals cannot easily apply for jobs they cannot negotiate their way through bureaucratic systems, they cannot read instructions on drug labels, they cannot read signage on roadways. In nearly all countries of the west, literacy is at 100%; in developing countries, illiteracy rates are alarmingly high. As a benchmark of educational status of developing countries, illiteracy is at the forefront of policymakers' concerns related to poverty (G1.1–G1.9).

Duration of Primary Education: The duration of compulsory primary education is an indicator of public educational standards within a country. Lower requirements for compulsory education are often not a reflection of the importance a society places on education, but of the limitations faced by communities such as lack of buildings and classroom space and an undersupply of trained teachers (G2.1–G2.3).

Children Not Expected to Reach Grade Five: This indicator represents number of children who have entered the first level of primary school but will not make it to grade five. A variety of reasons exist for this underachievement. Sometimes the reasons are personal and private: household responsibilities and subsistence work might require young children to work at home or in the field; sometimes religious or cultural traditions limit the extent of schooling allowed girl children. Public factors are also to blame: for instance, limited classroom space and limited teaching personnel may force some students (perhaps those of less promise) out before five years are up (G3.1–G3.3).

Gross Enrollment Ratio: Gross enrollment ratios compare the number of students attending a specific level of schooling (no matter what their age) to the number of people in the population at the applicable age group. It measures the portion of the population that is receiving an education at the primary, secondary, and tertiary (college) levels. As such, it is used to analyze the development and accessibility of all levels of education in a country (G4.1–G4.6). The indicator is given for women and men in two separate tables.

Pupil to Teacher Ratio: This statistic represents the average number of students for every teacher at the primary level. It measures the availability of teachers against the size of the population, and therefore can be considered a reflection of the adequacy of teachers and teacher-training programs in a particular country (G5.1–G5.4).

Public Education Expenditure as Percent of Gross National Product (GNP): This indicator is a benchmark statistic representing a cornerstone of public policy towards education. The statistic measures the total spent on both public education and subsidies for private edu-

cation against the total GNP, allowing for a comparison of educational spending to total economic capacity and output. Higher values reflect a greater emphasis by a government on education (G6.1–G6.4).

Public Education Expenditure per Capita as Percent of Gross National Product (GNP) per Capita: This indicator compares public education expenditure per capita to GNP per capita, thereby comparing the average amount of public education spending attributed to an individual to the average amount of total economic output attributed to an individual. It brings the analysis of public budget for education in relation to the total population and to the total output of country. Unfortunately, the data are unavailable for many of the countries of this study; therefore international comparisons are difficult to make (G7.1–G7.10).

G1.1 Adult Illiteracy Rate, 1980–1995—Low-Income Countries per World Bank

Country	1980	1985	1990	1995
Afghanistan	na	75.9	70.6	68.5
Angola	na	64.3	58.3	na
Armenia	na	na	na	na
Azerbaijan	na	na	na	na
Bangladesh	na	67.8	64.7	61.9
Benin	na	81.3	76.6	63.0
Bhutan	na	67.8	61.6	57.8
Bosnia and Herzegovina	na	na	na	na
Burkina Faso	na	85.5	81.8	80.8
Burundi	73.2	57.9	50.0	64.7
Cambodia	na	71.2	64.8	na
Cameroon	na	52.0	45.9	36.6
Central African Republic	67.0	68.5	62.3	40.0
Chad	na	77.0	70.2	51.9
China	na	31.8	26.7	18.5
Comoros	52.1	na	na	42.7
Congo, Dem. Rep. (Zaire)	na	34.1	na	33.0
Congo, Rep.	na	48.3	43.4	25.1
Cote d'Ivoire	65.0	51.3	46.2	59.9
Equatorial Guinea	63.0	55.1	49.8	na
Eritrea	na	na	na	na
Ethiopia	na	na	na	64.5
Gambia	79.9	79.7	72.8	61.4
Ghana	na	47.2	39.7	35.5
Guinea	na	83.2	76.0	64.1
Guinea-Bissau	na	69.8	63.5	45.1
Guyana	na	4.6	3.6	1.9
Haiti	na	52.1	47.0	55.0
Honduras	na	32.0	26.9	27.3
India	na	55.9	51.8	48.0
Kenya	52.9	35.0	31.0	21.9
Kyrgyzstan	na	na	na	na
Laos	na	56.0	na	43.4
Lesotho	na	26.4	na	28.7
Liberia	74.6	67.7	60.5	61.7
Madagascar	na	23.1	19.8	na
Malawi	na	58.8	na	43.6
Mali	na	77.3	68.0	69.0
Mauritania	na	72.5	66.0	62.3
Moldova	na	na	na	na
Mongolia	na	na	na	na
Mozambique	72.8	72.4	67.1	59.9
Myanmar (Burma)	na	22.0	19.4	16.9
Nepal	na	77.6	74.4	72.5
Nicaragua	13.0	na	na	34.3
Niger	na	78.5	71.6	86.4
Nigeria	na	57.3	49.3	42.9
Pakistan	na	69.0	65.2	62.2
Rwanda	na	54.6	49.8	39.5
Sao Tome and Principe	na	na	na	na
Senegal	na	67.9	61.7	66.9
Sierra Leone	na	86.7	79.3	68.6
Somalia	na	83.1	75.9	na
Sri Lanka	na	13.3	11.6	9.8
Sudan	na	75.6	72.9	53.9
Tajikistan	na	na	na	na
Tanzania	na	na	na	32.2
Togo	82.0	62.1	56.7	48.3

G1.1   Adult Illiteracy Rate, 1980–1995—Low-Income Countries per World Bank *(continued)*

Country	1980	1985	1990	1995
Uganda	na	57.2	51.7	38.2
Vietnam	na	15.6	12.4	6.3
Yemen	na	67.7	61.5	na
Zambia	47.5	32.6	27.2	21.8
Zimbabwe	na	37.7	33.1	14.9

Defintion: Illiteracy measures the inability to both read and write simple sentences concerning everyday life with some degree of accuracy. The illiteracy rate represents the percentage of adults (15 years and over) who are illiterate.

Source: World Bank, *World Development Indicators 1998*, Table 1.2; World Bank, *World Development Indicators 1998*, CD-ROM, Series: Illiteracy rate, adult total (SE.ADT.ILIT.ZS)

G1.2   Adult Illiteracy Rate, 1980–1995—Lower Middle-Income Countries per World Bank

Country	1980	1985	1990	1995
Albania	na	na	na	na
Algeria	na	51.4	42.6	38.4
Belarus	na	na	na	na
Belize	na	na	na	na
Bolivia	na	27.5	22.5	16.9
Botswana	na	30.0	26.4	30.2
Bulgaria	na	na	na	na
Cape Verde	52.6	na	na	28.4
Colombia	na	15.3	13.3	8.7
Costa Rica	na	8.2	7.2	5.2
Cuba	na	7.6	6.0	4.3
Djibouti	na	na	na	53.8
Dominica	na	na	na	na
Dominican Republic	na	19.6	16.7	17.9
Ecuador	na	17.0	14.2	9.9
Egypt	na	55.4	51.6	48.6
El Salvador	32.7	31.2	27.0	28.5
Estonia	na	na	na	na
Fiji	na	14.5	na	8.4
Georgia	na	na	na	na
Grenada	na	na	na	na
Guatemala	na	48.1	44.9	44.4
Indonesia	32.7	28.2	23.0	16.2
Iran	na	52.3	46.0	27.9
Iraq	na	47.6	40.3	42.0
Jamaica	na	2.0	1.6	15.0
Jordan	na	25.8	19.9	13.4
Kazakhstan	na	na	na	na
Kiribati	na	na	10.0	na
Latvia	na	na	na	na
Lebanon	na	23.2	19.9	15.0
Lithuania	na	na	na	na
Macedonia, FYRO	na	na	na	na
Maldives	na	na	na	6.8
Marshall Islands	na	na	9.3	na
Micronesia	na	na	na	na
Morocco	na	58.3	50.5	56.3
Namibia	na	na	na	na
North Korea, Dem. Rep.	na	na	na	na
Panama	14.4	13.6	11.9	9.2
Papua New Guinea	na	53.3	48.0	27.8
Paraguay	na	11.7	9.9	7.9

G1.2 Adult Illiteracy Rate, 1980–1995—Lower Middle-Income Countries per World Bank *(continued)*

Country	1980	1985	1990	1995
Peru	na	18.0	14.9	11.3
Philippines	16.7	12.3	10.3	5.4
Romania	na	na	na	na
Russia	na	na	na	na
Samoa	na	na	30.0	na
Solomon Islands	na	na	na	na
St. Vincent and the Grenadines	na	na	na	na
Suriname	na	7.3	5.1	7.0
Swaziland	na	32.1	na	23.3
Syria	na	40.9	35.5	29.2
Thailand	12.0	9.3	7.0	6.2
Tonga	na	na	na	na
Tunisia	53.5	42.4	32.0	33.3
Turkey	34.4	24.0	19.3	17.7
Turkmenistan	na	na	na	na
Ukraine	na	na	na	na
Uzbekistan	na	na	na	na
Vanuatu	na	na	30.0	na
Venezuela	na	14.3	8.0	8.9
Yugoslavia	na	9.2	7.3	na

Defintion: Illiteracy measures the inability to both read and write simple sentences concerning everyday life with some degree of accuracy. The illiteracy rate represents the percentage of adults (15 years and over) who are illiterate.

Source: World Bank, *World Development Indicators 1998*, Table 1.2; World Bank, *World Development Indicators 1998*, CD-ROM, Series: Illiteracy rate, adult total (SE.ADT.ILIT.ZS)

G1.3 Adult Illiteracy Rate, 1980–1995—Upper Middle-Income Countries per World Bank

Country	1980	1985	1990	1995
Antigua and Barbuda	na	na	na	na
Argentina	6.1	5.2	4.7	3.8
Bahrain	na	27.1	22.6	14.8
Barbados	na	na	na	2.6
Brazil	25.5	21.5	18.9	16.7
Chile	na	7.8	6.6	4.8
Croatia	na	na	na	na
Czech Republic	na	na	na	na
Gabon	na	43.9	39.3	36.8
Hungary	1.1	na	na	na
Libya	na	43.5	36.2	23.8
Malaysia	na	26.0	21.6	16.5
Malta	na	15.9	na	na
Mauritius	na	17.2	na	17.1
Mexico	17.3	15.3	12.7	10.4
Oman	na	na	na	na
Palau	na	na	na	na
Poland	na	na	na	na
Saudi Arabia	na	42.1	37.6	37.2
Seychelles	na	na	na	21.0
Slovakia	na	na	na	na
Slovenia	na	na	na	na
South Africa	na	na	na	18.2
St. Kitts & Nevis	na	na	na	na
St. Lucia	na	na	na	na
Trinidad & Tobago	5.1	3.9	na	2.1
Uruguay	na	4.7	3.8	2.7

Defintion: Illiteracy measures the inability to both read and write simple sentences concerning everyday life with some degree of accuracy. The illiteracy rate represents the percentage of adults (15 years and over) who are illiterate.

Source: World Bank, *World Development Indicators 1998*, Table 1.2; World Bank, *World Development Indicators 1998*, CD-ROM, Series: Illiteracy rate, adult total (SE.ADT.ILIT.ZS)

G1.4 Adult Female Illiteracy Rate, 1985–1995—Low-Income Countries per World Bank

Country	1985	1990	1995
Afghanistan	90.7	86.1	85.0
Angola	77.4	71.5	na
Armenia	na	na	na
Azerbaijan	na	na	na
Bangladesh	81.0	78.0	73.9
Benin	88.3	84.4	74.2
Bhutan	81.1	75.4	71.9
Bosnia and Herzegovina	na	na	na
Burkina Faso	93.8	91.1	90.8
Burundi	68.2	60.2	77.5
Cambodia	83.4	77.6	na
Cameroon	64.4	57.4	47.9
Central African Republic	80.7	75.1	47.6
Chad	87.5	82.1	65.3
China	44.7	38.2	27.3
Comoros	na	na	49.6
Congo, Dem. Rep. (Zaire)	46.8	na	32.3
Congo, Rep.	61.8	56.1	32.8
Cote d'Ivoire	65.7	59.8	70.0
Equatorial Guinea	68.8	63.0	31.9
Eritrea	na	na	na
Ethiopia	na	na	74.7
Gambia	89.5	84.0	75.1
Ghana	57.8	49.0	46.5
Guinea	91.6	86.6	78.1
Guinea-Bissau	81.9	76.0	57.5
Guyana	5.9	4.6	2.5
Haiti	58.1	52.6	57.8
Honduras	35.0	29.4	27.3
India	70.9	66.3	62.3
Kenya	46.8	41.5	30.0
Kyrgyzstan	na	na	na
Laos	24.2	na	55.6
Lesotho	15.5	na	37.7
Liberia	78.6	71.2	77.6
Madagascar	31.6	27.1	na
Malawi	69.2	na	58.2
Mali	84.6	76.1	76.9
Mauritania	84.2	78.6	73.7
Moldova	na	na	na
Mongolia	na	na	na
Mozambique	83.6	78.7	76.7
Myanmar (Burma)	31.4	27.7	22.3
Nepal	89.3	86.8	86.0
Nicaragua	na	na	33.4
Niger	88.7	83.2	93.4
Nigeria	68.9	60.5	52.7
Pakistan	82.3	78.9	75.6
Rwanda	67.9	62.9	48.4
Sao Tome and Principe	na	na	na
Senegal	80.7	74.9	76.8
Sierra Leone	93.8	88.7	81.8
Somalia	91.2	86.0	na
Sri Lanka	19.1	16.5	12.8
Sudan	90.3	88.3	65.4
Tajikistan	na	na	na
Tanzania	na	na	43.2
Togo	74.9	69.3	63.0

G1.4 Adult Female Illiteracy Rate, 1985–1995—Low-Income Countries per World Bank *(continued)*

Country	1985	1990	1995
Uganda	71.0	65.1	49.8
Vietnam	20.3	16.4	8.8
Yemen	79.5	73.7	na
Zambia	41.3	34.7	28.7
Zimbabwe	45.0	39.7	20.1

Defintion: The adult female illiteracy rate is the proportion of female adults aged 15 and above who are unable to both read and write simple sentences concerning everyday life with some degree of accuracy.

Source: World Bank, *World Development Indicators 1998*, CD-ROM, Series: Illiteracy rate, adult female (SE.ADT.ILIT.FE.ZS)

G1.5 Adult Female Illiteracy Rate, 1985–1995—Lower Middle-Income Countries per World Bank

Country	1985	1990	1995
Albania	na	na	na
Algeria	64.9	54.5	51.0
Belarus	na	na	na
Belize	na	na	na
Bolivia	35.5	29.3	24.0
Botswana	39.6	34.9	40.1
Bulgaria	na	na	na
Cape Verde	na	na	36.2
Colombia	16.3	14.1	8.6
Costa Rica	8.0	6.9	5.0
Cuba	8.9	7.0	4.7
Djibouti	na	na	67.3
Dominica	na	na	na
Dominican Republic	21.5	18.2	17.8
Ecuador	19.5	16.2	11.8
Egypt	70.5	66.2	61.2
El Salvador	34.7	30.0	30.2
Estonia	na	na	na
Fiji	19.1	na	10.7
Georgia	na	na	na
Grenada	na	na	na
Guatemala	56.2	52.9	51.4
Indonesia	36.5	32.0	22.0
Iran	63.7	56.7	34.2
Iraq	59.3	50.7	55.0
Jamaica	1.8	1.4	10.9
Jordan	38.0	29.7	20.6
Kazakhstan	na	na	na
Kiribati	na	na	na
Latvia	na	na	na
Lebanon	31.2	26.9	20.0
Lithuania	na	na	na
Macedonia, FYRO	na	na	na
Maldives	na	na	7.0
Marshall Islands	na	na	na
Micronesia	na	na	na
Morocco	70.5	62.0	69.0
Namibia	na	na	na
North Korea, Dem. Rep.	na	na	3.3
Panama	13.8	11.8	9.8
Papua New Guinea	68.0	62.2	37.3

G1.5 Adult Female Illiteracy Rate, 1985–1995—Lower Middle-Income Countries per World Bank (continued)

Country	1985	1990	1995
Paraguay	14.2	11.9	9.4
Peru	25.5	21.3	17.0
Philippines	12.7	10.5	5.7
Romania	na	na	na
Russia	na	na	na
Samoa	na	na	na
Solomon Islands	na	na	na
St. Vincent and the Grenadines	na	na	na
Suriname	7.6	5.3	9.0
Swaziland	34.3	na	24.4
Syria	56.5	49.2	44.2
Thailand	13.3	10.1	8.4
Tonga	na	na	na
Tunisia	52.7	43.7	45.4
Turkey	35.7	28.9	27.6
Turkmenistan	na	na	na
Ukraine	na	na	na
Uzbekistan	na	na	na
Vanuatu	na	na	na
Venezuela	11.7	16.8	9.7
Yugoslavia	14.6	11.9	na

Defintion: The adult female illiteracy rate is the proportion of female adults aged 15 and above who are unable to both read and write simple sentences concerning everyday life with some degree of accuracy.

Source: World Bank, *World Development Indicators 1998*, CD-ROM, Series: Illiteracy rate, adult female (SE.ADT.ILIT.FE.ZS)

G1.6 Adult Female Illiteracy Rate, 1985–1995—Upper Middle-Income Countries per World Bank

Country	1985	1990	1995
Antigua and Barbuda	na	na	na
Argentina	5.6	4.9	3.8
Bahrain	36.7	30.7	20.6
Barbados	na	na	3.2
Brazil	23.3	20.2	16.8
Chile	8.1	6.8	5.0
Croatia	na	na	na
Czech Republic	na	na	na
Gabon	56.9	51.5	46.7
Hungary	na	na	na
Libya	59.7	49.6	37.0
Malaysia	35.0	29.6	21.9
Malta	17.7	na	na
Mauritius	22.9	na	21.2
Mexico	18.0	14.9	12.6
Oman	na	na	na
Palau	na	na	na
Poland	na	na	na
Saudi Arabia	57.5	51.9	49.8
Seychelles	na	na	na
Slovakia	na	na	na
Slovenia	na	na	na
South Africa	na	na	18.3
St. Kitts & Nevis	na	na	na
St. Lucia	na	na	na
Trinidad & Tobago	5.2	na	3.0
Uruguay	4.9	4.1	2.3

Defintion: The adult female illiteracy rate is the proportion of female adults aged 15 and above who are unable to both read and write simple sentences concerning everyday life with some degree of accuracy.

Source: World Bank, *World Development Indicators 1998*, CD-ROM, Series: Illiteracy rate, adult female (SE.ADT.ILIT.FE.ZS)

G1.7 Adult Male Illiteracy Rate, 1985–1995—Low-Income Countries per World Bank

Country	1985	1990	1995
Afghanistan	62.0	55.9	52.8
Angola	50.4	44.4	na
Armenia	na	na	na
Azerbaijan	na	na	na
Bangladesh	55.5	52.9	50.6
Benin	74.0	68.3	51.3
Bhutan	55.2	48.7	43.8
Bosnia and Herzegovina	na	na	na
Burkina Faso	77.0	72.1	70.5
Burundi	46.6	39.1	50.7
Cambodia	58.7	51.8	na
Cameroon	38.9	33.7	25.0
Central African Republic	55.0	48.2	31.5
Chad	66.0	57.8	37.9
China	19.6	15.9	10.1
Comoros	na	na	35.8
Congo, Dem. Rep. (Zaire)	20.6	na	13.4
Congo, Rep.	34.0	30.0	16.9
Cote d'Ivoire	37.5	33.1	50.1
Equatorial Guinea	40.6	35.9	10.4
Eritrea	na	na	na
Ethiopia	na	na	54.5
Gambia	69.6	61.0	47.2
Ghana	36.3	30.0	24.1
Guinea	74.5	65.1	50.1
Guinea-Bissau	56.6	49.8	32.0
Guyana	3.3	2.5	1.4
Haiti	45.7	40.9	52.0
Honduras	29.0	24.5	27.4
India	41.8	38.2	34.5
Kenya	22.9	20.2	13.7
Kyrgyzstan	na	na	na
Laos	8.0	na	30.6
Lesotho	37.6	na	18.9
Liberia	57.3	50.2	46.1
Madagascar	14.2	12.3	na
Malawi	47.8	na	28.1
Mali	69.0	59.2	60.6
Mauritania	60.2	52.9	50.4
Moldova	na	na	na
Mongolia	na	na	na
Mozambique	60.6	54.9	42.3
Myanmar (Burma)	12.3	10.9	11.3
Nepal	66.2	62.4	59.1
Nicaragua	na	na	35.4
Niger	67.9	59.6	79.1
Nigeria	45.2	37.7	32.7
Pakistan	56.9	52.7	50.0
Rwanda	40.7	36.1	30.2
Sao Tome and Principe	na	na	na
Senegal	54.6	48.1	57.0
Sierra Leone	79.2	69.3	54.6
Somalia	73.3	63.9	na
Sri Lanka	7.6	6.6	6.6
Sudan	60.7	57.3	42.3
Tajikistan	na	na	na
Tanzania	na	na	20.6
Togo	48.6	43.6	33.0

G1.7 Adult Male Illiteracy Rate, 1985–1995—Low-Income Countries per World Bank *(continued)*

Country	1985	1990	1995
Uganda	42.9	37.8	26.3
Vietnam	10.4	8.0	3.5
Yemen	52.9	46.7	na
Zambia	23.3	19.2	14.4
Zimbabwe	30.2	26.3	9.6

Defintion: The adult male illiteracy rate is the proportion of male adults aged 15 and above who are unable to both read and write simple sentences concerning everyday life with some degree of accuracy.

Source: World Bank, *World Development Indicators 1998*, CD-ROM, Series: Illiteracy rate, adult male (SE.ADT.ILIT.MA.ZS)

G1.8 Adult Male Illiteracy Rate, 1985–1995—Lower Middle-Income Countries per World Bank

Country	1985	1990	1995
Albania	na	na	na
Algeria	37.3	30.2	26.1
Belarus	na	na	na
Belize	na	na	na
Bolivia	19.1	15.3	9.5
Botswana	18.5	16.3	19.5
Bulgaria	na	na	na
Cape Verde	na	na	18.6
Colombia	14.2	12.5	8.8
Costa Rica	8.4	7.4	5.3
Cuba	6.3	5.0	3.8
Djibouti	na	na	39.7
Dominica	na	na	na
Dominican Republic	17.8	15.2	18.0
Ecuador	14.5	12.2	8.0
Egypt	40.4	37.1	36.4
El Salvador	27.4	23.8	26.5
Estonia	na	na	na
Fiji	9.8	na	6.2
Georgia	na	na	na
Grenada	na	na	na
Guatemala	40.0	36.9	37.5
Indonesia	19.6	15.9	10.4
Iran	40.9	35.5	21.6
Iraq	36.2	30.2	29.3
Jamaica	2.2	1.8	19.2
Jordan	14.3	10.7	6.6
Kazakhstan	na	na	na
Kiribati	na	na	na
Latvia	na	na	na
Lebanon	14.1	12.2	10.0
Lithuania	na	na	na
Macedonia, FYRO	na	na	na
Maldives	na	na	6.7
Marshall Islands	na	na	na
Micronesia	na	na	na
Morocco	45.7	38.7	43.4
Namibia	na	na	na
North Korea, Dem. Rep.	na	na	0.7
Panama	13.5	11.9	8.6
Papua New Guinea	39.8	35.1	19.0
Paraguay	9.1	7.9	6.5
Peru	10.5	8.5	5.5
Philippines	11.8	10.0	5.0

G1.8 Adult Male Illiteracy Rate, 1985–1995—Lower Middle-Income Countries per World Bank *(continued)*

Country	1985	1990	1995
Romania	na	na	na
Russia	na	na	na
Samoa	na	na	na
Solomon Islands	na	na	na
St. Vincent and the Grenadines	na	na	na
Suriname	6.9	4.9	4.9
Swaziland	29.7	na	22.0
Syria	25.8	21.7	14.3
Thailand	5.3	3.9	4.0
Tonga	na	na	na
Tunisia	32.2	25.8	21.4
Turkey	12.4	10.3	8.3
Turkmenistan	na	na	na
Ukraine	na	na	na
Uzbekistan	na	na	na
Vanuatu	na	na	na
Venezuela	16.2	13.3	8.2
Yugoslavia	3.5	2.6	na

Defintion: The adult male illiteracy rate is the proportion of male adults aged 15 and above who are unable to both read and write simple sentences concerning everyday life with some degree of accuracy.

Source: World Bank, *World Development Indicators 1998*, CD-ROM, Series: Illiteracy rate, adult male (SE.ADT.ILIT.MA.ZS)

G1.9 Adult Male Illiteracy Rate, 1985–1995—Upper Middle-Income Countries per World Bank

Country	1985	1990	1995
Antigua and Barbuda	na	na	na
Argentina	4.9	4.5	3.8
Bahrain	21.5	17.9	10.9
Barbados	na	na	2.0
Brazil	19.7	17.5	16.7
Chile	7.4	6.5	4.6
Croatia	na	na	na
Czech Republic	na	na	na
Gabon	30.1	26.5	26.3
Hungary	na	na	na
Libya	29.9	24.6	12.1
Malaysia	16.8	13.5	10.9
Malta	14.0	na	na
Mauritius	11.3	na	12.9
Mexico	12.5	10.5	8.2
Oman	na	na	na
Palau	na	na	na
Poland	na	na	na
Saudi Arabia	30.6	26.9	28.5
Seychelles	na	na	na
Slovakia	na	na	na
Slovenia	na	na	na
South Africa	na	na	18.1
St. Kitts & Nevis	na	na	na
St. Lucia	na	na	na
Trinidad & Tobago	2.7	na	1.2
Uruguay	4.4	3.4	3.1

Defintion: The adult male illiteracy rate is the proportion of male adults aged 15 and above who are unable to both read and write simple sentences concerning everyday life with some degree of accuracy.

Source: World Bank, *World Development Indicators 1998*, CD-ROM, Series: Illiteracy rate, adult male (SE.ADT.ILIT.MA.ZS)

G2.1 Duration of Primary Education, 1995—Low-Income Countries per World Bank

Country	Percent	Country	Percent
Afghanistan	na	Laos	5
Angola	4	Lesotho	7
Armenia	4	Liberia	na
Azerbaijan	4	Madagascar	5
Bangladesh	5	Malawi	8
Benin	6	Mali	6
Bhutan	na	Mauritania	6
Bosnia and Herzegovina	na	Moldova	4
Burkina Faso	6	Mongolia	3
Burundi	6	Mozambique	5
Cambodia	5	Myanmar (Burma)	5
Cameroon	6	Nepal	5
Central African Republic	6	Nicaragua	6
Chad	6	Niger	6
China	5	Nigeria	6
Comoros	na	Pakistan	5
Congo, Dem. Rep. (Zaire)	6	Rwanda	7
Congo, Rep.	6	Sao Tome and Principe	na
Cote d'Ivoire	6	Senegal	6
Equatorial Guinea	na	Sierra Leone	7
Eritrea	5	Somalia	na
Ethiopia	6	Sri Lanka	5
Gambia	6	Sudan	8
Ghana	6	Tajikistan	4
Guinea	6	Tanzania	7
Guinea-Bissau	6	Togo	6
Guyana	na	Uganda	7
Haiti	6	Vietnam	5
Honduras	6	Yemen	9
India	5	Zambia	7
Kenya	8	Zimbabwe	7
Kyrgyzstan	4		

Defintion: Duration of primary education reflects the minimum number of grades (years) that a country's government requires for a child's primary schooling.

Source: World Bank, *World Development Indicators 1998*, Table 2.9, Education policy and infrastructure

G2.2 Duration of Primary Education, 1995—Lower Middle-Income Countries per World Bank

Country	Percent	Country	Percent
Albania	8	Lithuania	4
Algeria	6	Macedonia, FYRO	8
Belarus	4	Maldives	na
Belize	na	Marshall Islands	na
Bolivia	8	Micronesia	na
Botswana	7	Morocco	6
Bulgaria	4	Namibia	7
Cape Verde	na	North Korea, Dem. Rep.	4
Colombia	5	Panama	6
Costa Rica	6	Papua New Guinea	6
Cuba	6	Paraguay	6
Djibouti	na	Peru	6
Dominica	na	Philippines	6
Dominican Republic	8	Romania	4
Ecuador	6	Russia	3
Egypt	5	Samoa	na
El Salvador	9	Solomon Islands	na
Estonia	5	St. Vincent and the Grenadines	na
Fiji	na	Suriname	na
Georgia	4	Swaziland	na
Grenada	na	Syria	6
Guatemala	6	Thailand	6
Indonesia	6	Tonga	na
Iran	5	Tunisia	6
Iraq	6	Turkey	5
Jamaica	6	Turkmenistan	4
Jordan	10	Ukraine	4
Kazakhstan	4	Uzbekistan	4
Kiribati	na	Vanuatu	na
Latvia	4	Venezuela	9
Lebanon	6	Yugoslavia	4

Defintion: Duration of primary education reflects the minimum number of grades (years) that a country's government requires for a child's primary schooling.

Source: World Bank, *World Development Indicators 1998*, Table 2.9, Education policy and infrastructure

G2.3 Duration of Primary Education, 1995—Upper Middle-Income Countries per World Bank

Country	Percent	Country	Percent
Antigua and Barbuda	na	Mexico	6
Argentina	7	Oman	6
Bahrain	na	Palau	na
Barbados	na	Poland	8
Brazil	8	Saudi Arabia	6
Chile	8	Seychelles	na
Croatia	4	Slovakia	4
Czech Republic	4	Slovenia	4
Gabon	6	South Africa	7
Hungary	8	St. Kitts & Nevis	na
Libya	9	St. Lucia	na
Malaysia	6	Trinidad & Tobago	7
Malta	na	Uruguay	6
Mauritius	6		

Defintion: Duration of primary education reflects the minimum number of grades (years) that a country's government requires for a child's primary schooling.

Source: World Bank, *World Development Indicators 1998*, Table 2.9, Education policy and infrastructure

G3.1 Percentage of Children Not Reaching Grade Five, 1990–1995—Low-Income Countries per World Bank

Country	Percent	Country	Percent
Afghanistan	na	Kyrgyzstan	na
Angola	66.0	Laos	47.0
Armenia	na	Lesotho	40.0
Azerbaijan	7.0	Liberia	na
Bangladesh	53.0	Madagascar	72.0
Benin	23.5	Malawi	63.0
Bhutan	18.0	Mali	15.0
Bosnia and Herzegovina	na	Mauritania	28.0
Burkina Faso	39.0	Moldova	na
Burundi	26.0	Mongolia	na
Cambodia	50.0	Mozambique	65.0
Cameroon	34.0	Myanmar (Burma)	na
Central African Republic	35.0	Nepal	48.0
Chad	54.0	Nicaragua	51.0
China	12.0	Niger	18.0
Comoros	na	Nigeria	na
Congo, Dem. Rep. (Zaire)	47.0	Pakistan	52.0
Congo, Rep.	36.0	Rwanda	40.0
Cote d'Ivoire	27.0	Sao Tome and Principe	na
Equatorial Guinea	na	Senegal	12.0
Eritrea	21.0	Sierra Leone	na
Ethiopia	42.0	Somalia	na
Gambia	13.0	Sri Lanka	8.0
Ghana	20.0	Sudan	6.0
Guinea	20.0	Tajikistan	na
Guinea-Bissau	80.0	Tanzania	17.0
Guyana	na	Togo	50.0
Haiti	53.0	Uganda	45.0
Honduras	na	Vietnam	na
India	38.0	Yemen	na
Kenya	23.0	Zambia	na
		Zimbabwe	24.0

Defintion: This indicator shows the proportion of children, in percent format, starting primary school, but who will not reach grade 5 (in some cases, grade 4 if primary school is only four years). Data reflect estimates calculated over a set of 2-year periods, to compensate for students repeating grade levels.

Source: United Nations Development Programme, *Human Development Report 1997*, Table A2.1, Profile of Human Poverty

G3.2 Percentage of Children Not Reaching Grade Five, 1990–1995—Lower Middle-Income Countries per World Bank

Country	Percent	Country	Percent
Albania	8	Lithuania	6
Algeria	8	Macedonia, FYRO	5
Belarus	1	Maldives	7
Belize	32	Marshall Islands	na
Bolivia	40	Micronesia	na
Botswana	30.2	Morocco	20
Bulgaria	7	Namibia	18
Cape Verde	na	North Korea, Dem. Rep.	na
Colombia	41	Panama	18
Costa Rica	12	Papua New Guinea	29
Cuba	5	Paraguay	29
Djibouti	6	Peru	na
Dominica	7	Philippines	33
Dominican Republic	42	Romania	7
Ecuador	33	Russia	3
Egypt	2	Samoa	na
El Salvador	42	Solomon Islands	19
Estonia	0	St. Vincent and the Grenadines	na
Fiji	13	Suriname	na
Georgia	na	Swaziland	22
Grenada	na	Syria	8
Guatemala	na	Thailand	12
Indonesia	8	Tonga	na
Iran	10	Tunisia	8
Iraq	28	Turkey	11
Jamaica	4	Turkmenistan	na
Jordan	2	Ukraine	3
Kazakhstan	na	Uzbekistan	0
Kiribati	na	Vanuatu	na
Latvia	5	Venezuela	22
Lebanon	na	Yugoslavia	

Defintion: This indicator shows the proportion of children, in percent format, starting primary school, but who will not reach grade 5 (in some cases, grade 4 if primary school is only four years). Data reflect estimates calculated over a set of 2-year periods, to compensate for students repeating grade levels.

Source: United Nations Development Programme, *Human Development Report 1997*, Table A2.1, Profile of Human Poverty

G3.3 Percentage of Children Not Reaching Grade Five, 1990–1995—Upper Middle-Income Countries per World Bank

Country	Percent	Country	Percent
Antigua and Barbuda	na	Mexico	16
Argentina	na	Oman	4
Bahrain	1	Palau	na
Barbados	na	Poland	0
Brazil	30	Saudi Arabia	6
Chile	5	Seychelles	1
Croatia	2	Slovakia	3
Czech Republic	2	Slovenia	0
Gabon	50	South Africa	24
Hungary	2	St. Kitts & Nevis	na
Libya	na	St. Lucia	5
Malaysia	2	Trinidad & Tobago	5
Malta	0	Uruguay	6
Mauritius	0		

Defintion: This indicator shows the proportion of children, in percent format, starting primary school, but who will not reach grade 5 (in some cases, grade 4 if primary school is only four years). Data reflect estimates calculated over a set of 2-year periods, to compensate for students repeating grade levels.

Source: United Nations Development Programme, *Human Development Report 1997*, Table A2.1, Profile of Human Poverty

G4.1 Gross Female Enrollment Ratio, 1995, Combined Primary, Secondary, and Tertiary—Low-Income Countries per World Bank

Country	Percent	Country	Percent
Afghanistan	na	Laos	41.7
Angola	27.5	Lesotho	61.0
Armenia	83.0	Liberia	na
Azerbaijan	71.0	Madagascar	na
Bangladesh	30.9	Malawi	71.4
Benin	26.3	Mali	13.9
Bhutan	31.0	Mauritania	33.4
Bosnia and Herzegovina	na	Moldova	68.0
Burkina Faso	14.9	Mongolia	59.3
Burundi	20.1	Mozambique	20.5
Cambodia	54.0	Myanmar (Burma)	47.5
Cameroon	41.0	Nepal	42.6
Central African Republic	20.7	Nicaragua	65.7
Chad	16.7	Niger	10.7
China	61.5	Nigeria	43.7
Comoros	35.6	Pakistan	27.0
Congo, Dem. Rep. (Zaire)	na	Rwanda	na
Congo, Rep.	na	Sao Tome and Principe	na
Cote d'Ivoire	30.1	Senegal	27.9
Equatorial Guinea	64.0	Sierra Leone	23.7
Eritrea	25.1	Somalia	na
Ethiopia	15.1	Sri Lanka	67.9
Gambia	34.0	Sudan	28.8
Ghana	38.1	Tajikistan	67.0
Guinea	16.2	Tanzania	32.1
Guinea-Bissau	29.0	Togo	45.4
Guyana	65.8	Uganda	34.2
Haiti	28.0	Vietnam	55.8
Honduras	61.3	Yemen	26.9
India	46.5	Zambia	48.5
Kenya	50.9	Zimbabwe	65.3
Kyrgyzstan	74.0		

Definition: The gross enrollment ratio reflects the number of students attending school at a particular level of education, regardless of whether they belong to the applicable age group for that level of schooling. It is stated as a percentage of the population in the applicable age group for that educational level. It represents the total of all female students enrolled in primary, secondary, and tertiary (college and university) levels of education.

Source: United Nations Development Programme, *Human Development Report 1997*, Table 2, Gender-related development index

G4.2 Gross Female Enrollment Ratio, 1995, Combined Primary, Secondary, and Tertiary—Lower Middle-Income Countries per World Bank

Country	Percent	Country	Percent
Albania	60.0	Lithuania	72.0
Algeria	62.0	Macedonia, FYRO	61.0
Belarus	81.0	Maldives	71.0
Belize	na	Marshall Islands	na
Bolivia	63.5	Micronesia	na
Botswana	71.6	Morocco	40.6
Bulgaria	69.0	Namibia	84.9
Cape Verde	64.0	North Korea, Dem. Rep.	na
Colombia	70.7	Panama	73.1
Costa Rica	68.3	Papua New Guinea	33.9
Cuba	67.3	Paraguay	63.0
Djibouti	na	Peru	76.1
Dominica	na	Philippines	81.8
Dominican Republic	74.0	Romania	62.0
Ecuador	68.9	Russia	82.0
Egypt	63.4	Samoa	na
El Salvador	58.1	Solomon Islands	47.0
Estonia	74.0	St. Vincent and the Grenadines	na
Fiji	77.8	Suriname	71.0
Georgia	69.0	Swaziland	75.4
Grenada	na	Syria	57.8
Guatemala	41.7	Thailand	55.5
Indonesia	59.1	Tonga	na
Iran	62.6	Tunisia	66.4
Iraq	45.4	Turkey	53.7
Jamaica	68.9	Turkmenistan	90.0
Jordan	66.0	Ukraine	78.0
Kazakhstan	75.0	Uzbekistan	71.0
Kiribati	na	Vanuatu	na
Latvia	69.0	Venezuela	68.4
Lebanon	75.1	Yugoslavia	na

Definition: The gross enrollment ratio reflects the number of students attending school at a particular level of education, regardless of whether they belong to the applicable age group for that level of schooling. It is stated as a percentage of the population in the applicable age group for that educational level. It represents the total of all female students enrolled in primary, secondary, and tertiary (college and university) levels of education.

Source: United Nations Development Programme, *Human Development Report 1997*, Table 2, Gender-related development index

G4.3 Gross Female Enrollment Ratio, 1995, Combined Primary, Secondary, and Tertiary—Upper Middle-Income Countries per World Bank

Country	Percent	Country	Percent
Antigua and Barbuda	na	Mexico	72.1
Argentina	80.6	Oman	58.1
Bahrain	85.9	Palau	na
Barbados	79.1	Poland	80.0
Brazil	71.8	Saudi Arabia	54.4
Chile	72.1	Seychelles	na
Croatia	68.0	Slovakia	73.0
Czech Republic	70.0	Slovenia	76.0
Gabon	60.0	South Africa	82.9
Hungary	68.0	St. Kitts & Nevis	na
Libya	89.0	St. Lucia	na
Malaysia	62.0	Trinidad & Tobago	70.3
Malta	75.0	Uruguay	79.6
Mauritius	61.1		

Definition: The gross enrollment ratio reflects the number of students attending school at a particular level of education, regardless of whether they belong to the applicable age group for that level of schooling. It is stated as a percentage of the population in the applicable age group for that educational level. It represents the total of all female students enrolled in primary, secondary, and tertiary (college and university) levels of education.

Source: United Nations Development Programme, *Human Development Report 1997*, Table 2, Gender-related development index

G4.4 Gross Male Enrollment Ratio, 1995, Combined Primary, Secondary, and Tertiary—Low-Income Countries per World Bank

Country	Percent	Country	Percent
Afghanistan	na	Kyrgyzstan	71.0
Angola	31.8	Laos	57.5
Armenia	74.0	Lesotho	51.3
Azerbaijan	74.0	Liberia	na
Bangladesh	39.6	Madagascar	na
Benin	48.1	Malawi	79.7
Bhutan	31.0	Mali	22.3
Bosnia and Herzegovina	na	Mauritania	41.4
Burkina Faso	23.5	Moldova	66.0
Burundi	25.1	Mongolia	43.8
Cambodia	69.5	Mozambique	29.0
Cameroon	48.3	Myanmar (Burma)	46.4
Central African Republic	34.0	Nepal	66.6
Chad	37.2	Nicaragua	59.7
China	64.1	Niger	18.6
Comoros	41.8	Nigeria	53.9
Congo, Dem. Rep. (Zaire)	na	Pakistan	53.1
Congo, Rep.	na	Rwanda	na
Cote d'Ivoire	43.6	Sao Tome and Principe	na
Equatorial Guinea	64.0	Senegal	36.5
Eritrea	31.8	Sierra Leone	35.7
Ethiopia	24.1	Somalia	na
Gambia	42.6	Sri Lanka	64.7
Ghana	48.6	Sudan	33.1
Guinea	32.4	Tajikistan	70.0
Guinea-Bissau	29.0	Tanzania	33.4
Guyana	58.8	Togo	72.8
Haiti	29.6	Uganda	41.9
Honduras	56.2	Vietnam	57.7
India	60.1	Yemen	67.7
Kenya	51.8	Zambia	55.0
		Zimbabwe	69.7

Definition: The gross enrollment ratio reflects the number of students attending school at a particular level of education, regardless of whether they belong to the applicable age group for that level of schooling. It is stated as a percentage of the population in the applicable age group for that educational level. It represents the total of all male students enrolled in primary, secondary, and tertiary (college and university) levels of education.

Source: United Nations Development Programme, *Human Development Report 1997*, Table 2, Gender-related development index

G4.5 Gross Male Enrollment Ratio, 1995, Combined Primary, Secondary, and Tertiary—Lower Middle-Income Countries per World Bank

Country	Percent	Country	Percent
Albania	59.0	Lithuania	68.0
Algeria	66.7	Macedonia, FYRO	60.0
Belarus	79.0	Maldives	71.0
Belize	na	Marshall Islands	na
Bolivia	65.8	Micronesia	na
Botswana	69.0	Morocco	50.7
Bulgaria	64.0	Namibia	78.7
Cape Verde	64.0	North Korea, Dem. Rep.	na
Colombia	62.7	Panama	63.4
Costa Rica	59.0	Papua New Guinea	39.4
Cuba	62.1	Paraguay	61.1
Djibouti	na	Peru	72.0
Dominica	na	Philippines	70.9
Dominican Republic	63.6	Romania	62.0
Ecuador	64.3	Russia	75.0
Egypt	68.9	Samoa	na
El Salvador	52.5	Solomon Islands	47.0
Estonia	69.0	St. Vincent and the Grenadines	na
Fiji	74.9	Suriname	71.0
Georgia	68.0	Swaziland	77.7
Grenada	na	Syria	61.2
Guatemala	46.5	Thailand	49.4
Indonesia	61.3	Tonga	na
Iran	67.0	Tunisia	67.6
Iraq	55.1	Turkey	59.9
Jamaica	63.4	Turkmenistan	90.0
Jordan	66.0	Ukraine	75.0
Kazakhstan	71.0	Uzbekistan	75.0
Kiribati	na	Vanuatu	na
Latvia	66.0	Venezuela	58.0
Lebanon	66.1	Yugoslavia	

Definition: The gross enrollment ratio reflects the number of students attending school at a particular level of education, regardless of whether they belong to the applicable age group for that level of schooling. It is stated as a percentage of the population in the applicable age group for that educational level. It represents the total of all male students enrolled in primary, secondary, and tertiary (college and university) levels of education.

Source: United Nations Development Programme, *Human Development Report 1997*, Table 2, Gender-related development index

G4.6 Gross Male Enrollment Ratio, 1995, Combined Primary, Secondary, and Tertiary—Upper Middle-Income Countries per World Bank

Country	Percent	Country	Percent
Antigua and Barbuda	na	Mexico	66.1
Argentina	68.7	Oman	60.1
Bahrain	78.1	Palau	na
Barbados	73.7	Poland	79.0
Brazil	69.1	Saudi Arabia	55.1
Chile	64.7	Seychelles	na
Croatia	67.0	Slovakia	71.0
Czech Republic	69.0	Slovenia	72.0
Gabon	60.0	South Africa	75.4
Hungary	66.0	St. Kitts & Nevis	na
Libya	85.5	St. Lucia	na
Malaysia	60.0	Trinidad & Tobago	59.2
Malta	79.0	Uruguay	65.1
Mauritius	58.2		

Definition: The gross enrollment ratio reflects the number of students attending school at a particular level of education, regardless of whether they belong to the applicable age group for that level of schooling. It is stated as a percentage of the population in the applicable age group for that educational level. It represents the total of all male students enrolled in primary, secondary, and tertiary (college and university) levels of education.

Source: United Nations Development Programme, *Human Development Report 1997*, Table 2, Gender-related development index

G5.1 Pupil to Teacher Ratio, Primary Level, 1980–1995—Low-Income Countries per World Bank

Country	1980	1985	1990	1995
Afghanistan	31.6	37.3	41.2	na
Angola	na	31.3	31.9	na
Armenia	na	na	na	na
Azerbaijan	na	na	na	na
Bangladesh	53.6	47.0	63.0	na
Benin	47.5	33.0	36.2	na
Bhutan	na	na	na	na
Bosnia and Herzegovina	na	na	na	na
Burkina Faso	54.5	57.8	56.7	na
Burundi	36.6	56.2	66.9	na
Cambodia	43.8	37.5	32.6	45.0
Cameroon	51.5	50.8	51.1	46.3
Central African Republic	59.6	65.6	90.4	na
Chad	na	70.6	65.8	62.1
China	26.6	24.9	21.9	na
Comoros	46.2	34.8	36.5	na
Congo, Dem. Rep. (Zaire)	na	na	40.0	na
Congo, Rep.	54.4	61.4	66.5	na
Cote d'Ivoire	38.7	36.3	36.3	na
Equatorial Guinea	68.8	na	na	na
Eritrea	na	na	37.7	40.2
Ethiopia	63.9	48.1	36.1	na
Gambia	24.0	23.2	31.3	na
Ghana	28.8	23.2	29.1	na
Guinea	35.9	36.3	39.9	na
Guinea-Bissau	22.9	na	na	na
Guyana	33.5	29.4	na	na
Haiti	44.1	37.6	21.2	na
Honduras	36.7	na	na	na
India	54.9	57.9	60.6	na
Kenya	38.3	34.0	31.3	na

G5.1 Pupil to Teacher Ratio, Primary Level, 1980–1995—Low-Income Countries per World Bank *(continued)*

Country	1980	1985	1990	1995
Kyrgyzstan	27.8	19.1	16.0	16.6
Laos	29.8	24.9	28.2	na
Lesotho	48.0	55.4	54.5	na
Liberia	16.2	na	na	na
Madagascar	43.7	38.3	40.3	na
Malawi	64.6	61.0	61.1	62.5
Mali	42.4	34.0	41.8	65.6
Mauritania	41.5	50.6	44.7	51.8
Moldova	28.8	26.1	23.2	24.2
Mongolia	na	30.2	28.1	23.7
Mozambique	81.5	61.5	54.5	57.6
Myanmar (Burma)	51.6	51.1	36.5	na
Nepal	38.4	35.3	39.2	na
Nicaragua	35.5	33.3	33.3	na
Niger	41.5	37.4	41.7	na
Nigeria	37.2	44.1	39.0	na
Pakistan	36.5	39.3	42.2	na
Rwanda	59.2	56.2	57.4	na
Sao Tome and Principe	27.9	na	35.5	na
Senegal	45.7	46.5	52.9	na
Sierra Leone	33.1	38.9	33.9	na
Somalia	33.5	19.0	na	na
Sri Lanka	na	15.5	29.1	na
Sudan	33.7	34.7	34.0	na
Tajikistan	na	na	21.3	22.9
Tanzania	41.5	34.2	34.9	na
Togo	55.1	46.1	58.3	na
Uganda	33.6	34.5	29.4	na
Vietnam	38.6	34.5	35.1	34.9
Yemen	na	na	na	na
Zambia	48.6	49.4	44.0	na
Zimbabwe	43.9	39.5	35.8	na

Definition: The primary school pupil to teacher ratio is calculated by taking the number of pupils enrolled in primary school and dividing that figure by the number of primary school teachers (regardless of their teaching assignment). The ratio includes both public and private schools.

Source: World Bank, *World Development Indicators 1998*, Table 2.9; World Bank, *World Development Indicators 1998*, CD-ROM, Series: Pupil-teacher ratio, primary (SE.PRM.ENRL.TC.ZS)

G5.2 Pupil to Teacher Ratio, Primary Level, 1980–1995—Lower Middle-Income Countries per World Bank

Country	1980	1985	1990	1995
Albania	21.3	20.0	19.1	17.8
Algeria	35.2	27.8	27.7	27.3
Belarus	8.3	8.3	5.6	5.1
Belize	24.4	25.2	na	25.9
Bolivia	20.0	na	24.7	na
Botswana	32.3	32.0	31.7	na
Bulgaria	19.3	17.7	15.4	14.2
Cape Verde	40.1	38.8	34.4	na
Colombia	30.6	30.4	29.9	na
Costa Rica	27.7	31.5	31.9	na
Cuba	17.5	14.0	12.5	13.6
Djibouti	40.2	49.1	42.7	37.6
Dominica	na	15.3	29.2	19.7

G5.2 Pupil to Teacher Ratio, Primary Level, 1980–1995—Lower Middle-Income Countries per World Bank *(continued)*

Country	1980	1985	1990	1995
Dominican Republic	na	43.6	47.2	34.7
Ecuador	36.2	32.4	30.2	na
Egypt	na	31.9	24.9	25.1
El Salvador	48.0	na	na	na
Estonia	na	na	na	na
Fiji	28.3	29.0	33.6	na
Georgia	na	na	na	16.2
Grenada	23.3	na	na	na
Guatemala	33.8	36.6	na	na
Indonesia	32.4	25.3	23.2	na
Iran	na	21.9	31.4	31.9
Iraq	27.8	23.8	24.8	na
Jamaica	41.4	35.2	36.6	na
Jordan	31.8	31.3	25.1	na
Kazakhstan	na	25.7	21.3	na
Kiribati	30.4	29.2	28.6	na
Latvia	na	na	na	13.2
Lebanon	17.9	na	na	na
Lithuania	25.3	25.3	18.1	17.2
Macedonia, FYRO	22.5	21.1	20.6	19.8
Maldives	na	na	na	na
Marshall Islands	na	na	na	na
Micronesia	na	na	na	na
Morocco	38.2	27.8	27.1	28.3
Namibia	na	na	na	na
North Korea, Dem. Rep.	na	na	na	na
Panama	27.3	25.5	23.0	na
Papua New Guinea	31.4	na	31.7	38.5
Paraguay	27.4	25.1	24.7	na
Peru	37.5	34.8	29.1	na
Philippines	30.4	30.9	32.9	33.6
Romania	20.6	20.6	21.9	21.6
Russia	27.9	26.5	22.3	na
Samoa	23.0	na	na	na
Solomon Islands	25.1	25.9	19.4	na
St. Vincent and the Grenadines	na	19.4	19.7	na
Suriname	26.6	23.2	22.4	na
Swaziland	34.2	33.9	32.7	na
Syria	28.1	25.9	25.1	23.4
Thailand	24.7	19.3	22.1	na
Tonga	24.3	22.9	24.0	na
Tunisia	38.5	31.6	27.8	25.2
Turkey	26.6	31.2	30.4	na
Turkmenistan	na	na	na	na
Ukraine	45.2	42.4	33.4	na
Uzbekistan	24.1	24.1	24.1	20.6
Vanuatu	23.6	na	na	na
Venezuela	34.1	32.7	22.9	na
Yugoslavia				

Definition: The primary school pupil to teacher ratio is calculated by taking the number of pupils enrolled in primary school and dividing that figure by the number of primary school teachers (regardless of their teaching assignment). The ratio includes both public and private schools.

Source: World Bank, *World Development Indicators 1998*, Table 2.9; World Bank, *World Development Indicators 1998*, CD-ROM, Series: Pupil-teacher ratio, primary (SE.PRM.ENRL.TC.ZS).

G5.3 Pupil to Teacher Ratio, Primary Level, 1980–1995—Upper Middle-Income Countries per World Bank

Country	1980	1985	1990	1995
Antigua and Barbuda	na	na	na	na
Argentina	na	20.0	na	na
Bahrain	18.8	20.1	21.5	20.5
Barbados	26.6	20.9	17.8	na
Brazil	25.6	23.8	23.0	na
Chile	na	na	na	na
Croatia	na	19.2	18.6	17.5
Czech Republic	na	27.6	23.4	20.4
Gabon	45.1	45.8	na	na
Hungary	15.4	14.7	12.5	11.0
Libya	18.1	16.0	13.7	na
Malaysia	27.3	24.1	20.4	na
Malta	21.2	21.8	20.7	na
Mauritius	20.2	21.8	21.1	na
Mexico	39.1	33.6	30.5	28.7
Oman	23.2	26.6	27.5	26.1
Palau	na	na	na	na
Poland	21.3	17.9	16.3	16.0
Saudi Arabia	18.3	16.1	15.7	na
Seychelles	22.0	22.0	na	na
Slovakia	na	na	na	22.0
Slovenia	na	na	na	15.1
South Africa	27.2	na	na	na
St. Kitts & Nevis	na	22.1	22.2	na
St. Lucia	30.9	30.3	29.3	na
Trinidad & Tobago	23.9	22.1	26.0	na
Uruguay	22.4	25.1	21.9	na

Definition: The primary school pupil to teacher ratio is calculated by taking the number of pupils enrolled in primary school and dividing that figure by the number of primary school teachers (regardless of their teaching assignment). The ratio includes both public and private schools.

Source: World Bank, *World Development Indicators 1998*, Table 2.9; World Bank, *World Development Indicators 1998*, CD-ROM, Series: Pupil-teacher ratio, primary (SE.PRM.ENRL.TC.ZS)

G5.4 Pupil to Teacher Ratio, 1995, Worldwide Summary—Primary Level

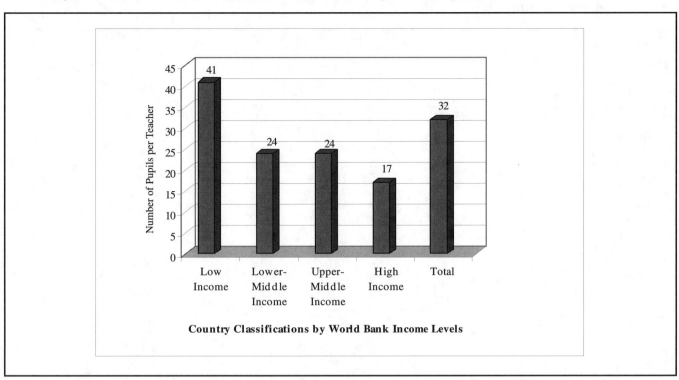

Source: World Bank, *World Development Indicators 1998*, Table 2.9; World Bank, *World Development Indicators 1998,* CD-ROM, Series: Pupil-teacher ratio, primary (SE.PRM.ENR2.TC.25)

G6.1 Public Expenditure on Education as Percent of GNP, 1980–1990—Low-Income Countries per World Bank

Country	1980	1985	1990
Afghanistan	2.0	na	na
Angola	na	na	na
Armenia	na	na	7.4
Azerbaijan	na	na	7.7
Bangladesh	1.5	1.9	2.0
Benin	na	na	na
Bhutan	na	na	na
Bosnia and Herzegovina	na	na	na
Burkina Faso	2.6	2.3	na
Burundi	na	2.5	3.4
Cambodia	na	na	na
Cameroon	3.2	3.0	3.4
Central African Republic	na	na	2.8
Chad	na	na	na
China	2.5	2.6	2.3
Comoros	na	na	na
Congo, Dem.Rep. (Zaire)	2.6	1.0	na
Congo, Rep.	7.0	na	5.7
Cote d'Ivoire	7.2	na	na
Equatorial Guinea	na	na	na
Eritrea	na	na	na
Ethiopia	na	na	na
Gambia	3.3	3.2	3.8
Ghana	3.1	2.6	3.1
Guinea	na	na	na
Guinea-Bissau	na	na	na

G6.1 Public Expenditure on Education as Percent of GNP, 1980–1990—Low-Income Countries per World Bank (continued)

Country	1980	1985	1990
Guyana	na	9.8	5.0
Haiti	1.5	1.2	1.4
Honduras	3.2	4.2	na
India	2.8	3.4	3.9
Kenya	6.8	6.4	6.7
Kyrgyzstan	7.2	7.9	8.5
Laos	na	na	na
Lesotho	5.1	4.3	3.7
Liberia	5.7	na	na
Madagascar	4.4	2.9	1.5
Malawi	3.4	3.5	3.3
Mali	3.8	3.7	na
Mauritania	na	na	na
Moldova	na	na	7.1
Mongolia	na	7.8	8.6
Mozambique	4.4	4.2	6.3
Myanmar (Burma)	1.7	2.0	na
Nepal	1.8	2.6	2.0
Nicaragua	3.4	6.8	na
Niger	3.1	na	na
Nigeria	na	1.2	0.9
Pakistan	2.0	2.5	2.6
Rwanda	2.7	na	na
Sao Tome and Principe	na	na	na
Senegal	na	na	na
Sierra Leone	3.8	2.4	na
Somalia	1.0	0.5	na
Sri Lanka	2.7	2.6	2.7
Sudan	4.8	na	na
Tajikistan	8.2	8.6	10.7
Tanzania	4.4	3.6	5.0
Togo	5.6	5.0	5.6
Uganda	1.2	na	1.5
Vietnam	na	na	na
Yemen	na	na	na
Zambia	4.5	4.7	2.6
Zimbabwe	6.6	na	10.5

Definition: Public expenditure on education is the percentage of a country's gross national product (GNP) attributed to public spending on public education in addition to subsidies given to private education. The figure applies to primary, secondary, and tertiary educational levels.

Source: World Bank, *World Development Indicators 1998*, Table 2.9; World Bank, *World Development Indicators 1998*, CD-ROM, Series: Public spending on education, total (SE.XPD.TOTL.GN.ZS)

G6.2 Public Expenditure on Education as Percent of GNP, 1980–1990—Lower Middle-Income Countries per World Bank

Country	1980	1985	1990
Albania	na	na	5.8
Algeria	7.8	8.5	5.7
Belarus	5.2	4.8	5.0
Belize	na	na	na
Bolivia	4.4	2.1	2.7
Botswana	na	6.8	7.6
Bulgaria	4.5	5.5	5.6
Cape Verde	na	3.6	na
Colombia	1.9	2.9	2.8
Costa Rica	7.8	4.5	4.6
Cuba	7.2	6.3	6.6
Djibouti	na	2.7	3.4
Dominica	na	na	na
Dominican Republic	2.2	1.8	na
Ecuador	5.6	3.7	na
Egypt	na	6.3	4.9
El Salvador	3.9	na	1.8
Estonia	na	na	na
Fiji	na	na	4.7
Georgia	na	na	na
Grenada	na	na	na
Guatemala	na	na	1.4
Indonesia	1.7	na	1.1
Iran	7.5	3.6	4.1
Iraq	3.0	4.0	na
Jamaica	7.0	5.8	5.4
Jordan	na	5.5	4.2
Kazakhstan	na	6.5	6.5
Kiribati	na	6.7	6.0
Latvia	3.3	3.4	3.8
Lebanon	na	na	na
Lithuania	5.5	5.3	4.8
Macedonia, FYRO	na	na	na
Maldives	na	na	6.3
Marshall Islands	na	na	na
Micronesia	na	na	na
Morocco	6.1	6.3	5.5
Namibia	na	na	7.9
North Korea, Dem. Rep.	na	na	na
Panama	4.8	4.8	5.2
Papua New Guinea	na	na	na
Paraguay	1.5	1.5	1.2
Peru	3.1	2.9	na
Philippines	1.7	1.4	2.9
Romania	3.3	2.2	2.8
Russia	3.5	3.2	3.5
Samoa	na	na	4.2
Solomon Islands	5.6	na	na
St. Vincent and the Grenadines	na	na	6.7
Suriname	6.7	9.4	8.1
Swaziland	6.1	5.9	na
Syria	4.6	6.1	4.2
Thailand	3.4	3.8	3.6
Tonga	na	4.4	na
Tunisia	5.4	5.9	6.2
Turkey	2.8	2.3	2.2
Turkmenistan	na	7.6	8.6

G6.2 Public Expenditure on Education as Percent of GNP, 1980–1990—Lower Middle-Income Countries per World Bank (continued)

Country	1980	1985	1990
Ukraine	5.6	5.2	5.2
Uzbekistan	6.4	7.5	9.5
Vanuatu	na	na	na
Venezuela	4.4	5.1	3.1
Yugoslavia			

Definition: Public expenditure on education is the percentage of a country's gross national product (GNP) attributed to public spending on public education in addition to subsidies given to private education. The figure applies to primary, secondary, and tertiary educational levels.

Source: World Bank, *World Development Indicators 1998*, Table 2.9; World Bank, *World Development Indicators 1998*, CD-ROM, Series: Public spending on education, total (SE.XPD.TOTL.GN.ZS)

G6.3 Public Expenditure on Education as Percent of GNP, 1980–1990—Upper Middle-Income Countries per World Bank

Country	1980	1985	1990
Antigua and Barbuda	3.0	na	na
Argentina	2.7	1.5	1.1
Bahrain	2.9	4.0	5.0
Barbados	6.5	na	7.9
Brazil	3.6	3.8	na
Chile	4.6	4.4	2.7
Croatia	na	na	na
Czech Republic	na	na	na
Gabon	2.7	4.5	na
Hungary	4.7	5.5	6.1
Libya	3.4	7.1	na
Malaysia	6.0	6.6	5.4
Malta	3.0	3.4	4.0
Mauritius	5.3	3.8	3.7
Mexico	4.7	3.9	4.0
Oman	2.1	4.0	3.5
Palau	na	na	na
Poland	na	4.9	na
Saudi Arabia	4.1	6.7	6.0
Seychelles	5.8	10.7	8.1
Slovakia	na	na	na
Slovenia	na	na	na
South Africa	na	na	6.5
St. Kitts & Nevis	5.2	5.8	2.7
St. Lucia	na	na	na
Trinidad & Tobago	4.0	6.1	4.0
Uruguay	2.3	2.8	3.1

Definition: Public expenditure on education is the percentage of a country's gross national product (GNP) attributed to public spending on public education in addition to subsidies given to private education. The figure applies to primary, secondary, and tertiary educational levels.

Source: World Bank, *World Development Indicators 1998*, Table 2.9; World Bank, *World Development Indicators 1998*, CD-ROM, Series: Public spending on education, total (SE.XPD.TOTL.GN.ZS)

G7.4 Public Expenditure on Education per Capita, Percent of GNP per Capita, 1980 and 1994—Secondary Level, Low-Income Countries per World Bank

Country	1980	1994	Country	1980	1994
Afghanistan	na	na	Kyrgyzstan	na	na
Angola	na	na	Laos	na	25.0
Armenia	na	na	Lesotho	na	51.0
Azerbaijan	na	na	Liberia	na	na
Bangladesh	na	23.0	Madagascar	35.6	na
Benin	na	22.0	Malawi	na	145.0
Bhutan	na	na	Mali	na	35.0
Bosnia and Herzegovina	na	na	Mauritania	na	59.0
Burkina Faso	na	na	Moldova	na	na
Burundi	na	69.0	Mongolia	na	34.0
Cambodia	na	na	Mozambique	na	na
Cameroon	na	na	Myanmar (Burma)	na	10.0
Central African Republic	na	na	Nepal	na	11.9
Chad	na	33.0	Nicaragua	na	na
China	na	14.0	Niger	na	na
Comoros	na	na	Nigeria	na	na
Congo, Dem. Rep. (Zaire)	na	na	Pakistan	na	na
Congo, Rep.	na	na	Rwanda	na	na
Cote d'Ivoire	113.0	na	Sao Tome and Principe	na	na
Equatorial Guinea	na	na	Senegal	na	na
Eritrea	na	na	Sierra Leone	na	na
Ethiopia	na	62.0	Somalia	na	na
Gambia	na	28.0	Sri Lanka	na	na
Ghana	na	na	Sudan	na	na
Guinea	na	38.0	Tajikistan	na	na
Guinea-Bissau	na	na	Tanzania	na	na
Guyana	na	na	Togo	na	42.0
Haiti	na	na	Uganda	na	na
Honduras	na	22.0	Vietnam	na	na
India	na	13.0	Yemen	na	na
Kenya	na	47.0	Zambia	na	9.0
			Zimbabwe	na	39.0

Definition: Public expenditure on education per capita is the percentage of a country's gross national product per capita (GNP/capita) attributed to public spending on public education in addition to subsidies given to private education. This indicator applies to secondary educational levels.

Source: World Bank, *World Development Indicators 1998*, Table 2.9; Series: Public spending on education, total (SE.XPD.TOTL.GN.ZS)

G7.5 Public Expenditure on Education per Capita, Percent of GNP per Capita, 1980 and 1994—Secondary Level, Lower Middle-Income Countries per World Bank

Country	1980	1994	Country	1980	1994
Albania	na	23	Lithuania	na	na
Algeria	na	na	Macedonia, FYRO	na	na
Belarus	na	na	Maldives	na	na
Belize	na	na	Marshall Islands	na	na
Bolivia	na	18	Micronesia	na	na
Botswana	na	na	Morocco	na	51
Bulgaria	na	na	Namibia	na	44
Cape Verde	na	na	North Korea, Dem.Rep.	na	na
Colombia	na	11	Panama	na	13
Costa Rica	na	19	Papua New Guinea	na	na
Cuba	na	na	Paraguay	na	11
Djibouti	na	na	Peru	na	na
Dominica	na	na	Philippines	na	na
Dominican Republic	na	5	Romania	na	7
Ecuador	na	15	Russia	na	na
Egypt	na	na	Samoa	na	na
El Salvador	na	5	Solomon Islands	na	na
Estonia	na	na	St. Vincent and the Grenadines	na	na
Fiji	na	na	Suriname	na	na
Georgia	na	na	Swaziland	na	na
Grenada	na	na	Syria	na	17
Guatemala	na	5	Thailand	na	11
Indonesia	na	na	Tonga	na	na
Iran	na	12	Tunisia	na	23
Iraq	na	na	Turkey	na	9
Jamaica	na	25	Turkmenistan	na	na
Jordan	na	na	Ukraine	na	na
Kazakhstan	na	na	Uzbekistan	na	na
Kiribati	na	na	Vanuatu	na	na
Latvia	na	na	Venezuela	na	na
Lebanon	na	na	Yugoslavia	na	na

Definition: Public expenditure on education per capita is the percentage of a country's gross national product per capita (GNP/capita) attributed to public spending on public education in addition to subsidies given to private education. This indicator applies to secondary educational levels.

Source: World Bank, *World Development Indicators 1998*, Table 2.9; World Bank, *World Development Indicators 1998*, CD-ROM, Series: Public spending on education, total (SE.XPD.TOTL.GN.ZS)

G7.6 Public Expenditure on Education per Capita, Percent of GNP per Capita, 1980 and 1994—Secondary Level, Upper Middle-Income Countries per World Bank

Country	1980	1994	Country	1980	1994
Antigua and Barbuda	na	na	Mauritius	na	na
Argentina	na	12	Mexico	na	20
Bahrain	na	na	Oman	na	23
Barbados	na	na	Palau	na	na
Brazil	11	na	Poland	na	19
Chile	na	9	Saudi Arabia	na	na
Croatia	na	na	Seychelles	na	na
Czech Republic	na	25	Slovakia	na	4
Gabon	na	na	Slovenia	na	24
Hungary	na	28	South Africa	na	na
Libya	na	na	St. Kitts & Nevis	na	na
Malaysia	na	22	St. Lucia	na	na
Malta	na	na	Trinidad & Tobago	na	17
			Uruguay	na	8

Definition: Public expenditure on education per capita is the percentage of a country's gross national product per capita (GNP/capita) attributed to public spending on public education in addition to subsidies given to private education. This indicator applies to secondary educational levels.

Source: World Bank, *World Development Indicators 1998*, Table 2.9; World Bank, *World Development Indicators 1998*, CD-ROM, Series: Public spending on education, total (SE.XPD.TOTL.GN.ZS)

G7.7 Public Expenditure on Education per Capita, Percent of GNP per Capita, 1980 and 1994—Tertiary Level, Low-Income Countries per World Bank

Country	1980	1994	Country	1980	1994
Afghanistan	na	na	Kyrgyzstan	na	49
Angola	na	na	Laos	na	55
Armenia	na	19	Lesotho	642.3	399
Azerbaijan	na	13	Liberia	na	na
Bangladesh	46.8	30	Madagascar	na	na
Benin	na	240	Malawi	1,136.70	979
Bhutan	na	na	Mali	na	522
Bosnia and Herzegovina	na	na	Mauritania	na	157
Burkina Faso	3,371.10	na	Moldova	na	na
Burundi	na	941	Mongolia	na	74
Cambodia	na	na	Mozambique	na	na
Cameroon	362.8	na	Myanmar (Burma)	na	21
Central African Republic	na	na	Nepal	271.9	156
Chad	na	234	Nicaragua	85.9	na
China	na	81	Niger	1,492.60	na
Comoros	na	na	Nigeria	344.6	na
Congo, Dem.Rep. (Zaire)	748.9	na	Pakistan	235.6	na
Congo, Rep.	na	224	Rwanda	na	na
Cote d'Ivoire	na	na	Sao Tome and Principe	na	na
Equatorial Guinea	na	na	Senegal	na	na
Eritrea	na	na	Sierra Leone	na	na
Ethiopia	na	592	Somalia	na	na
Gambia	na	235	Sri Lanka	62.2	64
Ghana	na	na	Sudan	440.6	na
Guinea	na	498	Tajikistan	29.7	39
Guinea-Bissau	na	na	Tanzania	2,195.3	na
Guyana	na	na	Togo	891.5	521
Haiti	65.3	na	Uganda	na	na
Honduras	72.1	59	Vietnam	na	na
India	na	78	Yemen	na	na
Kenya	808.2	540	Zambia	762.3	160
			Zimbabwe	259.8	234

Definition: Public expenditure on education per capita is the percentage of a country's gross national product per capita (GNP/capita) attributed to public spending on public education in addition to subsidies given to private education. This indicator applies to tertiary (college and university) educational levels.

Source: World Bank, *World Development Indicators 1998*, Table 2.9; World Bank, *World Development Indicators 1998*, CD-ROM, Series: Public spending on education, total (SE.XPD.TOTL.GN.ZS)

G7.8 Public Expenditure on Education per Capita, Percent of GNP per Capita, 1980 and 1994—Tertiary Level, Lower Middle-Income Countries per World Bank

Country	1980	1994	Country	1980	1994
Albania	na	36	Lithuania	na	51
Algeria	na	na	Macedonia, FYRO	na	na
Belarus	32.8	20	Maldives	na	na
Belize	na	na	Marshall Islands	na	na
Bolivia	na	67	Micronesia	na	na
Botswana	665.5	na	Morocco	na	74
Bulgaria	na	21	Namibia	na	86
Cape Verde	na	na	North Korea, Dem.Rep.	na	na
Colombia	41.1	29	Panama	29.1	47
Costa Rica	76.1	44	Papua New Guinea	na	na
Cuba	28.5	na	Paraguay	na	52
Djibouti	na	na	Peru	5.1	na
Dominica	na	na	Philippines	na	na
Dominican Republic	na	5	Romania	na	40
Ecuador	22.3	34	Russia	na	na
Egypt	na	108	Samoa	na	na
El Salvador	103.5	8	Solomon Islands	na	na
Estonia	na	40	St. Vincent and the Grenadines	na	na
Fiji	na	na	Suriname	na	na
Georgia	na	28	Swaziland	na	na
Grenada	na	na	Syria	na	na
Guatemala	na	33	Thailand	na	25
Indonesia	na	na	Tonga	na	na
Iran	na	62	Tunisia	193.9	89
Iraq	na	na	Turkey	107.7	51
Jamaica	166.6	193	Turkmenistan	na	na
Jordan	na	111	Ukraine	38.5	20
Kazakhstan	na	20	Uzbekistan	na	28
Kiribati	na	na	Vanuatu	na	na
Latvia	na	45	Venezuela	56.8	na
Lebanon	na	na	Yugoslavia	na	na

Definition: Public expenditure on education per capita is the percentage of a country's gross national product per capita (GNP/capita) attributed to public spending on public education in addition to subsidies given to private education. This indicator applies to tertiary (college and university) educational levels.

Source: World Bank, *World Development Indicators 1998*, Table 2.9; World Bank, *World Development Indicators 1998*, CD-ROM, Series: Public spending on education, total (SE.XPD.TOTL.GN.ZS)

G7.9 Public Expenditure on Education per Capita, Percent of GNP per Capita, 1980 and 1994—Tertiary Level, Upper Middle-Income Countries per World Bank

Country	1980	1994	Country	1980	1994
Antigua and Barbuda	na	na	Mexico	na	61.0
Argentina	10.4	17.0	Oman	na	na
Bahrain	na	na	Palau	na	na
Barbados	na	na	Poland	na	42.0
Brazil	0.1	na	Saudi Arabia	na	63.0
Chile	na	21.0	Seychelles	na	na
Croatia	na	na	Slovakia	na	39.0
Czech Republic	na	41.0	Slovenia	na	38.0
Gabon	na	na	South Africa	na	59.0
Hungary	75.3	73.0	St. Kitts & Nevis	na	na
Libya	na	na	St. Lucia	na	na
Malaysia	148.6	77.0	Trinidad & Tobago	55.1	77.0
Malta	na	na	Uruguay	na	28.4
Mauritius	163.0	na			

Definition: Public expenditure on education per capita is the percentage of a country's gross national product per capita (GNP/capita) attributed to public spending on public education in addition to subsidies given to private education. This indicator applies to tertiary (college and university) educational levels.

Source: World Bank, *World Development Indicators 1998*, Table 2.9; World Bank, *World Development Indicators 1998*, CD-ROM, Series: Public spending on education, total (SE.XPD.TOTL.GN.ZS)

G7.10 Public Expenditure on Education per Capita, Percent of GNP per Capita, 1994—World-wide Summary, All Levels of Education

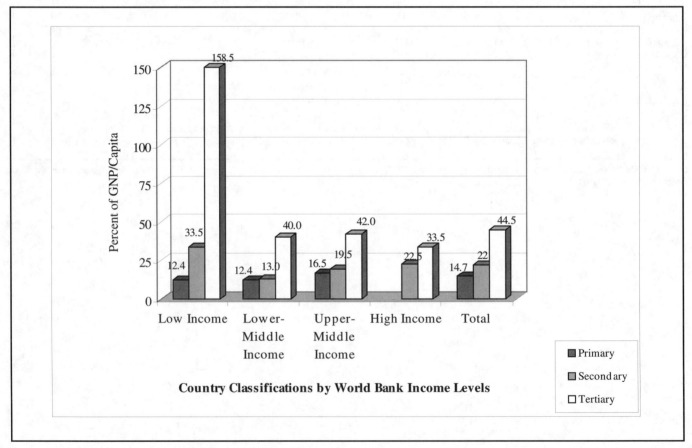

Source: World Bank, *World Development Indicators 1998*, Table 2.9

H. Nutrition and Food Supply

GENERAL OVERVIEW

This section presents data concerning various aspects of nutrition and food supply in poorer countries of the world. Including indicators that detail nutritional intake, food consumption, and food production capacities, it presents data on issues that are crucial to survival in developing countries.

Some of the material in this section comes from *The Sixth World Food Survey* by the United Nations' Food and Agriculture Organization (FAO), published in 1997. This survey is a valuable and sweeping study of food consumption and production conducted every 10 years; due to its comprehensive nature, it is an invaluable resource for students and researchers of poverty worldwide. The data presented in the survey cover the period from 1990 through 1992, so while they may appear to be dated, they are the latest data available from the FAO in this comprehensive format.

EXPLANATION OF INDICATORS

Daily Calorie Supply and Dietary Protein Supply per Capita: These are benchmark statistics in monitoring the nutritional adequacy of the food supply of countries worldwide. As a daily amount averaged out across the population, however, they say nothing about the variations that exist between different pockets of the population including rural-urban and income-class disparities. Still, they are invaluable in characterizing the overall nutritional sufficiency experienced by a population, and they allow for easy international comparisons (H1.1–H1.6).

Percent of Population Undernourished: As a reflection of the portion of a population that is undernourished, this statistic helps to quantify the extent of undernourishment suffered in a country. It measures the scope of food deprivation; therefore, it helps policymakers evaluate broad-based food policy initiatives (H2.1–H2.3).

Percent of Households Consuming Iodized Salt: Consumption of iodized salt is one of the most efficient ways to provide the body with the iodine it needs for good health and development. Iodine deficiency has a broad range of implications; it can cause a variety of developmental problems including mental retardation, paralysis of the lower limbs, and dwarfism. The importance of an adequate intake of iodine to pregnant women and their offspring cannot be overstated. Deficiency in iodine can cause miscarriage and stillbirth, and it is the most significant cause of preventable brain damage, mostly in utero. Recent efforts to iodize all salt intended for food intake have paid off; nevertheless, problems associated with the lack of iodine in the diet—especially brain damage—are still widespread. Monitoring the intake of this nutrient on a country-by-country basis is crucial to reversing the negative and preventable health problems caused by its deficiency (H3.1–H3.4).

Percent of Household Consumption of All Foods: This indicator reflects the share of household resources spent on food relative to other items. Generally, in poorer countries where the total income available for consumption of all goods and services is limited, the amount spent on necessities takes up a greater percentage of total income. Unfortunately in many of these poorer countries, systematic surveying of household consumption patterns is often unavailable. Whatever data are available from official sources have been included in the tables below. The chart at the end of this set shows data of those countries with a household food consumption share equalling less than 12%. Including some of the wealthiest countries of the world, the chart is intended as a backdrop for the poorer countries represented in the tables (H4.1–H4.4).

Cereal Yield: Cereal crops include wheat, rice, rye, oats, barley, corn (maize), and sorghum; they constitute the most important source of food for the majority of the world's population, especially people in poorer countries. These indicators represent the production of cereal crops per unit of land and therefore can reflect, among other things, the wealth of physical resources (land, water, etc.) and the efficiency of agricultural processes. The data extend across a 16-year time period from 1980–1996, allowing an analysis of recent trends in cereal production (H5.1–H5.4).

Food Production per Capita Index: This indicator measures the amount of food produced per capita against a base year of 1980. It either reflects an increase (indexes over 100) or decrease (indexes less than 100) over the base year, and therefore can help to analyze trends in recent food production capacity. It takes into account all food—cereals, as well as other plant-based foods (vegetables, fruit, edible roots, etc.) and livestock products (H6.1–H6.3).

Food Imports as Percent of Total Imports: Food imports as a share of overall imports can illuminate the reliance of a country on foodstuffs produced outside their boundaries. Since food is one of the basic necessities of life, an overreliance on food imports may put pressure on a country's entire economy, unless successful export industries exist to counterbalance and "pay" for food exports (H7.1–H7.4).

H1.1 Daily Calorie Supply per Capita, 1970 and 1995—Low-Income Countries per World Bank

Country	1970	1995	Country	1970	1995
Afghanistan	na	na	Laos	2,154	2,105
Angola	2,071	1,904	Lesotho	1,986	1,965
Armenia	na	na	Liberia	na	na
Azerbaijan	na	na	Madagascar	2,406	1,996
Bangladesh	2,177	2,001	Malawi	2,340	2,026
Benin	1,964	2,386	Mali	2,095	2,137
Bhutan	na	na	Mauritania	1,868	2,568
Bosnia and Herzegovina	na	na	Moldova	na	na
Burkina Faso	1,762	2,248	Mongolia	2,279	1,895
Burundi	2,094	1,741	Mozambique	1,886	1,675
Cambodia	2,059	1,996	Myanmar (Burma)	1,997	2,728
Cameroon	2,280	2,199	Nepal	1,933	2,367
Central African Republic	2,378	1,877	Nicaragua	2,411	2,308
Chad	2,183	1,917	Niger	1,992	2,135
China	2,000	2,708	Nigeria	2,254	2,497
Comoros	1,848	1,794	Pakistan	2,198	2,471
Congo, Dem. Rep. (Zaire)	2,158	1,870	Rwanda	na	na
Congo, Rep.	1,996	2,083	Sao Tome and Principe	na	na
Cote d'Ivoire	2,428	2,494	Senegal	2,546	2,365
Equatorial Guinea	na	na	Sierra Leone	2,419	1,992
Eritrea	na	na	Somalia	na	na
Ethiopia	na	na	Sri Lanka	2,229	2,302
Gambia	2,108	2,122	Sudan	2,167	2,310
Ghana	2,121	2,574	Tajikistan	na	na
Guinea	2,212	2,150	Tanzania	1,749	2,003
Guinea-Bissau	1,989	2,423	Togo	2,261	1,736
Guyana	2,224	2,388	Uganda	2,294	2,249
Haiti	na	na	Vietnam	2,122	2,438
Honduras	2,177	2,358	Yemen	1,763	2,013
India	2,078	2,382	Zambia	2,140	1,915
Kenya	2,180	1,980	Zimbabwe	2,222	1,961
Kyrgyzstan	na	na			

Note: Daily calorie supply per capita is the equivalent of the total net food supplies in a country, stated in terms of calories, divided by the population, and calculated on a daily basis.

Source: United Nations Development Programme, *Human Development Report 1998,* Table 14.

H1.2 Daily Calorie Supply per Capita, 1970 and 1995—Lower Middle-Income Countries per World Bank

Country	1970	1995	Country	1970	1995
Albania	na	na	Lithuania	na	na
Algeria	1,798	3,035	Macedonia, FYRO	na	na
Belarus	na	na	Maldives	1,428	2,211
Belize	2,265	2,776	Marshall Islands	na	na
Bolivia	2,000	2,189	Micronesia	na	na
Botswana	2,101	2,140	Morocco	2,404	3,140
Bulgaria	na	na	Namibia	2,149	2,093
Cape Verde	1,475	3,003	North Korea, Dem. Rep.	2,498	2,282
Colombia	2,042	2,749	Panama	2,236	2,462
Costa Rica	2,391	2,855	Papua New Guinea	1,920	2,273
Cuba	2,619	2,277	Paraguay	2,591	2,552
Djibouti	1,842	1,827	Peru	2,207	2,147
Dominica	2,012	2,982	Philippines	1,670	2,319
Dominican Republic	1,988	2,308	Romania	na	na
Ecuador	2,175	2,420	Russia	na	na
Egypt	2,352	3,315	Samoa	na	na
El Salvador	1,827	2,571	Solomon Islands	2,150	2,085
Estonia	na	na	St. Vincent and the Grenadines	2,295	2,397
Fiji	2,380	3,015	Suriname	2,177	2,521
Georgia	na	na	Swaziland	2,346	2,660
Grenada	2,185	2,630	Syria	2,317	3,295
Guatemala	2,100	2,298	Thailand	2,148	2,247
Indonesia	1,859	2,699	Tonga	na	na
Iran	1,994	2,945	Tunisia	2,221	3,173
Iraq	2,254	2,266	Turkey	2,991	3,577
Jamaica	2,483	2,615	Turkmenistan	na	na
Jordan	2,415	2,726	Ukraine	na	na
Kazakhstan	na	na	Uzbekistan	na	na
Kiribati	na	na	Vanuatu	2,412	2,499
Latvia	na	na	Venezuela	na	na
Lebanon	2,330	3,269	Yugoslavia	na	na

Note: Daily calorie supply per capita is the equivalent of the total net food supplies in a country, stated in terms of calories, divided by the population, and calculated on a daily basis.

Source: United Nations Development Programme, *Human Development Report 1998,* Table 14.

H1.3 Daily Calorie Supply per Capita, 1970 and 1995—Upper Middle-Income Countries per World Bank

Country	1970	1995	Country	1970	1995
Antigua and Barbuda	2,489	2,300	Mexico	2,698	3,116
Argentina	3,340	3,097	Oman	na	na
Bahrain	na	na	Palau	na	na
Barbados	2,805	3,155	Poland	na	na
Brazil	2,398	2,824	Saudi Arabia	1,872	2,736
Chile	2,619	2,713	Seychelles	1,826	2,311
Croatia	na	na	Slovakia	na	na
Czech Republic	na	na	Slovenia	na	na
Gabon	2,118	2,443	South Africa	2,807	2,865
Hungary	na	na	St. Kitts & Nevis	1,762	2,156
Libya	2,439	3,117	St. Lucia	1,954	2,757
Malaysia	2,518	2,765	Trinidad & Tobago	2,464	2,550
Malta	na	na	Uruguay	3,041	2,813
Mauritius	2,322	2,886			

Note: Daily calorie supply per capita is the equivalent of the total net food supplies in a country, stated in terms of calories, divided by the population, and calculated on a daily basis.

Source: United Nations Development Programme, *Human Development Report 1998,* Table 14.

H1.4 Dietary Protein Supply per Capita, 1990–1992—Low-Income Countries per World Bank

Country	Grams/Day 1990–1992	Country	Grams/Day 1990–1992
Afghanistan	47	Laos	61
Angola	41	Lesotho	65
Armenia	63	Liberia	34
Azerbaijan	79	Madagascar	51
Bangladesh	43	Malawi	54
Benin	59	Mali	62
Bhutan	na	Mauritania	80
Bosnia and Herzegovina	58	Moldova	90
Burkina Faso	63	Mongolia	73
Burundi	62	Mozambique	32
Cambodia	51	Myanmar (Burma)	64
Cameroon	49	Nepal	55
Central African Republic	37	Nicaragua	55
Chad	55	Niger	59
China	67	Nigeria	44
Comoros	na	Pakistan	57
Congo, Dem. Rep. (Zaire)	33	Rwanda	46
Congo, Rep.	48	Sao Tome and Principe	na
Cote d'Ivoire	51	Senegal	66
Equatorial Guinea	na	Sierra Leone	38
Eritrea	na	Somalia	49
Ethiopia	51	Sri Lanka	46
Gambia	56	Sudan	63
Ghana	45	Tajikistan	69
Guinea	53	Tanzania	51
Guinea-Bissau	na	Togo	53
Guyana	64	Uganda	52
Haiti	41	Vietnam	51
Honduras	56	Yemen	58
India	57	Zambia	52
Kenya	52	Zimbabwe	53
Kyrgyzstan	85		

Note: The indicator is calculated by translating the food commodities available for human consumption in a country into a total protein equivalent. This total is divided by the population and then calculated as a daily average. Protein supplies are reported in the unit of grams per day. Data are based on a three-year average.

Source: Food and Agriculture Organization (FAO), FAOSTAT database, http://apps.fao.org

H1.5 Dietary Protein Supply per Capita, 1990–1992—Lower Middle-Income Countries per World Bank

Country	Grams/Day 1990–1992	Country	Grams/Day 1990–1992
Albania	82	Macedonia, FYRO	60
Algeria	77	Maldives	na
Belarus	99	Marshall Islands	na
Belize	na	Micronesia	na
Bolivia	52	Morocco	83
Botswana	69	Namibia	62
Bulgaria	95	North Korea, Dem. Rep.	86
Cape Verde	na	Panama	59
Colombia	59	Papua New Guinea	50
Costa Rica	69	Paraguay	68
Cuba	66	Peru	50
Djibouti	na	Philippines	53
Dominica	na	Romania	95
Dominican Republic	50	Russia	90
Ecuador	52	Samoa	na
Egypt	87	Solomon Islands	na
El Salvador	62	St. Vincent and the Grenadines	na
Estonia	93	Suriname	63
Fiji	na	Swaziland	66
Georgia	69	Syria	84
Grenada	na	Thailand	53
Guatemala	57	Tonga	na
Indonesia	60	Tunisia	87
Iran	72	Turkey	101
Iraq	56	Turkmenistan	90
Jamaica	64	Ukraine	92
Jordan	77	Uzbekistan	79
Kazakhstan	91	Vanuatu	na
Kiribati	na	Venezuela	65
Latvia	89	Yugoslavia	82
Lebanon	86		
Lithuania	99		

Note: The indicator is calculated by translating the food commodities available for human consumption in a country into a total protein equivalent. This total is divided by the population and then calculated as a daily average. Protein supplies are reported in the unit of grams per day. Data are based on a three-year average.

Source: Food and Agriculture Organization (FAO), FAOSTAT database, http://apps.fao.org

H1.6 Dietary Protein Supply per Capita, 1990–1992—Upper Middle-Income Countries per World Bank

Country	Grams/Day 1990–1992	Country	Grams/Day 1990–1992
Antigua and Barbuda	na	Mexico	80
Argentina	97	Oman	na
Bahrain	na	Palau	na
Barbados	na	Poland	101
Brazil	64	Saudi Arabia	77
Chile	70	Seychelles	na
Croatia	67	Slovakia	95
Czech Republic	95	Slovenia	82
Gabon	63	South Africa	71
Hungary	95	St. Kitts & Nevis	na
Libya	79	St. Lucia	na
Malaysia	58	Trinidad & Tobago	63
Malta	na	Uruguay	83
Mauritius	68		

Note: The indicator is calculated by translating the food commodities available for human consumption in a country into a total protein equivalent. This total is divided by the population and then calculated as a daily average. Protein supplies are reported in the unit of grams per day. Data are based on a three-year average.

Source: Food and Agriculture Organization (FAO), FAOSTAT database, http://apps.fao.org

H2.1 Percent of Population Undernourished, 1969–71 and 1990–1992—Low-Income Countries per World Bank

Country	1969–71	1990–1992	Country	1969–71	1990–1992
Afghanistan	37	73	Laos	29	24
Angola	39	54	Lesotho	49	35
Armenia	na	na	Liberia	34	59
Azerbaijan	na	na	Madagascar	20	31
Bangladesh	23	34	Malawi	26	49
Benin	36	20	Mali	45	34
Bhutan	na	na	Mauritania	52	20
Bosnia and Herzegovina	na	na	Moldova	na	na
Burkina Faso	66	41	Mongolia	23	32
Burundi	42	50	Mozambique	55	66
Cambodia	13	29	Myanmar (Burma)	34	12
Cameroon	29	43	Nepal	45	29
Central African Republic	28	62	Nicaragua	22	25
Chad	40	61	Niger	48	37
China	45	16	Nigeria	26	38
Comoros	na	na	Pakistan	24	17
Congo, Dem. Rep. (Zaire)	36	39	Rwanda	35	47
Congo, Rep.	42	34	Sao Tome and Principe	na	na
Cote d'Ivoire	24	22	Senegal	24	30
Equatorial Guinea	na	na	Sierra Leone	34	55
Eritrea	na	na	Somalia	59	72
Ethiopia	59	65	Sri Lanka	21	26
Gambia	36	29	Sudan	36	37
Ghana	34	40	Tajikistan	na	na
Guinea	35	25	Tanzania	60	38
Guinea-Bissau	na	na	Togo	30	30
Guyana	22	24	Uganda	29	32
Haiti	56	69	Vietnam	24	25
Honduras	27	21	Yemen	51	24
India	36	21	Zambia	34	43
Kenya	33	46	Zimbabwe	35	41
Kyrgyzstan	na	na			

Note: The percent of undernourished population is the proportion of people in a country who do not receive an adequate amount of food and are undernourished as a result. Data are based on a three-year average.

Source: The Sixth World Food Survey, Food and Agriculture Organization (FAO), 1997, http://www.FAO.org

H2.2 Percent of Population Undernourished, 1969–71 and 1990–1992—Lower Middle-Income Countries per World Bank

Country	1969–71	1990–1992	Country	1969–71	1990–1992
Albania	na	na	Lithuania	na	na
Algeria	52	9	Macedonia, FYRO	na	na
Belarus	na	na	Maldives	na	na
Belize	na	na	Marshall Islands	na	na
Bolivia	43	40	Micronesia	na	na
Botswana	34	29	Morocco	23	10
Bulgaria	na	na	Namibia	36	35
Cape Verde	na	na	North Korea, Dem. Rep.	20	9
Colombia	38	18	Panama	12	19
Costa Rica	25	12	Papua New Guinea	27	10
Cuba	15	9	Paraguay	12	15
Djibouti	na	na	Peru	20	49
Dominica	na	na	Philippines	54	21
Dominican Republic	44	32	Romania	na	na
Ecuador	32	19	Russia	na	na
Egypt	24	6	Samoa	na	na
El Salvador	50	19	Solomon Islands	na	na
Estonia	na	na	St. Vincent	na	na
Fiji	na	na	Suriname	31	21
Georgia	na	na	Swaziland	26	13
Grenada	na	na	Syria	2	3
Guatemala	35	26	Thailand	28	26
Indonesia	34	12	Tonga	na	na
Iran	32	7	Tunisia	23	3
Iraq	21	21	Turkey	9	3
Jamaica	21	23	Turkmenistan	na	na
Jordan	11	3	Ukraine	na	na
Kazakhstan	na	na	Uzbekistan	na	na
Kiribati	na	na	Vanuatu	na	na
Latvia	na	na	Venezuela	25	20
Lebanon	27	5	Yugoslavia	na	na

Note: The percent of undernourished population is the proportion of people in a country who do not receive an adequate amount of food, and are undernourished as a result. Data are based on a three-year average.

Source: The Sixth World Food Survey, Food and Agriculture Organization (FAO), 1997, http://www.FAO.org

H2.3 Percent of Population Undernourished, 1969–71 and 1990–1992—Upper Middle-Income Countries per World Bank

Country	1969–71	1990–1992	Country	1969–71	1990–1992
Antigua and Barbuda	na	na	Mauritius	31	18
Argentina	4	9	Mexico	15	8
Bahrain	na	na	Oman	na	na
Barbados	na	na	Palau	na	na
Brazil	14	6	Poland	na	na
Chile	17	22	Saudi Arabia	51	12
Croatia	na	na	Seychelles	na	na
Czech Republic	na	na	Slovakia	na	na
Gabon	39	24	Slovenia	na	na
Hungary	na	na	South Africa	na	na
Libya	20	3	St. Kitts & Nevis	na	na
Malaysia	14	7	St. Lucia	na	na
Malta	na	na	Trinidad & Tobago	15	11
			Uruguay	3	8

Note: The percent of undernourished population is the proportion of people in a country who do not receive an adequate amount of food, and are undernourished as a result. Data are based on a three-year average.

Source: The Sixth World Food Survey, Food and Agriculture Organization (FAO), 1997, http://www.FAO.org

H3.1 Percent of Households Consuming Iodized Salt, 1992–1996—Low-Income Countries per World Bank

Country	Percent	Country	Percent
Afghanistan	na	Laos	90
Angola	10	Lesotho	73
Armenia	na	Liberia	na
Azerbaijan	na	Madagascar	1
Bangladesh	44	Malawi	58
Benin	35	Mali	9
Bhutan	96	Mauritania	3
Bosnia and Herzegovina	na	Moldova	na
Burkina Faso	23	Mongolia	42
Burundi	80	Mozambique	62
Cambodia	na	Myanmar (Burma)	14
Cameroon	86	Nepal	93
Central African Republic	65	Nicaragua	98
Chad	31	Niger	83
China	51	Nigeria	83
Comoros	na	Pakistan	19
Congo, Dem. Rep. (Zaire)	12	Rwanda	90
Congo, Rep.	na	Sao Tome and Principe	na
Cote d'Ivoire	na	Senegal	9
Equatorial Guinea	20	Sierra Leone	75
Eritrea	80	Somalia	na
Ethiopia	0	Sri Lanka	7
Gambia	0	Sudan	na
Ghana	10	Tajikistan	20
Guinea	37	Tanzania	74
Guinea-Bissau	na	Togo	1
Guyana	na	Uganda	69
Haiti	10	Vietnam	59
Honduras	85	Yemen	21
India	70	Zambia	90
Kenya	100	Zimbabwe	80
Kyrgyzstan	na		

Note: This indicator represents the total percent of households that consume, as a regular part of their diet, iodized salt.

Source: The State of the World's Children 1998, UNICEF's web site, http://www.unicef.org/sowc98/

H3.2 Percent of Households Consuming Iodized Salt, 1992–1996—Lower Middle-Income Countries per World Bank

Country	Percent	Country	Percent
Albania	na	Lithuania	na
Algeria	92	Macedonia, FYRO	100
Belarus	37	Maldives	na
Belize	90	Marshall Islands	na
Bolivia	92	Micronesia	na
Botswana	27	Morocco	na
Bulgaria	na	Namibia	80
Cape Verde	na	North Korea, Dem. Rep.	5
Colombia	90	Panama	92
Costa Rica	89	Papua New Guinea	na
Cuba	45	Paraguay	77
Djibouti	na	Peru	90
Dominica	na	Philippines	15
Dominican Republic	40	Romania	na
Ecuador	97	Russia	30
Egypt	0	Samoa	na
El Salvador	91	Solomon Islands	na
Estonia	na	St. Vincent and the Grenadines	na
Fiji	31	Suriname	na
Georgia	na	Swaziland	26
Grenada	na	Syria	36
Guatemala	64	Thailand	50
Indonesia	85	Tonga	na
Iran	82	Tunisia	98
Iraq	50	Turkey	18
Jamaica	100	Turkmenistan	0
Jordan	75	Ukraine	4
Kazakhstan	53	Uzbekistan	0
Kiribati	na	Vanuatu	na
Latvia	na	Venezuela	65
Lebanon	92	Yugoslavia	70

Note: This indicator represents the total percent of households that consume, as a regular part of their diet, iodized salt.

Source: The State of the World's Children 1998, UNICEF's web site, http://www.unicef.org/sowc98/

H3.3 Percent of Households Consuming Iodized Salt, 1992–1996—Upper Middle-Income Countries per World Bank

Country	Percent	Country	Percent
Antigua and Barbuda	na	Mexico	87
Argentina	90	Oman	35
Bahrain	na	Palau	na
Barbados	na	Poland	na
Brazil	95	Saudi Arabia	na
Chile	95	Seychelles	na
Croatia	100	Slovakia	na
Czech Republic	na	Slovenia	na
Gabon	na	South Africa	40
Hungary	na	St. Kitts & Nevis	na
Libya	90	St. Lucia	na
Malaysia	na	Trinidad & Tobago	na
Malta	na	Uruguay	na
Mauritius	0		

Note: This indicator represents the total percent of households that consume, as a regular part of their diet, iodized salt.

Source: The State of the World's Children 1998, UNICEF's web site, http://www.unicef.org/sowc98/

H3.4 Percent of Households Consuming Iodized Salt, 1992–1996—Worldwide Summary, Region by Region

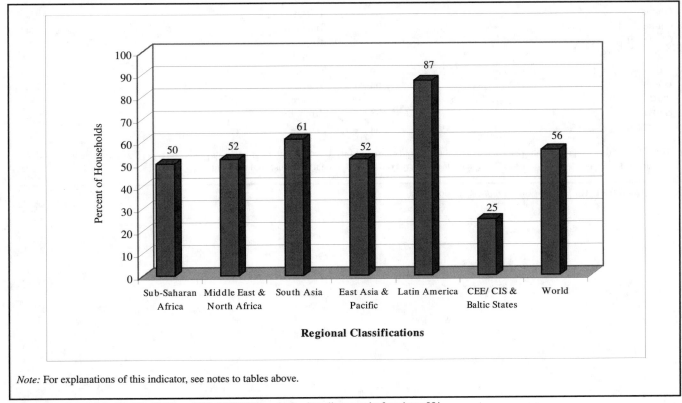

Note: For explanations of this indicator, see notes to tables above.

Source: The State of the World's Children 1998, UNICEF's web site, http://www.unicef.org/sowc98/

H4.1 Percent of Household Consumption of All Foods, 1996—Low-Income Countries per World Bank

Country	Percent	Country	Percent
Afghanistan	na	Laos	na
Angola	na	Lesotho	na
Armenia	na	Liberia	na
Azerbaijan	na	Madagascar	na
Bangladesh	41	Malawi	45
Benin	45	Mali	48
Bhutan	na	Mauritania	na
Bosnia and Herzegovina	na	Moldova	28
Burkina Faso	na	Mongolia	na
Burundi	na	Mozambique	na
Cambodia	na	Myanmar (Burma)	na
Cameroon	38	Nepal	37
Central African Republic	na	Nicaragua	na
Chad	na	Niger	na
China	na	Nigeria	48
Comoros	na	Pakistan	40
Congo, Dem. Rep. (Zaire)	na	Rwanda	na
Congo, Rep.	36	Sao Tome and Principe	na
Cote d'Ivoire	35	Senegal	52
Equatorial Guinea	na	Sierra Leone	48
Eritrea	na	Somalia	na
Ethiopia	na	Sri Lanka	38
Gambia	na	Sudan	na
Ghana	na	Tajikistan	na
Guinea	32	Tanzania	na
Guinea-Bissau	na	Togo	na
Guyana	na	Uganda	na
Haiti	na	Vietnam	40
Honduras	na	Yemen	na
India	na	Zambia	47
Kenya	38	Zimbabwe	28
Kyrgyzstan	na		

Note: This indicator represents the percentage of total household consumption (covering clothing, fuel, health care, etc. as well as food) spent on food. For the purposes of calculating this statistic, "all foods" include any type of food bought for household consumption.

Source: World Bank, *World Development Indicators 1998,* Table 4.10

H4.2 Percent of Household Consumption of All Foods, 1996—Lower Middle-Income Countries per World Bank

Country	Percent	Country	Percent
Albania	na	Lithuania	na
Algeria	na	Macedonia, FYRO	na
Belarus	16	Maldives	na
Belize	28	Marshall Islands	na
Bolivia	na	Micronesia	na
Botswana	25	Morocco	45
Bulgaria	15	Namibia	na
Cape Verde	na	North Korea, Dem. Rep.	na
Colombia	na	Panama	na
Costa Rica	na	Papua New Guinea	na
Cuba	na	Paraguay	na
Djibouti	na	Peru	na
Dominica	32	Philippines	33
Dominican Republic	na	Romania	24
Ecuador	na	Russia	18
Egypt	44	Samoa	na
El Salvador	na	Solomon Islands	na
Estonia	na	St. Vincent and the Grenadines	24
Fiji	30	Suriname	na
Georgia	na	Swaziland	27
Grenada	26	Syria	na
Guatemala	na	Thailand	23
Indonesia	45	Tonga	na
Iran	23	Tunisia	35
Iraq	na	Turkey	23
Jamaica	26	Turkmenistan	na
Jordan	na	Ukraine	21
Kazakhstan	na	Uzbekistan	na
Kiribati	na	Vanuatu	na
Latvia	na	Venezuela	na
Lebanon	na	Yugoslavia	na

Note: This indicator represents the percentage of total household consumption (covering clothing, fuel, health care, etc. as well as food) spent on food. For the purposes of calculating this statistic, "all foods" include any type of food bought for household consumption.

Source: World Bank, *World Development Indicators 1998,* Table 4.10

H4.3 Percent of Household Consumption of All Foods, 1996—Upper Middle-Income Countries per World Bank

Country	Percent	Country	Percent
Antigua and Barbuda	33	Mexico	na
Argentina	na	Oman	na
Bahrain	na	Palau	na
Barbados	na	Poland	20
Brazil	na	Saudi Arabia	na
Chile	na	Seychelles	na
Croatia	17	Slovakia	17
Czech Republic	15	Slovenia	13
Gabon	37	South Africa	na
Hungary	14	St. Kitts & Nevis	30
Libya	na	St. Lucia	39
Malaysia	na	Trinidad & Tobago	20
Malta	na	Uruguay	na
Mauritius	24		

Note: This indicator represents the percentage of total household consumption (covering clothing, fuel, health care, etc. as well as food) spent on food. For the purposes of calculating this statistic, "all foods" include any type of food bought for household consumption.

Source: World Bank, *World Development Indicators 1998,* Table 4.10

H4.4 Percent of Household Consumption of All Foods, 1996—For Countries with Food Consumption Shares Lower than Twelve Percent

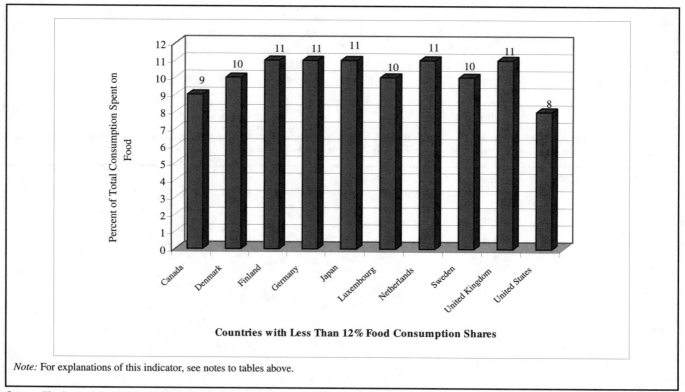

Note: For explanations of this indicator, see notes to tables above.

Source: The State of the World's Children 1998, UNICEF's web site, http://www.unicef.org/sowc98/

H5.1 Cereal Yield, Kilograms per Hectare, 1980–1996—Low-Income Countries per World Bank

Country	1980	1985	1990	1995	1996
Afghanistan	1349	1332	1201	1377	1156
Angola	618	449	321	356	559
Armenia	na	na	na	1415	1596
Azerbaijan	na	na	na	1458	1689
Bangladesh	2006	2149	2491	2593	2720
Benin	718	856	848	1045	1021
Bhutan	1425	1386	1083	1097	1097
Bosnia and Herzegovina	na	na	na	2841	2904
Burkina Faso	570	709	600	783	846
Burundi	1063	1152	1349	1287	1337
Cambodia	1256	1333	1450	1704	1729
Cameroon	864	1154	1241	1363	1367
Central African Republic	521	1078	771	777	826
Chad	547	615	557	586	616
China	na	na	na	na	na
Comoros	1058	1089	1281	1336	1335
Congo, Dem. Rep. (Zaire)	na	na	na	na	na
Congo, Rep.	827	757	887	937	938
Cote d'Ivoire	na	na	na	na	na
Equatorial Guinea	na	na	na	na	na
Eritrea	na	na	na	517	611
Ethiopia	1191	966	1276	na	na
Gambia	1325	1262	1008	1035	1120
Ghana	718	891	989	1427	1444
Guinea	955	895	940	1233	1353
Guinea-Bissau	699	1244	1531	1408	1357
Guyana	2953	3262	2943	3909	3716
Haiti	1016	1010	1027	934	917
Honduras	1132	1433	1468	1547	1450
India	1350	1592	1891	2144	2141
Kenya	1244	1641	1488	1867	1673
Kyrgyzstan	na	na	na	1621	2454
Laos	1422	2048	2309	2665	2464
Lesotho	960	721	1036	1362	1600
Liberia	1234	1253	1000	1120	1100
Madagascar	1682	1749	1945	2048	2055
Malawi	1187	1169	992	1293	1391
Mali	726	819	748	808	809
Mauritania	422	639	870	752	810
Moldova	na	na	na	3101	2846
Mongolia	517	1396	1097	737	726
Mozambique	596	531	474	596	825
Myanmar (Burma)	2600	2897	2762	3005	3048
Nepal	1687	1620	1920	1795	1927
Nicaragua	1572	1658	1524	1633	1702
Niger	457	425	215	323	342
Nigeria	1100	1258	1148	1163	1221
Pakistan	1613	1602	1766	2033	1960
Rwanda	1212	1226	1270	1632	1640
Sao Tome and Principe	1500	1517	1929	1875	2000
Senegal	547	820	795	874	853
Sierra Leone	1251	1254	1200	1145	1263
Somalia	465	747	793	378	489
Sri Lanka	2501	2961	2965	2079	2722
Sudan	671	561	461	446	624
Tajikistan	na	na	na	944	1539
Tanzania	1020	1367	1462	1419	1342
Togo	636	840	747	736	865

H5.1 Cereal Yield, Kilograms per Hectare, 1980–1996—Low-Income Countries per World Bank (continued)

Country	1980	1985	1990	1995	1996
Uganda	1491	1469	1498	1551	1572
Vietnam	2016	2697	3079	3569	3487
Yemen	1016	518	908	1105	943
Zambia	na	na	na	na	na
Zimbabwe	1185	1868	1625	532	1518

Note: Cereal yield is stated in kilograms per hectare of harvested land. The cereals covered include wheat, rice, maize, barley, oats, rye, millet, sorghum, buckwheat, and mixed grains.

Source: World Bank, *World Development Indicators 1998,* Table 3.3; World Bank, *World Development Indicators 1998,* CD-ROM, Series: Cereal Yield (AG.YLD.CREL.KG)

H5.2 Cereal Yield, Kilograms per Hectare, 1980–1996—Lower Middle-Income Countries per World Bank

Country	1980	1985	1990	1995	1996
Albania	2364	2901	2794	2708	2531
Algeria	760	912	575	830	1279
Belarus	na	na	na	2041	2174
Belize	1989	1516	1512	1824	1824
Bolivia	1117	1336	1341	1584	1646
Botswana	228	189	259	262	358
Bulgaria	3705	2915	3963	3054	1982
Cape Verde	531	401	335	308	327
Colombia	2415	2663	2475	2637	2743
Costa Rica	2924	2324	2736	3167	3896
Cuba	2547	2616	2423	1872	1872
Djibouti	na	1750	1667	1625	1250
Dominica	1438	1333	1364	1308	1308
Dominican Republic	2941	3805	3676	4112	4224
Ecuador	1640	1929	1724	1984	2153
Egypt	4094	4539	5703	5885	6499
El Salvador	1706	1809	1939	2027	2027
Estonia	na	na	na	1684	1987
Fiji	1926	2408	2181	2649	2649
Georgia	na	na	na	2079	1624
Grenada	894	951	1000	1000	1000
Guatemala	1449	1660	1998	1911	1940
Indonesia	2866	3513	3800	3843	3977
Iran	1067	1223	1445	1891	1772
Iraq	826	985	1061	714	644
Jamaica	1785	1857	1116	1362	1377
Jordan	933	615	1220	1283	973
Kazakhstan	na	na	na	504	651
Kiribati	na	na	na	na	na
Latvia	na	na	na	1685	2035
Lebanon	1745	1339	2000	1988	1850
Lithuania	na	na	na	1865	2391
Macedonia, FYRO	na	na	na	3007	2454
Maldives	850	1000	1000	1000	1000
Marshall Islands	na	na	na	na	na
Micronesia	na	na	na	na	na
Morocco	1019	1108	1120	446	1680
Namibia	377	322	461	180	268
North Korea, Dem. Rep.	3130	3950	3736	3449	3547
Panama	1539	1623	1867	1936	2354

H5.2 Cereal Yield, Kilograms per Hectare, 1980–1996—Lower Middle-Income Countries per World Bank *(continued)*

Country	1980	1985	1990	1995	1996
Papua New Guinea	2364	2299	1752	1698	1698
Paraguay	1508	1627	1836	2065	2200
Peru	1815	2328	2615	2644	3208
Philippines	1606	1841	2065	2280	2308
Romania	2994	3103	3011	3109	2454
Russia	na	na	na	1169	1323
Samoa	na	na	na	na	na
Solomon Islands	3685	2744	na	na	na
St. Vincent and the Grenadines	3313	3368	3490	3910	3910
Suriname	3960	3990	3765	3661	3661
Swaziland	1381	2046	1065	1269	2167
Syria	1438	938	749	1655	1793
Thailand	1911	2125	2009	2445	2446
Tonga	na	na	na	na	na
Tunisia	916	1085	1147	1142	1458
Turkey	1855	1931	2214	2041	2106
Turkmenistan	na	na	na	2852	682
Ukraine	na	na	na	2512	1997
Uzbekistan	na	na	na	1935	1738
Vanuatu	520	520	538	538	538
Venezuela	1914	2029	2362	2673	2668
Yugoslavia	**na**	**na**	**na**	**na**	**na**

Note: Cereal yield is stated in kilograms per hectare of harvested land. The cereals covered include wheat, rice, maize, barley, oats, rye, millet, sorghum, buckwheat, and mixed grains.

Source: World Bank, *World Development Indicators 1998,* Table 3.3; World Bank, *World Development Indicators 1998,* CD-ROM, Series: Cereal Yield (AG.YLD.CREL.KG)

H5.3 Cereal Yield, Kilograms per Hectare, 1980-1996—Upper Middle-Income Countries per World Bank

Country	1980	1985	1990	1995	1996
Antigua and Barbuda	1706	1900	1786	1607	1607
Argentina	1866	2438	2227	2805	2809
Bahrain	na	na	na	na	na
Barbados	2500	2500	2674	2500	2500
Brazil	1576	1828	1755	2512	2352
Chile	2059	2949	3620	4472	4265
Croatia	na	na	na	4368	4512
Czech Republic	na	na	na	4187	4217
Gabon	1692	1453	1583	1740	1805
Hungary	4806	5159	4521	4059	3690
Libya	387	595	674	689	685
Malaysia	2836	2754	2858	3081	3080
Malta	3196	3626	3500	2508	3488
Mauritius	2455	4741	4193	4339	4339
Mexico	2189	2431	2425	2436	2481
Oman	905	1038	2160	2180	2180
Palau	na	na	na	na	na
Poland	2337	2894	3284	3022	2973
Saudi Arabia	588	3471	4245	4407	3506
Seychelles	na	na	na	na	na
Slovakia	na	na	na	4109	4489
Slovenia	na	na	na	4989	5025
South Africa	2023	1606	1781	1245	2174
St. Kitts & Nevis	na	na	na	na	na
St. Lucia	700	692	696	714	714
Trinidad & Tobago	3202	2359	2826	3659	3659
Uruguay	1618	1841	2182	3088	3156

Note: Cereal yield is stated in kilograms per hectare of harvested land. The cereals covered include wheat, rice, maize, barley, oats, rye, millet, sorghum, buckwheat, and mixed grains.

Source: World Bank, *World Development Indicators 1998,* Table 3.3; World Bank, *World Development Indicators 1998,* CD-ROM, Series: Cereal Yield (AG.YLD.CREL.KG).

H5.4 Cereal Yield, Kilograms per Hectare, 1980–1996—Worldwide Summary

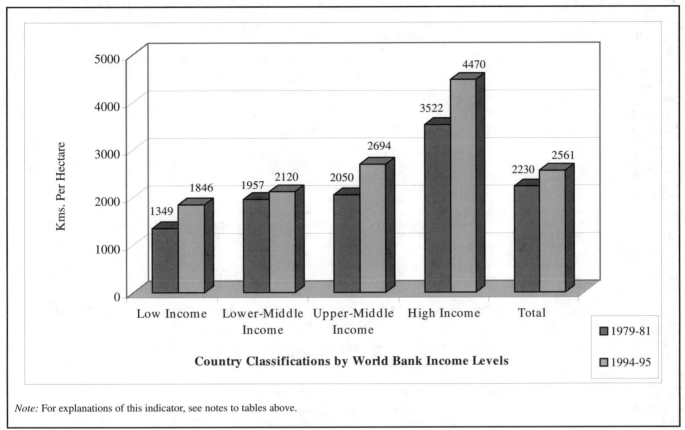

Note: For explanations of this indicator, see notes to tables above.

Source: World Bank, *World Development Indicators 1998,* Table 3.3; World Bank, *World Development Indicators 1998,* CD-ROM, Series: Cereal Yield (AG.YLD.CREL.KG)

H6.1 Food Production per Capita Index, 1996—Low-Income Countries per World Bank (Base Year 1980 = 100)

Country	1996 Index	Country	1996 Index
Afghanistan	na	Gambia	56
Angola	90	Ghana	122
Armenia	na	Guinea	79
Azerbaijan	na	Guinea-Bissau	118
Bangladesh	98	Guyana	125
Benin	131	Haiti	64
Bhutan	91	Honduras	73
Bosnia and Herzegovina	na	India	127
Burkina Faso	135	Kenya	91
Burundi	81	Kyrgyzstan	na
Cambodia	132	Laos	99
Cameroon	91	Lesotho	89
Central African Republic	99	Liberia	na
Chad	84	Madagascar	74
China	215	Malawi	78
Comoros	79	Mali	90
Congo, Dem. Rep. (Zaire)	84	Mauritania	82
Congo, Rep.	91	Moldova	na
Cote d'Ivoire	105	Mongolia	63
Equatorial Guinea	59	Mozambique	83
Eritrea	na	Myanmar (Burma)	125
Ethiopia	na	Nepal	112

H6.1 Food Production per Capita Index, 1996—Low-Income Countries per World Bank (Base Year 1980 = 100) *(continued)*

Country	1996 Index	Country	1996 Index
Nicaragua	78	Sudan	87
Niger	70	Tajikistan	na
Nigeria	143	Tanzania	80
Pakistan	122	Togo	108
Rwanda	na	Uganda	99
Sao Tome and Principe	75	Vietnam	149
Senegal	112	Yemen	77
Sierra Leone	85	Zambia	97
Somalia	na	Zimbabwe	85
Sri Lanka	87		

Note: The food production per capita index is the amount of food produced, figured on an average annual per capita basis, and expressed in relationship to the amount produced in the base year (1980). Food comprises all types: nuts, pulses, fruit, cereals, vegetables, sugar cane, sugar beets, starchy roots, edible oils, livestock, and livestock products.

Source: United Nations Development Programme, *Human Development Report 1998,* Table 14

H6.2 Food Production per Capita Index, 1996—Lower Middle-Income Countries per World Bank (Base Year 1980 = 100)

Country	1996 Index	Country	1996 Index
Albania	na	Lithuania	na
Algeria	116	Macedonia, FYRO	na
Belarus	na	Maldives	84
Belize	124	Marshall Islands	na
Bolivia	122	Micronesia	na
Botswana	95	Morocco	143
Bulgaria	na	Namibia	64
Cape Verde	114	North Korea, Dem. Rep.	na
Colombia	109	Panama	90
Costa Rica	112	Papua New Guinea	86
Cuba	66	Paraguay	124
Djibouti	70	Peru	124
Dominica	165	Philippines	94
Dominican Republic	91	Romania	na
Ecuador	118	Russia	na
Egypt	121	Samoa	83
El Salvador	92	Solomon Islands	65
Estonia	na	St. Vincent and the Grenadines	108
Fiji	105	Suriname	79
Georgia	na	Swaziland	76
Grenada	76	Syria	85
Guatemala	103	Thailand	106
Indonesia	146	Tonga	na
Iran	131	Tunisia	124
Iraq	72	Turkey	101
Jamaica	118	Turkmenistan	na
Jordan	113	Ukraine	na
Kazakhstan	na	Uzbekistan	na
Kiribati	na	Vanuatu	82
Latvia	na	Venezuela	102
Lebanon	164	Yugoslavia	na

Note: The food production per capita index is the amount of food produced, figured on an average annual per capita basis, and expressed in relationship to the amount produced in the base year (1980). Food comprises all types: nuts, pulses, fruit, cereals, vegetables, sugar cane, sugar beets, starchy roots, edible oils, livestock, and livestock products.

Source: United Nations Development Programme, *Human Development Report 1998,* Table 14

H6.3 Food Production per Capita Index, 1996—Upper Middle-Income Countries per World Bank (Base Year 1980 = 100)

Country	1996 Index	Country	1996 Index
Antigua and Barbuda	92	Mexico	101
Argentina	108	Oman	71
Bahrain	50	Palau	na
Barbados	87	Poland	na
Brazil	127	Saudi Arabia	134
Chile	143	Seychelles	97
Croatia	na	Slovakia	na
Czech Republic	na	Slovenia	na
Gabon	84	South Africa	79
Hungary	na	St. Kitts & Nevis	66
Libya	na	St. Lucia	123
Malaysia	149	Trinidad & Tobago	84
Malta	na	Uruguay	144
Mauritius	120		

Note: The food production per capita index is the amount of food produced, figured on an average annual per capita basis, and expressed in relationship to the amount produced in the base year (1980). Food comprises all types: nuts, pulses, fruit, cereals, vegetables, sugar cane, sugar beets, starchy roots, edible oils, livestock and livestock products.

Source: United Nations Development Programme, *Human Development Report 1998*, Table 14

H7.1 Food Imports as Percent of Total Imports, 1980–1996—Low-Income Countries per World Bank

Country	1980	1985	1990	1995	1996
Afghanistan	14.6	na	na	na	na
Angola	na	32.5	na	na	na
Armenia	na	na	na	na	na
Azerbaijan	na	na	na	na	na
Bangladesh	23.6	24.3	19.0	na	na
Benin	26.3	na	na	na	na
Bhutan	17.5	na	na	na	na
Bosnia and Herzegovina	na	na	na	na	na
Burkina Faso	20.5	na	na	na	na
Burundi	12.7	na	na	na	na
Cambodia	na	na	na	na	na
Cameroon	8.6	na	18.5	17.4	13.7
Central African Republic	20.9	na	na	15.6	12.3
Chad	23.0	na	na	24.0	na
China	na	na	8.7	7.0	5.9
Comoros	22.2	na	na	na	na
Congo, Dem. Rep. (Zaire)	9.4	20.6	na	na	na
Congo, Rep.	19.2	19.1	na	na	na
Cote d'Ivoire	na	na	na	na	na
Equatorial Guinea	36.4	na	na	na	na
Eritrea	na	na	na	na	na
Ethiopia	7.9	29.8	14.9	na	na
Gambia	25.9	na	na	na	na
Ghana	10.1	na	na	na	na
Guinea	11.9	na	na	na	na
Guinea-Bissau	20.0	na	na	na	na
Guyana	13.7	na	na	na	na
Haiti	21.5	na	na	na	na
Honduras	10.1	9.1	10.2	12.6	15.5
India	9.0	8.4	3.2	4.3	na

H7.1 Food Imports as Percent of Total Imports, 1980–1996—Low-Income Countries per World Bank *(continued)*

Country	1980	1985	1990	1995	1996
Kenya	7.7	9.7	9.3	na	na
Kyrgyzstan	na	na	na	18.3	20.9
Laos	na	na	na	na	na
Lesotho	na	na	na	na	na
Liberia	18.9	na	na	na	na
Madagascar	8.5	12.6	11.2	16.3	na
Malawi	7.5	7.6	8.7	13.9	na
Mali	19.1	na	25.5	na	na
Mauritania	29.6	na	na	na	na
Moldova	na	na	na	8.1	na
Mongolia	na	na	na	na	14.3
Mozambique	13.8	na	na	na	22.0
Myanmar (Burma)	6.5	na	na	na	na
Nepal	4.3	14.0	14.8	15.1	na
Nicaragua	15.4	9.5	19.3	17.9	18.7
Niger	14.3	na	na	na	na
Nigeria	15.1	18.5	na	na	na
Pakistan	13.0	18.9	17.4	17.7	15.2
Rwanda	10.0	na	na	na	na
Sao Tome and Principe	36.2	na	na	na	na
Senegal	24.6	na	28.7	32.5	na
Sierra Leone	23.7	na	na	na	na
Somalia	32.5	na	na	na	na
Sri Lanka	20.4	20.0	19.1	na	na
Sudan	25.9	16.9	na	na	na
Tajikistan	na	na	na	na	na
Tanzania	13.3	na	na	na	na
Togo	16.5	na	22.4	na	na
Uganda	11.2	na	na	na	na
Vietnam	36.7	na	na	na	na
Yemen	28.4	na	na	28.9	na
Zambia	5.4	na	na	na	na
Zimbabwe	6.4	5.0	3.7	6.0	10.4

Note: Data refer to goods sent from one country to another country to be sold for profit or traded. Food imports include food and live animals, beverages and tobacco, animal and vegetable oils and fats, oil seeds, oil nuts, and oil kernels.

Source: World Bank, *World Development Indicators 1998,* Table 4.5; World Bank, *World Development Indicators 1998,* CD-ROM, Series: Food Imports (TM.VAL.FOOD.ZS.UN)

H7.2 Food Imports as Percent of Total Imports, 1980–1996—Lower Middle-Income Countries per World Bank

Country	1980	1985	1990	1995	1996
Albania	na	na	na	na	na
Algeria	21.0	25.4	23.7	29.5	na
Belarus	na	na	na	na	na
Belize	24.8	26.9	23.5	19.1	20.3
Bolivia	18.9	18.3	11.5	9.6	10.5
Botswana	na	na	na	na	na
Bulgaria	na	na	na	na	na
Cape Verde	42.7	na	na	na	na
Colombia	11.7	9.5	7.1	9.4	na
Costa Rica	8.8	8.2	7.6	10.2	11.9
Cuba	na	na	na	na	na
Djibouti	42.7	29.6	29.9	na	na
Dominica	27.3	26.4	23.6	26.2	27.8
Dominican Republic	16.5	11.9	na	na	na
Ecuador	8.4	8.2	8.7	7.6	9.9
Egypt	32.4	27.1	31.5	28.4	29.5
El Salvador	17.7	15.5	14.2	14.8	17.0
Estonia	na	na	na	13.8	15.3
Fiji	16.3	18.8	14.7	na	na
Georgia	na	na	na	na	na
Grenada	32.9	27.3	28.0	na	na
Guatemala	7.6	9.2	10.2	11.9	14.3
Indonesia	12.7	6.9	5.1	8.8	10.8
Iran	20.9	na	na	na	na
Iraq	13.3	na	na	na	na
Jamaica	20.3	17.8	15.1	14.3	14.6
Jordan	18.2	18.8	26.1	20.8	na
Kazakhstan	na	na	na	na	na
Kiribati	40.1	32.6	31.4	na	na
Latvia	na	na	na	10.5	12.9
Lebanon	15.8	na	na	na	na
Lithuania	na	na	na	13.1	12.8
Macedonia, FYRO	na	na	na	na	na
Maldives	31.4	na	na	na	na
Marshall Islands	na	na	na	na	na
Micronesia	na	na	na	na	na
Morocco	19.8	17.5	9.8	19.5	18.9
Namibia	na	na	na	na	na
North Korea, Dem. Rep.	na	na	na	na	na
Panama	10.1	12.1	11.9	10.7	11.1
Papua New Guinea	21.0	18.7	18.4	na	na
Paraguay	11.4	9.7	8.0	18.5	20.7
Peru	19.8	19.5	23.6	13.5	16.6
Philippines	7.8	10.7	10.3	8.3	8.1
Romania	na	na	12.1	8.5	7.3
Russia	na	na	na	na	na
Samoa	24.8	na	27.1	na	na
Solomon Islands	14.4	20.9	na	na	na
St. Vincent and the Grenadines	35.2	na	na	na	na
Suriname	9.7	na	11.3	na	na
Swaziland	na	na	na	na	na
Syria	14.1	19.0	31.1	na	na
Thailand	5.2	5.2	5.0	3.8	na
Tonga	30.2	28.5	27.8	na	na
Tunisia	13.7	14.1	10.6	12.6	9.7
Turkey	3.5	5.2	8.3	7.0	6.5
Turkmenistan	na	na	na	na	na

H7.2 Food Imports as Percent of Total Imports, 1980–1996—Lower Middle-Income Countries per World Bank *(continued)*

Country	1980	1985	1990	1995	1996
Ukraine	na	na	na	na	na
Uzbekistan	na	na	na	na	na
Vanuatu	29.5	na	na	na	na
Venezuela	14.5	12.9	11.2	14.3	15.6
Yugoslavia	na	na	na	na	na

Note: Data refer to goods sent from one country to another country to be sold for profit or traded. Food imports include food and live animals, beverages and tobacco, animal and vegetable oils and fats, oil seeds, oil nuts, and oil kernels.

Source: World Bank, *World Development Indicators 1998,* Table 4.5; World Bank, World Development Indicators 1998, CD-ROM, Series: Food Imports (TM.VAL.FOOD.ZS.UN)

H7.3 Food Imports as Percent of Total Imports, 1980–1996—Upper Middle-Income Countries per World Bank

Country	1980	1985	1990	1995	1996
Antigua and Barbuda	12.7	na	na	na	na
Argentina	5.7	4.7	4.0	5.5	4.9
Bahrain	6.9	8.4	8.5	na	na
Barbados	17.9	15.0	17.4	18.3	17.7
Brazil	9.6	9.0	9.4	10.7	na
Chile	15.0	8.3	4.4	6.7	7.2
Croatia	na	na	na	11.8	11.2
Czech Republic	na	na	na	6.7	7.0
Gabon	19.1	na	na	na	19.1
Hungary	8.3	6.9	7.6	5.6	5.2
Libya	19.3	17.3	23.0	na	na
Malaysia	11.9	11.8	7.3	4.9	5.4
Malta	19.4	16.4	10.4	na	na
Mauritius	26.3	20.4	12.5	16.7	16.4
Mexico	16.1	12.4	14.6	6.3	na
Oman	15.2	13.5	18.5	20.3	na
Palau	na	na	na	na	na
Poland	14.0	10.1	7.7	9.5	10.1
Saudi Arabia	14.1	14.9	14.8	na	na
Seychelles	20.8	17.9	18.9	21.2	19.7
Slovakia	na	na	na	8.3	7.0
Slovenia	na	na	na	7.8	7.8
South Africa	2.9	6.1	na	6.7	6.4
St. Kitts & Nevis	na	na	na	na	na
St. Lucia	21.0	25.3	23.2	26.7	na
Trinidad & Tobago	11.1	22.9	19.4	13.2	13.5
Uruguay	7.9	7.0	6.9	10.4	10.9

Note: Data refer to goods sent from one country to another country to be sold for profit or traded. Food imports include food and live animals, beverages and tobacco, animal and vegetable oils and fats, oil seeds, oil nuts, and oil kernels.

Source: World Bank, World Development Indicators 1998, Table 4.5; World Bank, *World Development Indicators 1998,* CD-ROM, Series: Food imports (TM.VAL.FOOD.ZS.UN)

H7.4 Food Imports as Percent of Total Imports, 1980 and 1996—Worldwide Summary

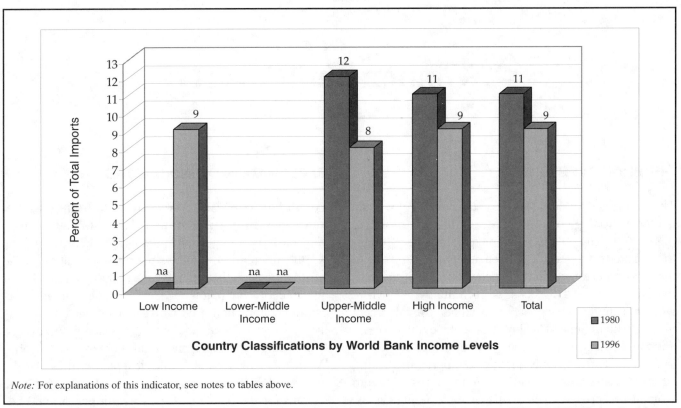

Note: For explanations of this indicator, see notes to tables above.

Source: World Bank, *World Development Indicators 1998,* Table 4.5; World Bank, *World Development Indicators 1998,* CD-ROM, Series: Food imports (TM.VAL.FOOD.ZS.UN)

I. Women and Poverty

GENERAL OVERVIEW

The factors and features specific to the poverty of women in the developing countries of the world are explored in this section. The poverty of women in developing countries has recently become an area of intense study due to the importance of women in the development of the family. The causes and effects of women in poverty—from women's literacy and education to women's involvement in family planning and health care—can be self-perpetuating and extend from women to their offspring.

Often, statistics on economic, demographic, health, education, and political participation patterns related to women are presented in terms of male-female gaps, which measure the indicator for the female population as a ratio against the value for the male population. Analyzed in this manner, the causes and effects of poverty can be viewed as part of a consistent and routine discrimination against women that is ingrained in many cultures and societies. Analyzing these statistical gaps not only reveals these patterns of discrimination but can offer goals in terms of lessening the gaps between men and women.

Other statistics in this section offer female to total population ratios—such as number of female teachers to total teachers. Such statistics allow students and researchers to monitor the activities and features of women's lives in terms of the total population. Still other indicators simply monitor aspects of life pertinent to women, such as childbirth—aspects that have a profound effect on the future prospects of families and children.

As primary caregivers, women can be the most intimate sponsors of direct human development and anti-poverty efforts. Therefore, to improve the outlook of women in poorer populations is to improve the prospects of the family as a whole and children in particular. Vigilant monitoring of the aspects of life that affect and are affected by women serves those efforts. This section offers students and researchers a starting point in such investigations.

EXPLANATION OF INDICATORS

Population Worldwide, According to Male, Female, and Age Group Breakdown: The first chart paints a very basic, yet important, demographic portrait of the world's population. It shows the total population of the world alongside the totals for men and women in broad age-category breakdowns. The graph reveals an interesting phenomenon: that while women outlive men, as the number of women in the "65 plus" category reveals, overall there are more men than women in the world. While this seems to defy biological possibilities—as the number of male and female births should be equal—the reasons for the discrepancy revolve in part around human involvement, including such factors as incomplete reporting of female population, female infanticides, or sex-related abortions (I1.1).

Sex Ratio: As with the above indicator, the sex ratio, which reports the number of males for every 100 females in a population, represents the slight imbalance in the world's population in favor of men. This gap is a primary demographic indicator of the composition of the world's population and the populations of individual countries (I2.1–I2.4).

Life Expectancy, Men Compared with Women: In nearly all nations throughout the world, women live longer than men. While the reasons for this are not clear, it is a fact borne out by extensive statistical monitoring across long periods of time; it is represented in the tables below for the poorer countries of the world. The data in these charts also reflect another significant trend—that the male-female gap in life expectancy in lower-income countries is much smaller than that in higher-income countries; that is, the life expectancy of women in low-income countries doesn't match that of more developed nations. Also, the overall life expectancy is astoundingly low in developing countries, revealed by the figures for male and female life expectancy. Reasons for this revolve around standards of living: less-advanced nutritional standards and poorer health conditions, for instance, have a clear impact on life expectancy in poor countries (I3.1–I3.7).

Women Age 60 and Above Compared with Men: This indicator reveals that more older women exist than older men. The implications for poorer communities of the world is that women, whose livelihood options are limited throughout their lives but especially in later years, face a greater possibility of income instability as they age (I4.1–4.4).

Total Fertility Rates, Historical Trends, and Average Annual Reduction: Fertility rates estimate the number of children a women is likely to have throughout her childbearing years given prevailing fertility trends. It can be used to calculate the size of a population at various points in the future. Reducing fertility rates is a primary objective of many developing countries, whose populations increase at very high rates, making the satisfaction of many basic human needs difficult due to the imbalance between demand on resources and resources available to meet those demands (I5.1–I5.7).

Births per 1,000 Women, Aged 15 to 19: This statistic is an indicator of early childbearing. Having children before age 20 limits the opportunities for young women in obtaining education and training, in employment options and involvement with the community, and in attending to their own physical development and health concerns before having to focus on that of dependent children. Monitoring and reducing the adolescent birth rate is important to the long-term human development needs of poor populations worldwide (I6.1–I6.3).

Average Age of Marriage for Women: This indicator represents the average age of a woman's first marriage. Like the indicator above, it is a potential indication of limited educational, employment, and health opportunities for young women, as the earlier a woman gets married the more likely she is to have children at an earlier age (I7.1–I7.3).

Maternal Mortality Ratio: Maternal mortality reflects the number of deaths of women during pregnancy and delivery compared with the number of live births within a given year. As such, it helps to monitor the status of a country's healthcare system, especially as it relates to women's health and reproductive concerns. In particular, lack of access to healthcare professionals and facilities during pregnancy and delivery can increase the risk to expectant mothers. The World Health Organization (WHO) says that, in regions with high maternal mortality, many maternal deaths are not reported, resulting in statistics that don't fully account for the incidence of maternal deaths (I8.1–I8.4).

Contraceptive Prevalence and Contraceptive Use, Methods Compared: Effective contraception allows women to limit the number of children they have and to gain some control over when they bear children. This control over birth patterns can help to improve the quality of the lives of women and the children they have. Advanced methods of birth control, such as IUDs, oral contraceptives (the pill), condoms, and diaphragms, are generally more reliable than traditional methods (I9.1–I9.6).

Whether Abortion Is Legal: The legal status of abortion is an important indicator of the potential health risks of and choices available to women in poorer countries. Often, if abortion is illegal, women will seek unprofessional and unauthorized means of terminating pregnancy, greatly increasing the possibility of health complications and death (I10.1–I10.3).

Anemia among Pregnant Women: Anemia can cause increased risk of hemorrhage during delivery along with reduced levels of productivity during pregnancy and increased possibility of unhealthy babies. This indicator is a sign of the adequacy of a country's health care system particularly as it relates to women's reproductive needs; it also signals the prevalence of health risks to women and their expected children—health risks that can be prevented by better health care and nutrition during pregnancy (I11.1–I11.3).

Pregnant Women Immunized against Tetanus: Tetanus (also called lockjaw) is an infectious disease that affects the nervous system and muscular control. Infection is caused by a toxin found in many natural sources, particularly in topsoil; therefore any open wound caused by something that may have had contact with the soil should be treated with an antitoxin. Regular immunizations against the toxin should also be given as a safeguard for each individual. Also, a pregnant woman can pass the disease to her fetus. Accordingly, tetanus represents a health threat to newborns, but one that can be avoided by immunizing women in their childbearing years. Monitoring the rate of immunization of women against tetanus helps to analyze the extent of this potential health risk (I12.1–I12.3).

Female to Male Enrollment Ratios: As a comparison of the enrollment of females to males at the primary and secondary levels, these indicators help to analyze the extent to which women's educational opportunities differ from men's. They are very significant for women in poverty, because increased educational opportunity could increase prospects for employment and income earning potential. Increased access to education, in particular at the primary level, also enhances the possibility that a woman will be literate, and reading and writing skills can help people to address many basic human needs (health care, for instance) that might be ignored without language skills (I13.1–I13.4).

Female Teachers as Percent of Total Teachers: The significance of this statistic lies in the fact that the teaching profession is one of the first occupations to be made accessible to women in countries that are undergoing modernization. Accordingly, teaching offers women a new means of economic advancement in many societies and the number of female teachers as a percent of all teachers reflects the extent of this potential growing economic opportunity. Further, women teachers offer important role models for girls; therefore, this statistic also indicates the extent of this significant long-term influence on women's development (I14.1–I14.6).

Females as Percent of Labor Force: The share of women in the total labor force shows how economically active women are in relation to males and to the total work force. It can be viewed as an indication of the level of economic opportunity open to women in a given country and the divergence between the economic prospects of men and women. This indicator does not account for women who work in the home; women homeworkers are often not considered economically active, but the contributions they make to household economics in satisfying the material needs of a family are crucial to poorer families in all societies (I15.1–I15.6).

Women in Legislatures, and in Ministerial and Sub-Ministerial Positions: These indicators are a measure of women's political power in a country. The data reflect the proportion of important government positions that are occupied by women. Having women in decision-making roles increases the chances that policymaking will be more sensitive to women's needs (I16.1–I16.6).

I1.1 Population Worldwide, 1997—Male, Female, and Age Group Breakdown

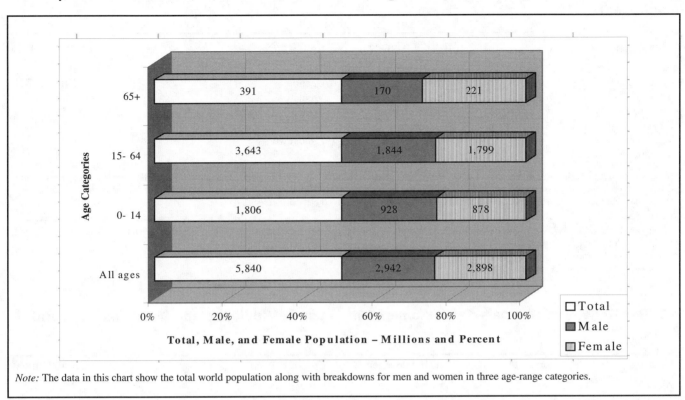

Note: The data in this chart show the total world population along with breakdowns for men and women in three age-range categories.

Source: International Data Base, U.S. Bureau of the Census, web site http://www.census.gov/ipc/www/idbnew.html

I2.1 Sex Ratio, Men Compared with Women, 1997—Low-Income Countries per World Bank

Country	Men/100 Women	Country	Men/100 Women
Afghanistan	95	Guinea-Bissau	103
Angola	102	Guyana	103
Armenia	106	Haiti	104
Azerbaijan	104	Honduras	98
Bangladesh	95	India	94
Benin	103	Kenya	100
Bhutan	99	Kyrgyzstan	104
Bosnia and Herzegovina	102	Laos	102
Burkina Faso	101	Lesotho	103
Burundi	105	Liberia	99
Cambodia	107	Madagascar	101
Cameroon	101	Malawi	102
Central African Republic	107	Mali	103
Chad	102	Mauritania	102
China	na	Moldova	109
Comoros	97	Mongolia	99
Congo, Dem. Rep. (Zaire)	102	Mozambique	102
Congo, Rep.	105	Myanmar (Burma)	101
Cote d'Ivoire	96	Nepal	98
Equatorial Guinea	103	Nicaragua	100
Eritrea	101	Niger	102
Ethiopia	99	Nigeria	102
Gambia	102	Pakistan	94
Ghana	101	Rwanda	103
Guinea	99	Sao Tome and Principe	102

I2.1 Sex Ratio, Men Compared with Women, 1997—Low-Income Countries per World Bank (continued)

Country	Men/100 Women	Country	Men/100 Women
Senegal	100	Togo	102
Sierra Leone	104	Uganda	101
Somalia	102	Vietnam	103
Sri Lanka	102	Yemen	99
Sudan	99	Zambia	103
Tajikistan	101	Zimbabwe	101
Tanzania	102		

Note: The sex ratio is calculated as the number of males per 100 females. If a value is greater than 100, there are more men than women in a country, while a value less than 100 indicates more women than men. The ratio is based on estimates and projections from the Population Division of the United Nations Secretariat, and national statistics collected by the Statistics Division of the United Nations Secretariat.

Source: The World's Women 1995: Trends and Statistics, Table 1-1; United Nations Web site, http://www.un.org/Depts/unsd/gender/1-1asi.htm
http://www.un.org/Depts/unsd/gender/1-1dev.htm
http://www.un.org/Depts/unsd/gender/1-1lat.htm
http://www.un.org/Depts/unsd/gender/1-1afr.htm

I2.2 Sex Ratio, Men Compared with Women, 1997—Lower Middle-Income Countries per World Bank

Country	Men/100 Women	Country	Men/100 Women
Albania	95	Lithuania	111
Algeria	98	Macedonia, FYRO	98
Belarus	113	Maldives	95
Belize	98	Marshall Islands	96
Bolivia	101	Micronesia	95
Botswana	104	Morocco	100
Bulgaria	105	Namibia	101
Cape Verde	113	North Korea, Dem. Rep.	100
Colombia	102	Panama	98
Costa Rica	98	Papua New Guinea	94
Cuba	99	Paraguay	98
Djibouti	103	Peru	102
Dominica	100	Philippines	99
Dominican Republic	97	Romania	103
Ecuador	99	Russia	114
Egypt	97	Samoa	91
El Salvador	104	Solomon Islands	94
Estonia	113	St. Vincent and the Grenadines	100
Fiji	97	Suriname	101
Georgia	109	Swaziland	108
Grenada	107	Syria	98
Guatemala	98	Thailand	100
Indonesia	100	Tonga	98
Iran	97	Tunisia	97
Iraq	97	Turkey	98
Jamaica	99	Turkmenistan	102
Jordan	95	Ukraine	115
Kazakhstan	106	Uzbekistan	102
Kiribati	103	Vanuatu	100
Latvia	119	Venezuela	99
Lebanon	105	Yugoslavia	101

Note: The sex ratio is calculated as the number of males per 100 females. If a value is greater than 100, there are more men than women in a country, while a value less than 100 indicates more women than men. The ratio is based on estimates and projections from the Population Division of the United Nations Secretariat, and national statistics collected by the Statistics Division of the United Nations Secretariat.

Source: The World's Women 1995: Trends and Statistics, Table 1-1; United Nations Web site, http://www.un.org/Depts/unsd/gender/1-1asi.htm
http://www.un.org/Depts/unsd/gender/1-1dev.htm
http://www.un.org/Depts/unsd/gender/1-1lat.htm
http://www.un.org/Depts/unsd/gender/1-1afr.htm

I2.3 Sex Ratio, Men Compared with Women, 1997—Upper Middle-Income Countries per World Bank

Country	Men/100 Women	Country	Men/100 Women
Antigua and Barbuda	na	Mexico	102
Argentina	104	Oman	88
Bahrain	75	Palau	88
Barbados	106	Poland	106
Brazil	102	Saudi Arabia	80
Chile	102	Seychelles	100
Croatia	107	Slovakia	105
Czech Republic	105	Slovenia	106
Gabon	102	South Africa	101
Hungary	109	St. Kitts & Nevis	104
Libya	92	St. Lucia	105
Malaysia	98	Trinidad & Tobago	90
Malta	102	Uruguay	105
Mauritius	100		

Note: The sex ratio is calculated as the number of males per 100 females. If a value is greater than 100, there are more men than women in a country, while a value less than 100 indicates more women than men. The ratio is based on estimates and projections from the Population Division of the United Nations Secretariat, and national statistics collected by the Statistics Division of the United Nations Secretariat.

Source: The World's Women 1995: Trends and Statistics, Table 1-1; United Nations Web site, http://www.un.org/Depts/unsd/gender/1-1asi.htm
http://www.un.org/Depts/unsd/gender/1-1dev.htm
http://www.un.org/Depts/unsd/gender/1-1lat.htm
http://www.un.org/Depts/unsd/gender/1-1afr.htm

I2.4 Sex Ratio, Worldwide Summary, 1997—With Age Breakdown

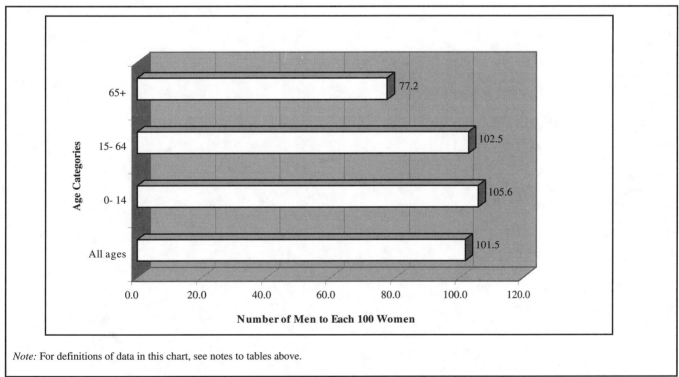

Note: For definitions of data in this chart, see notes to tables above.

Source: International Data Base, U.S. Bureau of the Census, web site http://www.census.gov/ipc/www/idbnew.html

I3.1 Life Expectancy at Birth, In Years, Men Compared with Women, 1996—Low-Income Countries per World Bank

Country	Men	Women	Difference
Afghanistan	na	na	na
Angola	45	48	3
Armenia	69	76	7
Azerbaijan	65	74	9
Bangladesh	57	59	2
Benin	52	57	5
Bhutan	na	na	na
Bosnia and Herzegovina	69	74	5
Burkina Faso	45	47	2
Burundi	45	48	3
Cambodia	52	55	3
Cameroon	55	58	3
Central African Republic	46	51	5
Chad	47	50	3
China	68	71	3
Comoros	na	na	na
Congo, Dem. Rep. (Zaire)	51	54	3
Congo, Rep.	49	54	5
Cote d'Ivoire	53	55	2
Equatorial Guinea	na	na	na
Eritrea	54	56	2
Ethiopia	48	51	3
Gambia	51	55	4
Ghana	57	61	4
Guinea	46	47	1
Guinea-Bissau	42	45	3
Guyana	na	na	na
Haiti	54	57	3
Honduras	65	69	4
India	62	63	1
Kenya	57	60	3
Kyrgyzstan	62	71	9
Laos	52	54	2
Lesotho	57	60	3
Liberia	na	na	na
Madagascar	57	60	3
Malawi	43	43	0
Mali	48	52	4
Mauritania	52	55	3
Moldova	64	71	7
Mongolia	64	67	3
Mozambique	44	46	2
Myanmar (Burma)	58	61	3
Nepal	57	57	0
Nicaragua	65	70	5
Niger	44	49	5
Nigeria	51	55	4
Pakistan	62	65	3
Rwanda	39	42	3
Sao Tome and Principe	na	na	na
Senegal	49	52	3
Sierra Leone	35	38	3
Somalia	na	na	na
Sri Lanka	71	75	4
Sudan	53	56	3
Tajikistan	66	72	6
Tanzania	49	52	3

I3.1 Life Expectancy at Birth, In Years, Men Compared with Women, 1996—Low-Income Countries per World Bank *(continued)*

Country	Men	Women	Difference
Togo	49	52	3
Uganda	43	43	0
Vietnam	66	70	4
Yemen	54	54	0
Zambia	44	45	1
Zimbabwe	55	57	2

Note: Life expectancy at birth is the number of years a newborn is expected to live given the existing demographic patterns. This figure is calculated for both male and female infants; the difference in years is also represented in the third column.

Source: World Bank, *World Development Indicators 1998*, Table 1.2 Quality of Life; *World's Women 1995;* United Nations Development Programme, *Human Development Report 1997*

I3.2 Life Expectancy at Birth, In Years, Men Compared with Women, 1996—Lower Middle-Income Countries per World Bank

Country	Men	Women	Difference
Albania	69	75	6
Algeria	68	72	4
Belarus	63	74	11
Belize	na	na	na
Bolivia	59	63	4
Botswana	50	53	3
Bulgaria	67	75	8
Cape Verde	na	na	na
Colombia	67	73	6
Costa Rica	75	79	4
Cuba	74	78	4
Djibouti	na	na	na
Dominica	na	na	na
Dominican Republic	69	73	4
Ecuador	67	73	6
Egypt	64	67	3
El Salvador	66	72	6
Estonia	63	76	13
Fiji	na	na	0
Georgia	69	77	8
Grenada	na	na	na
Guatemala	64	69	5
Indonesia	63	67	4
Iran	69	70	1
Iraq	60	63	3
Jamaica	72	77	5
Jordan	69	72	3
Kazakhstan	60	70	10
Kiribati	na	na	na
Latvia	63	76	13
Lebanon	68	71	3
Lithuania	65	76	11
Macedonia, FYRO	70	74	4
Maldives	na	na	na
Marshall Islands	na	na	na
Micronesia	na	na	na
Morocco	64	68	4
Namibia	55	57	2

I3.2 Life Expectancy at Birth, In Years, Men Compared with Women, 1996—Lower Middle-Income Countries per World Bank *(continued)*

Country	Men	Women	Difference
North Korea, Dem. Rep.	61	65	4
Panama	72	76	4
Papua New Guinea	57	58	1
Paraguay	68	74	6
Peru	66	71	5
Philippines	64	68	4
Romania	65	73	8
Russia	60	73	13
Samoa	na	na	na
Solomon Islands	na	na	na
St. Vincent and the Grenadines	na	na	na
Suriname	na	na	na
Swaziland	na	na	na
Syria	66	71	5
Thailand	67	72	5
Tonga	na	na	na
Tunisia	69	71	2
Turkey	66	71	5
Turkmenistan	62	69	7
Ukraine	62	73	11
Uzbekistan	66	72	6
Vanuatu	na	na	na
Venezuela	70	76	6
Yugoslavia	70	75	5

Note: Life expectancy at birth is the number of years a newborn is expected to live given the existing demographic patterns. This figure is calculated for both male and female infants; the difference in years is also represented in the third column.

Source: World Bank, *World Development Indicators 1998,* Table 1.2 Quality of Life; *World's Women 1995;* United Nations Development Programme, *Human Development Report 1997*

I3.3 Life Expectancy at Birth, In Years, Men Compared with Women, 1996—Upper Middle-Income Countries per World Bank

Country	Men	Women	Difference
Antigua and Barbuda	na	na	na
Argentina	69	77	8
Bahrain	na	na	na
Barbados	na	na	na
Brazil	63	71	8
Chile	72	78	6
Croatia	68	77	9
Czech Republic	70	77	7
Gabon	53	57	4
Hungary	65	75	10
Libya	66	70	4
Malaysia	70	74	4
Malta	na	na	na
Mauritius	68	75	7
Mexico	69	75	6
Oman	69	73	4
Palau	na	na	na
Poland	68	77	9
Saudi Arabia	69	71	2
Seychelles	na	na	na
Slovakia	69	77	8

I3.3 Life Expectancy at Birth, In Years, Men Compared with Women, 1996—Upper Middle-Income Countries per World Bank *(continued)*

Country	Men	Women	Difference
Slovenia	71	78	7
South Africa	62	68	6
St. Kitts & Nevis	na	na	na
St. Lucia	na	na	na
Trinidad & Tobago	70	75	5
Uruguay	70	77	7

Note: Life expectancy at birth is the number of years a newborn is expected to live given the existing demographic patterns. This figure is calculated for both male and female infants; the difference in years is also represented in the third column.

Source: World Bank, *World Development Indicators 1998*, Table 1.2 Quality of Life; *World's Women 1995;* United Nations Development Programme, *Human Development Report 1997*

I3.4 Life Expectancy at Birth, as Percent of Males, 1996—Low-Income Countries per World Bank

Country	Percent	Country	Percent
Afghanistan	102	Laos	106
Angola	107	Lesotho	105
Armenia	110	Liberia	107
Azerbaijan	112	Madagascar	105
Bangladesh	100	Malawi	100
Benin	110	Mali	107
Bhutan	106	Mauritania	108
Bosnia and Herzegovina	109	Moldova	113
Burkina Faso	104	Mongolia	105
Burundi	107	Mozambique	107
Cambodia	106	Myanmar (Burma)	105
Cameroon	106	Nepal	98
Central African Republic	111	Nicaragua	108
Chad	107	Niger	109
China	104	Nigeria	106
Comoros	102	Pakistan	103
Congo, Dem. Rep. (Zaire)	106	Rwanda	106
Congo, Rep.	110	Sao Tome and Principe	92
Cote d'Ivoire	106	Senegal	104
Equatorial Guinea	106	Sierra Leone	109
Eritrea	106	Somalia	106
Ethiopia	106	Sri Lanka	106
Gambia	107	Sudan	106
Ghana	105	Tajikistan	109
Guinea	102	Tanzania	106
Guinea-Bissau	107	Togo	106
Guyana	110	Uganda	105
Haiti	106	Vietnam	108
Honduras	107	Yemen	102
India	100	Zambia	102
Kenya	108	Zimbabwe	104
Kyrgyzstan	114		

Note: Life expectancy at birth is the number of years a newborn is expected to live given the existing demographic patterns. Female life expectancy represented as a percent of male life expectancy is calculated by dividing female life expectancy by that of the male population and multiplying by 100.

Source: State of the World's Children 1998; UNICEF Web site, Table 7; http://www.unicef.org/sowc98/

I3.5 Life Expectancy at Birth, as Percent of Males, 1996—Lower Middle-Income Countries per World Bank

Country	Percent	Country	Percent
Albania	109	Lithuania	117
Algeria	104	Macedonia, FYRO	106
Belarus	117	Maldives	97
Belize	104	Marshall Islands	na
Bolivia	107	Micronesia	95
Botswana	106	Morocco	106
Bulgaria	110	Namibia	104
Cape Verde	103	North Korea, Dem. Rep.	109
Colombia	107	Panama	106
Costa Rica	107	Papua New Guinea	102
Cuba	105	Paraguay	107
Djibouti	106	Peru	108
Dominica	96	Philippines	106
Dominican Republic	106	Romania	111
Ecuador	107	Russia	122
Egypt	105	Samoa	106
El Salvador	109	Solomon Islands	107
Estonia	117	St. Vincent and the Grenadines	92
Fiji	107	Suriname	107
Georgia	112	Swaziland	109
Grenada	na	Syria	108
Guatemala	108	Thailand	109
Indonesia	105	Tonga	93
Iran	101	Tunisia	103
Iraq	105	Turkey	108
Jamaica	107	Turkmenistan	111
Jordan	106	Ukraine	116
Kazakhstan	116	Uzbekistan	111
Kiribati	92	Vanuatu	106
Latvia	117	Venezuela	107
Lebanon	104	Yugoslavia	107

Note: Life expectancy at birth is the number of years a newborn is expected to live given the existing demographic patterns. Female life expectancy represented as a percent of male life expectancy is calculated by dividing female life expectancy by that of the male population and multiplying by 100.

Source: State of the World's Children 1998; UNICEF Web site, Table 7; http://www.unicef.org/sowc98/

I3.6 Life Expectancy at Birth, as Percent of Males, 1996—Upper Middle-Income Countries per World Bank

Country	Percent	Country	Percent
Antigua and Barbuda	92	Mexico	109
Argentina	110	Oman	106
Bahrain	106	Palau	na
Barbados	107	Poland	113
Brazil	113	Saudi Arabia	106
Chile	108	Seychelles	91
Croatia	112	Slovakia	113
Czech Republic	109	Slovenia	113
Gabon	108	South Africa	110
Hungary	114	St. Kitts & Nevis	93
Libya	106	St. Lucia	93
Malaysia	106	Trinidad & Tobago	107
Malta	107	Uruguay	109
Mauritius	110		

Note: Life expectancy at birth is the number of years a newborn is expected to live given the existing demographic patterns. Female life expectancy represented as a percent of male life expectancy is calculated by dividing female life expectancy by that of the male population and multiplying by 100.

Source: State of the World's Children 1998; UNICEF Web site, Table 7; http://www.unicef.org/sowc98/

I3.7 Life Expectancy at Birth, as Percent of Males, 1996 Worldwide Summary—Region by Region

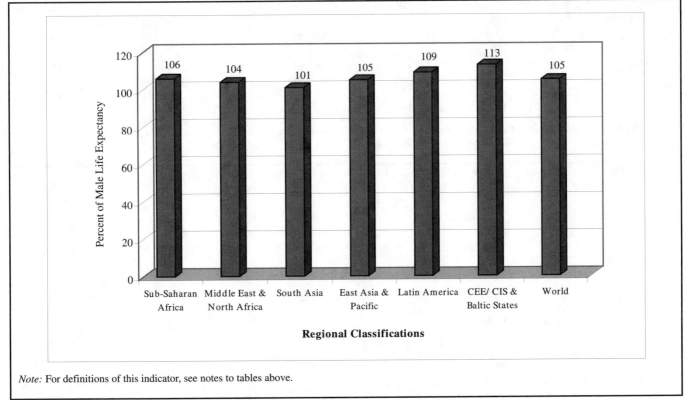

Note: For definitions of this indicator, see notes to tables above.

Source: State of the World's Children 1998; UNICEF Web site, Table 7; http://www.unicef.org/sowc98/

I4.1 Women Age 60 and Over, per 100 Men, 1996 and 2010 (projected)—Low-Income Countries per World Bank

Country	1996	2010 (proj.)	Country	1996	2010 (proj.)
Afghanistan	na	na	Laos	109	125
Angola	121	119	Lesotho	126	119
Armenia	138	143	Liberia	na	na
Azerbaijan	145	154	Madagascar	119	118
Bangladesh	82	95	Malawi	118	107
Benin	124	126	Mali	131	140
Bhutan	na	na	Mauritania	124	117
Bosnia and Herzegovina	na	na	Moldova	157	152
Burkina Faso	111	140	Mongolia	123	111
Burundi	151	147	Mozambique	126	120
Cambodia	174	159	Myanmar (Burma)	116	118
Cameroon	117	114	Nepal	97	101
Central African Republic	132	134	Nicaragua	117	116
Chad	123	121	Niger	123	130
China	101	100	Nigeria	130	127
Comoros	na	na	Pakistan	96	97
Congo, Dem. Rep. (Zaire)	130	123	Rwanda	122	125
Congo, Rep.	145	144	Sao Tome and Principe	na	na
Cote d'Ivoire	94	90	Senegal	111	111
Equatorial Guinea	na	na	Sierra Leone	130	131
Eritrea	114	110	Somalia	na	na
Ethiopia	122	111	Sri Lanka	106	120
Gambia	112	112	Sudan	116	110
Ghana	118	118	Tajikistan	131	124
Guinea	109	106	Tanzania	120	114
Guinea-Bissau	115	115	Togo	121	117
Guyana	na	na	Uganda	116	99
Haiti	119	129	Vietnam	136	142
Honduras	113	116	Yemen	126	148
India	106	106	Zambia	101	106
Kenya	114	114	Zimbabwe	112	103
Kyrgyzstan	156	146			

Note: This indicator states the ratio of the number of women age 60 and older to the number of men in that same age group. A higher-than-100 number indicates there are more women over 60 than men over 60 in that country.

Source: World Bank, *World Development Indicators 1998*, Table 2.1 Population; *World's Women 1995*, pp. 1-2

I4.2 Women Age 60 and Over, per 100 Men, 1996 and 2010 (projected)—Lower Middle-Income Countries per World Bank

Country	1996	2010 (proj.)	Country	1996	2010 (proj.)
Albania	118	114	Lithuania	175	176
Algeria	112	113	Macedonia, FYRO	118	119
Belarus	180	172	Maldives	na	na
Belize	na	na	Marshall Islands	na	na
Bolivia	120	123	Micronesia	na	na
Botswana	169	152	Morocco	114	127
Bulgaria	127	138	Namibia	120	115
Cape Verde	na	na	North Korea, Dem. Rep.	168	119
Colombia	109	125	Panama	103	105
Costa Rica	114	114	Papua New Guinea	103	109
Cuba	107	114	Paraguay	132	117
Djibouti	na	na	Peru	114	116
Dominica	na	na	Philippines	115	116
Dominican Republic	102	106	Romania	130	138
Ecuador	113	119	Russia	198	181
Egypt	116	114	Samoa	na	na
El Salvador	120	133	Solomon Islands	na	na
Estonia	187	191	St. Vincent and the Grenadines	na	na
Fiji	na	na	Suriname	na	na
Georgia	155	157	Swaziland	na	na
Grenada	na	na	Syria	108	120
Guatemala	108	117	Thailand	123	121
Indonesia	114	117	Tonga	na	na
Iran	79	84	Tunisia	102	117
Iraq	112	111	Turkey	113	119
Jamaica	121	122	Turkmenistan	143	133
Jordan	78	96	Ukraine	184	170
Kazakhstan	174	159	Uzbekistan	141	130
Kiribati	na	na	Vanuatu	na	na
Latvia	194	191	Venezuela	116	116
Lebanon	115	125	Yugoslavia	122	123

Note: This indicator states the ratio of the number of women age 60 and older to the number of men in that same age group. A higher-than-100 number indicates there are more women over 60 than men over 60 in that country.

Source: World Bank, *World Development Indicators 1998*, Table 2.1 Population; *World's Women 1995*, pp. 1-2

I4.3 Women Age 60 and Over, per 100 Men, 1996 and 2010 (projected)—Upper Middle-Income Countries per World Bank

Country	1996	2010 (proj.)	Country	1996	2010 (proj.)
Antigua and Barbuda	na	na	Mexico	120	125
Argentina	134	134	Oman	99	na
Bahrain	na	na	Palau	na	na
Barbados	na	na	Poland	151	149
Brazil	122	131	Saudi Arabia	92	na
Chile	134	130	Seychelles	na	na
Croatia	155	143	Slovakia	148	148
Czech Republic	145	133	Slovenia	160	138
Gabon	118	122	South Africa	142	140
Hungary	153	152	St. Kitts & Nevis	na	na
Libya	83	87	St. Lucia	na	na
Malaysia	117	114	Trinidad & Tobago	102	101
Malta	na	na	Uruguay	133	141
Mauritius	130	131			

Note: This indicator states the ratio of the number of women age 60 and older to the number of men in that same age group. A higher-than-100 number indicates there are more women over 60 than men over 60 in that country.

Source: World Bank, *World Development Indicators 1998*, Table 2.1, Population; *World's Women 1995*, pp. 1-2

I4.4 Women Age 60 and Over, per 100 Men, 1996 and 2010, Worldwide Summary—Comparison By Income Level per World Bank

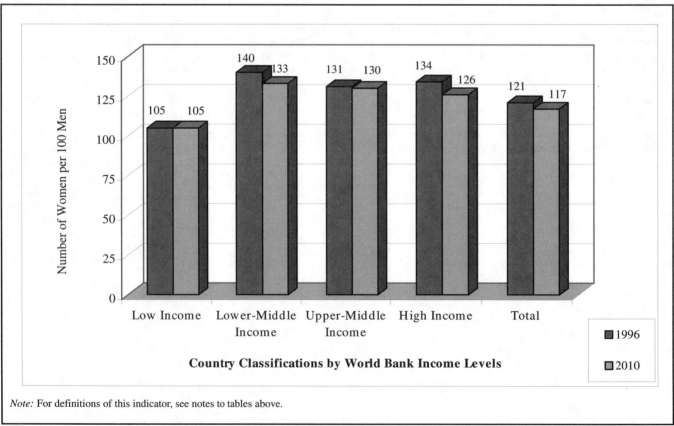

Note: For definitions of this indicator, see notes to tables above.

Source: World Bank, *World Development Indicators 1998*, Table 2.1, Population

I5.1 Total Fertility Rates, Recent Historical Trends, 1960–1996—Low-Income Countries per World Bank

Country	1960	1980	1996
Afghanistan	6.9	7.1	6.9
Angola	6.4	6.9	6.8
Armenia	4.5	2.4	1.8
Azerbaijan	5.5	3.3	2.4
Bangladesh	6.7	6.4	3.2
Benin	6.9	7.1	6.0
Bhutan	5.9	5.9	5.9
Bosnia and Herzegovina	4.0	2.1	1.4
Burkina Faso	6.7	7.8	6.7
Burundi	6.8	6.8	6.4
Cambodia	6.3	4.6	4.6
Cameroon	5.8	6.4	5.4
Central African Republic	5.6	5.8	5.1
Chad	6.0	5.9	5.6
China	5.7	2.9	1.8
Comoros	6.8	7.1	5.7
Congo, Dem. Rep. (Zaire)	6.0	6.6	6.4
Congo, Rep.	5.9	6.3	6.0
Cote d'Ivoire	7.2	7.4	5.3
Equatorial Guinea	5.5	5.7	5.6
Eritrea	6.6	6.1	5.5
Ethiopia	6.9	6.9	7.0
Gambia	6.4	6.5	5.3
Ghana	6.9	6.5	5.4
Guinea	7.0	7.0	6.7
Guinea-Bissau	5.1	5.7	5.5
Guyana	6.5	3.6	2.4
Haiti	6.3	5.3	4.7
Honduras	7.5	6.3	4.5
India	5.9	4.7	3.2
Kenya	8.0	7.8	5.0
Kyrgyzstan	5.1	4.1	3.3
Laos	6.2	6.7	6.7
Lesotho	5.8	5.7	5.0
Liberia	6.6	6.8	6.5
Madagascar	6.6	6.6	5.8
Malawi	6.9	7.6	6.8
Mali	7.1	7.1	6.8
Mauritania	6.5	6.3	5.1
Moldova	3.3	2.5	1.9
Mongolia	6.0	6.2	3.4
Mozambique	6.3	6.5	6.2
Myanmar (Burma)	6.0	5.1	3.4
Nepal	5.8	6.2	5.1
Nicaragua	7.3	6.2	4.0
Niger	7.3	8.1	7.2
Nigeria	6.5	6.5	6.1
Pakistan	6.9	6.8	5.2
Rwanda	7.5	8.3	6.2
Sao Tome and Principe	na	na	na
Senegal	7.0	6.9	5.8
Sierra Leone	6.2	6.5	6.2
Somalia	7.0	7.0	7.0
Sri Lanka	5.3	3.5	2.1
Sudan	6.7	6.5	4.7
Tajikistan	6.3	5.7	4.0

I5.1 Total Fertility Rates, Recent Historical Trends, 1960–1996—Low-Income Countries per World Bank (continued)

Country	1960	1980	1996
Tanzania	6.8	6.8	5.6
Togo	6.6	6.6	6.2
Uganda	6.9	7.0	7.1
Vietnam	6.1	5.1	3.1
Yemen	7.6	7.6	7.6
Zambia	6.6	7.1	5.6
Zimbabwe	7.5	6.4	4.8

Note: Total fertility rate signifies the total number of children projected to be born to a woman, if she lived through the end of an expected childbearing period (usually from age 15 to 49 years) and if she bore children at a rate in accordance with prevailing fertility rates corresponding to specific age groups.

Source: State of the World's Children 1998; UNICEF Web site, Table 8, http://www.unicef.org/sowc98

I5.2 Total Fertility Rates, Recent Historical Trends, 1960–1996—Lower Middle-Income Countries per World Bank

Country	1960	1980	1996
Albania	5.9	3.8	2.7
Algeria	7.3	6.8	4.0
Belarus	2.7	2.1	1.5
Belize	6.5	5.8	3.8
Bolivia	6.7	5.6	4.5
Botswana	6.8	6.1	4.6
Bulgaria	2.2	2.1	1.5
Cape Verde	7.0	6.5	3.7
Colombia	6.8	3.8	2.8
Costa Rica	7.0	3.7	3.0
Cuba	4.2	2.0	1.6
Djibouti	7.0	6.6	5.5
Dominica	na	na	na
Dominican Republic	7.4	4.3	2.9
Ecuador	6.7	5.1	3.2
Egypt	7.0	5.2	3.5
El Salvador	6.8	5.1	3.2
Estonia	2.0	2.1	1.4
Fiji	6.4	3.9	2.8
Georgia	2.9	2.3	2.0
Grenada	na	na	na
Guatemala	6.9	6.3	5.0
Indonesia	5.5	4.4	2.7
Iran	7.2	6.7	4.9
Iraq	7.2	6.5	5.4
Jamaica	5.4	3.8	2.5
Jordan	7.7	7.1	5.3
Kazakhstan	4.5	3.0	2.4
Kiribati	na	na	na
Latvia	1.9	2.0	1.5
Lebanon	6.3	4.0	2.9
Lithuania	2.5	2.1	1.6
Macedonia, FYRO	4.2	2.6	2.0
Maldives	7.0	6.9	6.8
Marshall Islands	na	na	na
Micronesia	na	na	na
Morocco	7.2	5.5	3.3
Namibia	6.0	5.9	5.0
North Korea, Dem. Rep.	5.8	2.8	2.1

I5.2 Total Fertility Rates, Recent Historical Trends, 1960–1996—Lower Middle-Income Countries per World Bank *(continued)*

Country	1960	1980	1996
Panama	5.9	3.8	2.7
Papua New Guinea	6.3	5.6	4.8
Paraguay	6.5	5.2	4.3
Peru	6.9	5.0	3.1
Philippines	6.9	4.9	3.7
Romania	2.3	2.4	1.4
Russia	2.6	2.0	1.4
Samoa	8.3	5.9	3.9
Solomon Islands	6.4	6.7	5.1
St. Vincent and the Grenadines	na	na	na
Suriname	6.6	3.8	2.5
Swaziland	6.5	6.3	4.6
Syria	7.3	7.4	4.2
Thailand	6.4	3.6	1.8
Tonga	na	na	na
Tunisia	7.1	5.3	3.0
Turkey	6.3	4.3	2.6
Turkmenistan	6.4	5.1	3.7
Ukraine	2.2	2.0	1.5
Uzbekistan	6.3	4.9	3.6
Vanuatu	7.2	5.4	4.5
Venezuela	6.6	4.2	3.1
Yugoslavia	2.7	2.3	1.8

Note: Total fertility rate signifies the total number of children projected to be born to a woman, if she lived through the end of an expected childbearing period (usually from age 15 to 49 years) and if she bore children at a rate in accordance with prevailing fertility rates corresponding to specific age groups.

Source: State of the World's Children 1998; UNICEF Web site, Table 8, http://www.unicef.org/sowc98

I5.3 Total Fertility Rates, Recent Historical Trends, 1960–1996—Upper Middle-Income Countries per World Bank

Country	1960	1980	1996
Antigua and Barbuda	na	na	na
Argentina	3.1	3.3	2.7
Bahrain	7.1	4.9	3.1
Barbados	4.5	2.1	1.7
Brazil	6.2	4.0	2.3
Chile	5.3	2.8	2.5
Croatia	2.3	2.0	1.6
Czech Republic	2.3	2.2	1.5
Gabon	4.1	4.4	5.3
Hungary	2.0	2.0	1.5
Libya	7.1	7.3	6.1
Malaysia	6.8	4.2	3.4
Malta	3.4	2.0	2.1
Mauritius	5.8	2.8	2.3
Mexico	6.9	4.8	2.9
Oman	7.2	7.2	7.2
Palau	na	na	na
Poland	3.0	2.3	1.7
Saudi Arabia	7.2	7.3	6.0
Seychelles	na	na	na
Slovakia	3.1	2.4	1.6
Slovenia	2.4	2.1	1.3
South Africa	6.5	4.9	3.9

I5.3 Total Fertility Rates, Recent Historical Trends, 1960–1996—Upper Middle-Income Countries per World Bank (continued)

Country	1960	1980	1996
St. Kitts & Nevis	na	na	na
St. Lucia	na	na	na
Trinidad & Tobago	5.1	3.3	2.2
Uruguay	2.9	2.7	2.3

Note: Total fertility rate signifies the total number of children projected to be born to a woman, if she lived through the end of an expected childbearing period (usually from age 15 to 49 years) and if she bore children at a rate in accordance with prevailing fertility rates corresponding to specific age groups.

Source: State of the World's Children 1998; UNICEF Web site, Table 8, http://www.unicef.org/sowc98

I5.4 Total Fertility Rates, Average Annual Reduction Rate, 1960–1996—Low-Income Countries per World Bank

Country	Percent, 1960–1980	Percent, 1980–1996	Country	Percent, 1960–1980	Percent, 1980–1996
Afghanistan	-0.1	0.2	Kyrgyzstan	1.1	1.4
Angola	-0.4	0.1	Laos	-0.4	0.0
Armenia	3.1	1.8	Lesotho	0.1	0.8
Azerbaijan	2.6	2.0	Liberia	-0.1	0.3
Bangladesh	0.2	4.3	Madagascar	0.0	0.8
Benin	-0.1	1.1	Malawi	-0.5	0.7
Bhutan	0.0	0.0	Mali	0.0	0.3
Bosnia and Herzegovina	3.2	2.5	Mauritania	0.2	1.3
Burkina Faso	-0.8	1.0	Moldova	1.4	1.7
Burundi	0.0	0.4	Mongolia	-0.2	3.8
Cambodia	1.6	0.0	Mozambique	-0.2	0.3
Cameroon	-0.5	1.1	Myanmar (Burma)	0.8	2.5
Central African Republic	-0.2	0.8	Nepal	-0.3	1.2
Chad	0.1	0.3	Nicaragua	0.8	2.7
China	3.4	3.0	Niger	-0.5	0.7
Comoros	-0.2	1.4	Nigeria	0.0	0.4
Congo, Dem. Rep. (Zaire)	-0.5	0.2	Pakistan	0.1	1.7
Congo, Rep.	-0.3	0.3	Rwanda	-0.5	1.8
Cote d'Ivoire	-0.1	2.1	Sao Tome and Principe	na	na
Equatorial Guinea	-0.2	0.1	Senegal	0.1	1.1
Eritrea	0.4	0.6	Sierra Leone	-0.2	0.3
Ethiopia	0.0	-0.1	Somalia	0.0	0.0
Gambia	-0.1	1.3	Sri Lanka	2.1	3.2
Ghana	0.3	1.2	Sudan	0.2	2.0
Guinea	0.0	0.3	Tajikistan	0.5	2.2
Guinea-Bissau	-0.6	0.2	Tanzania	0.0	1.2
Guyana	3.0	2.5	Togo	0.0	0.4
Haiti	0.9	0.8	Uganda	-0.1	-0.1
Honduras	0.9	2.1	Vietnam	0.9	3.1
India	1.1	2.4	Yemen	0.0	0.0
Kenya	0.1	2.8	Zambia	-0.4	1.5
			Zimbabwe	0.8	1.8

Note: Total fertility rate signifies the total number of children projected to be born to a woman, if she lived through the end of an expected childbearing period (usually from age 15 to 49 years) and if she bore children at a rate in accordance with prevailing fertility rates corresponding to specific age groups. This indicator—the average annual reduction rate (AARR)—measures the rate of reduction in fertility rates; it takes the annual changes in fertility rates and averages them across a specified time span.

Source: State of the World's Children 1998; UNICEF Web site, Table 8, http://www.unicef.org/sowc98

I5.5 Total Fertility Rates, Average Annual Reduction Rate, 1960–1996—Lower Middle-Income Countries per World Bank

Country	Percent, 1960–1980	Percent, 1980–1996	Country	Percent, 1960–1980	Percent, 1980–1996
Albania	2.2	2.1	Lithuania	0.9	1.7
Algeria	0.4	3.3	Macedonia, FYRO	2.4	1.6
Belarus	1.3	2.1	Maldives	0.1	0.1
Belize	0.6	2.6	Marshall Islands	na	na
Bolivia	0.9	1.4	Micronesia	na	na
Botswana	0.5	1.8	Morocco	1.3	3.2
Bulgaria	0.2	2.1	Namibia	0.1	1.0
Cape Verde	0.4	3.5	North Korea, Dem. Rep.	3.6	1.8
Colombia	2.9	1.9	Panama	2.2	2.1
Costa Rica	3.2	1.3	Papua New Guinea	0.6	1.0
Cuba	3.7	1.4	Paraguay	1.1	1.2
Djibouti	0.3	1.1	Peru	1.6	3.0
Dominica	na	na	Philippines	1.7	1.8
Dominican Republic	2.7	2.5	Romania	-0.2	3.4
Ecuador	1.4	2.9	Russia	1.3	2.2
Egypt	1.5	2.5	Samoa	1.7	2.6
El Salvador	1.4	2.9	Solomon Islands	-0.2	1.7
Estonia	-0.2	2.5	St. Vincent and the Grenadines	na	na
Fiji	2.5	2.1	Suriname	2.8	2.6
Georgia	1.2	0.9	Swaziland	0.2	2.0
Grenada	na	na	Syria	-0.1	3.5
Guatemala	0.5	1.4	Thailand	2.9	4.3
Indonesia	1.1	3.1	Tonga	na	na
Iran	0.4	2.0	Tunisia	1.5	3.6
Iraq	0.5	1.2	Turkey	1.9	3.1
Jamaica	1.8	2.6	Turkmenistan	1.1	2.0
Jordan	0.4	1.8	Ukraine	0.5	1.8
Kazakhstan	2.0	1.4	Uzbekistan	1.3	1.9
Kiribati	na	na	Vanuatu	1.4	1.1
Latvia	-0.3	1.8	Venezuela	2.3	1.9
Lebanon	2.3	2.0	Yugoslavia	0.8	1.5

Note: Total fertility rate signifies the total number of children projected to be born to a woman, if she lived through the end of an expected childbearing period (usually from age 15 to 49 years) and if she bore children at a rate in accordance with prevailing fertility rates corresponding to specific age groups. This indicator—the average annual reduction rate (AARR)—measures the rate of reduction in fertility rates; it takes the annual changes in fertility rates and averages them across a specified time span.

Source: State of the World's Children 1998; UNICEF Web site, Table 8, http://www.unicef.org/sowc98

I5.6 Total Fertility Rates, Average Annual Reduction Rate, 1960–1996—Upper Middle-Income Countries per World Bank

Country	Percent, 1960–1980	Percent, 1980–1996	Country	Percent, 1960–1980	Percent, 1980–1996
Antigua and Barbuda	na	na	Mauritius	3.6	1.2
Argentina	-0.3	1.3	Mexico	1.8	3.1
Bahrain	1.9	2.9	Oman	0.0	0.0
Barbados	3.8	1.3	Palau	na	na
Brazil	2.2	3.5	Poland	1.3	1.9
Chile	3.2	0.7	Saudi Arabia	-0.1	1.2
Croatia	0.7	1.4	Seychelles	na	na
Czech Republic	0.2	2.4	Slovakia	1.3	2.5
Gabon	-0.4	-1.2	Slovenia	0.7	3.0
Hungary	0.0	1.8	South Africa	1.4	1.4
Libya	-0.1	1.1	St. Kitts & Nevis	na	na
Malaysia	2.4	1.3	St. Lucia	na	na
Malta	2.7	-0.3	Trinidad & Tobago	2.2	2.5
			Uruguay	0.4	1.0

Note: Total fertility rate signifies the total number of children projected to be born to a woman, if she lived through the end of an expected childbearing period (usually from age 15 to 49 years) and if she bore children at a rate in accordance with prevailing fertility rates corresponding to specific age groups. This indicator—the average annual reduction rate (AARR)—measures the rate of reduction in fertility rates; it takes the annual changes in fertility rates and averages them across a specified time span.

Source: State of the World's Children 1998; UNICEF Web site, Table 8, http://www.unicef.org/sowc98

I5.7 Total Fertility Rates, Average Annual Reduction Rate, 1960–1996, Worldwide Summary—Region by Region

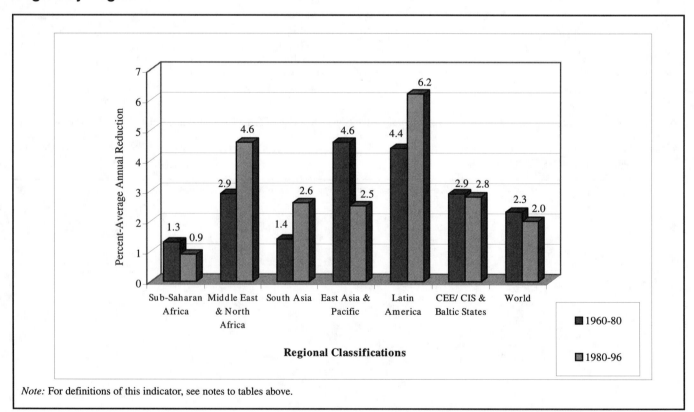

Note: For definitions of this indicator, see notes to tables above.

Source: State of the World's Children 1998; UNICEF Web site, Table 7; http://www.unicef.org/sowc98/

I6.1 Early Childbearing, Births per 1,000 Women, Aged 15–19, 1990–1995—Low-Income Countries per World Bank

Country	Births per 1,000	Country	Births per 1,000
Afghanistan	153	Laos	51
Angola	236	Lesotho	91
Armenia	52	Liberia	230
Azerbaijan	22	Madagascar	155
Bangladesh	138	Malawi	173
Benin	144	Mali	199
Bhutan	86	Mauritania	133
Bosnia and Herzegovina	31	Moldova	39
Burkina Faso	157	Mongolia	31
Burundi	60	Mozambique	131
Cambodia	12	Myanmar (Burma)	35
Cameroon	141	Nepal	92
Central African Republic	147	Nicaragua	149
Chad	192	Niger	219
China	5	Nigeria	150
Comoros	142	Pakistan	93
Congo, Dem. Rep. (Zaire)	231	Rwanda	60
Congo, Rep.	146	Sao Tome and Principe	na
Cote d'Ivoire	151	Senegal	155
Equatorial Guinea	192	Sierra Leone	212
Eritrea	140	Somalia	208
Ethiopia	169	Sri Lanka	34
Gambia	171	Sudan	59
Ghana	123	Tajikistan	36
Guinea	241	Tanzania	134
Guinea-Bissau	189	Togo	126
Guyana	66	Uganda	180
Haiti	54	Vietnam	45
Honduras	127	Yemen	102
India	116	Zambia	145
Kenya	110	Zimbabwe	129
Kyrgyzstan	45		

Note: This indicator reflects the number of births attributed to adolescent women, age 15 to 19. It is stated in terms of births per 1,000 women. Data refer to a single year between 1990 to 1995, most likely the most recent available year.

Source: The World's Women 1995: Trends and Statistics, Table 1-3; United Nations Web site, http://www.un.org/Depts/unsd/gender/1-3afr.htm
http://www.un.org/Depts/unsd/gender/1-3dev.htm
http://www.un.org/Depts/unsd/gender/1-3lat.htm
http://www.un.org/Depts/unsd/gender/1-3asi.htm

I6.2 Early Childbearing, Births per 1,000 Women, Aged 15–19, 1990–1995—Lower Middle-Income Countries per World Bank

Country	Births per 1,000	Country	Births per 1,000
Albania	14	Lithuania	26
Algeria	26	Macedonia, FYRO	44
Belarus	28	Maldives	71
Belize	117	Marshall Islands	99
Bolivia	82	Micronesia	na
Botswana	100	Morocco	37
Bulgaria	60	Namibia	111
Cape Verde	85	North Korea, Dem. Rep.	5
Colombia	80	Panama	91
Costa Rica	93	Papua New Guinea	23
Cuba	67	Paraguay	87
Djibouti	31	Peru	63
Dominica	na	Philippines	48
Dominican Republic	91	Romania	47
Ecuador	79	Russia	45
Egypt	62	Samoa	22
El Salvador	105	Solomon Islands	99
Estonia	33	St. Vincent and the Grenadines	na
Fiji	46	Suriname	62
Georgia	51	Swaziland	88
Grenada	na	Syria	57
Guatemala	123	Thailand	51
Indonesia	62	Tonga	28
Iran	96	Tunisia	17
Iraq	49	Turkey	59
Jamaica	95	Turkmenistan	22
Jordan	49	Ukraine	43
Kazakhstan	35	Uzbekistan	39
Kiribati	76	Vanuatu	75
Latvia	35	Venezuela	101
Lebanon	32	Yugoslavia	41

Note: This indicator reflects the number of births attributed to adolescent women, age 15 to 19. It is stated in terms of births per 1,000 women. Data refer to a single year between 1990 to 1995, most likely the most recent available year.

Source: The World's Women 1995: Trends and Statistics, Table 1-3; United Nations Web site, http://www.un.org/Depts/unsd/gender/1-3afr.htm
http://www.un.org/Depts/unsd/gender/1-3dev.htm
http://www.un.org/Depts/unsd/gender/1-3lat.htm
http://www.un.org/Depts/unsd/gender/1-3asi.htm

I6.3 Early Childbearing, Births per 1,000 Women, Aged 15–19, 1990–1995—Upper Middle-Income Countries per World Bank

Country	Births per 1,000	Country	Births per 1,000
Antigua and Barbuda	na	Mexico	77
Argentina	70	Oman	122
Bahrain	25	Palau	38
Barbados	51	Poland	28
Brazil	73	Saudi Arabia	124
Chile	56	Seychelles	77
Croatia	32	Slovakia	43
Czech Republic	42	Slovenia	28
Gabon	159	South Africa	72
Hungary	35	St. Kitts & Nevis	89
Libya	110	St. Lucia	114
Malaysia	29	Trinidad & Tobago	60
Malta	13	Uruguay	60
Mauritius	46		

Note: This indicator reflects the number of births attributed to adolescent women, age 15 to 19. It is stated in terms of births per 1,000 women. Data refer to a single year between 1990 to 1995, most likely the most recent available year.

Source: The World's Women 1995: Trends and Statistics, Table 1-3; United Nations Web site, http://www.un.org/Depts/unsd/gender/1-3afr.htm
http://www.un.org/Depts/unsd/gender/1-3dev.htm
http://www.un.org/Depts/unsd/gender/1-3lat.htm
http://www.un.org/Depts/unsd/gender/1-3asi.htm

I7.1 Average Age of Marriage for Women, 1985–1996—Low-Income Countries per World Bank

Country	Average Age	Country	Average Age
Afghanistan	17.8	India	18.7
Angola	na	Kenya	21.1
Armenia	na	Kyrgyzstan	na
Azerbaijan	na	Laos	na
Bangladesh	18.0	Lesotho	20.5
Benin	18.3	Liberia	19.7
Bhutan	na	Madagascar	20.3
Bosnia and Herzegovina	na	Malawi	17.8
Burkina Faso	17.4	Mali	16.4
Burundi	21.9	Mauritania	23.1
Cambodia	na	Moldova	22.7
Cameroon	19.7	Mongolia	na
Central African Republic	18.9	Mozambique	22.2
Chad	na	Myanmar (Burma)	22.4
China	22.4	Nepal	17.9
Comoros	19.5	Nicaragua	na
Congo, Dem. Rep. (Zaire)	20.0	Niger	16.3
Congo, Rep.	21.9	Nigeria	18.7
Cote d'Ivoire	18.9	Pakistan	19.2
Equatorial Guinea	na	Rwanda	na
Eritrea	na	Sao Tome and Principe	na
Ethiopia	17.1	Senegal	21.7
Gambia	na	Sierra Leone	23.8
Ghana	21.1	Somalia	21.2
Guinea	na	Sri Lanka	23.1
Guinea-Bissau	18.3	Sudan	28.2
Guyana	23.7	Tajikistan	21.5
Haiti	23.8	Tanzania	23.1
Honduras	na	Togo	na
		Uganda	na

I7.1 Average Age of Marriage for Women, 1985–1996—Low-Income Countries per World Bank (continued)

Country	Average Age	Country	Average Age
Vietnam	21.2	Zambia	na
Yemen	na	Zimbabwe	20.0

Note: This indicator represents the average age of a woman's first marriage including any woman who ever married throughout her life; the age group covered is 15 to 50. The indicator is derived from the proportions of women never married, and calculated incrementally from each five-year age group, covering the broad age group 15-50. The information most commonly comes from census or survey data and covers the years cited.

Source: The World's Women 1995: Trends and Statistics; United Nations Web site, Table 1-4, http://www.un.org/Depts/unsd/gender/1-4afr.htm
http://www.un.org/Depts/unsd/gender/1-4dev.htm
http://www.un.org/Depts/unsd/gender/1-4lat.htm
http://www.un.org/Depts/unsd/gender/1-4asi.htm

I7.2 Average Age of Marriage for Women, 1985–1996—Lower Middle-Income Countries per World Bank

Country	Average Age	Country	Average Age
Albania	na	Lithuania	na
Algeria	23.7	Macedonia, FYRO	22.7
Belarus	na	Maldives	17.5
Belize	23.9	Marshall Islands	21.0
Bolivia	22.1	Micronesia	23.3
Botswana	25.0	Morocco	22.3
Bulgaria	21.1	Namibia	na
Cape Verde	na	North Korea, Dem. Rep.	na
Colombia	22.6	Panama	25.7
Costa Rica	22.2	Papua New Guinea	21.9
Cuba	19.9	Paraguay	20.8
Djibouti	19.3	Peru	21.8
Dominica	na	Philippines	22.7
Dominican Republic	20.5	Romania	28.2
Ecuador	21.1	Russia	21.1
Egypt	22.0	Samoa	21.2
El Salvador	na	Solomon Islands	24.1
Estonia	na	St. Vincent and the Grenadines	31.4
Fiji	22.5	Suriname	24.1
Georgia	na	Swaziland	na
Grenada	29.4	Syria	25.0
Guatemala	20.5	Thailand	na
Indonesia	21.1	Tonga	20.3
Iran	19.7	Tunisia	22.3
Iraq	22.3	Turkey	25
Jamaica	29.7	Turkmenistan	21.5
Jordan	24.7	Ukraine	19.0
Kazakhstan	na	Uzbekistan	na
Kiribati	21.5	Vanuatu	na
Latvia	22.4	Venezuela	22.5
Lebanon	na	Yugoslavia	19.1

Note: This indicator represents the average age of a woman's first marriage including any woman who ever married throughout her life; the age group covered is 15 to 50. The indicator is derived from the proportions of women never married, and calculated incrementally from each five-year age group, covering the broad age group 15-50. The information most commonly comes from census or survey data and covers the years cited.

Source: The World's Women 1995: Trends and Statistics; United Nations Web site, Table 1-4, http://www.un.org/Depts/unsd/gender/1-4afr.htm
http://www.un.org/Depts/unsd/gender/1-4dev.htm
http://www.un.org/Depts/unsd/gender/1-4lat.htm
http://www.un.org/Depts/unsd/gender/1-4asi.htm

I7.3 Average Age of Marriage for Women, 1985–1996—Upper Middle-Income Countries per World Bank

Country	Average Age	Country	Average Age
Antigua and Barbuda	na	Mexico	20.6
Argentina	22.9	Oman	na
Bahrain	25.5	Palau	21.7
Barbados	na	Poland	23.8
Brazil	22.6	Saudi Arabia	15.6
Chile	23.6	Seychelles	23.7
Croatia	23.6	Slovakia	27.0
Czech Republic	na	Slovenia	na
Gabon	na	South Africa	20.1
Hungary	21.0	St. Kitts & Nevis	24.4
Libya	na	St. Lucia	31.3
Malaysia	23.5	Trinidad & Tobago	24.7
Malta	na	Uruguay	23.3
Mauritius	22.8		

Note: This indicator represents the average age of a woman's first marriage including any woman who ever married throughout her life; the age group covered is 15 to 50. The indicator is derived from the proportions of women never married, and calculated incrementally from each five-year age group, covering the broad age group 15-50. The information most commonly comes from census or survey data and covers the years cited.

Source: The World's Women 1995: Trends and Statistics; United Nations Web site, Table 1-4, http://www.un.org/Depts/unsd/gender/1-4afr.htm
http://www.un.org/Depts/unsd/gender/1-4dev.htm
http://www.un.org/Depts/unsd/gender/1-4lat.htm
http://www.un.org/Depts/unsd/gender/1-4asi.htm

I8.1 Maternal Mortality Ratio, Deaths per 100,000 Live Births, 1990–1996—Low-Income Countries per World Bank

Country	Deaths per 100,000 Births	Country	Deaths per 100,000 Births
Afghanistan	na	Honduras	220
Angola	1500	India	437
Armenia	21	Kenya	650
Azerbaijan	44	Kyrgyzstan	32
Bangladesh	850	Laos	650
Benin	500	Lesotho	610
Bhutan	na	Liberia	na
Bosnia and Herzegovina	na	Madagascar	660
Burkina Faso	930	Malawi	620
Burundi	1300	Mali	580
Cambodia	900	Mauritania	800
Cameroon	550	Moldova	33
Central African Republic	700	Mongolia	65
Chad	900	Mozambique	1500
China	115	Myanmar (Burma)	580
Comoros	na	Nepal	1500
Congo, Dem. Rep. (Zaire)	na	Nicaragua	160
Congo, Rep.	890	Niger	593
Cote d'Ivoire	600	Nigeria	1000
Equatorial Guinea	na	Pakistan	340
Eritrea	1400	Rwanda	1300
Ethiopia	1400	Sao Tome and Principe	na
Gambia	1100	Senegal	510
Ghana	740	Sierra Leone	1800
Guinea	880	Somalia	na
Guinea-Bissau	910	Sri Lanka	30
Guyana	na	Sudan	370
Haiti	600	Tajikistan	74

I8.1 Maternal Mortality Ratio, Deaths per 100,000 Live Births, 1990–1996—Low-Income Countries per World Bank *(continued)*

Country	Deaths per 100,000 Births	Country	Deaths per 100,000 Births
Tanzania	530	Yemen	1400
Togo	640	Zambia	230
Uganda	550	Zimbabwe	280
Vietnam	105		

Note: The maternal mortality ratio is derived from dividing the number of maternal deaths by the number of live births for a given year; it is expressed per 100,000 live births. Maternal deaths can result during pregnancy, delivery, and the complications thereof. However, the exact definition of maternal death can vary from case to case and between societies and countries. Further, it is not always clear from the original source of the data, particularly in relationship to the inclusion or exclusion of abortion-related deaths.

Source: World Bank, *World Development Indicators 1998,* Table 2.15, Reproductive Health; *State of the World's Children 1998*; UNICEF Web site, Table 8, http://www.unicef.org/sowc98; United Nations Development Programme, *Human Development Report 1997*

I8.2 Maternal Mortality Ratio, Deaths per 100,000 Live Births, 1990–1996—Lower Middle-Income Countries per World Bank

Country	Deaths per 100,000 Births	Country	Deaths per 100,000 Births
Albania	28	Lithuania	13
Algeria	140	Macedonia, FYRO	22
Belarus	22	Maldives	na
Belize	na	Marshall Islands	na
Bolivia	370	Micronesia	na
Botswana	250	Morocco	372
Bulgaria	20	Namibia	220
Cape Verde	na	North Korea, Dem. Rep.	na
Colombia	100	Panama	55
Costa Rica	55	Papua New Guinea	930
Cuba	36	Paraguay	190
Djibouti	na	Peru	280
Dominica	na	Philippines	208
Dominican Republic	110	Romania	41
Ecuador	150	Russia	53
Egypt	170	Samoa	na
El Salvador	300	Solomon Islands	na
Estonia	52	St. Vincent and the Grenadines	na
Fiji	na	Suriname	na
Georgia	19	Swaziland	na
Grenada	na	Syria	179
Guatemala	190	Thailand	200
Indonesia	390	Tonga	na
Iran	120	Tunisia	na
Iraq	310	Turkey	180
Jamaica	120	Turkmenistan	44
Jordan	150	Ukraine	30
Kazakhstan	53	Uzbekistan	24
Kiribati	na	Vanuatu	na
Latvia	15	Venezuela	200
Lebanon	300	Yugoslavia	12

Note: The maternal mortality ratio is derived from dividing the number of maternal deaths by the number of live births for a given year; it is expressed per 100,000 live births. Maternal deaths can result during pregnancy, delivery, and the complications thereof. However, the exact definition of maternal death can vary from case to case and between societies and countries. Further, it is not always clear from the original source of the data, particularly in relationship to the inclusion or exclusion of abortion-related deaths.

Source: World Bank, *World Development Indicators 1998,* Table 2.15, Reproductive Health; *State of the World's Children 1998*; UNICEF Web site, Table 8, http://www.unicef.org/sowc98; United Nations Development Programme, *Human Development Report 1997*

I8.3 Maternal Mortality Ratio, Deaths per 100,000 Live Births, 1990–1996—Upper Middle-Income Countries per World Bank

Country	Deaths per 100,000 Births	Country	Deaths per 100,000 Births
Antigua and Barbuda	na	Mauritius	112
Argentina	100	Mexico	110
Bahrain	na	Oman	na
Barbados	na	Palau	na
Brazil	160	Poland	10
Chile	180	Saudi Arabia	18
Croatia	12	Seychelles	na
Czech Republic	7	Slovakia	8
Gabon	500	Slovenia	5
Hungary	14	South Africa	230
Libya	220	St. Kitts & Nevis	na
Malaysia	43	St. Lucia	na
Malta	na	Trinidad & Tobago	90
		Uruguay	85

Note: The maternal mortality ratio is derived from dividing the number of maternal deaths by the number of live births for a given year; it is expressed per 100,000 live births. Maternal deaths can result during pregnancy, delivery, and the complications thereof. However, the exact definition of maternal death can vary from case to case and between societies and countries. Further, it is not always clear from the original source of the data, particularly in relationship to the inclusion or exclusion of abortion-related deaths.

Source: World Bank, *World Development Indicators 1998,* Table 2.15, Reproductive Health; *State of the World's Children 1998*; UNICEF Web site, Table 8, http://www.unicef.org/sowc98; United Nations Development Programme, *Human Development Report 1997*

I8.4 Maternal Mortality Ratio, Deaths per 100,000 Live Births, 1990–1996—Region by Region

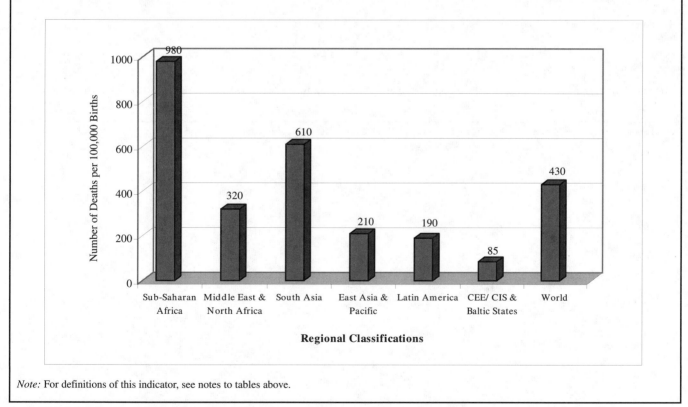

Note: For definitions of this indicator, see notes to tables above.

Source: State of the World's Children 1998; UNICEF Web site, Table 7; http://www.unicef.org/sowc98/

I9.1 Contraceptive Prevalence, Percent of Married Women, 1990–1997—Low-Income Countries per World Bank

Country	Percent	Country	Percent
Afghanistan	2		
Angola	1	Laos	19
Armenia	na	Lesotho	23
Azerbaijan	na	Liberia	6
Bangladesh	49	Madagascar	17
Benin	9	Malawi	22
Bhutan	19	Mali	7
Bosnia and Herzegovina	na	Mauritania	4
Burkina Faso	8	Moldova	na
Burundi	9	Mongolia	na
Cambodia	na	Mozambique	4
Cameroon	16	Myanmar (Burma)	17
Central African Republic	15	Nepal	29
Chad	1	Nicaragua	49
China	83	Niger	4
Comoros	21	Nigeria	6
Congo, Dem. Rep. (Zaire)	8	Pakistan	12
Congo, Rep.	na	Rwanda	21
Cote d'Ivoire	11	Sao Tome and Principe	10
Equatorial Guinea	na	Senegal	13
Eritrea	8	Sierra Leone	4
Ethiopia	4	Somalia	1
Gambia	12	Sri Lanka	66
Ghana	20	Sudan	8
Guinea	2	Tajikistan	na
Guinea-Bissau	1	Tanzania	16
Guyana	0	Togo	12
Haiti	18	Uganda	15
Honduras	47	Vietnam	65
India	41	Yemen	7
Kenya	33	Zambia	15
Kyrgyzstan	na	Zimbabwe	48

Note: This indicator represents the percentage of married women of childbearing age (most often considered between ages 15 and 49) who use, or whose partners use, any form of contraception.

Source: State of the World's Children 1998; UNICEF Web site, Table 7, http://www.unicef.org/sowc98/

I9.2 Contraceptive Prevalence, Percent of Married Women, 1990–1997—Lower Middle-Income Countries per World Bank

Country	Percent	Country	Percent
Albania	na	Lithuania	na
Algeria	57	Macedonia, FYRO	na
Belarus	50	Maldives	10
Belize	47	Marshall Islands	27
Bolivia	45	Micronesia	na
Botswana	33	Morocco	50
Bulgaria	76	Namibia	29
Cape Verde	15	North Korea, Dem. Rep.	na
Colombia	72	Panama	58
Costa Rica	75	Papua New Guinea	4
Cuba	70	Paraguay	50
Djibouti	na	Peru	64
Dominica	50	Philippines	40
Dominican Republic	64	Romania	57
Ecuador	57	Russia	na
Egypt	48	Samoa	21
El Salvador	53	Solomon Islands	25
Estonia	70	St. Vincent and the Grenadines	58
Fiji	32	Suriname	na
Georgia	na	Swaziland	21
Grenada	54	Syria	36
Guatemala	31	Thailand	74
Indonesia	55	Tonga	39
Iran	73	Tunisia	60
Iraq	18	Turkey	63
Jamaica	62	Turkmenistan	na
Jordan	35	Ukraine	na
Kazakhstan	59	Uzbekistan	56
Kiribati	28	Vanuatu	15
Latvia	na	Venezuela	49
Lebanon	55	Yugoslavia	na

Note: This indicator represents the percentage of married women of childbearing age (most often considered between ages 15 and 49) who use, or whose partners use, any form of contraception.

Source: State of the World's Children 1998; UNICEF Web site, Table 7, http://www.unicef.org/sowc98/

I9.3 Contraceptive Prevalence, Percent of Married Women, 1990–1997—Upper Middle-Income Countries per World Bank

Country	Percent	Country	Percent
Antigua and Barbuda	53	Mexico	53
Argentina	74	Oman	9
Bahrain	54	Palau	38
Barbados	55	Poland	75
Brazil	77	Saudi Arabia	na
Chile	43	Seychelles	na
Croatia	na	Slovakia	74
Czech Republic	69	Slovenia	na
Gabon	na	South Africa	50
Hungary	73	St. Kitts & Nevis	41
Libya	na	St. Lucia	47
Malaysia	48	Trinidad & Tobago	53
Malta	na	Uruguay	84
Mauritius	75		

Note: This indicator represents the percentage of married women of childbearing age (most often considered between ages 15 and 49) who use, or whose partners use, any form of contraception.

Source: State of the World's Children 1998; UNICEF Web site, Table 7, http://www.unicef.org/sowc98/

I9.4 Contraceptive Use, Methods Compared, 1986–1995—Low-Income Countries per World Bank

Country	Percent Using Any Method	Percent Using Modern Methods	Country	Percent Using Any Method	Percent Using Modern Methods
Afghanistan	na	na	Kyrgyzstan	31	na
Angola	na	na	Laos	19	15
Armenia	22	na	Lesotho	23	19
Azerbaijan	17	na	Liberia	6	5
Bangladesh	49	42	Madagascar	17	5
Benin	16	3	Malawi	22	14
Bhutan	19	na	Mali	7	5
Bosnia and Herzegovina	na	na	Mauritania	3	1
Burkina Faso	8	4	Moldova	22	na
Burundi	7	1	Mongolia	61	25
Cambodia	na	na	Mozambique	na	na
Cameroon	13	4	Myanmar (Burma)	17	14
Central African Republic	15	3	Nepal	29	26
Chad	na	na	Nicaragua	49	45
China	83	80	Niger	4	2
Comoros	21	11	Nigeria	6	4
Congo, Dem. Rep. (Zaire)	8	2	Pakistan	12	9
Congo, Rep.	na	na	Rwanda	21	13
Cote d'Ivoire	11	4	Sao Tome and Principe	na	na
Equatorial Guinea	na	na	Senegal	13	8
Eritrea	5	4	Sierra Leone	na	na
Ethiopia	4	3	Somalia	na	na
Gambia	12	7	Sri Lanka	66	44
Ghana	20	10	Sudan	8	7
Guinea	2	1	Tajikistan	21	na
Guinea-Bissau	na	na	Tanzania	18	13
Guyana	na	na	Togo	12	3
Haiti	18	13	Uganda	15	8
Honduras	47	35	Vietnam	65	44
India	41	37	Yemen	7	6
Kenya	33	27	Zambia	26	14
			Zimbabwe	48	42

Note: This indicator represents the percentage of married women of childbearing age (most often considered between ages 15 and 49) who use, or whose partners use, any form of contraception compared with those using modern methods of contraception, such as oral contraceptives (the pill), condoms, diaphragms, etc.

Source: The World's Women 1995: Trends and Statistics; United Nations Web site, Table 3-2, http://www.un.org/Depts/unsd/gender/3-2lat.htm
http://www.un.org/Depts/unsd/gender/3-2asi.htm
http://www.un.org/Depts/unsd/gender/3-2afr.htm
http://www.un.org/Depts/unsd/gender/3-2dev.htm

I9.5 Contraceptive Use, Methods Compared, 1986–1995—Lower Middle-Income Countries per World Bank

Country	Percent Using Any Method	Percent Using Modern Methods	Country	Percent Using Any Method	Percent Using Modern Methods
Albania	na	na	Lithuania	na	na
Algeria	52	49	Macedonia, FYRO	na	na
Belarus	50	42	Maldives	na	na
Belize	47	42	Marshall Islands	27	18
Bolivia	45	18	Micronesia	na	na
Botswana	33	32	Morocco	50	42
Bulgaria	na	na	Namibia	29	26
Cape Verde	na	na	North Korea, Dem. Rep.	62	53
Colombia	72	59	Panama	64	58
Costa Rica	75	65	Papua New Guinea	na	na
Cuba	70	67	Paraguay	56	41
Djibouti	na	na	Peru	64	41
Dominica	50	48	Philippines	40	25
Dominican Republic	64	59	Romania	57	14
Ecuador	57	46	Russia	32	na
Egypt	47	46	Samoa	34	34
El Salvador	53	48	Solomon Islands	na	na
Estonia	70	56	St. Vincent and the Grenadines	58	55
Fiji	40	40	Suriname	na	na
Georgia	17	na	Swaziland	20	17
Grenada	54	na	Syria	36	28
Guatemala	31	27	Thailand	74	72
Indonesia	55	52	Tonga	74	56
Iran	65	45	Tunisia	60	51
Iraq	14	10	Turkey	63	35
Jamaica	62	58	Turkmenistan	20	na
Jordan	35	27	Ukraine	23	na
Kazakhstan	59	46	Uzbekistan	56	51
Kiribati	37	27	Vanuatu	15	15
Latvia	na	na	Venezuela	52	40
Lebanon	na	na	Yugoslavia	na	na

Note: This indicator represents the percentage of married women of childbearing age (most often considered between ages 15 and 49) who use, or whose partners use, any form of contraception compared with those using modern methods of contraception, such as oral contraceptives (the pill), condoms, diaphragms, etc.

Source: The World's Women 1995: Trends and Statistics; United Nations Web site, Table 3-2, http://www.un.org/Depts/unsd/gender/3-2lat.htm
http://www.un.org/Depts/unsd/gender/3-2asi.htm
http://www.un.org/Depts/unsd/gender/3-2afr.htm
http://www.un.org/Depts/unsd/gender/3-2dev.htm

I9.6 Contraceptive Use, Methods Compared, 1986–1995—Upper Middle-Income Countries per World Bank

Country	Percent Using Any Method	Percent Using Modern Methods	Country	Percent Using Any Method	Percent Using Modern Methods
Antigua and Barbuda	53	51	Mauritius	75	49
Argentina	na	na	Mexico	53	45
Bahrain	53	30	Oman	9	8
Barbados	55	53	Palau	na	na
Brazil	77	70	Poland	na	na
Chile	30	na	Saudi Arabia	na	na
Croatia	na	na	Seychelles	na	na
Czech Republic	69	45	Slovakia	74	41
Gabon	na	na	Slovenia	na	na
Hungary	73	64	South Africa	50	48
Libya	na	na	St. Kitts & Nevis	41	37
Malaysia	48	31	St. Lucia	47	46
Malta	na	na	Trinidad & Tobago	53	44
			Uruguay	na	na

Note: This indicator represents the percentage of married women of childbearing age (most often considered between ages 15 and 49) who use, or whose partners use, any form of contraception compared with those using modern methods of contraception, such as oral contraceptives (the pill), condoms, diaphragms, etc.

Source: The World's Women 1995: Trends and Statistics; United Nations Web site, Table 3-2, http://www.un.org/Depts/unsd/gender/3-2lat.htm
http://www.un.org/Depts/unsd/gender/3-2asi.htm
http://www.un.org/Depts/unsd/gender/3-2afr.htm
http://www.un.org/Depts/unsd/gender/3-2dev.htm

I10.1 Whether Abortion Is Legal, 1994—Low-Income Countries per World Bank

Country	Yes or No	Country	Yes or No
Afghanistan	No	India	No
Angola	No	Kenya	No
Armenia	Yes	Kyrgyzstan	Yes
Azerbaijan	Yes	Laos	No
Bangladesh	No	Lesotho	No
Benin	No	Liberia	No
Bhutan	No	Madagascar	No
Bosnia and Herzegovina	Yes	Malawi	No
Burkina Faso	No	Mali	No
Burundi	No	Mauritania	No
Cambodia	No	Moldova	Yes
Cameroon	No	Mongolia	Yes
Central African Republic	No	Mozambique	No
Chad	No	Myanmar (Burma)	No
China	Yes	Nepal	No
Comoros	No	Nicaragua	No
Congo, Dem. Rep. (Zaire)	No	Niger	No
Congo, Rep.	No	Nigeria	No
Cote d'Ivoire	No	Pakistan	No
Equatorial Guinea	No	Rwanda	No
Eritrea	No	Sao Tome and Principe	No
Ethiopia	No	Senegal	No
Gambia	No	Sierra Leone	No
Ghana	No	Somalia	No
Guinea	No	Sri Lanka	No
Guinea-Bissau	No	Sudan	na
Guyana	No	Tajikistan	Yes
Haiti	No	Tanzania	No
Honduras	No	Togo	No

I10.1 Whether Abortion Is Legal, 1994—Low-Income Countries per World Bank *(continued)*

Country	Yes or No	Country	Yes or No
Uganda	No	Zambia	Yes
Vietnam	Yes	Zimbabwe	No
Yemen	No		

Note: This indicator states whether a country allows abortions to be performed. "Yes" indicates that abortion is legal in a country and "no" indicates that it is not. The specific circumstances under which "legal" abortions can be performed may vary from country to country.

Source: The World's Women 1995: Trends and Statistics; United Nations Web site, Table 1-3, http://www.un.org/Depts/unsd/gender/1-3afr.htm
http://www.un.org/Depts/unsd/gender/1-3dev.htm
http://www.un.org/Depts/unsd/gender/1-3lat.htm
http://www.un.org/Depts/unsd/gender/1-3asi.htm

I10.2 Whether Abortion Is Legal, 1994—Lower Middle-Income Countries per World Bank

Country	Yes or No	Country	Yes or No
Albania	Yes	Lithuania	Yes
Algeria	No	Macedonia, FYRO	Yes
Belarus	Yes	Maldives	No
Belize	Yes	Marshall Islands	No
Bolivia	No	Micronesia	na
Botswana	No	Morocco	No
Bulgaria	Yes	Namibia	No
Cape Verde	Yes	North Korea, Dem. Rep.	Yes
Colombia	No	Panama	No
Costa Rica	No	Papua New Guinea	No
Cuba	Yes	Paraguay	No
Djibouti	No	Peru	No
Dominica	No	Philippines	No
Dominican Republic	No	Romania	Yes
Ecuador	No	Russia	Yes
Egypt	No	Samoa	No
El Salvador	No	Solomon Islands	No
Estonia	Yes	St. Vincent and the Grenadines	No
Fiji	No	Suriname	No
Georgia	Yes	Swaziland	No
Grenada	No	Syria	No
Guatemala	No	Thailand	No
Indonesia	No	Tonga	na
Iran	No	Tunisia	Yes
Iraq	No	Turkey	Yes
Jamaica	No	Turkmenistan	Yes
Jordan	No	Ukraine	Yes
Kazakhstan	Yes	Uzbekistan	Yes
Kiribati	No	Vanuatu	No
Latvia	Yes	Venezuela	No
Lebanon	No	Yugoslavia	Yes

Note: This indicator states whether a country allows abortions to be performed. "Yes" indicates that abortion is legal in a country and "no" indicates that it is not. The specific circumstances under which "legal" abortions can be performed may vary from country to country.

Source: The World's Women 1995: Trends and Statistics; United Nations Web site, Table 1-3, http://www.un.org/Depts/unsd/gender/1-3afr.htm
http://www.un.org/Depts/unsd/gender/1-3dev.htm
http://www.un.org/Depts/unsd/gender/1-3lat.htm
http://www.un.org/Depts/unsd/gender/1-3asi.htm

I10.3 Whether Abortion Is Legal, 1994—Upper Middle-Income Countries per World Bank

Country	Yes or No	Country	Yes or No
Antigua and Barbuda	No	Mexico	No
Argentina	No	Oman	No
Bahrain	No	Palau	na
Barbados	Yes	Poland	No
Brazil	No	Saudi Arabia	No
Chile	No	Seychelles	No
Croatia	Yes	Slovakia	Yes
Czech Republic	Yes	Slovenia	Yes
Gabon	No	South Africa	No
Hungary	Yes	St. Kitts & Nevis	No
Libya	No	St. Lucia	No
Malaysia	No	Trinidad & Tobago	No
Malta	No	Uruguay	No
Mauritius	No		

Note: This indicator states whether a country allows abortions to be performed. "Yes" indicates that abortion is legal in a country and "no" indicates that it is not. The specific circumstances under which "legal" abortions can be performed may vary from country to country.

Source: The World's Women 1995: Trends and Statistics; United Nations Web site, Table 1-3, http://www.un.org/Depts/unsd/gender/1-3afr.htm
http://www.un.org/Depts/unsd/gender/1-3dev.htm
http://www.un.org/Depts/unsd/gender/1-3lat.htm
http://www.un.org/Depts/unsd/gender/1-3asi.htm

I11.1 Prevalence of Anemia in Pregnant Women, 1985–1995—Low-Income Countries per World Bank

Country	Percent	Country	Percent
Afghanistan		Laos	na
Angola	29	Lesotho	7
Armenia	na	Liberia	na
Azerbaijan	na	Madagascar	na
Bangladesh	53	Malawi	55
Benin	41	Mali	58
Bhutan	na	Mauritania	na
Bosnia and Herzegovina	na	Moldova	50
Burkina Faso	24	Mongolia	45
Burundi	68	Mozambique	58
Cambodia	na	Myanmar (Burma)	58
Cameroon	44	Nepal	65
Central African Republic	67	Nicaragua	36
Chad	37	Niger	41
China	52	Nigeria	55
Comoros	na	Pakistan	37
Congo, Dem. Rep. (Zaire)	76	Rwanda	na
Congo, Rep.	na	Sao Tome and Principe	na
Cote d'Ivoire	na	Senegal	26
Equatorial Guinea	na	Sierra Leone	na
Eritrea	na	Somalia	na
Ethiopia	42	Sri Lanka	39
Gambia	80	Sudan	36
Ghana	na	Tajikistan	50
Guinea	na	Tanzania	na
Guinea-Bissau	74	Togo	48
Guyana	na	Uganda	30
Haiti	38	Vietnam	52
Honduras	14	Yemen	na
India	88	Zambia	34
Kenya	35	Zimbabwe	na
Kyrgyzstan	na		

Note: This indicator represents the percent of pregnant women who have been classified as anemic. According to the World Health Organization (WHO), anemia, or iron deficiency, results when hemoglobin levels slip below 11 grams per deciliter.

Source: World Bank, *World Development Indicators 1998,* Table 2.16

I11.2 Prevalence of Anemia in Pregnant Women, 1985–1995—Lower Middle-Income Countries per World Bank

Country	Percent	Country	Percent
Albania	na	Lithuania	na
Algeria	42	Macedonia, FYRO	na
Belarus	na	Maldives	na
Belize	na	Marshall Islands	na
Bolivia	51	Micronesia	na
Botswana	na	Morocco	45
Bulgaria	na	Namibia	16
Cape Verde	na	North Korea, Dem. Rep.	na
Colombia	24	Panama	na
Costa Rica	28	Papua New Guinea	13
Cuba	47	Paraguay	29
Djibouti	na	Peru	53
Dominica	na	Philippines	48
Dominican Republic	na	Romania	31
Ecuador	17	Russia	30
Egypt	24	Samoa	na
El Salvador	14	Solomon Islands	na
Estonia	na	St. Vincent and the Grenadines	na
Fiji	na	Suriname	na
Georgia	na	Swaziland	na
Grenada	na	Syria	na
Guatemala	39	Thailand	57
Indonesia	64	Tonga	na
Iran	na	Tunisia	na
Iraq	18	Turkey	na
Jamaica	40	Turkmenistan	na
Jordan	na	Ukraine	na
Kazakhstan	11	Uzbekistan	na
Kiribati	na	Vanuatu	na
Latvia	na	Venezuela	29
Lebanon	na	Yugoslavia	na

Note: This indicator represents the percent of pregnant women who have been classified as anemic. According to the World Health Organization (WHO), anemia, or iron deficiency, results when hemoglobin levels slip below 11 grams per deciliter.

Source: World Bank, *World Development Indicators 1998,* Table 2.16

I11.3 Prevalence of Anemia in Pregnant Women, 1985–1995—Upper Middle-Income Countries per World Bank

Country	Percent	Country	Percent
Antigua and Barbuda	na	Mauritius	29
Argentina	26	Mexico	14
Bahrain	na	Oman	54
Barbados	na	Palau	na
Brazil	33	Poland	16
Chile	13	Saudi Arabia	na
Croatia	na	Seychelles	na
Czech Republic	23	Slovakia	na
Gabon	na	Slovenia	na
Hungary	na	South Africa	37
Libya	na	St. Kitts & Nevis	na
Malaysia	56	St. Lucia	na
Malta	na	Trinidad & Tobago	53
		Uruguay	20

Note: This indicator represents the percent of pregnant women who have been classified as anemic. According to the World Health Organization (WHO), anemia, or iron deficiency, results when hemoglobin levels slip below 11 grams per deciliter.

Source: World Bank, *World Development Indicators 1998,* Table 2.16

I12.1 Pregnant Women Immunized Against Tetanus, Percent, 1995–1996—Low-Income Countries per World Bank

Country	Percent	Country	Percent
Afghanistan	37	Kyrgyzstan	na
Angola	28	Laos	45
Armenia	na	Lesotho	10
Azerbaijan	na	Liberia	35
Bangladesh	72	Madagascar	33
Benin	75	Malawi	56
Bhutan	70	Mali	32
Bosnia and Herzegovina	na	Mauritania	28
Burkina Faso	27	Moldova	na
Burundi	33	Mongolia	na
Cambodia	36	Mozambique	61
Cameroon	12	Myanmar (Burma)	79
Central African Republic	15	Nepal	11
Chad	50	Nicaragua	96
China	13	Niger	31
Comoros	34	Nigeria	36
Congo, Dem. Rep. (Zaire)	20	Pakistan	54
Congo, Rep.	55	Rwanda	43
Cote d'Ivoire	22	Sao Tome and Principe	49
Equatorial Guinea	63	Senegal	34
Eritrea	23	Sierra Leone	65
Ethiopia	36	Somalia	28
Gambia	92	Sri Lanka	81
Ghana	9	Sudan	44
Guinea	43	Tajikistan	na
Guinea-Bissau	43	Tanzania	92
Guyana	56	Togo	43
Haiti	49	Uganda	55
Honduras	99	Vietnam	82
India	78	Yemen	55
Kenya	21	Zambia	48
		Zimbabwe	65

Note: This indicator represents the percent of pregnant women who have been immunized against tetanus. It is derived across two years.

Source: State of the World's Children 1998; UNICEF Web site, Table 7 and 3, http://www.unicef.org/sowc98/

I12.2 Pregnant Women Immunized Against Tetanus, Percent, 1995–1996—Lower Middle-Income Countries per World Bank

Country	Percent	Country	Percent
Albania	na	Lithuania	na
Algeria	34	Macedonia, FYRO	91
Belarus	na	Maldives	93
Belize	88	Marshall Islands	15
Bolivia	52	Micronesia	44
Botswana	61	Morocco	100
Bulgaria	na	Namibia	75
Cape Verde	4	North Korea, Dem. Rep.	95
Colombia	57	Panama	24
Costa Rica	90	Papua New Guinea	50
Cuba	61	Paraguay	69
Djibouti	39	Peru	51
Dominica	na	Philippines	47
Dominican Republic	96	Romania	na
Ecuador	25	Russia	na
Egypt	55	Samoa	96
El Salvador	69	Solomon Islands	63
Estonia	na	St. Vincent and the Grenadines	na
Fiji	100	Suriname	99
Georgia	na	Swaziland	65
Grenada	80	Syria	78
Guatemala	81	Thailand	88
Indonesia	75	Tonga	88
Iran	50	Tunisia	80
Iraq	65	Turkey	32
Jamaica	82	Turkmenistan	na
Jordan	41	Ukraine	na
Kazakhstan	na	Uzbekistan	na
Kiribati	41	Vanuatu	15
Latvia	64	Venezuela	60
Lebanon	na	Yugoslavia	na

Note: This indicator represents the percent of pregnant women who have been immunized against tetanus. It is derived across two years.

Source: State of the World's Children 1998; UNICEF Web site, Table 7 and 3, http://www.unicef.org/sowc98/

I12.3 Pregnant Women Immunized Against Tetanus, Percent, 1995-1996—Upper Middle-Income Countries per World Bank

Country	Percent	Country	Percent
Antigua and Barbuda	na	Mauritius	79
Argentina	63	Mexico	69
Bahrain	54	Oman	98
Barbados	100	Palau	55
Brazil	45	Poland	na
Chile	na	Saudi Arabia	60
Croatia	91	Seychelles	100
Czech Republic	na	Slovakia	na
Gabon	4	Slovenia	na
Hungary	na	South Africa	26
Libya	45	St. Kitts & Nevis	na
Malaysia	79	St. Lucia	na
Malta	na	Trinidad & Tobago	19
		Uruguay	13

Note: This indicator represents the percent of pregnant women who have been immunized against tetanus. It is derived across two years.

Source: State of the World's Children 1998; UNICEF Web site, Table 7 and 3, http://www.unicef.org/sowc98/

I13.1 Enrollment Ratios, Females as Percent of Males, 1990–1995, Primary and Secondary Schools—Low-Income Countries per World Bank

Country	Primary	Secondary	Country	Primary	Secondary
Afghanistan	51	34	Laos	75	61
Angola	92	na	Lesotho	112	148
Armenia	107	113	Liberia	55	39
Azerbaijan	96	98	Madagascar	96	100
Bangladesh	87	52	Malawi	90	67
Benin	50	41	Mali	64	55
Bhutan	61	29	Mauritania	81	58
Bosnia and Herzegovina	na	na	Moldova	99	104
Burkina Faso	65	50	Mongolia	106	140
Burundi	82	63	Mozambique	72	60
Cambodia	82	58	Myanmar (Burma)	96	100
Cameroon	90	69	Nepal	68	50
Central African Republic	63	35	Nicaragua	103	118
Chad	48	23	Niger	60	56
China	97	85	Nigeria	79	85
Comoros	85	81	Pakistan	45	52
Congo, Dem. Rep. (Zaire)	74	45	Rwanda	97	82
Congo, Rep.	na	na	Sao Tome and Principe	na	na
Cote d'Ivoire	76	52	Senegal	75	52
Equatorial Guinea	na	na	Sierra Leone	70	55
Eritrea	80	68	Somalia	53	56
Ethiopia	64	91	Sri Lanka	98	111
Gambia	71	52	Sudan	79	79
Ghana	84	64	Tajikistan	97	90
Guinea	49	33	Tanzania	97	83
Guinea-Bissau	55	44	Togo	66	35
Guyana	98	105	Uganda	80	57
Haiti	93	95	Vietnam	94	93
Honduras	101	128	Yemen	40	24
India	81	64	Zambia	93	61
Kenya	99	82	Zimbabwe	93	80
Kyrgyzstan	101	106			

Note: These indicators represent the percent of female enrollment in primary and secondary schools as a percent of male enrollment at those levels. Such enrollment covers attendance in public and private schools, but might exclude attendance in training programs and specialized schools. A higher value indicates that a larger number of females are enrolled at the pertinent level.

Source: State of the World's Children 1998, Table 7; UNICEF Web site, http://www.unicef.org/sowc98; United Nations Development Programme, *Human Development Report 1997*, Table A 2.2

I13.2 Enrollment Ratios, Females as Percent of Males, 1990–1995, Primary and Secondary Schools—Lower Middle-Income Countries per World Bank

Country	Primary	Secondary	Country	Primary	Secondary
Albania	101	103	Lebanon	96	111
Algeria	88	88	Lithuania	98	105
Belarus	97	105	Macedonia, FYRO	99	102
Belize	96	113	Maldives	98	100
Bolivia	91	85	Marshall Islands	na	na
Botswana	101	107	Micronesia	na	na
Bulgaria	95	106	Morocco	74	74
Cape Verde	98	93	Namibia	101	121
Colombia	102	119	North Korea, Dem. Rep.	94	na
Costa Rica	98	109	Papua New Guinea	85	65
Cuba	99	113	Paraguay	97	105
Djibouti	77	67	Peru	96	91
Dominica	na	na	Philippines	101	102
Dominican Republic	101	138	Romania	99	101
Ecuador	98	104	Russia	99	108
Egypt	87	87	Samoa	na	na
El Salvador	101	111	Solomon Islands	87	67
Estonia	97	98	St. Vincent and the Grenadines	na	na
Fiji	99	102	Suriname	97	116
Georgia	99	93	Swaziland	95	96
Grenada	na	na	Syria	90	82
Guatemala	88	92	Thailand	99	97
Indonesia	97	84	Tonga	na	na
Iran	93	82	Tunisia	92	91
Iraq	85	64	Turkey	93	66
Jamaica	99	113	Turkmenistan	na	na
Jordan	101	104	Ukraine	100	108
Kazakhstan	100	103	Uzbekistan	97	88
Kiribati	na	na	Vanuatu	102	78
Latvia	95	106	Venezuela	103	141
			Yugoslavia	104	103

Note: These indicators represent the percent of female enrollment in primary and secondary schools as a percent of male enrollment at those levels. Such enrollment covers attendance in public and private schools, but might exclude attendance in training programs and specialized schools. A higher value indicates that a larger number of females are enrolled at the pertinent level.

Source: State of the World's Children 1998, Table 7; UNICEF Web site, http://www.unicef.org/sowc98; United Nations Development Programme, *Human Development Report 1997*, Table A 2.2

I13.3 Enrollment Ratios, Females as Percent of Males, 1990–1995, Primary and Secondary Schools—Upper Middle-Income Countries per World Bank

Country	Primary	Secondary	Country	Primary	Secondary
Antigua and Barbuda	na	na	Mauritius	99	103
Argentina	99	107	Mexico	96	102
Bahrain	103	103	Oman	94	91
Barbados	101	89	Palau	na	na
Brazil	96	116	Poland	98	101
Chile	98	106	Saudi Arabia	95	82
Croatia	99	108	Seychelles	na	na
Czech Republic	100	104	Slovakia	100	106
Gabon	na	na	Slovenia	100	102
Hungary	100	105	South Africa	97	116
Libya	100	100	St. Kitts & Nevis	na	na
Malaysia	101	110	St. Lucia	na	na
Malta	97	89	Trinidad & Tobago	100	105
			Uruguay	99	119

Note: These indicators represent the percent of female enrollment in primary and secondary schools as a percent of male enrollment at those levels. Such enrollment covers attendance in public and private schools, but might exclude attendance in training programs and specialized schools. A higher value indicates that a larger number of females are enrolled at the pertinent level.

Source: State of the World's Children 1998, Table 7; UNICEF Web site, http://www.unicef.org/sowc98; United Nations Development Programme, *Human Development Report 1997*, Table A 2.2

I13.4 Enrollment Ratios, Females as Percent of Males, 1990–1995—Region by Region

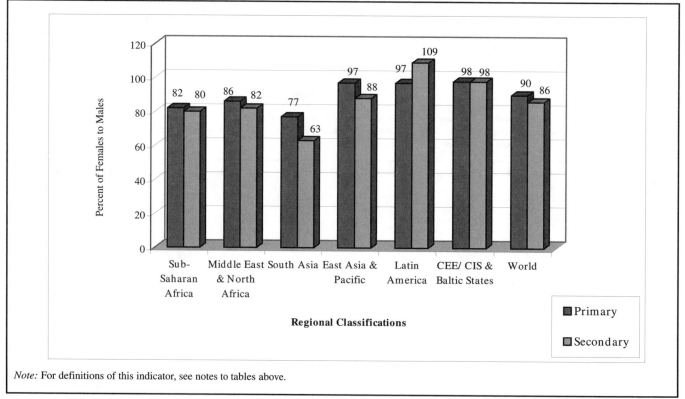

Note: For definitions of this indicator, see notes to tables above.

Source: State of the World's Children 1998; UNICEF Web site, Table 7; http://www.unicef.org/sowc98/

I14.1 Female Primary School Teachers, Percent of Total Teachers, 1980 and 1995—Low-Income Countries per World Bank

Country	1980	1995	Country	1980	1995
Afghanistan	na	na	Laos	30	42
Angola	na	na	Lesotho	75	79
Armenia	na	97	Liberia	na	na
Azerbaijan	na	83	Madagascar	na	56
Bangladesh	8	na	Malawi	32	38
Benin	23	24	Mali	20	23
Bhutan	na	na	Mauritania	9	20
Bosnia and Herzgovina	na	na	Moldova	96	97
Burkina Faso	20	24	Mongolia	na	91
Burundi	47	47	Mozambique	22	23
Cambodia	na	37	Myanmar (Burma)	54	67
Cameroon	20	32	Nepal	10	16
Central African Republic	25	na	Nicaragua	78	84
Chad	na	8	Niger	30	34
China	37	47	Nigeria	33	46
Comoros	na	na	Pakistan	32	na
Congo, Dem.Rep. (Zaire)	na	22	Rwanda	38	na
Congo, Rep.	25	36	Sao Tome and Principe	na	na
Cote d'Ivoire	15	18	Senegal	24	26
Equatorial Guinea	na	na	Sierra Leone	22	na
Eritrea	na	35	Somalia	na	na
Ethiopia	22	27	Sri Lanka	na	83
Gambia	34	34	Sudan	31	60
Ghana	42	na	Tajikistan	na	51
Guinea	14	25	Tanzania	37	43
Guinea-Bissau	24	na	Togo	21	14
Guyana	na	na	Uganda	30	32
Haiti	49	na	Vietnam	65	na
Honduras	74	73	Yemen	11	na
India	26	32	Zambia	40	43
Kenya	31	40	Zimbabwe	38	41
Kyrgyzstan	88	83			

Note: This indicator represents the share of primary school teachers that are women. It includes both full and part-time teachers.

Source: World Bank, *World Development Indicators 1998*, Table 2.12

I14.2 Female Primary School Teachers, Percent of Total Teachers, 1980 and 1995—Lower Middle-Income Countries per World Bank

Country	1980	1995	Country	1980	1995
Albania	50	60	Egypt	47	53
Algeria	37	44	El Salvador	65	na
Belarus	na	na	Estonia	na	89
Belize	na	na	Fiji	na	na
Bolivia	48	na	Georgia	na	94
Botswana	72	76	Grenada	na	na
Bulgaria	72	89	Guatemala	62	na
Cape Verde	na	na	Indonesia	33	52
Colombia	79	80	Iran	57	55
Costa Rica	79	na	Iraq	48	68
Cuba	75	81	Jamaica	87	89
Djibouti	na	na	Jordan	59	61
Dominica	na	na	Kazakhstan	na	97
Dominican Republic	na	71	Kiribati	na	na
Ecuador	65	68	Latvia	na	97

I14.2 Female Primary School Teachers, Percent of Total Teachers, 1980 and 1995—Lower Middle-Income Countries per World Bank *(continued)*

Country	1980	1995	Country	1980	1995
Lebanon	na	na	Samoa	na	na
Lithuania	97	98	Solomon Islands	na	na
Macedonia, FYRO	na	53	St. Vincent and the Grenadines	na	na
Maldives	na	na	Suriname	na	na
Marshall Islands	na	na	Swaziland	na	na
Micronesia	na	na	Syria	54	65
Morocco	30	38	Thailand	49	na
Namibia	na	65	Tonga	na	na
North Korea, Dem. Rep.	na	na	Tunisia	29	49
Panama	80	na	Turkey	41	44
Papua New Guinea	27	37	Turkmenistan	na	na
Paraguay	na	55	Ukraine	97	98
Peru	60	58	Uzbekistan	78	82
Philippines	80	na	Venezuela	83	75
Romania	70	84	West Bank & Gaza	na	48
Russia	98	98	Yugoslavia	na	75

Note: This indicator represents the share of primary school teachers that are women. It includes both full- and part-time teachers.

Source: World Bank, *World Development Indicators 1998,* Table 2.12

I14.3 Female Primary School Teachers, Percent of Total Teachers, 1980 and 1995—Upper Middle-Income Countries per World Bank

Country	1980	1995	Country	1980	1995
Antigua and Barbuda	na	na	Mexico	na	na
Argentina	92	na	Oman	34	50
Bahrain	na	na	Palau	na	na
Barbados	na	na	Poland	na	na
Brazil	85	na	Puerto Rico	na	na
Chile	na	72	Saudi Arabia	39	51
Croatia	73	89	Seychelles	na	na
Czech Republic	na	93	Slovakia	na	91
Gabon	27	44	Slovenia	na	92
Hungary	80	84	South Africa	na	58
Libya	47	na	St. Kitts & Nevis	na	na
Malaysia	44	59	Trinidad & Tobago	66	74
Malta	na	na	Uruguay	na	na
Mauritius	43	50			

Note: This indicator represents the share of primary school teachers that are women. It includes both full- and part-time teachers.

Source: World Bank, *World Development Indicators 1998,* Table 2.12

I14.4 Female Secondary School Teachers, Percent of Total Teachers, 1980 and 1995—Low-Income Countries per World Bank

Country	1980	1995	Country	1980	1995
Afghanistan	na	na	Kyrgyzstan	58	71
Angola	na	na	Laos	26	39
Armenia	na	85	Lesotho	48	51
Azerbaijan	na	na	Liberia	na	na
Bangladesh	7	na	Madagascar	na	na
Benin	na	na	Malawi	na	na
Bhutan	na	na	Mali	na	18
Bosnia and Herzegovina	na	na	Mauritania	8	10
Burkina Faso	na	18	Moldova	na	na
Burundi	18	na	Mongolia	na	67
Cambodia	na	28	Mozambique	27	19
Cameroon	18	25	Myanmar (Burma)	61	74
Central African Republic	12	na	Nepal	na	na
Chad	na	4	Nicaragua	na	56
China	25	36	Niger	22	23
Comoros	na	na	Nigeria	8	na
Congo, Dem.Rep. (Zaire)	na	na	Pakistan	30	na
Congo, Rep.	8	15	Rwanda	na	na
Cote d'Ivoire	na	na	Sao Tome and Principe	na	na
Equatorial Guinea	na	na	Senegal	15	15
Eritrea	na	13	Sierra Leone	21	na
Ethiopia	10	10	Somalia	na	na
Gambia	27	na	Sri Lanka	na	62
Ghana	21	na	Sudan	26	na
Guinea	10	12	Tajikistan	na	34
Guinea-Bissau	20	na	Tanzania	28	25
Guyana	na	na	Togo	13	11
Haiti	11	na	Uganda	20	na
Honduras	na	na	Vietnam	58	na
India	30	35	Yemen	na	na
Kenya	na	33	Zambia	na	na
			Zimbabwe	na	32

Note: This indicator represents the share of secondary school teachers that are women. It includes both full- and part-time teachers.

Source: World Bank, *World Development Indicators 1998,* Table 2.12

I14.5 Female Secondary School Teachers, Percent of Total Teachers, 1980 and 1995—Lower Middle-Income Countries per World Bank

Country	1980	1995	Country	1980	1995
Albania	46	51	Estonia	na	83
Algeria	na	45	Fiji	na	na
Belarus	na	na	Georgia	na	na
Belize	na	na	Grenada	na	na
Bolivia	na	na	Guatemala	na	na
Botswana	35	44	Indonesia	na	39
Bulgaria	64	75	Iran	32	46
Cape Verde	na	na	Iraq	42	55
Colombia	41	na	Jamaica	67	na
Costa Rica	57	na	Jordan	44	48
Cuba	50	61	Kazakhstan	na	74
Djibouti	na	na	Kiribati	na	na
Dominica	na	na	Latvia	na	81
Dominican Republic	na	50	Lebanon	na	na
Ecuador	38	44	Lithuania	85	82
Egypt	35	41	Macedonia, FYRO	na	52
El Salvador	24	na	Maldives	na	na

I14.5 Female Secondary School Teachers, Percent of Total Teachers, 1980 and 1995—Lower Middle-Income Countries per World Bank *(continued)*

Country	1980	1995	Country	1980	1995
Marshall Islands	na	na	St. Vincent and the Grenadines	na	na
Micronesia	na	na	Suriname	na	na
Morocco	na	32	Swaziland	na	na
Namibia	na	46	Syria	22	44
North Korea, Dem. Rep.	na	na	Thailand	57	na
Panama	55	na	Tonga	na	na
Papua New Guinea	34	35	Tunisia	na	36
Paraguay	na	65	Turkey	36	40
Peru	46	39	Turkmenistan	na	na
Philippines	na	na	Ukraine	na	na
Romania	53	65	Uzbekistan	48	49
Russia	76	79	Venezuela	na	na
Samoa	na	na	West Bank & Gaza	na	41
Solomon Islands	na	na	Yugoslavia	na	na

Note: This indicator represents the share of secondary school teachers that are women. It includes both full- and part-time teachers.

Source: World Bank, *World Development Indicators 1998,* Table 2.12

I14.6 Female Secondary School Teachers, Percent of Total Teachers, 1980 and 1995—Upper Middle-Income Countries per World Bank

Country	1980	1995	Country	1980	1995
Antigua and Barbuda	na	na	Mexico	na	na
Argentina	75	na	Oman	27	48
Bahrain	na	na	Palau	na	na
Barbados	na	na	Poland	na	na
Brazil	na	na	Puerto Rico	na	na
Chile	na	na	Saudi Arabia	33	49
Croatia	na	67	Seychelles	na	na
Czech Republic	na	72	Slovakia	na	75
Gabon	28	19	Slovenia	na	76
Hungary	61	67	South Africa	na	64
Libya	24	na	St. Kitts & Nevis	na	na
Malaysia	46	54	Trinidad & Tobago	52	56
Malta	na	na	Uruguay	na	na
Mauritius	39	44			

Note: This indicator represents the share of secondary school teachers that are women. It includes both full- and part-time teachers.

Source: World Bank, *World Development Indicators 1998,* Table 2.12

I15.1 Female Economic Activity Rate, as Percent of Males, 1995—Low-Income Countries per World Bank

Country	Percent	Country	Percent
Afghanistan	na	Laos	na
Angola	84	Lesotho	56
Armenia	87	Liberia	na
Azerbaijan	75	Madagascar	81
Bangladesh	76	Malawi	94
Benin	89	Mali	84
Bhutan	66	Mauritania	77
Bosnia and Herzegovina	na	Moldova	86
Burkina Faso	86	Mongolia	88
Burundi	91	Mozambique	92
Cambodia	104	Myanmar (Burma)	76
Cameroon	59	Nepal	68
Central African Republic	83	Nicaragua	54
Chad	78	Niger	77
China	87	Nigeria	55
Comoros	76	Pakistan	38
Congo, Dem. Rep. (Zaire)	73	Rwanda	93
Congo, Rep.	76	Sao Tome and Principe	54
Cote d'Ivoire	51	Senegal	74
Equatorial Guinea	na	Sierra Leone	54
Eritrea	89	Somalia	na
Ethiopia	70	Sri Lanka	54
Gambia	79	Sudan	40
Ghana	101	Tajikistan	76
Guinea	91	Tanzania	95
Guinea-Bissau	65	Togo	65
Guyana	48	Uganda	90
Haiti	73	Vietnam	94
Honduras	43	Yemen	39
India	50	Zambia	79
Kenya	86	Zimbabwe	79
Kyrgyzstan	84		

Note: The economic activity rate reflects all people in the work force who supply labor for the production of economic goods and services; it also includes employers and self-employed, members of producer cooperatives, and the armed forces. This indicator reflects the number of economically active women as a percent of the number of economically active men

Source: United Nations Development Programme, *Human Development Report 1997,* Table A2.2

I15.2 Female Economic Activity Rate, as Percent of Males, 1995—Lower Middle-Income Countries per World Bank

Country	Percent	Country	Percent
Albania	72	Egypt	41
Algeria	33	El Salvador	50
Belarus	84	Estonia	85
Belize	30	Fiji	39
Bolivia	59	Georgia	79
Botswana	81	Grenada	na
Bulgaria	89	Guatemala	36
Cape Verde	57	Indonesia	65
Colombia	59	Iran	33
Costa Rica	43	Iraq	23
Cuba	61	Jamaica	86
Djibouti	na	Jordan	28
Dominica	50	Kazakhstan	82
Dominican Republic	42	Kiribati	na
Ecuador	36	Latvia	85

I15.2 Female Economic Activity Rate, as Percent of Males, 1995—Lower Middle-Income Countries per World Bank *(continued)*

Country	Percent	Country	Percent
Lebanon	37	Solomon Islands	93
Lithuania	83	St. Vincent and the Grenadines	42
Macedonia, FYRO	na	Suriname	46
Maldives	77	Swaziland	55
Marshall Islands	na	Syria	36
Micronesia	na	Thailand	87
Morocco	na	Thailand	27
Namibia	68	Tonga	na
North Korea, Dem. Rep.	78	Tunisia	45
Panama	52	Turkey	57
Papua New Guinea	76	Turkmenistan	81
Paraguay	41	Ukraine	81
Peru	41	Uzbekistan	84
Philippines	60	Vanuatu	na
Romania	78	Venezuela	50
Russia	83	Yugoslavia	na
Samoa	na		

Note: The economic activity rate reflects all people in the work force who supply labor for the production of economic goods and services; it also includes employers and self-employed, members of producer cooperatives, and the armed forces. This indicator reflects the number of economically active women as a percent of the number of economically active men

Source: United Nations Development Programme, *Human Development Report 1997,* Table A2.2

I15.3 Female Economic Activity Rate, as Percent of Males, 1995—Upper Middle-Income Countries per World Bank

Country	Percent	Country	Percent
Antigua and Barbuda	na	Mexico	45
Argentina	43	Oman	19
Bahrain	31	Palau	na
Barbados	80	Poland	81
Brazil	53	Saudi Arabia	19
Chile	46	Seychelles	60
Croatia	72	Slovakia	87
Czech Republic	86	Slovenia	81
Gabon	78	South Africa	59
Hungary	74	St. Kitts & Nevis	na
Libya	28	St. Lucia	na
Malaysia	59	Trinidad & Tobago	56
Malta	35	Uruguay	65
Mauritius	46		

Note: The economic activity rate reflects all people in the work force who supply labor for the production of economic goods and services; it also includes employers and self-employed, members of producer cooperatives, and the armed forces. This indicator reflects the number of economically active women as a percent of the number of economically active men

Source: United Nations Development Programme, *Human Development Report 1997,* Table A2.2

I15.4 Women as Percent of Adult Labor Force, 1980–1995—Low-Income Countries per World Bank

Country	1980	1995	Country	1980	1995
Afghanistan	na	na	Kyrgyzstan	48	47
Angola	47	46	Laos	45	47
Armenia	48	48	Lesotho	38	37
Azerbaijan	47	44	Liberia	na	na
Bangladesh	42	42	Madagascar	45	45
Benin	47	48	Malawi	51	49
Bhutan	na	na	Mali	47	46
Bosnia and Herzegovina	33	na	Mauritania	45	44
Burkina Faso	48	47	Moldova	50	49
Burundi	50	49	Mongolia	46	46
Cambodia	56	53	Mozambique	49	48
Cameroon	37	38	Myanmar (Burma)	44	43
Central African Republic	48	47	Nepal	39	40
Chad	43	44	Nicaragua	28	36
China	43	45	Niger	45	44
Comoros	na	na	Nigeria	36	36
Congo, Dem. Rep. (Zaire)	45	44	Pakistan	23	27
Congo, Rep.	43	43	Rwanda	49	49
Cote d'Ivoire	32	33	Sao Tome and Principe	na	na
Equatorial Guinea	na	na	Senegal	42	43
Eritrea	47	47	Sierra Leone	36	36
Ethiopia	42	41	Somalia	na	na
Gambia	45	45	Sri Lanka	27	35
Ghana	51	51	Sudan	27	29
Guinea	47	47	Tajikistan	47	44
Guinea-Bissau	40	40	Tanzania	50	49
Guyana	na	na	Togo	39	40
Haiti	45	43	Uganda	48	48
Honduras	25	30	Vietnam	48	49
India	34	32	Yemen	33	29
Kenya	46	46	Zambia	45	45
			Zimbabwe	44	44

Note: This indicator represents the number of women active in the labor force as a share of the total labor force; it covers workers over 15 years of age. The labor force, according to the International Labor Organization (ILO), includes all people who supply labor in the production of goods and service, regardless of the venue in which those goods and services are used or sold: it can include subsistence work as well as work geared for the marketplace.

Source: World Bank, *World Development Indicators 1998,* Table 2.3

I15.5 Women as Percent of Adult Labor Force, 1980–1995—Lower Middle-Income Countries per World Bank

Country	1980	1995	Country	1980	1995
Albania	39	41	Lithuania	50	48
Algeria	21	25	Macedonia, FYRO	36	41
Belarus	50	49	Maldives	na	na
Belize	na	na	Marshall Islands	na	na
Bolivia	33	37	Micronesia	na	na
Botswana	50	46	Morocco	34	35
Bulgaria	45	48	Namibia	40	41
Cape Verde	na	na	North Korea, Dem. Rep.	45	45
Colombia	26	38	Panama	30	34
Costa Rica	21	30	Papua New Guinea	42	42
Cuba	31	38	Paraguay	27	29
Djibouti	na	na	Peru	24	29
Dominica	na	na	Philippines	35	37
Dominican Republic	25	29	Romania	46	44
Ecuador	20	27	Russia	49	49
Egypt	26	29	Samoa	na	na
El Salvador	27	35	Solomon Islands	na	na
Estonia	51	49	St. Vincent and the Grenadines	na	na
Fiji	na	na	Suriname	na	na
Georgia	49	46	Swaziland	na	na
Grenada	na	na	Syria	23	26
Guatemala	22	27	Thailand	47	46
Indonesia	35	40	Tonga	na	na
Iran	20	25	Tunisia	29	31
Iraq	17	18	Turkey	35	36
Jamaica	46	46	Turkmenistan	47	45
Jordan	15	22	Ukraine	50	49
Kazakhstan	48	47	Uzbekistan	48	46
Kiribati	na	na	Vanuatu	na	na
Latvia	51	50	Venezuela	27	33
Lebanon	23	28	Yugoslavia	38	42

Note: This indicator represents the number of women active in the labor force as a share of the total labor force; it covers workers over 15 years of age. The labor force, according to the International Labor Organization (ILO), includes all people who supply labor in the production of goods and service, regardless of the venue in which those goods and services are used or sold: it can include subsistence work as well as work geared for the marketplace.

Source: World Bank, *World Development Indicators 1998,* Table 2.3

I15.6 Women as Percent of Adult Labor Force, 1980-1995—Upper Middle-Income Countries per World Bank

Country	1980	1995	Country	1980	1995
Antigua and Barbuda			Mexico	27	31
Argentina	28	31	Oman	7	15
Bahrain	na	na	Palau	na	na
Barbados	na	na	Poland	45	46
Brazil	28	35	Saudi Arabia	8	14
Chile	26	32	Seychelles	na	na
Croatia	40	44	Slovakia	45	48
Czech Republic	47	47	Slovenia	46	46
Gabon	45	44	South Africa	35	37
Hungary	43	44	St. Kitts & Nevis	na	na
Libya	19	21	St. Lucia	na	na
Malaysia	34	37	Trinidad & Tobago	32	37
Malta	na	na	Uruguay	31	41
Mauritius	26	32			

Note: This indicator represents the number of women active in the labor force as a share of the total labor force; it covers workers over 15 years of age. The labor force, according to the International Labor Organization (ILO), includes all people who supply labor in the production of goods and service, irregardless of the venue in which those goods and services are used or sold: it can include subsistence work as well as work geared for the marketplace.

Source: World Bank, *World Development Indicators 1998,* Table 2.3

I16.1 Women in Legislative Body, as of January 1997, Percent of Lower House and Upper House—Low-Income Countries per World Bank

Country	Lower House Number of Seats	Lower House Percent	Upper House Number of Seats	Upper House Percent
Afghanistan				
Angola	220	9.5	na	na
Armenia	190	6.3	na	na
Azerbaijan	125	12.0	na	na
Bangladesh	330	9.1	na	na
Benin	83	7.2	na	na
Bhutan	150	2.0	na	na
Bosnia and Herzegovina	42	na	15	na
Burkina Faso	107	3.7	176	11.9
Burundi	na	na	na	na
Cambodia	120	5.8	na	na
Cameroon	180	12.2	na	na
Central African Republic	85	3.5	na	na
Chad	52	17.3	na	na
China	978	21.0	na	na
Comoros	43	0	na	na
Congo, Dem. Rep. (Zaire)	738	5.0	na	na
Congo, Rep.	125	1.6	60	3.3
Cote d'Ivoire	168	8.3	na	na
Equatorial Guinea	80	8.8	na	na
Eritrea	105	21.0	na	na
Ethiopia	550	2.0	117	na
Gambia	na	na	na	na
Ghana	200	na	na	na
Guinea	114	7.0	na	na
Guinea-Bissau	100	10.0	na	na
Guyana	65	20.0	na	na
Haiti	83	3.6	27	0
Honduras	128	7.8	na	na

I16.1 Women in Legislative Body, as of January 1997, Percent of Lower House and Upper House—Low-Income Countries per World Bank (continued)

Country	Lower House		Upper House	
	Number of Seats	Percent	Number of Seats	Percent
India	545	7.2	245	7.8
Kenya	202	3.0	na	na
Kyrgyzstan	70	1.4	35	11.4
Laos	85	9.4	na	na
Lesotho	65	4.6	33	24.2
Liberia	35	5.7	na	na
Madagascar	134	3.7	na	na
Malawi	177	5.6	na	na
Mali	129	2.3	na	na
Mauritania	79	1.3	56	0
Moldova	104	4.8	na	na
Mongolia	76	7.9	na	na
Mozambique	250	25.2	na	na
Myanmar (Burma)	na	na	na	na
Nepal	205	3.4	60	8.3
Nicaragua	93	10.8	na	na
Niger	83	na	na	na
Nigeria	na	na	na	na
Pakistan	na	na	87	3.4
Rwanda	70	17.1	na	na
Sao Tome and Principe	55	7.3	na	na
Senegal	120	11.7	na	na
Sierra Leone	80	6.3	na	na
Somalia	na	na	na	na
Sri Lanka	225	5.3	na	na
Sudan	400	5.3	na	na
Tajikistan	181	2.8	na	na
Tanzania	275	17.5	na	na
Togo	81	1.2	na	na
Uganda	276	18.1	na	na
Vietnam	395	18.5	na	na
Yemen	301	0.7	na	na
Zambia	155	9.7	na	na
Zimbabwe	150	14.7	na	na

Note: This indicator represents the number of women holding seats in the lower and upper house of a country's legislative body as a percent of the total number of seats in the respective houses.

Source: United Nations Web site, http://www.un.org/Depts/unsd/gender/6-1afr.htm
http://www.un.org/Depts/unsd/gender/6-1dev.htm
http://www.un.org/Depts/unsd/gender/6-1lat.htm
http://www.un.org/Depts/unsd/gender/6-1asi.htm

I16.2 Women in Legislative Body, as of January 1997, Percent of Lower House and Upper House—Lower Middle-Income Countries per World Bank

Country	Lower House		Upper House	
	Number of Seats	**Percent**	**Number of Seats**	**Percent**
Albania	140	12.1	na	na
Algeria	183	6.6	na	na
Belarus	260	na	na	na
Belize	29	3.4	8	37.5
Bolivia	130	6.9	27	3.7
Botswana	47	8.5	na	na
Bulgaria	240	13.3	na	na
Cape Verde	72	11.1	na	na
Colombia	163	11.7	102	6.9
Costa Rica	57	15.8	na	na
Cuba	589	22.8	na	na
Djibouti	65	0	na	na
Dominica	32	9.4	na	na
Dominican Republic	120	11.7	30	3.3
Ecuador	82	na	na	na
Egypt	454	2.0	na	na
El Salvador	84	10.7	na	na
Estonia	101	12.9	na	na
Fiji	70	4.3	34	8.8
Georgia	235	6.8	na	na
Grenada	15	20.0	13	na
Guatemala	80	12.5	na	na
Indonesia	500	12.6	na	na
Iran	248	4.0	na	na
Iraq	250	na	na	na
Jamaica	60	11.7	21	14.3
Jordan	80	1.3	40	5.0
Kazakhstan	67	13.4	47	8.5
Kiribati	41	0	na	na
Latvia	100	9.0	na	na
Lebanon	128	2.3	na	na
Lithuania	137	17.5	na	na
Macedonia, FYRO	120	3.3	na	na
Maldives	48	6.3	na	na
Marshall Islands	33	na	na	na
Micronesia	14	0	na	na
Morocco	333	0.6	na	na
Namibia	72	18.1	26	na
North Korea, Dem. Rep.	687	20.1	na	na
Panama	72	9.7	na	na
Papua New Guinea	109	0	na	na
Paraguay	80	2.5	45	11.1
Peru	120	10.8	na	na
Philippines	203	10.8	24	16.7
Romania	328	7.0	143	2.1
Russia	450	10.2	178	0.6
Samoa	49	4.1	na	na
Solomon Islands	47	2.1	na	na
St. Vincent and the Grenadines	21	9.5	na	na
Suriname	51	15.7	na	na
Swaziland	65	3.1	30	20.0
Syria	250	9.6	na	na
Thailand	393	5.6	260	8.1
Tonga	30	0	na	na
Tunisia	163	6.7	na	na
Turkey	550	2.4	na	na

I16.2 Women in Legislative Body, as of January 1997, Percent of Lower House and Upper House—Lower Middle-Income Countries per World Bank (continued)

Country	Lower House		Upper House	
	Number of Seats	Percent	Number of Seats	Percent
Turkmenistan	50	18.0	na	na
Ukraine	450	3.8	na	na
Uzbekistan	250	6.0	na	na
Vanuatu	50	na	na	na
Venezuela	203	5.9	50	8.0
Yugoslavia	138	na	40	2.5

Note: This indicator represents the number of women holding seats in the lower and upper house of a country's legislative body as a percent of the total number of seats in the respective houses.

Source: United Nations Web site, http://www.un.org/Depts/unsd/gender/6-1afr.htm
http://www.un.org/Depts/unsd/gender/6-1dev.htm
http://www.un.org/Depts/unsd/gender/6-1lat.htm
http://www.un.org/Depts/unsd/gender/6-1asi.htm

I16.3 Women in Legislative Body, as of January 1997, Percent of Lower House and Upper House—Upper Middle-Income Countries per World Bank

Country	Lower House		Upper House	
	Number of Seats	Percent	Number of Seats	Percent
Antigua and Barbuda	19	5.3	17	17.6
Argentina	257	25.3	72	2.8
Bahrain	na	na	na	na
Barbados	28	10.7	21	28.6
Brazil	513	6.6	81	7.4
Chile	120	7.5	46	6.5
Croatia	127	7.9	68	4.4
Czech Republic	200	15.0	81	na
Gabon	120	na	na	na
Hungary	386	11.4	na	na
Libya	750	na	na	na
Malaysia	192	7.8	69	17.4
Malta	69	5.8	na	na
Mauritius	66	7.6	na	na
Mexico	500	14.2	128	12.5
Oman	na	na	na	na
Palau	16	0	14	7.1
Poland	460	13.0	100	13
Saudi Arabia	na	na	na	na
Seychelles	33	27.3	na	na
Slovakia	150	14.7	na	na
Slovenia	90	7.8	na	na
South Africa	400	25	90	17.8
St. Kitts & Nevis	15	13.3	na	na
St. Lucia	18	0	11	36.4
Trinidad & Tobago	36	11.1	31	29.0
Uruguay	99	7.1	31	6.5

Note: This indicator represents the number of women holding seats in the lower and upper house of a country's legislative body as a percent of the total number of seats in the respective houses.

Source: United Nations Web site, http://www.un.org/Depts/unsd/gender/6-1afr.htm
http://www.un.org/Depts/unsd/gender/6-1dev.htm
http://www.un.org/Depts/unsd/gender/6-1lat.htm
http://www.un.org/Depts/unsd/gender/6-1asi.htm

I16.4 Women in Decision-Making Positions, 1996, Percent of Total Ministerial and Sub-Ministerial Positions—Low-Income Countries per World Bank

Country	Percent of Ministerial Positions	Percent of Sub-Ministerial Positions	Country	Percent of Ministerial Positions	Percent of Sub-Ministerial Positions
Afghanistan	0	0	Kyrgyzstan	10.5	12.0
Angola	10.7	1.8	Laos	0	6.4
Armenia	0	2.9	Lesotho	0	18.2
Azerbaijan	7.7	6.9	Liberia	3.7	10
Bangladesh	7.7	0	Madagascar	0	3.3
Benin	19.0	13.3	Malawi	3.6	4.7
Bhutan	12.5	0	Mali	10.0	0
Bosnia and Herzegovina	0	4.6	Mauritania	3.6	5.9
Burkina Faso	9.1	11.9	Moldova	0	7
Burundi	10.3	0	Mongolia	0	2.6
Cambodia	0	3.1	Mozambique	4.0	14.7
Cameroon	2.6	5.3	Myanmar (Burma)	0	0
Central African Republic	8.0	2.4	Nepal	0	0
Chad	8.7	0	Nicaragua	15.8	17.9
China	6.1	3.9	Niger	14.3	10
Comoros	6.2	0	Nigeria	7.7	5.6
Congo, Dem. Rep. (Zaire)	8.0	0	Pakistan	4.0	2.2
Congo, Rep.	7.4	5.3	Rwanda	8.3	12.5
Cote d'Ivoire	8.3	6.8	Sao Tome and Principe	0	16.7
Equatorial Guinea	4.8	5.0	Senegal	6.7	4.2
Eritrea	18.8	4.2	Sierra Leone	3.8	6.5
Ethiopia	6.7	9.6	Somalia	0	0
Gambia	18.8	19.0	Sri Lanka	13.0	9.6
Ghana	10.3	9.4	Sudan	2.4	1.3
Guinea	15.0	11.5	Tajikistan	3.7	3.9
Guinea-Bissau	8.0	13.2	Tanzania	10.5	8.9
Guyana	5.6	20.0	Togo	4.3	0
Haiti	29.4	15.8	Uganda	10.7	8.1
Honduras	10.0	15.9	Vietnam	7.0	4.4
India	3.2	6.2	Yemen	0	0
Kenya	3.4	6.6	Zambia	7.7	8.6
			Zimbabwe	8.3	14

Note: This indicator represents the number of women in decision-making positions in government, that is, those serving in ministerial and sub-ministerial level positions such as ministers or the equivalent, deputy or assistant ministers, secretaries of government departments and their deputies and assistants. It is represented as a percent of the total such positions.

Source: United Nations Web site, http://www.un.org/Depts/unsd/gender/6-2afr.htm
http://www.un.org/Depts/unsd/gender/6-2dev.htm
http://www.un.org/Depts/unsd/gender/6-2lat.htm
http://www.un.org/Depts/unsd/gender/6-2asi.htm

I16.5 Women in Decision-Making Positions, 1996, Percent of Total Ministerial and Sub-Ministerial Positions—Lower Middle-Income Countries per World Bank

Country	Percent of Ministerial Positions	Percent of Sub-Ministerial Positions	Country	Percent of Ministerial Positions	Percent of Sub-Ministerial Positions
Albania	5.3	14.0	Lithuania	0	6.8
Algeria	0	8.3	Macedonia, FYRO	8.7	25
Belarus	5.3	7.0	Maldives	5.6	14.1
Belize	0	8.8	Marshall Islands	na	na
Bolivia	0	8.3	Micronesia	na	na
Botswana	7.7	15.4	Morocco	0	1.4
Bulgaria	4.8	16.2	Namibia	8.7	12.3
Cape Verde	13.3	8.3	North Korea, Dem. Rep.	1.3	0.6
Colombia	12.5	22.6	Panama	16.7	6.5
Costa Rica	11.1	35.2	Papua New Guinea	na	na
Cuba	2.7	11.9	Paraguay	6.7	3.7
Djibouti	0	1.0	Peru	5.6	15.5
Dominica	18.2	26.5	Philippines	4.5	25.3
Dominican Republic	4.0	11.9	Romania	0	4.1
Ecuador	6.2	2.8	Russia	2.4	2.6
Egypt	3.1	4.5	Samoa	na	na
El Salvador	6.2	27.0	Solomon Islands	na	na
Estonia	0	16.8	St. Vincent and the Grenadines	20	18.8
Fiji	na	na	Suriname	0	17.6
Georgia	0	4.7	Swaziland	0	13.6
Grenada	21.4	23.1	Syria	6.8	1.7
Guatemala	13.3	22.2	Thailand	0	2.6
Indonesia	3.6	1.6	Tonga	na	na
Iran	0	0.5	Tunisia	2.9	10.9
Iraq	0	0	Turkey	2.9	5.6
Jamaica	5.6	18.4	Turkmenistan	3.1	0
Jordan	6.1	0	Ukraine	0	2.2
Kazakhstan	2.6	1.7	Uzbekistan	2.6	0
Kiribati	na	na	Vanuatu	na	na
Latvia	11.1	19.0	Venezuela	11.1	17.9
Lebanon	0	0	Yugoslavia	5.9	8.7

Note: This indicator represents the number of women in decision-making positions in government, that is, those serving in ministerial and sub-ministerial level in positions such as ministers or the equivalent, deputy or assistant ministers, secretaries of government departments and their deputies and assistants. It is represented as a percent of the total such positions.

Source: United Nations Web site, http://www.un.org/Depts/unsd/gender/6-2afr.htm
http://www.un.org/Depts/unsd/gender/6-2dev.htm
http://www.un.org/Depts/unsd/gender/6-2lat.htm
http://www.un.org/Depts/unsd/gender/6-2asi.htm

fined as falling below the median "weight-for-height" ratio of a population by a factor of two "standard deviations." Moderate or severe stunting is defined as falling below the median "height-for-age" ratio of a population by a factor of two "standard deviations" (J6.1–J6.3).

Total Goitre Rate: The total goitre rate indicates the number of children in the age group with a visible goitre, the swelling of the thyroid gland which can be seen as a growth in the neck. Resulting from an iodine deficiency, goitre is found throughout populations suffering from poor nutrition. It is widespread in poorer, developing countries (J7.1–J7.3).

Child Immunization Rates: These indicators represent the share of the children under one year of age who have been adequately vaccinated against measles, diphtheria (DPT), polio, and TB. In poorer countries, immunization rates are relatively lower than in wealthier countries. Standards of vaccination have been set by the Universal Child Immunization (UCI) Programme, which many countries adhere to and which provides funds and programming to implement its standards. The effects of international immunization efforts can be seen in the data presented in the tables below. The data available for 1980 are unfortunately not complete for all countries, but even with the figures that are available, comparison between 1980 and 1996 shows a marked increase in immunization rates. Much more work in child immunization remains to be done: for diseases that are controllable with vaccination, all children worldwide should be immunized, not only to add to their individual quality of life but to lessen the burden on health care systems (J8.1–J8.9).

Children Not in Primary School: Because most countries require children of primary school age (six to 11) to attend school, deviations from this standard requirement are important to monitor. In poorer countries, economic necessity often demands that children work rather than attend school; further, an inadequate number of teachers or inaccessible school and classroom space are other factors that can keep school-age children from attending school. Even countries that require attendance may lack sufficient resources to develop and maintain adequate educational infrastructure and professional teaching staffs (J9.1–J9.3).

Primary School Children Reaching Grade Five: This indicator estimates the share of children entering the first grade who will reach grade five. As with the indicator above, several factors are at play, both private and public, including economic pressure to satisfy household and family needs and inadequate or limited teaching staff and infrastructure (J10.1–J10.4).

Percent of Children in the Labor Force: This indicators represents the share of children ages 10 to 14 that are in the labor force. This group of workers, called the child labor class, constitutes a significant percentage of the total labor force in many poorer countries whose economies require many family members, regardless of age, to work and earn money. Indeed, the poorer the country, the larger the share of children who must work (J11.1–J11.3).

J1.1 Infant and Under-Five Mortality Rates, per 1,000 Live Births, Worldwide Summary, 1996—Comparison by Income Level per World Bank

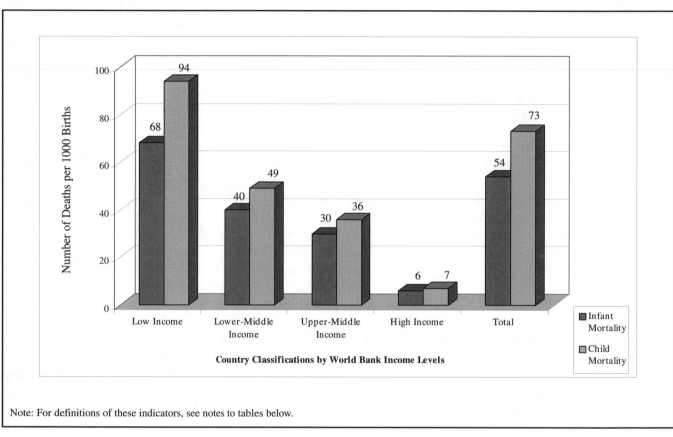

Note: For definitions of these indicators, see notes to tables below.

Source: World Bank, *World Development Indicators 1998*, Table 1.3

J1.2 Infant and Under-Five Mortality Rates, per 1,000 Live Births, Worldwide Summary, 1996— Region by Region

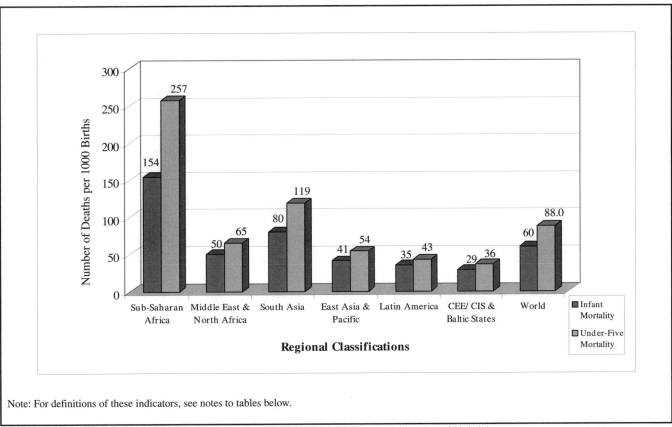

Note: For definitions of these indicators, see notes to tables below.

Source: The State of the World's Children 1998, Table 1, UNICEF Web site, http://www.unicef.org/sowc98/tab1b.htm

J1.3 Infant Mortality Rate, per 1,000 Live Births, Long-Range Trends, 1960–1996—Low-Income Countries per World Bank

Country	1960	1970	1980	1996
Afghanistan	215	na	na	na
Angola	208	178	153	124
Armenia	38	na	26	16
Azerbaijan	55	na	30	20
Bangladesh	151	140	132	77
Benin	184	148	120	87
Bhutan	175	na	na	na
Bosnia and Herzegovina	105	59	31	na
Burkina Faso	183	141	121	98
Burundi	151	138	121	97
Cambodia	146	161	201	105
Cameroon	156	126	94	54
Central African Republic	195	139	117	96
Chad	195	171	147	115
China	140	69	42	33
Comoros	165	na	na	na
Congo, Dem. Rep. (Zaire)	175	131	111	90
Congo, Rep.	143	101	89	90
Cote d'Ivoire	195	135	108	84
Equatorial Guinea	188	na	na	na
Eritrea	170	na	na	64
Ethiopia	175	158	155	109

J1.3 Infant Mortality Rate, per 1,000 Live Births, Long-Range Trends, 1960–1996—Low-Income Countries per World Bank *(continued)*

Country	1960	1970	1980	1996
Gambia	213	185	159	79
Ghana	126	111	100	71
Guinea	215	181	185	122
Guinea-Bissau	200	185	168	134
Guyana	100	na	na	na
Haiti	170	141	123	72
Honduras	137	110	70	44
India	144	137	116	65
Kenya	120	102	72	57
Kyrgyzstan	80	na	43	26
Laos	155	146	127	101
Lesotho	137	134	108	74
Liberia	190	na	na	na
Madagascar	219	181	138	88
Malawi	206	193	169	133
Mali	285	204	184	120
Mauritania	175	148	120	94
Moldova	64	na	35	20
Mongolia	128	102	82	53
Mozambique	163	171	155	123
Myanmar (Burma)	158	128	109	80
Nepal	212	166	132	85
Nicaragua	140	106	90	44
Niger	191	170	150	118
Nigeria	122	139	99	78
Pakistan	139	142	124	88
Rwanda	124	142	128	129
Sao Tome and Principe	na	na	na	na
Senegal	173	135	91	60
Sierra Leone	219	197	190	174
Somalia	175	na	na	na
Sri Lanka	90	53	34	15
Sudan	125	118	94	74
Tajikistan	95	na	58	32
Tanzania	142	129	108	86
Togo	158	134	110	87
Uganda	133	109	116	99
Vietnam	147	104	57	40
Yemen	230	186	141	98
Zambia	126	106	90	112
Zimbabwe	109	96	82	56

Note: The infant mortality rate indicates the number of deaths of infants (children under one year old) and is stated in terms of the number of deaths per 1,000 live births. The above indicators show the infant mortality rates for each of the given years.

Source: World Bank, *World Development Indicators 1998*, Table 1.3 and Table 2.7

J1.4 Infant Mortality Rate, per 1,000 Live Births, Long-Range Trends, 1960–1996—Lower Middle-Income Countries per World Bank

Country	1960	1970	1980	1996
Albania	112	66	47	37
Algeria	152	139	98	32
Belarus	37	na	16	13

J1.4 Infant Mortality Rate, per 1,000 Live Births, Long-Range Trends, 1960–1996—Lower Middle-Income Countries per World Bank *(continued)*

Country	1960	1970	1980	1996
Belize	74	na	na	na
Bolivia	152	153	118	67
Botswana	117	95	69	56
Bulgaria	49	27	20	16
Cape Verde	110	na	na	na
Colombia	82	74	45	25
Costa Rica	80	62	20	12
Cuba	39	39	20	8
Djibouti	186	na	na	na
Dominica	na	na	na	na
Dominican Republic	102	98	74	40
Ecuador	115	100	67	34
Egypt	189	158	120	53
El Salvador	130	103	81	34
Estonia	40	20	17	10
Fiji	71	na	na	na
Georgia	52	na	25	17
Grenada	na	na	na	na
Guatemala	140	106	81	41
Indonesia	127	118	90	49
Iran	145	131	92	36
Iraq	117	102	80	101
Jamaica	58	43	21	12
Jordan	97	na	41	30
Kazakhstan	55	na	33	25
Kiribati	na	na	na	na
Latvia	35	21	20	16
Lebanon	65	50	48	31
Lithuania	52	24	20	10
Macedonia, FYRO	120	na	54	16
Maldives	158	na	na	na
Marshall Islands	na	na	na	na
Micronesia	na	na	na	na
Morocco	135	128	99	53
Namibia	129	118	90	61
North Korea, Dem. Rep.	85	51	32	56
Panama	67	47	32	22
Papua New Guinea	137	112	67	62
Paraguay	66	55	50	24
Peru	142	108	81	42
Philippines	77	66	52	37
Romania	69	49	29	22
Russia	48	na	22	17
Samoa	134	na	na	na
Solomon Islands	120	na	na	na
St. Vincent and the Grenadines	na	na	na	na
Suriname	70	na	na	na
Swaziland	157	na	na	na
Syria	136	96	56	31
Thailand	103	73	49	34
Tonga	na	na	na	na
Tunisia	170	121	69	30
Turkey	163	144	109	42
Turkmenistan	100	na	54	41
Ukraine	41	22	17	14
Uzbekistan	84	na	47	24

J1.4 Infant Mortality Rate, per 1,000 Live Births, Long-Range Trends, 1960–1996—Lower Middle-Income Countries per World Bank *(continued)*

Country	1960	1970	1980	1996
Vanuatu	141	na	na	na
Venezuela	53	53	36	22
Yugoslavia	87	54	33	14

Note: The infant mortality rate indicates the number of deaths of infants (children under one year old) and is stated in terms of the number of deaths per 1,000 live births. The above indicators show the infant mortality rates for each of the given years.

Source: World Bank, *World Development Indicators 1998*, Table 1.3 and Table 2.7

J1.5 Infant Mortality Rate, per 1000 Live Births, Long-Range Trends, 1960–1996—Upper Middle-Income Countries per World Bank

Country	1960	1970	1980	1996
Antigua and Barbuda	na	na	na	na
Argentina	60	52	35	22
Bahrain	130	na	na	na
Barbados	74	na	na	na
Brazil	115	95	67	36
Chile	107	77	32	12
Croatia	70	na	21	9
Czech Republic	22	21	16	6
Gabon	171	138	116	87
Hungary	51	36	23	11
Libya	160	122	79	25
Malaysia	73	45	30	11
Malta	37	na	na	na
Mauritius	62	60	32	17
Mexico	103	72	51	32
Oman	164	119	41	18
Palau	na	na	na	na
Poland	62	33	21	12
Saudi Arabia	170	119	65	22
Seychelles	na	na	na	na
Slovakia	33	25	21	11
Slovenia	37	24	15	5
South Africa	89	79	67	49
St. Kitts & Nevis	na	na	na	na
St. Lucia	na	na	na	na
Trinidad & Tobago	61	52	35	13
Uruguay	48	46	37	18

Note: The infant mortality rate indicates the number of deaths of infants (children under one year old) and is stated in terms of the number of deaths per 1,000 live births. The above indicators show the infant mortality rates for each of the given years.

Source: World Bank, *World Development Indicators 1998*, Table 1.3 and Table 2.7

J1.6 Under-Five Mortality Rate, per 1,000 Live Births, Long-Range Trends, 1960–1996—Low-Income Countries per World Bank

Country	1960	1970	1980	1996
Afghanistan	360	na	280	257
Angola	345	na	261	292
Armenia	48	na	28	30
Azerbaijan	75	na	52	45

J1.6 Under-Five Mortality Rate, per 1,000 Live Births, Long-Range Trends, 1960–1996—Low-Income Countries per World Bank *(continued)*

Country	1960	1970	1980	1996
Bangladesh	247	237	211	112
Benin	310	256	176	140
Bhutan	300	na	227	127
Bosnia and Herzegovina	155	na	38	17
Burkina Faso	318	278	246	158
Burundi	255	233	193	176
Cambodia	217	na	330	170
Cameroon	264	215	173	102
Central African Republic	343	238	180	164
Chad	325	na	206	149
China	209	115	65	47
Comoros	248	na	167	122
Congo, Dem. Rep. (Zaire)	302	245	210	207
Congo, Rep.	220	na	125	108
Cote d'Ivoire	300	237	170	150
Equatorial Guinea	316	na	243	173
Eritrea	250	na	195	120
Ethiopia	280	239	213	177
Gambia	375	na	250	107
Ghana	213	187	155	110
Guinea	380	na	300	210
Guinea-Bissau	336	na	290	223
Guyana	126	na	90	83
Haiti	260	221	200	134
Honduras	204	170	101	35
India	236	202	177	111
Kenya	202	156	112	90
Kyrgyzstan	115	na	73	50
Laos	235	na	200	128
Lesotho	203	190	168	139
Liberia	288	na	235	235
Madagascar	364	na	216	164
Malawi	365	347	290	217
Mali	500	na	300	220
Mauritania	330	na	175	183
Moldova	88	na	52	32
Mongolia	185	na	112	71
Mozambique	280	281	280	214
Myanmar (Burma)	237	179	146	150
Nepal	315	232	195	116
Nicaragua	209	165	143	57
Niger	320	na	320	320
Nigeria	204	na	196	191
Pakistan	226	183	161	136
Rwanda	210	209	218	170
Sao Tome and Principe	na	na	na	80
Senegal	300	279	218	127
Sierra Leone	385	360	301	284
Somalia	294	na	246	211
Sri Lanka	130	100	52	19
Sudan	210	176	145	116
Tajikistan	140	na	94	76
Tanzania	240	218	176	144
Togo	267	na	175	125
Uganda	224	na	180	141
Vietnam	219	na	105	44

J1.6 Under-Five Mortality Rate, per 1,000 Live Births, Long-Range Trends, 1960–1996—Low-Income Countries per World Bank (continued)

Country	1960	1970	1980	1996
Yemen	340	na	198	105
Zambia	213	181	149	202
Zimbabwe	181	137	125	73

Note: This indicator reflects the likelihood that, under the prevailing mortality rates for the age group, a newborn will die before he or she turns five. It is stated as the number of likely deaths per 1,000 live births.

Source: World Bank, *World Development Indicators 1998*, Table 1.3 for 1970 data; *The State of the World's Children 1998*, Table 8; UNICEF Web site, http://www.unicef.org/sowc98, for other years

J1.7 Under-Five Mortality Rate, per 1000 Live Births, Long-Range Trends, 1960–1996—Lower Middle-Income Countries per World Bank

Country	1960	1970	1980	1996
Albania	151	na	57	40
Algeria	255	192	139	39
Belarus	47	na	26	18
Belize	104	na	70	44
Bolivia	252	243	170	102
Botswana	170	146	94	50
Bulgaria	70	na	25	19
Cape Verde	164	na	95	73
Colombia	130	113	58	31
Costa Rica	112	85	29	15
Cuba	54	43	22	10
Djibouti	289	na	199	157
Dominica	na	na	na	20
Dominican Republic	149	127	92	56
Ecuador	180	140	101	40
Egypt	282	235	175	78
El Salvador	210	161	120	40
Estonia	52	na	25	16
Fiji	97	na	42	24
Georgia	70	na	44	29
Grenada	na	na	na	31
Guatemala	204	168	140	56
Indonesia	216	172	128	71
Iran	233	191	126	37
Iraq	171	123	83	122
Jamaica	76	64	39	11
Jordan	139	107	64	25
Kazakhstan	74	na	57	45
Kiribati	na	na	na	76
Latvia	44	na	26	20
Lebanon	85	na	40	40
Lithuania	70	na	25	18
Macedonia, FYRO	177	na	69	30
Maldives	258	na	129	76
Marshall Islands	na	na	na	92
Micronesia	na	na	na	27
Morocco	220	187	152	74
Namibia	206	na	114	77
North Korea, Dem. Rep.	120	na	43	30
Panama	104	68	31	20

J1.7 Under-Five Mortality Rate, per 1,000 Live Births, Long-Range Trends, 1960–1996—Lower Middle-Income Countries per World Bank *(continued)*

Country	1960	1970	1980	1996
Papua New Guinea	204	na	112	112
Paraguay	90	76	61	34
Peru	234	178	126	58
Philippines	107	82	69	38
Romania	82	na	36	25
Russia	65	na	36	25
Samoa	210	na	100	53
Solomon Islands	185	na	56	29
St. Vincent and the Grenadines	na	na	na	23
Suriname	96	na	52	31
Swaziland	233	na	151	97
Syria	201	128	73	34
Thailand	148	102	58	38
Tonga	na	na	na	23
Tunisia	254	201	100	35
Turkey	219	201	133	47
Turkmenistan	150	na	95	78
Ukraine	53	na	28	24
Uzbekistan	122	na	78	60
Vanuatu	225	na	110	53
Venezuela	70	62	42	28
Yugoslavia	120	na	44	22

Note: This indicator reflects the likelihood that, under the prevailing mortality rates for the age group, a newborn will die before he or she turns five. It is stated as the number of likely deaths per 1,000 live births.

Source: World Bank, *World Development Indicators 1998*, Table 1.3, for 1970 data; *The State of the World's Children 1998*, Table 8; UNICEF Web site, http://www.unicef.org/sowc98, for other years

J1.8 Under-Five Mortality Rate, per 1,000 Live Births, Long-Range Trends, 1960–1996—Upper Middle-Income Countries per World Bank

Country	1960	1970	1980	1996
Antigua and Barbuda	na	na	nana	22
Argentina	72	71	38	25
Bahrain	203	na	42	22
Barbados	90	na	29	12
Brazil	177	135	92	52
Chile	138	97	35	13
Croatia	98	na	23	11
Czech Republic	25	na	19	7
Gabon	287	na	194	145
Hungary	57	na	26	12
Libya	269	na	118	61
Malaysia	105	na	42	13
Malta	42	na	17	11
Mauritius	84	83	42	23
Mexico	148	111	87	32
Oman	280	na	95	18
Palau	na	na	39	35
Poland	70	na	24	14
Saudi Arabia	292	na	85	30
Seychelles	na	na	na	19
Slovakia	40	na	23	11
Slovenia	45	na	18	6

J1.8 Under-Five Mortality Rate, per 1,000 Live Births, Long-Range Trends, 1960–1996—Upper Middle-Income Countries per World Bank *(continued)*

Country	1960	1970	1980	1996
South Africa	126	na	91	66
St. Kitts & Nevis	na	na	na	38
St. Lucia	na	na	na	22
Trinidad & Tobago	73	55	40	17
Uruguay	56	56	43	22

Note: This indicator reflects the likelihood that, under the prevailing mortality rates for the age group, a newborn will die before he or she turns five. It is stated as the number of likely deaths per 1,000 live births.

Source: World Bank, *World Development Indicators 1998*, Table 1.3, for 1970 data; *The State of the World's Children 1998*, Table 8; UNICEF Web site, http://www.unicef.org/sowc98, for other years

J1.9 Child Mortality Rate, per 1,000 Females, per 1,000 Males, 1996—Low-Income Countries per World Bank

Country	Female	Male	Country	Female	Male
Afghanistan	na	na	Laos	na	na
Angola	na	na	Lesotho	na	na
Armenia	na	na	Liberia	na	na
Azerbaijan	na	na	Madagascar	82	85
Bangladesh	62	47	Malawi	114	126
Benin	90	89	Mali	138	136
Bhutan	na	na	Mauritania	na	na
Bosnia and Herzegovina	na	na	Moldova	na	na
Burkina Faso	110	107	Mongolia	na	na
Burundi	114	101	Mozambique	na	na
Cambodia	na	na	Myanmar (Burma)	na	na
Cameroon	75	64	Nepal	na	na
Central African Republic	64	63	Nicaragua	na	na
Chad	na	na	Niger	232	212
China	11	10	Nigeria	102	118
Comoros	na	na	Pakistan	37	22
Congo, Dem. Rep. (Zaire)	na	na	Rwanda	73	87
Congo, Rep.	na	na	Sao Tome and Principe	na	na
Cote d'Ivoire	na	na	Senegal	80	96
Equatorial Guinea	na	na	Sierra Leone	na	na
Eritrea	69	82	Somalia	na	na
Ethiopia	na	na	Sri Lanka	9	10
Gambia	79	83	Sudan	63	62
Ghana	62	63	Tajikistan	na	na
Guinea	112	122	Tanzania	52	59
Guinea-Bissau	na	na	Togo	90	75
Guyana	na	na	Uganda	72	82
Haiti	58	59	Vietnam	na	na
Honduras	na	na	Yemen	47	41
India	42	29	Zambia	93	96
Kenya	33	33	Zimbabwe	26	26
Kyrgyzstan	na	na			

Note: This indicator reflects the likelihood that, under the prevailing mortality rates for the age group, a child will die between the ages of one and five. It is stated as the number of likely deaths per 1,000 female children and per 1,000 male children.

Source: World Bank, *World Development Indicators 1998*, Table 2.17

J1.10 Child Mortality Rate, per 1,000 Females, per 1,000 Males, 1996—Lower Middle-Income Countries per World Bank

Country	Female	Male	Country	Female	Male
Albania	15	15	Lithuania	na	na
Algeria	na	na	Macedonia, FYRO	na	na
Belarus	na	na	Maldives	na	na
Belize	na	na	Marshall Islands	na	na
Bolivia	47	53	Micronesia	na	na
Botswana	16	18	Morocco	19	21
Bulgaria	na	na	Namibia	34	30
Cape Verde	na	na	North Korea, Dem. Rep.	na	na
Colombia	7	7	Panama	na	na
Costa Rica	na	na	Papua New Guinea	na	na
Cuba	na	na	Paraguay	12	10
Djibouti	na	na	Peru	31	29
Dominica	na	na	Philippines	25	28
Dominican Republic	20	18	Romania	5	7
Ecuador	9	12	Russia	2	3
Egypt	28	22	Samoa	na	na
El Salvador	20	17	Solomon Islands	na	na
Estonia	na	na	St. Vincent and the Grenadines	na	na
Fiji	na	na	Suriname	na	na
Georgia	na	na	Swaziland	na	na
Grenada	na	na	Syria	na	na
Guatemala	24	22	Thailand	11	11
Indonesia	27	30	Tonga	na	na
Iran	na	na	Tunisia	19	19
Iraq	na	na	Turkey	14	12
Jamaica	na	na	Turkmenistan	na	na
Jordan	6	6	Ukraine	na	na
Kazakhstan	7	8	Uzbekistan	na	na
Kiribati	na	na	Vanuatu	na	na
Latvia	na	na	Venezuela	na	na
Lebanon	na	na	Yugoslavia	na	na

Note: This indicator reflects the likelihood that, under the prevailing mortality rates for the age group, a child will die between the ages of one and five. It is stated as the number of likely deaths per 1,000 female children and per 1,000 male children.

Source: World Bank, *World Development Indicators 1998*, Table 2.17

J1.11 Child Mortality Rate, per 1,000 Females, per 1,000 Males, 1996—Upper Middle-Income Countries per World Bank

Country	Female	Male	Country	Female	Male
Antigua and Barbuda	na	na	Mexico	17	15
Argentina	na	na	Oman	17	13
Bahrain	na	na	Palau	na	na
Barbados	na	na	Poland	2	2
Brazil	9	8	Saudi Arabia	na	na
Chile	2	3	Seychelles	na	na
Croatia	na	na	Slovakia	na	na
Czech Republic	2	2	Slovenia	na	na
Gabon	na	na	South Africa	na	na
Hungary	2	2	St. Kitts & Nevis	na	na
Libya	5	6	St. Lucia	na	na
Malaysia	4	4	Trinidad & Tobago	3	4
Malta	na	na	Uruguay	na	na
Mauritius	na	na			

Note: This indicator reflects the likelihood that, under the prevailing mortality rates for the age group, a child will die between the ages of one and five. It is stated as the number of likely deaths per 1,000 female children and per 1,000 male children.

Source: World Bank, *World Development Indicators 1998*, Table 2.17

J2.1 Average Annual Rate of Reduction, Under-Five Mortality Rates, 1960–1980 and 1980–1996—Low-Income Countries per World Bank

Country	1960–1980	1980–1996	Country	1960–1980	1980–1996
Afghanistan	1.3	0.5	Kyrgyzstan	2.3	2.4
Angola	1.4	-0.7	Laos	0.8	2.8
Armenia	2.7	-0.4	Lesotho	0.9	1.2
Azerbaijan	1.8	0.9	Liberia	1.0	0.0
Bangladesh	0.8	4.0	Madagascar	2.6	1.7
Benin	2.8	1.4	Malawi	1.1	1.8
Bhutan	1.4	3.6	Mali	2.6	1.9
Bosnia and Herzegovina	7.0	5.0	Mauritania	3.2	-0.3
Burkina Faso	1.3	2.8	Moldova	2.6	3.0
Burundi	1.4	0.6	Mongolia	2.5	2.8
Cambodia	-2.1	4.1	Mozambique	0.0	1.7
Cameroon	2.1	3.3	Myanmar (Burma)	2.4	-0.2
Central African Republic	3.2	0.6	Nepal	2.4	3.2
Chad	2.3	2.0	Nicaragua	1.9	5.7
China	5.9	2.0	Niger	0.0	0.0
Comoros	2.0	2.0	Nigeria	0.2	0.1
Congo, Dem.Rep. (Zaire)	1.8	0.1	Pakistan	1.7	1.1
Congo, Rep.	2.8	0.9	Rwanda	-0.2	1.6
Cote d'Ivoire	2.8	0.8	Sao Tome and Principe	na	na
Equatorial Guinea	1.3	2.1	Senegal	1.6	3.4
Eritrea	1.2	3.0	Sierra Leone	1.2	0.4
Ethiopia	1.4	1.2	Somalia	0.9	1.0
Gambia	2.0	5.3	Sri Lanka	4.6	6.3
Ghana	1.6	2.1	Sudan	1.9	1.4
Guinea	1.2	2.2	Tajikistan	2.0	1.3
Guinea-Bissau	0.7	1.7	Tanzania	1.6	1.3
Guyana	1.7	0.5	Togo	2.1	2.1
Haiti	1.3	2.5	Uganda	1.1	1.5
Honduras	3.5	6.6	Vietnam	3.7	5.4
India	1.4	2.9	Yemen	2.7	4.0
Kenya	2.9	1.4	Zambia	1.8	1.9
			Zimbabwe	1.8	3.4

Note: This indicator represents the average annual rate of reduction, stated as a percent in a country's under-five mortality rate, over the periods specified.

Source: The State of the World's Children 1998, Table 8; UNICEF Web site, http://www.unicef.org/sowc98/ and gopher://gopher.unicef.org/11/.s598sowcch2

J2.2 Average Annual Rate of Reduction, Under-Five Mortality Rates, 1960–1980 and 1980–1996—Lower Middle-Income Countries per World Bank

Country	1960–1980	1980–1996	Country	1960–1980	1980–1996
Albania	4.9	2.2	Macedonia, FYRO	4.7	5.2
Algeria	3.0	7.9	Maldives	3.5	3.3
Belarus	3.0	2.3	Marshall Islands	na	na
Belize	2.0	2.9	Micronesia	na	na
Bolivia	2.0	3.2	Morocco	1.8	4.5
Botswana	3.0	3.9	Namibia	3.0	2.5
Bulgaria	5.1	1.7	North Korea, Dem. Rep.	5.1	2.3
Cape Verde	2.7	1.7	Panama	6.0	2.7
Colombia	4.0	3.9	Papua New Guinea	3.0	0.0
Costa Rica	6.8	4.0	Paraguay	1.9	3.7
Cuba	4.5	4.7	Peru	3.1	4.8
Djibouti	1.9	1.5	Philippines	2.2	3.7
Dominica	na	na	Romania	4.1	2.2
Dominican Republic	2.4	3.1	Russia	3.0	2.3
Ecuador	2.9	5.8	Samoa	3.7	4.0
Egypt	2.4	5.1	Solomon Islands	6.0	4.1
El Salvador	2.8	6.9	St. Vincent and the Grenadines	na	na
Estonia	3.7	2.8	Suriname	3.0	3.3
Fiji	4.2	3.5	Swaziland	2.2	2.7
Georgia	2.3	2.6	Syria	5.1	4.8
Grenada	na	na	Thailand	4.7	2.6
Guatemala	1.9	5.7	Tonga	na	na
Indonesia	2.6	3.7	Tunisia	4.7	6.6
Iran	3.1	7.7	Turkey	2.5	6.5
Iraq	3.6	-2.4	Turkmenistan	2.3	1.2
Jamaica	3.4	7.8	Ukraine	3.2	1.0
Jordan	3.9	5.9	Uzbekistan	2.2	1.6
Kazakhstan	1.3	1.5	Vanuatu	3.6	4.6
Kiribati	na	na	Venezuela	2.6	2.6
Latvia	2.6	1.6	Yugoslavia	5.0	4.3
Lebanon	3.8	0.0			
Lithuania	5.1	2.1			

Note: This indicator represents the average annual rate of reduction, stated as a percent in a country's under-five mortality rate, over the periods specified.

Source: The State of the World's Children 1998, Table 8; UNICEF Web site, http://www.unicef.org/sowc98/ and gopher://gopher.unicef.org/11/.s598sowcch2

J2.3 Average Annual Rate of Reduction, Under-Five Mortality Rates, 1960–1980 and 1980–1996—Upper Middle-Income Countries per World Bank

Country	1960–1980	1980–1996	Country	1960–1980	1980–1996
Antigua and Barbuda	na	na	Mexico	2.7	6.3
Argentina	3.2	2.6	Oman	5.4	10.4
Bahrain	7.9	4.0	Palau	na	0.7
Barbados	5.7	5.5	Poland	5.3	3.6
Brazil	3.3	3.6	Saudi Arabia	6.2	6.5
Chile	6.9	6.2	Seychelles	na	na
Croatia	7.2	4.6	Slovakia	2.7	4.7
Czech Republic	1.4	6.6	Slovenia	4.6	6.8
Gabon	2.0	1.8	South Africa	1.6	2.0
Hungary	3.9	4.8	St. Kitts & Nevis	na	na
Libya	4.1	4.1	St. Lucia	na	na
Malaysia	4.6	7.3	Trinidad & Tobago	3.0	5.3
Malta	4.6	2.8	Uruguay	1.3	4.1
Mauritius	3.4	3.9			

Note: This indicator represents the average annual rate of reduction, stated as a percent in a country's under-five mortality rate, over the periods specified.

Source: The State of the World's Children 1998, Table 8; UNICEF Web site, http://www.unicef.org/sowc98/ and gopher://gopher.unicef.org/11/.s598sowcch2

J2.4 Average Annual Rate of Reduction (AARR), Under-Five Mortality Rates, Worldwide Summary, 1996–2000—Region by Region

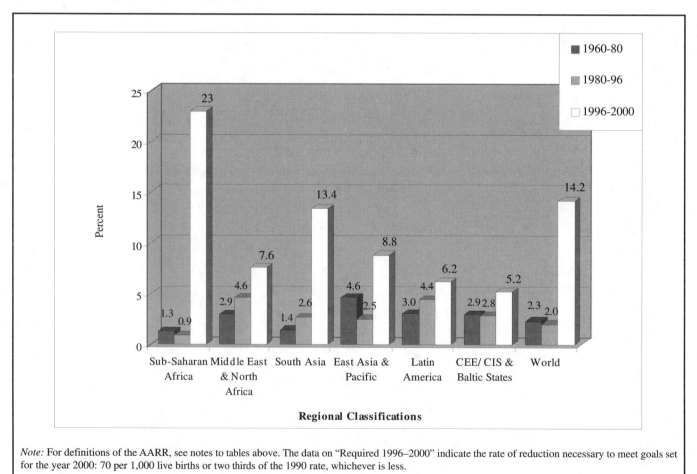

Note: For definitions of the AARR, see notes to tables above. The data on "Required 1996–2000" indicate the rate of reduction necessary to meet goals set for the year 2000: 70 per 1,000 live births or two thirds of the 1990 rate, whichever is less.

Source: The State of the World's Children 1998, Table 8, UNICEF Web site, http://www.unicef.org/sowc98/tab1b.htm

J3.1 Low Birth-Weight Babies, Percent of Births, 1989–1995—Low-Income Countries per World Bank

Country	Percent	Country	Percent
Afghanistan	na	Laos	18
Angola	19	Lesotho	11
Armenia	na	Liberia	na
Azerbaijan	na	Madagascar	10
Bangladesh	34	Malawi	20
Benin	10	Mali	17
Bhutan	na	Mauritania	11
Bosnia and Herzegovina	na	Moldova	na
Burkina Faso	21	Mongolia	10
Burundi	na	Mozambique	20
Cambodia	na	Myanmar (Burma)	16
Cameroon	13	Nepal	26
Central African Republic	15	Nicaragua	15
Chad	na	Niger	15
China	6	Nigeria	16
Comoros	na	Pakistan	25
Congo, Dem. Rep. (Zaire)	15	Rwanda	17
Congo, Rep.	16	Sao Tome and Principe	na
Cote d'Ivoire	14	Senegal	11
Equatorial Guinea	na	Sierra Leone	17
Eritrea	na	Somalia	na
Ethiopia	16	Sri Lanka	17
Gambia	10	Sudan	15
Ghana	17	Tajikistan	na
Guinea	21	Tanzania	14
Guinea-Bissau	20	Togo	20
Guyana	na	Uganda	na
Haiti	15	Vietnam	17
Honduras	9	Yemen	19
India	33	Zambia	13
Kenya	16	Zimbabwe	14
Kyrgyzstan	na		

Note: This indicator represents the percent of infants born within the specified date range who are classified as "low birth-weight." Low birth-weight signifies a weight, measured immediately after birth, of less than 2,500 grams, or (5.5 pounds).

Source: World Bank, *World Development Indicators 1998,* Table 2.16

J3.2 Low Birth-Weight Babies, Percent of Births, 1989–1995—Lower Middle-Income Countries per World Bank

Country	Percent	Country	Percent
Albania	7	Lithuania	na
Algeria	9	Macedonia, FYRO	na
Belarus	5	Maldives	na
Belize	na	Marshall Islands	na
Bolivia	10	Micronesia	na
Botswana	8	Morocco	9
Bulgaria	6	Namibia	12
Cape Verde	na	North Korea, Dem. Rep.	na
Colombia	9	Panama	10
Costa Rica	7	Papua New Guinea	23
Cuba	8	Paraguay	8
Djibouti	na	Peru	11
Dominica	na	Philippines	na
Dominican Republic	16	Romania	na
Ecuador	13	Russia	na
Egypt	12	Samoa	na
El Salvador	11	Solomon Islands	na
Estonia	na	St. Vincent and the Grenadines	na
Fiji	na	Suriname	na
Georgia	na	Swaziland	na
Grenada	na	Syria	8
Guatemala	14	Thailand	13
Indonesia	14	Tonga	na
Iran	12	Tunisia	10
Iraq	15	Turkey	8
Jamaica	11	Turkmenistan	na
Jordan	7	Ukraine	5
Kazakhstan	na	Uzbekistan	na
Kiribati	na	Vanuatu	na
Latvia	na	Venezuela	9
Lebanon	na	Yugoslavia	na

Note: This indicator represents the percent of infants born within the specified date range who are classified as "low birth-weight." Low birth-weight signifies a weight, measured immediately after birth, of less than 2,500 grams, or (5.5 pounds).

Source: World Bank, *World Development Indicators 1998,* Table 2.16

J3.3 Low Birth-Weight Babies, Percent of Births, 1989–1995—Upper Middle-Income Countries per World Bank

Country	Percent	Country	Percent
Antigua and Barbuda	na	Mexico	12
Argentina	7	Oman	10
Bahrain	na	Palau	na
Barbados	na	Poland	8
Brazil	11	Saudi Arabia	na
Chile	7	Seychelles	na
Croatia	8	Slovakia	6
Czech Republic	6	Slovenia	6
Gabon	10	South Africa	na
Hungary	9	St. Kitts & Nevis	na
Libya	5	St. Lucia	na
Malaysia	8	Trinidad & Tobago	10
Malta	na	Uruguay	8
Mauritius	8		

Note: This indicator represents the percent of infants born within the specified date range who are classified as "low birth-weight." Low birth-weight signifies a weight, measured immediately after birth, of less than 2,500 grams, or (5.5 pounds).

Source: World Bank, *World Development Indicators 1998*, Table 2.16

J4.1 Births Attended by Trained Health Personnel, Percent of Births, 1990–1996—Low-Income Countries per World Bank

Country	Percent	Country	Percent
Afghanistan	9	Laos	na
Angola	15	Lesotho	40
Armenia	na	Liberia	58
Azerbaijan	na	Madagascar	57
Bangladesh	14	Malawi	55
Benin	45	Mali	24
Bhutan	15	Mauritania	40
Bosnia and Herzegovina	na	Moldova	na
Burkina Faso	42	Mongolia	99
Burundi	19	Mozambique	25
Cambodia	47	Myanmar (Burma)	57
Cameroon	64	Nepal	9
Central African Republic	46	Nicaragua	61
Chad	15	Niger	15
China	84	Nigeria	31
Comoros	52	Pakistan	19
Congo, Dem. Rep. (Zaire)	na	Rwanda	26
Congo, Rep.	na	Sao Tome and Principe	86
Cote d'Ivoire	45	Senegal	46
Equatorial Guinea	58	Sierra Leone	25
Eritrea	21	Somalia	2
Ethiopia	14	Sri Lanka	94
Gambia	44	Sudan	69
Ghana	44	Tajikistan	na
Guinea	31	Tanzania	53
Guinea-Bissau	27	Togo	54
Guyana	90	Uganda	38
Haiti	21	Vietnam	95
Honduras	88	Yemen	16
India	34	Zambia	51
Kenya	45	Zimbabwe	69
Kyrgyzstan	na		

Note: This indicator shows the percent of births during which a trained health care professional has been present. These professionals can include doctors, nurses, medical and physician's assistants, and other health care workers who have been trained to provide pre- and post-natal care for both mother and newborn.

Source: *The State of the World's Children 1998*, Table 7; UNICEF Web site, http://www.unicef.org/sowc98

J4.2 Births Attended by Trained Health Personnel, Percent of Births, 1990–1996—Lower Middle-Income Countries per World Bank

Country	Percent	Country	Percent
Albania	99	Lithuania	na
Algeria	77	Macedonia, FYRO	na
Belarus	100	Maldives	90
Belize	77	Marshall Islands	na
Bolivia	47	Micronesia	90
Botswana	78	Morocco	40
Bulgaria	100	Namibia	68
Cape Verde	30	North Korea, Dem. Rep.	100
Colombia	85	Panama	86
Costa Rica	93	Papua New Guinea	20
Cuba	90	Paraguay	66
Djibouti	79	Peru	56
Dominica	96	Philippines	53
Dominican Republic	96	Romania	100
Ecuador	64	Russia	na
Egypt	46	Samoa	95
El Salvador	87	Solomon Islands	87
Estonia	na	St. Vincent and the Grenadines	73
Fiji	96	Suriname	91
Georgia	na	Swaziland	55
Grenada	81	Syria	67
Guatemala	35	Thailand	71
Indonesia	36	Tonga	92
Iran	77	Tunisia	69
Iraq	54	Turkey	76
Jamaica	82	Turkmenistan	na
Jordan	87	Ukraine	100
Kazakhstan	99	Uzbekistan	na
Kiribati	72	Vanuatu	86
Latvia	na	Venezuela	69
Lebanon	45	Yugoslavia	na

Note: This indicator shows the percent of births during which a trained professional health care professional has been present. These professionals can include doctors, nurses, medical and physician's assistants, and other health care workers who have been trained to provide pre- and post-natal care for both mother and newborn.

Source: The State of the World's Children 1998, Table 7; UNICEF Web site, http://www.unicef.org/sowc98

J4.3 Births Attended by Trained Health Personnel, Percent of Births, 1990–1996—Upper Middle-Income Countries per World Bank

Country	Percent	Country	Percent
Antigua and Barbuda	90	Mexico	77
Argentina	97	Oman	87
Bahrain	97	Palau	90
Barbados	98	Poland	99
Brazil	88	Saudi Arabia	82
Chile	98	Seychelles	99
Croatia	na	Slovakia	na
Czech Republic	na	Slovenia	na
Gabon	80	South Africa	82
Hungary	99	St. Kitts & Nevis	100
Libya	76	St. Lucia	99
Malaysia	94	Trinidad & Tobago	98
Malta	na	Uruguay	96
Mauritius	97		

Note: This indicator shows the percent of births during which a trained professional health care professional has been present. These professionals can include doctors, nurses, medical and physician's assistants, and other health care workers who have been trained to provide pre- and post-natal care for both mother and newborn.

Source: The State of the World's Children 1998, Table 7; UNICEF Web site, http://www.unicef.org/sowc98

J5.1 Prevalence of Child Malnutrition, Percent of Children Under Five, 1990–1996—Low-Income Countries per World Bank

Country	Percent	Country	Percent
Afghanistan	na	Laos	40
Angola	35	Lesotho	21
Armenia	na	Liberia	na
Azerbaijan	10	Madagascar	32
Bangladesh	68	Malawi	28
Benin	24	Mali	31
Bhutan	na	Mauritania	48
Bosnia and Herzegovina	na	Moldova	na
Burkina Faso	33	Mongolia	12
Burundi	38	Mozambique	47
Cambodia	38	Myanmar (Burma)	31
Cameroon	15	Nepal	49
Central African Republic	23	Nicaragua	24
Chad	na	Niger	43
China	16	Nigeria	35
Comoros	na	Pakistan	40
Congo, Dem. Rep. (Zaire)	34	Rwanda	29
Congo, Rep.	24	Sao Tome and Principe	na
Cote d'Ivoire	24	Senegal	22
Equatorial Guinea	na	Sierra Leone	29
Eritrea	41	Somalia	na
Ethiopia	48	Sri Lanka	38
Gambia	17	Sudan	34
Ghana	27	Tajikistan	na
Guinea	24	Tanzania	29
Guinea-Bissau	23	Togo	25
Guyana	na	Uganda	26
Haiti	28	Vietnam	45
Honduras	18	Yemen	30
India	66	Zambia	29
Kenya	23	Zimbabwe	16
Kyrgyzstan	na		

Note: This indicator reflects the percentage of children under five years of age whose weight deviates from the standard for their age, which is based on both a standard weight for height and a standard height for age.

Source: World Bank, *World Development Indicators 1998*, Table 2.16

J5.2 Prevalence of Child Malnutrition, Percent of Children Under Five, 1990–1996—Lower Middle-Income Countries per World Bank

Country	Percent	Country	Percent
Albania	na	Lithuania	na
Algeria	10	Macedonia, FYRO	na
Belarus	na	Maldives	na
Belize	na	Marshall Islands	na
Bolivia	16	Micronesia	na
Botswana	27	Morocco	10
Bulgaria	na	Namibia	26
Cape Verde	na	North Korea, Dem. Rep.	na
Colombia	8	Panama	7
Costa Rica	2	Papua New Guinea	30
Cuba	8	Paraguay	4
Djibouti	na	Peru	11
Dominica	na	Philippines	30
Dominican Republic	6	Romania	6
Ecuador	17	Russia	3
Egypt	9	Samoa	na
El Salvador	11	Solomon Islands	na
Estonia	na	St. Vincent and the Grenadines	na
Fiji	na	Suriname	na
Georgia	na	Swaziland	na
Grenada	na	Syria	na
Guatemala	33	Thailand	13
Indonesia	40	Tonga	na
Iran	16	Tunisia	9
Iraq	12	Turkey	10
Jamaica	10	Turkmenistan	na
Jordan	10	Ukraine	na
Kazakhstan	1	Uzbekistan	4
Kiribati	na	Vanuatu	na
Latvia	na	Venezuela	5
Lebanon	9	Yugoslavia	na

Note: This indicator reflects the percentage of children under five years of age whose weight deviates from the standard for their age, which is based on both a standard weight for height and a standard height for age.

Source: World Bank, *World Development Indicators 1998,* Table 2.16

J5.3 Prevalence of Child Malnutrition, Percent of Children Under Five, 1990–1996—Upper Middle-Income Countries per World Bank

Country	Percent	Country	Percent
Antigua and Barbuda	na	Mexico	14
Argentina	2	Oman	14
Bahrain	na	Palau	na
Barbados	na	Poland	na
Brazil	7	Saudi Arabia	na
Chile	1	Seychelles	na
Croatia	na	Slovakia	na
Czech Republic	1	Slovenia	na
Gabon	15	South Africa	9
Hungary	na	St. Kitts & Nevis	na
Libya	5	St. Lucia	na
Malaysia	23	Trinidad & Tobago	7
Malta	na	Uruguay	4
Mauritius	15		

Note: This indicator reflects the percentage of children under five years of age whose weight deviates from the standard for their age, which is based on both a standard weight for height and a standard height for age.

Source: World Bank, *World Development Indicators 1998*, Table 2.16

J6.1 Children Under Five Suffering from Underweight, Wasting, and Stunting, 1990–1997—Low-Income Countries per World Bank

Country	Percent of Under-Five Underweight	Percent of Under-Five Wasting	Percent of Under-Five Stunted
Afghanistan	na	na	na
Angola	na	na	na
Armenia	na	na	na
Azerbaijan	na	na	na
Bangladesh	56	18	55
Benin	na	na	na
Bhutan	38	4	56
Bosnia and Herzegovina	na	na	na
Burkina Faso	30	13	29
Burundi	37	9	43
Cambodia	40	8	38
Cameroon	14	3	24
Central African Republic	27	7	34
Chad	na	na	na
China	16	na	na
Comoros	26	8	34
Congo, Dem. Rep. (Zaire)	34	10	45
Congo, Rep.	24	4	21
Cote d'Ivoire	24	8	24
Equatorial Guinea	na	na	na
Eritrea	44	16	38
Ethiopia	48	8	64
Gambia	na	na	na
Ghana	27	11	26
Guinea	26	12	32
Guinea-Bissau	23	na	na
Guyana	18	na	na
Haiti	28	8	32
Honduras	18	2	40

J6.1   Children Under Five Suffering from Underweight, Wasting, and Stunting, 1990–1997—Low-Income Countries per World Bank *(continued)*

Country	Percent of Under-Five Underweight	Percent of Under-Five Wasting	Percent of Under-Five Stunted
India	53	18	52
Kenya	23	8	34
Kyrgyzstan	na	na	na
Laos	40	11	47
Lesotho	16	5	44
Liberia	na	na	na
Madagascar	34	7	50
Malawi	30	7	48
Mali	27	11	49
Mauritania	23	7	44
Moldova	na	na	na
Mongolia	12	2	26
Mozambique	27	5	55
Myanmar (Burma)	43	8	45
Nepal	47	11	48
Nicaragua	12	2	24
Niger	36	16	32
Nigeria	36	9	43
Pakistan	38	na	na
Rwanda	29	4	48
Sao Tome and Principe	17	5	26
Senegal	22	7	23
Sierra Leone	29	9	35
Somalia	na	na	na
Sri Lanka	38	16	24
Sudan	34	13	33
Tajikistan	na	na	na
Tanzania	27	6	42
Togo	19	na	34
Uganda	26	5	38
Vietnam	45	12	47
Yemen	39	na	39
Zambia	28	6	53
Zimbabwe	16	6	21

Note: These indicators represent the number of children under five years of age suffering, either moderately or severely, from being underweight, from wasting, and from stunting. Moderate or severe underweight is defined as falling below the median weight of a population by a factor of two "standard deviations." Moderate or severe wasting is defined as falling below the median "weight-for-height" ratio of a population by a factor of two "standard deviations." Moderate or severe stunting is defined as falling below the median "height-for-age" ratio of a population by a factor of two "standard deviations."

Source: The State of the World's Children 1998, Table 2; UNICEF Web site, http://www.unicef.org/sowc98, <s>Source:

J6.2   Children Under Five Suffering from Underweight, Wasting, and Stunting, 1990–1997—Lower Middle-Income Countries per World Bank

Country	Percent of Under-Five Underweight	Percent of Under-Five Wasting	Percent of Under-Five Stunted
Albania	na	na	na
Algeria	13	9	18
Belarus	na	na	na
Belize	na	na	na
Bolivia	8	1	29
Botswana	15	na	44
Bulgaria	na	na	na

J6.2 Children Under Five Suffering from Underweight, Wasting, and Stunting, 1990–1997—Lower Middle-Income Countries per World Bank *(continued)*

Country	Percent of Under-Five Underweight	Percent of Under-Five Wasting	Percent of Under-Five Stunted
Cape Verde	19	3	26
Colombia	8	1	15
Costa Rica	2	na	na
Cuba	na	1	na
Djibouti	23	11	22
Dominica	5	2	6
Dominican Republic	6	1	11
Ecuador	17	2	34
Egypt	15	6	25
El Salvador	11	1	23
Estonia	na	na	na
Fiji	na	na	na
Georgia	na	na	na
Grenada	na	na	na
Guatemala	27	3	50
Indonesia	11	na	4
Iran	16	7	19
Iraq	12	3	22
Jamaica	10	4	6
Jordan	9	2	16
Kazakhstan	8	3	16
Kiribati	na	na	na
Latvia	na	na	na
Lebanon	na	na	na
Lithuania	na	na	na
Macedonia, FYRO	na	na	na
Maldives	39	16	30
Marshall Islands	na	na	na
Micronesia	na	na	na
Morocco	9	2	23
Namibia	26	9	28
North Korea, Dem. Rep.	na	na	na
Panama	7	1	9
Papua New Guinea	35	na	na
Paraguay	4	0	17
Peru	8	1	26
Philippines	30	8	33
Romania	na	na	na
Russia	na	na	na
Samoa	na	na	na
Solomon Islands	na	na	na
St. Vincent and the Grenadines	na	na	na
Suriname	na	na	na
Swaziland	10	1	30
Syria	13	9	21
Thailand	26	6	22
Tonga	na	na	na
Tunisia	9	4	23
Turkey	10	na	na
Turkmenistan	na	na	na
Ukraine	na	na	na
Uzbekistan	na	na	na
Vanuatu	20	na	19
Venezuela	6	2	6
Yugoslavia	na	na	na

Note: These indicators represent the number of children under five years of age suffering, either moderately or severely, from being underweight, from wasting, and from stunting. Moderate or severe underweight is defined as falling below the median weight of a population by a factor of two "standard deviations." Moderate or severe wasting is defined as falling below the median "weight-for-height" ratio of a population by a factor of two "standard deviations." Moderate or severe stunting is defined as falling below the median "height-for-age" ratio of a population by a factor of two "standard deviations."

Source: The State of the World's Children 1998, Table 2; UNICEF Web site, http://www.unicef.org/sowc98,

J6.3 Children Under Five Suffering from Underweight, Wasting, and Stunting, 1990–1997—Upper Middle-Income Countries per World Bank

Country	Percent of Under-Five Underweight	Percent of Under-Five Wasting	Percent of Under-Five Stunted
Antigua and Barbuda	10	10	0
Argentina	na	na	na
Bahrain	na	na	na
Barbados	5	4	7
Brazil	6	2	11
Chile	1	0	3
Croatia	na	na	na
Czech Republic	na	na	na
Gabon	na	na	na
Hungary	na	na	na
Libya	5	3	15
Malaysia	23	na	na
Malta	na	na	na
Mauritius	16	15	10
Mexico	14	6	22
Oman	23	13	23
Palau	na	na	na
Poland	na	na	na
Saudi Arabia	na	na	na
Seychelles	6	2	5
Slovakia	na	na	na
Slovenia	na	na	na
South Africa	9	3	23
St. Kitts & Nevis	na	na	na
St. Lucia	na	na	na
Trinidad & Tobago	7	4	5
Uruguay	7	na	16

Note: These indicators represent the number of children under five years of age suffering, either moderately or severely, from being underweight, from wasting, and from stunting. Moderate or severe underweight is defined as falling below the median weight of a population by a factor of two "standard deviations." Moderate or severe wasting is defined as falling below the median "weight-for-height" ratio of a population by a factor of two "standard deviations." Moderate or severe stunting is defined as falling below the median "height-for-age" ratio of a population by a factor of two "standard deviations."

Source: The State of the World's Children 1998, Table 2; UNICEF Web site, http://www.unicef.org/sowc98,

J7.1 Total Goitre Rate, Percent of Age Group, 6-11 Years, 1985–1994—Low-Income Countries per World Bank

Country	Percent	Country	Percent
Afghanistan	20	Laos	25
Angola	7	Lesotho	43
Armenia	10	Liberia	6
Azerbaijan	20	Madagascar	24
Bangladesh	50	Malawi	13
Benin	24	Mali	29
Bhutan	25	Mauritania	na
Bosnia and Herzegovina	na	Moldova	na
Burkina Faso	16	Mongolia	28
Burundi	42	Mozambique	20
Cambodia	15	Myanmar (Burma)	18
Cameroon	26	Nepal	44
Central African Republic	63	Nicaragua	4
Chad	15	Niger	9
China	20	Nigeria	10
Comoros	na	Pakistan	32
Congo, Dem.Rep. (Zaire)	9	Rwanda	49
Congo, Rep.	8	Sao Tome and Principe	na
Cote d'Ivoire	6	Senegal	12
Equatorial Guinea	na	Sierra Leone	7
Eritrea	na	Somalia	7
Ethiopia	31	Sri Lanka	14
Gambia	na	Sudan	20
Ghana	10	Tajikistan	20
Guinea	55	Tanzania	37
Guinea-Bissau	19	Togo	22
Guyana	na	Uganda	7
Haiti	4	Vietnam	20
Honduras	9	Yemen	32
India	9	Zambia	51
Kenya	7	Zimbabwe	42
Kyrgyzstan	20		

Note: The total goitre rate reflects the share of children, ages six to eleven, with a visible or palpable goitre. A swelling of the thyroid gland, goitre can be seen as a growth at the front of the neck. It indicates a deficiency of iodine.

Source: The State of the World's Children 1998, Table 2; UNICEF Web site, http://www.unicef.org/sowc98

J7.2 Total Goitre Rate, Percent of Age Group, 6–11 Years, 1985-1994—Lower Middle-Income Countries per World Bank

Country	Percent	Country	Percent
Albania	41	Macedonia, FYRO	na
Algeria	9	Maldives	24
Belarus	22	Marshall Islands	na
Belize	0	Micronesia	na
Bolivia	21	Morocco	20
Botswana	8	Namibia	35
Bulgaria	20	North Korea, Dem. Rep.	na
Cape Verde	na	Panama	13
Colombia	7	Papua New Guinea	30
Costa Rica	4	Paraguay	49
Cuba	10	Peru	36
Djibouti	na	Philippines	15
Dominica	na	Romania	10
Dominican Republic	5	Russia	na
Ecuador	10	Samoa	na
Egypt	5	Solomon Islands	na
El Salvador	25	St. Vincent and the Grenadines	na
Estonia	na	Suriname	na
Fiji	na	Swaziland	na
Georgia	20	Syria	73
Grenada	na	Thailand	8
Guatemala	20	Tonga	na
Indonesia	28	Tunisia	4
Iran	30	Turkey	36
Iraq	7	Turkmenistan	20
Jamaica	na	Ukraine	10
Jordan	na	Uzbekistan	18
Kazakhstan	20	Vanuatu	na
Kiribati	na	Venezuela	11
Latvia	na	Yugoslavia	na
Lebanon	15		
Lithuania	na		

Note: The total goitre rate reflects the share of children, ages six to eleven, with a visible or palpable goitre. A swelling of the thyroid gland, goitre can be seen as a growth at the front of the neck. It indicates a deficiency of iodine.

Source: The State of the World's Children 1998, Table 2; UNICEF Web site, http://www.unicef.org/sowc98

J7.3 Total Goitre Rate, Percent of Age Group, 6–11 Years, 1985-1994—Upper Middle-Income Countries per World Bank

Country	Percent	Country	Percent
Antigua and Barbuda	na	Mexico	3
Argentina	8	Oman	10
Bahrain	na	Palau	na
Barbados	na	Poland	10
Brazil	14	Saudi Arabia	na
Chile	9	Seychelles	na
Croatia	na	Slovakia	na
Czech Republic	na	Slovenia	na
Gabon	5	South Africa	2
Hungary	na	St. Kitts & Nevis	na
Libya	6	St. Lucia	na
Malaysia	20	Trinidad & Tobago	na
Malta	na	Uruguay	na
Mauritius	0		

Note: The total goitre rate reflects the share of children, ages six to eleven, with a visible or palpable goitre. A swelling of the thyroid gland, goitre can be seen as a growth at the front of the neck. It indicates a deficiency of iodine.

Source: The State of the World's Children 1998, Table 2; UNICEF Web site, http://www.unicef.org/sowc98

J8.1 One-Year-Olds Fully Immunized against DPT, Percent of Total, 1980 and 1995–1996—Low-Income Countries per World Bank

Country	1980	1995-1996	Country	1980	1995-1996
Afghanistan	na	31	Laos	na	28
Angola	6	42	Lesotho	56	58
Armenia	na	86	Liberia	na	45
Azerbaijan	na	95	Madagascar	48	73
Bangladesh	0	66	Malawi	58	90
Benin	na	80	Mali	na	29
Bhutan	na	87	Mauritania	18	50
Bosnia and Herzegovina	na	88	Moldova	na	97
Burkina Faso	2	48	Mongolia	76	90
Burundi	38	63	Mozambique	56	60
Cambodia	na	75	Myanmar (Burma)	4	88
Cameroon	5	46	Nepal	8	51
Central African Republic	13	53	Nicaragua	15	78
Chad	1	19	Niger	6	33
China	58	95	Nigeria	na	28
Comoros	na	60	Pakistan	2	77
Congo, Dem. Rep. (Zaire)	18	36	Rwanda	17	98
Congo, Rep.	42	47	Sao Tome and Principe	na	66
Cote d'Ivoire	na	55	Senegal	na	62
Equatorial Guinea	na	64	Sierra Leone	13	65
Eritrea	na	46	Somalia	na	21
Ethiopia	3	67	Sri Lanka	46	90
Gambia	80	97	Sudan	1	79
Ghana	7	51	Tajikistan	na	93
Guinea	na	48	Tanzania	59	85
Guinea-Bissau	9	56	Togo	na	82
Guyana	na	83	Uganda	9	68
Haiti	3	34	Vietnam	4	94
Honduras	31	93	Yemen	1	59
India	31	89	Zambia	83	83
Kenya	na	46	Zimbabwe	39	80
Kyrgyzstan	na	82			

Note: This indicator represents the share of one-year-olds immunized against diphtheria (DPT). It is expressed as a percent of the total in the age group.

Source: World Bank, *World Development Indicators 1998*, Table 2.14, 1985 data; *The State of the World's Children 1998*, Table 3; UNICEF Web site, http://www.unicef.org/sowc98, for other years

J8.2 One-Year-Olds Fully Immunized against DPT, Percent of Total, 1980 and 1995–1996—Lower Middle-Income Countries per World Bank

Country	1980	1995–1996	Country	1980	1995–1996
Albania	94	98	Macedonia, FYRO	na	93
Algeria	33	75	Maldives	na	95
Belarus	na	95	Marshall Islands	na	74
Belize	na	85	Micronesia	na	83
Bolivia	11	76	Morocco	43	95
Botswana	64	83	Namibia	na	70
Bulgaria	97	100	North Korea, Dem. Rep.	50	96
Cape Verde	na	73	Panama	47	93
Colombia	15	92	Papua New Guinea	32	55
Costa Rica	86	84	Paraguay	17	80
Cuba	67	100	Peru	14	72
Djibouti	na	49	Philippines	47	70
Dominica	na	100	Romania	na	98
Dominican Republic	35	58	Russia	na	87
Ecuador	10	88	Samoa	na	95
Egypt	84	77	Solomon Islands	na	72
El Salvador	43	100	St. Vincent and the Grenadines	na	100
Estonia	84	90	Suriname	na	80
Fiji	na	97	Swaziland	na	70
Georgia	na	58	Syria	13	96
Grenada	na	80	Thailand	49	94
Guatemala	43	73	Tonga	na	95
Indonesia	0	91	Tunisia	36	91
Iran	32	96	Turkey	42	84
Iraq	13	94	Turkmenistan	na	80
Jamaica	34	92	Ukraine	53	94
Jordan	30	99	Uzbekistan	na	89
Kazakhstan	na	94	Vanuatu	na	67
Kiribati	na	79	Venezuela	56	57
Latvia	na	64	Yugoslavia	90	91
Lebanon	4	94			
Lithuania	na	91			

Note: This indicator represents the share of one-year-olds immunized against diphtheria (DPT). It is expressed as a percent of the total in the age group.

Source: World Bank, *World Development Indicators 1998*, Table 2.14, 1985 data; *The State of the World's Children 1998*, Table 3; UNICEF Web site, http://www.unicef.org/sowc98, for other years

J8.3 One-Year-Olds Fully Immunized against DPT, Percent of Total, 1980 and 1995–1996—Upper Middle-Income Countries per World Bank

Country	1980	1995-1996	Country	1980	1995-1996
Antigua and Barbuda	na	100	Mexico	41	83
Argentina	41	83	Oman	18	100
Bahrain	na	98	Palau	na	100
Barbados	na	88	Poland	96	95
Brazil	40	75	Saudi Arabia	41	93
Chile	94	92	Seychelles	na	100
Croatia	na	91	Slovakia	na	98
Czech Republic	na	97	Slovenia	na	98
Gabon	14	41	South Africa	74	73
Hungary	99	100	St. Kitts & Nevis	na	100
Libya	60	96	St. Lucia	na	88
Malaysia	58	90	Trinidad & Tobago	24	89
Malta	na	84	Uruguay	53	89
Mauritius	87	90			

Note: This indicator represents the share of one-year-olds immunized against diphtheria (DPT). It is expressed as a percent of the total in the age group.

Source: World Bank, *World Development Indicators 1998*, Table 2.14, 1985 data; *The State of the World's Children 1998*, Table 3; UNICEF Web site, http://www.unicef.org/sowc98, for other years

J8.4 One-Year-Olds Fully Immunized against Measles, Percent of Total, 1980 and 1995–1996—Low-Income Countries per World Bank

Country	1980	1995–1996	Country	1980	1995–1996
Afghanistan	na	42	Laos	na	62
Angola	26	65	Lesotho	49	82
Armenia	na	89	Liberia	na	44
Azerbaijan	na	99	Madagascar	na	68
Bangladesh	0	59	Malawi	49	89
Benin	na	74	Mali	na	35
Bhutan	na	86	Mauritania	45	53
Bosnia and Herzegovina	na	88	Moldova	na	98
Burkina Faso	23	54	Mongolia	na	88
Burundi	30	50	Mozambique	32	67
Cambodia	na	72	Myanmar (Burma)	na	86
Cameroon	16	46	Nepal	2	45
Central African Republic	12	46	Nicaragua	15	78
Chad	na	28	Niger	19	59
China	78	97	Nigeria	55	45
Comoros	na	48	Pakistan	1	78
Congo, Dem. Rep. (Zaire)	18	41	Rwanda	42	76
Congo, Rep.	49	42	Sao Tome and Principe	na	57
Cote d'Ivoire	na	65	Senegal	na	60
Equatorial Guinea	na	61	Sierra Leone	36	79
Eritrea	na	38	Somalia	na	33
Ethiopia	4	54	Sri Lanka	na	86
Gambia	71	89	Sudan	1	75
Ghana	16	53	Tajikistan	na	80
Guinea	na	49	Tanzania	45	81
Guinea-Bissau	na	53	Togo	na	39
Guyana	na	91	Uganda	22	66
Haiti	na	31	Vietnam	1	96
Honduras	35	91	Yemen	2	51
India	0	81	Zambia	na	93
Kenya	na	38	Zimbabwe	56	77
Kyrgyzstan	na	80			

Note: This indicator represents the share of one-year-olds immunized against measles. It is expressed as a percent of the total in the age group.

Source: World Bank, *World Development Indicators 1998*, Table 2.14, 1985 data; *The State of the World's Children 1998*, Table 3; UNICEF Web site, http://www.unicef.org/sowc98, for other years

J8.5 One-Year-Olds Fully Immunized against Measles, Percent of Total, 1980 and 1995–1996—Lower Middle-Income Countries per World Bank

Country	1980	1995–1996	Country	1980	1995–1996
Albania	90	92	Lithuania	na	96
Algeria	17	68	Macedonia, FYRO	na	90
Belarus	na	74	Maldives	na	94
Belize	na	81	Marshall Islands	na	69
Bolivia	13	87	Micronesia	na	90
Botswana	63	82	Morocco	17	93
Bulgaria	98	93	Namibia	na	61
Cape Verde	na	66	North Korea, Dem. Rep.	29	60
Colombia	14	95	Panama	47	92
Costa Rica	60	86	Papua New Guinea	1	44
Cuba	48	94	Paraguay	19	81
Djibouti	na	47	Peru	21	71
Dominica	na	100	Philippines	9	72
Dominican Republic	29	78	Romania	83	94
Ecuador	24	79	Russia	na	95
Egypt	78	85	Samoa	na	96
El Salvador	45	97	Solomon Islands	na	67
Estonia	74	86	St. Vincent and the Grenadines	na	100
Fiji	na	94	Suriname	na	78
Georgia	na	63	Swaziland	na	59
Grenada	na	85	Syria	13	95
Guatemala	23	69	Thailand	na	85
Indonesia	0	92	Tonga	na	94
Iran	39	95	Tunisia	65	86
Iraq	35	97	Turkey	27	84
Jamaica	12	99	Turkmenistan	na	66
Jordan	29	98	Ukraine	na	96
Kazakhstan	na	97	Uzbekistan	na	81
Kiribati	na	64	Vanuatu	na	61
Latvia	na	82	Venezuela	50	64
Lebanon	na	85	Yugoslavia	95	81

Note: This indicator represents the share of one-year-olds immunized against measles. It is expressed as a percent of the total in the age group.

Source: World Bank, *World Development Indicators 1998*, Table 2.14, 1985 data; *The State of the World's Children 1998*, Table 3; UNICEF Web site, http://www.unicef.org/sowc98, for other years

J8.6 One-Year-Olds Fully Immunized against Measles, Percent of Total, 1980 and 1995–1996—Upper Middle-Income Countries per World Bank

Country	1980	1995–1996	Country	1980	1995–1996
Antigua and Barbuda	na	100	Mexico	35	75
Argentina	58	100	Oman	22	98
Bahrain	na	95	Palau	na	100
Barbados	na	100	Poland	92	91
Brazil	56	74	Saudi Arabia	8	92
Chile	87	96	Seychelles	na	98
Croatia	na	91	Slovakia	na	99
Czech Republic	na	97	Slovenia	na	91
Gabon	na	38	South Africa	74	76
Hungary	99	100	St. Kitts & Nevis	na	100
Libya	65	92	St. Lucia	na	95
Malaysia	11	81	Trinidad & Tobago	na	88
Malta	na	51	Uruguay	50	85
Mauritius	34	61			

Note: This indicator represents the share of one-year-olds immunized against measles. It is expressed as a percent of the total in the age group.

Source: World Bank, *World Development Indicators 1998*, Table 2.14, 1985 data; *The State of the World's Children 1998*, Table 3; UNICEF Web site, http://www.unicef.org/sowc98, for other years

J8.7 One-Year-Olds Fully Immunized against Polio and TB, Percent of Total, 1980 and 1995–1996—Low-Income Countries per World Bank

Country	Polio	TB	Country	Polio	TB
Afghanistan	31	47	Kyrgyzstan	81	90
Angola	42	74	Laos	33	62
Armenia	97	82	Lesotho	58	55
Azerbaijan	97	90	Liberia	45	84
Bangladesh	66	88	Madagascar	73	87
Benin	80	90	Malawi	82	95
Bhutan	86	98	Mali	30	70
Bosnia and Herzegovina	86	97	Mauritania	50	93
Burkina Faso	48	61	Moldova	99	98
Burundi	63	77	Mongolia	90	92
Cambodia	76	90	Mozambique	60	83
Cameroon	46	54	Myanmar (Burma)	87	92
Central African Republic	53	94	Nepal	48	73
Chad	19	40	Nicaragua	86	93
China	96	97	Niger	33	63
Comoros	57	89	Nigeria	32	49
Congo, Dem. Rep. (Zaire)	36	51	Pakistan	77	93
Congo, Rep.	47	50	Rwanda	98	93
Cote d'Ivoire	55	68	Sao Tome and Principe	61	85
Equatorial Guinea	64	99	Senegal	62	80
Eritrea	46	52	Sierra Leone	65	77
Ethiopia	67	87	Somalia	21	43
Gambia	97	99	Sri Lanka	91	88
Ghana	52	65	Sudan	80	96
Guinea	48	59	Tajikistan	96	96
Guinea-Bissau	58	72	Tanzania	80	96
Guyana	83	88	Togo	82	63
Haiti	34	68	Uganda	67	96
Honduras	94	100	Vietnam	94	95
India	90	96	Yemen	59	59
Kenya	43	56	Zambia	81	100
			Zimbabwe	80	74

Note: This indicator represents the share of one-year-olds immunized against polio and TB (tuberculosis). It is expressed as a percent of the total in the age group.

Source: World Bank, *World Development Indicators 1998*, Table 2.14, 1985 data; *The State of the World's Children 1998*, Table 3; UNICEF Web site, http://www.unicef.org/sowc98, for other years

J8.8 One-Year-Olds Fully Immunized against Polio and TB, Percent of Total, 1980 and 1995–1996—Lower Middle-Income Countries per World Bank

Country	Polio	TB	Country	Polio	TB
Albania	100	94	Lithuania	93	98
Algeria	75	94	Macedonia, FYRO	94	98
Belarus	94	93	Maldives	95	98
Belize	85	90	Marshall Islands	75	88
Bolivia	76	90	Micronesia	81	50
Botswana	81	67	Morocco	95	96
Bulgaria	94	98	Namibia	71	79
Cape Verde	73	80	North Korea, Dem. Rep.	58	60
Colombia	93	98	Panama	93	100
Costa Rica	84	91	Papua New Guinea	57	78
Cuba	93	99	Paraguay	81	89
Djibouti	49	58	Peru	66	93
Dominica	100	100	Philippines	67	82
Dominican Republic	48	98	Romania	97	100
Ecuador	89	100	Russia	97	97
Egypt	77	91	Samoa	95	98
El Salvador	100	100	Solomon Islands	72	71
Estonia	93	99	St. Vincent and the Grenadines	100	100
Fiji	99	100	Suriname	79	na
Georgia	82	30	Swaziland	71	68
Grenada	80	na	Syria	96	100
Guatemala	73	76	Thailand	94	98
Indonesia	90	99	Tonga	93	99
Iran	97	90	Tunisia	91	86
Iraq	95	99	Turkey	83	69
Jamaica	92	98	Turkmenistan	83	88
Jordan	99	na	Ukraine	95	92
Kazakhstan	98	93	Uzbekistan	99	95
Kiribati	82	100	Vanuatu	68	72
Latvia	77	100	Venezuela	73	90
Lebanon	94	na	Yugoslavia	94	97

Note: This indicator represents the share of one-year-olds immunized against polio and TB (tuberculosis). It is expressed as a percent of the total in the age group.

Source: World Bank, *World Development Indicators 1998*, Table 2.14, 1985 data; *The State of the World's Children 1998*, Table 3; UNICEF Web site, http://www.unicef.org/sowc98, for other years

J8.9 One-Year-Olds Fully Immunized against Polio and TB, Percent of Total, 1980 and 1995–1996—Upper Middle-Income Countries per World Bank

Country	Polio	TB	Country	Polio	TB
Antigua and Barbuda	100	na	Mexico	84	97
Argentina	90	100	Oman	100	96
Bahrain	98	na	Palau	100	100
Barbados	85	na	Poland	95	94
Brazil	73	90	Saudi Arabia	93	91
Chile	92	96	Seychelles	100	100
Croatia	91	90	Slovakia	98	98
Czech Republic	98	96	Slovenia	98	99
Gabon	41	54	South Africa	72	95
Hungary	100	100	St. Kitts & Nevis	98	na
Libya	96	99	St. Lucia	88	89
Malaysia	90	97	Trinidad & Tobago	90	na
Malta	92	96	Uruguay	89	98
Mauritius	90	87			

Note: This indicator represents the share of one-year-olds immunized against polio and TB (tuberculosis). It is expressed as a percent of the total in the age group.

Source: World Bank, *World Development Indicators 1998*, Table 2.14, 1985 data; *The State of the World's Children 1998*, Table 3; UNICEF Web site, http://www.unicef.org/sowc98, for other years

J9.1 Children Not in Primary School, Percent of Total, 1993–1995—Low-Income Countries per World Bank

Country	Percent	Country	Percent
Afghanistan	na	Kyrgyzstan	0
Angola	na	Laos	9
Armenia	na	Lesotho	35
Azerbaijan	na	Liberia	na
Bangladesh	38	Madagascar	na
Benin	48	Malawi	0
Bhutan	na	Mali	75
Bosnia and Herzegovina	na	Mauritania	44
Burkina Faso	71	Moldova	na
Burundi	48	Mongolia	25
Cambodia	na	Mozambique	61
Cameroon	24	Myanmar (Burma)	na
Central African Republic	42	Nepal	na
Chad	na	Nicaragua	14
China	1	Niger	77
Comoros	47	Nigeria	na
Congo, Dem. Rep. (Zaire)	na	Pakistan	na
Congo, Rep.	39	Rwanda	24
Cote d'Ivoire	48	Sao Tome and Principe	na
Equatorial Guinea	na	Senegal	46
Eritrea	69	Sierra Leone	na
Ethiopia	na	Somalia	na
Gambia	45	Sri Lanka	na
Ghana	na	Sudan	na
Guinea	63	Tajikistan	na
Guinea-Bissau	44	Tanzania	52
Guyana	na	Togo	22
Haiti	74	Uganda	na
Honduras	10	Vietnam	na
India	na	Yemen	na
Kenya	9	Zambia	25
		Zimbabwe	0

Note: This indicator reflects the number of children not attending primary school. It is stated as a percent of the total children in the pertinent age group.

Source: United Nations Development Programme, *Human Development Report 1997*, Table A 2.2

J9.2 Children Not in Primary School, Percent of Total, 1993–1995—Lower Middle-Income Countries per World Bank

Country	Percent	Country	Percent
Albania	4	Maldives	na
Algeria	5	Marshall Islands	na
Belarus	14	Micronesia	na
Belize	1	Morocco	28
Bolivia	9	Namibia	8
Botswana	4	North Korea, Dem. Rep.	na
Bulgaria	10	Panama	na
Cape Verde	0	Papua New Guinea	na
Colombia	15	Paraguay	11
Costa Rica	8	Peru	13
Cuba	4	Philippines	0
Djibouti	68	Romania	8
Dominica	na	Russia	7
Dominican Republic	19	Samoa	na
Ecuador	na	Solomon Islands	na
Egypt	11	St. Vincent and the Grenadines	na
El Salvador	21	Suriname	na
Estonia	76	Swaziland	5
Fiji	1	Syria	9
Georgia	18	Thailand	na
Grenada	na	Thailand	17
Guatemala	42	Tonga	na
Indonesia	3	Tunisia	3
Iran	3	Turkey	6
Iraq	21	Turkmenistan	na
Jamaica	0	Ukraine	na
Jordan	11	Uzbekistan	na
Kazakhstan	na	Vanuatu	26
Kiribati	na	Venezuela	12
Latvia	16	Yugoslavia	na
Lebanon	na		
Lithuania	na		
Macedonia, FYRO	15		

Note: This indicator reflects the number of children not attending primary school. It is stated as a percent of the total children in the pertinent age group.

Source: United Nations Development Programme, *Human Development Report 1997,* Table A 2.2

J9.3 Children Not in Primary School, Percent of Total, 1993–1995—Upper Middle-Income Countries per World Bank

Country	Percent	Country	Percent
Antigua and Barbuda	na	Mexico	0
Argentina	5	Oman	29
Bahrain	0	Palau	na
Barbados	22	Poland	3
Brazil	10	Saudi Arabia	38
Chile	13	Seychelles	na
Croatia	18	Slovakia	na
Czech Republic	15	Slovenia	0
Gabon	na	South Africa	4
Hungary	7	St. Kitts & Nevis	na
Libya	3	St. Lucia	na
Malaysia	na	Trinidad & Tobago	11
Malta	0	Uruguay	5
Mauritius	5		

Note: This indicator reflects the number of children not attending primary school. It is stated as a percent of the total children in the pertinent age group.

Source: United Nations Development Programme, *Human Development Report 1997,* Table A 2.2

J10.1 Primary School Children Reaching Grade Five, Percentage of Students, 1990–1995—Low-Income Countries per World Bank

Country	Percent	Country	Percent
Afghanistan	43	Kyrgyzstan	92
Angola	34	Laos	53
Armenia	na	Lesotho	79
Azerbaijan	na	Liberia	na
Bangladesh	47	Madagascar	28
Benin	61	Malawi	94
Bhutan	82	Mali	86
Bosnia and Herzegovina	na	Mauritania	63
Burkina Faso	79	Moldova	93
Burundi	74	Mongolia	na
Cambodia	50	Mozambique	47
Cameroon	66	Myanmar (Burma)	na
Central African Republic	24	Nepal	52
Chad	28	Nicaragua	47
China	92	Niger	77
Comoros	45	Nigeria	80
Congo, Dem. Rep. (Zaire)	64	Pakistan	48
Congo, Rep.	54	Rwanda	60
Cote d'Ivoire	73	Sao Tome and Principe	na
Equatorial Guinea	na	Senegal	81
Eritrea	79	Sierra Leone	na
Ethiopia	51	Somalia	na
Gambia	87	Sri Lanka	98
Ghana	80	Sudan	94
Guinea	54	Tajikistan	na
Guinea-Bissau	20	Tanzania	83
Guyana	93	Togo	71
Haiti	47	Uganda	55
Honduras	na	Vietnam	na
India	62	Yemen	na
Kenya	68	Zambia	na
		Zimbabwe	90

Note: This indicator shows the percentage of primary school students, those who enter the first grade, who will stay through the fifth grade.

Source: The State of the World's Children 1998, Table 4; UNICEF Web site, http://www.unicef.org/sowc98

J10.2 Primary School Children Reaching Grade Five, Percentage of Students, 1990–1995—Lower Middle-Income Countries per World Bank

Country	Percent	Country	Percent
Albania	82	Macedonia, FYRO	99
Algeria	95	Maldives	93
Belarus	98	Marshall Islands	na
Belize	70	Micronesia	na
Bolivia	60	Morocco	78
Botswana	89	Namibia	76
Bulgaria	95	North Korea, Dem. Rep.	na
Cape Verde	na	Panama	82
Colombia	58	Papua New Guinea	59
Costa Rica	89	Paraguay	71
Cuba	94	Peru	na
Djibouti	82	Philippines	70
Dominica	84	Romania	99
Dominican Republic	58	Russia	na
Ecuador	77	Samoa	na
Egypt	98	Solomon Islands	81
El Salvador	58	St. Vincent and the Grenadines	na
Estonia	97	Suriname	na
Fiji	87	Swaziland	78
Georgia	98	Syria	91
Grenada	na	Thailand	88
Guatemala	na	Tonga	92
Indonesia	90	Tunisia	92
Iran	90	Turkey	95
Iraq	72	Turkmenistan	na
Jamaica	96	Ukraine	54
Jordan	98	Uzbekistan	na
Kazakhstan	na	Vanuatu	61
Kiribati	90	Venezuela	78
Latvia	96	Yugoslavia	100
Lebanon	na		
Lithuania	98		

Note: This indicator shows the percentage of primary school students, those who enter the first grade, who will stay through the fifth grade.

Source: The State of the World's Children 1998, Table 4; UNICEF Web site, http://www.unicef.org/sowc98

J10.3 Primary School Children Reaching Grade Five, Percentage of Students, 1990–1995—Upper Middle-Income Countries per World Bank

Country	Percent	Country	Percent
Antigua and Barbuda	na	Mauritius	99
Argentina	na	Mexico	85
Bahrain	94	Oman	96
Barbados	na	Palau	na
Brazil	70	Poland	100
Chile	92	Saudi Arabia	94
Croatia	98	Seychelles	97
Czech Republic	99	Slovakia	97
Gabon	50	Slovenia	98
Hungary	98	South Africa	65
Libya	na	St. Kitts & Nevis	na
Malaysia	94	St. Lucia	96
Malta	97	Trinidad & Tobago	95
		Uruguay	96

Note: This indicator shows the percentage of primary school students, those who enter the first grade, who will stay through the fifth grade.

Source: The State of the World's Children 1998, Table 4; UNICEF Web site, http://www.unicef.org/sowc98

J10.4 Primary School Children Reaching Grade Five and Secondary Enrollment Ratios, 1990–1995—Worldwide Summary, Region by Region

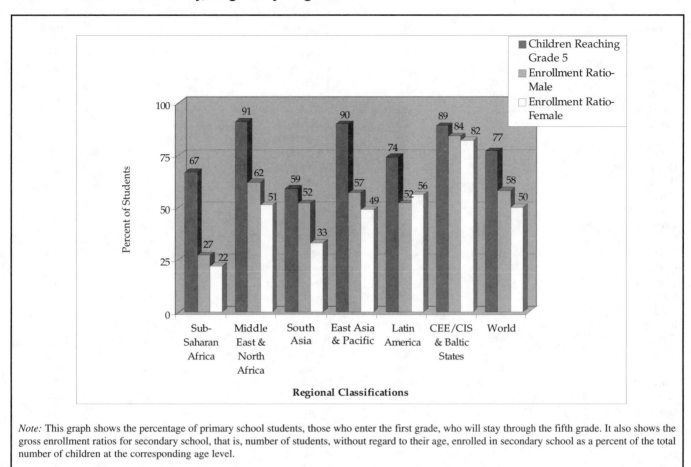

Note: This graph shows the percentage of primary school students, those who enter the first grade, who will stay through the fifth grade. It also shows the gross enrollment ratios for secondary school, that is, number of students, without regard to their age, enrolled in secondary school as a percent of the total number of children at the corresponding age level.

Source: The State of the World's Children 1998, Table 4, UNICEF Web site, http://www.unicef.org/sowc98

J11.1 Children (Ages 10-14) in Labor Force, Percent of Total Age Group, 1980 and 1996—Low-Income Countries per World Bank

Country	1980	1996	Country	1980	1996
Afghanistan	na	na	Laos	31	27
Angola	30	27	Lesotho	28	22
Armenia	0	0	Liberia	na	na
Azerbaijan	0	0	Madagascar	40	35
Bangladesh	35	30	Malawi	45	34
Benin	30	27	Mali	61	54
Bhutan	na	na	Mauritania	30	24
Bosnia and Herzegovina	1	na	Moldova	3	0
Burkina Faso	71	50	Mongolia	4	2
Burundi	50	49	Mozambique	39	34
Cambodia	27	24	Myanmar (Burma)	28	24
Cameroon	34	25	Nepal	56	45
Central African Republic	39	31	Nicaragua	19	14
Chad	42	38	Niger	48	45
China	30	11	Nigeria	29	25
Comoros	na	na	Pakistan	23	17
Congo, Dem. Rep. (Zaire)	33	29	Rwanda	43	42
Congo, Rep.	27	26	Sao Tome and Principe	na	na
Cote d'Ivoire	28	20	Senegal	43	31
Equatorial Guinea	na	na	Sierra Leone	19	15
Eritrea	44	39	Somalia	na	na
Ethiopia	46	42	Sri Lanka	4	2
Gambia	44	36	Sudan	33	29
Ghana	16	13	Tajikistan	0	0
Guinea	41	33	Tanzania	43	39
Guinea-Bissau	43	38	Togo	36	28
Guyana	na	na	Uganda	49	45
Haiti	33	25	Vietnam	22	8
Honduras	14	8	Yemen	26	20
India	21	14	Zambia	19	16
Kenya	45	41	Zimbabwe	37	29
Kyrgyzstan	0	0			

Note: This indicator reflects the number of children, ages 10 to 14, in the labor force. It is stated as a percent of the total children in that age group.

Source: World Bank, *World Development Indicators 1998*, Table 2.3, Labor Force Structure

J11.2 Children (Ages 10-14) in Labor Force, Percent of Total Age Group, 1980 and 1996—Lower Middle-Income Countries per World Bank

Country	1980	1996	Country	1980	1996
Albania	4	1	Lithuania	0	0
Algeria	7	1	Macedonia, FYRO	1	0
Belarus	0	0	Maldives	na	na
Belize	na	na	Marshall Islands	na	na
Bolivia	19	14	Micronesia	na	na
Botswana	26	16	Morocco	21	5
Bulgaria	0	0	Namibia	34	21
Cape Verde	na	na	North Korea, Dem. Rep.	3	0
Colombia	12	6	Panama	6	3
Costa Rica	10	5	Papua New Guinea	28	19
Cuba	0	0	Paraguay	15	7
Djibouti	na	na	Peru	4	2
Dominica	na	na	Philippines	14	8
Dominican Republic	25	16	Romania	0	0
Ecuador	9	5	Russia	0	0
Egypt	18	11	Samoa	na	na
El Salvador	17	15	Solomon Islands	na	na
Estonia	0	0	St. Vincent and the Grenadines	na	na
Fiji	na	na	Suriname	na	na
Georgia	0	0	Swaziland	na	na
Grenada	na	na	Syria	14	5
Guatemala	19	16	Thailand	25	15
Indonesia	13	9	Tonga	na	na
Iran	14	4	Tunisia	6	0
Iraq	11	3	Turkey	21	23
Jamaica	0	0	Turkmenistan	0	0
Jordan	4	1	Ukraine	0	0
Kazakhstan	0	0	Uzbekistan	0	0
Kiribati	na	na	Vanuatu	na	na
Latvia	0	0	Venezuela	4	1
Lebanon	5	0	Yugoslavia	0	0

Note: This indicator reflects the number of children, ages 10 to 14, in the labor force. It is stated as a percent of the total children in that age group.

Source: World Bank, *World Development Indicators 1998*, Table 2.3, Labor Force Structure

J11.3 Children (Ages 10-14) in Labor Force, Percent of Total Age Group, 1980 and 1996—Upper Middle-Income Countries per World Bank

Country	1980	1996	Country	1980	1996
Antigua and Barbuda	na	na	Mexico	9	6
Argentina	8	4	Oman	6	0
Bahrain	na	na	Palau	na	na
Barbados	na	na	Poland	0	0
Brazil	19	16	Saudi Arabia	5	0
Chile	0	0	Seychelles	na	na
Croatia	0	0	Slovakia	0	0
Czech Republic	0	0	Slovenia	0	0
Gabon	29	18	South Africa	1	0
Hungary	0	0	St. Kitts & Nevis	na	na
Libya	9	0	St. Lucia	na	na
Malaysia	8	3	Trinidad & Tobago	1	0
Malta	na	na	Uruguay	4	2
Mauritius	5	3			

Note: This indicator reflects the number of children, ages 10 to 14, in the labor force. It is stated as a percent of the total children in that age group.

Source: World Bank, *World Development Indicators 1998*, Table 2.3, Labor Force Structure

K. Cities

GENERAL OVERVIEW

This section investigates the extent and intensity of urbanization in less-developed countries of the world. It also presents data on the specific living conditions in some of the most populous urban areas in those countries.

Urbanization is a feature of the landscape of many countries, not only the world's less-developed nations. The reasons for this revolve primarily around economic opportunity and the nature of economic development, which tends to grow in clustered pockets of enterprise. As economic development occurs, infrastructure development follows to match the growing needs of producers and workers who serve the new enterprises. The tendency for enterprises to develop close to one another intensifies in less-developed countries whose economies are at early stages of development. Often these urban areas develop rapidly, leaving infrastructure—such as housing stocks, sanitation systems, and water supplies—to catch up.

Inadequately controlled urbanization of poorer countries of the world is of great concern among policymakers at national and international levels. Basic health and environmental issues top the list of concerns; further problems revolve around quality-of-life questions, such as crime and personal security, adequate living space, and other infrastructure problems. The data presented below offer an introduction to these issues; with this basic information the student and researcher can formulate further questions and launch extended investigations.

EXPLANATION OF INDICATORS

Population in Urban Centers of More than One Million: Concerns about urbanization for less-developed nations usually focus on the tendency of some urban areas to grow disproportionately, as compared with other population centers and areas of a country. Development efforts often try to encourage a more even economic development. This indicator represents the share of a country's population that is concentrated in very large cities—those whose population exceeds one million. It measures the extent to which uneven economic development and extreme urbanization have occurred and the extent to which a country's population relies on urban centers for its livelihood (K1.1–K1.4).

Population in Largest City, Percent of Urban Population: This indicator takes the above question—the uneven settlement of people in urban areas—a step further. It measures the imbalance between urban areas themselves, and the extent to which demographic and economic concentration is centered on a single, huge population center within a country (K2.1–K2.4).

Profile of Metropolitan Areas: The chapter presents quality-of-life data for 29 cities in less-developed countries throughout the world. The tables cover any city that is located within low- and middle-income countries (as classified by the World Bank) whose population exceeds four million (K3.1–K3.29).

K1.1 Population in Urban Centers of More than One Million—Percent of Total Population, 1980, 1996 and 2015 (proj.), Low-Income Countries per World Bank

Country	1980	1996	2015
Afghanistan	na	na	
Angola	13	20	30
Armenia	34	34	41
Azerbaijan	26	25	29
Bangladesh	5	10	15
Benin	na	na	na
Bhutan	na	na	na
Bosnia and Herzgovina	na	na	na
Burkina Faso	na	na	na.
Burundi	na	na	na
Cambodia	na	na	na
Cameroon	6	19	14
Central African Republic	na	na	na
Chad	na	na	na
China	8	11	14
Comoros	na	na	na
Congo, Dem. Rep. (Zaire)	na	10	na
Congo, Rep.	na	39	na
Cote d'Ivoire	15	20	31
Equatorial Guinea	na	na	na
Eritrea	na	na	na
Ethiopia	3	4	6
Gambia	na	na	na
Ghana	9	10	14
Guinea	12	24	35
Guinea-Bissau	na	na	na
Guyana	na	na	na
Haiti	13	21	27
Honduras	na	na	na
India	6	10	12
Kenya	5	7	14
Kyrgyzstan	na	na	na
Laos	na	na	na
Lesotho	na	na	na
Liberia	na	na	na
Madagascar	na	na	na
Malawi	na	na	na
Mali	na	na	na
Mauritania	na	na	na
Moldova	na	na	na
Mongolia	na	na	na
Mozambique	6	13	20
Myanmar (Burma)	7	9	13
Nepal	na	na	na
Nicaragua	23	26	33
Niger	na	na	na
Nigeria	6	11	15
Pakistan	11	18	23
Rwanda	na	na	na
Sao Tome and Principe	na	na	na
Senegal	18	21	31
Sierra Leone	na	na	na
Somalia	na	na	naaa
Sri Lanka	na	na	na
Sudan	6	9	14
Tajikistan	na	na	na
Tanzania	5	6	9

K1.1 Population in Urban Centers of More than One Million—Percent of Total Population, 1980, 1996 and 2015 (proj.), Low-Income Countries per World Bank (continued)

Country	1980	1996	2015
Togo	na	na	na
Uganda	na	na	na
Vietnam	5	6	9
Yemen	na	na	na
Zambia	9	15	23
Zimbabwe	na	13	na

Note: This indicator reflects the share of a country's population that live in urban centers whose population exceeds than one million people.

Source: World Bank, *World Development Indicators 1998*, Table 3.10

K1.2 Population in Urban Centers of More than One Million—Percent of Total Population, 1980, 1996 and 2015 (proj.), Lower Middle-Income Countries per World Bank

Country	1980	1996	2015
Albania	na	na	na
Algeria	11	13	16
Belarus	14	17	20
Belize	na	na	na
Bolivia	14	17	19
Botswana	na	na	na
Bulgaria	12	14	20
Cape Verde	na	na	na
Colombia	22	34	30
Costa Rica	na	na	na
Cuba	20	20	22
Djibouti	na	na	na
Dominica	na	na	na
Dominican Republic	25	58	36
Ecuador	14	28	31
Egypt	23	25	25
El Salvador	na	22	na
Estonia	na	na	na
Fiji	na	na	na
Georgia	22	25	31
Grenada	na	na	na
Guatemala	na	21	na
Indonesia	7	9	16
Iran	13	22	24
Iraq	26	29	21
Jamaica	na	na	na
Jordan	29	29	34
Kazakhstan	6	8	10
Kiribati	na	na	na
Latvia	na	na	na
Lebanon	na	46	na
Lithuania	na	na	na
Macedonia, FYRO	na	na	na
Maldives	na	na	na
Marshall Islands	na	na	na
Micronesia	na	na	na
Morocco	11	17	22
Namibia	na	na	na
North Korea, Dem. Rep.	10	11	13
Panama	na	na	na

K1.2 Population in Urban Centers of More than One Million—Percent of Total Population, 1980, 1996 and 2015 (proj.), Lower Middle-Income Countries per World Bank *(continued)*

Country	1980	1996	2015
Papua New Guinea	na	na	na
Paraguay	na	23	na
Peru	26	28	33
Philippines	12	15	15
Romania	9	9	10
Russia	16	19	20
Samoa	na	na	na
Solomon Islands	na	na	na
St. Vincent and the Grenadines	na	na	na
Suriname	na	na	na
Swaziland	na	na	na
Syria	28	28	36
Thailand	10	11	16
Tonga	na	na	na
Tunisia	17	19	26
Turkey	17	25	25
Turkmenistan	na	na	na
Ukraine	14	16	18
Uzbekistan	11	10	12
Vanuatu	na	na	na
Venezuela	16	28	28
Yugoslavia	11	11	15

Note: This indicator reflects the share of a country's population that live in urban centers whose population exceeds than one million people.

Source: World Bank, *World Development Indicators 1998*, Table 3.10

K1.3 Population in Urban Centers of More than One Million—Percent of Total Population, 1980, 1996 and 2015 (proj.), Upper Middle-Income Countries per World Bank

Country	1980	1996	2015
Antigua and Barbuda	na	na	na
Argentina	35	41	36
Bahrain	na	na	na
Barbados	na	na	na
Brazil	27	33	34
Chile	33	34	36
Croatia	na	na	na
Czech Republic	12	12	13
Gabon	na	na	na
Hungary	19	20	21
Libya	38	34	77
Malaysia	7	6	7
Malta	na	na	na
Mauritius	na	na	na
Mexico	27	27	25
Oman	na	na	na
Palau	na	na	na
Poland	18	18	19
Saudi Arabia	19	22	22
Seychelles	na	na	na
Slovakia	na	na	na
Slovenia	na	na	na
South Africa	12	34	24
St. Kitts & Nevis	na	na	na

K1.3 Population in Urban Centers of More than One Million—Percent of Total Population, 1980, 1996 and 2015 (proj.), Upper Middle-Income Countries per World Bank (continued)

Country	1980	1996	2015
Papua New Guinea	na	na	na
St. Lucia	na	na	na
Trinidad & Tobago	na	na	na
Uruguay	42	42	41

Note: This indicator reflects the share of a country's population that live in urban centers whose population exceeds than one million people.

Source: World Bank, *World Development Indicators 1998*, Table 3.10

K1.4 Population in Urban Centers of More than One Million, Worldwide Summary, 1990, 1996, and 2015 (proj.)—Comparison By Income Level per World Bank

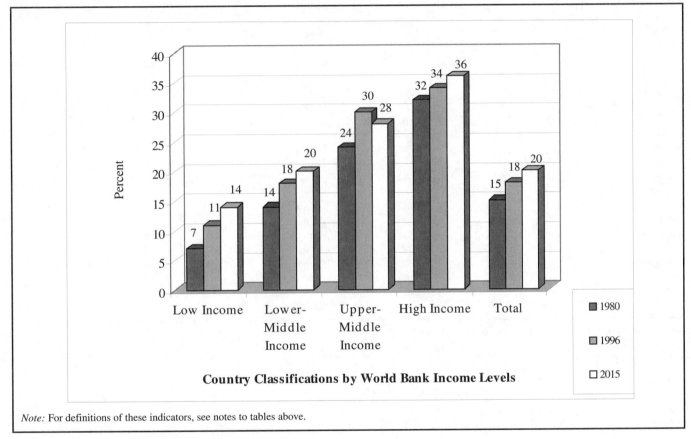

Note: For definitions of these indicators, see notes to tables above.

Source: World Bank, *World Development Indicators 1998*, Table 3.10

K2.1 Population in Largest City as Percent of Urban Population, 1980 and 1995—Low-Income Countries per World Bank

Country	1980	1995	Country	1980	1995
Afghanistan	na	na	Laos	na	na
Angola	63	62	Lesotho	na	na
Armenia	51	50	Liberia	na	na
Azerbaijan	48	44	Madagascar	30	25
Bangladesh	33	39	Malawi	na	na
Benin	na	na	Mali	40	35
Bhutan	na	na	Mauritania	na	na
Bosnia and Herzegovina	na	na	Moldova	na	na
Burkina Faso	44	50	Mongolia	na	na
Burundi	na	na	Mozambique	47	38
Cambodia	na	na	Myanmar (Burma)	27	33
Cameroon	19	22	Nepal	na	na
Central African Republic	na	na	Nicaragua	42	41
Chad	40	58	Niger	na	na
China	6	4	Nigeria	23	23
Comoros	na	na	Pakistan	22	22
Congo, Dem. Rep. (Zaire)	28	34	Rwanda	na	na
Congo, Rep.	67	65	Sao Tome and Principe	na	na
Cote d'Ivoire	44	46	Senegal	47	47
Equatorial Guinea	na	na	Sierra Leone	na	na
Eritrea	na	na	Somalia	na	na
Ethiopia	30	28	Sri Lanka	na	na
Gambia	na	na	Sudan	31	27
Ghana	30	27	Tajikistan	na	na
Guinea	65	81	Tanzania	30	24
Guinea-Bissau	na	na	Togo	na	na
Guyana	na	na	Uganda	42	40
Haiti	55	64	Vietnam	27	25
Honduras	32	38	Yemen	na	na
India	5	6	Zambia	23	34
Kenya	32	24	Zimbabwe	39	40
Kyrgyzstan	na	na			

Note: This indicator reflects the share of population living in the largest city against the total urban population of a country.

Source: World Bank, *World Development Indicators 1998,* Table 3.10

K2.2 Population in Largest City as Percent of Urban Population, 1980 and 1995—Lower Middle-Income Countries per World Bank

Country	1980	1995	Country	1980	1995
Albania	na	na	Lithuania	na	na
Algeria	25	24	Macedonia, FYRO	na	na
Belarus	24	24	Maldives	na	na
Belize	na	na	Marshall Islands	na	na
Bolivia	30	28	Micronesia	na	na
Botswana	na	na	Morocco	26	23
Bulgaria	20	21	Namibia	na	na
Cape Verde	na	na	North Korea, Dem. Rep.	18	18
Colombia	20	23	Panama	62	66
Costa Rica	61	55	Papua New Guinea	na	na
Cuba	29	27	Paraguay	51	43
Djibouti	na	na	Peru	39	39
Dominica	na	na	Philippines	33	24
Dominican Republic	50	65	Romania	18	17
Ecuador	30	27	Russia	8	8
Egypt	38	37	Samoa	na	na
El Salvador	40	48	Solomon Islands	na	na
Estonia	na	na	St. Vincent and the Grenadines	na	na
Fiji	na	na	Suriname	na	na
Georgia	42	43	Swaziland	na	na
Grenada	na	na	Syria	34	28
Guatemala	29	53	Thailand	59	55
Indonesia	18	13	Tonga	na	na
Iran	26	19	Tunisia	35	31
Iraq	39	28	Turkey	23	19
Jamaica	na	na	Turkmenistan	na	na
Jordan	49	39	Ukraine	7	8
Kazakhstan	12	13	Uzbekistan	28	24
Kiribati	na	na	Vanuatu	na	na
Latvia	49	50	Venezuela	22	16
Lebanon	55	52	Yugoslavia	24	20

Note: This indicator reflects the share of population living in the largest city against the total urban population of a country.

Source: World Bank, *World Development Indicators 1998*, Table 3.10

K2.3 Population in Largest City as Percent of Urban Population, 1980 and 1995—Upper Middle-Income Countries per World Bank

Country	1980	1995	Country	1980	1995
Antigua and Barbuda	na	na	Mexico	31	25
Argentina	43	39	Oman	na	na
Bahrain	na	na	Palau	na	na
Barbados	na	na	Poland	16	14
Brazil	16	13	Saudi Arabia	16	17
Chile	41	41	Seychelles	na	na
Croatia	28	37	Slovakia	na	na
Czech Republic	18	18	Slovenia	na	na
Gabon	na	na	South Africa	12	12
Hungary	34	31	St. Kitts & Nevis	na	na
Libya	38	39	St. Lucia	na	na
Malaysia	16	11	Trinidad & Tobago	na	na
Malta	na	na	Uruguay	49	46
Mauritius	na	na			

Note: This indicator reflects the share of population living in the largest city against the total urban population of a country.

Source: World Bank, *World Development Indicators 1998*, Table 3.10

K2.4 Population in Largest City as Percent of Urban Population, 1980 and 1995—Comparison By Income Level per World Bank

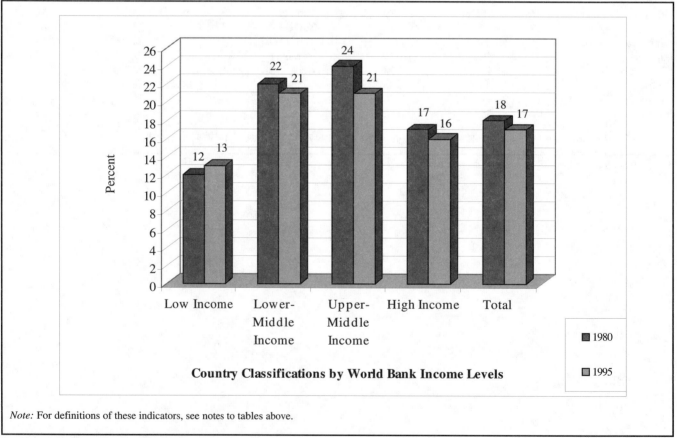

Note: For definitions of these indicators, see notes to tables above.

Source: World Bank, *World Development Indicators 1998*, Table 3.10

K3.1 Profile of Metropolitan Areas: Baghdad, Iraq

Indicator	Value
Population	4,400,000
Public Safety: Murders Per 1,000,000 People	na
Food Costs: Percent Income Spent on Food	45
Living Space: Persons Per Room	2.2
Housing Standards: Percent Homes with Water/Electricity	98
Communications: Telephones Per 100 People	7
Education: Percent Children in Secondary School	85 de
Public Health: Infant Deaths Per 1,000 Live Births	40
Peace and Quiet: Levels of Ambient Noise (1-10)	7
Traffic Flow: Miles per Hour in Rush Hour	31.1
Clean Air: Alternate Pollution Measures	na

Note: "de" indicates that the data are estimated
Clean air statistic cited is the lowest of the following three measures:
ppm D_3 = one-hour concentration of ozone, in parts per million
days SPM = number of days with concentrations of suspended particulate matter over World Health Organization's (WHO's) standard
days SO_2 = number of days with concentrations of sulfur dioxide over WHO's standard

Source: Population Crisis Committee, "Cities: Life in the World's 100 Largest Metropolitan Areas"

K3.2 Profile of Metropolitan Areas: Bangalore, India

Indicators	Value
Population	4,100,000
Public Safety: Murders Per 1,000,000 People	2.8
Food Costs: Percent Income Spent on Food	62
Living Space: Persons Per Room	2.8
Housing Standards: Percent Homes with Water/Electricity	67
Communications: Telephones Per 100 People	2
Education: Percent Children in Secondary School	60
Public Health: Infant Deaths Per 1,000 Live Births	48
Peace and Quiet: Levels of Ambient Noise (1-10)	4
Traffic Flow: Miles per Hour in Rush Hour	16
Clean Air: Alternate Pollution Measures	na

K3.3 Profile of Metropolitan Areas: Bangkok, Thailand

Indicators	Value
Population	7,000,000
Public Safety: Murders Per 1,000,000 People	7.6
Food Costs: Percent Income Spent on Food	36
Living Space: Persons Per Room	3.2
Housing Standards: Percent Homes with Water/Electricity	76
Communications: Telephones Per 100 People	12
Education: Percent Children in Secondary School	71
Public Health: Infant Deaths Per 1,000 Live Births	27
Peace and Quiet: Levels of Ambient Noise (1-10)	7
Traffic Flow: Miles per Hour in Rush Hour	13
Clean Air: Alternate Pollution Measures	97 days SPM

Notes and Source for all Metropolitan Area tables: [see above]

K3.4 Profile of Metropolitan Areas: Beijing, China

Indicators	Value
Population	7,040,000
Public Safety: Murders Per 1,000,000 People	2.5
Food Costs: Percent Income Spent on Food	52
Living Space: Persons Per Room	1.2
Housing Standards: Percent Homes with Water/Electricity	89
Communications: Telephones Per 100 People	2
Education: Percent Children in Secondary School	97
Public Health: Infant Deaths Per 1,000 Live Births	11
Peace and Quiet: Levels of Ambient Noise (1-10)	4
Traffic Flow: Miles per Hour in Rush Hour	25.7
Clean Air: Alternate Pollution Measures	272 days SPM

Note: "de" indicates that the data are estimated
Clean air statistic cited is the lowest of the following three measures:
ppm D_3 = one-hour concentration of ozone, in parts per million
days SPM = number of days with concentrations of suspended particulate matter over World Health Organization's (WHO's) standard
days SO_2 = number of days with concentrations of sulfur dioxide over WHO's standard

Source: Population Crisis Committee, "Cities: Life in the World's 100 Largest Metropolitan Areas"

K3.5 Profile of Metropolitan Areas: Bogota, Colombia

Indicators	Value
Population	4,640,000
Public Safety: Murders Per 1,000,000 People	21.1
Food Costs: Percent Income Spent on Food	22
Living Space: Persons Per Room	1.5
Housing Standards: Percent Homes with Water/Electricity	89
Communications: Telephones Per 100 People	18
Education: Percent Children in Secondary School	80
Public Health: Infant Deaths Per 1,000 Live Births	19
Peace and Quiet: Levels of Ambient Noise (1-10)	4
Traffic Flow: Miles per Hour in Rush Hour	12.4
Clean Air: Alternate Pollution Measures	na

K3.6 Profile of Metropolitan Areas: Bombay, India

Indicators	Value
Population	12,900,000
Public Safety: Murders Per 1,000,000 People	3.2
Food Costs: Percent Income Spent on Food	57
Living Space: Persons Per Room	4.2
Housing Standards: Percent Homes with Water/Electricity	85
Communications: Telephones Per 100 People	5
Education: Percent Children in Secondary School	49 de
Public Health: Infant Deaths Per 1,000 Live Births	59
Peace and Quiet: Levels of Ambient Noise (1-10)	5
Traffic Flow: Miles per Hour in Rush Hour	10.4
Clean Air: Alternate Pollution Measures	100 days SPM

Notes and Source for all Metropolitan Area tables: [see above]

K3.7 Profile of Metropolitan Areas: Buenos Aires-La Plata, Argentina

Indicators	Value
Population	12,400,000
Public Safety: Murders Per 1,000,000 People	7.6
Food Costs: Percent Income Spent on Food	40
Living Space: Persons Per Room	1.3
Housing Standards: Percent Homes with Water/Electricity	86
Communications: Telephones Per 100 People	14
Education: Percent Children in Secondary School	51
Public Health: Infant Deaths Per 1,000 Live Births	21
Peace and Quiet: Levels of Ambient Noise (1-10)	3
Traffic Flow: Miles per Hour in Rush Hour	29.8
Clean Air: Alternate Pollution Measures	.0560 ppm O_3

Note: "de" indicates that the data are estimated
Clean air statistic cited is the lowest of the following three measures:
ppm D_3 = one-hour concentration of ozone, in parts per million
days SPM = number of days with concentrations of suspended particulate matter over World Health Organization's (WHO's) standard
days SO_2 = number of days with concentrations of sulfur dioxide over WHO's standard

Source: Population Crisis Committee, "Cities: Life in the World's 100 Largest Metropolitan Areas"

K3.8 Profile of Metropolitan Areas: Cairo, Egypt

Indicators	Value
Population	11,000,000
Public Safety: Murders Per 1,000,000 People	56.4
Food Costs: Percent Income Spent on Food	47
Living Space: Persons Per Room	1.5
Housing Standards: Percent Homes with Water/Electricity	94
Communications: Telephones Per 100 People	3
Education: Percent Children in Secondary School	53
Public Health: Infant Deaths Per 1,000 Live Births	53
Peace and Quiet: Levels of Ambient Noise (1-10)	7
Traffic Flow: Miles per Hour in Rush Hour	12.4
Clean Air: Alternate Pollution Measures	na

K3.9 Profile of Metropolitan Areas: Calcutta, India

Indicators	Value
Population	12,800,000
Public Safety: Murders Per 1,000,000 People	1.1
Food Costs: Percent Income Spent on Food	60
Living Space: Persons Per Room	3
Housing Standards: Percent Homes with Water/Electricity	57
Communications: Telephones Per 100 People	2
Education: Percent Children in Secondary School	49 de
Public Health: Infant Deaths Per 1,000 Live Births	46
Peace and Quiet: Levels of Ambient Noise (1-10)	4
Traffic Flow: Miles per Hour in Rush Hour	13.3
Clean Air: Alternate Pollution Measures	268 days SPM

Notes and Source for all Metropolitan Area tables: [see above]

K3.10 Profile of Metropolitan Areas: Delhi-New Delhi, India

Indicators	Value
Population	9,800,000
Public Safety: Murders Per 1,000,000 People	4.1
Food Costs: Percent Income Spent on Food	40
Living Space: Persons Per Room	2.4
Housing Standards: Percent Homes with Water/Electricity	66
Communications: Telephones Per 100 People	5
Education: Percent Children in Secondary School	49
Public Health: Infant Deaths Per 1,000 Live Births	40
Peace and Quiet: Levels of Ambient Noise (1-10)	5
Traffic Flow: Miles per Hour in Rush Hour	14
Clean Air: Alternate Pollution Measures	294 days SPM

Note: "de" indicates that the data are estimated

Clean air statistic cited is the lowest of the following three measures:

ppm D_3 = one-hour concentration of ozone, in parts per million

days SPM = number of days with concentrations of suspended particulate matter over World Health Organization's (WHO's) standard

days SO_2 = number of days with concentrations of sulfur dioxide over WHO's standard

Source: Population Crisis Committee, "Cities: Life in the World's 100 Largest Metropolitan Areas"

K3.11 Profile of Metropolitan Areas: Dhaka, Bangladesh

Indicators	Value
Population	4,300,000
Public Safety: Murders Per 1,000,000 People	2.4
Food Costs: Percent Income Spent on Food	63
Living Space: Persons Per Room	3.1
Housing Standards: Percent Homes with Water/Electricity	73
Communications: Telephones Per 100 People	2
Education: Percent Children in Secondary School	37
Public Health: Infant Deaths Per 1,000 Live Births	108
Peace and Quiet: Levels of Ambient Noise (1-10)	4
Traffic Flow: Miles per Hour in Rush Hour	21.4
Clean Air: Alternate Pollution Measures	na

K3.12 Profile of Metropolitan Areas: Istanbul, Turkey

Indicators	Value
Population	6,500,000
Public Safety: Murders Per 1,000,000 People	3.5
Food Costs: Percent Income Spent on Food	60
Living Space: Persons Per Room	1.6
Housing Standards: Percent Homes with Water/Electricity	89
Communications: Telephones Per 100 People	18
Education: Percent Children in Secondary School	67
Public Health: Infant Deaths Per 1,000 Live Births	59
Peace and Quiet: Levels of Ambient Noise (1-10)	7
Traffic Flow: Miles per Hour in Rush Hour	11.2
Clean Air: Alternate Pollution Measures	na

Notes and Source for all Metropolitan Area tables: [see above]

K3.13 Profile of Metropolitan Areas: Jakarta, Indonesia

Indicators	Value
Population	9,900,000
Public Safety: Murders Per 1,000,000 People	5.3
Food Costs: Percent Income Spent on Food	45
Living Space: Persons Per Room	3.4
Housing Standards: Percent Homes with Water/Electricity	85
Communications: Telephones Per 100 People	3
Education: Percent Children in Secondary School	77
Public Health: Infant Deaths Per 1,000 Live Births	45
Peace and Quiet: Levels of Ambient Noise (1-10)	6
Traffic Flow: Miles per Hour in Rush Hour	16.3
Clean Air: Alternate Pollution Measures	173 days SPM

Note: "de" indicates that the data are estimated
Clean air statistic cited is the lowest of the following three measures:
ppm D_3 = one-hour concentration of ozone, in parts per million
days SPM = number of days with concentrations of suspended particulate matter over World Health Organization's (WHO's) standard
days SO_2 = number of days with concentrations of sulfur dioxide over WHO's standard

Source: Population Crisis Committee, "Cities: Life in the World's 100 Largest Metropolitan Areas"

K3.14 Profile of Metropolitan Areas: Johannesburg, South Africa

Indicators	Values
Population	4,600,000
Public Safety: Murders Per 1,000,000 People	19.8
Food Costs: Percent Income Spent on Food	na
Living Space: Persons Per Room	5
Housing Standards: Percent Homes with Water/Electricity	28
Communications: Telephones Per 100 People	6 de
Education: Percent Children in Secondary School	25
Public Health: Infant Deaths Per 1,000 Live Births	22
Peace and Quiet: Levels of Ambient Noise (1-10)	3
Traffic Flow: Miles per Hour in Rush Hour	38.8
Clean Air: Alternate Pollution Measures	.1200 ppm O_3

K3.15 Profile of Metropolitan Areas: Karachi, Pakistan

Indicators	Values
Population	7,300,000
Public Safety: Murders Per 1,000,000 People	5.7
Food Costs: Percent Income Spent on Food	43
Living Space: Persons Per Room	3.3
Housing Standards: Percent Homes with Water/Electricity	75
Communications: Telephones Per 100 People	2
Education: Percent Children in Secondary School	65
Public Health: Infant Deaths Per 1,000 Live Births	97
Peace and Quiet: Levels of Ambient Noise (1-10)	9
Traffic Flow: Miles per Hour in Rush Hour	17.6
Clean Air: Alternate Pollution Measures	.0900 ppm O_3

Notes and Source for all Metropolitan Area tables: [see above]

K3.16 Profile of Metropolitan Areas: Lagos, Nigeria

Indicators	Value
Population	4,000,000
Public Safety: Murders Per 1,000,000 People	na
Food Costs: Percent Income Spent on Food	58
Living Space: Persons Per Room	5.8
Housing Standards: Percent Homes with Water/Electricity	50
Communications: Telephones Per 100 People	1
Education: Percent Children in Secondary School	31
Public Health: Infant Deaths Per 1,000 Live Births	85
Peace and Quiet: Levels of Ambient Noise (1-10)	7
Traffic Flow: Miles per Hour in Rush Hour	17.4
Clean Air: Alternate Pollution Measures	na

Note: "de" indicates that the data are estimated
Clean air statistic cited is the lowest of the following three measures:
ppm D_3 = one-hour concentration of ozone, in parts per million
days SPM = number of days with concentrations of suspended particulate matter over World Health Organization's (WHO's) standard
days SO_2 = number of days with concentrations of sulfur dioxide over WHO's standard

Source: Population Crisis Committee, "Cities: Life in the World's 100 Largest Metropolitan Areas"

K3.17 Profile of Metropolitan Areas: Lima, Peru

Indicators	Value
Population	5,400,000
Public Safety: Murders Per 1,000,000 People	na
Food Costs: Percent Income Spent on Food	70
Living Space: Persons Per Room	2.3
Housing Standards: Percent Homes with Water/Electricity	82
Communications: Telephones Per 100 People	2
Education: Percent Children in Secondary School	55
Public Health: Infant Deaths Per 1,000 Live Births	34
Peace and Quiet: Levels of Ambient Noise (1-10)	7
Traffic Flow: Miles per Hour in Rush Hour	3.7
Clean Air: Alternate Pollution Measures	na

K3.18 Profile of Metropolitan Areas: Madras, India

Indicators	Value
Population	5,600,000
Public Safety: Murders Per 1,000,000 People	1.1
Food Costs: Percent Income Spent on Food	33
Living Space: Persons Per Room	2.9
Housing Standards: Percent Homes with Water/Electricity	76
Communications: Telephones Per 100 People	2
Education: Percent Children in Secondary School	56
Public Health: Infant Deaths Per 1,000 Live Births	44
Peace and Quiet: Levels of Ambient Noise (1-10)	8
Traffic Flow: Miles per Hour in Rush Hour	13
Clean Air: Alternate Pollution Measures	na

Notes and Source for all Metropolitan Area tables: [see above]

K3.19 Profile of Metropolitan Areas: Manila, Philippines

Indicators	Values
Population	9,200,000
Public Safety: Murders Per 1,000,000 People	30.5
Food Costs: Percent Income Spent on Food	38
Living Space: Persons Per Room	3
Housing Standards: Percent Homes with Water/Electricity	91
Communications: Telephones Per 100 People	9
Education: Percent Children in Secondary School	67
Public Health: Infant Deaths Per 1,000 Live Births	36
Peace and Quiet: Levels of Ambient Noise (1-10)	4
Traffic Flow: Miles per Hour in Rush Hour	7.2
Clean Air: Alternate Pollution Measures	24 days SO_2

Note: "de" indicates that the data are estimated
Clean air statistic cited is the lowest of the following three measures:
ppm D_3 = one-hour concentration of ozone, in parts per million
days SPM = number of days with concentrations of suspended particulate matter over World Health Organization's (WHO's) standard
days SO_2 = number of days with concentrations of sulfur dioxide over WHO's standard

Source: Population Crisis Committee, "Cities: Life in the World's 100 Largest Metropolitan Areas"

K3.20 Profile of Metropolitan Areas: Mexico City, Mexico

Indicators	Values
Population	19,400,000
Public Safety: Murders Per 1,000,000 People	27.6
Food Costs: Percent Income Spent on Food	41
Living Space: Persons Per Room	1.9
Housing Standards: Percent Homes with Water/Electricity	94
Communications: Telephones Per 100 People	6
Education: Percent Children in Secondary School	62
Public Health: Infant Deaths Per 1,000 Live Births	36
Peace and Quiet: Levels of Ambient Noise (1-10)	6
Traffic Flow: Miles per Hour in Rush Hour	8
Clean Air: Alternate Pollution Measures	.4050 ppm O_3

K3.21 Profile of Metropolitan Areas: Moscow, Russia

Indicators	Values
Population	13,200,000
Public Safety: Murders Per 1,000,000 People	7
Food Costs: Percent Income Spent on Food	33
Living Space: Persons Per Room	1.3
Housing Standards: Percent Homes with Water/Electricity	100
Communications: Telephones Per 100 People	39
Education: Percent Children in Secondary School	100
Public Health: Infant Deaths Per 1,000 Live Births	20
Peace and Quiet: Levels of Ambient Noise (1-10)	6
Traffic Flow: Miles per Hour in Rush Hour	31.5
Clean Air: Alternate Pollution Measures	na

Notes and Source for all Metropolitan Area tables: [see above]

K3.22 Profile of Metropolitan Areas: Rio de Janeiro, Brazil

Indicators	Values
Population	10,975,000
Public Safety: Murders Per 1,000,000 People	36.6
Food Costs: Percent Income Spent on Food	26
Living Space: Persons Per Room	0.8
Housing Standards: Percent Homes with Water/Electricity	92
Communications: Telephones Per 100 People	8
Education: Percent Children in Secondary School	55
Public Health: Infant Deaths Per 1,000 Live Births	40
Peace and Quiet: Levels of Ambient Noise (1-10)	7
Traffic Flow: Miles per Hour in Rush Hour	18.6
Clean Air: Alternate Pollution Measures	11 days SPM

Note: "de" indicates that the data are estimated
Clean air statistic cited is the lowest of the following three measures:
ppm D_3 = one-hour concentration of ozone, in parts per million
days SPM = number of days with concentrations of suspended particulate matter over World Health Organization's (WHO's) standard
days SO_2 = number of days with concentrations of sulfur dioxide over WHO's standard

Source: Population Crisis Committee, "Cities: Life in the World's 100 Largest Metropolitan Areas"

K3.23 Profile of Metropolitan Areas: St. Petersburg, Russia

Indicators	Values
Population	5,900,000
Public Safety: Murders Per 1,000,000 People	7.3
Food Costs: Percent Income Spent on Food	32
Living Space: Persons Per Room	1.5
Housing Standards: Percent Homes with Water/Electricity	100
Communications: Telephones Per 100 People	31
Education: Percent Children in Secondary School	93
Public Health: Infant Deaths Per 1,000 Live Births	19
Peace and Quiet: Levels of Ambient Noise (1-10)	5
Traffic Flow: Miles per Hour in Rush Hour	30.8
Clean Air: Alternate Pollution Measures	na

K3.24 Profile of Metropolitan Areas: Santiago, Chile

Indicators	Values
Population	4,700,000
Public Safety: Murders Per 1,000,000 People	7.4
Food Costs: Percent Income Spent on Food	42
Living Space: Persons Per Room	1.3
Housing Standards: Percent Homes with Water/Electricity	91
Communications: Telephones Per 100 People	9
Education: Percent Children in Secondary School	86
Public Health: Infant Deaths Per 1,000 Live Births	16
Peace and Quiet: Levels of Ambient Noise (1-10)	7
Traffic Flow: Miles per Hour in Rush Hour	16.8
Clean Air: Alternate Pollution Measures	.3990 ppm O_3

Notes and Source for all Metropolitan Area tables: [see above]

K3.25 Profile of Metropolitan Areas: Sao Paulo, Brazil

Indicators	Values
Population	17,200,000
Public Safety: Murders Per 1,000,000 People	26
Food Costs: Percent Income Spent on Food	50
Living Space: Persons Per Room	0.8
Housing Standards: Percent Homes with Water/Electricity	100
Communications: Telephones Per 100 People	16
Education: Percent Children in Secondary School	67
Public Health: Infant Deaths Per 1,000 Live Births	37
Peace and Quiet: Levels of Ambient Noise (1-10)	6
Traffic Flow: Miles per Hour in Rush Hour	15
Clean Air: Alternate Pollution Measures	0.1549 ppm 0_3

Note: "de" indicates that the data are estimated
Clean air statistic cited is the lowest of the following three measures:
ppm D_3 = one-hour concentration of ozone, in parts per million
days SPM = number of days with concentrations of suspended particulate matter over World Health Organization's (WHO's) standard
days SO_2 = number of days with concentrations of sulfur dioxide over WHO's standard

Source: Population Crisis Committee, "Cities: Life in the World's 100 Largest Metropolitan Areas"

K3.26 Profile of Metropolitan Areas: Shanghai, China

Indicators	Values
Population	9,185,000
Public Safety: Murders Per 1,000,000 People	2.5
Food Costs: Percent Income Spent on Food	55
Living Space: Persons Per Room	2
Housing Standards: Percent Homes with Water/Electricity	95
Communications: Telephones Per 100 People	4
Education: Percent Children in Secondary School	94
Public Health: Infant Deaths Per 1,000 Live Births	14
Peace and Quiet: Levels of Ambient Noise (1-10)	5
Traffic Flow: Miles per Hour in Rush Hour	15.3
Clean Air: Alternate Pollution Measures	16 days SO^2 sa

K3.27 Profile of Metropolitan Areas: Shenyang, China

Indicators	Values
Population	4,040,000
Public Safety: Murders Per 1,000,000 People	2.3
Food Costs: Percent Income Spent on Food	52
Living Space: Persons Per Room	2.5
Housing Standards: Percent Homes with Water/Electricity	66
Communications: Telephones Per 100 People	3
Education: Percent Children in Secondary School	83
Public Health: Infant Deaths Per 1,000 Live Births	13
Peace and Quiet: Levels of Ambient Noise (1-10)	6
Traffic Flow: Miles per Hour in Rush Hour	16
Clean Air: Alternate Pollution Measures	146 days SO^2

Notes and Source for all Metropolitan Area tables: [see above]

K3.28 Profile of Metropolitan Areas: Tehran, Iran

Indicators	Values
Population	8,100,000
Public Safety: Murders Per 1,000,000 People	na
Food Costs: Percent Income Spent on Food	na
Living Space: Persons Per Room	1.3
Housing Standards: Percent Homes with Water/Electricity	84
Communications: Telephones Per 100 People	na
Education: Percent Children in Secondary School	58
Public Health: Infant Deaths Per 1,000 Live Births	54
Peace and Quiet: Levels of Ambient Noise (1-10)	5
Traffic Flow: Miles per Hour in Rush Hour	7.5
Clean Air: Alternate Pollution Measures	174 days SPM

Note: "de" indicates that the data are estimated
Clean air statistic cited is the lowest of the following three measures:
ppm D_3 = one-hour concentration of ozone, in parts per million
days SPM = number of days with concentrations of suspended particulate matter over World Health Organization's (WHO's) standard
days SO_2 = number of days with concentrations of sulfur dioxide over WHO's standard

Source: Population Crisis Committee, "Cities: Life in the World's 100 Largest Metropolitan Areas"

K3.29 Profile of Metropolitan Areas: Tianjin, China

Indicators	Values
Population	5,625,000
Public Safety: Murders Per 1,000,000 People	2.5
Food Costs: Percent Income Spent on Food	52
Living Space: Persons Per Room	1.2
Housing Standards: Percent Homes with Water/Electricity	82
Communications: Telephones Per 100 People	4
Education: Percent Children in Secondary School	71
Public Health: Infant Deaths Per 1,000 Live Births	15
Peace and Quiet: Levels of Ambient Noise (1-10)	5
Traffic Flow: Miles per Hour in Rush Hour	20.2
Clean Air: Alternate Pollution Measures	1900 ppm O_3 sa

Notes and Source for all Metropolitan Area tables: [see above]

L1.1 Aid per Capita, Worldwide Summary, 1991 and 1996—Comparison By Income Level per World Bank

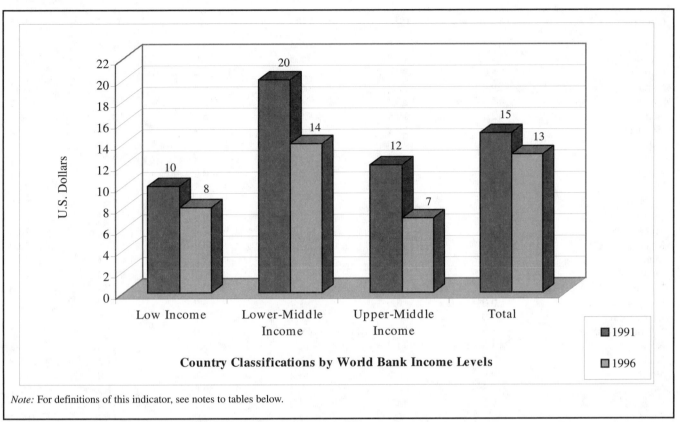

Note: For definitions of this indicator, see notes to tables below.

Source: World Bank, *World Development Indicators 1998*, Table 6.11

L1.2 Aid per Capita in United States Dollars, 1975–1996—Low-Income Countries per World Bank

Country	1975	1980	1985	1990	1995	1996
Afghanistan	5.1	2.0	0.9	6.7	9.1	9.5
Angola	0.8	7.5	11.4	29.2	38.8	49.0
Armenia	0.0	0.0	0.0	0.0	57.9	78.1
Azerbaijan	0.0	0.0	0.0	0.0	14.5	14.0
Bangladesh	13.5	14.8	11.5	19.0	10.7	10.3
Benin	18.0	26.0	23.3	56.8	51.4	52.0
Bhutan	4.6	17.0	44.6	79.8	106.2	87.2
Bosnia and Herzgovina	na	na	na	na	na	na
Burkina Faso	14.4	30.5	24.8	37.2	46.9	39.2
Burundi	13.1	28.4	29.3	48.4	46.0	31.7
Cambodia	11.5	43.3	1.7	4.8	56.5	44.1
Cameroon	14.9	30.5	15.3	38.9	33.4	30.2
Central African Republic	27.5	48.0	40.1	85.7	51.2	49.9
Chad	17.4	7.9	36.0	55.7	37.1	46.2
China	0.0	0.1	0.9	1.8	2.9	2.2
Comoros	na	129.0	124.8	107.3	88.1	79.3
Congo, Dem. Rep. (Zaire)	8.8	15.8	9.7	24.0	4.4	3.7
Congo, Rep.	38.8	55.1	35.4	95.8	47.6	158.8
Cote d'Ivoire	14.9	25.7	11.8	57.6	86.7	67.4
Equatorial Guinea	9.8	42.4	54.8	175.7	84.6	75.7
Eritrea	na	na	0.0	0.0	42.0	42.5
Ethiopia	4.1	5.6	16.4	19.9	15.7	14.6

L1.2 Aid per Capita in United States Dollars, 1975–1996—Low-Income Countries per World Bank (continued)

Country	1975	1980	1985	1990	1995	1996
Gambia	14.4	84.6	66.3	108.6	42.8	33.6
Ghana	12.8	17.8	15.5	37.9	38.3	37.3
Guinea	5.9	20.0	23.1	51.4	63.1	43.7
Guinea-Bissau	29.8	73.3	65.2	136.8	108.9	164.4
Guyana	13.8	56.1	34.1	212.6	106.4	171.5
Haiti	12.1	19.6	25.5	26.6	101.9	51.1
Honduras	17.0	28.1	61.7	88.3	69.3	60.2
India	2.6	3.2	2.1	1.7	1.9	2.0
Kenya	9.4	23.9	21.5	50.8	27.4	22.2
Kyrgyzstan	0.0	0.0	0.0	0.0	62.8	50.7
Laos	12.9	12.7	10.3	37.5	67.9	71.6
Lesotho	25.3	68.8	59.6	79.9	58.0	53.0
Liberia	12.9	52.0	41.1	46.0	45.1	73.5
Madagascar	11.2	26.4	18.6	34.2	22.8	26.6
Malawi	12.1	23.3	15.7	59.4	44.5	50.0
Mali	24.4	40.5	50.9	57.6	56.1	50.5
Mauritania	49.6	113.5	117.0	119.7	101.5	117.3
Moldova	0.0	0.0	0.0	0.0	15.4	8.6
Mongolia	0.0	0.0	1.7	5.9	84.3	80.5
Mozambique	2.0	14.0	22.2	71.2	63.2	51.2
Myanmar (Burma)	1.9	9.1	9.2	4.0	3.4	1.2
Nepal	3.5	11.3	14.2	22.9	20.3	18.2
Nicaragua	17.1	78.8	31.9	89.2	151.2	211.8
Niger	29.9	30.8	46.2	52.0	29.9	27.7
Nigeria	1.3	0.5	0.4	2.6	1.9	1.7
Pakistan	9.3	14.3	8.0	10.1	6.3	6.6
Rwanda	20.7	30.1	29.6	42.2	111.1	100.2
Sao Tome and Principe	8.2	42.7	122.0	488.3	638.2	347.3
Senegal	29.2	47.5	45.3	112.3	80.5	68.1
Sierra Leone	6.1	28.0	18.1	15.7	45.8	42.2
Somalia	27.7	64.5	44.9	57.3	20.2	9.3
Sri Lanka	11.3	26.4	29.6	43.0	30.7	27.0
Sudan	16.5	33.4	52.6	34.4	8.8	8.4
Tajikistan	0.0	0.0	0.0	0.0	11.1	19.1
Tanzania	18.6	36.5	22.2	46.1	29.7	29.3
Togo	18.3	34.7	36.8	74.2	46.9	39.2
Uganda	4.3	8.9	12.7	41.1	43.3	34.6
Vietnam	7.3	4.2	1.9	2.9	11.2	12.3
Yemen	34.1	66.9	38.9	34.2	11.5	16.5
Zambia	17.9	55.4	48.1	61.8	226.6	66.6
Zimbabwe	0.7	23.4	28.5	34.9	44.7	33.3

Note: This indicator reflects total assistance given to a country divided by its population. It includes both official development assistance (ODA) and official aid. ODA is granted by authoritative agencies of the members of the Development Assistance Committee (DAC) and includes all net disbursements of loans and grants. Official aid, also under the auspices of the DAC, is the total of loans and grants given to certain countries including the "transition economies" of Eastern Europe and the former Soviet Union; it also includes aid to advanced developing countries, as designated by the DAC.

Source: World Bank, *World Development Indicators 1998*, Table 6.11

L1.3 Aid per Capita in United States Dollars, 1975–1996—Lower Middle-Income Countries per World Bank

Country	1975	1980	1985	1990	1995	1996
Albania	0.0	0.0	0.0	3.4	55.8	67.6
Algeria	10.9	9.4	7.9	10.5	11.1	10.8
Belarus	0.0	0.0	0.0	0.0	21.6	7.1
Belize	66.1	100.0	131.1	160.3	74.8	81.5
Bolivia	11.9	31.7	33.4	84.3	99.4	112.0
Botswana	67.5	117.7	89.6	116.3	63.6	54.6
Bulgaria	0.0	0.0	0.0	1.8	13.5	20.3
Cape Verde	31.3	222.8	224.5	325.3	295.7	308.9
Colombia	3.4	3.2	2.0	2.9	6.3	6.7
Costa Rica	15.4	28.3	105.9	75.7	7.5	-2.0
Cuba	2.3	3.3	1.8	4.8	5.9	6.2
Djibouti	167.8	259.1	208.4	376.3	176.8	157.5
Dominica	110.0	241.3	228.4	269.3	328.9	582.2
Dominican Republic	6.1	21.9	32.5	14.2	15.8	13.3
Ecuador	10.2	5.8	14.9	15.9	20.6	22.3
Egypt	60.8	33.9	37.8	103.7	34.8	37.3
El Salvador	10.1	21.2	73.7	69.0	54.1	54.6
Estonia	0.0	0.0	0.0	0.0	39.2	42.5
Fiji	33.3	56.9	45.3	68.5	54.6	56.5
Georgia	0.0	0.0	0.0	0.0	38.6	58.8
Grenada	30.4	34.8	381.1	151.4	106.9	106.6
Guatemala	6.6	10.5	10.4	22.1	20.2	19.8
Indonesia	5.2	6.4	3.7	9.8	7.2	5.7
Iran	-0.2	0.8	0.4	2.0	3.1	2.7
Iraq	6.0	0.7	1.7	3.5	15.8	18.1
Jamaica	12.4	59.0	73.2	113.4	42.5	23.5
Jordan	234.5	585.0	203.3	280.2	127.5	119.1
Kazakhstan	0.0	0.0	0.0	0.0	3.5	7.5
Kiribati	107.3	327.0	186.2	283.9	193.4	161.2
Latvia	0.0	0.0	0.0	0.0	25.3	31.5
Lebanon	5.0	78.9	25.3	71.3	47.2	57.1
Lithuania	0.0	0.0	0.0	0.0	48.3	24.1
Macedonia, FYRO	na	na	na	na	40.1	53.3
Maldives	23.4	134.2	50.0	101.0	226.1	127.8
Marshall Islands	0.0	0.0	0.0	0.0	695.5	1279.5
Micronesia	na	0.0	0.0	0.0	723.2	1036.7
Morocco	13.8	46.3	35.4	43.7	18.7	24.1
Namibia	0.0	0.0	5.3	91.1	122.4	119.0
North Korea, Dem. Rep.	0.0	0.0	0.3	0.4	0.6	1.9
Panama	19.0	23.4	31.9	41.1	18.7	33.5
Papua New Guinea	111.8	105.6	74.6	107.7	86.7	87.5
Paraguay	13.8	9.7	13.6	13.4	30.3	19.6
Peru	4.9	11.7	16.3	18.7	17.9	16.9
Philippines	4.2	6.2	8.4	20.4	12.6	12.3
Romania	0.0	0.0	0.0	10.5	12.2	9.7
Russia	0.0	0.0	0.0	1.7	0.0	0.0
Samoa	89.5	164.5	120.2	299.9	252.6	189.3
Solomon Islands	114.9	191.0	75.9	141.4	123.2	109.7
St. Vincent and the Grenadines	64.7	98.2	53.8	140.5	426.1	237.6
Suriname	144.6	230.5	26.9	152.3	180.5	256.9
Swaziland	34.0	88.0	37.6	71.5	61.7	33.0
Syria	90.7	194.9	58.9	56.4	24.7	15.5
Thailand	2.1	9.0	9.0	14.3	14.6	13.9
Tonga	36.7	173.4	140.0	309.4	400.2	328.9
Tunisia	34.9	36.4	22.4	48.2	7.9	13.8
Turkey	2.1	21.4	3.6	21.7	4.9	3.7
Turkmenistan	0.0	0.0	0.0	0.0	5.8	5.2

L1.3 Aid per Capita in United States Dollars, 1975–1996—Lower Middle-Income Countries per World Bank (continued)

Country	1975	1980	1985	1990	1995	1996
Ukraine	0.0	0.0	0.0	5.6	6.2	7.5
Uzbekistan	0.0	0.0	0.0	0.0	3.6	3.8
Vanuatu	126.5	381.5	167.3	338.8	271.8	180.8
Venezuela	1.5	1.0	0.6	4.1	2.2	2.0
Yugoslavia	na	na	na	4.5	50.2	64.4

Note: This indicator reflects total assistance given to a country divided by its population. It includes both official development assistance (ODA) and official aid. ODA is granted by authoritative agencies of the members of the Development Assistance Committee (DAC) and includes all net disbursements of loans and grants. Official aid, also under the auspices of the DAC, is the total of loans and grants given to certain countries including the "transition economies" of Eastern Europe and the former Soviet Union; it also includes aid to advanced developing countries, as designated by the DAC.

Source: World Bank, *World Development Indicators 1998*, Table 6.11

L1.4 Aid per Capita in United States Dollars, 1975–1996—Upper Middle-Income Countries per World Bank

Country	1975	1980	1985	1990	1995	1996
Antigua and Barbuda	33.3	91.8	45.2	72.8	34.8	181.8
Argentina	0.9	0.7	1.3	5.6	6.5	7.9
Bahrain	95.8	466.5	170.4	272.5	84.3	9.1
Barbados	21.2	55.8	28.1	11.2	-1.9	17.2
Brazil	1.5	0.7	0.9	1.1	2.3	2.5
Chile	12.4	-0.9	3.3	8.3	11.2	14.1
Croatia	na	na	na	na	11.3	28.0
Czech Republic	0.0	0.0	0.0	0.3	14.3	11.8
Gabon	101.7	80.3	75.2	137.9	131.7	112.5
Hungary	0.0	0.0	0.0	6.5	0.0	18.2
Libya	1.9	5.4	1.4	4.6	1.7	1.9
Malaysia	8.2	9.8	14.6	26.2	5.7	-22.0
Malta	101.5	43.1	53.2	10.4	25.0	193.5
Mauritius	32.8	34.3	26.2	84.1	19.9	17.3
Mexico	1.0	0.8	1.9	1.9	4.3	3.1
Oman	49.2	152.4	55.7	40.6	27.5	28.3
Palau	na	na	na	na	na	na
Poland	0.0	0.0	0.0	34.7	0.1	21.5
Saudi Arabia	0.8	1.6	2.3	2.8	1.2	1.5
Seychelles	124.2	333.9	329.4	513.4	172.4	247.6
Slovakia	0.0	0.0	0.0	0.3	18.4	26.4
Slovenia	na	na	na	na	26.5	41.3
South Africa	na	na	na	0.0	10.4	9.6
St. Kitts & Nevis	34.4	137.4	105.3	188.2	96.8	170.7
St. Lucia	78.6	67.9	51.2	81.1	303.5	245.3
Trinidad & Tobago	5.2	4.3	5.6	14.7	19.9	13.0
Uruguay	4.4	3.4	1.6	17.4	25.9	16.1

Note: This indicator reflects total assistance given to a country divided by its population. It includes both official development assistance (ODA) and official aid. ODA is granted by authoritative agencies of the members of the Development Assistance Committee (DAC) and includes all net disbursements of loans and grants. Official aid, also under the auspices of the DAC, is the total of loans and grants given to certain countries including the "transition economies" of Eastern Europe and the former Soviet Union; it also includes aid to advanced developing countries, as designated by the DAC.

Source: World Bank, *World Development Indicators 1998*, Table 6.11

L2.1 Aid Dependency Ratio, Aid as Percent of GNP, 1991 and 1996—Low-Income Countries per World Bank

Country	1991	1996	Country	1991	1996
Afghanistan	na	na	Laos	13.9	18.2
Angola	9.6	15.8	Lesotho	12.1	8.7
Armenia	0.1	18.2	Liberia	na	na
Azerbaijan	0	3.0	Madagascar	17.9	9.1
Bangladesh	8.1	3.9	Malawi	24.6	23.2
Benin	14.5	13.5	Mali	19.2	19.4
Bhutan	na	na	Mauritania	20.6	26.4
Bosnia and Herzegovina	na	na	Moldova	0	2.1
Burkina Faso	15.2	16.5	Mongolia	24.2	21.3
Burundi	22.4	18.1	Mozambique	83.8	59.8
Cambodia	5.6	14.5	Myanmar (Burma)	na	na
Cameroon	4.5	4.9	Nepal	12	8.9
Central African Republic	12.8	16.1	Nicaragua	64.1	57.1
Chad	20.2	26.9	Niger	16.5	13.2
China	0.5	0.3	Nigeria	1.1	0.6
Comoros	na	na	Pakistan	2.9	1.4
Congo, Dem. Rep. (Zaire)	5.7	2.8	Rwanda	19.9	51.2
Congo, Rep.	5.9	22.9	Sao Tome and Principe	na	na
Cote d'Ivoire	6.9	9.9	Senegal	12.0	11.6
Equatorial Guinea	na	na	Sierra Leone	14.8	21.2
Eritrea	na	na	Somalia	na	na
Ethiopia	20.6	14.3	Sri Lanka	10.1	3.6
Gambia	31.6	13.4	Sudan	12.3	na
Ghana	13.6	10.5	Tajikistan	0	5.6
Guinea	13.6	7.8	Tanzania	24.9	15.6
Guinea-Bissau	49.4	67.5	Togo	12.9	12.0
Guyana	na	na	Uganda	20.4	11.3
Haiti	5.6	14.4	Vietnam	2.5	4.0
Honduras	10.5	9.2	Yemen	6.2	4.9
India	1.1	0.6	Zambia	27.7	18.6
Kenya	12.1	6.8	Zimbabwe	6.3	5.2
Kyrgyzstan	0	13.9			

Note: This indicator reflects total assistance given to a country as a percent of its GNP. It includes both official development assistance (ODA) and official aid. ODA is granted by authoritative agencies of the members of the Development Assistance Committee (DAC) and includes all net disbursements of loans and grants. Official aid, also under the auspices of the DAC, is the total of loans and grants given to certain countries including the "transition economies" of Eastern Europe and the former Soviet Union; it also includes aid to advanced developing countries, as designated by the DAC.

Source: World Bank, *World Development Indicators 1998*, Table 6.11

L2.2 Aid Dependency Ratio, Aid as Percent of GNP, 1991 and 1996—Lower Middle-Income Countries per World Bank

Country	1991	1996	Country	1991	1996
Albania	29.0	8.0	Lithuania	0	1.2
Algeria	0.8	0.7	Macedonia, FYRO	0	5.3
Belarus	0.5	0.4	Maldives	na	na
Belize	na	na	Marshall Islands	na	na
Bolivia	10.8	13.3	Micronesia	na	na
Botswana	3.4	1.7	Morocco	4.6	1.8
Bulgaria	3.2	1.9	Namibia	6.9	5.7
Cape Verde	na	na	North Korea, Dem. Rep.	na	na
Colombia	0.3	0.3	Panama	1.9	1.1
Costa Rica	3.2	-0.1	Papua New Guinea	10.8	8
Cuba	na	na	Paraguay	2.4	1.0
Djibouti	na	na	Peru	2.2	0.7
Dominica	na	na	Philippines	2.3	1
Dominican Republic	0.9	0.8	Romania	1.1	0.6
Ecuador	2.2	1.5	Russia	0.1	0.0
Egypt	14.3	3.3	Samoa	na	na
El Salvador	5.6	3.1	Solomon Islands	na	na
Estonia	0.3	1.4	St. Vincent and the Grenadines	na	na
Fiji	na	na	Suriname	na	na
Georgia	0	7.1	Swaziland	na	na
Grenada	na	na	Syria	3.0	1.4
Guatemala	2.1	1.4	Thailand	0.7	0.5
Indonesia	1.5	0.5	Tonga	na	na
Iran	0.2	0.1	Tunisia	2.8	0.7
Iraq	na	na	Turkey	1.1	0.1
Jamaica	4.9	1.4	Turkmenistan	0	0.5
Jordan	23.8	7.2	Ukraine	0.5	0.9
Kazakhstan	0.4	0.6	Uzbekistan	0	0.4
Kiribati	na	na	Vanuatu	na	na
Latvia	0	1.6	Venezuela	0.1	0.1
Lebanon	2.7	1.8	Yugoslavia	na	na

Note: This indicator reflects total assistance given to a country as a percent of its GNP. It includes both official development assistance (ODA) and official aid. ODA is granted by authoritative agencies of the members of the Development Assistance Committee (DAC) and includes all net disbursements of loans and grants. Official aid, also under the auspices of the DAC, is the total of loans and grants given to certain countries including the "transition economies" of Eastern Europe and the former Soviet Union; it also includes aid to advanced developing countries, as designated by the DAC.

Source: World Bank, *World Development Indicators 1998*, Table 6.11

L2.3 Aid Dependency Ratio, Aid as Percent of GNP, 1991 and 1996—Upper Middle-Income Countries per World Bank

Country	1991	1996	Country	1991	1996
Antigua and Barbuda	na	na	Mexico	0.1	0.1
Argentina	0.2	0.1	Oman	0.2	0.6
Bahrain	na	na	Palau	na	na
Barbados	na	na	Poland	0	0.6
Brazil	0	0.1	Saudi Arabia	0	0
Chile	0.4	0.3	Seychelles	na	na
Croatia	0	0.7	Slovakia	1.1	0.7
Czech Republic	0.9	0.2	Slovenia	0	0.4
Gabon	3	2.6	South Africa	0	0.3
Hungary	2	0.4	St. Kitts & Nevis	na	na
Libya	na	na	St. Lucia	na	na
Malaysia	0.6	-0.5	Trinidad & Tobago	0	0.3
Malta	na	na	Uruguay	0.5	0.3
Mauritius	2.4	0.5			

Note: This indicator reflects total assistance given to a country as a percent of its GNP. It includes both official development assistance (ODA) and official aid. ODA is granted by authoritative agencies of the members of the Development Assistance Committee (DAC) and includes all net disbursements of loans and grants. Official aid, also under the auspices of the DAC, is the total of loans and grants given to certain countries including the "transition economies" of Eastern Europe and the former Soviet Union; it also includes aid to advanced developing countries, as designated by the DAC.

Source: World Bank, *World Development Indicators 1998*, Table 6.11

L2.4 Aid Dependency Ratio, Aid as Percent of GNP, Worldwide Summary, 1991 and 1996—Comparison By Income Level per World Bank

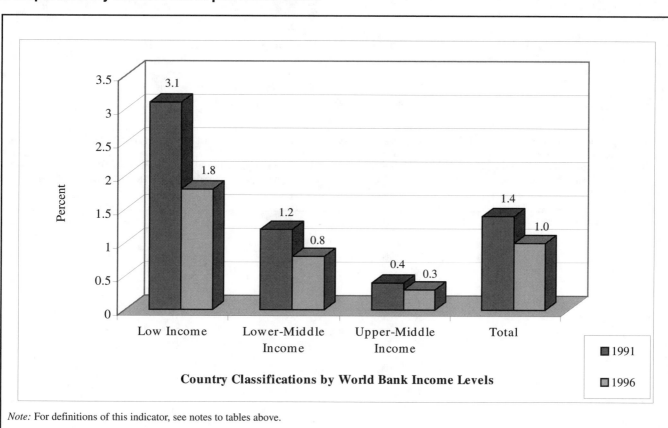

Note: For definitions of this indicator, see notes to tables above.

Source: World Bank, *World Development Indicators 1998*, Table 6.11

L2.5 Aid Dependency Ratio, Aid as Percent of Gross Domestic Investment, 1991 and 1996—Low-Income Countries per World Bank

Country	1991	1996	Country	1991	1996
Afghanistan	na	na	Laos	na	59.8
Angola	51.5	72	Lesotho	27.6	11.6
Armenia	0.2	146.8	Liberia	na	na
Azerbaijan	2.3	11.9	Madagascar	161.3	87.8
Bangladesh	70.2	23.2	Malawi	119.6	132.4
Benin	98.6	77.5	Mali	83	71.7
Bhutan	na	na	Mauritania	108.4	113.8
Bosnia and Herzgovina	na	na	Moldova	0	7.3
Burkina Faso	73.7	64.8	Mongolia	80.8	93
Burundi	154	203.2	Mozambique	163.4	111.5
Cambodia	59.3	70	Myanmar (Burma)	na	na
Cameroon	25	28.4	Nepal	58.8	38.8
Central African Republic	99.8	280.7	Nicaragua	239.8	174.5
Chad	274	134.9	Niger	176.4	134.8
China	1.5	0.8	Nigeria	4.1	3.2
Comoros	na	na	Pakistan	15.9	7.3
Congo, Dem. Rep. (Zaire)	94	38.5	Rwanda	166.8	371.9
Congo, Rep.	24.9	29.6	Sao Tome and Principe	na	na
Cote d'Ivoire	82	66.1	Senegal	94.8	68.3
Equatorial Guinea	na	na	Sierra Leone	123.3	223.2
Eritrea	na	na	Somalia	na	na
Ethiopia	287.8	67.6	Sri Lanka	43.3	13.9
Gambia	157.2	62.6	Sudan	94.9	na
Ghana	84.2	55.2	Tajikistan	0	20.3
Guinea	77.5	57.6	Tanzania	86.7	84.8
Guinea-Bissau	144.9	304.3	Togo	73.7	85.4
Guyana	na	na	Uganda	132.3	68.3
Haiti	49.4	2,117.20	Vietnam	16.5	14.2
Honduras	40	28.6	Yemen	37.4	17.1
India	4.8	2.1	Zambia	237.4	120.2
Kenya	53.9	32.4	Zimbabwe	23.9	27.6
Kyrgyzstan	0	69.2			

Note: This indicator reflects total assistance given to a country as a percent of its gross domestic investment. It includes both official development assistance (ODA) and official aid. ODA is granted by authoritative agencies of the members of the Development Assistance Committee (DAC) and includes all net disbursements of loans and grants. Official aid, also under the auspices of the DAC, is the total of loans and grants given to certain countries including the "transition economies" of Eastern Europe and the former Soviet Union; it also includes aid to advanced developing countries, as designated by the DAC. Gross domestic investment reflects the amount of capital investment in a country and includes expenditures on increases to fixed assets and net increases in inventory.

Source: World Bank, *World Development Indicators 1998*, Table 6.11

L2.6 Aid Dependency Ratio, Aid as Percent of Gross Domestic Investment, 1991 and 1996—Lower Middle-Income Countries per World Bank

Country	1991	1996	Country	1991	1996
Albania	470.0	40.0	Lithuania	0.1	5.5
Algeria	2.4	2.5	Macedonia, FYRO	0	26
Belarus	1.8	1.5	Maldives	na	na
Belize	na	na	Marshall Islands	na	na
Bolivia	74.0	71.6	Micronesia	na	na
Botswana	10.9	6.8	Morocco	19.5	8.6
Bulgaria	12.8	12.7	Namibia	38.8	29.4
Cape Verde	na	na	North Korea, Dem. Rep.	na	na
Colombia	1.9	1.4	Panama	9.1	3.7
Costa Rica	12.3	-0.3	Papua New Guinea	38.2	27.7
Cuba	na	na	Paraguay	10.1	4.5
Djibouti	na	na	Peru	12.6	2.9
Dominica	na	na	Philippines	11.5	4.4
Dominican Republic	3.8	3.3	Romania	4.0	2.4
Ecuador	9.1	7.8	Russia	0.3	0
Egypt	64.2	19.7	Samoa	na	na
El Salvador	36.0	19.3	Solomon Islands	na	na
Estonia	1	5.4	St. Vincent and the Grenadines	na	na
Fiji	na	na	Suriname	na	na
Georgia	0	121.1	Swaziland	na	na
Grenada	na	na	Syria	18.6	na
Guatemala	14.8	10.7	Thailand	1.7	1.1
Indonesia	5.0	1.6	Tonga	na	na
Iran	0.5	na	Tunisia	10.5	2.7
Iraq	na	na	Turkey	4.7	0.5
Jamaica	16.7	5.1	Turkmenistan	0	na
Jordan	84.9	20.0	Ukraine	1.7	3.8
Kazakhstan	0.1	2.6	Uzbekistan	0	2.1
Kiribati	na	na	Vanuatu	na	na
Latvia	0.1	8.4	Venezuela	0.3	0.4
Lebanon	15.4	5.9	Yugoslavia	na	na

Note: This indicator reflects total assistance given to a country as a percent of its gross domestic investment. It includes both official development assistance (ODA) and official aid. ODA is granted by authoritative agencies of the members of the Development Assistance Committee (DAC) and includes all net disbursements of loans and grants. Official aid, also under the auspices of the DAC, is the total of loans and grants given to certain countries including the "transition economies" of Eastern Europe and the former Soviet Union; it also includes aid to advanced developing countries, as designated by the DAC. Gross domestic investment reflects the amount of capital investment in a country and includes expenditures on increases to fixed assets and net increases in inventory.

Source: World Bank, *World Development Indicators 1998*, Table 6.11

L2.7 Aid Dependency Ratio, Aid as Percent of Gross Domestic Investment, 1991 and 1996— Upper Middle-Income Countries per World Bank

Country	1991	1996	Country	1991	1996
Antigua and Barbuda	na	na	Mauritius	8.3	1.8
Argentina	1.1	0.5	Mexico	0.4	0.4
Bahrain	na	na	Oman	0.9	5.0
Barbados	na	na	Palau	na	na
Brazil	0.2	0.3	Poland	0	3
Chile	1.5	1.0	Saudi Arabia	0.2	0.1
Croatia	0	4.7	Seychelles	na	na
Czech Republic	3.2	0.6	Slovakia	3.4	2.0
Gabon	10.0	11.0	Slovenia	0	1.9
Hungary	9.2	1.5	South Africa	0	1.6
Libya	na	na	St. Kitts & Nevis	na	na
Malaysia	1.7	-1.1	St. Lucia	na	na
Malta	na	na	Trinidad & Tobago	-0.2	2.0
			Uruguay	4.3	2.3

Note: This indicator reflects total assistance given to a country as a percent of its gross domestic investment. It includes both official development assistance (ODA) and official aid. ODA is granted by authoritative agencies of the members of the Development Assistance Committee (DAC) and includes all net disbursements of loans and grants. Official aid, also under the auspices of the DAC, is the total of loans and grants given to certain countries including the "transition economies" of Eastern Europe and the former Soviet Union; it also includes aid to advanced developing countries, as designated by the DAC. Gross domestic investment reflects the amount of capital investment in a country and includes expenditures on increases to fixed assets and net increases in inventory.

Source: World Bank, *World Development Indicators 1998*, Table 6.11

L2.8 Aid Dependency Ratio, Aid as Percent of Gross Domestic Investment, Worldwide Summary, 1991 and 1996—Comparison By Income Level per World Bank

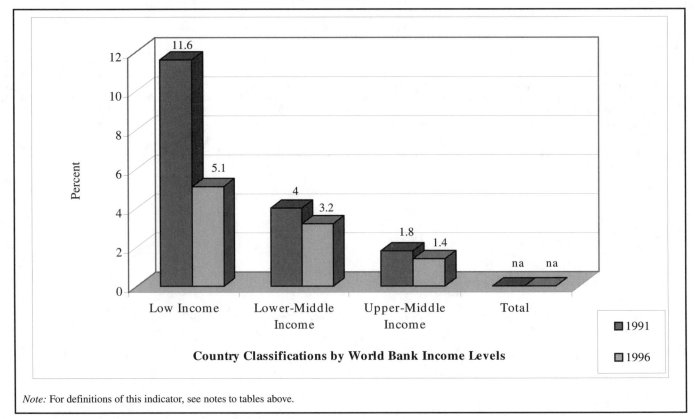

Note: For definitions of this indicator, see notes to tables above.

Source: World Bank, *World Development Indicators 1998*, Table 6.11

L3.1 Government Expenditure Allocated to Health and Education, Percent of Total, 1990–1996—Low-Income Countries per World Bank

Country	Health	Education	Country	Health	Education
Afghanistan	na	na	Kyrgyzstan	na	na
Angola	6	15	Laos	na	na
Armenia	na	na	Lesotho	13	21
Azerbaijan	na	na	Liberia	5	11
Bangladesh	5	11	Madagascar	6	11
Benin	6	31	Malawi	7	12
Bhutan	8	10	Mali	2	9
Bosnia and Herzgovina	na	na	Mauritania	4	23
Burkina Faso	7	17	Moldova	na	na
Burundi	4	16	Mongolia	4	7
Cambodia	na	na	Mozambique	5	10
Cameroon	5	18	Myanmar (Burma)	4	12
Central African Republic	na	na	Nepal	5	14
Chad	8	8	Nicaragua	13	15
China	0	2	Niger	na	na
Comoros	na	na	Nigeria	1	3
Congo, Dem. Rep. (Zaire)	1	1	Pakistan	1	2
Congo, Rep.	na	na	Rwanda	5	26
Cote d'Ivoire	4	21	Sao Tome and Principe	na	na
Equatorial Guinea	na	na	Senegal	na	na
Eritrea	na	na	Sierra Leone	10	13
Ethiopia	5	14	Somalia	1	2
Gambia	7	12	Sri Lanka	6	10
Ghana	7	22	Sudan	na	na
Guinea	3	11	Tajikistan	na	na
Guinea-Bissau	1	3	Tanzania	6	8
Guyana	na	na	Togo	5	20
Haiti	na	na	Uganda	2	15
Honduras	10	19	Vietnam	na	na
India	2	2	Yemen	5	21
Kenya	5	19	Zambia	14	15
			Zimbabwe	8	24

Note: These indicators reflect the total public expenditures on health and the total on education as a share of total government expenditures. It covers all public moneys spent including subsidies to private education and health/medical enterprises. Statistics on central government budgets and finance are accounted for in the country's local currency, which is then converted into U.S. dollars using the official exchange rate for the year.

Source: The State of the World's Children 1998, Table 6, UNICEF, UNICEF's web site http://www.unicef.org/sowc98/

L3.2 Government Expenditure Allocated to Health and Education, Percent of Total, 1990–1996—Lower Middle-Income Countries per World Bank

Country	Health	Education	Country	Health	Education
Albania	6	2	Lithuania	7	7
Algeria	na	na	Macedonia, FYRO	na	na
Belarus	2	18	Maldives	8	16
Belize	13	20	Marshall Islands	na	na
Bolivia	6	19	Micronesia	na	na
Botswana	5	21	Morocco	3	18
Bulgaria	3	4	Namibia	10	22
Cape Verde	na	na	North Korea, Dem. Rep.	na	na
Colombia	5	19	Panama	18	17
Costa Rica	21	17	Papua New Guinea	8	15
Cuba	23	10	Paraguay	7	22
Djibouti	na	na	Peru	5	16
Dominica	na	na	Philippines	3	16
Dominican Republic	10	12	Romania	8	10
Ecuador	11	18	Russia	2	2
Egypt	2	12	Samoa	na	na
El Salvador	8	13	Solomon Islands	na	na
Estonia	17	9	St. Vincent and the Grenadines	13	17
Fiji	9	18	Suriname	na	na
Georgia	na	na	Swaziland	na	na
Grenada	10	17	Syria	3	9
Guatemala	11	19	Thailand	8	22
Indonesia	3	10	Tonga	7	13
Iran	9	16	Tunisia	6	17
Iraq	na	na	Turkey	3	12
Jamaica	7	11	Turkmenistan	na	na
Jordan	8	16	Ukraine	na	na
Kazakhstan	na	na	Uzbekistan	na	na
Kiribati	na	na	Vanuatu	na	na
Latvia	6	15	Venezuela	10	20
Lebanon	na	na	Yugoslavia	na	na

Note: These indicators reflect the total public expenditures on health and the total on education as a share of total government expenditures. It covers all public moneys spent including subsidies to private education and health/medical enterprises. Statistics on central government budgets and finance are accounted for in the country's local currency, which is then converted into U.S. dollars using the official exchange rate for the year.

Source: The State of the World's Children 1998, Table 6, UNICEF, UNICEF's web site http://www.unicef.org/sowc98/

L3.3 Government Expenditure Allocated to Health and Education, Percent of Total, 1990–1996 — Upper Middle-Income Countries per World Bank

Country	Health	Education	Country	Health	Education
Antigua and Barbuda	na	na	Mexico	3	27
Argentina	2	5	Oman	6	13
Bahrain	9	13	Palau	na	na
Barbados	na	na	Poland	na	na
Brazil	5	3	Saudi Arabia	6	14
Chile	12	15	Seychelles	8	12
Croatia	15	7	Slovakia	na	na
Czech Republic	17	12	Slovenia	na	na
Gabon	na	na	South Africa	na	na
Hungary	8	3	St. Kitts & Nevis	na	na
Libya	na	na	St. Lucia	na	na
Malaysia	6	22	Trinidad & Tobago	na	na
Malta	11	12	Uruguay	6	7
Mauritius	9	17			

Note: These indicators reflect the total public expenditures on health and the total on education as a share of total government expenditures. It covers all public moneys spent including subsidies to private education and health/medical enterprises. Statistics on central government budgets and finance are accounted for in the country's local currency, which is then converted into U.S. dollars using the official exchange rate for the year.

Source: The State of the World's Children 1998, Table 6, UNICEF, UNICEF's web site http://www.unicef.org/sowc98/

L3.4 Government Expenditure Allocated to Capital Development, Percent of Total, 1980 and 1995—Low-Income Countries per World Bank

Country	1980	1995	Country	1980	1995
Afghanistan	na	na	Kyrgyzstan	na	na
Angola	na	na	Laos	na	na
Armenia	na	na	Lesotho	na	30
Azerbaijan	na	na	Liberia	na	na
Bangladesh	na	na	Madagascar	na	35
Benin	na	na	Malawi	48	na
Bhutan	na	na	Mali	9	na
Bosnia and Herzgovina	na	na	Mauritania	na	na
Burkina Faso	19	na	Moldova	na	na
Burundi	46	42	Mongolia	na	23
Cambodia	na	na	Mozambique	na	na
Cameroon	33	8	Myanmar (Burma)	24	49
Central African Republic	6	na	Nepal	na	na
Chad	na	na	Nicaragua	19	33
China	na	na	Niger	49	na
Comoros	na	na	Nigeria	na	na
Congo, Dem. Rep. (Zaire)	20	3	Pakistan	17	18
Congo, Rep.	45	na	Rwanda	35	na
Cote d'Ivoire	28	na	Sao Tome and Principe	na	na
Equatorial Guinea	na	na	Senegal	8	na
Eritrea	na	na	Sierra Leone	20	24
Ethiopia	15	19	Somalia	na	na
Gambia	48	23	Sri Lanka	40	21
Ghana	10	15	Sudan	23	na
Guinea	na	na	Tajikistan	na	na
Guinea-Bissau	na	na	Tanzania	40	na
Guyana	na	na	Togo	27	na
Haiti	20	na	Uganda	13	na
Honduras	na	na	Vietnam	na	na
India	12	11	Yemen	na	11
Kenya	23	19	Zambia	11	34
			Zimbabwe	5	13

Note: These indicators reflect the total public expenditures on capital expenses as a share of total government expenditures. It covers all public moneys spent to purchase fixed assets (equipment, furniture, etc.), land, intangible assets, nonmilitary, non-financial assets, and capital grants. Statistics on central government budgets and finance are accounted for in the country's local currency, which is then converted into U.S. dollars using the official exchange rate for the year.

Source: World Bank, *World Development Indicators 1998*, Table 4.13

L3.5 Government Expenditure Allocated to Capital Development, Percent of Total, 1980 and 1995—Lower Middle-Income Countries per World Bank

Country	1980	1995	Country	1980	1995
Albania	na	18	Lithuania	na	10
Algeria	na	na	Macedonia, FYRO	na	na
Belarus	na	na	Maldives	na	na
Belize	na	na	Marshall Islands	na	na
Bolivia	na	19	Micronesia	na	na
Botswana	32	16	Morocco	31	na
Bulgaria	na	4	Namibia	na	15
Cape Verde	na	na	North Korea, Dem. Rep.	na	na
Colombia	31	18	Panama	18	11
Costa Rica	21	8	Papua New Guinea	15	11
Cuba	na	na	Paraguay	24	15
Djibouti	na	na	Peru	23	17
Dominica	na	na	Philippines	26	15
Dominican Republic	31	42	Romania	33	13
Ecuador	16	21	Russia	na	5
Egypt	20	19	Samoa	na	na
El Salvador	16	12	Solomon Islands	na	na
Estonia	na	7	St. Vincent and the Grenadines	na	na
Fiji	na	na	Suriname	na	na
Georgia	na	na	Swaziland	na	na
Grenada	na	na	Syria	37	38
Guatemala	42	26	Thailand	23	33
Indonesia	47	46	Tonga	na	na
Iran	22	33	Tunisia	30	20
Iraq	na	na	Turkey	28	8
Jamaica	na	na	Turkmenistan	na	na
Jordan	29	19	Ukraine	na	na
Kazakhstan	na	na	Uzbekistan	na	na
Kiribati	na	na	Vanuatu	na	na
Latvia	na	4	Venezuela	22	16
Lebanon	na	18	Yugoslavia	na	na

Note: These indicators reflect the total public expenditures on capital expenses as a share of total government expenditures. It covers all public moneys spent to purchase fixed assets (equipment, furniture, etc.), land, intangible assets, nonmilitary, non-financial assets, and capital grants. Statistics on central government budgets and finance are accounted for in the country's local currency, which is then converted into U.S. dollars using the official exchange rate for the year.

Source: World Bank, *World Development Indicators 1998*, Table 4.13

L3.6 Government Expenditure Allocated to Capital Development, Percent of Total, 1980 and 1995—Upper Middle-Income Countries per World Bank

Country	1980	1995	Country	1980	1995
Antigua and Barbuda	na	na	Mexico	32	12
Argentina	na	7	Oman	21	15
Bahrain	na	na	Palau	na	na
Barbados	na	na	Poland	na	3
Brazil	8	2	Saudi Arabia	na	na
Chile	10	16	Seychelles	na	na
Croatia	na	8	Slovakia	na	na
Czech Republic	na	12	Slovenia	na	na
Gabon	na	na	South Africa	14	9
Hungary	13	na	St. Kitts & Nevis	na	na
Libya	na	na	St. Lucia	na	na
Malaysia	35	23	Trinidad & Tobago	39	10
Malta	na	na	Uruguay	8	6
Mauritius	17	17			

Note: These indicators reflect the total public expenditures on capital expenses as a share of total government expenditures. It covers all public moneys spent to purchase fixed assets (equipment, furniture, etc.), land, intangible assets, nonmilitary, non-financial assets, and capital grants. Statistics on central government budgets and finance are accounted for in the country's local currency, which is then converted into U.S. dollars using the official exchange rate for the year.

Source: World Bank, *World Development Indicators 1998*, Table 4.13

L3.7 Government Expenditure Allocated to Military, Percent of Total, 1985 and 1995—Low-Income Countries per World Bank

Country	1985	1995	Country	1985	1995
Afghanistan	na	na	Laos	na	na
Angola	na	na	Lesotho	na	2.5
Armenia	na	na	Liberia	na	na
Azerbaijan	na	na	Madagascar	8.0	5.0
Bangladesh	13.0	9.9	Malawi	5.8	3.5
Benin	na	8.6	Mali	8.1	na
Bhutan	na	na	Mauritania	25	9.3
Bosnia and Herzgovina	na	na	Moldova	na	na
Burkina Faso	18.7	12.0	Mongolia	13.1	7.0
Burundi	20.8	24.8	Mozambique	38.0	na
Cambodia	na	na	Myanmar (Burma)	na	na
Cameroon	8.3	10.2	Nepal	6.2	5.8
Central African Republic	6.4	na	Nicaragua	26.2	5.3
Chad	6.1	na	Niger	5	7.9
China	23.8	18.5	Nigeria	9.4	3.5
Comoros	na	na	Pakistan	28.1	25.3
Congo, Dem. Rep. (Zaire)	na	na	Rwanda	9.4	23.3
Congo, Rep.	9.2	na	Sao Tome and Principe	na	na
Cote d'Ivoire	na	na	Senegal	8.8	na
Equatorial Guinea	na	na	Sierra Leone	5.0	28.9
Eritrea	na	na	Somalia	na	na
Ethiopia	28.9	9.2	Sri Lanka	8.4	15.7
Gambia	na	na	Sudan	na	37.6
Ghana	7.2	5.8	Tajikistan	na	na
Guinea	na	na	Tanzania	12.8	8.4
Guinea-Bissau	4.7	na	Togo	6.9	10.2
Guyana	na	na	Uganda	15.6	13.3
Haiti	7.5	21.6	Vietnam	na	10.9
Honduras	14	8.7	Yemen	na	na
India	15.7	12.7	Zambia	na	12.6
Kenya	8.4	6.2	Zimbabwe	14.4	10.5
Kyrgyzstan	na	na			

Note: These indicators reflect the total public expenditures on military as a share of total government expenditures. It covers all public moneys spent including subsidies to private education and health/medical enterprises. Statistics on central government budgets and finance are accounted for in the country's local currency, which is then converted into U.S. dollars using the official exchange rate for the year.

Source: World Bank, *World Development Indicators 1998*, Table 5.7

L3.8 Government Expenditure Allocated to Military Percent of Total, 1985 and 1995—Lower Middle-Income Countries per World Bank

Country	1985	1995	Country	1985	1995
Albania	10.9	3.2	Lithuania	na	2.1
Algeria	6.3	6.9	Macedonia, FYRO	na	na
Belarus	na	na	Maldives	na	na
Belize	na	na	Marshall Islands	na	na
Bolivia	22.6	9.5	Micronesia	na	na
Botswana	5.8	12.7	Morocco	20.0	13.8
Bulgaria	32.5	6.3	Namibia	na	5.5
Cape Verde	na	na	North Korea, Dem. Rep.	na	na
Colombia	10.3	16.2	Panama	6.4	5.3
Costa Rica	2.8	2.7	Papua New Guinea	4.5	5.6
Cuba	na	na	Paraguay	11.9	7.3
Djibouti	na	na	Peru	36.3	9.3
Dominica	na	na	Philippines	9.5	8.5
Dominican Republic	8.0	9.1	Romania	20	11.2
Ecuador	16.9	18.3	Russia	na	na
Egypt	22.1	13.7	Samoa	na	na
El Salvador	29.1	7.4	Solomon Islands	na	na
Estonia	na	2.9	St. Vincent and the Grenadines	na	na
Fiji	na	na	Suriname	na	na
Georgia	na	na	Swaziland	na	na
Grenada	na	na	Syria	na	na
Guatemala	17	14.2	Thailand	19.7	15.2
Indonesia	10.3	8.9	Tonga	na	na
Iran	na	na	Tunisia	8.8	6.3
Iraq	na	na	Turkey	17.9	17.6
Jamaica	1.8	1.4	Turkmenistan	na	na
Jordan	39.7	21.7	Ukraine	na	7.8
Kazakhstan	na	na	Uzbekistan	na	na
Kiribati	na	na	Vanuatu	na	na
Latvia	na	na	Venezuela	9.2	6.3
Lebanon	na	9.7	Yugoslavia	na	na

Note: These indicators reflect the total public expenditures on military as a share of total government expenditures. It covers all public moneys spent including subsidies to private education and health/medical enterprises. Statistics on central government budgets and finance are accounted for in the country's local currency, which is then converted into U.S. dollars using the official exchange rate for the year.

Source: World Bank, *World Development Indicators 1998*, Table 5.7

L3.9 Government Expenditure Allocated to Military, Percent of Total, 1985 and 1995 —Upper Middle-Income Countries per World Bank

Country	1985	1995	Country	1985	1995
Antigua and Barbuda	na	na	Mauritius	0.8	1.6
Argentina	12.4	27.0	Mexico	2.6	5.1
Bahrain	na	na	Oman	42.3	33.9
Barbados	na	na	Palau	na	na
Brazil	2.1	3.9	Poland	40.7	5.4
Chile	11.4	17.5	Saudi Arabia	27.0	41.0
Croatia	na	32	Seychelles	na	na
Czech Republic	na	6.6	Slovakia	na	6.8
Gabon	6.6	9.6	Slovenia	na	3.5
Hungary	15.3	4.6	St. Kitts & Nevis	na	na
Libya	na	na	St. Lucia	na	na
Malaysia	10.7	12.4	Trinidad & Tobago	na	na
Malta	na	na	Uruguay	10.6	7.3

Note: These indicators reflect the total public expenditures on military as a share of total government expenditures. It covers all public moneys spent including subsidies to private education and health/medical enterprises.

Source: World Bank, *World Development Indicators 1998*, Table 5.7

L3.10 Government Expenditure Allocations, Worldwide Summary, 1991 and 1996—Region by Region

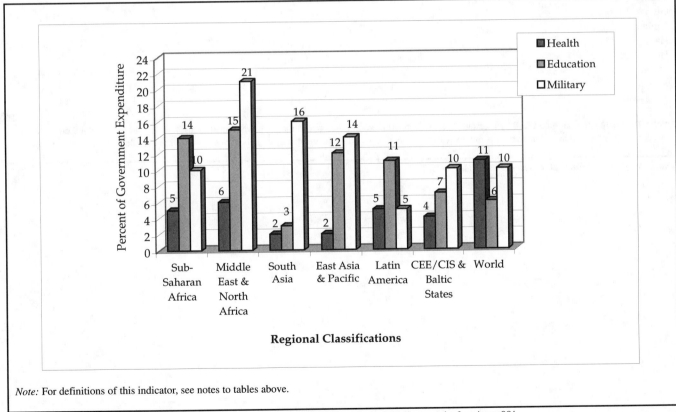

Note: For definitions of this indicator, see notes to tables above.

Source: The State of the World's Children 1998, Table 6, UNICEF, UNICEF's web site http://www.unicef.org/sowc98/

L4.1 Total Debt as Percent of GDP, 1995—Low-Income Countries per World Bank

Country	1995	Country	1995
Afghanistan	na	Laos	na
Angola	na	Lesotho	na
Armenia	na	Liberia	na
Azerbaijan	na	Madagascar	118.4
Bangladesh	na	Malawi	na
Benin	na	Mali	na
Bhutan	na	Mauritania	na
Bosnia and Herzgovina	na	Moldova	na
Burkina Faso	na	Mongolia	na
Burundi	105.0	Mozambique	na
Cambodia	na	Myanmar (Burma)	na
Cameroon	139.6	Nepal	66.2
Central African Republic	na	Nicaragua	na
Chad	na	Niger	na
China	na	Nigeria	na
Comoros	na	Pakistan	na
Congo, Dem. Rep. (Zaire)	214.1	Rwanda	na
Congo, Rep.	na	Sao Tome and Principe	na
Cote d'Ivoire	na	Senegal	na
Equatorial Guinea	na	Sierra Leone	114.1
Eritrea	na	Somalia	na
Ethiopia	na	Sri Lanka	94.6
Gambia	na	Sudan	na
Ghana	na	Tajikistan	na
Guinea	na	Tanzania	na
Guinea-Bissau	na	Togo	na
Guyana	na	Uganda	na
Haiti	na	Vietnam	na
Honduras	na	Yemen	na
India	52.2	Zambia	161.8
Kenya	na	Zimbabwe	69.5
Kyrgyzstan	na		

Note: Total debt is the amount owed by a country's central government to other governments, private institutions, and individuals. It is the gross amount owed by government, that is, the amount is not decreased by amounts owed *to* the government. This indicator states the total debt as a percent of GDP.

Source: World Bank, *World Development Indicators 1998*, Table 4.12

L4.2 Total Debt as Percent of GDP, 1995—Lower Middle-Income Countries per World Bank

Country	1995	Country	1995
Albania	35.3	Macedonia, FYRO	na
Algeria	na	Maldives	na
Belarus	na	Marshall Islands	na
Belize	na	Micronesia	na
Bolivia	62.9	Morocco	na
Botswana	11.5	Namibia	na
Bulgaria	na	North Korea, Dem.Rep.	na
Cape Verde	na	Panama	na
Colombia	na	Papua New Guinea	43.0
Costa Rica	na	Paraguay	12.8
Cuba	na	Peru	45.9
Djibouti	na	Philippines	61.1
Dominica	na	Romania	na
Dominican Republic	na	Russia	na
Ecuador	na	Samoa	na
Egypt	na	Solomon Islands	na
El Salvador	27.7	St. Vincent and the Grenadines	na
Estonia	na	Suriname	na
Fiji	na	Swaziland	na
Georgia	na	Syria	na
Grenada	na	Thailand	4.6
Guatemala	na	Tonga	na
Indonesia	30.9	Tunisia	57.7
Iran	na	Turkey	41.4
Iraq	na	Turkmenistan	na
Jamaica	na	Ukraine	na
Jordan	90.2	Uzbekistan	na
Kazakhstan	na	Vanuatu	na
Kiribati	na	Venezuela	na
Latvia	16.0	Yugoslavia	na
Lebanon	77.9		
Lithuania	na		

Note: Total debt is the amount owed by a country's central government to other governments, private institutions, and individuals. It is the gross amount owed by government, that is, the amount is not decreased by amounts owed *to* the government. This indicator states the total debt as a percent of GDP.

Source: World Bank, *World Development Indicators 1998*, Table 4.12

L4.3 Total Debt as Percent of GDP, 1995—Upper Middle-Income Countries per World Bank

Country	1995	Country	1995
Antigua and Barbuda	na	Mexico	40.9
Argentina	na	Oman	31.3
Bahrain	na	Palau	na
Barbados	na	Poland	57.9
Brazil	na	Saudi Arabia	na
Chile	19	Seychelles	na
Croatia	32.5	Slovakia	na
Czech Republic	15.5	Slovenia	na
Gabon	na	South Africa	57.4
Hungary	na	St. Kitts & Nevis	na
Libya	na	St. Lucia	na
Malaysia	42.8	Trinidad & Tobago	53.5
Malta	na	Uruguay	26.3
Mauritius	33.7		

Note: Total debt is the amount owed by a country's central government to other governments, private institutions, and individuals. It is the gross amount owed by government, that is, the amount is not decreased by moneys owed *to* the government. This indicator states the total debt as a percent of GDP.

Source: World Bank, *World Development Indicators 1998*, Table 4.12

L5.1 Total Debt Interest as Percent of Current Revenue, 1995—Low-Income Countries per World Bank

Country	1995	Country	1995
Afghanistan	na	Laos	na
Angola	na	Lesotho	na
Armenia	na	Liberia	na
Azerbaijan	na	Madagascar	59.9
Bangladesh	na	Malawi	na
Benin	na	Mali	na
Bhutan	na	Mauritania	na
Bosnia and Herzgovina	na	Moldova	na
Burkina Faso	na	Mongolia	1.7
Burundi	7.7	Mozambique	na
Cambodia	na	Myanmar (Burma)	na
Cameroon	23.0	Nepal	na
Central African Republic	na	Nicaragua	15.8
Chad	na	Niger	na
China	na	Nigeria	na
Comoros	na	Pakistan	28.8
Congo, Dem. Rep. (Zaire)	1.0	Rwanda	na
Congo, Rep.	na	Sao Tome and Principe	na
Cote d'Ivoire	na	Senegal	na
Equatorial Guinea	na	Sierra Leone	20.4
Eritrea	na	Somalia	na
Ethiopia	16.8	Sri Lanka	28.1
Gambia	na	Sudan	na
Ghana	20.5	Tajikistan	na
Guinea	na	Tanzania	na
Guinea-Bissau	na	Togo	na
Guyana	na	Uganda	na
Haiti	na	Vietnam	na
Honduras	na	Yemen	17.1
India	33.6	Zambia	8.7
Kenya	31.7	Zimbabwe	23.4
Kyrgyzstan	na		

Note: This indicator represents the total amount of interest required to service government debt as a share of current government revenue. Interest includes payments due to domestic and foreign entities and residents. Total debt is the amount owed by a country's central government to other governments, private institutions, and individuals. It is the gross amount owed by government, that is, the amount is not decreased by amounts owed *to* the government.

Source: World Bank, *World Development Indicators 1998*, Table 4.12

L5.2 Total Debt Interest as Percent of Current Revenue, 1995—Lower Middle-Income Countries per World Bank

Country	1995	Country	1995
Albania	11.1	Lithuania	1.8
Algeria	na	Macedonia, FYRO	na
Belarus	na	Maldives	na
Belize	na	Marshall Islands	na
Bolivia	14.1	Micronesia	na
Botswana	1.7	Morocco	na
Bulgaria	41.2	Namibia	2.4
Cape Verde	na	North Korea, Dem. Rep.	na
Colombia	10.5	Panama	6.9
Costa Rica	21.4	Papua New Guinea	12.2
Cuba	na	Paraguay	5.6
Djibouti	na	Peru	19.9
Dominica	na	Philippines	21.5
Dominican Republic	5.8	Romania	4.4
Ecuador	21.8	Russia	17.0
Egypt	25.8	Samoa	na
El Salvador	11.3	Solomon Islands	na
Estonia	0.6	St. Vincent and the Grenadines	na
Fiji	na	Suriname	na
Georgia	na	Swaziland	na
Grenada	na	Syria	na
Guatemala	11.1	Thailand	1.8
Indonesia	8.9	Tonga	na
Iran	0	Tunisia	12.4
Iraq	na	Turkey	15.2
Jamaica	na	Turkmenistan	na
Jordan	10	Ukraine	na
Kazakhstan	na	Uzbekistan	na
Kiribati	na	Vanuatu	na
Latvia	3.6	Venezuela	29.0
Lebanon	59.8	Yugoslavia	na

Note: This indicator represents the total amount of interest required to service government debt as a share of current government revenue. Interest includes payments due to domestic and foreign entities and residents. Total debt is the amount owed by a country's central government to other governments, private institutions, and individuals. It is the gross amount owed by government, that is, the amount is not decreased by amounts owed *to* the government.

Source: World Bank, *World Development Indicators 1998*, Table 4.12

L5.3 Total Debt Interest as Percent of Current Revenue, 1995—Upper Middle-Income Countries per World Bank

Country	1995	Country	1995
Antigua and Barbuda	na	Mexico	18.5
Argentina	11.3	Oman	7.8
Bahrain	na	Palau	na
Barbados	na	Poland	11.8
Brazil	75.6	Saudi Arabia	na
Chile	3.4	Seychelles	na
Croatia	3.3	Slovakia	na
Czech Republic	3.2	Slovenia	na
Gabon	na	South Africa	22.3
Hungary	na	St. Kitts & Nevis	na
Libya	na	St. Lucia	na
Malaysia	12.1	Trinidad & Tobago	18.3
Malta	na	Uruguay	5.9
Mauritius	11.5		

Note: This indicator represents the total amount of interest required to service government debt as a share of current government revenue. Interest includes payments due to domestic and foreign entities and residents. Total debt is the amount owed by a country's central government to other governments, private institutions, and individuals. It is the gross amount owed by government, that is, the amount is not decreased by amounts owed *to* the government.

Source: World Bank, *World Development Indicators 1998*, Table 4.12

L6.1 Overall Budget Deficit, as Percent of GDP, 1980 and 1995—Low-Income Countries per World Bank

Country	1980	1995	Country	1980	1995
Afghanistan	na	na	Laos	na	na
Angola	na	na	Lesotho	na	6.4
Armenia	na	na	Liberia	na	na
Azerbaijan	na	na	Madagascar	na	-1.6
Bangladesh	2.5	na	Malawi	-15.9	na
Benin	na	na	Mali	-4.5	na
Bhutan	na	na	Mauritania	na	na
Bosnia and Herzgovina	na	na	Moldova	na	na
Burkina Faso	0.2	na	Mongolia	na	-3.5
Burundi	-3.9	-3.7	Mozambique	na	na
Cambodia	na	na	Myanmar (Burma)	1.2	-4.1
Cameroon	0.5	0.2	Nepal	-3.0	-4.6
Central African Republic	-3.5	na	Nicaragua	-6.8	-0.6
Chad	na	na	Niger	-4.7	na
China	na	-1.8	Nigeria	na	na
Comoros	na	na	Pakistan	-5.7	-4.8
Congo, Dem. Rep. (Zaire)	-0.8	0	Rwanda	-1.7	-7.4
Congo, Rep.	-5.2	na	Sao Tome and Principe	na	na
Cote d'Ivoire	-10.8	na	Senegal	0.9	na
Equatorial Guinea	na	na	Sierra Leone	-11.8	-6.1
Eritrea	na	na	Somalia	na	na
Ethiopia	-3.1	-5.9	Sri Lanka	-18.3	-8.3
Gambia	-4.5	3.7	Sudan	-3.3	na
Ghana	-4.2	-2.6	Tajikistan	na	na
Guinea	na	na	Tanzania	na	na
Guinea-Bissau	na	na	Togo	-2.0	na
Guyana	na	na	Uganda	-3.1	na
Haiti	-4.7	na	Vietnam	na	na
Honduras	na	na	Yemen	na	-5.5
India	-6.5	-6.0	Zambia	-18.5	-7.2
Kenya	-4.5	-3.4	Zimbabwe	-10.9	-10.7
Kyrgyzstan	na	na			

Note: This indicator represents total government revenue, including official grants, minus total government spending and lending (less repayments). A negative number shows deficit and a positive number reflects government surplus.

Source: World Bank, *World Development Indicators 1998*, Table 4.12

L6.2 Overall Budget Deficit, as Percent of GDP, 1980 and 1995—Lower Middle-Income Countries per World Bank

Country	1980	1995	Country	1980	1995
Albania	na	-9.0	Lithuania	na	-5.3
Algeria	na	na	Macedonia, FYRO	na	na
Belarus	na	na	Maldives	na	na
Belize	na	na	Marshall Islands	na	na
Bolivia	na	-2.5	Micronesia	na	na
Botswana	-0.2	2.8	Morocco	-9.7	na
Bulgaria	na	-5.3	Namibia	na	-4.5
Cape Verde	na	na	North Korea, Dem. Rep.	na	na
Colombia	-1.8	-0.5	Panama	-5.2	2.9
Costa Rica	-7.4	-2.9	Papua New Guinea	-1.9	-4.1
Cuba	na	na	Paraguay	0.3	1.2
Djibouti	na	na	Peru	-2.4	-1.3
Dominica	na	na	Philippines	-1.4	0.6
Dominican Republic	-2.6	0.8	Romania	0.5	-2.5
Ecuador	-1.4	0	Russia	na	-4.4
Egypt	-6.3	0.3	Samoa	na	na
El Salvador	-5.7	-0.1	Solomon Islands	na	na
Estonia	na	0	St. Vincent and the Grenadines	na	na
Fiji	na	na	Suriname	na	na
Georgia	na	na	Swaziland	na	na
Grenada	na	na	Syria	-9.7	-1.7
Guatemala	-3.4	-0.7	Thailand	-4.9	2.9
Indonesia	-2.3	2.2	Tonga	na	na
Iran	-13.8	1.4	Tunisia	-2.8	-3.2
Iraq	na	na	Turkey	-3.1	-4.1
Jamaica	-15.5	na	Turkmenistan	na	na
Jordan	-9.3	1.1	Ukraine	na	na
Kazakhstan	na	na	Uzbekistan	na	na
Kiribati	na	na	Vanuatu	na	na
Latvia	na	-4.2	Venezuela	0	-3.7
Lebanon	na	-15.7	Yugoslavia	na	na

Note: This indicator represents total government revenue, including official grants, minus total government spending and lending (less repayments). A negative number shows deficit and a positive number reflects government surplus.

Source: World Bank, *World Development Indicators 1998*, Table 4.12

L6.3 Overall Budget Deficit, as Percent of GDP, 1980 and 1995—Upper Middle-Income Countries per World Bank

Country	1980	1995	Country	1980	1995
Antigua and Barbuda	na	na	Mexico	-3.0	-0.5
Argentina	-2.6	-1.1	Oman	0.4	-10.1
Bahrain	na	na	Palau	na	na
Barbados	na	na	Poland	na	-2.0
Brazil	-2.4	-9.4	Saudi Arabia	na	na
Chile	5.4	2.5	Seychelles	na	na
Croatia	na	-0.9	Slovakia	na	na
Czech Republic	na	0.4	Slovenia	na	na
Gabon	6.1	na	South Africa	-2.3	-5.9
Hungary	-2.8	na	St. Kitts & Nevis	na	na
Libya	na	na	St. Lucia	na	na
Malaysia	-6.0	2.3	Trinidad & Tobago	7.4	0.2
Malta	na	na	Uruguay	0	-1.3
Mauritius	-10.3	-1.2			

Note: This indicator represents total government revenue, including official grants, minus total government spending and lending (less repayments). A negative number shows deficit and a positive number reflects government surplus.

Source: World Bank, *World Development Indicators 1998*, Table 4.12

Index

This index offers access to information relating to the three lowest income categories employed by the World Bank in their country classification system: low-income countries, lower middle-income countries, and upper middle-income countries. The countries included in each category are listed below.

You can use this index in several ways: 1) by looking up one of the income categories, under which are listed all the tables included for each category, 2) by looking up a specific indicator, such as one-year-olds fully immunized against DPT, which will then send you to three tables, each of which itemizes the data for one of the three income categories, or 3) by looking up a more general subject, such as immunization, under which you will find specific indicators, such as one-year-olds immunized against DPT and one-year-olds immunized against measles.

Low-Income Countries (per World Bank)

Afghanistan	Congo, Rep.	Lesotho	Sao Tome and Principe
Angola	Cote d'Ivoire	Liberia	Senegal
Armenia	Equatorial Guinea	Madagascar	Sierra Leone
Azerbaijan	Eritrea	Malawi	Somalia
Bangladesh	Ethiopia	Mali	Sri Lanka
Benin	Gambia	Mauritania	Sudan
Bhutan	Ghana	Moldova	Tajikistan
Bosnia and Herzegovina	Guinea	Mongolia	Tanzania
Burkina Faso	Guinea-Bissau	Mozambique	Togo
Burundi	Guyana	Myanmar (Burma)	Uganda
Cambodia	Haiti	Nepal	Vietnam
Cameroon	Honduras	Nicaragua	Yemen
Central African Republic	India	Niger	Zambia
Chad	Kenya	Nigeria	Zimbabwe
China	Kyrgyzstan	Pakistan	
Comoros	Laos	Rwanda	
Congo, Dem. Rep. (Zaire)			

Lower Middle-Income Countries (per World Bank)

Albania	El Salvador	Macedonia, FYRO	St. Vincent and the Grenadines
Algeria	Estonia	Maldives	Suriname
Belarus	Fiji	Marshall Islands	Swaziland
Belize	Georgia	Micronesia	Syria
Bolivia	Grenada	Morocco	Thailand
Botswana	Guatemala	Namibia	Tonga
Bulgaria	Indonesia	North Korea, Dem. Rep.	Tunisia
Cape Verde	Iran	Panama	Turkey
Colombia	Iraq	Papua New Guinea	Turkmenistan
Costa Rica	Jamaica	Paraguay	Ukraine
Cuba	Jordan	Peru	Uzbekistan
Djibouti	Kazakhstan	Philippines	Vanuatu
Dominica	Kiribati	Romania	Venezuela
Dominican Republic	Latvia	Russia	Yugoslavia
Ecuador	Lebanon	Samoa	
Egypt	Lithuania	Solomon Islands	

Upper Middle-Income Countries (per World Bank)

Antigua and Barbuda	Czech Republic	Mexico	Slovenia
Argentina	Gabon	Oman	South Africa
Bahrain	Hungary	Palau	St. Kitts & Nevis
Barbados	Libya	Poland	St. Lucia
Brazil	Malaysia	Saudi Arabia	Trinidad & Tobago
Chile	Malta	Seychelles	Uruguay
Croatia	Mauritius	Slovakia